Cognitive Psychology

Fifth Edition

Cognitive Psychology

Fifth Edition

John B. Best

Eastern Illinois University

Brooks/Cole • Wadsworth

I(T)P® An International Thomson Publishing Company

Belmont • Albany • Bonn • Boston • Cincinnati • Detroit • Johannesburg • London • Madrid
Melbourne • Mexico City • New York • Pacific Grove • Paris • Singapore • Tokyo • Toronto • Washington

Sponsoring Editor: *Marianne Taflinger*
Marketing Team: *Alicia Barelli/Christine Davis/Aaron Eden*
Editorial Assistants: *Scott Brearton/Rachael Bruckman*
Production Editor: *Tessa McGlasson Avila*
Manuscript Editor: *David Lynch*
Permissions Editor: *The Permissions Group*
Art Editor: *Lisa Torri*

Interior Illustration: *Suffolk Technical Illustrators*
Interior Design: *Rita Naughton*
Cover Design: *Bill Stanton*
Cover Photo: *PhotoDisc*
Indexer: *Nancy Humphreys*
Typesetting: *Carlisle Communications, Ltd.*
Cover Printing: *Phoenix Color Corp.*
Printing and Binding: *R. R. Donnelley/ Crawfordsville*

For more information, contact:

WADSWORTH PUBLISHING COMPANY
10 Davis Drive
Belmont, CA 94002
USA

International Thomson Publishing Europe
Berkshire House 168-173
High Holborn
London WC1V 7AA
England

Thomas Nelson Australia
102 Dodds Street
South Melbourne, 3205
Victoria, Australia

Nelson Canada
1120 Birchmount Road
Scarborough, Ontario
Canada M1K 5G4

International Thomson Editores
Seneca 53
Col. Polanco
México, D. F., México 11560

International Thomson Publishing GmbH
Königswinterer Strasse 418
53227 Bonn
Germany

International Thomson Publishing Asia
60 Albert Street
#15-01 Albert Complex
Singapore 189969

International Thomson Publishing Japan
Hirakawacho Kyowa Building, 3F
2-2-1 Hirakawacho
Chiyoda-ku, Tokyo 102
Japan

Printed in the United States of America

10   9   8   7   6   5   4   3   2

Library of Congress Cataloging-in-Publication Data

Best, John B.
    Cognitive psychology / John B. Best. —5th ed.
        p.   cm.
    Includes bibliographical references and index.
    ISBN 0-534-35417-3
    1. Cognitive psychology.   I. Title
    BF311.B485   1998
    153—dc21
                             98-40566
                                CIP

In memory of my daughter Adrienne

Related Titles

Psychology of Language, third edition, by David W. Carroll
Exploring the Mind: Readings in Cognitive Psychology, by Lloyd K. Komatsu
Psychology: The Adaptive Mind, by James S. Nairne
Human Memory: An Introduction to Research, Data, and Theory, by Ian Neath

Forthcoming

Mind, Brain, and Computer, by Lloyd K. Komatsu

Brief Contents

Contents

Chapter 4   Memory as Recomputation and Correspondence   130

Part V   *Language*   *237*

Chapter **9**   **Language Acquisition and Cognitive Development   316**

Preface

To the Student

Cognitive psychology is not a very old scientific discipline, but it has changed a lot in its brief existence, and it continues to develop at an astonishing pace. To an author, this explosion of knowledge presents both opportunities and problems. It's certainly an exciting time to be a cognitive psychologist, and communicating the theories and findings of cognitive psychology to a student such as yourself, who is hearing it for the first time, is an exciting opportunity for an author. However, one of the problems resulting from the pace of change and sheer volume of material is that any book such as this one must be simply an "introduction" to the field. If I were to include coverage of every topic of interest to cognitive psychologists, the result would be an unmanageable volume from which no professor, no matter how skillful, could teach, or which no student, no matter how dedicated, could assimilate.

As it stands, there will be plenty to keep you busy. I've tried to be mindful of that, and I've incorporated into the book some features that I hope will enable you to learn the material in as painless a manner as possible. Each chapter begins with an overview. In the overviews, I've used an anecdote as a springboard into the questions and issues of the chapter. Each chapter contains summary sections at various points—sometimes these are explicitly labeled, and sometimes they can simply be found at the conclusion of the chapter's major headings. These should offer breathing spaces and logical starting and stopping places within the chapter if you don't want to try to read the chapter in just one sitting. One of my objectives in writing the book is to show you how cognitive psychologists think about attacking a problem, and how they analyze it. I believe that the material will be easier for you to assimilate if you understand something about the methods and approach that cognitive psychologists use. To get these points across, I've included in most of the chapters a "Focus on Research" section. Some of the findings in the Focus sections may be redundant with those of the text, but the main point is to shine a light on the theorizing and methodology that cognitive psychologists use.

Each chapter closes with some Concluding Comments. The comments are intended as a summary, but I didn't want them to be simply a rehash of the material in the chapter. So, although the concluding comments summarize the chapter, I also intended them to point out some implications of that chapter's material, to examine how certain "themes" or ideas in cognitive psychology are reworked in different areas, and so on. Following the Concluding Comments is a list of key terms that were used in the chapter. Most of the key terms also appear in the Glossary. I recommend that you learn the definitions of all the key terms. Finally, many of the chapters include a section called "Using Your Knowledge of Cognition." Sometimes students complain that the material in cognitive psychology is rather abstract and, by implication, alien or remote. The point of the Using Your Knowledge sections is to show you that cognitive psychology can be applied, sometimes without much difficulty, to many issues that arise during a typical day.

Finally, I'd like to invite you to enjoy your course in cognition! If the course has the same reputation at your school that it does at mine, then this may not be a course that you have been particularly looking forward to taking. But while I think that the course can be challenging, I view it as a positive challenge. If you learn this material, I think you will be doing yourself a big favor both in terms of building a solid foundation for later study in any area of psychology, and in providing yourself with knowledge you may use to operate your own cognitive system at a higher level. As you can see, I'm optimistic that you will get a lot out of this course!

To the Professor

My intention is that the book be used by upper-division students who are taking their first course in cognition. The book can be covered comfortably in a semester-long course, although I do not cover the entire book in my own semester-long course. Some knowledge of research methods, experimental design, and statistics is presupposed, but most of the experiments in the book are described in enough detail that student readers who have not had those courses will be able to read the book and maintain good comprehension. Although almost every chapter contains some references to previous and future chapters, the chapters nevertheless can stand on their own, and so the sequence implied by the table of contents is just a suggestion.

Users of previous editions will find that there have been quite a few changes—in fact, too many to list here. I'll limit myself to describing only the major foci of change. Chapter 1 is now focused on what I've described as three "levels of analysis": The mental, the neural, and the cognitive. In Chapter 2, there is more coverage of the "pop-out" phenomenon, and there is coverage of the recognition by components model (Biederman). The work of David Marr is also described in Chapter 2. The chapter on cognitive processes in vision has been deleted in this edition. The material on memory (Chapters 3 and 4) has been organized explicitly around two alternative views: the view that memory is the result of some sort of storage and the view that memory is the result of a recomputation, or reconstruction at retrieval time. Chapter 4 now includes a lengthy discussion of J.R. Anderson's ACT-R theory. Chapter 6 includes more discussion of the relationship between connectionist models and actual cognitive neural science processes. Cognitive neuropsychology also plays a greater role in Chapter 7 than it did previously. Chapter 8 now includes material on dyslexia, and relates difficulties in reading to other cognitive processes used in communication, specifically with regard to speaking and listening. Chapter 9, the developmental chapter, now includes material on childrens' theory of mind. Chapter 10, the reasoning chapter, now includes material on the neuropsychology of "higher" cognitive processes—this kind of material is seldom seen in a first book. The discussion of deontic reasoning has been expanded, and there is a discussion of reasoning about causal influences, which includes a description of the Cheng model. Chapter 11 deals with concepts and categories and is new to this edition. Chapter 12, the problem-solving chapter, now includes a discussion of some recent work in the production and use of operators in moving through the problem space.

To help you get the most out of this text, an *Instructor's Manual* contains chapter overviews; demonstrations; a resource list of approximately 20 annotated, correlated websites; about 50 test items per chapter; transparency masters with approximately 80 figures from the text; and computer software correlation for the *Mel-Lab, Mindscope, Superlab, MacLaboratory,* and *Psyscope* programs.

Also available through your ITP representative is *Thomson World Class Learning*™ *Testing Tool,* a fully integrated suite of test creation, delivery, and classroom management tools. This invaluable set of tools includes *World Class Test* and *Test Online* and *World Class Manager* software. The program provides text-specific testing options designed to offer instructors greater flexibility. A complete description of each component and a self-running demonstration can be found at *www. worldclasslearning.com.*

Acknowledgments

This is the first edition of the book to have been produced by Brooks/Cole, and their excellent editorial staff made sure that the transition went very smoothly. I'd like to thank my senior acquisitions editor, Marianne Taflinger, who spent major portions of her time with me, and who was very patient, especially in academic year 1997-98 when I served as the chairperson of our Psychology Department. I thank Tessa McGlasson, production editor, for shepherding the book through production with a minimum of hassle. David Lynch, copyeditor, has done a prodigious job of cleaning up the writing and catching my all-too-numerous errors: he has earned my humble thanks. In addition, Jennifer Wilkinson has enthusiastically supported and guided me in the production of the ancillaries, and I thank her warmly as well.

A number of specialists have given willingly of their time and talent by reviewing the previous edition, and by reviewing portions of the current edition too. Their comments have proved invaluable to me to making the book the best it can be. They are:

Thomas R. Alley, Clemson University

Ian Begg, McMaster University

Jill Booker, Queen's University

Patrick Brown, University of Western Ontario

Brian Butler, Queen's University

Judith Goggin, University of Texas at El Paso

Peter Graf, University of British Columbia

Donald Homa, Arizona State University

Jacqueline Johnson, University of Virginia

Julian Keith, University of North Carolina at Wilmington

Mustaq Khan, University of Western Ontario

Stuart Klapp, California State University Hayward

Ray Majeres, Western Illinois University

Harvey Marmurek, University of Guelph

Ian Neath, Purdue University

David G. Payne, State University of New York at Binghamton

Kerri Pickel, Ball State University

William Prinzmetal, University of California Berkeley

Steven Smith, Texas A & M University

L.G. Standing, Bishop's University

Jim Staszewski, Carnegie Mellon University

Aimee Surprenant, Purdue University

Edward Vela, California State University at Chico

Jerry Vost, Saint Norbert College

When I started the revision process back in the summer of 1996, the chairperson of our department was Fred L. Yaffe. I'd like to thank Fred for his consideration in assigning my teaching duties, and for all his support in helping to keep my lab functional and operational. When I became the chairperson in June of 1997, and I saw all that the position entailed, my gratitude for Fred's work on my behalf increased geometrically. In addition to our former chair, I would like to thank all of the nineteen Psychology faculty at EIU for their encouragement, and for being so stimulating and so great to work with.

At EIU, I've been grateful for the support and hard work of my graduate assistants: Mike DeBoer (1994-95), Lisa Ballinger (1995-96) and Jenelle Thompson (1996-97). And in addition to the graduate students, I was fortunate to have Jeffrey Dick work with me as an undergraduate assistant.

Finally, how can I thank my family enough? To my wife, Lorraine, and our sons, Frank and Matthew: As you know, producing this edition has tried my patience and exhausted me at times. Thanks for being the greatest family anyone could ever ask for.

John B. Best

Introduction

Preceding each section in this book is a part opener describing some issues that are dealt with in the section. These part openers also provide a preliminary orientation to the material by describing some key phrases or concepts that are designed to help you organize the material as you read.

You may get more out of this introduction if you understand that much of this chapter deals with "approaches" to cognition, and that these approaches are built on metaphors. Cognitive psychology has two commonly used approaches. The information-processing approach has as its metaphorical base the idea that "the mind works like a computer," and the connectionist approach's metaphorical base is the idea that "the mind works like a brain." Let's briefly consider what each of these metaphorical statements may mean.

It is intuitively obvious to many students that minds and computers have similarities. Both humans and computers have memories that are organized in particular ways, and both are capable of following directions line by line. Computers and people are similar in some less obvious ways, too. Both humans and computers *represent* information internally. In other words, they take in information from the world in one form (keystrokes or mouse-clicks for computers, senses for humans) and store it in some other form. Once stored, this information can be altered by the computer's program, or in the humans, by cognitive processes. Cognitive processes become the equivalent of mental programs according to the information-processing approach. These processes operate on the information we have stored, modifying it to suit our current purposes.

Obvious though the computer–mind similarity is, the brain–mind metaphor underlying the connectionist approach is even more obvious to many students— so obvious, in fact, that many think this metaphor is simply a trivial cliché. But we should resist the temptation to dismiss the connectionist approach. Theorists and researchers point out that digital computers do one thing at a time; the advantage of such machines is their incredible speed. But my cognitive system and yours are not at all like this image. Compared to computing machines, our cognitive systems are much, much slower. But they have an awesome advantage nevertheless. Our cognitive systems can do more than one thing at a time; in fact, they are usually doing more than one thing at a time. This fact suggests that our cognitive systems, like our brains, work as *parallel* (many things at once) machines, rather than as *serial* (one thing at a time) machines as computers do.

If you keep this distinction in mind as you wend your way through this chapter, I think you'll get a good grasp of why cognitive psychologists approach specific problems as they do. One other thing: I hope you don't feel you need to decide which of these perspectives is "right" and which is "wrong." Both the information-processing and the connectionist approach have their uses, as we'll see directly.

CHAPTER 1

Cognitive Psychology: Definitions, Roots, and Metaphors

Overview

Last week I did something that I thought was very strange. After supper, I told my wife that I was going to the grocery store to buy milk, and she asked me, as long as I was going out, to return a book to the library. Some minutes intervened while I did other chores, and then I finally got going, almost forgetting the book, then remembering to put it on the passenger seat beside me in the car. The weather had turned quite a bit colder in the past week, and so I thought I could go to the grocery store first, leaving the milk in the car

3

while I returned the book, without the milk being spoiled by warm temperatures. Having made this plan, I sort of put my mind on automatic pilot while I drove. I bought the milk, put it on the front seat next to the book, drove to the library, got out, went around to the passenger side, grabbed an object, walked into the library, walked all the way to the circulation desk, and met the somewhat quizzical eyes of the librarian before I realized that I had the milk, not the book. I sheepishly retreated and brought back the correct object a few minutes later.

On the drive home, I tried to figure out why I had made that mistake. At first, I couldn't come up with an answer. Milk gallons and books don't look alike; they don't have similar functions; and the objects weren't the same temperature, or the same weight. How then could I get them confused? To answer this question, we must realize first that my cognitive system created internal representations of both the milk and the book, and second that these internal representations have properties all their own. Some of the properties are based on what I know about the object in question; hence, these properties are stable and more or less unchanging. For example, I know that milk is food and that a book is not food, and these characteristics are part of my permanent internal representation of these objects. But some of the properties of the internal representation refer to characteristics that the object may possess temporarily, but not permanently. That is, our cognitive system seems to have a batch of "temporary files" into which an object can be placed for the time being, probably for the sake of some convenience. In these files the object may be represented by characteristics that it probably does not have permanently.

Essentially, this is how I explained my mistake to myself: In my daydreaming, automatic-pilot state, both the objects on the front seat were represented simply as "things on the front seat" and were not "tagged" with their complete and permanent specification. Given that two things were on the seat, I think I had about a 50% chance of carrying the wrong object into the library.

From this example arise several questions and themes that are dealt with in this chapter, and that will come into play again and again throughout this book. What is the relationship between cognition and conscious awareness? How can human knowledge be described and explained? Are cognitive processes really as "modular" or as separate from one another as they seem to be in this example? We'll begin exploring these issues in this chapter.

In this chapter we also consider some of the many origins of cognitive psychology. Its roots are to be found in (among other places) linguistics, computer science, neurology, and human factors research. You may be surprised to find that cognitive psychology has a relatively short history. Although the problems it investigates are ancient, nearly all of its founding figures are still alive.

In addition, we examine in this chapter two approaches to the problems of cognitive psychology: the information-processing approach and the connectionist approach. As we'll see, these approaches differ fundamentally in their assumptions about human cognition, although they don't necessarily differ in their predictions about human cognition. The chapter concludes with a description of some research methods and techniques that cognitive psychologists use.

*I*ntroduction to Cognitive Psychology

You're already doing them—engaging in a number of distinct cognitive processes, that is. In fact, to be human is to engage in these processes. Anytime we read something in order to understand it, anytime we try to remember where we've left something, anytime we solve a word problem in algebra, we're using our cognitive processes. But the list doesn't stop there: Even when we're not conscious of using those processes, they are still operating. Paying attention to a lecture is an example. You may not be conscious of the cognition required to pay attention; you just do it. But paying attention to something is a complicated bit of cognitive business, no matter how easy or effortless it seems to us. In fact, all the rest of the words in this book (130,000 or so) are really just meant to explain that complexity. In a way, I'm aware that the rest of the book is just an elaboration of the points that I make in this paragraph.

Neisser's Definition of Cognition

In 1967, Ulric Neisser published the now-classic textbook *Cognitive Psychology*, in which he offers this definition: "Cognitive psychology refers to all processes by which the sensory input is transformed, reduced, elaborated, stored, recovered, and used." Let's explore the definition's terms. Neisser has cognition beginning with sensory input. Our cognitive processes are always *about* something; our senses bring energy from the physical world outside our bodies into our neural and cognitive systems, where it will be further worked on. This is what Neisser means when he asserts that the sensory input must be transformed. Physical energy from the world must be converted into a pattern of neural events—a kind of neural energy—that can be used as the basis for all subsequent cognitive processing. Once the physical energy in the sensory stimulus has been transformed into a pattern of neural events, then any physical stimulus that has not been transformed may be lost for good. This is the transformation that takes place when our cognitive system reduces sensory input.

This reduction in sensory input means that neural and cognitive processes may not preserve every aspect of the sensory world, in which we are constantly bathed with potential stimuli. The reduction isn't necessarily bad, because most of the energy in the physical world is not necessarily informative and doesn't need to be transformed in the first place. For example, without looking back, what was the first word in the first sentence in the Overview? Take a guess, and then look back. Did you get the correct answer? If you did, great; if not, I'm not too surprised. When you read that sentence, at some level you knew it was unlikely that any specific word would be important to remember. It's true that for a brief period, right after reading the sentence, you could have told me the first word. But very soon this information was no longer present, and you could no longer recover it. Would you say you "forgot" this information—specifically, the first word in the Overview? *Forgetting* is a word that covers a number of processes. My preference would be to say that your cognitive system reduced this information. As you continued to read the Overview, and to try to make sense of it, your cognitive system subjected each sentence to a number of analyses. These analyses resulted in creating a representation of the Overview, just as they are now creating a representation of this paragraph, and ultimately of the entire chapter and book. (But don't worry, you don't have to create a representation of the whole book today—we won't have the whole book's representation until the end of the term.) As you continued to work your way through the Overview, that representation changed and evolved as you continued to try to determine the Overview's main points. I think of the information about specific wording as something like notes that you jot down on the spur of the moment to organize your thoughts. You probably will make more extensive and refined notes later, and you probably will discard the spontaneously created notes. For a time, the notes are a good representation of your thoughts, but as your thoughts change, the notes change, too.

Elaboration is the other side of the reduction coin. Whereas reduction means discarding information, elaboration means connecting information. When we elaborate a representation, we take that specific representation and relate it to more specific or general representations. The result is that, unlike reduction, which eliminates some aspects of a representation from further processing, elaboration may add *more* information to the current representation. For example, each movie in the *Star Wars* series begins with a screen that announces: "A long time ago, in a galaxy far, far, away . . . ."

When he saw Episode IV ("A New Hope") for the first time, my younger son, then seven years old, was confused by this message. "But the movie was in the future," he said, "why did they say it happened a long time ago?" Maybe others found this message odd too. I had a somewhat different interpretation of the initial message. What does it remind you of? To me, the initial screen immediately suggests a kind of "fairy tale" or fable. That is, in many or most of these children's stories, the initial sentence begins, "A long time ago, there lived a man who . . . ." Almost every one of these stories is an entertaining adventure at one level. At another level, however, these stories are almost always teaching devices. That is, they have a point or moral. Moreover, the point is about human behavior and the appropriate or correct way to treat others in our dealings with them, or about correctible failings within ourselves. So it is with the *Star Wars* series. That is (as it turns out at the end), it is a fable, and it has a point. Notice that nowhere is any of this description stated directly. Rather, my use of my cognitive system enabled me to elaborate this line of reasoning from the cue given initially, and thus I added all this information to the movie as it unfolded. That my son was apparently unable to appreciate this point, though he has heard plenty of fables in his life, suggests that this cognitive process may have a developmental aspect. It is probable that children elaborate information too, but the elaboration is bound to differ from that done by adults.

A question now arises about the function of elaboration: Why go to all the trouble of elaborating this information? The function of elaboration by our cognitive system is to establish a context for the representation in question. This context includes any other representations, permanent or temporary, which are used to identify or interpret the incoming representation. For example, going back to the *Star Wars* example, I used my knowledge of fables to help me interpret the movie, and to understand what the movie was about. As we'll see throughout this book, a representation's elaboration has a lot do with what eventually is understood and remembered. For a brief practical application of this theory, I suggest that you be mindful of two things. First, greater elaboration probably leads to deeper understanding of material than does no elaboration. When learning, then, always ask yourself questions about the relationship between the incoming representation and other knowledge that you already have ("What is this like? What does it remind me of?"). Second, the context that you elaborate probably has some consequences for later learning and retrieval. Some contexts may facilitate later learning and retrieval, and others may not. Be careful of the context that you generate. I like to tell students that they should try to be mindful that the context they establish at learning time will help only to the extent they can reestablish that context at test time. A context that is hard to reestablish at test time may not be as helpful as one that is somewhat easier to reestablish at that time.

In the next words in the definition, Neisser addresses the cognitive system's ability to store and recover information. We usually think of these cognitive processes as corresponding to our "memory." It certainly seems that we can hang on for long periods to some of the representations that we create, and we can certainly recover many of them with ease. When we get to the chapters on memory, however, we'll see other ways to think about memory than simply storing a representation. Perhaps the most important word in Neisser's definition of cognitive psychology is the last. Cognition creates representations that are *used* by people. Here, we see that to Neisser and modern cognitive psychologists, cognition has a functional value: it enables people to accomplish some things that would be difficult to accomplish, to put it mildly, without it.

Levels of Analysis: The Mental, the Neural, the Cognitive

Neisser's definition is focused on cognition as a set of processes that produces a set of events. When you elaborate a representation, you may pay attention to the incoming information in order to classify it, and you may use your memory to store it. Thus the representation is the initial object of attentional processes, and so it becomes a kind of attentional event; then it was classified, and the representation now becomes a thing that has been categorized, and so on. What kind of events are these cognitive representations? This is a good question, and the answer will require some time and thought on your part.

To begin, I'd like you to consider that part of yourself you call your mind. Some synonyms will do just as well for this demonstration: You can think of your mind as your consciousness, or your awareness. Let's engage in a little mental exercise: I'd like you to think now of the house or other dwelling in which you spent most of your childhood. When you are ready, I'd like you to answer a simple question: How many windows did this house have in front? Do you know the answer to this question? Most people can answer with surprising ease and speed, which is remarkable when you think about it. How did you go about answering the question about the windows? If you are like most people you produced, at my request, a mental image of this house. This image corresponds to something like a mental picture. That is, in your mind's eye, you may have been aware that a view of the house was suddenly arrayed before you. In addition, this array has some surprising properties, which correspond to an actual picture. To answer the question, most of my students tell me, and I think they are telling me the truth, that they were able to "scan" their mental images, and while scanning, count the windows in the front of the house. We refer to this image, and its properties, as existing at a mental level of analysis. At this mental level you can deliberately engage in some operations on the content of your mind, and this is what you were doing when you were scanning and counting the windows. The image may have other properties, too: Can you tell me the color of the house? How far from the street the house sat? I'm sure these and other properties are available to you.

You know, however, that there really is no picture inside your head, or anywhere else: The image is *like* a picture, but it is not one. What then is the image and what accounts for its presence? Well, to begin to answer that question we need to talk about the activity of your central nervous system, your brain. That is, if we were to, without warning, deprive you completely of your brain, we would also deprive you (we believe) of the ability to produce and sustain such images, along with depriving you of just about every other psychologically interesting characteristic. This statement doesn't answer the question about what exactly the image is, but it gets us started: The image is an experience of particular types, or particular patterns, or maybe particular places, of neural activity. Let's put it in other words: When we say that your image is an experience of particular kinds of neural activity, we're suggesting that your brain is capable of producing some neural events that are "constructable." Such neural events may not "feel" like neural events, but that is what they are. From this perspective, your mind is not like some corporate executive high up in an office building making decisions and giving orders. Rather, from the standpoint that we are describing here, the existence of your (human) mind is nature's way of telling you that your human brain is operational. The image of your house that is in your mind is not something that is different from the neural events that comprise it. Instead, the image is just and only just those neural events, but considered from a mental rather than a neural perspective.

Could we find the image, this set of neural events, if we went looking into the image-holder's brain? Well, it might not be that easy, and we'll get into some of the conceptual problems with this tactic a little later in this chapter. But for now, let's analyze the language with which some neuroscientist in the future might describe the image, assuming that its neural basis, or substrate, could be identified. The first and most important point to realize is that if the image could be identified at the neural level, its description would be in neural terms. That is, the neuroscientist would talk about the image in terms of the number of specific neurons, their locations, their pattern of firing, their interconnections, the transmitter substances present, and so on. Do you see what we've done here? We've taken one event (the image) and discussed it at two levels: first at an "experiential" level, which you call your mind, and second at a concrete or physical level, which you call your brain. When we talk about the image at the experiential level, we use terms that are appropriate for that level, mental terms that describe properties of our awareness. But when we talk about the image at the neural level, we use terms that are appropriate there, which describe neural processes and events. Both levels are real, and, as descriptions, exist independently even when their contents are about the "same thing."

If you look back at the heading for this section you'll see that it refers to a mental, a neural, and a cognitive level. We've discussed the mental and neural levels. To see where the cognitive level fits in, let's think about the house image once more. How long did you live in the house that you imagined? If it was several years or more, then we have an interesting phenomenon to deal with. When people photograph something, they usually raise the camera to their eye to look through the viewfinder, and the resulting photograph shows the effects of the person's height; that is, the camera angle changes as a function of the photographer's height. Thus, two photographs taken in the same place by people of different heights will look somewhat different. If you lived in one house for even a few years, then your height inevitably changed, maybe by a lot.

What I'm about to propose is not doable at this time, but if we could somehow convert your neural events into some kind of electronic code and read it, we might be able to make your image visible on a computer screen. And if we could make your image visible to others, then it too would presumably have a camera angle, as a real photograph does. But if you lived in one house long enough, what would this camera angle be? You might have a number of images from which to choose. At your mental level of analysis, you were not aware of making any decision about how your image would look. But a part of you apparently did make that decision, even though you were not aware of it. And making the camera-angle decision was not the only one that was made in depicting the image.

When you retrieved or constructed your image, were you aware of the time of year that was depicted in the image (were the leaves on the trees, or was snow on the ground)? As you can see, even though you were not aware of it, these decisions had to be made at some level. Therefore, some part of "you" or some part of your system (and it doesn't seem to be part of your mind) had to engage in several discrete activities. It had to first "find" any or all of the stored representations of your house, then it had to "decide" on the characteristics of the image that would be depicted, and finally it had to "construct" an image that was the one of which you became aware. It's true that these activities were taking place at the neural level. Thus some specific neural events may be the ones responsible for the finding, the deciding, and the constructing of the image, and we could describe these activities as neural if we so wished. We could also describe these neural events in an abstract way, however, just as we've done here.

That is, when we talk about some part of you "finding" the images, "deciding" which characteristics to incorporate in the image, and "constructing" or making the image appear, we are not using neural terms to describe these activities, and we're not using mental terms, either (because you weren't aware of any of these things). We are, though, using abstract language, and by that I mean words that are not tied to any one type of neural operation, to describe those neural processes. When we use abstract terms to describe such neural processes, we are offering a description at the cognitive level of analysis, and the part of you that engaged in such processes was your cognitive system.

Briefly restated: The cognitive level of analysis is an abstract specification of the events taking place at the neural level. Just as the neural and mental levels of analysis are real, the cognitive level is real. Anytime we use abstract labels that are not tied to any one neural event, labels that include words like "deciding," "attending," "storing," "retrieving," and a host of others, we are describing the activities of the neural system; that is, your brain, although we are not using neural labels explicitly.

Figure 1.1 is an attempt to depict the relationship among the mental, neural, and cognitive levels of analysis.

Figure 1.1 A representation of three levels of analysis.

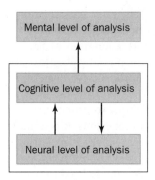

As Figure 1.1 shows, neural information can be described abstractly, and when we do so we are speaking of a cognitive analysis. Moreover, it also shows that cognitive events (like mental events) are always based on underlying neural events. That is why the cognitive events are shown in the same box as the neural events, and also why all the arrows coming up from the neural events project completely into the cognitive level. From this perspective, then, there are no "wasted" or pointless neural events; all, or just about all, neural events are cognitive events.

Not all cognitive events, however, are mental events, explaining why the mental level is enclosed in a box by itself, and why not all the cognitive arrows project into the mental box. Certainly we are sometimes aware of our cognitive processes. Any time we are conscious of searching our memories to remember something or trying to solve a difficult calculus problem, we are conscious of our cognition. But at numerous other times we do not become conscious or aware of our cognitive processes. Then we can talk about events at the cognitive level of analysis that have no correspondence with anything in our minds. In other words, the diagram raises the possibility of cognition without awareness or mentality.

Some of these effects were seen in a study by Bonebakker et al. (1996). The subjects were patients who were about to undergo surgery under a general anesthetic. The subjects heard several lists of words that were presented both preoperatively and intraoperatively (that is, during the surgery, when the subjects presumably had no awareness). Following the operation, the subjects were given a word-completion task in which they were given the first two or three letters of a word that was presented under anesthesia. They were asked to complete this stem with the first word that came to mind, excluding a preoperatively presented distractor. The subjects were significantly more likely to complete the word stem with the letters of a word presented during the operation than they were to complete it with the letters from a distractor word. The subjects had no conscious recollection of the operation, or of hearing the word lists (although they knew the lists would be played while they were under the anesthetic). Moreover, the subjects were not very confident about their answers. Although no trace of the memory appeared at the mental level of analysis, this finding suggests that, at the neural and cognitive level of analysis, the person's cognitive and neural systems continued to transform incoming sensory stimulation, as described in Neisser's definition. The Bonebakker et al. study dramatically demonstrates this effect because it shows that even when people temporarily have no mind at all (that is, we hope and presume that general anesthetic disables any consciousness), they still have cognition.

This discussion of levels of analysis implies that many phenomena can be analyzed or addressed at all three levels. To understand this, let's look at a specific phenomenon, that of attention. At a mental level, you can describe the consciousness experience you have when you are paying attention to something, versus when you are not paying attention. First, if you haven't been paying attention, you can tell because you are aware that your mind has not been focused on the stimulus. Second, when you do pay attention, you have the experience, or feeling, that you are picking up more information about the source of stimulation than when you are not paying attention. At a neural level we may be able to talk about specific patterns in brain activity that are characteristically observed when a person is paying attention. For example, a positive pattern of brain activity may occur within 300 milliseconds (msec) after an unusual or unexpected stimulus is presented. This pattern, called P300, is sometimes interpreted as a "novelty response" by the brain, and it shows that somehow the brain is "tracking" incoming sensory stimulation. Thus, when an unexpected stimulus is observed, the brain responds in a characteristic way. At a cognitive level; that is, at an abstract level, how can we describe these phenomena? As we'll see in Chapter 2, cognitive psychologists have wondered about the number of separate stimuli that can be tracked by the system, the length of time that such stimuli can be tracked, and the amount of knowledge about the stimuli that humans acquire by such tracking. The result of such study by cognitive psychologists might be a theory postulating that paying attention in general is something like spending money for things. That is, just as you can spend a little money on a lot of things, or a lot of money for a few things, so too you can pay a little attention to a lot of stimuli, or a lot of attention to just a few stimuli. Of course this is not actually what is going on at the neural level (and here it's fun to imagine what a neuron could say if a neuron could talk: "We don't have any money down here, bub. We just fire or we don't fire, get it?"). Rather, realize that a cognitive psychologist is striving to specify the outcome of these neural events at a higher and more general level of analysis.

Kinds of Knowledge and Types of Processing

Although the term *knowledge* encompasses a vast territory, we can get some idea about the lay of the land by looking at a few examples of knowledge in use. Consider the knowledge that Tamara has about her computer. She knows that, as she types, each keystroke contributes to a pattern of electrons called a *file*, and she knows that this file can be stored in various ways, such as on the computer's hard drive. This knowledge can be useful in operating the computer, as in recovering the file and editing it. But Tamara probably doesn't know how to fix her hard drive if it crashes. In contrast with her knowledge about computers, consider Tamara's knowledge about bicycle riding. She knows how to ride her own mountain bike, and she thinks she could also ride just about any other mountain bike. Tamara is certain that she would retain this knowledge even if several years elapsed without her riding a bicycle. Although she has knowledge about how to ride a bicycle, she can't explain what she does to keep her balance, how she makes a turn without falling over, and so on. About the computer, Tamara has some knowledge that she can describe verbally, but she has little practical knowledge. About the bicycle, the situation is reversed. Tamara rides the bicycle well, but she can't describe what she does very thoroughly.

Cognitive psychologists use two terms to describe these two seemingly different kinds of knowledge: **declarative knowledge** and **procedural knowledge.** Declarative knowledge refers to factual information that is somewhat static (i.e., unchanging), the organization of which is often apparent to us, and which is usually describable. Let's take these items one at a time. Declarative knowledge often takes the form of a series of related facts. For example, the description of Tamara's computer knowledge listed a series of facts that are agreed upon by others who are familiar with computers. Even when our declarative knowledge is wrong, it's still expressible in this factual format, as would be true for someone who said, for example, that *Apollo 11* was the first Apollo spacecraft to land on the moon. In this definition, static means stationary or unchanging. I know that Abraham Lincoln was the sixteenth president of the United States. The chance is excellent that I'll retain this knowledge to the end of my life, and I can't think of anything that would improve my grasp of this fact. We can control the organization of declarative knowledge in a very real sense. To see how, suppose I were to ask you to develop a system that we might use to categorize sports. How would you go about it?

You might start by dividing all sporting activities into two categories: those which involve a ball and those which don't. Then, you might proceed to further divide each of those categories into team versus individual sports.

In contrast with declarative knowledge, procedural knowledge refers to the knowledge underlying skillful actions, and it tends to be dynamic (i.e., changing). The organization of procedural knowledge is not very clear to us, nor is procedural knowledge usually very describable. It is more easily *shown* to someone than it is *told*. Using the bicycle example again, biking is an action that is best understood as a skill. When Tamara was six, she acquired this skill by falling off her bike numerous times. Acquiring a skill often seems to involve making and detecting errors. Unlike my knowledge about Lincoln's presidency, Tamara's skill in bicycle riding continues to improve, as does her typing ability and her tennis serve. If Tamara were to stop doing any of these things for an extended period, her knowledge of how to do them would apparently decline. The knowledge probably wouldn't disappear altogether, but nevertheless, procedural knowledge is dynamic in the sense that, with additional experience, we continue to improve; without it, the knowledge begins to decline.

The distinction between these two kinds of knowledge might best be summed up in the phrases "knowing how" and "knowing that." "Knowing how" refers to nonverbal knowledge of procedures that a person engages in to accomplish some objective. Whenever we hit a backhand, ride our bicycles, or make pancakes, we're using procedural knowledge to achieve some objective. "Knowing that" refers to knowledge that can be described more or less completely in a series of declarative sentences. When we describe how to program a computer or explain the workings of a camera, we're expressing declarative knowledge.

Cognitive psychologists have wondered about the relationship between declarative and procedural knowledge. Many—perhaps most—of our daily activities involve both kinds of knowledge. Nevertheless, a question that a cognitive psychologist might entertain concerns the cognitive codes in which procedural and declarative knowledge are represented: Are these codes fundamentally different from each other? If they are, then how does the brain know (in advance) what sorts of knowledge it will represent as a procedural-knowledge code and what sorts as a declarative-knowledge code? We'll try to answer that question later in the book.

The procedural–declarative distinction isn't the only one we can apply to our knowledge. Let's consider the generality of our knowledge. Even though you and I have actually shared only the sentences that you've read in this book, nevertheless there are many bits of knowledge that both you and I have in common and that we can retrieve effortlessly. For example, we both know the alphabet; we know that "thirty days has September"; and we both know that a home run scores at least one run in baseball. But you know many things that I don't, and I know and can retrieve easily many things that you couldn't possibly know (such as how many miles I have on my car, or how many pairs of maroon socks I own). Cognitive psychologists refer to the general knowledge about the properties of words and concepts that is shared by many as **semantic knowledge** or semantic memory (Tulving, 1972). Knowledge that each individual has that is based on his or her own experience, and thus is linked to a specific time or place, is referred to as **episodic knowledge,** or episodic memory.

Like the procedural–declarative distinction we looked at earlier, this division of knowledge raises interesting questions. One issue is the possibility of converting episodic to semantic memory. How many specific experiences are required to convert some portion of our episodic knowledge to semantic knowledge? Do you know what a hard-boiled egg tastes like? If the answer is yes, then how many did you have to eat before you could describe their taste? As an alternative possibility, it could be that semantic knowledge is something of an illusion: Maybe we really don't have knowledge "in general" about words or concepts. This would be true if, when I asked you the question about hard-boiled eggs, you retrieved simply the taste of the last hard-boiled egg that you ate.

We've talked about some of the terms that cognitive psychologists might use to describe human knowledge, but cognitive psychologists also use various terms to talk about the varieties of cognitive processing that people can bring to bear on a task. A good way to begin this discussion is to talk about the phenomenon of attention.

A complete discussion of attention is reserved for later, but right now, attention can briefly be defined as the concentration and focusing of mental activity (Matlin, 1983). In the dim light of morning, I must pay attention to the pair of socks that I get out of the drawer, lest I select a pair that doesn't go with the rest of my clothes. Paying attention seems to accentuate, or enhance, the sensory input that has been focused on. Thus, when I pay attention to eating my Black Forest torte, the flavor seems much more intense than it does when I pay attention instead to what my dinner companion is saying.

Attention is such a hallmark of our mental lives that it would be tempting to conclude that allocating attention is necessary to initiate any other cognitive processing. Such a conclusion would be erroneous, however. Evidence from our daily lives, which is supported by experimental findings, suggests that cognitive processes can sometimes be initiated and sustained with little or no selective attention paid to them. Have you ever driven on an interstate highway while daydreaming about the events in your life, only to realize an hour later that you're not sure if you've already passed your exit? During the hour that you spent daydreaming, your cognitive processes continued to work because you made an untold number of decisions about passing other cars, maintaining speed, and so on. Yet these decisions did not seem to require any conscious effort.

Effortful cognitive processes that seem to require attention to initiate and sustain them are referred to as **controlled processes.** Processes that seem to be initiated and run without conscious allocation of attention are referred to as **automatic processes.** Like the procedural–declarative knowledge distinction we have already examined, the automatic–controlled distinction allows cognitive psychologists to describe the type of cognitive processing that is taking place.

One form of the automatic–controlled distinction applies to the phenomenon of retrieval. **Explicit memory** refers to situations in which a person is aware of using cognitive processes in an effort to retrieve something, or is otherwise conscious of being reminded. Such use of memory can be thought of as a controlled memory process. But numerous other situations show that our cognitive and neural systems sometimes retrieve things even though we are not aware of using our memories (Roediger, 1990). This phenomenon is referred to as **implicit memory,** and such memories seem much like automatic memory processing.

For example, subjects who are given a list of common words such as "table" may be asked to recall them after a specified interval. At retrieval time, the subjects "try" to remember the words, and this is a straightforward example of explicit memory. As you might expect, subjects in such situations usually recall some but not all of the words that were presented. Here's what happens next. The subjects leave the laboratory, but instead of going home, they go into another laboratory where they are given a "word-guessing game" that asks them to fill in the letters in a partially blanked-out word (such as _a b_e). Some of the words in the game are from the first list of words that the subjects were asked to recall; some are new words. Surprisingly, we find that the subjects are more likely to succeed on the partially blanked-out items from the first list than they are on new items. Also, the subjects in such situations frequently fill in the blanks successfully on items that they could not explicitly recall a short time earlier. Notice that the second task is not treated by the subjects as a "memory task"; very seldom does the subject become aware that some of the elements were presented before. Rather, we see here that the subject's memory is showing the effects of its prior exposure to a set of words, even though the person is not explicitly trying to recall those words.

The topics that a cognitive psychologist may investigate are discussed in the next section. In the meantime, let's summarize what has been discussed so far. Cognitive psychologists study questions about the representation of human knowledge and its use as seen in human action. They have devised terminology to describe both the knowledge used (that is, whether it is declarative or procedural, episodic or semantic) and the processing used (controlled and explicit processing, or automatic and implicit processing).

Topics in Cognitive Psychology

You may have gotten the impression that cognitive psychologists study anything they please, because practically every human activity requires some sort of knowledge. Technically, you would be right. In practice, however, cognitive psychologists are more likely to investigate specific sorts of mental events rather than others. Complete agreement will never be reached about which specific mental events should be studied, but at least some consensus exists about subject matters that are truly cognitive. This section provides an annotated list of some cognitive topics, along with the questions that cognitive psychologists may ask about those topics. Neither the list of topics nor the questions associated with them should be regarded as complete, but both are typical.

1. **Attention.**   We've already looked briefly at the phenomenon of mental focusing. The issue of attention is loaded with practical significance. You've no doubt heard people say that a person can pay attention to only one thing at a time. Yet various situations commonly demand that we attend to more than one thing simultaneously. For example, in class, I expect my students to listen to me. At the same time, I expect them to take accurate notes. If the "one thing at a time" theory is correct, I'm doing my students a disservice that compromises their ability to learn the material. On the other hand, maybe the students are so practiced that these two tasks—listening and writing—no longer require attention. The cognitive psychologist is often interested in the attentional demands that a task makes on a person. If a task is sufficiently demanding, do we pay attention to that task alone, or can we always divide our attention among various tasks?

2. **Pattern recognition.**   Survival often depends upon our ability to correctly interpret ambiguous sensory input. While driving home in the fog, we have to pay attention to the road so that we can correctly categorize, and evade, anything that suddenly looms out. This process of making sense out of sensory input goes on, however, even when the situation is not life threatening. For example, while writing this book I made numerous typing errors. In my case, detecting typing errors involves looking at my computer's screen and determining whether the patterns of pixels (points of light) are the appropriate ones. In other words, I have to determine, from the sensory input, whether the pixels have been organized in the right way.

3. **Memory.**   We observe regularities in our own behavior as a function of the experiences that we have had. This simple fact implies that we (and others in whom we observe similar regularities) must possess a means for keeping copies of those experiences; otherwise, our experiences would be of no benefit to us. Many questions about memory fascinate cognitive psychologists, and so the list of questions here is by no means complete. Cognitive psychologists are interested in how knowledge is organized in memory. How does the memory of our personal experiences fit in with what we have learned about the world in general? Are procedural and declarative knowledge organized similarly in our memories? What has happened to forgotten memories? Are they still present somewhere in our minds, or have they truly been lost?

4. **Organization of knowledge.**   Related to questions of memory storage are questions about the *form* of the stored material. If we maintain that this stored material is knowledge, then the question we are asking comes down to describing the form of knowledge. Going back to a distinction we made earlier, psychologists have been interested in describing the forms of both procedural and declarative knowledge. Cognitivists do not now have much

in the way of clear ideas about how procedural knowledge is stored, or even how to write a formal theory showing how it *could* be stored. But the situation is a lot different for declarative knowledge. Here, cognitive scientists have developed several theoretical perspectives using both the information-processing and connectionist approaches.

5. **Language.**   As we shall see, the phenomenon of language has been subjected to intense scrutiny by cognitive psychologists. There are many obvious issues to be studied here, including the role of experience in acquiring language, how normal and abnormal language develop, and so on. Apart from these developmental issues, there are many unresolved controversies about the very nature of language. We have a great deal of linguistic knowledge, and some of this knowledge (e.g., knowledge about pronunciation, knowledge about word order) seems to be expressible in the form of rules. Does this mean that the linguistically competent adult possesses a set of rules that governs pronunciation and word order? Some linguists have argued that it does. Some have claimed too that the organization of such rules is itself subject to inherent limitations in our mental capabilities. According to such a view, therefore, discovering the rules of language is equivalent to discovering the rules of thought itself. It's interesting to imagine what might be going on if it turns out that our cognitive systems do not follow linguistic rules. For example, it's just possible that, although our linguistic knowledge may be *described* as following a system of rules, our language use may not actually be *governed* by those rules, or by any other set of formal rules. This distinction, that of rule-describable versus rule-governed actions, pervades much of cognitive psychology. We'll explore its implications in several chapters.

6. **Reasoning.**   You may have taken a course in logic only to find that the principles of correct reasoning often were not intuitively obvious, and that some were downright confusing. To the extent that your experience is a common one, what does this say about naturally occurring human reasoning? Are people inherently illogical? This state of affairs would be unsatisfying, and such a proposition seems illogical itself. If it couldn't put two and two together, what would be the good in having a great cognitive system capable of accurate pattern recognition, vivid imagery, and amazingly complex verbal reports? Our experience with logic tells us that people are not necessarily intuitively logical, but our experience in the real world tells us that people are not inaccurate reasoners, either. This evidence suggests that people are perhaps using some other (nonlogical) system of reasoning that produces the correct outcome frequently enough to be useful in the real world. This possibility leads to a question: If naturally occurring human reasoning is illogical, then what is its nature?

7. **Problem solving.**   You solve problems, most of them small ones, all day long. Every time you recognize that some deficiency in the current situation needs to be remedied, you begin to engage in problem solving. Usually the first step is to define a goal that would remedy the current situation. Are you

hungry right now? Food would be the goal if you were. As soon as the goal is established, you use your cognitive system to plan steps that will accomplish the goal (What do you feel like eating? Where can you get that food? How will you get there? How long will it take? How much money will be required?). Answering these questions will result in a plan, or series of steps that will take you to your goal (you believe), and thus solve your problem. In numerous situations we recognize a goal that we would like to attain, and so we begin to plan steps to take us there. Cognitive psychologists are very interested in these processes for planning and executing plans. For example, where do plans come from? That is, when I'm faced with a problem, how do I use information from my memory, and other knowledge, to formulate a goal? We see variations too among people in problem solving. How is it that some people are able to plan effectively; that is, to come up with a series of steps, which if executed will attain the goal, but others plan poorly or not at all?

8. **Classification, concepts, and categorization.**   Our conceptual knowledge, whether about concrete things such as computers, cars, or stereos, or about abstract entities such as truth, seems fundamental to us. When I tell you that it's cold today, and so I'll have to put on my coat before leaving for home, I can be sure that, if you were to see the garment I'm looking at right now, you too would identify it as an example of a "coat." Without the ability to organize incoming information into such "slots" we would probably be at a total loss to use any other cognitive process. Yet numerous questions are raised by our ability to classify objects. Were you born with the bases for all the concepts that you have, or did you develop those concepts as a result of your experience? If the former, it suggests some limitations on both the number and possibly the nature of the concepts that you could form. If the latter, then we would like to know more about the role of specific experiences in producing such general knowledge.

Mental events can be viewed in many other ways, too. For example, one could look at the roles that others play in the formation of one's own mind. Similarly, an investigator could study dreams and other phenomena that seem to have a strong mental component. Cognitive psychologists usually don't, however, take social factors into account in their study of cognition, nor do they usually study dreams. Further, cognitive psychologists have tended to deemphasize individual differences in mental events. Of all the variables that might be considered cognitive, cognitive psychologists usually consider only a small part. This realization raises a question: What factors were responsible for molding the field into its present shape? Answering this question requires delving into psychology's history.

Roots of Cognitive Psychology

Speculation about the nature of mental events has been active for at least 2000 years, but not until the formal beginnings of academic psychology in the past century were such investigations treated from an empirical standpoint. When Wilhelm

Wundt (1832–1920) founded a psychological laboratory in Leipzig in 1879, he was determined to carry out a program of research designed to establish psychology as a natural science (Hilgard, 1987). Although Wundt referred to his theoretical position as voluntarism, in the United States his theoretical orientation became known as **structuralism.**

Describing mental events as having structure implies that mentality or awareness can be viewed as a set of organized elements, and Wundt adhered to this position. According to Wundt, the mind was an active agent involved in combining or, more accurately, synthesizing basic mental elements. Wundt had fond hopes for the "new science" of psychology: He hoped to show that basic mental processes could be observed and recorded.

Accordingly, Wundt trained his human subjects in an exacting technique known as *introspection,* which literally means "looking into." The introspectionist was supposed to look into his or her own mind. In practice, the introspectionist was to report orally the first associations that entered his or her awareness when a stimulus word or image was presented. Ideally, these reports were to be expressed in words that were as close as possible to the raw sensory input. Wundt hoped that, by analyzing the subjects' reports, the laws of mental operation could be discovered.

What happened? When asked to introspect about the idea *dog,* Wundt's subjects reported generalized doglike images, often accompanied by kinesthetic sensations such as the feel of holding a dog on a leash, running away from a ferocious dog, or even being bitten by a dog. From a series of such reports, Wundt became convinced that the technique of introspection could be used, if liberally supported by more "behavioral" measures, as a sort of window on the active, synthetic mental processes that underlie all other mental activity. Keep in mind that the stimuli used in Wundt's experiments tended to be fairly "simple" ones that usually produced only a brief and fleeting experience. Second, recognize that the introspective technique invariably produced imagery.

One aspect of Wundt's work that was to have fateful implications for cognitive psychology was his decision to divide the subject matter of psychology into two classes. Wundt believed that the development of mental life was so deeply influenced by culture and language that "higher" mental processes, such as thinking, which depend upon language and culture, could not be studied successfully using the fairly limited observational techniques of the laboratory (Leahey, 1987). Accordingly, Wundt did not investigate what we might call "thought processes" in the lab. Rather, he believed that the higher mental processes could best be studied by observing the mental products of an entire culture or society, as such a society had developed. For this purpose, Wundt argued that a historical or anthropological viewpoint, rather than the experimental approach, would be called for. For Wundt, then, the study of thinking processes per se was included in the study of what he referred to as *Volkerpsychologie* ("folk psychology"). Wundt undertook such an enterprise toward the end of his career (Wundt, 1900–1920).

Although Wundt's influence on the new science of psychology was considered strong, a group of researchers in the university town of Würzburg soon began to chafe under the constraints imposed by the Leipzig school. The Würzburgers, led by Oswald Kulpe, began to apply the experimental technique to the problem of thought. Consider this "problem" and introspectionist report:

Poem. In what larger category does it belong?

Once again, immediately a full understanding of the [question]. Then again an intensive glance, the symbolic fixation of that which is sought: then at once, the flitting memory of art, poetry, and so on appeared. The word *art,* I think, in auditory-motor terms. Then the thought that I cannot subsume poetry under art but only under artistic production. With this, I am certain, no words and images: then I said, "work of art." (Humphrey, 1963, p. 137)

Although the style of the report and its terminology are somewhat old-fashioned, the introspectionist seems to be using controlled processes ("an intensive glance") to describe knowledge that many of us would regard as procedural rather than declarative. That is, most of us would have a hard time telling somebody what exactly had been going on in our minds when we categorized a stimulus. Regarding Wundt's structural position, the important implication of this report is that its author is certain that no images were involved in its production. From reports such as this one, Kulpe and his circle went on to develop the doctrine of *imageless thought.* This position refers to the idea that some mental events could not be classified according to any accompanying sensory content. The issue of the underlying form of thought is still very much with us, as we shall see in the chapters on memory.

From this brief description of Wundt's work, and the response it drew, it's hard to see how such reports could form the basis for modern cognitive psychology. Yet, although Wundt focused on some topics and ignored others, much work by contemporary cognitive psychologists is clearly related to his ideas. For example, Wundt realized that attention was an important component in cognition. He also recognized that mental events could be described as concepts that were formed through experience. Studies in concept formation have been one of the foundations of modern cognitive psychology. Wundt's notion that mental events were related to one another also foreshadowed modern work in an area known as *semantic memory.* In retrospect, it seems clear that the experimental psychology developed by Wundt and challenged by the Würzburgers had a number of commonalities with contemporary cognitive psychology.

The train of thought that Wundt initiated jumped the track in this country, however. American psychologists were dismayed that Wundt's methods produced findings that were neither reproducible nor observable—two characteristics that seemed necessary for any science of psychology. American psychologists soon turned to behaviorism as their principal theory. For the first fifty to sixty years in this century, many—perhaps most—American psychologists strongly believed that this theory was essentially the only correct approach to erecting a science of behavior. Renewed interest in mental events began to take place in the United States around 1960. In the next sections we describe some of the events that led American psychologists to question their behavioristic beliefs.

Human Factors Research During World War II

The field of **human factors research** deals with the problems in human–machine interactions, particularly with regard to improving human skills and performance. This field formed during World War II, when it became clear that the advanced technology then being developed required improvements in the layout and design of instrumentation. Nowhere was the problem of human use of instrumentation more critical than in aviation.

Broadbent's Studies   In his work at the Applied Psychology Research Unit, Donald Broadbent found that human workers were guided by the information, or "feedback," as it was called, given to them by machines. For pilots, Broadbent observed that not all the information being displayed was used by the pilot to fly the aircraft. Rather, some instruments were monitored more diligently than others. Broadbent also found that oftentimes too much information was displayed; the pilots were unable to attend to all of it at once. Instead, the pilots had to focus on successive gauges—a procedure that required a substantial amount of time.

Broadbent's work has several implications. First, he countered the idea that humans wait passively for stimuli to impinge upon them. Rather, he found, the pilots and other technical personnel actively sought out information, a finding that was somewhat troublesome for the then-popular behaviorist theories. Second, human information processing seemed quite similar to the *servomechanisms* (automatic devices) controlling the complex machines. That is, as each servomechanism responds to a particular kind of information and in a particular way, so too can the human information-processing system be thought of as a collection of such mechanisms. For the individual human operator, one key problem then became allocating attention to direct the information processing of such mental servomechanisms. The title of one of Broadbent's postwar papers, "A Mechanical Model for Human Attention and Immediate Memory" (1954), indicates how far this new approach to human performance could be taken.

Computing Machinery

In discussing Broadbent's studies, we alluded to the concept of **information.** Broadbent's interest in this term was typical given the spirit of the times. Shortly before World War II, several thinkers—notably Shannon—attempted to define the concept of information mathematically. Shannon reasoned that the function of information was to reduce the uncertainty in particular future events. Specifically, if we imagine future possible events as occupying a range, or space, and then find out that this range has been constrained by exactly half (that is, half the future events are no longer possible), then our uncertainty about these future events has been reduced. We know that half of them cannot take place, and so we have to worry only about the remaining half. How much information have we received? Shannon defined a bit of information as the amount needed to reduce the number of possible outcomes by exactly half. Let's consider an illustration. Suppose Maria tells Bill that she's thinking of a specific square on a chessboard, and Bill's task is to determine which square Maria has in mind. To determine which square Maria is thinking of, Bill is allowed to ask her questions about the chessboard that can be answered with a yes or a no. Further suppose that Bill is trying to figure out the correct square with a minimum of questions. How would he proceed? A chessboard has sixty-four squares, and so to get one bit of information, Bill needs to ask a question that eliminates thirty-two squares from further consideration. One way for him to do so is to ask if the square is in the top half of the board. If Maria said yes, Bill would restrict his search to the top half of the board. If she said no, Bill would know that the square was in the bottom half of the board, and he would begin to search there. Subsequent searches would consist of dividing the appropriate half of the board into halves again, and so on. If Bill did this search efficiently, determining the square Maria had in mind would require that he ask six questions.

As Shannon phrased it, representing a particular square on a chessboard requires six bits of information. Phrased in a slightly different way, a string of six *Y*s or *N*s like this—*YYNYYN*—represents a particular square on a chessboard. Moreover, every square on the chessboard could be represented by some such string. Shortly after World War II, it became clear to a number of thinkers, including John von Neuman, that a machine capable of creating and storing such strings also would be capable of symbolically representing a wide variety of phenomena. With the publication of *Cybernetics* by Wiener in 1948, Shannon's information theory was formally welded with Broadbent's servomechanism theory, and the development of general-purpose computers was just around the corner. Some computing hardware was developed late in the 1930s, although the real power of the digital computer was not exploited until programming languages such as FORTRAN came along early in the 1950s.

Psychologists were fascinated with the digital computer for several reasons. First, computers showed that complex actions could be broken down into a series of yes or no decisions. This capability was important because it indicated that, theoretically, no matter how complex a human's knowledge or information, it could be represented by a code that was simply a **binary code.** When used as an adjective, *binary* refers to information that is expressible in two elements. If a computer could be given correct feedback as it worked its way through each step in a binary code, then a computing machine could (again, theoretically) duplicate the behavior of a person, no matter how complex that behavior. This invention led psychologists to develop models of behavior based on the ideas of feedback and binary operations. One of these systems was developed by Miller, Galanter, and Pribram (1960) in their famous *Plans and the Structure of Behavior.* They conceived of human action as represented by components they called TOTE units. The acronym stands for Test Operate Test Exit.

Figure 1.2 shows the workings of a famous TOTE unit; this one is designed to drive nails. In the first stage, the nail is *tested.* If it sticks up, then the process must *operate* by swinging the hammer down on the nail. After the operate stage, the process must again test the nail. If the nailhead is now flush with the surface, then the process may exit, going on to something else.

The beauty of this system is that TOTE units can be built upon one another hierarchically, with increasingly general TOTE units near the top of the hierarchy. For example, a building contractor might be endowed with an extremely general TOTE unit for house construction, which might consist of several more specific TOTE units for wall construction, each of which might contain a nail-driving TOTE unit like the one just described. Imagining that humans are governed by such TOTE units does not furnish proof that humans *are* made up of them. Nevertheless, *Plans and the Structure of Behavior* was extremely persuasive because it demonstrated that the feedback and mechanism approach to human actions could have tremendous explanatory power—power that was strong enough to challenge the behavioristic account.

Figure 1.2   A TOTE unit. *Source:* From Miller, 1960.

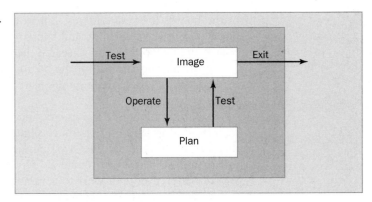

Psychologists became fascinated with computers for another reason, too—one that you may have already guessed. From one perspective, computers could be thought of as nothing more than gigantic collections of vacuum tubes. The computer's power was awesome, but each vacuum tube couldn't do much: It was either on or off. The machine's power was derived from its speed in altering the on-off pattern of the vacuum tubes and from having so many of them. Given what was known about neurology at that time, it seemed reasonable to compare the activity of the vacuum tube with the *action potential,* or firing, of the individual neuron. If the analogy were continued, it seemed clear that the complexity of human action depended on the speed of neural events (the action potential could take place 1000 times per second) and on humans being endowed with billions of such neurons. In retrospect, it's not surprising that early computers were often referred to as "giant electronic brains." This name reflects the fond hope many early computer scientists had that the machines would do more than simply mimic the action of the nervous system; they would duplicate it.

Linguistics

Almost all our utterances have a purpose: to communicate something. For thousands of years, scholars have been interested in both what people say and when they say it. In the past century or so, the study of speaking and listening has become decidedly psychological in tone. That is, many thinkers have realized that speech and hearing acts are closely intertwined and that both acts are influenced by the distinctly psychological process of perception. Language, however, is not always studied from a psychological perspective. Linguistics is the discipline that studies the structure of language. **Psycholinguistics** is the study of language from a psychological rather than a linguistic perspective. Rather than focus on speech and hearing, the linguist attempts to understand the *organization* of language, its regularities that seem more or less universal. Language seems intimately bound to thought. The linguist hopes that, by discovering the organizing principles in language, the laws of thought also will be revealed.

Skinner's Book and Chomsky's Rebuttal   One classic problem in studying language is its acquisition. How do children learn to comprehend speech and produce grammatically correct utterances? The behavioristic perspective in psychology was firmly established by the time B. F. Skinner undertook a behavioristic analysis of language acquisition in 1936. Skinner created a phonograph record consisting of random groupings of sounds. The record had been made by recording natural speech and then editing the utterances so that the placement and ordering of the sounds were no longer typical. Skinner played this record—known as a verbal summator—for his subjects, and he noticed that people read into the sounds, interpreting them as actual words. This phenomenon impressed Skinner. The verbal summator demonstrated that nothing was inherently special about linguistic sounds, and, Skinner argued, that meant language sounds could be studied as examples of operant behavior. Skinner reasoned that the same laws that governed the learning of other operant behaviors should govern the learning of language.

Consider a child who makes a request of a parent, which is followed by the parent's response. A behavioristic theory of language would state that this verbal behavior was learned, because the parent reinforced the child for producing the utterance by complying with it. If a one-year-old holds up his cup and says "More!" the parent is reinforcing the child's utterance by providing him with more apple juice. Skinner called this function of language the **mand function.** Manded utterances are reinforced through compliance. Children must learn when to make the appropriate mands and which mands will be followed by a reward. According to Skinner, the latter problem boiled down to a case of discrimination learning. That is, the child plays a sort of naming game with the parent, during which words gradually become restricted to their appropriate referents. The child may point to a red book and say "Red?" to which the parent may respond affirmatively. If the child then points to a blue book and says "Red?" the parent will respond with a no, and, presumably, the child will learn that the operant *red* does not apply to the shape of the object but rather to some other feature. Proceeding in this way, the child eventually learns which cues must be present before the operant *red* will be rewarded; namely, that *red* refers to the color of an object. The child is in a position similar to that of Skinner's pigeons, which would be reinforced for doing a behavior under some conditions but not under others. For the child as well as for the pigeon, the task consists of discriminating the relevant features that signal when a behavior will be reinforced. Skinner referred to this recognition of the appropriate discriminative cues as the **tact function** of language.

As Skinner understood the problem of language acquisition, children go on tacting and manding their way through the first several years of their lives, gradually improving in emitting linguistic utterances. The publication of these ideas in Skinner's *Verbal Behavior* (1957) was not well received by linguists, however. Noam Chomsky (1959) published a detailed and relentlessly critical review that seemed to devastate Skinner's claims.

First, Chomsky described the problem of creativity in language. Some people have estimated that the number of humans who have ever lived is 40 to 50 billion. This number being so large, you might think that everything you could say has already been uttered by somebody, somewhere, sometime. This assumption is wrong. Constructing a completely novel remark is easy:

Sophomores are limiculous.

Limiculous is an adjective referring to creatures whose habitat is mud. I'm sure that no one has ever applied that adjective to sophomores before. The problem for the behaviorist is explaining what enabled me to construct the remark. Because I've never created that remark before, no reinforcement could have existed for my constructing it. Simply, the mand function of language does not appear powerful enough to explain novel remarks.

Chomsky also described problems with the tact function. He uses the tact function to explain particular responses to particular stimuli, as when we respond to a piece of music by saying "Beethoven" or respond to a building by saying "Wright." In such situations, we have learned to discriminate when to emit particular verbal behaviors; namely, in the presence of particular stimulus characteristics of the music or of the building. For example, when we see a painting and respond "Dutch," we are responding to particular characteristics of that painting—that is, particular stimuli that presumably exist in the world. But Chomsky maintains:

> Suppose instead of saying "Dutch" we said "Clashes with the wallpaper, I thought you liked abstract work, never saw it before, tilted, hanging too low, beautiful, hideous, remember our camping trip last summer?" or whatever else might come into our minds when looking at a picture. . . . Skinner could only say that each of these responses is under the control of some other stimulus property of the physical object. . . . But the word *stimulus* has lost all objectivity in this usage. Stimuli are no longer part of the outside physical world: They are driven back into the organism. We identify the stimulus when we hear the response. It is clear from such examples, which abound, that the talk of *stimulus control* simply disguises a complete retreat to mentalistic psychology. (Chomsky, 1959) (Emphasis in original.)

In this instance, Chomsky points out that the behavioristic account of language is no more scientific that the mentalistic accounts it had supplanted a half century earlier. The behaviorist's frustrating problem is that the tact function is not powerful enough to explain why particular utterances are produced at particular times. The notion of stimulus control is no help because, as Chomsky points out, it's not possible to specify what the stimulus is until we hear the subject's response. In other words, the idea that characteristics of the world signal us to produce specific remarks seems false, because it's not possible to specify in advance which characteristics of the world did the signaling.

Neurocomputing

Earlier, I mentioned that many psychologists immediately after World War II were impressed with the apparent similarity between computing machines and the human nervous system. It was during this time that D. O. Hebb (1949) put a novel slant on this comparison by reversing its usual direction. Rather than think of the ways in which a computer might be like a nervous system, Hebb wondered about the ways in which a nervous system could compute things. Hebb theorized that "learning" could be defined as a succession of changes in the neurological states that a given brain could enter, or compute, as a function of its experiences with certain types of stimuli. That is, as a brain processed certain types of stimuli (and remember, each such processing event means that the brain must represent the stimuli as some sort of pattern of neural firing, or neural code), the activities involved in this processing resulted in structural changes in the brain. What are structural changes? Structural changes are essentially changes in the connections among neurons—that is, changes in the number and nature of the neuron's synapses with other neurons. Specifically, Hebb formulated this principle, which describes how these changes might occur:

> When an axon of cell A is near enough to excite cell B and repeatedly or persistently takes part in firing it, some growth process or metabolic change takes place in one or both cells such that A's efficiency, as one of the cells firing B, is increased. (Hebb, 1949, p. 50)

Expressed simplistically, if two ideas become associated in your mind, then according to Hebb, some rather large collection of neurons has now achieved some synaptic connection with some other large collection of neurons.

The next person to explore this idea was Rosenblatt (1958). In his view, the nervous system could be divided into three "layers." These layers are shown in Figure 1.3. The first layer consists of neurons, whose job is to bring information in from the physical world. These are the sensory neurons, and they are shown in the drawing leading away from the area called the retina. Rosenblatt used the term *retina* because he was most interested in describing visual information processing. But the same logic applies to all sensory systems. The sensory neurons communicate with the neurons in the next layer (the projection layer). The neurons located there are called association neurons or association cells.

If you've taken a course in physiological psychology, you probably remember that neurons can have many "styles" of communicating. In some cases, we say that a particular neuron can have an excitatory connection with an adjacent neuron. We mean that when the first neuron "fires," or sends its electrochemical impulse along its axon, the second neuron, which receives this impulse, also has a tendency to "fire." But there is another style of communication among neurons. In some cases, when the first neuron fires, it produces a chemical reaction in the second neuron that makes the second neuron *resist* firing. We refer to this type of connection as inhibitory. Thus the firing of some neurons can produce firing in adjacent neurons (this is the type of relationship that Hebb discussed), but neurons can also exert an inhibitory relationship on other neurons.

Understanding this concept is important in understanding the activity of the association cells. In Rosenblatt's view, some of the sensory neurons had excitatory connections with a particular association cell, but other sensory neurons might have

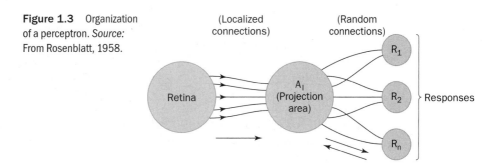

Figure 1.3 Organization of a perceptron. *Source:* From Rosenblatt, 1958.

inhibitory connections with the same cell. Under these circumstances, the association cell becomes a kind of "decision maker." If you put yourself in the place of the association cell, you'll see what I mean. As the association cell, will you "fire" your impulse in response to the activity of the sensory cells that are communicating with you? It depends on how many of the cells have excitatory connections and how many have inhibitory connections. Of all the cells communicating with you, if there are more excitatory sensory neurons than inhibitory cells, then you will "decide" to fire your impulse. But if there are more inhibitory cells than excitatory cells, then you will refrain from firing your impulse.

Now we have one more layer of cells to discuss: the response cells. Just as the sensory neurons communicate with the association cells in either excitatory or inhibitory styles, so too the association cells can have excitatory or inhibitory connections with the response cells. Thus the response cell is a decision maker too. Just as the association cell listens (metaphorically) to all the sensory neurons that communicate with it and decides if the sum of the sensory inputs is excitatory or inhibitory, so too the response cells keep track of all the association cells communicating with them. If the net response (that is, the sum of the excitatory and inhibitory connections) is positive (more excitatory than inhibitory), then the response cell fires, but if the net response is negative (more inhibitory than excitatory), then the response cell remains silent.

In our discussion so far we have pointed out the similarities between the association cells and the response cells, but there is one important difference between them. The association cells have no influence on the firing of the sensory cells, but the response cells *can* influence the firing of the association cells. The specific pattern goes like this: When association cells activate a response cell, the response cell in turn has excitatory connections back to the association cells that activated it. But with any association cell that did not contribute to the activation of the response cell, the response cell has *inhibitory* connections. What function does this relationship serve? This pattern of excitatory and inhibitory connections from the response cell back to the association cell means that the response cell functions as a kind of "amplifier": it has excitatory connections with cells that have excitatory connections with it. Rosenblatt named such a system of artificial neurons a *perceptron*. The perceptron was the first attempt to develop an abstract model of the nervous system that showed how a system with neural characteristics could actually compute things. Although subsequent research (Minsky & Papert, 1969) showed that our nervous systems must be much more complicated than Rosenblatt's analysis indicated, this first attempt was nevertheless important.

We've explored four historical antecedent areas—human factors research, computer technology, psycholinguistics, and neurocomputing—to find the roots of modern cognitive psychology. In the 1960s, the strands of research and intellectual activity suggested by these roots came together. In 1967, Ulric Neisser published his eagerly awaited *Cognitive Psychology*, which synthesisized many of the ideas that had been percolating in different areas. In 1970, further synthesis occurred when the academic journal *Cognitive Psychology* began publication. These publications marked the reemergence of cognition as a fixture in the American psychological landscape.

Contemporary Cognitive Psychology

Two Approaches to Cognition

A couple of times in this introduction I've alluded to the "approaches" that a cognitive psychologist might use in studying some specific problem. In this section we'll discuss the two main approaches: the **information-processing approach** and the **connectionist approach.** As you'll see, each approach has clear links with the historical roots that we have covered. For example, the information-processing approach is squarely rooted in the emergence of the computing machine; in fact, information-processing psychologists sometimes argue that the mind works like a computer. The information-processing approach can also trace its lineage back to the work in human factors. This research demonstrated that humans actively seek information about the world, and that the plans and goals that humans formed for the world were based on the information they sought and found. Like adherents of the information-processing approach, connectionists seek to develop computational models of cognition, and in this sense they can also trace their intellectual ancestry back to the early workers in computer science. Unlike the approach taken by information-processing adherents, however, connectionists' work is intimately linked to historical roots in neurocomputing and therefore is very much neuronally inspired. Hence, connectionists, it is said, have adopted the "brain metaphor," whereas information-processing psychologists have adopted the "computer metaphor." In the next sections, we explore these distinctions further.

Information-Processing Approach   The information-processing approach is based on the idea that many of our cognitive processes occur **serially** and **sequentially.** When we say that our cognitive processes occur serially, we mean that they occur in a one-thing-at-a-time way. For example, if you've heard it said that "you can pay attention to only one thing at time," the speaker was espousing a serial position toward cognition. Serial processing is the kind of processing that occurs in most computers. A computer armed with a modern central processing chip can make transformations of incoming data with blinding speed, but fundamentally, at any given time, the computer's central processing unit is engaged in doing exactly one and only one computation.

When information-processing theorists say that cognition occurs sequentially, they emphasize the notion that cognitive processes seem to occur in a definable order, with some processes preceding others in time. Thus, if I'm given these numbers to add up:

$$896$$
$$+495$$

I'll look first at the 6 and the 5, add them, write the unit's number in the sum below the 5, put the "carry" (1) above the 9, and so on. I didn't always know how to do this adding, but now I say that the knowledge I have about addition is just this type of sequential processing knowledge that I describe in the preceding sentence.

We need to deal with a couple of issues about the information-processing position. The first can be illustrated by raising a question that my students sometimes ask of me: Because the information-processing viewpoint is necessarily abstract, why use it to study cognitive processes, especially when it might be possible to study the underlying neural processes directly? In other words, the students seem to suggest that we simply cut to the chase and study the neural processes themselves. What stops us? Information-processing theorists might argue that an abstract analysis is necessary because of discoverability problems at the neural level. It's true that specific relationships may always be discoverable between specific neural activities or locations, and particular cognitive or mental events. In fact, as we'll see in the language chapters, a few such relationships have been discovered. Despite this reservation, however, cognitive psychologists working in the information-processing tradition maintain that there are no guarantees that a general, discoverable neural representation inevitably underlies all specific cognitive events. Moreover, these cognitivists make several points to buttress their contention. First, they argue, we have to be aware that our brains are not identical, and so specifying what is similar about the *function* of, let's say, my brain vis-à-vis yours may be impossible. Now, it may be that my brain obeys functional laws that relate my neural events to my cognitive events, and this state of affairs may be true for your brain as well. But there may be no principled (i.e., rule-based) way to relate the functioning of my brain to that of yours. That is, the only operative principle may be, "Each person's brain coordinates the functioning of that person's neural events to that person's mental events."

The second issue raised by cognitivists working within the information-processing approach has to do with translatability. Information-processing psychologists use certain language to talk about mental events, and the language they use necessarily differs from that neurologists use to talk about neural events. It may be that the reality of the phenomenon in question (be it neural or cognitive) is simply bound into the language used to describe it and thus cannot be translated into other terms. Let me give you an example of this phenomenon. In your studies of mathematics, you may have encountered the imaginary number, i, the square root of minus one. Mathematicians use this number all day long as a valid mathematical object, and so its existence can hardly be doubted. What would happen if you approached a mathematician and asked him or her what number i would be if i were a real number instead of an imaginary one? The mathematician might reply unkindly that it's a silly question. Imaginary numbers are valid and real in their realm, but they have no reality outside that realm. Despite our intuitions to the contrary, it might be exactly this state of affairs that governs neural and cognitive events. The validity of each type of event may be unimpeachable within its realm, but each type of event may have no validity outside that realm.

Cognitive psychologists usually divide the human information-processing system into components, as shown in Figure 1.4. This differentiation is based in part on the supposition that some cognitive acts seem quite different from others.

The first component in the information-processing system is the sensory system, where the cognitive code is created. In this system, specific aspects of the environment are detected and their organization is begun. After the cognitive code is created by the sensory system, it is passed on to the memory. As Figure 1.4 shows, cognitive psychologists distinguish between the permanent memory, sometimes referred to as the inactive memory, and the working memory. The permanent memory can be considered a vast depository of both declarative and procedural knowledge. The permanent memory is a storehouse not only of facts but also of skills and motor programs that enable us to move and speak. Under some conditions, the central processor allocates attention to the working memory. When it does so, elements that have been passed into the permanent memory become activated, and at this juncture the cognitive code can be elaborated and modified.

Working memory is a kind of workbench for cognitive codes. As Figure 1.4 shows, working memory is the site where goals can be established. These goals sometimes include the modification of a cognitive code. For example, in problem solving, the cognitive code might consist of representations of both possible solutions and possible operations that might be done to produce a solution. When solving problems, the central processor might use the working memory as a site to systematically match up possible solutions with possible operations to see if a fit can be achieved and the problem solved. The central processor's task is to formulate goals. Once the goal is formulated, the central processor must develop a plan for accomplishing the goal. When the central processor is dealing with multiple goals (which it probably is in most real-life situations), a priority listing of goals must be established. When this has been done, the central processor must allocate attention to the cognitive processes involved to monitor their progress. The central processor uses working, or active memory to keep track of its place in the plan, and from this site in the working memory, the response system is controlled.

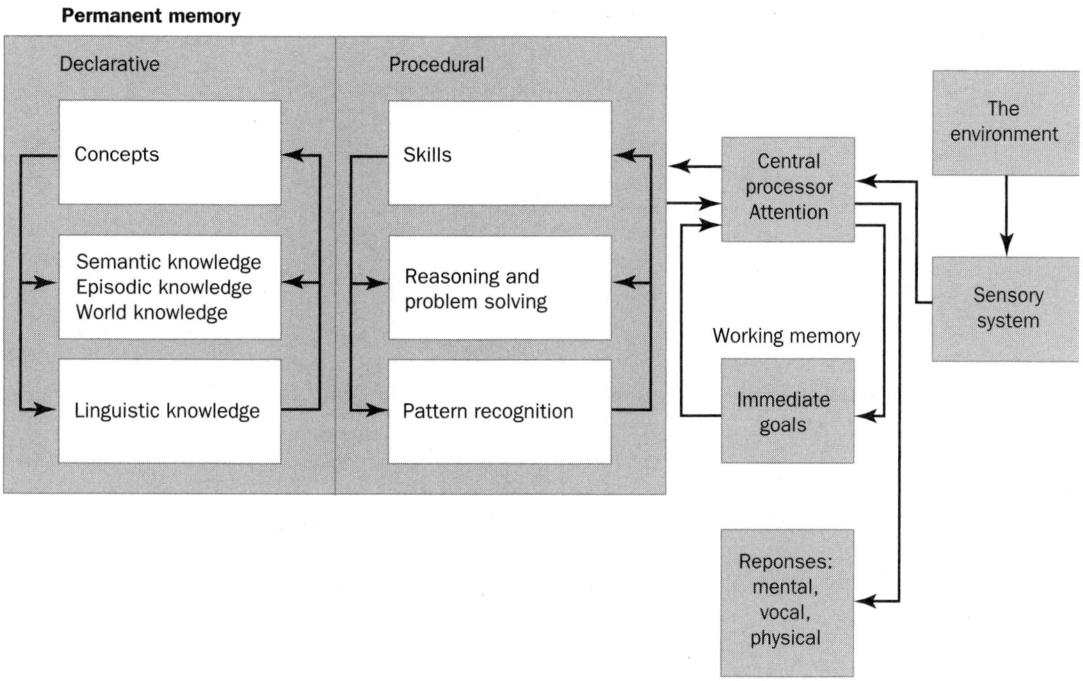

Figure 1.4   The human information-processing system.

Let's use Figure 1.4 as the basis for an everyday example, that of hitting a forehand drive in tennis. First, the environment offers the tennis player information about the flight of the ball—information that would be picked up primarily by the visual and auditory systems (top tennis pros such as Pete Sampras listen to the sound of the ball as it leaves the racquet's strings). Presumably, the player's central processor has allocated attention to processes that recognize and categorize the opponent's shot. This categorization is important; it lets the tennis pro know where to go to be in position for the return. A second function of the categorization is that it affords the pro an opportunity to determine what kind of point is being played. If the ball is hit short, the pro has knowledge about the various patterns of play (a drop-shot return, a cross-court volley, and so on) that can be attempted from a short ball. Following the categorization, the central processor begins to allocate attention to the opponent's movements. Here, the goal is to determine an effective placement for the return shot. Is the opponent coming to the net? If so, then a passing shot down the line could be the right response. While this has been going on, several automatic processes have been initiated. The pro uses automatic and procedural running programs stored in his or her permanent memory to move quickly from his or her present position to the desired position on the court. Once there, the pro attempts to hit the forehand drive, and to do so he or she uses the procedural-knowledge program described earlier in this chapter.

We can sum up this discussion of information-processing systems by listing and describing the principles underlying the information-processing approach (Massaro & Cowan, 1993; Palmer & Kimchi, 1986). In general, the information-processing approach to cognition emphasizes these five qualities:

1. Informational description
2. Recursive decomposition
3. Flow continuity
4. Flow dynamics
5. Physical embodiment

Let's go through these terms one at a time. Informational description simply means that, according to information-processing theorists, both the environment in which we live and our mental processing of it can be characterized by the amounts and types of information they contain. Recursive decomposition means that cognitive processes can be thought of as consisting of simpler cognitive processes (which can be thought of as still simpler cognitive processes). The idea underlying recursive decomposition is that our cognitive processes are hierarchically arranged, and by clever and careful experimentation, we may be able to discern the nature of this hierarchy. The flow continuity principle asserts that information goes forward in time; whatever input information is needed to carry out a cognitive process can be found in the outputs of the cognitive processes that feed into it. The principle of flow dynamics asserts that, because mental and cognitive processes coexist with the chemical and electrical events in the neural system, and because these neural events take time, then no mental process can occur instantaneously. All mental or cognitive processes must involve the passage of some time, even if that time is only a few thousandths of a second. The physical embodiment principle refers to the idea that all cognitive processes take place in a physical system—for humans, a neural system. This last principle has an important implication, and is easily overlooked by people who are just beginning to study cognition. Let's phrase the implication as a question: If cognitive processes are abstract, then how can something abstract be housed in a physical system? The answer is that the information in the system must be represented by physical events. For example, in the word "boat," the knowlege you have about what the word means is abstract, but this knowledge must be represented in the cognitive and neural system by a pattern of specific neural events. Thus, the knowledge that we have must be housed in the physical system in the form of "representations."

Connectionist Approach   Whereas the information-processing approach to the study of cognition is described as an abstract analysis, connectionists emphasize the neural and mathematical bases in their approach (Churchland, 1989). Thus connectionists do *not* see their models as necessarily abstract; in fact, they frequently maintain that connectionist models (sometimes equivalent expressions such as "distributed" or "neural-network" are used) are "neurally inspired" (Rumelhart & McClelland, 1986). This doesn't mean that connectionists spend their days rooting around in nervous systems; the neural systems they study often are idealized nervous systems that are expressed in the form of mathematical and computerized models. But it's also true that connectionists usually strongly attempt to show that the actual nervous system could carry out computations that are similar to their idealized systems, thus suggesting that the actual nervous system may behave in ways congruent with the idealized systems.

As you might figure, connectionists don't always agree with some of the positions raised by information-processing theorists. For example, if you look back to Figure 1.4, you'll see that information-processing psychologists may talk about "control" of the system housed in some "central processor." But this language is all Greek to a connectionist. If the central processor controls the cognitive system, can the central processor do this controlling without having some sort of control system within itself? And if it does, does this control system within the central processor have its own central processor? To a connectionist, saying that the cognitive system is controlled by a central processor isn't much of an answer, because it just pushes the problem of control one step deeper into the system. Besides this logical conundrum, connectionists say that the nervous system doesn't work in the way that information-processing theory implies. You can look all you want for the kinds of control structures implied by information-processing theory, but you'll seldom, if ever, find them. As connectionists point out, there are no executive neurons that "know" more than other neurons and hence direct their underlings' activity. In fact, the central nervous system, in many ways, is not a hierarchy at all. Neurons sometimes facilitate, sometimes inhibit the activity of other neurons, and the pattern of neural activity thus produced may change dramatically with a change in the stimuli presented to the system. Where there was a facilitative relationship, there may now be an inhibitory one, and vice versa. Our view of neural activity suggests that there are few, if any, "boss neurons."

Connectionists also point out problems with the serial-processing assumption made by information-processing theorists—the idea that cognitive processes occur one step at a time. Connectionists point out that many significant cognitive operations can be accomplished in one second or so (Feldman, 1985). But if we consider that the basic neuron takes several milliseconds to operate and that the operating speed of these units is the "speed limit" of the brain, then we see that the cognitive system must accomplish its goals within relatively few "time steps"—one hundred or so steps is the suggested number (Feldman, 1985). As the connectionists point out, the problem here is that it's extremely difficult to write a computer program that is able to accomplish in only one hundred serial elementary operations what our cognitive systems are routinely capable of doing. For the connectionists, this limitation means that any attempts to model the cognitive processes in the human must be based on *parallel,* not serial, processing. In other words, our brains and our cognitive systems must routinely do more than one thing at a time.

What can we say in summary about these two approaches to cognition? We can see that the information-processing approach to cognition emphasizes an abstract, serial analysis of cognitive processes. The information-processing approach implies that some cognitive processes direct other processes hierarchically and that the cognitive system as a whole has a "modular" organization. That is, it has parts, or subunits, which seem to be more or less separate from one another. The connectionist approach emphasizes a neuronally based, parallel-processing view. The connectionist approach maintains that neurons do not typically stand in a hierarchic relationship with other neurons. Moreover, connectionists argue that the cognitive system is not actually modular, either, meaning that it really can't be broken down into parts. In each cognitive act, the neural and cognitive systems work as entire units, not as systems of cooperating components. Describing how the neural and cognitive systems work as units requires a lengthier discussion than we have time for here. Suffice it to say that throughout the book we'll pose many examples of both approaches in operation.

Methods in Cognitive Psychology

We've seen something of the topics discussed in cognitive psychology, and we've received an orientation to the terms and background in the field. One more task remains for us to accomplish in this chapter: to understand something about the methods and techniques used by cognitive psychologists.

Throughout this textbook we cite studies from which cognitive psychologists infer the characteristics of our cognitive functioning. Cognitive psychologists often use an experimental approach to their subject, which involves manipulating some independent variable and observing changes produced in a dependent variable. The listing of things that have served as dependent variables in psychological studies is endless, but cognitive psychologists are fond of two classes of events for this purpose: patterns of errors and reaction times to complex stimuli.

Consider a person who wishes to say the phrase "a current argument" as part of an utterance but says instead "an arrent curgument." This error, which is authentic (Fromkin, 1971; Garrett, 1982), tells us a great deal about the cognitive processes involved in speech. How would we describe what has taken place? First, we say that a syllable switch has taken place. The first syllable of "current" has been switched with the first syllable of "argument." From this observation, we might conclude that the human mind builds words by assembling them syllable by syllable. We might go on to theorize that, before being completely assembled, each planned word is held in a group of slots marked First Syllable, Second Syllable, and so on. To assemble the word, a cognitive program draws the contents of the first slot and follows it with the contents of the second slot, and so on. If a mistake is going to occur, presumably it's because this program can't recognize which slots go with which other slots. Consequently, this program can't tell if an error is being made in the assembly process, because it apparently doesn't know the meaning of the words. This is what seems to be happening here, because there's no such thing as a "curgument."

In English, we use the indefinite article *a* before consonants and *an* before vowels. Although the person in our example intended to use *a,* the assembly error has resulted in a vowel sound being placed where the consonant sound was intended. We notice that this error has been rectified in the actual utterance: The *a* has been changed to *an.* What can we conclude from this switch? Apparently, the program that determines the sounds in our utterances must operate after the program that assembles the syllables. If the program that determined the sound of utterances went first, then the person would have said "a arrent curgument"; but such errors do not occur.

A second common approach consists of measuring reaction times to the presentation of stimuli. The work of Meyer and Schvaneveldt (1971) illustrates this approach well. They hypothesized that conceptually related words would be recognized as words faster than unrelated words would. To test this assertion, they presented their subjects with pairs of related and unrelated words. They also presented pairs of nonwords. The subjects' task was to decide as quickly as possible if both elements in a pair were words, and, if so, they were to say yes. If an element in the pair was a nonword, subjects were instructed to say no. Table 1.1 shows the findings. The positive pairs (those in which the subject was to respond yes) are of particular interest. When the words were related, subjects responded 85 milliseconds (msec) faster than they did when the words were unrelated. Although this difference may not seem like much (and we would probably not be *aware* of such a difference), a 10% difference in processing time is usually accepted as substantial by many cognitive psychologists. If one group requires about 1500 msec to carry out a task, and a second group requires about 1550 msec to carry out some variation of the task, such a difference wouldn't pique our curiosity. If the 50-msec difference between the groups occurred against a base rate of 500 msec, however, then we would be curious.

Table 1.1   Examples of the Pairs Used to Demonstrate Associative Pairing

Positive Pairs		Negative Pairs		
Unrelated	*Related*	*First Nonword*	*Second Nonword*	*Both Nonwords*
Nurse	Bread	Plame	Wine	Plame
Butter	Butter	Wine	Plame	Reab
940 msec	855 msec	904 msec	1087 msec	884 msec

Source: From Meyer and Schvaneveldt, 1971.

What can we gather from the Meyer and Schvaneveldt findings? From the substantial difference in processing time, we might state that recognizing a word seems to facilitate recognizing and reading a related word. Such a finding tells us that words are probably recognized at least in part by their *context*.

A third method, used by both information-processing theorists and connectionists, is the use of computers to model or simulate cognitive and neural processes. This approach has advantages. For one thing, it forces the theorist or researcher to be explicit about his or her theory. For many years, psychological theories have been plagued with fuzziness resulting from reliance on natural language. But when a psychological theory is embodied or translated into a computer program, this fuzziness is immediately exposed because fuzzy programs don't run. A second advantage stems from the intriguing fact that sometimes cognitive tasks that appear very different from one another can be simulated with programs that seem rather similar in the programs' data structures and basic operations. This fact may (repeat, *may*) suggest that the cognitive processes and operations underlying these different tasks are actually similar. This similarity could prove to be advantageous because, from a scientific perspective, such a finding might enable cognitivists to entertain some hope of producing something like a "unified" theory of cognition. A unified theory of cognition would mean that when a system, human or artificial, did something requiring knowledge or intelligence, we would expect to see similarities in its operation because a unified theory implies that there is only one form of intelligence or knowledge, and this form is always expressed in programs having certain features. This would be a dramatic breakthrough, if it occurred.

Let's go through some of the steps in building such a program. First, data are gathered from human subjects on some task that requires cognitive operations. Typically, the data are gathered from humans who are relatively new to the task, although sometimes data are gathered from experts. The data can be of the types that we have seen; that is, either error patterns or reaction times. In building a program, the researcher may gather data by asking the subjects to verbalize, or think out loud, as they do the task. A tape recording is made of each subject as he or she engages in the task, and this tape, called a protocol, is then analyzed intensively to observe commonalities in storing, retrieving, or using data in the task. The commonalities observed in the protocols are then used as a basis for program writing.

As an example of this methodology, let's consider some work by Larkin (1989). Larkin was interested in the cognitive processes underlying the solving of algebra equations such as this:

$$-3 - 4(2x - 9) = 7 + 5x$$

Larkin's program, the Display-Based Solver (DiBS), solves these kinds of problems by first putting each of the terms into a relationship with other terms. This setting of relationships is called a "data structure," and the DiBS data structure for this problem is shown in the first part of Table 1.2. This solution won't be too meaningful yet, but notice that the data structure does have a goal. It lists where we "want" the terms in the equation to wind up ultimately—on the left or on the right side. The second part of Table 1.2 lists the operations that the program goes through; this list is called the "trace" of the program. The data structure that has been created enables DiBS to treat

Table 1.2   Trace of DiBS Solution of a Linear Equation

(A)   The Initial Data Structure

Name	Type	Value	Below	Want__Below
p1	term	−3	lhs	rhs
p2	term		lhs	
p3	factor	−4	p2	rhs
p4	factor		p2	
p5	term	2	p4	lhs
p6	term	−9	p4	rhs
p7	term	7	rhs	rhs
p8	term	5	rhs	lhs

(B)   Trace of the Solving Process

p1		p3		p5		p6		p7		p8
−3	+	−4	(2x	+	−9	=	7	+	5x

1. put__an__object__where__it__wants__to__be__alg
p1, value −3 wants to be below rhs
moving p1 below rhs

2. combine__add
combining terms of value −3 and −7 on rhs

3. put__an__object__where__it__wants__to__be__alg
p8, value 5 wants to be below lhs
moving p8 below lhs

	p2			
		p4		
p8	p3	p5	p6	p7
−5x +	−4	(2x +	−9)	=10

4. uncover__alg
taking apart the mixed term p2 with coefficient −4 and
number 2 and x__term −9

p8		p5		p6		p7
−5x	+	−8x	+	36	=	10

5. combine__add
combining terms of value −5 and −8 on lhs

6. put__an__object__where__it__wants__to__be__alg
p6, value 36 wants to be below rhs
moving p8 below rhs

7. combine__add
combining terms of value −36 and 10 on rhs

p5		p7
−13x +		−26

8. last__x__term
dividing both sides by −13

9. done__alg
all variables are below lhs
and all numbers are below rhs only two terms remain
therefore done

Source: From Larkin, 1989.

sets of variables as groups. For example, in operation 4, DiBS gets ready to take apart the group $-4(2x - 9)$. Operation 3 has shown that DiBS has represented this group of elements, called p2, as two subgroups (p3 and p4), and the subgroup p4 is in turn broken down into two elements (p5 and p6). Representing the data in this way tells DiBS that to break down this group, you have to multiply (-4) by (-9) to get (positive) 36. In other words, this data structure enables DiBS to duplicate human knowledge about the role of parentheses in solving equations. But suppose the novice human didn't understand yet that the group, $-4(2x - 9)$, had to be treated in this way? That is, suppose that such a person simply understood the equation to be a string of symbols that had no higher relationships to one another?

It turns out that one error novices frequently make in this type of problem is this (Sleeman, 1982):

$$\text{From the initial equation } -3 - 4(2x - 9) = 7 + 5x$$
$$\text{novices get } -3 - 4(2x) = 5x + 16$$
$$\text{or } -3 - 4(2x) = 5x - 2$$

The error that is made depends on whether the human literally just takes the -9 across the equals sign, or whether the human incorrectly adds $+9$ to both sides of the equation. We've seen that DiBS can get the right answer, but can it duplicate these errors? Yes, if some changes are made in the initial data structure, then DiBS treats the equation as simply a string of symbols, rather than as symbols that must be grouped in certain ways, and when this is done, then DiBS makes the same errors that human novices do.

Ecological Validity

Although cognitive psychologists usually bring their subjects into the laboratory for study, during the 1970s a movement was afoot to increase the **ecological validity** of research in cognition. This term, which was popularized by Neisser (1976), refers to the quest for theories of cognition that describe people's use of knowledge in real, everyday, culturally significant situations. Although this quest doesn't restrict the researcher's use of the laboratory, the emphasis on ecological validity does mean that the contemporary cognitive psychologist seeks to gather data and findings in ways that mesh naturally with the sorts of things that people actually use their cognitive systems to accomplish. In other words, memorizing a list of words, when done in a cognitive psychologist's laboratory, may not tell us much about some of the really interesting capabilities of human memory, because memorizing lists of unrelated words is a kind of task that humans do only in highly constrained or unnatural situations. We'd like to know how people go about using their memory systems for things that are believed to require use of memory. Thus, a contemporary cognitive psychologist may be much more interested in how a person goes about trying to study, learn, and remember a textbook chapter than he or she would be in learning how many words a subject can remember from a list that was presented once.

The emphasis on ecological validity has a special implication for the nonspecialist reader. It means that much of what you are about to read should be useful to you. I can't promise that you'll be able to use everything that you read in this book, or that the applications will be obvious. But my hope is that, after you study human reasoning, for example (Chapter 11), your reasoning will improve. Perhaps after you study the material on problem solving (Chapter 12), you'll become more successful at detecting and avoiding some of the pitfalls that hinder creative thinking. Similarly, after you study memory (Chapters 4 and 5), I'm optimistic that you'll be able to use the material to improve your retention and retrieval. As long as you keep in mind that the theories presented are the current best guess about their respective phenomena and are not absolute truths, I'm confident that your studies in this book will be rewarded with both practical skills and deeper appreciation of your mind's complexity.

Concluding Comments and Suggestions for Further Reading

At the end of each chapter, I'll offer some commentary on the material that was presented in an effort to foster your integration and learning of it. I'll also present titles of some books and articles that you may wish to read if you're interested in learning more about the topics that are covered in that chapter.

If you wish to learn more about the methodology of research in cognition, try Kintsch, Miller, and Polson, *Methods and Tactics in Cognitive Science* (1984). If you are particularly interested in computer applications in cognitive science, try the chapter by Aitkenhead and Slack (1985). Students who would like to find out more about the nuts and bolts of the information-processing approach would benefit by reading the excellent collection of chapters edited by Klahr and Kotovsky (1989). The chapter by Massaro and Cowan (1993) is also a very good overview of the information-processing approach. The research on connectionism in the last few years could fill a good-sized library all by itself. Anderson and Rosenfeld (1988) edited a good collection of basic papers (many of them are very difficult to read). The books edited by Grossberg (1988) and by Nadel, Cooper, Culicover, and Harnish (1989) have a strong connectionist and biological orientation. Clark (1989) covers the information-processing and connectionist viewpoints from a philosophical perspective.

Focus on Research
Uh oh! I breaked it!

If you've ever been in the company of a three- or four-year-old for any length of time, chances are that you have heard him or her produce a characteristic error called an overregularization. One of the commonest forms of overregularization occurs when a child takes an irregular verb, such as *sing* or *break,* and simply adds an "-ed" ending to the present tense of the verb to express something that happened in the past. Notice that this choice seems logical enough: If today I eat and sing, then yesterday, I eated and singed. It happens, however, that these forms are not correct and therefore children who produce them are telling us something about themselves; namely, that whatever it is they have learned about language at that time in their lives, it is strong enough to make them say something they have almost certainly not heard adults say very often. This finding leads to a question: Where do these errors come from? If they are not imitating adults, then what factors are responsible for these mistakes?

Marcus (1996) has carried out an analysis that provides us with an answer, and incidentally is a good example of using error analysis to illustrate cognitive processes in action. Marcus theorized that children must use their knowledge of rules and their memory to produce language. This approach is embodied in his "rule and memory" model, which has three components. First, as humans acquire language, they build a default rule to form the past tense of a verb. This rule states that you add -ed to a verb to form the past tense. Like other default rules, such as those pertaining to computer operations, this default rule operates if and only if there are no explicit instructions anywhere in the cognitive system to override it. The second component is the memory. If a verb is irregular, then its past-tense form is stored in the child's memory. The memory is accurate in the

sense that an irregular form is always stored. Thus, if the child hears an adult say, "Uh oh, I broke it," then the child will store this correct past-tense form. The child's memory may not, however, always succeed at retrieval time. When a child wants to talk about an episode in the past in which something was broken, he or she may not succeed in retrieving the stored form. The third component stipulates the order of precedence. If the child does succeed in retrieving the correctly stored form, then he or she will always say it. But if the correctly stored irregular form is not retrieved, then the child will revert to the default rule: Add -ed. This is when the child says "I breaked it," or "I goed," or one that my younger son actually produced, "I forgetted how to say it."

This position makes a number of predictions. First, it predicts that, as time goes by, children should tend to reduce the number of overregularization errors they produce. To support this prediction, Marcus and his colleagues gathered information from CHILDES (MacWhinney & Snow, 1985), which is a database consisting of spontaneous vocalizations by dozens of children. They analyzed 11,521 past-tense utterances, and found, as predicted, that with time children tend to reduce the number of overregularizations they produce. Figure 1.5 shows these effects in three children: Adam, Sarah, and Eve. The dotted lines show the percentage of correct past-tense use. As you can see, we find a lot of variability in the three children, but in general, at no overall time do the overregularizations actually predominate. In other words, even an individual child seldom or never prefers to use the incorrect, overregularized form. Rather, when a child commits an overregularization error, these data suggest that the error occurs as a result of some limitation in performance (such as memory), rather than from learning an inaccu-

Focus on Research

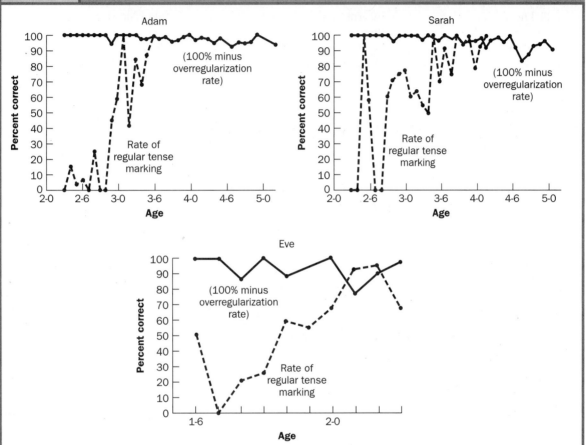

Figure 1.5 Overregularization and regular tense marking in three children as a function of age. In each panel, the heavy line plots the percentage of overregularization subtracted from 100%, and the dashed line plots the percentage of regular-past-tense contexts in which the child has successfully supplied the regular past tense. *Source:* From Marcus, 1996.

rate grammatical rule. This finding in turn suggests that children who get more chances to hear the correct form of the verb (perhaps because their parents use that verb more often than other verbs) should be more likely to use the correct past tense of the verb, presumably because these children are more likely to remember the correct past tense, compared to children who haven't heard that verb as often. This prediction was also supported by the data: For nearly all the children studied, the more often the parent used a specific irregular verb, the more likely his or her child was to use the irregular past-tense form too.

Key Terms

Declarative knowledge
Procedural knowledge
Semantic knowledge
Episodic knowledge
Controlled processes
Automatic processes
Explicit memory

Implicit memory
Structuralism
Human factors research
Information
Binary code
Psycholinguistics
Mand function

Tact function
Information-processing approach
Connectionist approach
Serial processing
Sequential processing
Ecological validity

Perception

Cognitive psychologists refer to a large number of cognitive processes as "perceptual," and many of them are basic to your understanding in the rest of this book. Perceptual processes are those that take sensory input and transform it into a more abstract code. We know that our senses respond to forms of physical energy. In our nervous systems, a code is created in which aspects of the physical energy are preserved. For example, you probably remember from your introductory psychology course that the rods and cones in our retinas preserve aspects of electromagnetic radiation. But I'm not aware of what my rods and cones are doing; in describing the visual world, I use terms like *light* and *color*. These are psychological terms that correspond to, but are not equivalent to, the sensory information. What does this statement mean? It means that some other intervening processes have taken the sensory code—the neurological information being relayed by the rods and cones—and converted it into another code that gives rise to my awareness of the psychological experiences of light and color. These intervening processes are perceptual.

Cataloguing all such processes would be incredibly lengthy, but we know about some of them intuitively. For example, we know that we can direct our sensory capabilities, which is referred to as the phenomenon of attention. To some extent we can aim all our senses at sensory stimulation by turning our heads to look or by reaching out and touching. We can even get ready to hear something. Whenever we aim our senses, perception seems to occur faster. We also recognize that perceptual processes sometimes seem to occur in sequential order. This sequence implies a sort of hierarchy of processing. For example, in order to read, we must organize groups of lines into letters, groups of letters into words, and groups of words into meaning. This kind of hierarchy suggests that some perceptual processes occur earlier than others in the processing of information. After all, how can we know the meaning of a sentence before we know the letters in the alphabet?

Important as sensory information is for perception, it can't be the whole story. If I look out to the parking lot on a bright day, my rods and cones nicely pick up reflected radiation from an object, which my perceptual processes elaborate until I recognize the pattern as a car. But I can still recognize the car on a foggy day or at night, when my rods and cones are not providing my perceptual processes with the same quality of information. How can this be? You may already have guessed the answer. In addition to using sensory information to perceive, I use my knowledge of the world to make inferences about the sensory information I can expect to encounter. What else would be in the parking lot, if not a car?

We see, then, that perception involves two distinct types of cognitive operations. Perception is achieved by a combination of cognitive processes—some that begin by elaborating the sensory code and others that are inferential and begin with our knowledge of the world. Keep this interplay in mind as you read this chapter.

CHAPTER 2

Attention and Object Recognition

*O*verview

You may have had an experience similar to this one. One morning I was driving to school over an almost deserted rural highway, when the radio station I was listening to began playing one of my favorite symphonic pieces. I was enjoying every minute of it, turning up the radio louder and louder to get the full effect. Everything was going fine until something flickering in my rearview mirror caught my eye. To my horror, I suddenly discovered behind me the flashing red lights of the sheriff's patrol car! I was going almost 70 miles per hour.

When I thought about the episode later, in a calmer frame of mind, I realized that the incident revealed several characteristics of our information-processing systems. For example, it's possible for us to concentrate our senses on particular sources of stimulation to gather information about them, but this concentration is always partial and never total, no matter how intense our concentration seems. Consequently, when other sources of stimulation present themselves, our concentration may shift to these new stimuli and leave the old ones behind. When I finally saw the flashing red lights in my rearview mirror, I stopped hearing the music—despite its overpowering volume. Not every new stimulus that presents itself, however, provokes this shift in concentration. As I blasted along the highway, deaf to everything but the music, I didn't bother shifting my attention to count the number of crows perched on the fenceposts. Why did I notice the flashing red lights but not the crows? In other words, what do some stimuli have that enable them to provoke the shift in concentration that other stimuli don't have? This question is not adequately answered by responding that familiar stimuli don't provoke the shift whereas terri-

fying stimuli do. This answer is unacceptable because, presumably, I didn't know that the patrol car *was* the patrol car, and therefore it was not terrifying until *after* I had shifted my concentration to the rearview mirror. As you can see, the episode is considerably more complicated than it initially appears to be.

In this chapter we examine the concept of attention—a mental phenomenon that cognitive psychologists have used to describe and explain concentration and its shifts. We'll review several studies of **selective attention** and we'll consider several theoretical models that have been erected to explain the findings in such studies. Generally speaking, we can divide the research into two phases. In the first phase of theory building, which took place in the 1950s, attention was commonly thought of as a bottleneck in the information-processing system. According to this concept, stimuli cannot be fully processed unless they are attended to, and our attentional mechanisms are limited to processing only a small amount of the stimulation bombarding us. In the second phase of theory building, which has taken place in the last twenty or so years, this conception has been supplemented with a view of attention as allocation of resources. We'll consider this position and examine one of its implications; namely, that highly overlearned tasks require allocating few cognitive resources. In such a state of affairs, cognitive processes can take place without conscious guidance; this is referred to as automatic processing.

The function of attention is to bring cognitive processes to bear on external stimuli so that information can be gathered about them. Going back to the patrol car once again: Once my attention was focused, I detected characteristics in the stimuli (the lights and their color) that enabled me to recognize and then categorize the vehicle. This chapter closes with a discussion of the role of context, or surrounding stimulation, as it influences object recognition. One final point: After the officer pulled me over and asked me why I was going so fast, I told him the truth, and he let me off with a warning. I resolved to pay more attention to my driving and less to the radio.

What Is Attention?

Definitions

Providing a concise definition of attention is difficult because the word has been used in so many ways. For example, when you take a test, you have to attend to it, which implies that you have the ability to focus your mental effort on specific stimuli while excluding other stimuli from consideration. One important aspect of attention, therefore, is its **selectivity.** If a professor advises you to pay attention to a question and you do, your actions indicate that you have the ability to shift the focus of mental effort from one stimulus to another. In this case, you were able to change the focus of your efforts from one question on the test to another, and this ability seems to be under your control. That is, the shift in attention doesn't seem to be demanded by the stimulus alone (because you could choose to ignore your professor's instructions). Such facts tell us that not only is the focus of mental effort shiftable, but also some cognitive process must decide the timing and direction of the shift. If you go to a bar after the test to debrief with your friends, you might pay attention to their conversation and watch an episode of your favorite soap opera at the same time. This ability indicates that we apparently can maintain more than one focus of mental effort simultaneously. The focus of mental effort not only is selective and shiftable but also can be divided into parts. As a general definition, therefore, attention refers to the concentration and focusing of mental effort (Matlin, 1983)—a focus that is selective, shiftable, and divisible.

Problems in Defining Attention

When we focus mental effort on a task, the action seems to be under our conscious control. That is, we consciously decide which stimuli will be selectively focused upon and which will be excluded. Understanding attention would be much easier if all such selection decisions were made consciously, but unfortunately they don't seem to be. For example, if a friend takes a long car trip with you, you will pay attention to your friend's speech. This effort is a conscious decision to focus mental effort on particular stimuli. At the same time, you will continue to drive the car appropriately, which involves focusing mental effort selectively on continually changing highway conditions. But this sort of focusing, although continuing, probably is not done with any awareness of the many decisions that are being made.

The role of awareness seemingly creates problems for defining attention. Why? If awareness is not required for selection and shifts in mental effort, then attention is not under conscious control, because such shifts and selections would take place without any decision making that we were aware of. On the other hand, if awareness *is* required for attention, then attention is not selective, because to shift attention under those circumstances, we would already have had to be aware of all the stimuli around us.

A couple of difficult questions can now be formulated. Under what circumstances is attention truly under conscious control, and when is it truly selective? To arrive at a preliminary answer to these questions, we'll explore the results of several **dichotic listening** studies that made up the first wave of research in this area.

Studies of Selective Attention

Early studies of selective attention often involved dichotic presentation of material. The subject wore stereo headphones, and into each ear a different message was transmitted. The subject was told to attend to only one ear and to make sure this instruction was carried out; the subject was requested to *shadow* the attended ear. **Shadowing** involves listening to the message in the attended ear and repeating it aloud as soon as possible after hearing it. Assuming the subject makes no errors in shadowing the attended ear, the technique seems a good way of ensuring selective focusing on a message.

Using the dichotic listening procedure, Cherry (1953) found that subjects had remarkably little difficulty with the shadowing technique. They made few errors in shadowing the attended ear. Cherry was also interested in what the subjects remembered about the message in the *unattended* ear. He found that the subjects could accurately report whether the unattended message had been a human voice or a noise, and they could also report whether the voice had been a man's or a woman's, apparently by pitch. In other words, the subjects seemed to have some knowledge about the physical or acoustic properties of the unattended message. They seemed, however, to have little knowledge about the *meaning* of the unattended message. For example, the subjects were unable to detect the language used by the voice in the unattended ear, and they were not able to recognize words that had been presented in the unshadowed ear thirty-five times (Moray, 1959).

Forty years ago, such studies were widely interpreted as indicating that attention was highly selective. We became conscious of what was attended to. Moreover, the focus of attention was thought to be consciously directed so that little unattended information could enter our consciousness. According to such a viewpoint, subjects would have difficulty doing two demanding tasks simultaneously because, as they focused on one task, they were no longer conscious of the events taking place in the second task. Consequently, some information would be lost no matter how quickly the subjects attempted to alternate between the two tasks, and so their performance on both tasks would inevitably decline.

Mowbray's (1953) study supports this position. Mowbray instructed his subjects to attend to two messages simultaneously. The subjects heard one story while silently reading a second story whose content was unrelated to the story presented aurally. Subjects then took a test measuring comprehension of both stories. The subjects almost always comprehended one of the stories substantially better than the other; the subject's poorer score was usually at the chance, or guessing, level.

*B*ottleneck Theories of Attention

Filter Theory

Broadbent (1958) developed a theory of attention attempting to account for the findings by Cherry and Mowbray. Broadbent proposed that the focus of attention is determined by three components: a **selective filter,** which led to a channel of limited capacity, which in turn led to a detection device. These components are represented in Figure 2.1.

The sensory register, or sensory information store, is discussed more fully in Chapter 4. This register is a memory of stimuli that have recently been presented. Stimuli are stored in sensory memory in one of several channels, each channel corresponding loosely to a different sensory modality. Although the duration of this memory is brief, its contents are thought to be exact representations of the original stimuli. While they are stored in the sensory register, the stimuli are subjected to a **preattentive analysis** (Neisser, 1967), which determines some of their physical characteristics, such as pitch and intensity. As a result of this preattentive analysis, the selective filter determines which stimuli will undergo further processing. The stimuli not selected are essentially tuned out; no further elaboration of them takes place.

Figure 2.1   Three models of attention and capacity in sensory processing. *Source:* Copyright © 1973 by the Psychonomic Society, Inc. Adapted by permission of the publisher and author.

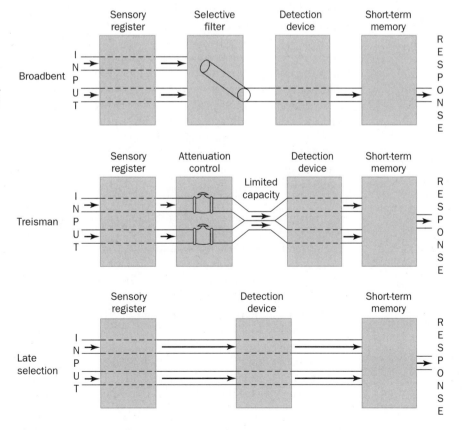

Following their selection, the stimuli are shunted along a limited-capacity channel to the detection device. The channel's relatively limited capacity has important implications for the human information processor. If asked to pay attention to several demanding tasks simultaneously, the shunting channel lacks the capacity to carry all the incoming information simultaneously to the detection device. Instead, the selective filter switches as rapidly as possible among the channels in the sensory register, in each case taking the information that has been loaded into that channel and transferring it to the shunting channel. This process explains why Broadbent's viewpoint is referred to as a *bottleneck* theory. A great deal of information can be stored simultaneously in the sensory channels, but evacuating information from the sensory register is laborious and must be done serially—that is, one channel at a time.

Information in the shunting channel is transferred to the detection device, where the information's *meaning* is analyzed. According to Broadbent's position, we "know" only about stimuli that make it past the selective filter. Information that was stopped at that stage is subjected only to a preattentive analysis, which is incapable of determining the stimulus's meaning.

This theory provides a reasonable account of Cherry's and Mowbray's findings. Recall that Mowbray (1953) found that subjects could apparently extract the meaning of only one story when two had been presented—one visually, the other aurally. In this case, the decrement in performance was produced by the selective filter's inability to switch rapidly enough between the auditory and visual channels. While information from one channel in the sensory register was extracted and loaded into the shunting channel, information in other channels of the sensory register could not be evacuated. As we'll see in Chapter 4, the sensory storage has large capacity; however, material in sensory storage has an extremely short "shelf life." If the information stored there is not extracted in a short time, it begins to decay. This is why the subject could not answer questions about the information stored in the unselected channel. By the time the shunting channel was switched back to this information, it had decayed. Because the subjects gave the information in the blocked channel only a preattentive analysis, they were unable to answer questions about the passage's meaning.

Regarding Cherry's findings: The filter is tuned to accept information from the shadowed ear; this information is loaded into the shunting channel and ultimately processed for meaning by the detection device. Material that is presented in the nonshadowed ear has a different fate. Because the filter is never opened to the nonshadowed ear, none of this material is transferred to the shunting channel and detection device. Consequently, the subjects in Cherry's study were able to report only the physical characteristics of the nonshadowed message. These characteristics were determined by the preattentive analysis.

It's possible, however, to demonstrate that Broadbent's theory of attention, although convincing, cannot be completely correct. Moray (1959) found that subjects sometimes recognized that their names had been uttered in the nonshadowed message. According to Broadbent's theory, this recognition should not have happened. Names are meaningful to their owners, but the analysis of meaning is supposedly carried out by the detection device, which nonshadowed material never enters.

Similarly, Treisman (1960) reported that subjects could shadow the semantic content (i.e., the meaning) of a message even when the message was played into the non-

Figure 2.2 An illustration of Treisman's (1960) shadowing study. *Source:* From Matlin, 1983.

shadowed ear. Treisman instructed her subjects to shadow one ear, into which was played a meaningful message. The nonshadowed ear received a random string of words. Sometime in the delivery, the semantic content switched ears, as shown in Figure 2.2. At the same time, the random words were switched into the shadowed ear. Although the subjects had been instructed to shadow a particular ear, many of them ignored this instruction and shadowed the meaningful *message* instead. This finding indicated to Treisman that the subjects must have had some knowledge about the semantic content of the nonshadowed message.

In other studies, Treisman (1964a, 1964b) demonstrated that a message's semantic content is analyzed fairly early in the human information-processing system. Treisman used the dichotic listening procedure once again, telling her subjects to shadow a message. The message in the nonshadowed ear was to be ignored. Unknown (initially) to the subjects, the messages were identical. The nonshadowed message was started either slightly ahead of or slightly behind the shadowed message, and during the presentation, the nonshadowed message was speeded up or slowed down to synchronize it with the shadowed message. The critical variables were whether the subjects detected that the two messages were the same and, if so, the time interval between the two messages when detection occurred.

Treisman found that all the subjects detected that the two messages were the same. When the shadowed message led the unshadowed message, detection occurred when the messages were still 4.5 seconds apart. When the unshadowed message led the shadowed message, detection did not typically take place until the messages were much closer, about 1.4 seconds apart. The difference in times probably reflects the extent to which the material has been processed. The shadowed message is processed by the detection device and is passed on to the short-term, or working, memory. Consequently, a fairly durable representation is created that enables the subject to compare and match the content of the working memory with the nonshadowed ear even when the messages are 4.5 seconds apart. Presumably, however, the nonshadowed message never leaves the sensory register, and its representation is far less durable than that of the shadowed message. When the nonshadowed ear leads the shadowed ear, the subject probably won't be able to detect that the two messages are identical until the shadowed message is brought within the memory span of the auditory channel of the sensory register. This span has been estimated as about 1 or 2 seconds long. This finding seems to indicate that a semantic analysis of the sensory register is carried out, which is contrary to the predictions in Broadbent's model.

Attenuation Theory

Accordingly, Treisman proposed a modification for the basic theory, which is known as the **attenuation model.** According to this theory, incoming stimuli might undergo three kinds of analysis, or tests. The first test analyzes the physical properties of the stimuli. For auditory stimuli, the physical properties are equivalent to acoustic properties such as pitch and intensity. The second test determines whether the stimuli are linguistic and, if so, groups them into syllables and words. The final test recognizes the words and assigns meaning to them. All three tests are not necessarily carried out on all incoming stimuli. Rather, the processing is continued until the competing stimuli can be disentangled from one another.

Disentangling competing stimuli sometimes requires little processing. If you're talking to a man at a party, and the people standing and talking nearby happen to be women, the stimuli can be sorted out by the first test. Under these circumstances, you would probably not become aware of the semantic content of the women's speech, because the semantic content of their conversation had not been processed. If the first test fails to disentangle the stimuli, then a second-level test must be carried out. For example, a friend called one day to tell me about the breakup of his latest romance. Unfortunately, he called in the middle of an exciting football game. Because the acoustic differences between the two messages were minimal, a second-level test based on syllables and words had to be carried out to separate the two messages. In this case, I *did* become aware of some of the words used in both messages. That is, my subjective report of the incoming stimuli was something like this:

> So then she says to me Washington, first and goal on the two!

According to Treisman, what takes place in such circumstances is not a complete tuning out of the nonshadowed message, à la Broadbent, but rather an attenuation (turning down) of some messages that have been sorted out following the results of the tests. Figure 2.1 graphically compares Treisman's model with Broadbent's.

The attenuation model differs from the filter model in two ways. First, the filter model postulates that the basis of selective attention is a fairly crude analysis of the physical characteristics of the incoming stimuli. The attenuation model maintains that the preattentive analysis is much more complex and may even consist of semantic processing. Second, the filter in the filter theory is an all-or-none affair. Whatever is not selected is tuned out completely. The attenuation model, however, supposes that non-selected channels are not completely shut off but are simply turned down or damped.

These distinctions are consistent with the findings of Cherry and Kruger (1983), who studied the selective attention abilities of learning-disabled (LD) children. In their task, children aged seven to nine years were required to point to the appropriate picture of a word that was presented in one channel of stereo headphones. In the other ear, the children were presented with one of three distractors: a nonlinguistic, nonsemantic sound called *white noise* (a hissing sound); backward speech, which is linguistic but nonsemantic; or forward speech, which is both linguistic and semantic. When subjected to a distractor, the performance of the LD children was substantially worse than that of normal-achieving children. The discrepancy in performance between the exceptional and normal children was greatest when the semantic distractor was used.

Treisman would argue that this finding indicates that the LD children's preattentive analysis includes semantic analysis of the nonshadowed message. Also, such a finding suggests that LD children's problems stem at least in part from apparent inability to control the attenuation of nonshadowed messages. The LD children apparently can't completely damp the nonshadowed (and unwanted) competing stimuli. Incidentally, the Cherry and Kruger study is a good way to demonstrate how a cognitive analysis might help in understanding and possibly treating a practical problem.

Late-Selection Theory

Although Treisman's theory provides a good account for many of the phenomena associated with selective attention, it has a serious shortcoming. Specifically, it seems too complicated. The theory postulates that the preattentive analysis is almost as complete as the attentive analysis. If that's so, then what's the point in doing the preattentive analysis in the first place? A simpler alternative to the Treisman position was originally proposed by Deutsch and Deutsch (1963).

These theorists argued that the bottleneck in selective attention occurs later in the processing of information than the Treisman theory proposed. Whereas Treisman maintained that the preattentive analysis determines what information is selected for further processing, Deutsch and Deutsch argued that almost all the incoming stimuli are sent on for further processing. When the information reaches working memory, selection for further processing takes place at that site. This viewpoint is referred to as the **late-selection** position because the selection for further processing is made in working memory rather than earlier, in the channels of sensory memory. Figure 2.1 compares the late-selection position with the models of Broadbent and Treisman.

The late-selection model predicts that all incoming stimuli are processed. Consequently, subjects should recognize information under almost any circumstances, even when information is presented to a nonshadowed ear. This assertion was tested in a study by Lewis (1970). In a dichotic listening task, subjects were told to shadow words that were presented in one ear and to ignore anything presented in the nonshadowed ear. Words also were presented in the nonshadowed ear. These words were sometimes semantically unrelated to the words being shadowed, and on other occasions the nonshadowed words were synonyms of the shadowed words. Lewis measured the latency between presentation of the shadowed word and the subject's vocal response. He found that presenting a nonshadowed synonym produced a delay in the subject's response, which was not observed when the nonshadowed stimulus was an unrelated word.

This finding is not consistent with either model of early selection. If the filter theory was completely correct, the nature of the word should not have increased the latency of response, because the nonshadowed ear supposedly is completely tuned out. The attenuation model argues that nonshadowed words are turned down. Although the meaning of nonshadowed words might sometimes intrude on the shadowed message, semantic relationships such as synonymity should not. In Lewis's study, the subjects had recognized a semantic relationship between the messages in the nonshadowed and shadowed ears.

As explained by Norman (1968), the late-selection model operates in this way. All information is transmitted to the working memory, but this transmission is different from that proposed by Broadbent or Treisman. Rather than describe the transmission as a serial (one step at a time) process, the transmission is thought to be in parallel (all at once, as shown in Figure 2.1). Because the capacity of the working memory is limited, parallel transmission strains the operation of working memory. Not all the information sent there can be stored. In working memory, a judgment is made about the material's importance (this point is discussed later in the chapter). Material that has been judged important is elaborated more fully, in turn creating a more durable representation of the information that may eventually enter permanent memory (Watanabe, 1980). Anything not important is not elaborated or rehearsed, and consequently is forgotten. According to this view, the act of shadowing per se is not what determines what we attend to and consequently become aware of. Rather, the patterns that are formed and recognized in our working memory become the basis for our awareness.

A study by MacKay (1973) illustrates these points. The subjects were told to shadow sentences that were grammatically correct but semantically ambiguous. For example, the subjects might shadow the sentence "They were throwing stones at the bank." This sentence could refer to individuals who were standing beside a river throwing stones into it, or it could refer to individuals who were throwing stones at a financial institution. A word that might steer the subject toward resolution of the ambiguity was presented at the appropriate time in the subject's nonshadowed ear. In this case, when the subject shadowed *bank*, either *money* or *river* was presented in the nonshadowed ear. After a number of such sentences, the subjects were given a memory task in which they were asked to recognize the sentences they had shadowed. In some cases, the subjects were given forms of the sentence that were congruent with the word that had been presented in the nonshadowed ear. In other cases, the forms of the sentences were not congruent with the word presented in the nonshadowed ear.

You can probably predict the findings of this study. Subjects tended to remember having shadowed sentences that were congruent with the word presented in the nonshadowed ear. In the preceding sentence, for example, the subject might remember having shadowed the sentence "They were throwing stones at the financial institution" if the word *money* had been presented in the nonshadowed ear. But the subject would not remember this sentence as previously shadowed if *river* had been presented in the nonshadowed ear.

Another finding from the MacKay study might be more difficult to predict. When the subjects were asked to indicate which words had been presented in the nonshadowed ear, they could not remember which words they had heard. This finding is somewhat curious. The meaning of the nonshadowed words had been processed, although apparently only a fragile code had been created—so fragile that it no longer survived by the end of the presentation. The subjects therefore did not remember the nonshadowed words on the memory test.

Earlier I referred to the importance of the information entering the working memory. A major implication of the Deutsch and Deutsch (1963) and Norman

(1968) position is that working memory can be preset to determine the value of incoming stimuli, and the evaluation of the incoming material can be consciously controlled even if unimportant information does not itself enter consciousness. These contentions were explored in a complex and provocative study by Johnston and Heinz (1978).

These researchers argued that by carrying out different sorts of tests on the material in working memory humans could control the extent to which unattended stimuli are processed. They also reasoned that some tests should be carried out before others. Specifically, it's sensible to assume that a subject would carry out a sensory (or physical) analysis before a semantic analysis. Why? Because in many ways, a semantic analysis is much more effortful than a sensory analysis. A semantic analysis is more effortful because more knowledge is required to carry it out. If you think about this statement for a minute, you'll see what I mean. I can carry out some physical analyses of foreign languages, but I can't carry out a semantic analysis because my knowledge is too limited. Johnston and Heinz argued that, if the sensory tests provided enough information to disentangle the competing stimuli, the subjects would be unwilling to engage in the semantic test. So far, this reasoning should remind you of Treisman's theory. Treisman, however, described these tests as ways of attenuating unwanted stimulation, whereas Johnston and Heinz had a different objective. They maintained that the processing capability of working memory is limited. Consequently, if the subject were required to carry out several tests to recognize and categorize incoming information, the subject would have little processing capability left over to deal with another ancillary task, and his or her performance on this secondary task should thus be poor. Remember, however, that the nature and extent of the evaluation are thought to be under conscious control. If the subject determines that incoming stimuli can be categorized without a complete semantic analysis, some of the working memory's processing capability should be available for executing the secondary task. In that case, performance on the ancillary task should be reasonable. To sum up, performance on some ancillary task should be poor if the primary task requires a semantic analysis. Performance on the ancillary task may not be poor, however, if the primary task does not require a semantic analysis. Let's see how this reasoning was enacted in the Johnston and Heinz (1978) study.

Subjects were asked to shadow messages that differed from the nonshadowed message in physical characteristics, semantic aspects, or both. Messages of low physical discriminability were produced by having the same male voice recite both messages. Messages of high physical discriminability were created by using a male voice to recite one message and a female voice to recite the other. Semantic aspects varied in two ways. Messages of low semantic discriminability were created by reciting lists of items drawn from the same category. For example, two lists of types of furniture might be played into stereo-headphone channels. Messages of high semantic discriminability were formed by reciting lists of items drawn from different categories (such as a list of furniture types and a list of fruits). While subjects were shadowing one message in the familiar dichotic listening task, they were also required to detect and respond to changes in a light's brightness. This was the ancillary task.

The researchers were interested in whether changes in the shadowing task affect the subject's ability to detect and respond to changes in brightness. If the subject does not have control over analyzing the incoming stimuli, the differences in physical or semantic aspects of the messages should have no effect on the subject's ability to do the ancillary task. Why? Because if the subject has no control over the analysis, the entire analysis must be carried out regardless of whether it is necessary. Whatever the processing demands in the full analysis, they would be constant across all the combinations of physical and semantic discriminability; hence, the subject would be left with a constant amount of processing ability to carry out the secondary task.

If the subject does have control over the analysis, however, a different prediction follows. For example, if the messages were discriminable by sensory characteristics, we might expect that the subject wouldn't bother carrying out the semantic analysis. If the semantic analysis were not carried out, the processing capabilities of working memory would not be as taxed, and the subject would be able to devote some of these capabilities to processing the ancillary task. If the messages were low in physical discriminability, the subject would be compelled to carry out the effortful semantic analysis to keep up with the message to be shadowed. Then we would look for a decrement in performance on the ancillary task.

The results of the study supported Johnston and Heinz's reasoning. Regardless of the messages' semantic discriminability, the subjects' reaction times on the ancillary task were much faster in the high physical discriminability condition than they were in the low physical discriminability condition. That is, when the messages had high physical discriminability, the subjects were able to rapidly detect and respond to changes in the light's brightness even when the messages were semantically similar. When the full (i.e., semantic) analysis had to be carried out, Johnston and Heinz found that the subjects had little processing capability left over to carry out the ancillary task. This decreased capability was reflected in their slower reaction times and reduced shadowing accuracy in that condition. In other words, when the messages were low in physical discriminability and the subjects had to engage in the semantic analysis, they became slower at detecting and responding to changes in the light's brightness.

Intrachapter Summary and Interpretation

For several pages we have dealt with several bottleneck theories of attention, each seeming to supplant its predecessor. Along the way, many findings have been mentioned. Now is the time for us to try to organize these findings into a coherent picture.

We have seen that Broadbent and Treisman thought of attention as a filter that operated in the earliest stages of human information processing to screen out stimuli. Treisman argued specifically that a complex preattentive analysis was carried out early in the processing of information. Surviving information was sent serially along a limited-capacity channel for recognition. Late-selection theorists such as Deutsch and Deutsch postulated that all information is sent on in parallel to a recognition device. This change in viewpoint paved the way for another major change in our conceptualization of attention; namely, that we can consciously control attentional analysis even though the results of such analysis may not enter our consciousness (MacKay, 1973; Johnston & Heinz, 1978). As these researchers point out, the subject's intention can be critical in determining what material we become conscious of, which means that we have to consider what strategic factors might be involved in the subject's processing (Lowe & Mitterer, 1982). Paradoxically, however, the intention to process incoming information doesn't ensure that we will become aware of that material for any meaningful length of time. According to the late-selection view, we will process as much as necessary to disentangle the competing stimuli. When the stimuli have been sorted out, we'll elaborate the material we wish to keep, thus creating a more durable representation. Anything not elaborated will be forgotten.

These findings superficially suggest that attention can be compared to a funnel—a constricted point in the information-processing system through which all incoming material must pass. More recent studies suggest, however, that such an analogy is somewhat misleading. Rather, we might think of attention as a spotlight that comes equipped with a controllable lens. Because this lens is under our control, we can narrow the beam to a pencil point of light, and then the object of scrutiny comes under intense and highly focused illumination. On the other hand, we can open up the lens and illuminate several objects at once, although less intensely than before. Notice that the wattage of the light does not change. What changes is the way in which we apply the light's power.

These "spotlight" effects have been explored by Palmer (1990). Palmer's subjects viewed stimuli consisting of one, two, or four horizontal lines that were presented for 100 msec; when four lines were presented, they were always presented in the same spatial location relative to the subject's viewpoint. These horizontal lines are referred to as the "study stimuli"; that is, the subject was supposed to inspect and "study" them while they were on view. The number of lines in the study stimulus is referred to as the "set size." For example, when only one line was presented, we say the set size was 1. After seeing the lines, subjects waited a 2000-msec interstimulus interval, after which a test stimulus appeared for 100 msec. The test stimulus consisted of a horizontal line appearing in the same location as one of the lines in the study stimulus; when the study stimulus consisted of only one line, the test stimulus's line appeared in the same location as the line of the study stimulus. The subject's task was to determine if the test stimulus was longer than the corresponding line of the study stimulus. This task was not "speeded"; the subjects could take as long as they wanted to make up their mind. The dependent measure in this study was the difference in line length between study and test stimuli required for the subject to accurately detect any differences in the two lines. From the research we have gone over, we might expect that if indeed the spotlight is weaker when we are forced to examine a greater number of stimuli, then we might expect that the discrepancy in line length would have to be made correspondingly greater when the set size was 4, compared with when it was only 1, for the subjects to detect the difference in length between study and test stimuli. Notice that this study also has an interesting memory component because, in addition to paying attention to the lines in the study stimulus, the subjects had to remember how long each line was for 2000 msec to respond accurately.

Palmer (1990) found that set size had a very reliable and pronounced effect on the difference in line length required for detection. For example, when the set size was 2, subjects required about a 40 percent greater discrepancy in line lengths between study and test stimuli to detect the length difference, compared with that required when the set size was 1. When set size 4 was compared with set size 1, the difference was about 100 percent. In other words, if subjects could detect a difference in line lengths with a certain accuracy when the set size was 1, increasing the set size up to 4 would mean the difference in line lengths would have to be doubled for the subjects to detect the difference with the same accuracy. Palmer's studies show us just how much weaker in intensity the attentional spotlight gets when the number of stimuli in the input condition is increased.

Alternatives to Filter Theories: Capacity Models

The second phase in theory building in attention began with a reconceptualization of the problem, which occurred with the publication of Kahneman's (1973) book *Attention and Effort.* Partly from everyday examples such as driving a car and simultaneously carrying out a conversation, Kahneman argued that the location of the bottleneck in selective attention tasks seemed less important than understanding what the task itself demanded of the person. For example, because driving and talking are usually not highly demanding tasks, we can do both simultaneously. Driving in heavy traffic, however, is more demanding than driving on the open interstate, and so we would expect that conversation might break down during heavy traffic conditions.

Rather than talk about funneling stimuli along some limited-capacity channel, Kahneman maintained that attention could be understood as a set of cognitive processes for categorizing and recognizing stimuli. These **cognitive resources** were limited. To fully recognize a stimulus, resources were required; and if the stimulus was complex, many resources would be required. If several complex stimuli were presented simultaneously, the resources might be quickly used up; and if additional stimuli were presented to the person whose resources were used up, these newcomers would go unprocessed (and unnoticed). But the situation need not be so bleak. Kahneman postulated that incoming stimuli don't grab the resources all on their own. Instead, the cognitive system features a stage in which resources are allocated to process incoming stimuli. As Johnston and Heinz (1978) point out, allocation of cognitive resources is flexible and under our control. Rather than being slaves to incoming stimuli, we are able to shift limited resources to important stimuli.

Figure 2.3 depicts Kahneman's model. Notice that for this model he does not assume that the number of resources is completely fixed. Rather, the pool of resources available at any one time is determined partly by the individual's arousal level. The greater the level of arousal, the greater the pool of resources, at least up to a certain point. Beyond that point, increases in arousal may result in a decrease in the number of available resources. Which incoming stimuli have resources devoted to them is determined by the system's **allocation policy.** This policy is set by enduring dispositions and momentary intentions. *Enduring dispositions* are tendencies that many creatures have for processing loud noises, sudden motions, bright colors, and other unusual events. One enduring disposition of mature humans is the tendency to process our own names. *Momentary intentions* are situational dispositions to allocate cognitive resources to a source of incoming stimulation.

The **cognitive capacity** model makes several predictions, which we'll attempt to deal with. First, the capacity model assumes that the interference produced by competing sources of stimulation is nonspecific. That is, any problems that we may have in doing two things at once are not produced because the tasks interfere with each

Figure 2.3 A capacity model for attention. *Source:* From Kahneman, 1973.

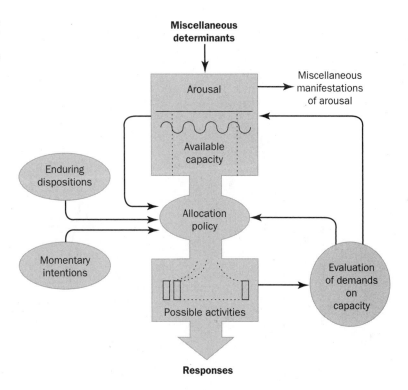

other, but rather because the tasks require more resources than we have available. Accordingly, the capacity model predicts that we will be able to do two things at once as long as these activities don't exceed the number of available resources. The second prediction follows from the first: Performance on one task will decline if we try to do a second task simultaneously when the sum total of the processing demands exceeds capacity. The third prediction states that the allocation policy is flexible and can be altered to suit the demands of the incoming stimuli. We have already looked at one study that bears on the third prediction. Recall that Johnston and Heinz (1978) demonstrated that their subjects would tailor their analyses of incoming information to the minimal depth necessary to shadow the message. If the subjects could shadow the message by using only a sensory analysis, which presumably requires fewer cognitive resources than the semantic analysis, then they would do that.

A study by Posner and Boies (1971) provides support for the first two predictions. Their subjects were required to do simultaneous tasks. The primary task (the one to which the subjects were told to devote their attention) was letter matching. Following the visual presentation of a warning signal, the subjects were shown a letter, such as a *T,* for a brief (50-msec) interval. After a 1-sec delay, the subjects were shown a second letter, and their task was to indicate as quickly as possible whether the second letter was the same as or different from the first. The subjects indicated their responses by pressing one of two buttons. If the second letter was the same as the first, subjects were supposed to tap a button with their right index fingers. If the second letter was different from the first, subjects used the right middle finger to tap.

Figure 2.4   The procedure and results of the experiment on simultaneous letter matching and tone detection: (*a*) sequence of events in a single trial (numbers designate points at which tones were presented intermittently); (*b*) time required to detect the tones at various points during the trials. *Source:* From Posner & Boies, 1971.

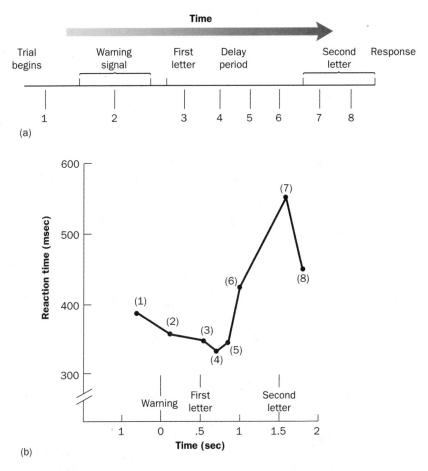

The second task was an auditory detection task. On some trials, a tone was presented via stereo headphones. Here, the subjects were told to tap a key with the left index finger as quickly as possible when they heard a tone. I'm sure you've already figured out that the procedure leaves a little to be desired, because the handedness of the subjects influences their ability to respond quickly to the tone. Consequently, we'll have to be extra careful in interpreting the findings in this experiment.

Figure 2.4 shows the sequence of stimuli presentation and the results of the study. Point 1 shows the average response time on the tone-detection task when the tone was presented prior to the warning signal. This point serves as a basis for comparison when the tone is presented later in the sequence. If the tone is presented before any of the letters are shown to the subjects, a reasonable assumption is that the subjects can devote all their resources to processing the tone. Consequently, any increase in response time to the tone when it is presented later is apparently the result of the subject's allocation of resources to the primary task. Notice in Figure 2.4 that the response time to the tone decreased somewhat during and immediately following the warning signal. One function of the warning signal is to increase the subject's alertness and arousal, which produces a corresponding increase in the available resources. At point (4), the graph of the response time is at its lowest point. This response, however, occurs immediately after the first letter has been presented and recognized.

This finding substantiates the first prediction by the Kahneman model: The subjects were able to process competing stimuli when the total demand did not exceed the available capacity. The arousal effects of the warning signal are not durable, and during the delay period, the subject must extract the first letter's code from sensory memory and develop a more durable representation in working memory. This procedure accounts for the increase in reaction time seen at point (6). The greatest increases in reaction time, however, are seen at points (7) and (8). At those points, the second letter has been presented and the subject is occupied with categorizing, recognizing, and judging it. These activities soak up most of the subject's available resources, leaving too few to process the tone quickly. This finding substantiates the second prediction in Kahneman's model: Performance of the auditory detection task declined when the processing demands exceeded capacity.

Some Questions About Capacity Models

Kahneman's capacity model is designed to supplement rather than supplant the bottleneck position. Whereas the bottleneck position postulates that incoming stimuli always compete for space on the shunting channel and therefore always interfere with each other, the capacity model assumes that the demands made by stimuli do not compete. That is, as long as sufficient resources are available, all the incoming stimuli can be accommodated. One question arises right away in comparing the two approaches about the interactions among incoming stimuli: Do they compete, or don't they? Cognitive psychologists have hedged their bets. A reasonable assumption is that some stimuli do interfere with each other, meaning that some tasks are truly incompatible. In those cases, some version of the bottleneck viewpoint is necessary to explain the processing. Posner and Boies (1971) demonstrated, however, that simultaneous tasks can be comfortably handled in some situations. There, the capacity model seems to be a reasonable explanation of events.

A second question is more problematic: the resources. Exactly what are they? No one knows the answer to this question with any certainty. Some researchers, though, have maintained that the resources are basic and elemental operations in the nervous system. Several researchers have attempted to establish a link between these operations and cerebral architecture.

For example, Dawson and Schell (1982, 1983) had their subjects shadow a list of unrelated words presented via stereo headphones. A separate list of semantically unrelated words was presented over the nonshadowed channel. Occasionally presented in the nonshadowed ear was one of a series of words that had previously been paired with a painful electric shock. We would expect such words to be processed even when they were presented on the nonshadowed channel, because we have an enduring disposition to process events that may signal onset of pain. Dawson and Schell found this to be the case. Skin responses known as **electrodermal responses** (EDRs) were elicited by presenting shock-associated words in the nonshadowed channel. But now the plot thickens intriguingly. You probably know that the cortex in the brain is divided into two hemispheres. Each hemisphere controls one side of the body. Hemispheric control over the body, however, is *contralateral,* or opposite sided, meaning that the left hemisphere controls the right-hand side of the body and vice versa. In most people, one hemisphere—typically the left—dominates.

Dawson and Schell found that when shock-associated words were presented to the right ear (whose neural pathway winds up in the left hemisphere), EDRs were observed only on trials in which the subject showed independent indications of attentional shifts. These independent indications included errors in shadowing and increased latency in shadowing the attended word. When the shock-associated words were presented to the left ear, however, EDRs were observed even on trials in which no independent indications of attentional shifts were shown. What to make of this result? The hemispheres apparently differ in the resources available to them, or in their allocation policies. For the dominant hemisphere, processing the significant word may require more of its resources, thus overloading capacity and producing increased latency in shadowing the attended channel. For the nondominant hemisphere, perhaps fewer or different resources are required to do the same thing. Indeed, Dawson and Schell (1983) hypothesize that each hemisphere may have a partially independent pool of processing capabilities.

This contention is explored in a study by Mathieson, Sainsbury, and Fitzgerald (1990). Their subjects participated in a dichotic listening task in which the subjects heard lists composed of consonants (i.e., speech sounds), emotional nonspeech sounds (e.g., crying), or combinations of both. After hearing pairs of such stimuli, subjects were asked to state the ear in which a specific stimulus had been played. The researchers found that the subjects were more accurate when nonspeech sounds were played into the left ear and when speech sounds were played into the right ear, regardless of whether the list the subject heard was composed of just speech sounds, just nonspeech sounds, or both classes of stimuli. Although the findings by Dawson and Schell and Mathieson et al. have not gone unchallenged (Walker & Ceci, 1983), each hemisphere may nevertheless have a pool of resources that work in a way that is consistent with what we know about laterality effects.

Demanding Stimuli: What Grabs Our Attention?

The capacity model of attention that we've been considering over the last few pages seems to emphasize the control that we have over our attention. And certainly we do have quite a bit of control; for example, I can decide to start paying attention to a source of stimulation, and I can decide to stop. I can even "get ready" to pay attention to something. But the experiences that we have in the world tell us that at many times our attention is not so much allocated as grabbed: Advertisers seem to know how to create arrangements of stimuli that refuse to stay in the background. Like it or not, these stimuli manage to get into the spotlight of our attention and stay there for at least a little while. What are the characteristics of these attention grabbers?

We need a little background information first. Cognitivists have known for some time that when humans are asked to search for a previously specified target (such as a letter) in a field of similar objects (such as other letters), then increasing the number of letters in the field that must be searched produces an increase in the time that people need to find the target. This increase is referred to as the *display-size effect*. And this choice makes sense: If you're searching for a specific letter, and the display has only two letters, you should be able to determine whether or not the target is present in that field much faster than if the display has 100 letters. Why? The answer is that, even though we can allocate attention to tasks that we want to do, making the judgment about each letter in the display size apparently must take place serially, or almost serially; it's certainly a processing-intensive task. When several potential targets are added to an array, we must allocate some attention to scanning each of them and to making a separate decision for each.

But sometimes the display-size effect is not observed. Consider when the target differs from all the other objects in the display field on some very salient dimension, such as color. Suppose you're instructed to search for a letter, and this target letter is shown to you printed in red ink. Then you are shown the display containing both the target and the distractors. If the target is printed in red ink and all the distractors in green ink, two findings are observed. First, the target is not hard to find, and, second, the display-size effect is negligible. A target that differs from all the distractors on some salient dimension is referred to as a *featural singleton* (Yantis, 1993). A featural singleton seems to "pop out" of the display without any apparent allocation of attention. Now a *featural singleton* actually has two things going for it. First, the featural singleton is the target, or contains the target. Second, the featural singleton is different from all the other stimuli. This raises a natural question: What happens when a stimulus is different from all other stimuli, but is nevertheless not the target?

Theeuwes (1992) shows that, under some circumstances, people have a difficult time not allocating attention to a featural singleton, even when the singleton does not contain information about the target. Figure 2.5 shows the materials that Theeuwes used. The subjects were told to report the orientation of the line (horizontal or vertical) inside the circle. All the other lines in the display were surrounded by diamonds. The circular shape was a reliable form singleton that would presumably pop out, enabling the subjects to quickly report the orientation of the line inside it. On half the trials, all the diamonds were the same color (green). But on the other half, one of the diamonds was red; it was called the distractor condition. Therefore, the trials in which a distractor was present had two singletons: the helpful form singleton that we've described, and the irrelevant, and useless, color singleton that the subjects might as well ignore if they could. We want to know whether the presence of an irrelevant featural singleton (the single red diamond) slowed the subjects in reporting the orientation of the line in the circle. As the bottom half of Figure 2.5 shows, this is exactly what happened. When an irrelevant color distractor appeared in the array, the subjects' reaction time increased significantly. In addition, you can see the beginning of a display-size effect in the distractor conditions. That is, when the display size consists of nine geometric forms, the subjects are slowed by the irrelevant distractor significantly more than they are when the irrelevant distractor appears in a display size of only five geometric forms. Thus, when observers search an array for singletons, their attention is apparently grabbed by any area of the array that has a singleton.

In all the studies we have talked about so far, the subjects knew that a singleton of some sort would appear and they knew that at least some singletons are helpful. This knowledge implies that the singleton becomes part of the subjects' attentional

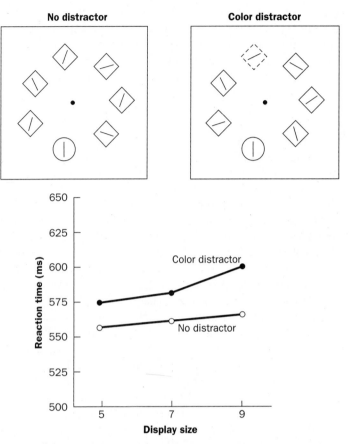

Figure 2.5 Effect of irrelevant singletons when the target is a singleton. Top: Sample displays from the form condition of Theeuwes's visual search task, which requires the observer to report the orientation of the single nonoblique line segment. Green lines are shown as solid, red lines as dotted. The target line segment is always inside the green circle, which is a form singleton here. The left panel shows no distractor singleton. The right panel shows a red distractor singleton. Bottom: Reaction time as a function of display size for the distractor and no-distractor conditions. Reaction time is slower when there is a color distractor than when there is not, suggesting that the color singleton cannot be ignored. *Source:* From Theeuwes, 1992.

set. What happens when the subjects do not know if processing the featural singleton will be helpful or harmful? That is, what happens when the singleton is not part of the subject's attentional set? Yantis and Jonides (1990) investigated this condition by presenting their subjects with arrays of letters, one of which was different from all the others in color or brightness. In this study, however, the singleton, whether a different-colored singleton or a brighter singleton, was no more likely to be the target than any of the other letters in the array. In this study, the display-size effect returned: Now, when the subjects had to search among many letters, the time required to find the target increased, even when the target was a singleton! The conclusion is that salient singletons can capture attention, but only when the singletons are somehow relevant to the perceiver's goals. When the singletons are not relevant, then they don't necessarily grab any more attention than do other stimuli in the array. It's as if people can "tune" their cognitive systems to meet their goals efficiently. Thus, when people know that the singleton may be helpful (because the target is always a singleton), then singletons are processed "first," and the display-size effect is not seen. But the mere presence of singletons is not enough to grab attention. In this situation, it's as if the cognitive system is saying, "All right, sometimes there are unique stimuli in this array, but I'm not going to bother processing them first, because they are not necessarily helpful." Under these circumstances, the display-size effect makes its return.

Other theorists have taken a different approach to featural singletons. Instead of simply buying into a notion that some visual searches are done in parallel, thus producing the "pop-out" phenomenon, and others are done serially, some researchers have wondered how ultimately useful this distinction is.

For example, to look at serial and parallel visual searches, Wolfe (1998) rounded up just about all the data gathered in his laboratory over 10 years. The resulting data set was huge, representing performance by about 650 subjects, each of whom underwent something like 500 to 1500 trials. The whole data set consisted of nearly 1 million visual search trials. Some of the data were produced by visual search tasks that are thought to be clearly serial, such as looking for an S among mirror-reversed Ss, and other data were produced by visual searches that are thought to be parallel, such as color-feature searches.

Before we discuss the findings, let's discuss what should happen if we make a graph of performance on such search tasks. Suppose we have a task in which the subject has to find the normal S among an array of mirror-reversed Ss. Generally speaking, the normal S will not pop out of this array; the current thinking is that, if you are a subject in such a study, you have to look for the normal S by scanning each of the elements in the whole array and making a decision about each one, until you find the normal S, at which time you stop searching and press the appropriate key. We would expect therefore that this task should show the display-size effect—the more elements in the array, the longer it takes to find the target. As a final step, we could also graph the time that the subject spent searching as a function of the number of elements in the array. If the subject spent 250 msec actually searching when the array size was 10, and 500 msec searching when the array size was 20, we can say with some confidence that the subject spends about 25 msec/item searching, and the slope of the line on the graph will be positive. Now let's consider a pop-out task such as searching for a blue S among other Ss that are red. We would probably find no display-size effect: it wouldn't matter whether the array size was 10 or 20. The search time per item would be constant, and negligible (typically less than 10 msec/item), and the slope of a line of search time as a function of items in the array would be flat. What would you expect if you were to make a composite graph of all the slopes in all the studies? It might be reasonable to expect that the resulting graph would be bimodal: one mode centering on the mean of the serial searches, and one lower mode centering on the fast, parallel searches.

This is a neat distinction; the only problem is that, as Wolfe found when he looked at his huge data set, it just doesn't happen in that way. Looking at the data over thousands and thousands of trials, in a number of searches, no bimodal distribution of slopes appears such as we would expect to see if two kinds of searches were going on. In fact, when all the slopes from all the studies are graphed together, the distribution of slopes from varied tasks is unimodal (it has only one point). The modal slope value is around 15 msec/item. If all visual search processes were either serial or parallel (which is where the pop-out phenomenon is supposed to come from) then the graph of the slope of reaction time per item from dozens of experiments should show bimodalism. Here are just a couple of Wolfe's (1998) own summary points:

1. The overall distribution of search slopes is unimodal and provides no support for a simple, data-driven division of searches into "serial" and "parallel" (or anything else).
8. Your favorite theory of visual search is wrong. So is mine. No current model of visual search generates the pattern of results in this data set. This is not to say that no current model could do so. Models must be adjusted to fit this new picture of reality (Wolfe, 1998, p. 38).

It will be fun to see how this issue plays out over the next few years. In the meantime, findings like these have some theorists questioning the varieties of attentional phenomena that will be required to explain them. We'll turn to that issue in the next section.

Attention: One Process or Two?

When we are "paying attention" to a stimulus, we are not conscious of using more than one attentional process. As we saw in Chapter 1, however, we may not be aware of all the cognitive processes that are constantly going on within us. This lack raises a question about the number of attentional processes that the cognitive system is able to call upon to process a stimulus: Is there just one process called "attention"? Or are there a number of attentional processes that might be used at different times in processing a stimulus?

Some research by Johnston, McCann, and Remington (1995) provides an interesting response to this question, but before we can appreciate their study and its findings, we need some background knowledge. Over the last few decades, cognitive psychologists have developed several techniques and procedures for studying attention; we have seen some of them in this chapter. Among some of the others that cognitive psychologists have made use of is a technique known as the spatial-cuing paradigm. In spatial-cuing studies, a signal or cue appears on a portion of the computer screen. Following the cue, a set of additional stimuli appears on the screen. In some trials, a target stimulus may appear at the location specified by the cue, and we call this a validly cued trial. On other occasions, the target stimulus may not appear at the location suggested by the cue (and now we have to go "hunting" to see if the target has been presented). This would be an invalidly cued trial. As you can predict, the typical finding in such studies is that humans respond much more quickly and much more accurately to targets that have been validly cued than they do to targets that have been invalidly cued. The explanation for this finding is that the cue directs the subject's attention to a point in space. At that point, humans are able to erect a movable "attentional window" through which stimuli that are selected for further processing can be accessed and processed. This explanation focuses on the selective aspects of attention, and consequently it is thought that this attentional window is erected relatively early in processing information. Another procedure that cognitive psychologists have used makes use of an attentional phenomenon called the **psychological refractory period** (PRP). "Refractory" here means "unable to respond." In studies using the PRP paradigm, humans are hit with two kinds of tasks, and they are asked to make two judgments as quickly as they can. For example, they may be given a musical tone and a briefly presented letter almost simultaneously. Their task may be to identify the letter as quickly as they can, and also to judge the pitch of the tone as quickly as possible. If enough time is allowed between the two tasks, subjects can do both of them with reasonable accuracy, showing that the tasks do not interfere with each other. But when the tasks are given very close together in time, then human performance suffers on whichever task is given second in the sequence, delaying performance on it by several hundred milliseconds. The explanation will seem reasonable. When the two tasks requiring different judgments are given close together in time, their processing demands overlap: We cannot start processing the second task until we are ready to begin paying attention to it, and we cannot do that until we have "cleared the first task" out of our systems. In this case, the attention that is required is not erecting an attentional window, but rather the attention required to process the stimuli themselves, which does not occur until a later stage in information processing. When the findings of both literatures are put together, they suggest that there is an early form of attention (Johnston et al. call it **input attention**), and a later form of attention called **central attention.** Their position is that input attention is needed to do spatial-cuing tasks, and central attention is needed in PRP tasks, and that these forms of attention operate at different times. How can that claim be substantiated?

Johnston et al. suggest that the differences in attentional processing and their order can be made clear by the "locus-of-slack" method (McCann & Johnston, 1992). "Locus" means "place" or "point," and "slack" implies "delay," and so the locus-of-slack method is a way of determining the point or place of delay in a series of cognitive processes. The locus-of-slack method can best be understood with a metaphor. Imagine a project that is accomplished in a series of steps that must be done in a specified order, such as, perhaps, constructing a building. The first steps may involve excavating, pouring the foundation, constructing steelwork, and so on. Let's also assume that prior steps must be completed before the later steps can be begun, as they would have to be in this example. For the building to be completed on time, each step must be completed promptly. A delay at any stage will be reflected in the project's completion date. In other words, if you were responsible for completing the building on time, and if you were to get a call from the steelwork contractor telling you that he or she has been delayed on another job and cannot come to your job site for four days, then you can add four days to the project's completion date. And for four days, no work is going on at your site (this is the slack time). Now let's imagine one more twist in this scenario. Suppose, after you get the call from the steelwork contractor, the concrete contractor stops in to tell you that the foundation work is more complicated than expected and thus it too will take longer than planned. Remember that the foundation comes before steel construction. If the foundation chief tells you the delay will be four days, then at least you can console yourself that this second four-day delay will not additionally delay the project, because of the four-day "slack" period already created by the steel delay. In other words, the steel delay has created a four-day slack period into which any additional problems that come before the steel work are simply "absorbed into slack."

This expression describes the means that Johnston et al. used to determine the timing of input and central attention. If a cognitive task's difficulty is increased so that additional time is required for that task, then we should be able to measure that increase in reaction time, and this increase corresponds to the "slack" created by the steelwork delay in the building example. If we simultaneously increase the difficulty in another cognitive task, but we observe no overall increase in processing time for the two tasks, then we can conclude that this other task must come *before* the initial task because its increase in complexity apparently has been absorbed into slack, just like the foundation work given in the example. But if, on the other hand, increases in complexity in the second task add to the overall time required to do both tasks, then we say that the additional task must come after the initial task, because its delays have not been absorbed into slack.

Johnston et al. (1995) conducted two studies; we'll have space here to describe only the first. In their first study, they investigated the timing of central attention as seen using the PRP technique. Subjects were given two tasks, with unpredictable time intervals between the tasks. The first task was an auditory discrimination task, and the instructions given to the subjects emphasized performance on the task. Subjects heard either a 300-Hz tone (to which they were to respond "low" as quickly and as accurately as they could), or a 900-Hz tone, to which they were told to respond with the word "high." Second was a letter-recognition task, in two versions. In the easy version, the subjects were shown a fixation point, at which one of two letters subsequently appeared: either an A or an H. Subjects were instructed to press one of two keys as quickly as they could for either letter. In the hard version of this task, the letters were distorted (see Figure 2.6 for a depiction of the distorted A and distorted H). Figure 2.6 shows the reaction times (RTs) for the two tasks graphed as a function of **stimulus onset asynchrony** (SOA—a good expression to know because it will crop up in several chapters). Stimulus onset asynchrony refers to the time differential between the two tasks. If the time difference between the auditory beep and the appearance of the letters was 50 msec (the briefest time difference in the current study), then we say that SOA was 50 msec.

What does this evidence tell us about the timing of the two kinds of attention? First, we would say that the two tasks (auditory discrimination and letter recognition) clearly show the effects of a bottleneck for central attention. When SOA was short (50 msec), performance on letter recognition increased by almost 250 msec, up to 725 msec, compared to letter-recognition performance when SOA was long. For example, at 600 msec SOA, letter recognition required only about 475 msec (on average). This finding tells us that when very little time came between presentations of the two tasks (i.e., SOA was short), letter recognition had to wait its turn for auditory discrimination to be completed before being completed itself. Second, and even more important, you'll notice an interaction effect between SOA and the difficulty of Task 2. Visually, you can discern this effect because the dashed lines in Task 2 are not perfectly parallel for the easy and hard versions of Task 2. When SOA was long (600 msec), the difficulty of Task 2 produced an effect: It took 27 msec longer to do the hard version

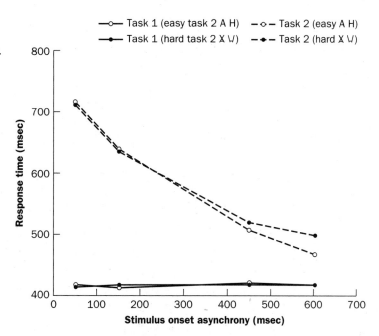

Figure 2.6 Response-time results from the Johnston et al. experiment. Solid lines show Task 1 response times, and dashed lines show Task 2 response times, as a function of stimulus onset asynchrony and whether Task 2 used normal (easy) or distorted (hard) letters. *Source:* From Johnson et al., 1995.

of Task 2 at an SOA of 600 msec than it did to do the easy version of Task 2 at that SOA. But when SOA was brief, difficulty in Task 2 didn't matter—the RTs were almost the same for both the easy and difficult versions of the task. We say therefore that the effect of letter difficulty (Task 2) was completely absorbed into slack at short SOAs. Now remember that because central attention is required to do Task 1, and because difficulty in letter recognition is absorbed into slack at short SOAs, letter recognition as a stage in cognitive processing must take place *before* central attention is placed on Task 1, just switching the directional arrow around. This finding in turn implies that central attention takes place after the delay in processing caused by the letter distortion.

In their second study, Johnston et al. reached an opposite conclusion for input attention. Using the spatial-cuing procedure, they found that letter difficulty was never absorbed into slack, suggesting that input attention was always required to do letter recognition. These combined effects are shown in their model depicted in Figure 2.7. There you can see that a little slack occurs after Stage C, where the letter recognition gets accomplished, and it is just this slack into which the difficulty in letter recognition was absorbed in this study. Other researchers have looked at the interaction between these attentional processes and other cognitive processes such as those involved in memory (e.g., Pashler, 1994) and suggest that these diverse attentional processes probably have some strong implications for what specific information can be stored and retrieved.

Relationship Between Practice and Attention

Our first efforts at doing a complex task often seem clumsy and uncoordinated, regardless of the resources we allocate to them. When my tennis teacher first showed

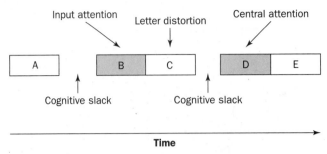

Figure 2.7   Stages-in-processing diagram for a dual-locus model of attention. Input attention is required for Stage B to begin; central attention is required for Stage D to begin. Letter identification is carried out in Stage C, which occurs after the stage in which input attention operates, but before the stage in which central attention operates. *Source:* From Johnston et. al., 1995.

me the correct service grip, stance, and movement, my initial thought was, I'll never do it right. Indeed, my first attempts were not promising. Thousands of serves later, I still don't have it right, although I've improved dramatically and objectively my serve is reasonably decent. This little tale is more than another illustration of practice-makes-reasonably-decent, however. As I practiced this task, I became aware that I no longer had to allocate all my attentional resources to monitoring kinesthetic sensations from my body and coordinating them with the toss of the ball. Using language described in Chapter 1, my tennis serve has gradually become both procedural (I no longer remember the steps in serving that my teacher made me memorize) and somewhat automatic as well. That is, although I'm aware of when it's time to serve in a match, I'm not in conscious control of running off the service program in my brain.

This everyday example has important implications for cognitive psychologists because it suggests that practice on a task reduces the resources needed to process the stimuli associated with doing the task. If practice were continued indefinitely, the performance not only would improve but also would become more automatic, requiring fewer and fewer cognitive resources. As fewer resources were allocated to the task, the subject's awareness would have a smaller and smaller role in initiating and executing the task. At the endpoint (which is probably seldom reached in everyday life), performance on the task would become truly automatic, requiring virtually no resources and leaving no conscious trace of its execution. This point is important. Recall from our discussion on the capacity model of attention that several sources of stimulation can be processed simultaneously as long as their demands do not exceed the supply of resources. Now we see that one way of solving the problem of attending to different sources of stimulation is to practice attending and doing one of the tasks, thus reducing the resources needed to process the task and leaving the remaining resources free to be allocated among the other tasks.

A second and perhaps controversial point is this: If practice reduces the resources needed to process incoming stimuli, then there are no demanding tasks, only unpracticed ones. In other words, if the attentional demands of a task can be reduced by practice, then our ability to attend to different sources of stimulation is limited not by our cognitive resources, but rather by the time in which we have to practice the tasks. In the next section we consider the question of automatic processing.

*A*utomaticity

Hasher and Zacks (1979) comment that two pathways lead to automatic processing. One is heredity, the other is learning. One implication of this position is striking: Hasher and Zacks argue that physical activities and mental events share the same pathway to **automaticity.** That is, mental actions, such as those involved in perception and memory, can be treated as though they were similar to motor skills. The same sort of repetition and drill that improve motor skills should also improve cognitive skills.

Schneider and Shiffrin (1977; Shiffrin & Schneider, 1977) show that complex but highly practiced perceptual analyses can be done automatically. They also demonstrate that such analyses will become automatic with practice even if they are not initially done in that way. Schneider and Shiffrin (1977) gave their subjects a set of letters or numbers that they called a memory set and instructed them to determine if any elements in the memory set appeared on slides that were presented for brief periods. This set of slides was varied in two ways. They might have one, two, or four characters printed on them— a factor called frame size. The relationship between the characters on the slides and the memory-set characters was the second variable. In the varied mapping condition, the subject was given a memory set consisting of one or more letters. All the characters to be searched were also letters. In the consistent mapping condition, the subject was given a memory set consisting of numbers. The elements to be searched through, however, were still all letters, unless the memory set number appeared on one of the slides. If one of the memory set numbers did appear, it was the only number present in the entire set of twenty slides. If after scanning the set of slides, the subjects had detected an element in the memory set, they were told to respond yes. If the subjects believed that no elements in the memory set were presented, they were instructed to respond no.

Figure 2.8 shows two examples of their trials. A good way to encode this study is to remember that, in the varied mapping conditions, the subject is searching for a letter among other letters, and in the consistent mapping condition, the subject is searching for a number among letters. Schneider and Shiffrin were interested in how quickly subjects could scan this set of slides while maintaining 95 percent accuracy—that is, saying yes or no and being correct 95 percent of the time.

The findings in this study are shown in Figure 2.9. Examine them and make your own interpretation. Considering the hits (trials in which the subject correctly said yes), we see that subjects could quickly scan the slides in the consistent mapping condition and still maintain 95 percent accuracy. That is, when looking for a number among letters, subjects required only 80 msec per slide to accurately process the information. Indeed, apparently the only variable in the consistent mapping condition that affected the subjects was frame time—the time in which subjects were allowed to view each slide. In the varied mapping condition, however, results differed.

Let's compare the same presentation (memory set size = 1, frame size = 2) across the two mapping conditions. As we've seen, subjects could achieve the accuracy criterion when viewing the slides for only 80 msec in the consistent mapping condition. Subjects required 200 msec to achieve the same accuracy, however, in the

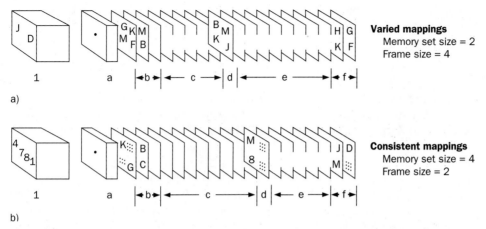

a)

b)

Figure 2.8   The two detection conditions in Schneider and Shiffrin's experiments: the varied mapping condition and the consistent mapping condition. On each trial the sequence of events was: presenting the memory set: (*a*) a fixation point; (*b*) three dummy frames that never contain the target; (*c*) distractor frames; (*d*) frame containing the target; (*e*) more distractor frames; (*f*) dummy frames that never contain the target. *Source:* From Schneider & Schiffrin, 1977.

Figure 2.9   Results of Schneider and Shiffrin's experiments. Subjects' performance in the varied mapping condition showed the effects of frame time, frame size, and memory-set size. In the consistent mapping condition, performance was affected only by frame time. *Source:* From Schneider & Shiffrin, 1977.

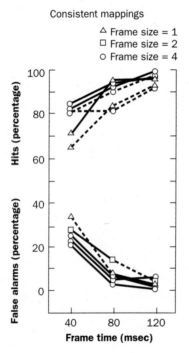

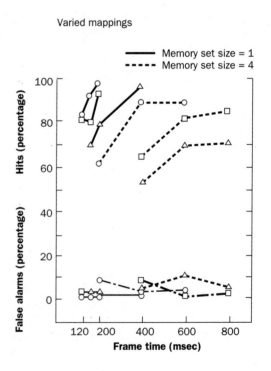

varied mapping condition; that is, when they were looking for a letter among other letters. Schneider and Shiffrin reasoned that processing letters during the search for a number is automatic, requiring virtually no allocation of resources. Searching for a letter among letters, though, is not automatic. This process is controlled and requires attention. If this reasoning is accurate, we would expect that frame size should not affect processing speed in the consistent mapping condition. That is, if you're looking for a number among letters, how many letters are on each slide doesn't matter, because the recognition processes are automatic and fast. But frame size should affect processing speed in the varied mapping condition. To maintain high accuracy, the subjects must scan each letter individually, and the more letters there are, the longer this search will take. This hypothesis was substantiated. Increases in the frame size had little effect on the subject's processing time in the consistent mapping condition, but similar changes produced substantial increases in processing speed in the varied mapping condition.

Shiffrin and Schneider (1977) demonstrated, however, that the search for a target letter in an array of letters can be done automatically if this task is practiced. Subjects were given a target letter that was always drawn from a particular set (B, C, D, G, F, H, J, K, L), and they were asked to scan a series of slides in which the distractor elements were always letters drawn from a different set (R, S, T, V, W, X, Y, Z). Although it took more than 2000 trials, the subjects nevertheless eventually performed as well on this varied mapping task as they did on the consistent mapping task in the previous experiment. This finding supports a point made earlier about the demands made by difficult tasks. As discussed, practice can tame difficult or time-consuming recognition tasks. Practice not only smooths the performance of motor and cognitive tasks but also reduces the resources that need to be allocated to process the information.

A similar point was made by Hirst, Spelke, Reaves, Caharack, and Neisser (1980). Their two subjects attempted to read and take dictation simultaneously. During the reading-only trials, the subjects read short stories, which were followed by tests of reading comprehension. This procedure was done to establish a baseline for reading rate and ability. The dictation task consisted of writing down short sentences, such as "The dog got free," which were slowly (thirty words per minute) presented to the subjects. During the reading–dictation trials, the subjects simultaneously read and took dictation. In the initial trials, the dictation task interfered with reading, resulting in slower speeds and poorer comprehension. After approximately 100 sessions, the subjects were able to take the dictation without its interfering with their reading. Their scores during the reading-dictation trials equaled the reading scores earned during the reading-only trials. Other evidence suggests that the subjects also comprehended the dictated sentences even though they had not been instructed to try to remember them. This second finding suggests that the two individuals in the study were carrying out two semantic analyses simultaneously.

One of the interesting and important questions raised in these studies is the length of time or, more accurately, the amount of experience with the stimuli, required for a cognitive process to be run automatically. Let's consider what might be involved. Logan (1990) draws an analogy between automaticity, generally speaking, and children's knowledge of addition facts. Asking an adult for the sum of 9 plus 6 produces a fast, effortless, and correct response, but small children must laboriously compute the answer. Now, suppose each time the child works that problem a residue or trace of the answer is left in the child's memory, and moreover, suppose residues accumulate with each solving of a problem. From the standpoint of the child's cognitive system, then, answering the question "What is 9 plus 6?" initiates a sort of race between the computational procedures and memory processes that look at the residues and try to figure out the answer from them. At first, the computational procedures will win this race every time, but each time the race is run, the residual trace gets stronger and stronger. Eventually the memory processes become faster than the computational procedure. According to this view, every instance of a response adds to the memory trace, and this view suggests that we set foot on the pathway to automaticity as soon as we begin to make the same type of response to specific stimuli.

To support these contentions, Logan (1990) carried out studies using lexical decision tasks as the basic paradigm. In a lexical decision task, a stimulus, either a word or a nonword, is presented to the subject visually. The subject is asked to decide as quickly as possible whether the stimulus is a word or a nonword, and the subjects indicate their choices by pressing keys. It's been known that when a stimulus in a lexical decision task, either a word or a nonword, is presented a second time, the subjects respond faster than they did to the first presentation. This phenomenon is called repetition priming. What happens when words and nonwords are presented several more times? Logan (1990) found that although the initial decision time for nonwords was in the neighborhood of 670 or so msec, the decision time after two repetitions was 70 to 100 msec less, and after ten presentations it had declined by about 150 msec compared with the initial response time. Given that 340 words and 340 nonwords were used as the stimuli in this study, it's clear that the subjects were not getting faster simply because of a "response set." That is, the number of stimuli in the study rules out the idea that the subjects were getting faster because they were saying to themselves something like, "I just have a hunch the next stimulus is going to be a nonword." Logan's findings suggest that automaticity is not some binary condition (we either have it or we don't) nor is it a terminal state (we're as automatic as we're going to be on some tasks). Rather, findings like these suggest that automaticity is a matter of some degree, and they also suggest that as soon as we begin to make the same class of response with some stimuli, we have begun to attain a measure of automatic processing.

Intrachapter Summary and Interpretation

In the second phase of theory building in the area of attention, Kahneman and others advance the idea that attention consists of a group of cognitive processes that can be allocated systematically to deal with incoming information. Demanding tasks require more resources than do less demanding tasks, but only unpracticed demanding tasks do so. With practice, the mental effort required to do demanding tasks decreases, and if practice is continued, the processing of a task may become automatic.

Capacity models should be thought of as complementing the bottleneck theories. Although as we have seen, humans often seem able to process competing stimuli simultaneously, parallel processing cannot be done in some situations. An obvious example is that purely physical limitations, resulting from the way your body is constructed, make it impossible to simultaneously attend to visual stimulation in front of you and behind you.

It is simply not known how much incoming stimuli compete for allocation of resources. To the extent that they do compete, bottleneck theories seem to account well for the fate of victorious stimuli—those which make it aboard the shunting channel. In the numerous cases in which competition seems absent, the capacity model seems a reasonable explanation. Another way of viewing this distinction was offered by Norman and Bobrow (1975). Certain difficult tasks were described as being data limited. We've all had the experience of trying to tune in a faraway radio station. Trying to catch the station's signal against the background of static consumes many of our resources as we try to make the fine discriminations necessary to tune in the station. Our processing of this auditory stimulus is limited by the poor data: the signal is weak. We tend to become single-minded as we fiddle with the tuner. An appropriate description is that the signal passes through a bottleneck into a detection device, where we extract as much information as possible from it. **Data-limited processes** can be contrasted with **resource-limited processes.** As the name implies, tasks must have resources allocated to them before they can be processed, and when we're out of resources, we're out.

Object Recognition

One of our cognitive systems' goals is to recognize and categorize incoming stimuli. How is this task accomplished? We deal with several theoretical accounts in this section.

Template-Matching Theory

When I was a child, one of my favorite playthings was a stencil that allowed me to trace geometric objects and letters. To my juvenile eyes, the traced capital letters looked far better than the irregular letters I produced freehand. I was much impressed with the timelessness of such letters. The *A* that I traced one day was identical to the previous day's *A,* which could easily be verified by putting the stencil over the traced *A* and seeing that only the correct *A* parts were visible.

Some researchers propose that human pattern recognition is achieved similarly. To recognize a pattern, such as the letter *T,* incoming information is compared with stored codes, called *templates,* until a good fit is found between the incoming information and the stored codes. Presumably, the best fit will be achieved when the incoming information matches the template for *T.* The incoming information will then be recognized and labeled *T.*

Figure 2.10 shows a template-matching system engaged in a series of hits and misses for the letter *A.* Early proponents of this view were cheered by the news that such a system could recognize letters. For example, if you take out your checkbook and look at the computer digits printed at the bottom of each check, you'll notice that they have been made highly distinguishable from one another. These differences apparently are necessary to permit the digits' recognition by machine.

The template-matching theory has two strikes against it. First, such a system is inefficient. Banking firms care little if their recognition machines slap (figuratively) as many as ten templates onto each digit before recognizing it, because only ten digits exist, and the machines can rapidly compare the input with the templates. Humans, however, must be able to recognize infinitely varied patterns, and they don't have the luxury of waiting until a match is achieved.

Figure 2.10 Examples of template-matching attempts: (*a*) through (*c*), successful attempts; (*d*) through (*h*), failed attempts. *Source:* From Neisser, 1967.

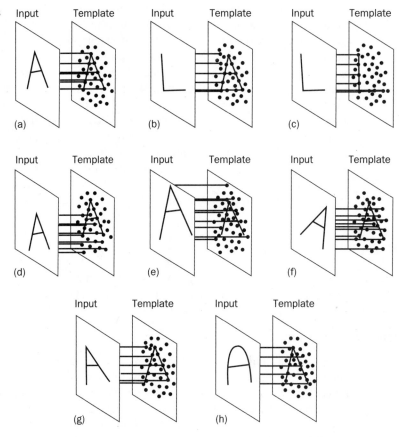

Second, template-matching systems are extremely inflexible, but human pattern recognition is successful despite great diversity of input. Notice in example (h) in Figure 2.10 that the input is clearly recognizable as an *A*, but the template system fails to recognize the stimulus because this *A* isn't the right kind of input. That is, strictly speaking, the template-recognition device can recognize stimuli only when their size and orientation permit a match. This method of recognition has its limitations. If I showed you an upside-down *A*, you would no doubt recognize it as a perfectly good example of an *A* despite its being upside down. A recognition device endowed with only a template-matching analysis, however, would draw a blank. These weaknesses have proved fatal for template-matching theories. Fortunately, a promising alternative is known.

Feature-Detection Theory

Earlier I mentioned that, as a child, I was never completely happy with the block letters that I drew freehand. I was dissatisfied with their irritating variability. Perhaps my annoyance was misplaced, because my ability to judge letters as one or another type indicates that I had detected that each example of a letter had something in common with all the other examples of that letter. The question is, what did each letter have in common with others?

Consider the letter *H*. It has two approximately vertical lines that are about the same length. Both of these vertical lines begin and end more or less in the same place, relative to the border of the page. An *H* has a horizontal line that intersects the two vertical lines, more or less at their midpoints. I have just provided a sort of checklist of things that an *H* must have. This list is not exhaustive; the relative lengths of the horizontal and vertical lines probably have additional stipulations. Nevertheless, a system endowed with the checklist just mentioned could scan a character, finding which items on the checklist the character had and which it did not. If a character had all the items on the checklist, the system would conclude that the character was an *H*. Thus, characters like these:

would not be called *H*s.

Feature analysis is the name given to this approach to the problem of pattern recognition. The basic assumption is that all complex stimuli are composed of distinctive and separable parts known as *features*. Pattern recognition is accomplished by counting the presence or absence of the features, and comparing the count with a tabulation of the features associated with different labels. Naturally, the success of the approach hinges on the decomposability of stimuli. Gibson (1969) demonstrated that features can apparently be tabulated, at least for letters.

Figure 2.11 lists presumed critical features. Notice that letters similar in appearance, such as *E* and *F*, share many features. This similarity leads to the expectation that, when errors in letter recognition take place, letters should be mistaken for letters with which they share features. This hypothesis has been confirmed many times (Geyer & DeWald, 1973; Garner, 1979). Other support for the feature-analysis model is supplied by Neisser (1964). Neisser gave his subjects blocks of letters such as those shown in Figure 2.12. The subjects were told to scan the blocks as quickly as they could to find the target letter, *Z*. Try it. Like most of Neisser's subjects, you probably located the *Z* much more quickly in block (1) than you did in block (2). Let's consider the implications of this finding.

The basic premise in the feature-analysis position is that cases of mistaken identity should occur among letters that share features. Thus, one might expect more such confusions when searching for *Z* in block (2), because the letters in block (2) share features with *Z*. Consequently, we should expect reduced accuracy of performance when subjects seek a target in feature-similar backgrounds as opposed to feature-dissimilar backgrounds. Neisser reported faster performance, however, when the subjects searched for a target in a feature-dissimilar background than when they sought the same target in the context of letters with similar features.

The implications of this discovery have not been lost on cognitive psychologists, who contend that this distinction indicates that features must be analyzed in steps, or stages. That is, in the first stage, the features are extracted from the stimulus and recorded. After this step is accomplished, the count, or comparison of the target letter with the background letter, is carried out. If the number of features in common is large, then the component in the system that is doing the counting will require more time, as Neisser said. This is another reason the feature-analysis model is a more persuasive account of pattern recognition than the template-matching theory. Template matching is an all-or-none theory. If the incoming stimulus matches some template, recognition is accurate and complete. If the incoming stimulus does not match some template, then the recognizer will presumably be left completely in the dark. The power of the feature-analysis point of view lies in its ability to explain both accuracy and latency of recognition. Incidentally, Neisser's subjects practiced tasks of this type for ten days. By now, you should be able to predict which changes had taken place in the subjects' performances by the tenth day.

Figure 2.11 Critical features of letters. *Source:* From Gibson, 1969.

Features	A	E	F	H	I	L	T	K	M	N	V	W	X	Y	Z	B	C	D	G	J	O	P	R	Q	S	U
Straight																										
Horizontal	+	+	+	+		+	+								+				+							
Vertical		+	+	+	+	+	+	+	+	+				+		+		+				+	+			
Diagonal /	+							+	+		+	+	+	+	+											
Diagonal /	+							+	+	+	+	+	+	+									+	+		
Curve																										
Closed																+		+			+	+	+	+		
Open *V*														+												+
Open *H*																	+		+						+	
Intersection	+	+	+	+		+	+							+		+						+	+	+		
Redundancy																										
Cyclic change		+							+		+						+								+	
Symmetry	+	+		+	+		+	+	+		+	+	+	+		+	+	+			+					+
Discontinuity																										
Vertical	+		+	+	+	+	+	+	+					+								+	+			
Horizontal		+	+			+	+							+												

Figure 2.12 Lists used to study feature analysis in a high-speed search task. *Source:* From Neisser, 1964.

(1)	(2)
ODUGQR	IVMXEW
QCDUGO	EWVMIX
CQOGRD	EXWMVI
QUGCDR	IXEMWV
URDCQO	VXWEMI
GRUQDO	MXVEWI
DUZGRO	XVWZEI
UCGROD	MWXVIE
DQRCGU	VIMEXW
QDOCGU	EXVWIM

A whimsical stage model of feature analysis was offered by Selfridge (1959). Called Pandemonium, his system described pattern recognition as taking place in stages that were carried out by highly specialized cognitive processes. Each process was referred to as a demon. In the first stage, the image demons are responsible for converting the physical stimulus into some sort of cognitive representation acceptable to the other demons. Next, the feature demons analyze the representation, with each one looking for his or her feature (horizontal lines, intersections, and so on). Next, the results of the feature count are posted for the cognitive demons. Each cognitive demon looks for his or her array of features. With every appropriate feature that a cognitive demon sees posted, his or her noisemaking increases a notch. Finally, the decision demon listens to the resulting pandemonium and judges which demon is shouting loudest; presumably, that is the incoming stimulus.

Recognition by Components

Biederman (1987; Biederman & Cooper, 1991; Biederman, Cooper, Hummel, & Fiser, 1993) has developed a model based on the idea that object recognition can be accomplished by breaking down a complex object's form into its simpler component shapes. His recognition by components model (RBC) is illustrated in Figure 2.13. The simple geometric forms on the left are labeled "geons," which stands for "geometric ion." In Biederman's theory, geons are really like atoms or molecules that can be assembled in numerous ways to make different objects (to me, the comparison with Lego® building bricks is irresistible). Like features in feature-detection theory, geons are primitives, but here they are volumetric primitives: primitives of shapes rather than lines or angles. The right-hand side in Figure 2.13 shows how the geons can be combined to form everyday objects. As this illustration shows, the relationship of the geons to each other is critical in determining the object's identity. Attached to the side of a cylinder, a partial loop makes the object a cup; attached across the top of the cylinder, the object becomes a bucket.

According to Biederman's model, we recognize an object by perceiving or "recovering" its underlying geons. If enough information is present to permit us to

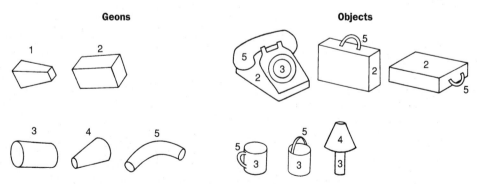

Figure 2.13 Left: Some geons. Right: Some objects created from the geons on the left. The numbers on the objects indicate which geons are present. Notice that recognizable objects can be formed by combining just two or three geons. Also notice that the relations between the geons matter, as illustrated by the cup and the pail. *Source:* Based on Biederman, 1985.

Figure 2.14   Although the object depicted in the top panel of this figure is masked, its geons are still visible, and so the object is recognizable. But in the bottom panel, the geons themselves are masked, and so the object is not recognizable. *Source:* Based on Biederman, 1985.

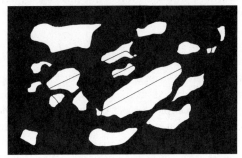

detect the geons, then we should be able to perceive the object. But if the information is presented to us in a way that does not permit us to detect the individual geons, then we will not be able to recognize the object. Biederman tested this assertion with displays like those shown in Figure 2.14. In the top panel the object is masked by the irregularly shaped dark blobs. Even though more than 50% of the object is obscured, the geons are still visible; consequently recognition of the object by the subjects was good (it's a flashlight). The bottom panel shows the same object, also obscured by a mask that covers more than 50% of its contours. Here, however, the geons are not recoverable, and the object is not recognizable. If you examine the two panels, you'll see that the intersections of the contours are still visible in the top panel, which enables the cognitive system to determine the "edge," and therefore the identity of the geons.

Object Recognition: A Computational View

One question you may have after reading about the RBC model is "Where do geons come from?" That is, how is the cognitive system able to put line segments together to form volumetric primitives in the first place? This was a question that the theorist David Marr took up in his classic work, *Vision* (1982). Marr proposed a way to an answer that was at once radical but eminently sensible: Human vision should be understood as an answer to a problem, here the problem of relaying a form of energy from the external world to the internal world of our cognitive systems. The goal of vision was to deliver enough information of the right kind to enable construction of a rep-

Table 2.1   Representational Framework for Deriving Shape Information from Images

Name	Purpose	Primitives
Image(s)	Represents intensity.	Intensity value at each point in the image
Primal sketch	Makes explicit important information about the two-dimensional image, primarily the intensity changes there and their geometrical distribution and organization.	Zero-crossings Blobs Terminations and discontinuities Edge segments Virtual lines Groups Curvilinear organization Boundaries
2 ½-D sketch	Makes explicit the orientation and rough depth of the visible surfaces, and contours of discontinuities in these quantities in a viewer-centered coordinate frame.	Local surface orientation (the "needles" primitives) Distance from viewer Discontinuities in depth Discontinuities in surface orientation
3-D model representation	Describes shapes and their spatial organization in an object-centered coordinate frame, using a modular hierarchic representation that includes volumetric primitives (i.e., primitives that represent the volume of space that a shape occupies) as well as surface primitives.	3-D models arranged hierarchically, each one based on a spatial configuration of a few sticks or axes, to which volumetric or surface shape primitives are attached

Source: From Marr, 1982.

resentation that is useful to its creator. Marr made two important points about this representation. First, it must be possible to create such a representation computationally, using only the information available to the photoreceptors in the retina, and, second, this representation could not be created in one step. Marr did not completely accomplish the computational or mathematical specification of visual information before his untimely death, but he made some vital statements about the steps that could be used to accomplish representation of information about shapes and objects from activity by the retina alone. Table 2.1 shows the series of representations that the visual system creates in his theory, along with the purpose for each representation and the features or primitives that are used at each level.

We won't be able to go too deeply into each of these stages, but I will try to explain some of the primitive terms. At the image, or retinal, level the intensity of each point in the retina corresponds to a mathematical depiction of the local region's brightness or darkness. You may have seen a kind of television set called "black and white" (my eight-year-old can't believe they were all like this once upon a time). Every small region on the screen is a mapping of the real world in one dimension only—brightness. If a region in the real world is very bright, it may be mapped as a region with a high value, let's say $+10$, on the screen. If a region in the real world is black, then it is mapped as a region with the lowest value, let's say -10 on the screen. If you wanted to take the time, you could photograph an object, convert the photo to such a numeric representation, put each number in a square on a piece of graph paper, and ask another person to blacken the squares. If you did this exercise appropriately, after the person had colored in all the squares on the graph paper, you should be able to "see" the object that was in the original photo. One of Marr's points is that our visual systems simply have no more information than this to start with, and so all our visual experiences must be based in some way on such an intensity mapping.

At the next level, the primitives consist of, among other things, zero crossings and blobs. A zero crossing is a change in intensity from mostly dark to mostly bright. In our example, if two adjacent squares had the values -1 and 0, or 0 and $+1$, we would say that the brightness had "crossed" the zero point at the border of those two squares. A series of such identical zero crossings would be a "line" or "edge segment." I'll try to show what one would look like typographically:

-1	-1	-1	-1	-1
$+1$	$+1$	$+1$	$+1$	$+1$

There would be a very faint horizontal line running "between" the positive and negative numbers. If the numbers above were -10 (instead of -1) and $+10$ instead of $+1$, then you would have a very abrupt series of adjacent zero crossings, and therefore a very clearly defined, high-contrast line. A blob is an enclosed region differing in brightness or darkness. Let's see if we can create one:

$+10$	$+10$	$+10$	$+10$	$+10$
$+10$	$+10$	-10	$+10$	$+10$
$+10$	-10	-10	-10	$+10$
$+10$	$+10$	-10	$+10$	$+10$
$+10$	$+10$	$+10$	$+10$	$+10$

It would be a black diamond shape on a white background. If the -10s were all zeros, then we would have a gray rather than black diamond shape, but it would still be a blob.

At a higher level, the 2½-D sketch is an attempt to use the information about zero crossings, edge segments, blobs, and so on to determine information about shading, and then to use shading information in an effort to compute information about shape. At the highest level, the 3-D representation, we see that the shape information from the 2½-D representation is used to compute the volumetric primitives similar to those used in the Biederman model. Notice in Table 2.1 that these volumetric primitives are based on edges, and these edges can be represented as sticks or axes.

The idea that in computing volumetric principles we can be aided by computing an underlying stick figure based on major axes was investigated by Ling and Sanocki (1995). They argued that if volumetric primitives such as geons are based on stick or

Figure 2.15 The three airplanes used as targets in the Ling and Sanocki study. *Source:* From Ling and Sanocki, 1995.

axis computation, object recognition should be facilitated if people are supplied the axes prior to trying to recognize the object in question. Their subjects were briefly shown one of the three targets depicted in Figure 2.15.

The leftmost target shows the major axes superimposed on the target, to give you an idea about what the major axes would look like for the airplane's volumetric primitives. The axes, however, were not directly superimposed on any target in the study. Notice that the major axes are truly a computational event by the cognitive system: they are not ever "visible" in the real world. Marr's theory suggests that at the final stage in information processing such axes are computed from the information that is visible, to aid in object recognition. Preceding each target was a "priming" stimulus that was shown briefly. Panel (a) in Figure 2.16 shows the priming stimuli that were used. After the specific target disappeared in that trial, the subjects were shown all three airplanes and asked to choose which one had been briefly shown. The dependent variable in this study was recognition accuracy. Notice that the recognition task really requires subjects to recognize the windows in the airplane, because that is the only difference among the three targets. The theory argues that, if the priming stimulus facilitates the computation in object recognition, it should facilitate recognition of all the "lower-level" features that make up the target as well. Consequently, even though the geons that make up the plane are the same for each, presenting the major axes should still facilitate target recognition, if Marr's theory is correct.

Panel (b) in Figure 2.16 shows the results of the study. As you can see, showing the major axes, or the edge of the plane, primed target recognition (approximately 70% accuracy under those conditions) compared to showing subjects a circle or frame outline of the plane (60% accuracy). These findings support the predictions made by Marr's theory. Object recognition can be understood as being computed in steps or stages. That priming subjects with the major axes of an object facilitates their recognizing that object suggests that at some stage in building a representation of an object, the geon's major axis is also computed.

Context

When we talk about the role of context in cognitive psychology, we mean the role that information surrounding a target might have in using a specific cognitive process. Have you ever met a person you know in a place where you did not expect to see him or her? You may have experienced a brief but perceptible delay in being able to recall the person's name. Why? The answer is that we typically use context, or surrounding information, such as that occurring in the situation where we usually encounter the person, whenever we perceive, recognize, and name people.

Figure 2.16   Primes (a) and results (b) from the Ling and Sanocki study. Line thickness of the primes was 1 pixel in all except the major-axis prime, which had a thickness of 2 pixels. The numbers in parentheses indicate the number of pixels in each prime. Standard error bars for percentages correct are shown in (b).

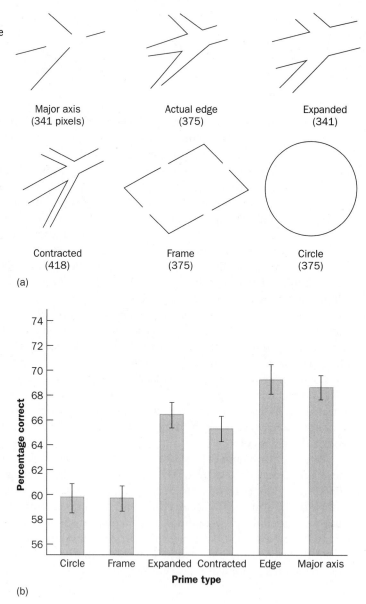

(a)

(b)

In almost every case of object recognition, contextual information is probably used at the same time as feature-analytic information or geon information is being processed. Look at the ambiguous characters at the top of Figure 2.17. Notice how the surrounding information, letters or numbers, "clarifies" the meaning of the ambiguous characters, turning them into the word "is" in one drawing and the number "15" in another.

The contrast between feature analysis and contextual analysis is sometimes described by cognitive psychologists as data-driven versus conceptually driven process-

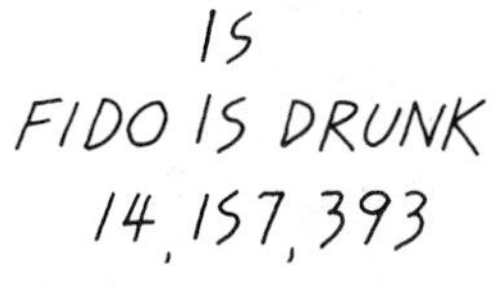

IS

FIDO IS DRUNK

14,157,393

Figure 2.17 The stimulus above the handwriting can be interpreted as either "15" or "is," depending on its context. The meaning of a stimulus is often determined in part by its context. *Source:* From *Psychology Today,* 3rd ed. Copyright 1975 by Random House, Inc.

ing (Lindsay & Norman, 1977). **Data-driven processes** operate from the bottom up, gathering and processing information in small pieces, which are later assembled in working memory. **Conceptually driven processes** operate from the top down and can be considered expectations or plans. Conceptually driven processes gulp in large amounts of information while making deductions and filling in the gaps. In letter recognition, conceptually driven processes are generated from our general knowledge of which letters are likely candidates to begin words, which combinations of letters are likely, and so on.

One reason for this dual processing is efficiency. If object recognition were accomplished solely and strictly by feature analysis, or individual geon processing, it would certainly require a great deal of cognitive effort and time. Let's examine an example from letter recognition and reading. If each letter has five features, and a page of typed text has about 300 words of five letters each, reading each page will require about 7500 individual feature detections (this exercise is based on an example appearing in Anderson, 1980). A typical college reader can read 250 words per minute, which necessitates more than 100 feature detections per second. If you think back to the varied-mapping condition in the Schneider and Shiffrin (1977) study, it seems unlikely that people could process that much information in real time, suggesting that context or surrounding information must also be used.

The effects of context on letter recognition were investigated by Reicher (1969) and Wheeler (1970). The basic finding, known as the **word superiority effect,** is that subjects are better able to identify a letter accurately when it appears in the context of a word than when it appears by itself or in a string of random letters. For example, Wheeler (1970) briefly presented to his subjects a letter or a word. They were then shown either two letters or two words, and were asked to determine which had been presented earlier. A letter trial consisted of showing a letter (*D*) and then two letters (*D, G*). The word trial consisted of a word (*WIND*) and then two words (*WIND, WING*). Wheeler found that recognition was about 10 percent better in the word condition, meaning that subjects were better able to discriminate *D* from *G* when these letters appeared in the context of a word.

Using Your Knowledge of Cognition
The "Pop-Out" Phenomenon

In this section, I present a question whose answer we might explore using a demonstration or miniexperiment. Using the knowledge that you have gained from the relevant sections in the text, you'll be able to follow along to see how cognitive scientists go about investigating and explaining various phenomena. In this section we explore some questions on the function of attention: What does paying attention do for us, anyway?

To see how attention works, and what it might do for us, prepare these materials and then try them out on a friend. First, get a couple of markers of clearly distinguishing colors—let's say red and blue. Then, on a plain sheet of paper, make one blue straight-line letter, like *T*, one red curved-line letter, such as *S*, and one red *T*. Then on a second sheet, scatter around these stimuli: One blue *T*, 14 red *S*s, and 15 red *T*s. Then ask a friend to locate the blue figure on each page as quickly as possible and notice if there seems to be a time difference. If your friend did as expected, there was no time difference in either version of the task; the blue figure seems to "pop out" (Treisman & Gelade, 1980) whether it is placed in the context of two distractors or twenty-nine. According to Treisman and her colleagues (Treisman & Gelade, 1980; Treisman and Gormican, 1988; Treisman, 1990), this experiment demonstrates that isolated features such as color are processed in parallel (that is, simultaneously) without any focusing of attention. This kind of processing results from the same sort of preattentive analysis that we saw in Treisman's earlier work. Now, prepare these materials and try this next task on a friend. Make a third display consisting of one blue *T*, 9 red *T*s, 10 blue *S*s, and 10 red *S*s. Now ask a friend to try to find the blue *T* on the first sheet of paper, and then on the third sheet of paper. Observe the time required to do these tasks. If your friend does as expected, it will take him or her substantially longer to find the blue *T* on the third piece of paper, compared with the first display, even though both pieces of paper have the same number of distractors (29). How come? According to Treisman, the time increases because searching for a blue *T* on the third piece of paper involves looking not just for a single feature but for a combination, or conjunction, of features. That is, the "blueness" is a feature, and the "*T*-ness" is also a set of features. In Treisman's terminology, on the third piece of paper you must search for the blue *T* at the object level, rather than at the featural level. Searching at the object level requires that the features, which are processed separately in the preattentive analysis, be combined or integrated. According to Treisman, this step requires a second analysis in the form of selective attention that integrates or "glues" (that's Treisman's metaphorical term) the separate features together. Selective attention operates serially, not in parallel, which means that selective attention will require more time than the preattentive analysis. That's why there can be no pop-out phenomenon when the search is at the object level instead of the feature level. What then does attention do for us? By paying attention to stimuli we integrate otherwise separate features and are therefore able to distinguish and search for stimuli at the object level.

Concluding Comments and Suggestions for Further Reading

I began this chapter by posing a question about the qualities that the stimulus must have to provoke a shift in attention. As you now know, phrasing the question in this way was slightly misleading. First, ascribing to the stimulus all the power to provoke an attentional shift is incorrect, because in addition to data-driven processes are conceptually driven processes. As the influence of context on the ambiguous figure showed us, pattern recognition is often propelled by our expectations. Things are seen or not seen, heard or not heard, depending upon whether they are congruent with the expectation in force. Second, to speak about shifts in attention is sometimes misleading. Over the last decade and a half, many cognitive psychologists have adopted the position that attention consists of resource allocation. It's unlikely that any action would be so engrossing that all processing resources would be allocated to it (strategically speaking, smart systems always keep a reserve). Thus some resources will be allocated to processing many of the stimuli surrounding us. Will we necessarily become aware of the stimuli we process? As we have seen, the answer appears to be no. The processing of stimuli depends in part upon enduring dispositions of the cognitive system. Many of these dispositions are under conscious control in that the incoming information's analysis can be altered. The results of the analysis, however, may not necessarily enter awareness. Shiffrin and Dumais (1981) point out that the relationship between attention and awareness is problematic. The results of automatic processing frequently don't enter consciousness, and even the results of controlled processing may not enter consciousness in all circumstances.

In pattern recognition, feature analysis is apparently a powerful method for detecting regularities in stimulation. The elements of stimulation that serve as features are at least partly constrained by biological need and neuronal architecture.

The student who wishes to pursue these topics further should read Kahneman's (1973) book, which has an excellent review of the literature on the first phase in theory building. The original papers by Broadbent (1958) and Treisman (1960) are classics. A good outline of the second phase in theory construction is in Posner and Snyder (1975). Advanced state-of-the-art work in this area can be found in the series of monographs called *Attention and Performance*. A first-rate summary of the findings on automaticity is in Shiffrin and Dumais (1981), and also in Schneider, Dumais, and Shiffrin (1984). Lindsay and Norman (1977) provide a readable account of pattern recognition by humans; Horn (1986) covers the question of pattern recognition by machines.

In the chapter I mention that learning-disabled children may have attentional deficits of some sort. There has been some movement to link several childhood disorders, including hyperactivity, learning disability, and some forms of organic brain dysfunction, to an underlying attentional problem called attentional deficit disorder (ADD). Koppel (1979) presented an early view on this topic. This movement has apparently sparked a lively controversy among diagnosticians and theorists. Kuehne, Kehle, and McMahon (1987) argue that ADD children can be differentiated from children with specific learning disabilities. In other words, ADD is just that—an attentional problem, not a catchall category. Other researchers have argued, however,

Focus on Research
Automaticity, Skill, and Awareness

The distinction between automatic and controlled processes is a matter of degree. As we improve a skill, automatization proceeds gradually, and the amount of control required gradually recedes.

The course of skill acquisition has been known to psychologists for a long time. Snoddy (1926) studied the acquisition of skill on a mirror-tracing task. This task usually involves subjects guiding a pencil through a geometric shape while watching the reflection of their hands in a mirror. The subjects improved, but the rate of improvement is what's particularly interesting. If we plot the time required to do the task as a function of trials (holding errors constant), we expect to see a decline. Snoddy plotted the *logarithm* of time as a function of the *logarithm* of the number of trials. When this

log-log plot was created for individual subjects, Snoddy observed that the line of best fit was a perfectly straight line! Figure 2.18 shows how the log-log plot would look for a hypothetical subject.

You should notice two important points here. First, the subject's improvement continued through the whole set of trials; there was no endpoint at which improvement ceased. Second, if you consider the amount of improvement (in time) from any one point on the X axis to any other point, you know that, in the future, ten times as many trials will be required to produce similar improvement.

Cognitive psychologists have since demonstrated that this log-log law holds not only for motor or perceptual skills but also for higher cognitive

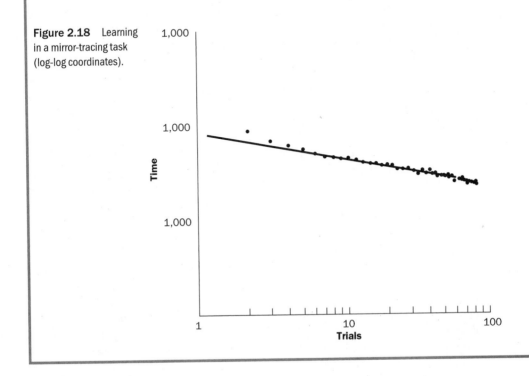

Figure 2.18 Learning in a mirror-tracing task (log-log coordinates).

Focus on Research

processes. For example, Newell and Rosenbloom (1981) studied how skill is acquired in a solitaire card game called Stair. Here are the rules:

> Stair involves laying out all 52 cards face up from a shuffled deck, in 8 *columns* (four with 7 rows, four with 6 rows). There are also four *spots* (initially empty), each of which can hold only one card. The aim is to build four stacks, ace to king, one for each suit, by moving cards around under typical solitaire constraints. A card in a spot or at the bottom of a column may be moved: (1) to a spot, if it is empty; (2) to a stack, if the card is the next in order building up; or (3) to the bottom of another column, if the card is the next lower in the same suit (e.g., the six of spades appended to the seven of spades). (Newell & Rosenbloom, 1981)

You might wish to try playing this game a few times while charting your progress. Notice that this is a game of perfect information. Although a perceptual component is involved (a player might overlook a card) and a weak component of motor learning, this game is nevertheless primarily one of intellectual skill. That is, the subject's ability to analyze the initial layout determines victory. Newell and Rosenbloom's subject played 500 hands of Stair. He got better, winning about 28% of his initial hands and about 40% of his final hands. In addition, the log-log law held for the time involved in playing (regardless of whether the hand was won or lost). For winning hands, the subject started out requiring about 1000 seconds. By the end, 500 hands later, this time had been reduced to about 550 seconds. All intermediate points fell close to the straight line established by the two end points, when the log of time was plotted as a function of the log of hand number.

Although playing this intellectual game had not become automatic, it was apparently on its way to becoming so. The implication of this finding is extremely interesting: With enough practice, the most challenging intellectual tasks could become automatic, requiring little or no awareness.

that hyperactivity is a frequent companion disorder with ADD. Cantwell and Baker (1987) present evidence arguing for two forms of ADD: those which also include hyperactivity (ADDH) and those without such an involvement. Lorys, Hynd, and Lahey (1990) found no evidence, however, that this distinction can be supported by neurological and cognitive tests.

*K*ey Terms

Selective attention
Selectivity
Dichotic listening
Shadowing
Selective filter
Preattentive analysis
Attenuation model
Late selection

Cognitive resources
Allocation policy
Cognitive capacity
Electrodermal responses
Psychological refractory period
Input attention
Central attention
Stimulus onset asynchrony

Automaticity
Data-limited processes
Resource-limited processes
Data-driven processes
Conceptually driven processes
Word superiority effect

PART THREE

Memory

Putting our memory systems to work is as natural to us as breathing, but just because it's easy doesn't mean memory is a simple function. When you learn and remember something, what exactly has taken place? From antiquity onward, philosophers and psychologists have sought to explain the phenomenon by invoking metaphorical (familiar) comparisons. Memory has been compared to a storehouse or library for more than 2500 years. More recently, Roediger (1980) searched the modern literature on memory for similar uses of metaphor to help understand memory. As it turns out, the storehouse metaphor lives on, along with many of the more than 35 others that he was able to identify.

In the next two chapters, you'll learn about several such tools and their histories. In contemporary psychology, the storehouse or warehouse metaphor has its roots in pathfinding research by the German psychologist Herman Ebbinghaus (1885). As you'll see in Chapter 3, Ebbinghaus invented a still-useful technique for estimating our ability to use our memories to retain or "save" material we have learned. His work was so influential that many contemporary theorists can trace their intellectual lineage to his ideas. The "Ebbinghaus tradition" emphasizes the memory system's ability to "keep" or "store" things. Further, researchers who espouse this viewpoint frequently argue that once material has been learned and stored, some version, or at least some portion of that learning, always remains within memory. These theorists believe that failure to retrieve something, which we all experience daily, is just the result of the memory system's inability to "find" something that has been stored. Just as a library book can be misshelved, keeping the would-be borrower from retrieving it, according to this tradition, something forgotten is really something that the memory has failed to find. Further, such forgetting results in a deficit from that which was originally presented. If you send me to the grocery store for five items, I may come back with only four, forgetting the fifth.

The Ebbinghaus tradition in memory research is not the only one. In the 1930s, the British psychologist Sir Frederick Bartlett's investigations proved as influential as Ebbinghaus's. You'll read about his work in more detail in Chapter 4, but for now we can report that Bartlett documented several interesting properties in his subject's retrieval failures. First, like Ebbinghaus, Bartlett found that passing time usually results in less and less material that can subsequently be retrieved. But material that was retrieved could not always be understood as a simple deficit from material that had originally been presented to the subject. In fact, some subjects retrieved factual material that had not been presented in the first place. These specific retrievals represented additions to the subject's memory rather than deficits. Thus, if I behave like one of Bartlett's subjects, sending me to the grocery store for five items may result in my returning with five items, but one of them may not be an item you asked for. Besides these interesting "intrusion" errors, Bartlett noticed that his subjects made frequent and subtle "adjustments" to the material originally presented. Just about every one of these adjustments modified the original material so that it made more sense to the person doing the learning and retrieval. For example, if I have experience in whitewater rafting, and as a subject in a study I'm asked to read and remember a story about friends who went kayaking, I may convert the unfamiliar kayaking to the more familiar (to me) rafting. At retrieval time, if I'm asked to say what the friends were doing on the turbulent mountain river, I may say "rafting," showing that I've converted the original material to something perhaps more relevant for me. From his investigations, Bartlett believed that memories were not stored in pure, isolated, static form. Memories were inevitably mixed with knowledge acquired previously to create a representation stitching together bits and pieces of several experiences. Unlike the Ebbinghaus tradition, emphasizing *quantity* of our memories—"How much do we retain about our experiences?"—the Bartlett tradition evaluates our memory's *quality*—"What was the content of the person's memory?"

Modern cognitive psychology works these two traditions into complementary accounts of memory. On the one hand, cognitive psychologists have erected numerous storage models of memory over the last thirty years, and we investigate those in Chapter 3. More recently, cognitive psychologists have revisited the Bartlett perspective and are again reviewing how we use memory. They describe how memory is a "recomputation" of events and treat its action as a "correspondence" (Koriat & Goldsmith, 1996). We explore this view in Chapter 4. Which view is right? In fact, I hope you'll *not* frame the question in that way, but rather ask how useful each perspective is in explaining types of memory phenomena.

C H A P T E R   3

Memory as Storage

*O*verview

We expect to remember some events in our lives but forget others. But there are some periods of our lives from which most, if not all events are routinely forgotten. What is your earliest memory? If you are like most people, you remember nothing from your first two or three years. An exercise demonstrates this general absence of memories from the first few years of life: If you have a sibling or siblings, determine your age in years and months at the time they were born. If you were then two years and seven months old, we denote that age 2:7. Most people cannot remember a sibling's birth if it occurred when they were 3:6 or younger. Try to remember your siblings' births. My brother was born when I was 2:8. I have absolutely no recollection of his birth; it just seems he's always been around. On the other hand, I was 6:6 when my sister was born, and I remember vividly the circumstances leading up to her birth (as I can all the subsequent episodes with her crying, wetting, spitting up, and so on that go along with a newborn). One potentially interesting variable here is my brother's recalling our sister's birth. He was 3:8 at the time, slightly older than the theoretical threshold, suggesting that he may have had some recollection about the event. Without tipping him off on the details, I sent him an e-mail the other day to ask if he remembered her birth. (We're both well into our forties now.) Here is how he responded:

"Do I remember? One of the only things I remember was that Dad made lunch. Split-pea soup and grilled ham and cheese sandwiches. Of course we didn't eat the soup. I don't think we ate the sandwiches, either. I don't really remember much else. Hell, I'm lucky if I remember yesterday. Hope the new edition of the book goes well."

It seems that my father's actually cooking something is about all my brother can retrieve.

This general absence of memory in the first years of life is *infantile amnesia,* which we'll study along with its implications later in this chapter. The phenomenon presents something of a puzzle for memory theorists and researchers. If memories should be understood as things that have been stored, then why do so few people remember much from their first few years? This puzzle might be resolved if memory systems of two- and three-year-olds were not at all operational. But toddlers and preschoolers do have functional memories. It's clear that a three-year-old can remember some things that happened six months earlier. Where did those memories go?

In this chapter, we examine the memory phenomenon from this **storage** perspective. Much of the material here follows the information-processing metaphor, which describes memory as a system with both structural and process components. By "structural," we mean that memories seem to differ markedly in their content, characteristics, and organization. Consider the *duration* of a memory. If I'm distracted while trying to memorize something unfamiliar to me, the memory will seem to evaporate; it is fragile. Others seem much more lasting. It's as if different memories are stored in different locations, and their properties seem to reflect the storage locations in which they are housed. We can hang on to a memory stored in the permanent location, but it seems the memory must go through a temporary location first. By "process" we mean the cognitive operations that transferred and altered the memories stored in different locations.

The information-processing viewpoint has undergone a great deal of theoretical development over the past 30 years, shifting the structural or process emphasis back and forth as new findings have come to light. Let's inspect this shifting and see why cognitive psychologists have modified some aspects of the theory. A good grounding in theory will help us understand the reasonings behind the research battles. Many cognitive psychologists have worked hard, dramatically building our knowledge about this subject so filled with complexity.

The Ebbinghaus Tradition

Most of the research reported here relies on Hermann Ebbinghaus, whose work demands our attention, however briefly, because he is recognized as the first to investigate memory empirically. Here is how he went about it.

First, recognize that Ebbinghaus believed in associationism, a doctrine of mind very prominent in his day (Leahey & Harris, 1985). The ideas in your head, associationists maintain, are all somehow "attached" to each other by an association. Strictly speaking, everything you've learned is precisely defined by its pattern of associations. Ebbinghaus realized that if he wanted to study memory in its "purest" form, he would need to learn material that was completely divorced from anything currently in his mind. He began by making up material to learn and remember; specifically, a stimulus known as a "nonsense syllable." In this syllable a consonant is followed by a vowel and concludes with another consonant. The three-letter combination must be pronounceable and must not form an actual German word. Some candidates were SAB and GEN. Ebbinghaus, a stickler for experimental precision (Baddeley, 1990), controlled his study of each nonsense syllable with a metronome set to beat every 2 or 2.5 seconds, depending on the study. Further, he made sure that his attempts to learn the lists of syllables occurred at the same time each day. He would focus on a new syllable at each metronome beat until he could recite the entire thirteen- or sixteen-syllable list twice without error. This level of performance represented his learning criterion. Each complete pass through the list was called a learning trial, and the first bit of information that Ebbinghaus recorded was the number of trials required to achieve his criterion. After learning each list he waited a set period, from 20 minutes to 31 days, before attempting to retrieve that list. At retrieval time Ebbinghaus would record if his retention was still perfect—that is, at criterion. If his retention no longer reached the criterion after the memory interval, Ebbinghaus would fire up his trusty metronome and relearn the list back up to the criterion. He would then record how many relearning trials it took to restore his memory to the criterion.

To determine how effective his memory had been during the retention interval, Ebbinghaus devised an objective scoring method. To estimate how much his memory had retained, or "saved," during the retention period, he applied this equation:

$$\text{Savings score} = \left[\frac{\text{Original trials} - \text{Relearning trials}}{\text{Original trials}} \right] 100$$

The savings score is thus a retention score. Let's consider some examples. Suppose that after a time Ebbinghaus found that he retained a list at criterion. The number of relearning trials would be zero; none were required. Given that the number of relearning trials is equal to zero, the equation reduces to original trials divided by original trials (thus equaling 1), multiplied by 100, giving a savings score of 100. Thus, 100 indicates that he had retained all the original material. On the other hand, suppose that after a retention interval the number of relearning trials was equal to the number of original trials; that is, Ebbinghaus took just as many trials to relearn the list as he had taken to learn it in the first place. The number in the numerator would then be zero, and the savings score would thus be zero. These examples establish the theoretical minimum and maximum values (actually, the minimum could be less than zero, but it never was). Zero indicates that nothing was retained in memory; 100 means that everything was retained. Any number between these two points indicates partial retention and partial loss. Ebbinghaus's classic findings are shown in Figure 3.1. As the graph shows, the loss from memory begins to occur almost immediately. In fact, Ebbinghaus demonstrated that much, perhaps most, of the forgetting that will ever take place comes in the first hour after learning. Second, Ebbinghaus demonstrated that the rate of loss is not constant, as commonly believed more than a century ago. Rather, he showed that the rate of loss, precipitous initially, levels out eventually. His third point (related to the second), demonstrated that relearning was always easier than the initial learning had been. Even one month later, fewer relearning trials were always required to return to criterion than the original number. This finding suggested to Ebbinghaus, and to innumerable memory researchers since, that at least some of the material originally learned always remained in memory.

Figure 3.1   Rate of forgetting for lists of nonsense syllables over a 31-day period, as found by Ebbinghaus (1885). Retention score determined by the savings method, which bases degree of retention on number of trials required to relearn lists after various intervals.

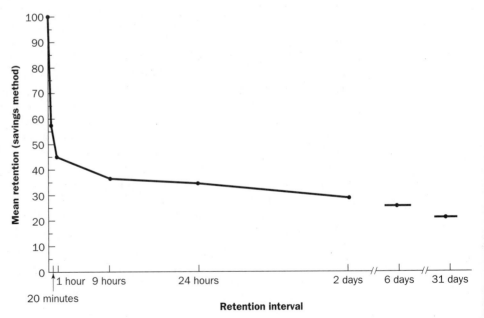

In the next section, we move forward nearly eighty years from Ebbinghaus's time, but as you'll see, recent theorists still believe that memories are stored somehow, somewhere, within the person.

Information-Processing Position

Approximately thirty years ago, an information-processing theory of memory was developed (Atkinson & Shiffrin, 1968; Waugh & Norman, 1965), which we now survey. In the theory memory or a system of related components, each called a storage, is capable of processing types of representations called **cognitive codes.** The theory also holds that cognitive codes can be transferred from storage to storage by **control processes.** One of the storages is the **sensory register,** where our feature-detection and pattern-recognition processes rapidly produce a cognitive code that can be stored briefly. The sensory register does not depend on resource allocation, meaning that we do not have to pay attention to incoming stimuli to have a cognitive code in sensory storage; it happens automatically. One implication in this theory is that the sensory register's **capacity** must be large, because it is assumed that all incoming stimulation is stored at least briefly. The sensory register is also thought to be **modality specific:** part of the storage is devoted to visual stimuli, part to auditory stimuli, and, presumably, other parts to each of the remaining senses. Material does not last long in sensory storage; visual stimuli remain there about 250 to 300 msec, and auditory stimuli are kept perhaps ten times that long. Material stored in the sensory register is affected by passing time. Within the durations just mentioned, codes in sensory storage simply **decay,** which refers to the loss of cognitive codes whose disappearance is produced strictly by passing time. To transfer the cognitive code from the sensory register, a person must allocate some resources to evacuate the information before it fades.

Information-processing theorists believe that cognitive codes are next transferred to the **short-term storage** component. Short-term storage (STS) differs from the sensory register in several ways. First, STS capacity is assumed to be quite limited (Miller, 1956). Second, information in STS is organized in a cognitive code that is acoustic, verbal, or linguistic. This organization applies even when the incoming information (i.e., the material evacuated from sensory storage) has been presented visually. Third, material can reside in STS much longer than it can in sensory storage. The duration of unrehearsed material in STS is about 30 seconds. Short-term storage and sensory storage are similar in one aspect, however. In both, material that is not elaborated and transferred decays.

Codes stored in STS can be transferred to **long-term storage** (LTS), whose capacity, like that of the sensory register, is extremely large. The control process that permits coded material to transfer between these two storages is **rehearsal,** which has many meanings in cognitive psychology. For the time being, let's restrict its meaning to cognitive operations that seem to have these two functions. First, rehearsal applies to procedures that maintain the code's vitality in STS. As long as the STS code is occasionally refreshed by rehearsal, it can apparently reside there for long periods. Second, rehearsal refers to operations that build up a corresponding code for the STS material in LTS. In a sense, then, information in STS is not transferred intact to LTS.

Figure 3.2   Structure of the memory system. *Source:* From Atkinson & Shiffrin, 1968.

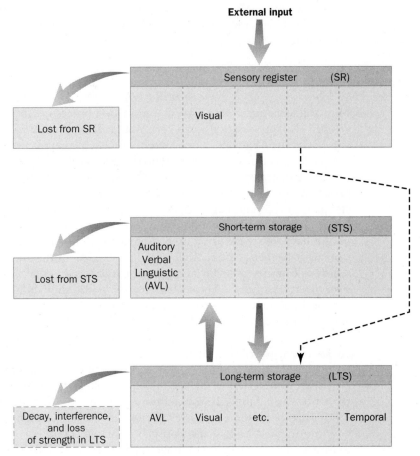

Instead, rehearsal duplicates a representation of the STS material in LTS. We're familiar with the subjective experience that often accompanies rehearsal. When we try to retain an unfamiliar bit of knowledge, we often say it to ourselves over and over again. Whether rehearsal depends on this kind of subvocal speech is currently controversial (Klatzky, 1980). Once stored in LTS, the code is believed to be permanent. Failures to retrieve information that has been transferred to LTS result from other codes that seem to block or inhibit the memory we're searching for. In other words, cognitive codes can sometimes interfere with each other. In STS, cognitive codes are organized by acoustic or verbal properties. In LTS, the organization is different. Once there, material is organized semantically—that is, by its meaning. Figure 3.2 summarizes the relationships between these storages.

In introducing the information-processing theory I've pointed out that the storages differ in capacity, duration, and operating characteristics. Next, I describe each of these storages in greater depth and examine some of the evidence for the claims you saw in the introduction. I withhold criticism until later so that we can appreciate the theory's strengths.

Sensory Storage

Sperling (1960) conducted some classic studies on sensory storage, demonstrating that people seem to have an extremely accurate and complete memory for visual stimulation, although this memory's duration is brief. Sperling found that if four or fewer letters were presented by tachistoscope (a device for presenting visual stimuli briefly) for 50 msec, subjects' retrieval of the elements was good, often approaching 100%. Moreover, Sperling found that the way in which the stimuli were arranged on the tachistoscope slide didn't seem to affect the subjects' retrieval. It didn't matter if six elements were presented in one row or in two rows of three elements. Either way, the subjects retrieved an average of four elements. Similarly, the number of elements in the array didn't seem to affect retrieval. When the array had nine or more elements, subjects still retrieved only about four of them. Finally, even when exposure time was increased dramatically, up to about .5 second, the number of elements retrieved stayed constant. This last finding indicates that the upper limit of retrieved items was not imposed by any difficulty in *seeing* the items—half a second is plenty of time for that. Instead, the difficulty in reporting elements from arrays of greater than four may have been produced by memory loss, raising a question: What was the memory deficit? Was it capacity (the initial storage being overloaded by more than four items) or duration (the items not remaining in the initial register long enough to get them out and into more durable storage)?

To settle these issues, Sperling abandoned the **whole-report technique,** in which he had asked the subjects to retrieve as much as they could from the array. In his next series of studies, Sperling substituted the **partial-report technique.** The subjects were now required to report only elements from the preceding display. The display consisted of an array of letters and digits arranged in three rows of four elements each. The subjects had to report only one row. Unlike the whole-report technique, however, in which the subjects could begin responding as soon as the slide had been presented, in the partial-report technique the subjects could not begin responding until they heard a musical tone signaling the row that was to be reported. A high-pitched tone told them to report the top row in the array, a medium-pitched tone specified the middle row, and so on. Because the tones were presented at random, the subjects could not know which of the three would be heard in any trial. From a subject's perspective, here was the order of events: First, the subject saw the array for 50 msec. Then the array was turned off and the subject waited until the tone was heard. This delay, the **interstimulus interval,** was originally set at 50 msec. During this time the subjects relied upon memory to hang on to as much of the original array as they could. Finally, at the end of the interstimulus interval, a tone was sounded and the subject began responding. Sperling found that the subjects' accuracy was good: most could retrieve all four of the signaled elements. This finding may seem predictable for the results of the whole-report studies, but with a difference. In the partial-report procedure, the subjects did not know in advance which row they would have to report. That subjects were accurate in reporting any signaled row strongly suggests that they had all twelve elements of the array stored in memory during the interstimulus interval.

Sperling's next task was to determine how long the elements were stored. He increased the interval and found that retention was good until the interval was increased to about 250 msec. At 300 msec, the subjects seemed to be guessing. If they correctly anticipated which row would be signaled, they could report it. If they misjudged the row to be signaled, though, they couldn't say much about what had been presented. Sperling interpreted this finding straightforwardly. The information-processing system seemingly held all incoming visual stimulation in a memory or buffer for an ultra-brief period. This memory was considered complete in that all aspects of the original stimulation were present in the storage. The storage content was considered *precate-gorical* (Crowder & Morton, 1969; Long, 1980), meaning that the information had not yet been transformed into the acoustic or semantic codes characterizing STS and LTS organization. Sperling elaborated his original findings with a visual-perception theory, arguing that visual information is recognized, elaborated, and rehearsed after the sensory stage. The subjects could not report more than four or five letters from the initial array because they had to recognize and transfer contents of the sensory memory to a more durable location from which they could be reported. Clearly, some time is required, and the transfer problem is worsened because the items apparently have to be transferred serially. By the time four items have been extracted from the sensory register, the remaining contents have decayed.

In 1967, Neisser named this brief visual memory the **icon.** The sensory register is not restricted to visual events alone. The **echo** is the appropriate name for auditory stimulation stored in the sensory register. Presumably, each sense contributes an accurate copy of the recent stimulation of sensory storage, although the icon and the echo have been investigated more than the other sensory memories.

Short-Term Storage

These studies suggest that visual information presented for less than 200 msec is held until a more durable cognitive code can be made, and that this more durable storage is called short-term storage.

Our STS is often called a mental workbench (Klatzky, 1980). Items from other storages can be transferred onto this workbench, where they can be "worked on," meaning that the material can be elaborated or transformed in various ways. The workbench analogy has other implications, too. Like a real workbench, our short-term memories have limited space, implying that we can work on only a few things simultaneously. Just as a real task on a workbench requires our concentration, working on material in STS also seems to require allocation of cognitive resources (Atkinson & Shiffrin, 1968). For these and other reasons, the content of the short-term store has sometimes been equated with the boundaries of our consciousness.

Basic Findings   The classic study of STS was conducted by Peterson and Peterson (1959). First, they demonstrated that subjects could retrieve a three-consonant trigram (e.g., MBN) with no difficulty after thirty seconds. In the next phase, subjects were asked to recall only one trigram, but during the retention interval they had to perform a distractor task. The task the Petersons chose was counting backward out loud by threes, starting from a three-digit number given to the subject right after the trigram. From the subject's perspective, each trial involved hearing the trigram, then hearing a three-digit number, let's say 987, then counting back-

Figure 3.3 Results of the experiment on forgetting in short-term memory, showing that recall decreases as a function of the retention interval. *Source:* From Peterson & Peterson, 1959.

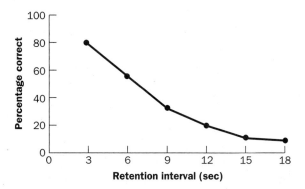

ward as quickly as possible, 987, 984, 981, 978 . . . until a retrieval cue was given. The subject then attempted to recall the trigram. Figure 3.3 shows the findings. Notice that the probability of retrieving the trigram decreases to about 10% after only 15 to 18 seconds, far less than that observed when the subjects were not given a distractor task. Clearly, that task prevented them from carrying out an important operation on their "workbenches"—namely, rehearsal.

As discussed earlier, rehearsal seems to refresh or regenerate the STS content, and without it, the material disappears. Because the distractor task seemed to prevent rehearsal, it was reasonable for the Petersons to interpret the retrieval failures as produced by decay.

This was a landmark finding because cognitive psychologists had known for some time that decay was not necessarily a major reason for failure of retrieval over long intervals (Jenkins & Dallenbach, 1924). Now that simple decay was demonstrably responsible for retrieval failures when the retention interval was short, the argument for two storages had a firm basis: the mechanism that produced forgetting. Decay caused forgetting from STS, but forgetting from LTS was caused by **interference,** the blocking that some memories can impose on others. This line of reasoning also explained some aspects of the well-known **serial-position effect.**

Suppose we present a list with forty common nouns to our subjects at the rate of one noun per second. Immediately after, we ask the subjects to recall as many of the nouns as they can. Would you expect the recall probability for each noun to be equal? As you may know, that's not what happens. When a lengthy list is presented with such a free-recall procedure, the subject's responses are predictable. Nouns presented first and those presented last tend to be recalled with greater frequency than those presented in the middle (Deese & Kaufman, 1957; Murdock, 1962). A noun's position in the sequence affects its likelihood of being recalled. The serial-position effect has two components. The **primacy component** applies to the nouns presented first (whose memory is therefore oldest), which are recalled better than items whose presentation occurred in midlist. The **recency component** describes the greater likelihood of an item's retrieval when it is near the end. These effects are observed because the subjects are retrieving the words from separate storages. When the subjects began seeing or hearing the list, their STSs were mostly empty, and so a great deal of rehearsal could be spent on each word as it entered the storage. Because the initial words were thoroughly rehearsed, we would expect them to develop into a more lasting representation in LTS. As the STS gradually became loaded to capacity, though, the subjects had less time to rehearse each new incoming word, and the probability of making a permanent representation was correspondingly diminished. Because material had to spend time in STS before it could be transferred to LTS, the most recently presented nouns should be found in STS. This account suggests that subjects may not retrieve the material in the same chronological order in which it was presented. Instead, they may spill the content of their STS first, because it is prone to decay. Indeed, if you get a chance to observe subjects' behavior in a free-recall situation, you'll see that their response pattern is characteristic. When the list has been presented and the cue is given to recall as many words as possible, the subjects first write down the words just presented, then they retrieve the words presented first, and finally, they jot down whatever else they can retrieve from the middle of the list.

If this retrieval pattern truly reflects storage in two independent locations, then apparently it should be possible to design an experiment that influences retrieval from one location but not the other. Such a study was carried out by Postman and Phillips (1965). In one group of conditions, lists of ten, twenty, or thirty words were presented at the rate of one word per second. Recall was measured immediately after presentation. The top part of Figure 3.3 (labeled "0 sec") shows the findings from this phase in the study. Notice that the serial-position effect is much stronger when the list is twenty or thirty words long than when it consists of only ten words. For the ten-word list, the probability of recalling the middle words approached 50%, a preliminary indication that the capacity of STS must be almost that size. The reasoning here is that if we made the list so short that it could all fit into STS, then we would expect the retrieval in the free-recall procedure to be good—in the 70% to 80% range. The observed retrieval probabilities for the middle words are close enough to those figures to enable us to infer that they've just recently been dropped from STS and begun their decay.

In the experiment's second phase, Postman and Phillips varied the procedure used by Peterson and Peterson. The words were presented as before, but the subjects were not permitted to recall the words immediately after the presentation. Instead, they were given a three-digit number from which they were to count backward by threes. After 30 seconds, they were given the recall cue. What should we expect? The theory predicts that the distractor task should affect the content of STS but not LTS. We'd expect that the subjects would have some difficulty dumping the content of their STSs, because after 30 seconds of decay, that content should be long gone. The distractor task should not, however, affect content or retrieval of any words that had already been transferred to LTS. Consequently, if the subjects are truly retrieving the words from two separate storages, we should expect that the distractor task would affect the recency component but not the primacy component. As shown in the bottom half of Figure 3.4, this is exactly the effect Postman and Phillips found, and it has been replicated on several occasions (Atkinson & Shiffrin, 1968).

The Code in Short-Term Storage   As discussed earlier, the content of the sensory register has no real organization, meaning that it is more or less untransformed by the cognitive system. The sensory register is simply a copy of the stimuli in close to their raw

Figure 3.4 Probability of correct recall as a function of serial position for free verbal recall with test following 0 sec and 30 sec of intervening arithmetic. *Source:* From Postman & Phillips, 1965.

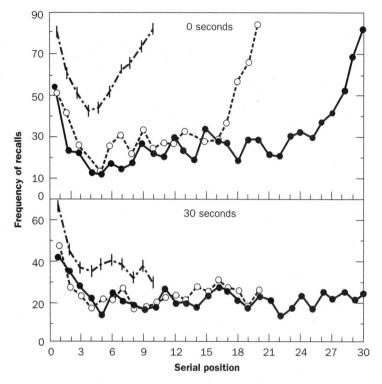

form. The content of STS, however, is highly transformed or coded by the cognitive system. What is this code?

Wickelgren (1965) aurally presented to his subjects a series of letters, and their task was to remember as many letters as they could. When the errors were analyzed, Wickelgren found that the subjects tended to substitute letters that sounded like those they had forgotten: A *D* might be substituted for a *T,* and an *A* for a *K.* Notice that these substitution errors are not caused by alphabetic proximity, nor are they visual confusions. This finding suggests that the code in STS is acoustic.

This finding was reinforced by Conrad (1964), who wished to more explicitly test the acoustic-cue hypothesis. In this study, the letters were presented to the subjects visually as well as aurally. Conrad found that, even when substitution errors were made for letters that had been presented visually, the error indicated the confusion had been acoustic. In other words, a *V* might be substituted for a *B* but not for a *U.*

This finding was complicated somewhat by Hintzman (1965, 1967), who maintained that such errors were not acoustic but were produced by the kinesthetic feedback the subjects got as they articulated the letters subvocally during the retention interval. His analysis of substitution errors, which were made against a background of white noise, indicated that such errors were explainable by the letter's voicing qualities (whether or not the vocal cords vibrated during the letter's production) and by place of articulation (where the tongue points during sounding). These qualities are closely related to the letter's sound, but Hintzman's findings suggest that the code in

STS is verbal or linguistic rather than simply acoustic. Clearing up this issue has proved difficult (Atkinson & Shiffrin, 1968), which is why STS is sometimes referred to as the AVL storage. The code seems to be acoustic, verbal, or linguistic.

Capacity of Short-Term Storage   Determining STS capacity has proved difficult. Before examining some studies, let's consider one difficulty. Pinning down a storage's capacity has been a tricky task, partly because different theorists mean different things by this term (Craik & Lockhart, 1972). For example, we can discuss a memory location's *storage* capacity, which means we're trying to describe how much information that component in the system can *hold*. On the other hand, we can discuss the *attentional,* or processing, capacity of storage, focusing on *how much can be done* on the information storage (Zechmeister & Nyberg, 1982). Going back to the workbench analogy, storage capacity defines how many items can be physically placed on the workbench, whereas processing capacity specifies how many separate operations (such as nailing things together or painting them) can be done on those items in some unit of time. Establishing which factor dominates in limiting STS capacity is hard because we never see the workbench except in the form of the subject's verbal reports or other behaviors.

Regardless of which definition of capacity we adopt, though, we know that STS capacity is limited. In his famous paper, Miller (1956) suggested that the short-term store capacity was seven, plus or minus two items. Exactly what an "item" is can be debated, however. Suppose you are given a list of unrelated digits at the rate of one per second, and you are asked to repeat the list in the original order. If you're like most college students, you'll show high accuracy in repeating a list of about seven or eight digits. This experiment is an easy way to demonstrate the so-called memory span and is the basis for Miller's "magic" number seven. Suppose you're given this list, however:

1, 4, 9, 2, 1, 7, 7, 6, 1, 9, 4, 1

Because the list has twelve digits, technically we shouldn't expect good retrieval. But if you're an American, you'd probably have no trouble remembering all twelve digits, because they can be grouped into three clusters of four digits each. Each cluster represents a year in which a historical event significant to Americans occurred, and it is formed by **chunking.** A chunk is a unit of information organized according to a rule or correspondence to some familiar pattern. Substantial evidence indicates that chunks are the items that fill up STS (Zechmeister & Nyberg, 1982).

Murdock (1961) demonstrated that three words would decay in STS at about the same rate as three letters. But during the same period, one word would show relatively little decay. If individual letters were the relevant items in STS, then three letters should show more decay than one word. Similarly, three words should decay much more quickly than three letters. Murdock's findings indicate that the organizational unit in STS is the chunk. When three unrelated letters are entered in STS, they are stored as three chunks. When the letters are related because they form a word, then the word becomes the organizational unit and occupies one chunk.

Long-Term Storage

In this section we consider two lines of evidence traditionally used to support the idea of a long-term storage (LTS), which is the ultimate repository for our knowledge.

First, we know that the memory code seems to change as a function of its time in the memory system. Second, evidence from the neuropsychological literature points to a distinction between STS and LTS.

Semantic Codes in Long-Term Storage   If we show subjects a list of words and ask them to recall the words several hours later, we'll see that they typically make **intrusion errors**—they recall words that were not on the list. These intrusions are interesting. The relationship between intruding word and left-out word is almost always *semantic;* that is, based on shared meaning. In other words, if the original word on the list was *boat,* the intruder is much more likely to be *ship* than *bud* or *boar* (Baddeley & Dale, 1966). These intrusions are far different from those occurring in STS, which tend to be acoustic.

Neuropsychological Findings   When you suffer a painful shock induced by physical, electrical, or chemical stimuli, you're likely to be unable to recall events immediately before the trauma (Russell & Nathan, 1946). In extreme cases, memory for events that happened up to an hour before the trauma may be absent. From the time you regain consciousness, your memory appears to function normally; events occurring after the accident are processed typically. Usually you regain the formerly wiped-out memories in a characteristic sequence. The oldest wiped-out memories (those furthest "in front" of the accident) are recovered first. Subsequently, you recover memories that are closer and closer in time to the accident. This type of memory loss is **retrograde amnesia.** What produces it?

If memories are transferred from STS to LTS, then we would expect the memory code to be particularly fragile at the time of transfer. Memories just transferred or just about to be transferred would be especially likely to be disrupted. Those whose transfer had already occurred might be a little hardier and better able to survive the traumatic shock.

These considerations were addressed by Chorover and Schiller (1965), who studied passive avoidance conditioning in rats. They placed the animal on a small platform raised several inches from the cage's floor. When the animal stepped onto the floor, it received an electroconvulsive shock (ECS). Chorover and Schiller varied the time delay between the animal's stepping down and the ECS. They reasoned that if the memories were truly being transferred and were thus disruptible, then the rat should show poor avoidance learning when the interval between stepping down and ECS was brief. This reasoning also implies that avoidance learning should improve if the delay between stepping down and ECS was increased, because the rat's memory system would already have transferred the memory into LTS and secured it. After exposing the rats to the ECS, Chorover and Schiller returned them to the experimental chamber 24 hours later for a memory trial. Their hypotheses were supported: If the ECS had been administered within 10 seconds of the rat's stepping down on the learning trial, then the rat showed a significantly shorter step-down latency in the memory trial than rats that were shocked more than 10 seconds after stepping down, or rats that hadn't been shocked at all. The interpretation seems to be that the rats shocked early (within 10 seconds) were more likely to have the memory of stepping down wiped out by the ECS. Consequently, when placed in the experimental chamber 24 hours later, they duplicated their error and stepped down again. The rats shocked late knew better than to take this step. They were more likely to remember what had happened to them 24 hours ago, and so they were cautious about stepping down from the platform. Chorover and Schiller concluded that the retrograde amnesia gradient was about 10 seconds, during which transfer of memories from STS to LTS could be disrupted.

Summary of the Information-Processing Position

Memory can be thought of as a system with interlocking but separate storages. Each storage has a different capacity, each is organized differently, and the mechanism that produces forgetting also differs. The sensory register is a large-capacity storage that retains sensory stimulation in raw form, meaning that no apparent code exists for material stored in the sensory register. Material stored here decays. For visual stimuli, the decay period is about 250 msec. The STS is a somewhat more durable storage capable of holding material for about 30 seconds. Material here is organized acoustically, and STS capacity is limited to about seven chunks. Unrehearsed material in STS decays. LTS holds our permanent memories. Its capacity is extremely large, and it can apparently hold material indefinitely. Material in LTS is organized semantically and is subject to interference by other memories.

Contemporary Versions of the Multistore Model

Over the past thirty years, some cognitive psychologists have continued to elaborate on distinctions in the information-processing model. They argue that empirical evidence clearly suggests that our cognitive systems may not include a structure that corresponds exactly to STS; nevertheless, a component in our cognitive systems produces the **primary memory,** and some other component produces the **secondary memory** (Shiffrin, 1993). That is, when we discuss our primary memories, we mean that empirically, some memories are very sensitive to temporal activation. That is, they may quickly depart and no longer be retrievable by us. Second, some component in our cognitive system is very sensitive to capacity limitations. If it is overloaded, some information is lost. Finally, some part of our cognitive systems seems to be the repository for our control processes. That is, searching for information is an act that itself seems to be limited by capacity: I can ask you to retrieve information about an event in your life, and you may succeed. But if I ask you to retrieve ten events from your life, you will no doubt fail, even though all ten events may be stored. What produces the retrieval failure? Contemporary multistore theorists would argue that it is your primary memory, however it may be constructed, which has been overburdened in this task.

In the next several sections we explore this distinction between primary and secondary memory. We consider some content for each component, and how each may be organized.

Search of Associative Memory (SAM)

We next look at a highly simplified "teaching" version of the search of associative memory (SAM) model (Raajmakers & Shiffrin, 1981). From this perspective, the "memory" for any specific thing, such as the memory for a word appearing in a list of words, is stored in related pieces. These pieces may consist of knowledge and earlier relationships that are stored in LTS, as well as coding processes and other operations taking place in STS (Healy & McNamara, 1996).

Once the memory is stored in LTS, it is accessed by retrieval cues or prompts that are given at retrieval time. Each cue is associated with each item in memory, depending on the cue's ability to prompt the item back out of LTS, and presumably back into STS, where it can be reported. Some "high-strength" cues may be very effective in carrying this prompting. Other cues may be much weaker in prompting retrieval of a specific memory. For example, if two items on such a list are rehearsed at about the same time in STS, then a cue stored with the first of these two stimuli may gain cuing strength in prompting the second stimulus—even though it has not been explicitly associated with that item on the list (Healy & McNamara, 1996). If I'm trying to remember something and you give me additional information, a cue, to prompt me, I may not retrieve the stimulus you were trying to prompt, but I may now be able to retrieve something related to it. I'll probably use the expression "that reminds me . . ." in this situation. Although I failed to retrieve what I was looking for in my LTS, I did succeed in getting something else out and again placed in my STS. When we look at a computational example for SAM, we'll see this phenomenon demonstrated.

Let's say a subject in a study is given a list of paired-associated words such as "boat–dog," and is asked to learn and remember the word "dog." The subject's memory for this word will consist of several pieces or components: whatever the subject manages to encode and store about the context, the word "dog" itself, the associations that are present, including association to the paired-associate "boat," and any other associations he or she formed to any other words on the list. The entire memory for "dog" is stored as a memory "image." (But don't fall into the trap of thinking that anything is visual about this representation; "image" just happens to be the word chosen to describe what is stored.) Here is an example showing how the memory image for "dog" might be represented in SAM. In showing this representation, and in the model's operation, I've changed some notation and procedures to make this concept more understandable to someone just beginning to study cognitive psychology, but the model's flavor is still here.

S(CT—Wdog)
S(Wboat—Wdog)
S(W1—Wdog)
. . .
S(Wn—Wdog)

The top element shows whatever has been stored (S) about the association between the context at retrieval time, or "test time" (CT), and the word (W) the subject is trying to remember ("dog"). The next element shows what has been stored specifically about the association between the words "boat" and "dog." The next elements show any associations that may have been stored relating "dog" to each of the other words in the list. Here the remaining words are shown as "1" through "n." In an actual study, the subject would have as many images as necessary to account for the words in the list, which could easily be twenty or more items. We're assuming that each paired associate produces exactly one image, but this assumption may not always be valid.

Some studies have shown that an image may sometimes represent considerably more information than is carried by one word (Shiffrin, Murname, Gronlund, & Roth, 1989).

As we've seen earlier in this chapter, almost all accounts of retrieval talk about how important cues are, and SAM is no exception. What types of cues drive retrieval, and how are they represented? Let's consider this set:

[C W1 W2 . . . Wn]

Here, C might represent the context at encoding time. Each of the other terms represents one of the prompt words in the list, and one of those words represents our prompt "boat." To show how these prompts affect the images, let's make up numbers that will show the differing "strengths" of the various associations. In the actual model, the association's strength varies as a function of both the encoding strategy and the time the subject spent working on the encoding in working memory. For our example, we use numbers from 0 to 9, with 0 representing essentially no association, and 9 a maximally strong association. Also, we set this problem up so that two cues are being used to activate the images stored in memory, and we assume that we'll consider the effects on only three of the images in a list. Just keep in mind that all the images are affected when cued, not just three or any other arbitrary number. Now, a preliminary question: How can we show cuing's effects on the images representing the memory of words in a list? One way of doing that is to use matrix algebra: By premultiplying each of the images with a subset of all the cues that could be given, we get a product that might represent that image's "activation level." If an image's activation level is higher than some preset threshold, then we say the system has "retrieved" that image, an act analogous to human retrieval of a memory. Our hypothetical example, with two cues from the cue list and three images stored in memory, might look like this:

$$[9\ 0\ 0\ 0\ 1]\qquad \begin{vmatrix}4\\1\\1\\1\\2\end{vmatrix}\quad \begin{vmatrix}2\\3\\3\\1\\3\end{vmatrix}\quad \begin{vmatrix}0\\1\\1\\1\\9\end{vmatrix}$$

Using the cues to multiply the first image, we get: $[\ (9 \times 4) + (0 \times 1) + (0 \times 1) + (0 \times 1) + (1 \times 2)]$, which equals 38, and this result becomes the strength of the activated image in memory. Treating the other two images in the same way, we get activation strengths of 21 and 9. Does this mean that the system would "remember" the first image? The answer is yes, if an activation strength of 38 is higher than the system's preset threshold criterion. If that criterion were set at, let's say, 30, then the system would retrieve the first image. Of course, if the criterion were set below 20, then the system would retrieve two images, but it's certainly possible to imagine an outcome such as this. For example, the subject might hear the cue "boat" and retrieve its correct paired associate, "dog." But the subject might also retrieve another word (maybe "tree") and recognize that "tree" also appeared somewhere in the list of words. In looking over the numbers I made up to illustrate SAM, you may get the idea that I stacked the deck, in the sense that the "same" image would always be retrieved no matter what the numbers were. But if you play around with the numbers a little, you'll see that it's possible for any specific image to be retrieved under the right circumstances. Remember, we used a sample of only two cues from a listing of cues, substituting zeros for the cues that weren't being used. If we had used different cues, which might have had different associative strengths, then we might well have gotten the system to retrieve a different image.

I admit that I find SAM and models like it fascinating, but sometimes my students are a little skeptical about the usefulness of such formal models. They argue that it is not possible to test or verify them. I appreciate the skepticism, but I think SAM, and many similar models, can handle that criticism. Can you think of some implications of this model that we could test? One implication is that the more cuing information a subject has, the more likely it is that the subject will select a cue that has a large associative strength with some specific part of the image the subject is trying to retrieve. In other words, if we go back to real human data, SAM should lead us to expect that the larger the number of cues that are given from a list of paired associates, the greater the likelihood that a person will retrieve a specific word. It's true that the more cues given, the higher the activation of all the images in memory (because each cue that's given independently affects each image that has been stored). But all things being equal, a greater number of cues increases the likelihood that one of those cues will have a high associative strength with some element in the image that a person is trying to retrieve. Hence, that image would stand a greater chance of being retrieved as a result of prompting with a greater number of cues. And this is the phenomenon we observe in human cued recall—a phenomenon that can be well accounted for by SAM.

*P*rimary-Memory Models

In this section we take up primary memory explicitly. One of the most important issues we'll deal with is the best way to understand and describe how primary memory operates. When we examined the information-processing model, the evidence pointed to a cognitive structure with highly definable and predictable characteristics in its capacity, the form of its representational code, and so on. Is our notion of an STS the best response to the evidence that we can make? Some theorists have suggested otherwise. We'll consider an alternative viewpoint on the primary-memory phenomenon known as the "working-memory" model.

Working-Memory Models and Short-Term Storage   The concept of primary memory as a "working" memory suggests that primary memory should not be thought of as a unitary "box" that changes any material placed there into an auditory or verbal representation. Working-memory theorists argue that primary memory instead refers to a collection of cognitive processes that can engage in a number of separable operations on incoming material.

Baddeley (1982, 1983, 1990; Baddeley & Lewis, 1981) designed a model that typifies this thinking. Figure 3.5 diagrams his approach. The central executive functions like a limited-capacity attentional system, similar to those discussed in Chapter 2. This system is responsible for directing the activities of the various "slave" systems, two of which are shown. Baddeley makes it clear that future research may carve additional peripheral

Figure 3.5   A simplified representation of the working-memory model. *Source:* Copyright 1983 by The Royal Society. Adapted by permission of the publisher and author.

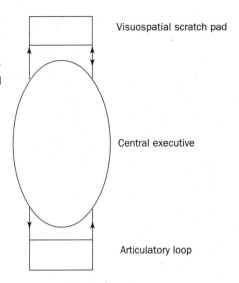

Visuospatial scratch pad

Central executive

Articulatory loop

systems away from the executive function. But for now the two subsystems shown—the **articulatory loop** and the **visuospatial scratch pad**—are the only ones about which much is known.

The articulatory loop is a component in working memory consisting of two parts: a phonological input store and an articulatory rehearsal process that may involve something like subvocal speech. The phonological store operates like the acoustic-verbal-linguistic storage that we saw in the Atkinson-Shiffrin model. Essentially, incoming verbal material is coded and stored by its sounds, or its articulatory (oral-motor) properties. As conceived by Baddeley, however, the articulatory loop can explain retrieval facts that were problematic for previous viewpoints. Consider this phenomenon: It has been known for some time that retrieval of visually presented items such as numbers can be degraded by simultaneously presenting spoken text. This degradation occurs even when the subject is told to ignore the spoken material. The text's semantic properties are not influential (nonsense syllables are just as disruptive as speech). But phonological properties are critical: a blast of ignored white noise doesn't have nearly the degrading effect that ignored speech does (Salame & Baddeley, 1982). This phenomenon is referred to as the **unattended speech effect.** Now, if subvocal rehearsal is prevented by requiring the subject to repeat the same word over and over, then mysteriously, the unattended speech effect disappears. The subject's memory for visually presented letters is not impaired by simultaneously presenting spoken text, but only if the subject repeats a word over and over while the spoken text is being presented.

The model explains this effect in this way: All spoken material has direct access to the phonological storage. Typically, when material is presented visually, it is recoded, or transformed, into a phonological representation and is thus able to take advantage of the phonological store. The visual materials are recorded into a phonological representation in the normal course of events, thus aiding their retrieval. When the subject is exposed to the spoken text, however, this material makes its way

Figure 3.6 The task for studying spatial and verbal memory coding, devised by Brooks (1967). *Source:* Copyright 1983 by The Royal Society. Adapted by permission of the publisher and author.

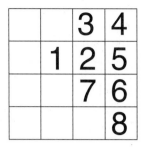

Spatial material

In the starting square put a 1.
In the next square to the right put a 2.
In the next square up put a 3.
In the next square to the right put a 4.
In the next square down put a 5.
In the next square down put a 6.
In the next square to the left put a 7.
In the next square down put an 8.

Nonsense material

In the starting square put a 1.
In the next square to the quick put a 2.
In the next square to the good put a 3.
In the next square to the quick put a 4.
In the next square to the bad put a 5.
In the next square to the bad put a 6.
In the next square to the slow put a 7.
In the next square to the bad put an 8.

into the phonological store, taking it out of action for the recoded visual stimuli. Therefore, retrieval of the visual material is hampered. Repeating the word, however, blocks the spoken text's obligatory entry into the phonological store. This step in turn paves the way for the executive to recode the visual material into the phonological store, enhancing retrieval of the visual material.

Figure 3.6 shows a task originally devised by Brooks (1967) to study the effects of spatial working memory. The subject was given the series of statements and was asked to repeat them. When the subjects were given the spatial statements, those on the left, they were able to recode them into a path through the matrix of cells; hence, the statements could be remembered as a visual pattern. The nonspatial statements held the same quantity of information as did the spatial statements, except that they could not be recoded so easily. Brooks found that the spatial statements were retained better when presented auditorily rather than visually, whereas the reverse was true for nonspatial sequences. Brooks suggested that representing the spatial sequence relies upon a visuospatial coding that interferes with processing visual stimuli such as written text. Moreover, the interference is bidirectional: processing visual stimuli interferes with the visuospatial coding of a spatial sequence. Baddeley and his colleagues further theorized that the interference is produced by spatial conflicts: Reading text requires involvement by the scratch pad in a spatial task; namely, directing the eye movements in order to encode the text into working memory. Of course, the spatial statements also demand spatial encoding, thus producing a conflict because the two tasks are both trying to make their way into the scratch pad's storage register.

In an experiment designed to test these ideas, Baddeley and his colleagues had their subjects engage in the memory task just described while simultaneously tracking a target visually on a computer's screen. In one condition, the target was actually moving in a sine-wave pattern on the screen. In a second condition, the target was stationary, but the background was moving, creating the illusion of target motion. In another condition, both the background and target were moving. Because the stimuli in the retention task were presented auditorily, we would expect that the subjects would perform better on the spatial version of the task, and this expectation was confirmed. When the subjects' eyes were fixed (i.e., when the background alone was moving), they retained 70% of the spatial sequences and 68% of the nonsense sequences. When the subjects' eyes were moving, with or without a moving background, however, the subjects retained only 52% of the spatial sequences and 63% of the nonsense sequences. In other words, moving one's eyes while doing the nonsense version of the task knocked performance down only 5%. But eye movements produced an 18% performance decrement on the spatial version of the task.

Let's summarize. Baddeley's work indicates that the working memory is probably not simply a passive, single register. Rather, retrieval from working memory involves applying several cognitive processes, extracting material from related but somewhat independent registers.

Against this view, though, theorists with the traditional STS orientation have produced some findings that cannot be explained so easily from the working-memory position (Cowan, 1994; Cowan, Wood, & Born, 1994). First, to understand these studies, we must know about the word-length effect in memory. In a typical STM experiment, subjects are given a list of stimuli and are asked to retrieve all they can from the list, either immediately or after a distractor, such as the one we saw in the Peterson and Peterson task. The maximum number of stimuli that we can retrieve is referred to as the memory span. The word-length effect applies to lists consisting of words. For such lists, memory span is increased if the words are shorter and easier to pronounce than longer words that are more difficult to pronounce. The conventional explanation for this finding is that shorter words can be rehearsed more extensively in memory simply because they don't require as much time to rehearse.

In one study Cowan et al. (1992) demonstrated that increased rehearsal time in buffer could not be the whole story in the word-length effect. Rather, they hypothesized that subjects were losing part of their memory content while they reported other elements that were stored. In other words, during the time the subject required to simply report a longer word, more material would be lost in memory than when a shorter word was reported. To support this hypothesis, they carried out a study in which subjects saw a printed list that might begin with long or short words, and might end with either long or short words. At the end of each list, subjects received a cue signaling them to report the elements in either forward or backward order. Before we go to the findings, let's think about the effect this manipulation might have. If the subject is losing memory at report time; that is, while speaking, then length of the word that is to be reported first should more strongly affect likelihood of retrieval than should length of the words to be reported later. If you were a subject and you saw a long word at the end of the list, its presence shouldn't influence your likelihood of retrieval if you were cued to report the words in forward order, because the other, presumably smaller words could still be reported quickly before you got to the large word at the end. But if you were cued to report this list in backward order, then we should expect the long word to have an effect, because while you are taking the time to say the long word, other material is being lost from your memory. Looking at Figure 3.7, we can see that this is precisely the effect that Cowan et al. found. When the long word

Figure 3.7 Proportion correct as a function of length of words in the first two (left-hand panels) and the last two (right-hand panels) of five serial positions (S.P.). Results are shown separately for forward recall (top panels) and backward recall (bottom panels). The length of the third (middle) word varied randomly in each condition, and filler lists prevented subjects from detecting a pattern. Length effects were significant only for length of words in whichever half of the list was to be recalled first (top-left and bottom-right panels). *Source:* From Cowan, 1994.

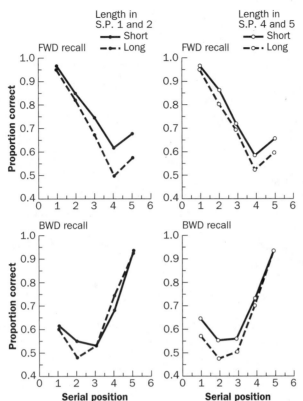

was in the early serial position, and forward recall was cued, then subjects had relatively low recall for the short words in the late serial positions. But when the long word occupied the late serial positions and backward recall was cued, the subjects had trouble retrieving the short words in the early serial positions.

In a subsequent study the researchers took this finding one step further. As you'll recall, when subjects are given a distractor task to do before they report the content of their memories, their performance is generally worsened. What might the effects of such a distractor task be on the word-length effect? According to the view that we have a separate STS with limited duration, the word-length effect should vanish. During the time the distractor task is being processed, all the information in STS is being lost; consequently, the presence of long or short words occupying particular serial locations should not have any overall effect. Notice that this is not necessarily the same prediction that the working-memory model might make. Cowan (1994) reported that the findings supported the notion that we have a separate storage that is used for immediate memory tasks. When short words were cued first, they were recalled with higher probability than were long words, as long as no distraction task was included. When the distraction task was imposed, though, no advantage appeared for recall probability in cuing the short words first.

*D*istinction Between Primary and Secondary Memory—Blurring the Line

Throughout this chapter we've assumed the distinction between primary and secondary memory, or between STS and LTS. Although we've seen a substantial body of evidence supporting such a distinction, and although this difference has a long history in American academic psychology, going back at least as far as James (1890/1983), some theorists and researchers nevertheless have determined that the theoretically postulated differences between STS and LTS are not always observed in careful experiments. Second, some researchers have suggested that numerous cognitive processes seem to work in exactly the same way regardless of whether the task seems to require primary or secondary memory (e.g., see Crowder, 1993, for a discussion of these and related issues). In this section we focus on the theoretical bases for the distinction between STS and LTS, but I think the discussion has broader implications. That is, as I think you'll see, from the standpoint of memory as a storage phenomenon, we may have reason to question whether the human cognitive system has two or more such storage locations.

Coding in STS: Is It Always Acoustic or Phonetic?

You may recall that the information-processing theory strongly states that our STM takes all incoming information and converts it into a phonetic or acoustic code. This position suggests that either semantic information should not be available to the cognitive system when it is occupied with an STM task, or if such information is available, it should at least not influence processing of material in STM. Shulman (1971, 1972) examined how semantic information influenced an STM task. His subjects underwent trials, each of which had this format: First, the subjects saw a list of ten words that were presented for 500 msec each. The tenth word was followed by the probe word, and the subjects had to tell whether the probe matched a word on the ten-item list. The match varied from trial to trial, however. On some trials, a *match* meant that the subject had to report if the probe was identical to one of the words appearing on the list. On the other trials, a match would be achieved if the probe word was a synonym for one of the words appearing in the list. The subject did not know in advance which trials would be synonym trials and which would be identity trials; the type of trial was signaled by flashing an *S* or an *I* just before the probe word appeared.

Before we go on to the findings in this study, let's review implications of this procedure. If the subject has only acoustic information available in STS, then no confusions should arise about the probe word when it has only a semantic relationship to the words on the list. That is, we would not expect subjects to mistake the probe word as identical to a word on the list when it was a synonym for one of the words on the list. If such confusions are observed, they must be based on a semantic, not an acoustic similarity, meaning that some semantic knowledge must be available to the subjects in STS. Figure 3.8 shows the findings. When an identity match was signaled and the probe was a word that was not semantically related to the words on the list, the proportion of errors was .11. When an identity match was signaled, and the probe was a word that was a synonym of one of the words in the list, however, the proportion of

Figure 3.8 Proportion of correct identity matches (II) and synonym matches (SS), as well as proportion of times subjects mistakenly said yes to a synonym when an identity match was requested (IS) as a function of serial position. *Source:* From Shulman, 1972.

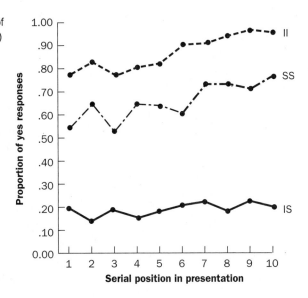

errors increased dramatically to .19 (this is the line on the graph labeled "IS"). Notice, too, that the proportion of such errors as a function of serial position in presentation remained constant. If an acoustic code dominated, or even lay alongside the semantic information, we would expect to see a reduction in errors when the probe was a synonym for the three or four items most recently presented. Presumably, these items would be most likely to be coded acoustically and therefore most resistant to confusion. That such a reduction was not observed suggests that the semantic information was more than simply available to the subjects. Rather, it suggests that the subjects had coded the words on the list by their semantic properties.

Notice that Shulman's subjects were not left to their own devices in forming a code. The task must have encouraged them to form a semantic representation of the list. Indeed, ample evidence suggests that when subjects are left to their own devices in a short-term task, their representations are likely to be somewhat acoustic (Drewnowski, 1980). Drewnowski and Murdock (1980) presented findings showing that intrusion errors for monosyllabic words stored in STS are primarily acoustic (echoing Conrad, 1964). When dissyllabic words were presented either visually or aurally, however, the intrusion errors could not be well explained purely by acoustics. Instead, Drewnowski and Murdock found that the intrusions were made according to the syllabic stress pattern, the phonemic class of the initial and final syllables, and the identity of the stressed vowel. Recall Atkinson and Shiffrin's comment on how difficult it was to separate acoustic from linguistic codes. The Drewnowski and Murdock findings seem to amplify the idea that the cognitive system produces various codes early and perhaps almost simultaneously. Thus, many cognitive psychologists are reluctant to use coding differences as a basis for establishing separate long- and short-term storages, and have taken instead to studying how these various codes arise and transform (Horton & Mills, 1984).

Mechanism of Forgetting   The difference in forgetting mechanisms—decay in STS, interference in LTS—has also been used as a basis for claiming that these storages are truly separate. Unfortunately, this distinction has been under a cloud for some time. Early critics of the original Peterson and Peterson finding pointed out that the possibility of interference from trial to trial had not been completely controlled for. According to this argument, the act of storing one trigram in STS may have interfered with ability to store the trigrams presented on later trials. As more and more trigrams were presented on successive trials, a reasonable supposition was that interference might increase from one trial to the next. If this putative explanation was correct, then the results the Petersons observed were produced not by decay but by interference by earlier trials in later trials. The Petersons defended themselves against this charge by saying that if this explanation were true, then the subjects' performance should get worse on successive trials on the counting-backward task. But it didn't. Performance on the first trial and the *n*th trial were essentially the same. This rebuttal seemed sound until Keppel and Underwood (1962) read the Petersons' procedure section closely and noticed that the Petersons had given their subjects two practice trials. Keppel and Underwood wondered if interference might have been induced on those trials. When the study was replicated without the practice trials, they found that a buildup of interference occurred across trials. Retention was better on trial 1 than on trial 2, which in turn was better than retention on the third and subsequent trials. Keppel and Underwood's study concluded that at least some interference seems to be involved in forgetting from STS.

Capacity Differences Between Short-Term and Long-Term Storage   We've seen that one foundation of the information-processing viewpoint of memory rests on apparent differences in capacity between STS and LTS. Specifically, the theory argues that STS has a rather small capacity, but LTS has a large, or perhaps even infinite capacity. But is this distinction valid? In this section we take a closer look at the chunking phenomenon and we'll see that both the existence of chunking and the relative ease with which most people do it may argue against the idea of necessary differences in STS and LTS capacities. That is, it's possible to learn to chunk information rather well, so well in fact that apparent capacity of STS balloons greatly.

In the literature on memory, this effect is perhaps seen most clearly in the S.F. case (Ericsson, Chase, & Faloon, 1980). An undergraduate with normal memory ability, S.F. agreed to participate in an extended study on memory skills. Three to five times a week, for about an hour each session, S.F. was read sequences of random digits at one digit per second. His task was to recall the sequence. If he succeeded, he was read another list that was one digit longer than the preceding one. Over approximately 1½ years, S.F. logged 230 hours hearing and recalling random digit sequences. During this period, his memory span (the number of random digits he could recite correctly) increased from a very typical 7 digits to a phenomenal 80 digits! It happened that S.F. was a talented distance runner who used his knowledge of this sport as a particularly effective mnemonic device to organize 3- and 4-digit groups of numbers as times that might be achieved in races. Thus, the sequence 3492 might be encoded as 3 minutes, 49.2 seconds—nearly record time in the mile. The power of this mnemonic is seen in a demonstration that Ericsson et al. carried out after S.F. had about two months of practice. Then S.F. was presented with a sequence of digits that could not be easily coded as race times. His performance dropped almost to his beginning level. On the other hand, when a sequence of digits was given that could all be easily represented as running times, S.F.'s performance increased by a dramatic 22%.

S.F.'s impressive memory performance raises a question: By chunking, is it possible to keep up to 80 distinct elements in short-term storage? Ericsson and his coworkers didn't think so. To show why, the researchers analyzed the structure of S.F.'s recall. First, realize that in retrieving the digits, S.F. did not recite them at a constant rate or speed. Rather, he seemed to retrieve a number of digits very quickly, then pause before reciting another group of digits. Based in part on the amount of time that S.F. hesitated between retrieving digits, Ericsson et al. determined that he used a three-level hierarchy in retrieving the random strings. This structure is shown below:

$$444\ 444 \qquad 333\ 333 \qquad 444 \qquad 333 \qquad 444 \qquad 5$$

Thus, S.F. began by arranging the digits into groups of four, the first level of organization. For example, if a string began with the digits "8," "3," "3," "2," these digits were grouped together, and are represented by the very leftmost 4 in the structure above. Then he used units of this sort to form a group of three such strings (accounting for the first set of 4s). This was the second level of organization and accounted for the first 12 digits. After a short pause he produced another set of 12 digits in the same way. These first 24 digits formed a "supergroup" and made up the third level of organization. After a longer pause he grouped the next set of 18 digits into a supergroup that was based on subgroups of 3, rather than 4 digits. He continued with this pattern, using groups of 3 or 4 digits as the basic unit of organization.

Two interesting observations about this organization: First, the basic size of the groups was always 3 to 5 digits, well within the traditional memory-span limit. Second, S.F. made use of his "normal" short-term storage, as you can see in the group of 5 digits at the end of the sequence. These five digits were not translated into running times; they were simply left in S.F.'s rehearsal buffer in an acoustic format. It might appear that he was maintaining 80 items in his short-term memory, but according to Ericsson et al., he really wasn't. Rather, S.F. was using a mnemonic device to impose a hierarchic organization on this material. Findings like those produced by S.F. tell cognitive psychologists that we really can't use memory span as a good indication of STM capacity.

Summing Up the Distinction   If you're like me, you probably have a strong intuition that you have two memory systems; one for the stimuli that are currently present, but out of your immediate focus, and a second for information that you had to learn, but whose learning took place long ago. This won't be the last time in going through this book that we see that our intuitions about our cognitive systems may not be completely correct. In fact it is not necessary to postulate two separate systems to account for most memory phenomena. No data mandate the two separate memory systems that seem, intuitively, so obvious. This conclusion leaves us with a question, though: Is it possible to describe what it is that the cognitive and neural systems are doing when they produce the events that seem to us like STM or LTM retrieval?

Several theorists have written (Cowan, 1993; Crowder, 1993), that the cognitive and neural systems must be doing something different when they retrieve briefly stored material than when they retrieve information that has been held for a long time. Let's consider what the central nervous system might be doing when a stimulus is being held in STM. According to many views, when stimuli are being held in STM the central nervous system maintains a consistent pattern or arrangement of neural activity—we might call this pattern the "posture" of the brain. Obviously, you cannot maintain this posture forever, if only because new incoming stimuli constantly demand to be processed, and doing so requires instantiating a new pattern of activity congruent with encoding these new stimuli. In effect, the brain goes on to a new posture with the processing of these incoming stimuli. According to this view, as long as the brain is maintaining a posture, the stimuli that produced that posture, whether they are currently visible or not, are nevertheless still being represented and thus can still be retrieved. To store something longer, the implication is that your brain must achieve a different configuration or pattern of neural activity. Whatever the pattern, this view implies two brain postures for stored material: one posture that occurs immediately as the material is converted to a neural code, and a second reflecting a more durable neural coding. If such a view is accurate, the first posture represents the brain activity that gives rise to our experience of STM, whereas the second posture refers to the brain activity that produces our experience of LTM.

Cowan (1993) apparently had in mind a similar view of the STM–LTM distinction. Cowan refers to STM as a hierarchic concept bearing at least two components. The first refers to elements in LTM that are currently activated. Thus such elements may be reconverted from whichever posture the neural system uses for durable storage back into the posture the brain used to represent those elements when it first encoded them. A second component in STM refers to activated elements that are currently the focus of attention. This second component in STM may provide us with our subjective experience of STM; namely, that STM consists of things of which we are currently "thinking" or which are currently "on our minds." Today I cannot comment on the accuracy of this viewpoint; obviously more time and research will be needed before we completely understand the relationship between the cognitive and neural systems.

Contents of Secondary Memory

When we looked into the information-processing model of memory, we saw its stipulation that once material was transferred to LTM, it was organized semantically. Obviously, this organization leaves open quite a few possibilities about the specific knowledge that is stored in LTM, and its organization. In this section we consider the long-term memory.

The Permastore   How long would you expect to remember something that you've learned? Clearly, you want to remember it long enough to do you some good. But beyond the period in which you believe you will use the knowledge, how much will be retained?

Bahrick's (1984) attempt to answer this question involved hundreds of subjects who learned Spanish over as many as fifty years. These people were asked to estimate both how well they had learned the material at the time they were studying Spanish, and how much they had rehearsed the material or used it since they had studied it. Subjects were then given a retention test, and their performance was then correlated with their active rehearsal of Spanish in the years since they had studied it, and with their self-reported mastery during their studies. Bahrick found that, overall, active rehearsal of Spanish was rather low for this group of people and in general was not highly correlated with performance on the Spanish retention test. Self-reported estimates of learning and involvement with other Romance languages, however, were both highly correlated with retention scores. This finding suggests that even for people who had not bothered to keep up with their foreign languages for decades, for those who had learned Spanish well in school, there was a strong correlation with retention even after fifty years had elapsed. From this and similar findings (e.g., Bahrick, Hall, Goggin, Bahrick, & Berger, 1994), Bahrick has developed the "permastore" concept and suggests that once material is truly learned and mastered, it endures more or less intact until the person's death. Notice that the permastore clearly includes semantic knowledge, but the suggestion is that it may include much more than that.

Other researchers have produced similar findings. Conway, Cohen, and Stanhope (1991) studied long-term retention for, of all things, material learned in a cognitive psychology course. They found, like Bahrick, that after an initial fall-off in knowledge in the first four years after taking the course, subjects reached an asymptote that remained stable for eight years. The implication is that whatever the subjects remembered about the cognitive psychology course after four years, they could be pretty sure they would continue to remember indefinitely. In a follow-up investigation, Conway et al. (1992) looked at the components in the students' performance most accurately predicting their long-term retention. Interestingly, they found that the student's grade in the course was not a good predictor of how much would be retained over the study's twelve-year interval. When they analyzed this finding in greater depth (Conway et al., 1992) they found, however, that the student's course grade was based on several components in performance. Among these components was performance on examinations, including the final exam. Other components included grades on elements that Conway et al. referred to as "coursework," which might consist of written reports on books, journal articles, or research reports. Conway et al. found that final-examination grades did not correlate with long-term retention, but coursework grades did. I think their explanation for their finding may interest you (assuming that you are a "student" reader). Conway et al. argued that exam grades reflect how well the student actually uses knowledge during learning, and so this kind of performance may contribute little to duration of the knowledge in memory. On the other hand, the coursework grades reflect the student's understanding and comprehension of the material at the time of learning, which is just the learning we would expect to be durable, given Bahrick's findings. If Conway et al. are right, then we are led to the intriguing proposition that grades given in courses may not necessarily predict efficiently how much knowledge the student will be able to retrieve from present courses in the future.

Episodic and Semantic Memory

As we've seen, we seem to have a semantic component in our permanent memory, but we have not yet considered how that memory may be organized. We'll spend a great deal of time describing this semantic memory component in Chapters 5 and 6. Here, though, our objective is to understand more about this semantic component in the context of other systems that theoretically reside in permanent memory.

Tulving (1972, 1983) proposed distinguishing between two types of permanent memory. **Episodic memories** were autobiographical, personal, and sensitive to context effects. These memories were organized by time and place of occurrence and could frequently be described according to their perceptual characteristics. Episodic memory could be contrasted with **semantic memory,** which housed general, encyclopedic knowledge of the world and language. Semantic memory was organized by class membership and other abstract principles such as sub- or superordination. In other words, semantic memory seemed to consist of facts that could be organized hierarchically. For example, I know that dogs and cats are both mammals, but they can be grouped together in a superordinate category—chordates—along with other animals that are not mammals. Semantic memory was composed of knowledge that had no specific temporal or spatial referent, and was therefore not sensitive to context. Although Tulving (1972) pointed out that these two systems do interact with each other, he felt that each system probably has its own encoding, storage, and retrieval laws.

Some evidence supports Tulving's contentions, at least to a degree. Kihlstrom (1980) reported episodic and semantic memory dissociation for normal subjects who were in a hypnotic state. The subjects were hypnotized and then memorized a list of unrelated words. Following the learning session, the subjects were given a posthypnotic suggestion that they would not be able to remember the memorized list until they got a specific retrieval cue. Following that, the subjects were told that they would now have to supply free associations to words given by the experimenter. These priming words were deliberately chosen because they had a high probability of eliciting the list words that the subjects had memorized. Subjects performed well on this task, indicating that the hypnotic state had not affected their general (i.e., semantic) knowledge of the words' meanings. Even after they had recited many of the words on the list, however, the subjects maintained that they were unable to retrieve the items studied. Yet when the retrieval cue mentioned in the posthypnotic suggestion was finally given, the subjects' retrieval was close to perfect.

Salasoo, Shiffrin, and Feustel (1985) investigated semantic and episodic effects in word recognition. Recognizing words that have been briefly presented appears to involve semantic memory, and true to expectations, subjects typically identify, name, and make decisions about actual words faster than they do for pronounceable nonwords. Episodic effects also appear, however. Consider how we identify a grammatically acceptable but completely novel nonword. Presumably, such a stimulus has no representation in semantic memory because the subject has never encountered it before and it doesn't mean anything anyway. It has been shown, though, that identification of such a stimulus is enhanced upon its *second* presentation, even when the delay between initial and second presentations is quite lengthy. This **repetition effect** is clearly the result of episodic memory. Salasoo et al. wondered how much the two memory systems contributed to each of these phenomena: How many episodic presentations were necessary before identification of a grammatically correct nonword equaled that of a familiar, semantically based actual word? They found that about five such presentations were required to enable subjects to identify a nonword as accurately as they did a word. They also found that these episodic effects were quite durable. They brought their subjects back into the lab one year after the original study. Subjects still showed the effects of repetition; their identification performance for previously seen nonwords, previously seen words, and new words was similar and superior to their performance for new nonwords.

Flashbulb Memories   The memories that result when we find that a highly unexpected and emotionally charged event has taken place are called flashbulb memories (Winograd & Killinger, 1983). They have been described as examples of extreme episodic memories (Houston, 1986). In some ways, such memories seem to obey the normal laws of retrieval. For example, they can seldom be cued by a chronological prompt. Can you retrieve one newsworthy event that happened, let's say, in January 1986? Most people can't. In other ways, however, these memories are unusual. One curious thing about them is the detail they seem to hold. Where were you when you learned about the *Challenger* space-shuttle disaster? Who were you with? How did you find out? Many people can answer these questions, and they believe their answers are quite accurate. (The event took place in January 1986, by the way.) Some argue that it's the highly charged emotional flavor of flashbulb memories that gives them their seemingly indelible, accurate quality. Intuitively, this account is appealing, but the scientific literature simply doesn't support it. First, as Wagenaar's findings show, pleasant and unpleasant memories do show differential probabilities of retrieval, but only for a year or so. After that, very pleasant memories were no more likely to be retrieved than were neutral or very unpleasant memories. Now the emotionally charged memories may *appear* to be indelible and accurate, but probably we use the same fallible inferential-retrieval strategies with both emotional and nonemotional memories.

Neisser and Harsch (1992) demonstrated this effect in studying people's memories about the *Challenger* disaster. While the rest of the nation sat transfixed and disbelieving in front of their television sets, Neisser and Harsch got busy and prepared a questionnaire, which they administered to 106 subjects the next morning. Among other things, the subjects were asked to answer five questions about how they heard the news: where they were, what they were doing, who told them, what time that occurred, and so on. Thirty-two months after the incident, 44 subjects agreed to complete the questionnaire again. When the results of the follow-up were compared to the answers on the original questionnaire (which were presumably accurate), it became clear that the subjects' memories about the incident had dimmed. Of the 220 potentially recallable facts produced by the subjects on the morning after the explosion, their later recall efforts were at least partially wrong on more than 150 items. Fully 25% of the subjects misremembered all five attributes on their original questionnaires. Notice that the accuracy of any one subject's memory did not correlate with his or her confidence in that memory. Some subjects were quite confident that an incorrect retrieval was accurate. Weaver (1993) subsequently demonstrated that this confidence may be the special characteristic of flashbulb memories. In a classroom demonstration, Weaver asked his students to encode everything they could about a truly ordinary event: the circumstances surrounding the occasion when they next saw their roommates. The students had this encounter and completed a detailed questionnaire with items about what they were wearing when they saw the roommate, the time of day, and so on. These events occurred on Wednesday, January 16, 1991. By coincidence, on that very day, President Bush announced that Iraq was being bombed, commencing the hostilities now known as the Gulf War. Before the next class period on Friday, January 18, 1991, Weaver prepared another questionnaire, designed to assess students' recollection about the circumstances in this disturbing and dramatic national development. After they completed this questionnaire, Weaver could be pretty sure that he had two accurate measures of his students' memories about two specific events in their lives, one recording a private and mundane occurrence, the other a public and emotional one. Weaver followed up this round of questionnaires with two more: one in April 1991, about three months after the bombing began, and a final one in January 1992, one year after Desert Storm began. Table 3.1 shows how accurate the subjects' recall was as a proportion of questions answered correctly, and also their self-reported confidence in their accuracy on a three-point scale, with greater numbers indicating greater confidence. In Table 3.1, the pattern of results clearly suggests that, at both the three-month and one-year follow-ups, the students were no more accurate in recalling details about the dramatic flashbulb event than they were about the boring everyday event. But the results also show that the students clearly believed the emotional, flashbulb memories were more accurate than the everyday memories. They appear to have experienced misplaced confidence in their own memory systems because, with passing time, their memory of public events was no more accurate than their recall about private ones.

Infantile Amnesia   In the Overview we saw that most people typically report that they have no real recall (that is, detailed, specific, and coherent memories) about events that took place before they were three or four years old. In the 1990s, some psychologists attempted to move back this onset—that is, the age after which earlier events will eventually be forgotten—to earlier in the child's life, say age two (Usher & Neisser, 1993), but this effort has been strenuously criticized (Loftus, 1993). Regardless of the age at which it begins, however, the phenomenon creates a problem for pure-storage theo-

Table 3.1   Composite Memory and Confidence Scores Averaged Across All Events for Each Subject in April 1991 and January 1992

	Public Event		Personal Event	
Time	*Accuracy*	*Confidence*	*Accuracy*	*Confidence*
January 1991		2.79		2.82
April 1991	.71	2.35	.62	1.98
January 1992	.69	2.35	.71	2.06

Source: From Weaver, 1994.

rists. That is, if you believe that coherent, specific memories are the result of something that has been transferred to LTM, and that it can stay in there permanently, then knowing that hardly anyone can retrieve events from their first years suggests that children don't have long-term memory. But it's easy to demonstrate that they do, as another anecdote will show effectively. When our younger son was about 3:3, it happened that we invited a well-known psychologist from another university, and his wife, to join us for dinner in our home. The event was somewhat unusual for us. At the dinner we introduced our younger son to our guests, and spoke their names. Some six months later, I asked our son if remembered that occasion and the professor's name. He said he did, and with no other prompting, he also produced the professor's wife's full name (which was different from her husband's). We hadn't rehearsed their names during the six-month interval (to the best of my knowledge), and so the implication is that the guests' names were retained for at least that period, which suggests in turn that the preschooler's memory system was operating in some sense. Now for the rest of the story: When he was about seven, I asked my son again if he remembered the dinner or the guests' names. Can you predict his response? You're right; consistent with everything we've learned about memory, he had no recollection whatsoever about the episode.

These effects have been empirically demonstrated numerous times. Fivush and Hammond (1990) show that before age three, children can render detailed accounts about specific, salient events in their lives, such as Halloween. Further, they demonstrate (Hammond & Fivush, 1991) that children at age four can produce detailed accounts of trips to Disney World when the children were only two. In general, though, these events can no longer be retrieved beyond kindergarten or first grade; no one is sure why. Those who believe the storage metaphor is more than a metaphor may point to very important differences in brain-hemispheric development, including increased lateralization in brain function, which takes place during the early school years. Other important differences could appear in how children themselves think about their own memories. This is the position taken by Perner (1991, 1992). Perner asked three- and four-year-olds to watch an everyday object being placed in a box. Other children were told the object that was in the box; still others neither saw nor heard what object was in the box. The children were then asked if they knew what was in the box. The correct answer for the children who saw the object placed in the box, or heard about it, was yes. For the rest of the children, the correct answer was no. All the children answered this question correctly. Perner then asked the children to explain how they knew the answer. Somewhat to Perner's surprise, only the four-year-olds could tell how they knew, explaining that they had seen the object or not, or had been told or not. The three-year-olds didn't have an explanation. Moreover, this difference in responses could not be attributed solely to any linguistic or motivational differences between the children of different ages. Perner's explanation involved the encodings made by the younger children. He suggested that children at this age may be able to encode an event, but simultaneously not be able to encode it in such a way as to indicate that they had experienced that event. The result is that a child at age two or three may have memories, but may have no way of verifying that the memory was actually an experience.

Comments on Episodic and Semantic Memory   Now for a brief comment on some implications of autobiographical memory (or "everyday" memory as it's sometimes called). From the standpoint of ecological validity (Neisser, 1978), research on flashbulb memories and autobiographical memory generally is healthy because it anchors the scientific study of memory on our everyday experience. Such a viewpoint implies a natural linkage between the scientific enterprise and our everyday lives: The scientific study of memory *should* help us answer questions about why we remember or forget what we do. On the other hand, some cognitivists have maintained that emphasizing ecological validity leads to studies that must have very low generalizability (Banaji & Crowder, 1989). That is, they argue that asking subjects about the *Challenger* disaster, for example, might answer questions about how accurate memory about that incident is, but such an approach tells us next to nothing about what people remember in a general sense. Banaji and Crowder (1989) go on to suggest that only laboratory studies (frequently rather low in ecological validity) can provide theories and findings that are generalizable.

Another important point questions the precision of the terms "episodic memory" and "autobiographical memory." As they are used here, autobiographical memory is described as a kind of episodic memory, implying that all autobiographical memories are episodic. This definition does not mean, however, that all episodic memory is autobiographical. In fact, we can be pretty sure that many episodic memories are not, and will not become autobiographical memories. Nelson (1993) makes this point by comparing what she had for lunch yesterday with the first time she delivered a research paper at a scientific conference. You may be able to retrieve (today) what you ate for lunch yesterday, but it's unlikely that you will be able to do so for an extended period into the future, unless your lunch yesterday was something very special. On the other hand, you probably will be able to retrieve for a long time a personal milestone such as your first job interview. This distinction implies that autobiographical memories may start out being "normal" or everyday episodic memories. But unless something occurs to somehow "elevate" them, such memories will not become part of our personal life stories.

For the student, we can say that findings in autobiographical or everyday memory studies are interesting, and that cognitivists are still sorting out how such findings relate to "mainstream" laboratory results.

Intrachapter Summary and Interpretation

We've seen ample evidence that for some things we've learned, especially things that we learned with reasonably high understanding, a very durable representation seems to appear in the cognitive system. Looking at the specifics about this organization suggests that people build their knowledge from their personal experiences. We've also seen, however, that our memories are very fallible. Although we may be confident that an event that happened some time ago did happen in just the way we remember, we've seen that this confidence is frequently misplaced. Individuals who may want to make the storage metaphor more than a metaphor face the puzzling phenomenon of infantile amnesia (among other puzzling things that this view would have to deal with). If children have operative memories, suggesting that these are durable memories that are being stored, then why can't such memories be retrieved at all later in life? Notice that it is the generality and completeness of the infantile amnesia phenomenon that produces a problem. If we could all remember even a few things from our early lives, or if some of us could remember a lot of information from infancy, then cognitive psychologists might be able to explain away infantile amnesia as simply individual differences in retrieval or some other variable rather than a problem with storage. But that's not what we observe; infantile amnesia means hardly anyone remembers anything prior to age three or four.

Storage at the Neural Level

When we looked at the information-processing position, we saw evidence suggesting that if the neural system is disrupted by electric shock when a memory is being encoded, or transferred to LTM, then it is likely that the memory itself will be lost or weakened. Findings such as this one clearly show that the cognitive system and the neural system are related, but such findings do not explicitly describe how the neural system goes about storing something. Understanding how that can be done is our task in the next section.

Karl Lashley's Work

Karl Lashley was born in 1890 and earned his Ph.D. in zoology from Johns Hopkins University in 1914. He had studied there with John B. Watson, whose research on learning had developed from Ivan Pavlov's ideas. Pavlov had produced a fairly specific notion about the neurological changes underpinning learning. Specifically, he believed learning was accompanied by structural changes in the brain. Parts of the brain that had not communicated neurally prior to learning were associated during learning, and this association took the form of a physical, neural connection. Once formed, the association could not be uncoupled; however, the association did depend upon the continued integrity of the neural connection. If the connection was destroyed, whatever had been learned was lost.

Lashley (1929, 1950) set out to prove this theory. His method was simplicity itself. Rats were trained to run one in a set of mazes varying in difficulty from easy to hard. After the rats were proficient at running the mazes, Lashley systematically cut the cortex of each rat, making the cut in a different location in each rat's brain. Lashley's thinking was that some of the cuts should interrupt the critical connections in the rats' brains, and the rats should show memory deficits in learning the mazes. But Lashley's expectation proved inaccurate. No matter where the cut was made, the rats still performed up to par, regardless of the maze's difficulty. Although Lashley may have missed the critical connection in every animal, the possibility is remote. Far more likely is Lashley's conclusion, namely that learning and memory don't seem to involve specific connections in the brain.

A second experiment reinforced this finding. Lashley once again trained his rats to run complicated mazes. Some rats had had varying amounts of their cerebral cortexes removed prior to the training. The remainder of the rats' brains were intact. The learning rate for the brain-damaged rats was indeed slower than that of the intact rats. Moreover, the performance decrement was more or less proportional to the quantity of brain tissue that had been removed. Again, the location from which the tissue had been taken was not relevant. When lesions were made in the brains of the intact rats, Lashley observed that their performance was similar to that of the original brain-damaged group.

From these and other studies, Lashley formulated two principles in brain organization:

1. **Mass Action.**   "The efficiency of performance of an entire complex function may be reduced in proportion to the extent of brain injury" (Lashley, 1929). Mass action means that the brain works en masse. If a small quantity of brain tissue is removed, the brain can cope; but if a lot is removed, deficits will occur.

2. **Equipotentiality.**   Equipotentiality means that all parts of the brain are created equal, at least for learning and memory. No one part of the brain seems to be more important than another for memory storage.

We can summarize Lashley's findings by saying about memory that the amount of brain tissue removed is far more important than the location from which it is removed. That is, if a small amount of tissue is removed, the location doesn't matter, and probably no apparent memory loss will result. If a large quantity of tissue is removed, the location still doesn't matter, and memory loss will probably result.

Do not assume, however, that location of damage in the brain is unimportant. A relatively small quantity of damage to language or vision centers can produce an irremediable disability. In other words, the principle of equipotentiality may be true for humans up to a point. Some areas of specialization are found within the human brain, though. If these areas are destroyed in an adult, complete recovery is almost impossible.

Evidence from PET Scans

Lashley's research suggests that it is not useful to think of the brain as storing specific memories in the form of specific structural changes that are made at specific points in the cortex. Contemporary researchers have shown, though, that Lashley's conclusion does not rule out the search for specific sites or locations on the brain's surface where specific memory processes may occur. These researchers argue rightly that many improvements in technology in the past seventy years allow us to view the brain's operation in great detail. One such technique involves positron emission tomography, or PET scans.

To produce a PET scan of a functioning human brain, the subject is injected with a solution of water and a radioactive isotope called a tracer. In cognitive neuroscience, one commonly used tracer is oxygen 15, an isotope whose half-life is only 2 minutes. When the tracer is injected, it is taken up by the subject's bloodstream and enters the brain, usually within 15 seconds (Awh et al., 1996). Once there, the tracer emits positrons, which collide with electrons in the brain to produce photons. These photons register on an array of sensors surrounding the subject's head. Thus, by measuring the site of photon registration, the researchers are able to directly measure such important variables as oxygen use, glucose metabolism, and blood flow; the latter measure usually gives the best picture of moment-to-moment transitions in the brain's activity (Nyberg, Cabeza, & Tulving, 1996).

Buckner (1996) has used this technique to find evidence supporting the hemispheric encoding/retrieval asymmetry (HERA) model (Tulving, Kapur, Crai, Moscovitch, & Houle, 1994). The HERA model stipulates that the right prefrontal cortical areas are more involved in episodic retrieval than are the left prefrontal cortical areas. The arrangement is reversed for semantic retrieval, however. Now the left prefrontal areas are more involved than the right areas. Bucker first considered performance on two semantic-retrieval tasks. In the first task, subjects were given three-letter cues that were called word stems. The subject was to complete each word. Thus if given the stem "cou," the subject might generate "couple" or "courage." When subjects are scanned while they do this task, we see that many areas in the brain are used, especially in reading the text and producing a speech code. Besides these areas, Buckner found one that was always active in the left prefrontal cortex. This is the area labeled *1* in Figure 3.9, panel *a*. This area in the brain does not always become active in every task. Thus, it does not typically become active if the subject is simply told to speak out loud out a word that has been read, such as "couple." Buckner also looked at the effect of another semantic memory task, this time retrieving a word that has a specific meaning. Here subjects might be asked to search their memories for a word that meant "extreme happiness," perhaps retrieving "joy." When they were given this type of task, subjects showed a left-hemisphere activity pattern somewhat different from that seen in the stem-completion results. In word retrieval based on meaning, the subjects' brains were active in another area, labeled *2* in Figure 3.9, panel *a*. This activity occurred in addition to that in site *1*. From findings such as these, Buckner concluded that the left prefrontal cortex must be involved when the subject accesses semantic word knowledge. The second area becomes involved when subjects must go beyond this stage to access the meaning beyond simple knowledge of the word itself. Buckner and colleagues (Buckner et al., 1995) next looked at retrieval from episodic memory. Subjects studied a list of words, one of which might be "courage." After the study period and a delay, they were given the first three letters in the words (e.g., "cou"), and were asked to recall the specific study items. Although this procedure is superficially similar to the semantic-retrieval task, the subjects' experience with the list of words suggests that the cue will trigger an episodic search because the cue is actually a portion from one of the words that was studied. As the left-hand portion in panel *b* shows, the left hemisphere is still active in this task because this version of the task continues to require semantic word knowledge. As the right-hand side of panel *b* in Figure 3.9 shows, however, we also see differences. The right hemisphere's prefrontal cortex, which has been relatively quiet in the processing tasks until now, becomes active at a site labeled *3* in panel *b*. This site is silent during the purely semantic tasks, which suggests that it is processing the personally experienced component in this memory.

Other researchers have used PET scans to provide additional evidence on the location of memory functions. Awh and colleagues (1996) show that some distinctions in Baddeley's (1992) model of working memory; namely, the distinction between a phonological store that houses the speech and language code and a rehearsal mechanism that refreshes and maintains these contents, may be a distinction also honored in the cortex. Using a letter-recognition task that required subjects to maintain four

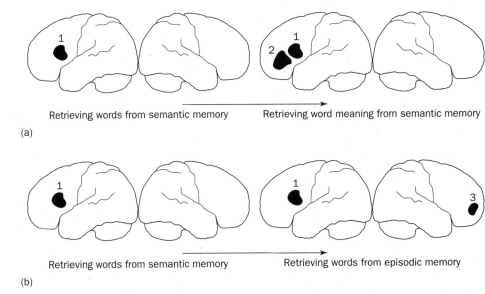

Figure 3.9   Three sets of tasks are depicted to illustrate memory-related activation of separate prefrontal areas. Each pair of hemispheres shows left and right lateralized activations from one task image, with activations indicated by shading. (*a*) Activations across two tasks relying on verbal semantic retrieval are illustrated. Two separate areas in the left prefrontal cortex (labeled *1* and *2*) are activated differentially across the two tasks (see text). (*b*) A comparison between a task relying on verbal semantic retrieval and one relying on verbal episodic retrieval. This comparison reveals a specific right anterior prefrontal area activated only during episodic retrieval (labeled *3*) (see text).

letters for 3 seconds, they found activity in the lower frontal lobe in the left hemisphere, very close in fact to the area in the brain responsible for producing the speech plan that we use when we speak. Awh et al. concluded that this is the area responsible for rehearsing the content of working memory. In addition to these frontal areas, however, heightened activation levels were observed in the left parietal lobe; that is, much farther back in the brain. As the researchers report, this area has been implicated in verbal short-term memory storage in a number of studies (McCarthy & Warrington, 1990; Vallar & Shallice, 1990). For example, among stroke victims, lesions in this site are frequently associated with deficits in verbal short-term memory, suggesting that such contents are stored in the left parietal lobe.

Evidence from MRI Scans

Cognitive neuroscientists have applied techniques other than PET scans to gather information about the neural system's structure and functioning during memory-driven tasks. Functional magnetic resonance imaging (fMRI) studies detect changes in the magnetic state of the blood in the brain. Because such changes in magnetic state depend on degree of oxygenation at that locus, and because changes in oxygenation can be used to infer changes in regional cerebral blood flow (rCBF), fMRI offers cognitive neuroscientists an opportunity to corroborate the findings in PET-scan studies.

Generally they do gain such corroboration. As an example, we consider work by Gabrieli and colleagues (Gabrieli et al., 1996). Four right-handed males participated in the neural-imaging portion of the study; the subjects' handedness ensured that they were left-hemisphere dominant. In one task, these subjects were given lists of words, half of them designating abstractions (TRUST), and the other half designating concrete objects (CHAIR). Half the words appeared in uppercase (capital) letters, and the other half in lowercase ("love"). The subjects were required to make one of two judgments about the words as they appeared. For some lists, they were to make a perceptual encoding, judging whether the word appeared in upper- or lowercase letters (subjects indicated their responses by squeezing a ball wired to a computer that recorded the change in pressure: during the fMRI scanning procedure, the subject was to remain immobile). For some lists, subjects made a semantic encoding responding to the word's abstractness or concreteness. The fMRI results support the PET-scan findings almost completely, increasing our confidence in the model that seems to be forming. When the subjects were asked to make a semantic judgment, the left prefrontal lobe once again lit up, suggesting a high level of activation. This activity was not observed when the subjects were required to make only a perceptual judgment. Let's put the findings in context: If you're a subject in the study and are asked to make a judgment on the concreteness of the word "love," you must contact some sort of semantic representation, and it looks as if the left prefrontal cortex is strongly implicated. Given the same word, "love," and asked to make only a perceptual judgment, however, no neural representation of meaning has to be accessed, and so the left prefrontal cortex simply stays at its normal, baseline level of activity.

Concluding Comments and Suggestions for Further Reading

How might we sum up our tour of memory from the storage-metaphor perspective? We started with the first empirical demonstration on loss of material from memory; that is, work by Hermann Ebbinghaus. His work in general had a salutary and productive effect on the study of memory, leading as it did to the information-processing theory of memory developed some eighty years later. The information-processing position was strongly anchored in the Ebbinghaus tradition, and thus information-processing theorists believed strongly that the abstract specifications in the model, such as short-term memory, were in fact simply ways of talking about changes at the neural level of analysis. We went on to consider modern incarnations of the information-processing model, such as SAM, and saw that such accounts can still be persuasive in accounting for numerous behavioral findings.

We then expanded our scope to look at other ways in which we might characterize the storage components or content of those components. For example, we saw that dividing memory into STS and LTS is but one way in which we might handle the distinction between primary and secondary memory. Other approaches, too, have come up. Researchers have devised an alternative to STS called "working memory." Similarly, some have suggested that the content of the secondary memory consists of a "permastore" (and isn't this just like the model of memory that Ebbinghaus erected?). At the same time as some researchers emphasized the durability of material that had been stored, others chose to consider the organizational principles that might govern the permanent memory. We considered dividing the permanent memory into two types; episodic memory reflecting our personal experiences, and semantic memory based on general knowledge. We also considered the idea that some permanent or temporary memories may consist of a visual or spatial format, and others are fundamentally verbal or linguistic.

Finally we considered evidence that the storage metaphor may be more than a metaphor. Although Karl Lashley's research shows us that it is unlikely that specific areas in the cortex are the basis for specific memories, contemporary researchers show rather convincingly that specific sites in the brain are associated with specific cognitive processes underlying memory. I think we should be careful not to oversell the findings from the PET and fMRI studies: we still have no evidence that specific sites in the brain are structurally or functionally altered in specific ways that correspond to that person's learning or memory. But I think it is fair to describe PET and MRI studies as showing the possibility of detailed linkages between the neural and cognitive systems. Thus, when cognitive psychologists distinguish between episodic and semantic memory, they are working at an abstract level of specification. When neurological evidence supports that distinction, however, as it seems to, then cognitive psychologists may be in a position to suggest that the neurological system seems to honor a distinction that we have made at the abstract level. This use of high-tech instrumentation, such as that seen in this chapter, is sure to increase in the future, enhancing the possibility of finding further linkages between cognitive and neural processes.

Students who are interested in these issues could begin with the Atkinson and Shiffrin (1968) article to learn more about the information-processing position. A fine textbook-level introduction to the entire subject of memory is Parkin (1993). The volume by Baddeley (1990) is written at a similar level and focused on his study of working memory. The academic and scientific journal entitled simply *Memory* carries articles written for the specialist on many topics. Students who would like a good grounding in the episodic/semantic distinction would be well served by reading Tulving's own writings (1983, 1985, 1986). To see how his theory has been converted into a neuroscience program of research, I recommend Nyberg, Cabeza, and Tulving (1996). Another look at the neural-science perspective underlying memory can be had in McGaugh, Weinberger, and Lynch (1995). On autobiographical memory, I commented on the rather negative viewpoint of Banaji and Crowder (1989), and their cogent article makes for interesting reading. In the January 1991 issue of *American Psychologist,* rebuttals appeared, and, along with books by Neisser (1982) and Ross (1992), these readings offer the student an opportunity to hear both sides of the issue. Also worth reading are the edited volume by Neisser and Winograd (1988) and an introduction to the literature on autobiographical memory by Conway (1990).

Using Your Knowledge of Cognition
Dating a Past Event

Ask some of your friends to determine, as best they can, the month and year in which the former National Football League player O. J. Simpson was apprehended following his famous low-speed chase on the streets of Los Angeles (it was in June 1994). Ask them to think out loud as they try to retrieve the date. We have several strategies for making this determination. Let's consider a couple. You might respond to the question: "Approximately how many years ago was that? Four or five? Then I think it was the summer between my junior and senior years in high school. I worked in a warehouse that summer. Is that right? Let's see, can I remember talking about the chase with anyone I was working with?" Let's contrast that approach with another retrieval attempt. "Okay, well, I remember I had a conversation with somebody I think I was working with at my sum-

mer job between junior and senior years in high school. I had that job only one year, and so that would make it four years ago."

Do you notice any difference in the two hypothetical approaches? Using the first strategy, we estimate when the event occurred and then treat this event as a hypothesis for which evidence can be gathered either to support or refute it. Using the second strategy, we rely on memory to retrieve an image or a moment, and then attempt to place this moment chronologically. Although each of these strategies is theoretically plausible, if you do this exercise, I think you'll find that very few people use the first. Instead, people seem to rely too heavily on the accuracy of their memories in retrieving a specific conversation, or reaction, "observing" this memory, and finally, dating it.

Key Terms

Storage
Cognitive codes
Control processes
Sensory register
Capacity
Modality specific
Decay
Short-term storage
Long-term storage
Rehearsal
Whole-report technique

Partial-report technique
Interstimulus interval
Icon
Echo
Interference
Serial-position effect
Primacy component
Recency component
Chunking
Intrusion errors
Retrograde amnesia

Primary memory
Secondary memory
Articulatory loop
Visuospatial scratch pad
Unattended speech effect
Infantile amnesia
Episodic memory
Semantic memory
Repetition effect

C H A P T E R   4

Memory as Recomputation and Correspondence

*O*verview

I'm something of a night owl, and so I often stay up at night after the rest of my family has gone to bed. When the time comes for me to turn in too, I have a routine, making sure that the lights are all turned off, the thermostat is turned down, the doors are locked, and so on. Lying in bed before I go to sleep, sometimes the thought occurs to mentally check to make sure that I've really done each of the elements in the routine. I've found that my memory then gives me little or no help. Oh, it's easy to produce a mental event in which I can see the door, the dead-bolt handle, and my hand turning it. The problem I have is that I really can't tell if the event that I'm producing actually happened, or if my current mental event is simply some generic cut-and-paste representation in which bits of memories are stitched together in the way that they actually occur most of the time. Because I know in advance that my attempts to mentally check to see if I really did lock the door usually are unsuccessful, I've learned to ignore the voice in my head that says, "You'd better check the door again" even when I go on to imagine the story in next day's newspaper quoting our home's burglar: "It was the easiest job in the world—they didn't even have their door locked!" For most of us, that's the end of the story: Our memories have failed us by not keeping separate events in our experiences from those in our imaginations, but such failures are simply an annoying part of everyday life. Parenthetically, however, I add that for individuals who have obsessive-compulsive disorder (OCD), these unbidden, unwelcome thoughts are much more intrusive than they are for normal people, and such thoughts cannot be dismissed so easily (Brown, Kosslyn, Breiter, Baer, & Jenike, 1994).

Apart from providing us with a window on what it would be like to have OCD, these memory failures are theoretically interesting. We think of memory failure as the kind of event in which we try to remember something and come up empty. In Chapter 3, we saw other types of memory failure, in which the failure results not from not finding something, but rather from finding something

that's wrong. In this chapter we explore this subject further, and we'll see that, as my anecdote suggests, our memory systems often, in response to an explicit demand to retrieve something, offer us a mental event whose status is frankly unclear, even to us.

As you may have discerned from the chapter title, and this Overview, this chapter is something of a counterpoise to my premise in Chapter 3. There, we saw that cognitive psychologists have built numerous accounts of memory phenomena on the notion that our memories are devices that store representations of our experiences. These models offer impressive accounts of human behavior for learning and retrieving lists of words or digits. But when we looked in more detail, we saw two contrary facts. First, most people don't very often use their memories for learning lists. Second, we saw that the storage metaphor does not explain some of the phenomena that occur when people use memory in more typical ways, such as remembering the content of a meeting, especially an emotional one.

And so we look at an alternative. As a general perspective in this chapter, we consider an explanation for much of this more common use of memory in a way that doesn't necessarily involve storage (although you'll see plenty of list learning in this chapter too). This viewpoint has a number of names, such as "constructive" or "recomputational" models, or "correspondence" accounts (Koriat & Goldsmith, 1996). These labels too are metaphors, just as storage is, but here the idea is that people are using whatever it is they retrieve in trying to create a coherent "story" about their experiences.

The Bartlett Tradition

In introducing Part II on memory, I described two perspectives on memory research: the Ebbinghaus tradition, an extension of the storage metaphor, and the Bartlett tradition. F. C. Bartlett's approach differed from Ebbinghaus's in several ways. Where Ebbinghaus and his followers emphasized the quantity of material that could be held in memory, Bartlett and current researchers who emulate his approach are likely to focus on the quality of the material retrieved. The Ebbinghaus position implies that memory is a somewhat passive occurrence, at least for things that have been transferred to permanent memory. But the Bartlett position emphasizes instead that our memories are continually changing, and the accounts that we render about our experiences are always changing. A pure-storage position implies that memory works more or less in isolation from the other cognitive system processes. But the Bartlett approach is likely to emphasize that a person's knowledge, goals, motives, and reasoning may all be crucial in determining the content of any specific memory.

Bartlett carried out many studies in England in the 1930s. In 1932, he published *Remembering,* recounting his findings using both his friends and Cambridge University undergraduates as subjects. Bartlett's interest was how meaningful material is stored and maintained, and so his subjects studied a potpourri of folk tales, fables, American Indian hieroglyphics, and so on. After briefly reading or studying the material, followed by a fifteen-minute break, the subjects were asked to retrieve it. Bartlett often used serial reproduction, which means that a subject might be asked to retrieve the same material over and over again. The retention intervals were often irregular, depending on when Bartlett could prevail on one of his friends to attempt another retrieval. Some were long suffering: a few tried to retrieve material they had studied ten years earlier. With serial reproduction, Bartlett hoped to measure the progressive deteriorations and distortions in the subjects' memories. His best-known story is reproduced in Table 4.1.

To get the same experience as one of Bartlett's subjects, read the story twice, take a fifteen-minute break, then write the story from memory as accurately as you can. Having done that, compare your efforts with those of Bartlett's subjects, whose results are shown in Table 4.2.

Bartlett was perhaps most interested in the subjects' errors, which strongly suggest that they were actively reconstructing the story during their retrieval attempts. We can see many effects of this reconstruction. The Cambridge undergraduates frequently altered the story to make it more consistent with their knowledge. They would recall the canoe as simply a boat, and the natives as having gone fishing. This second error is particularly telling. If we assume that the activity was encoded as abstract but related facts such as "requires a boat," "is done on a lake," and "is done to get food," and we ask an English student to name the activity, the student may well respond with the answer most plausible in England: fishing. Bartlett saw that many of the subjects' transformations and distortions were attempts to make the story more coherent and rational—at least, for students immersed in British culture.

Table 4.1 The "War of the Ghosts" Story

Read this American Indian folk tale, take a 15-minute break, and then attempt to reproduce the story by writing it down from memory.

One night two young men from Egulac went down to the river to hunt seals, and while they were there it became foggy and calm. Then they heard war-cries, and they thought, "Maybe this is a war-party." They escaped to the shore, and hid behind a log. Now canoes came up, and they heard the noise of paddles, and saw one canoe coming up to them. There were five men in the canoe, and they said:

"What do you think? We wish to take you along. We are going up the river to make war on the people."

One of the young men said, "I have no arrows."

"Arrows are in the canoe," they said.

"I will not go along. I might be killed. My relatives do not know where I have gone. But you," he said, turning to the other, "may go with them."

One of the young men went, but the other returned home.

And the warriors went on up the river to a town on the other side of Kalama. The people came down to the water and began to fight, and many were killed. But presently the young man heard one of the warriors say, "Quick, let us go home: that Indian has been hit." Now he thought, "Oh, they are ghosts." He did not feel sick, but they said he had been shot.

The canoes went back to Egulac, and the young man went ashore to his house, and made a fire. And he told everybody, saying, "Behold, I accompanied the ghosts, and we went to fight. Many of our fellows were killed, and many of those who attacked us were killed. They said I was hit, and I did not feel sick."

He told it all, and then he became quiet. When the sun rose he fell down. Something black came out of his mouth. His face became contorted. The people jumped up and cried.

He was dead.

Source: From Bartlett, 1932.

Schemas

Bartlett invokes the **schema** to describe the subject's errors. For Bartlett, the schema was "an active organization of past reactions or past experiences" (Bartlett, 1932). As Bartlett understood it, the subject was more or less unable to separate encoded facts from the previous schema at retrieval time. Consequently, schema-based facts were "remembered" at retrieval time along with whatever was left of the encoded facts.

Context

The Bartlett tradition focuses explicitly on the knowledge and processing that the person brings to bear at retrieval time. Over the next several sections we deal with a related issue, the knowledge and processing that we use to help learn, understand, and remember any sort of material in the first place. We use **context** in the broadest possible way to describe any environmental or internal stimulus that may be present at the same time as we are trying to learn and remember anything. Thus, if your stereo is playing when you are studying for the test in cognitive psychology, the background music is a contextual variable, and even the content of the songs may be important contextually. The room in which you study, its temperature, the cognitive processes

Table 4.2 Attempts by One of Bartlett's (1932) Subjects to Reproduce the "War of the Ghosts" Story

First recall, attempted about 15 minutes after hearing the story:

Two young men from Egulac went out to hunt seals. They thought they heard war-cries, and a little later they heard the noise of the paddling of canoes. One of these canoes, in which there were five natives, came forward towards them. One of the natives shouted out, "Come with us: we are going to make war on some natives up the river." The two young men answered, "We have no arrows." "There are arrows in our canoes," came the reply. One of the young men then said: "My folk will not know where I have gone"; but, turning to the other, he said: "But you could go." So the one returned whilst the other joined the natives.

The party went up the river as far as a town opposite Kalam, where they got on land. The natives of that part came down to the river to meet them. There was some severe fighting, and many on both sides were slain. Then one of the natives that had made the expedition up the river shouted, "Let us return: the Indian has fallen." Then they endeavored to persuade the young man to return, telling him that he was sick, but he did not feel as if he were. Then he thought he saw ghosts all around him.

When they returned, the young man told all his friends of what had happened. He described how many had been slain on both sides.

It was nearly dawn when the young man became very ill; and at sunrise a black substance rushed out of his mouth, and the natives said one to another: "He is dead."

Second recall, attempted about four months later:

There were two men in a boat, sailing towards an island. When they approached the island, some natives came running towards them, and informed them that there was fighting going on on the island, and invited them to join. One said to the other, "You had better go. I cannot very well, because I have relatives expecting me, and they will not know what has become of me. But you have no one to expect you." So one accompanied the natives, but the other returned.

Here there is a part I can't remember. What I don't know is how the man got to the fight. However, anyhow the man was in the midst of the fighting, and was wounded. The natives endeavored to persuade the man to return, but he assured them that he had not been wounded.

I have an idea that his fighting won the admiration of the natives.

The wounded man ultimately fell unconscious. He was taken from the fighting by the natives.

Then, I think it is, the natives describe what happened, and they seem to have imagined seeing a ghost coming out of his mouth. Really it was a kind of materialization of his breath. I know this phrase was not in the story, but that is the idea I have. Ultimately the man died at dawn the next day.

Third recall, about six and a half years later:

1. Brothers.
2. Canoe.
3. Something black from mouth.
4. Totem.
5. One of the brothers died.
6. Cannot remember whether one slew the other or was helping the other.
7. Were going on a journey, but why I cannot remember.
8. Party in war canoe.
9. Was the journey a pilgrimage for filial or religious reasons?
10. Am now sure it was a pilgrimage.
11. Purpose had something to do with totem.
12. Was it on a pilgrimage that they met a hostile party and one brother was slain?
13. I think there was a reference to a dark forest.
14. Two brothers were on a pilgrimage, having something to do with a totem in a canoe, up a river flowing through a dark forest. While on their pilgrimage they met a hostile party of Indians in a war canoe. In the fight one brother was slain, and something black came from his mouth.
15. Am not confident about the way the brother died. May have been something sacrificial in the manner of his death.
16. The cause of the journey had both something to do with a totem, and with filial piety.
17. The totem was the patron god of the family and so was connected with filial piety.

Source: From Bartlett, 1932.

that you use to remember the material, all are contextual variables that will influence the type, content, and ultimately, retrievability of the memory you make. Such variables, whose operation we'll detail in this section, support some of the essential tenets in the Bartlett position, in that they show the memory system is active at the point of initial contact with the target material. Thus the memory system begins its work of transforming and processing incoming material as soon as you try to learn and remember. How do such contextual variables affect memory?

This question was explored in an early study by Light and Carter-Sobell (1970). They gave their subjects sentences in which a phrase had been emphasized (e.g., "The boy earned a GOOD GRADE on the test"). Subjects were told that when they had all the sentences, a memory test would ask them to recognize the emphasized noun but not the adjective. The recognition task had several conditions. For some subjects the noun was presented once again with the same adjective (i.e., "good grade"). In other conditions the noun was presented with a different, but nevertheless meaningful, adjective. The subject might see the phrase "steep grade." Either way, the task was to report whether or not *grade* had been presented in a sentence.

This manipulation produced a dramatic effect. Subjects correctly recognized the nouns 64 percent of the time when they were presented in their original context. But the accuracy was only 27% when the nouns were presented in a different context. Light and Carter-Sobell also found that accuracy was superior even when the noun was presented with an adjective not previously seen as long as it established the same context as the original adjective. Accuracy was not substantially diminished when the noun was shown in a context such as "bad grade."

This study is important for several reasons. First, as we saw in the levels-of-processing literature, it demonstrates that a stimulus such as a word is not a rigidly fixed thing that can be encoded in only one way (Hulse, Deese, & Egeth, 1975). Instead, almost every stimulus apparently has many properties, from which we choose the ones that will be a basis for the encoding. Second, the context produces its biasing effects, even though the context itself apparently is not encoded. In other words, the subjects were obviously influenced by the semantic content of the adjectives even though they were told that the adjectives weren't important and no apparent attempt was made to encode them.

One implication is that the physical environment, which after all is the ultimate context in which all encoding takes place, influences the subject's representation even though aspects of the environment are not themselves encoded. These effects were explored in two studies. Smith, Glenberg, and Bjork (1978) had their subjects study lists of paired-associate words under different physical conditions. In the first condition, the subjects learned the lists in a large but windowless off-campus room. The experimenter was dressed in jacket and tie, and the lists were presented visually. In the second condition the subjects learned the lists in a small room on campus. The experimenter (the same person in both conditions) was dressed informally, and the lists were presented by tape recorder. The day after the subjects learned the lists, they took a memory test in which they were given one of the paired associates and asked to recall its mate. Half the subjects took the memory test in the same room where they learned the list; the other half tried to recall the paired associates in the other room. The results were impressive. Subjects tested in the same room in which they had learned the list recalled 59% of the paired associates. When tested in the other room, however, their recall dropped to 46%.

We should be somewhat cautious in interpreting these findings, because further research by Glenberg indicates that, although context can be a significant factor in retention, it can be mitigated by other retrieval cues. In short, the situation is more complex than originally thought. The study nevertheless makes an important point: If the subjects had been graded on their performance, their drop-off would have meant the difference between an A and a B, which leads to another necessary and practical point: If teachers are serious about getting optimal performance from their students, then tests and finals should always be given in the same classroom in which the class meetings took place.

Levels of Processing

As you'll recall, by the end of Chapter 3 we had seen that cognitive psychologists were becoming convinced that complete understanding of memory would not result from specifying the characteristics of the separate memory buffers. Indeed, cognitivists were instead trying to understand the many ways in which it might be possible to encode a stimulus. Craik and Lockhart (1972) were among the earliest researchers to express this viewpoint. They rejected the idea that memory's location determined its characteristics. Rather than think of the stimulus to be remembered as a fixed object with distinct properties that were altered as it moved through a rigid system of storages and buffers, Craik and Lockhart maintained that the stimulus could be processed in various ways. An individual could bring sensory processes to bear on a stimulus and extract from it its physical characteristics. On the other hand, the person had control over other cognitive processes capable of extracting and encoding acoustic or semantic features of the stimulus. Craik and Lockhart viewed this as a continuum of progressively deeper cognitive processing—deeper in the sense that more background knowledge is required to carry out a semantic analysis of a word than an acoustic analysis. Material stored in memory—the memory code—acquired its semantic or acoustic properties not because it was being stored in specific locations but because it had been processed in ways that were under the person's control. The memory code is therefore a record of the cognitive processes that have been performed on it. In summary, each approach to processing produced a cognitive code that could be evaluated along a continuum of depth. Generally, the greater the semantic analysis (the more meaning extracted from the stimulus), the greater the **depth of processing.**

Craik (1979) stated that the levels-of-processing model has two main postulates. First, semantic analysis results in a deeper and thus more meaningful code than does nonsemantic analysis. Second, the deeper the code, the more durable the memory. Thus forgetting is simply a function of depth of processing: we forget things that we have not processed semantically. To these postulates I add corollaries. First, be aware that we're not dealing with a multiple-storage model. That is, we have no notion about transfer of memories from one storage location to another. Second, and correspondingly, we see no capacity limitations. Evidence that seems to indicate the need for different storages with differing capacities (such as the memory-span phenomenon) can be interpreted as processing limitations. Another implication is that durability of a memory is somewhat independent of the time spent processing. A great deal of time spent processing material at a nonsemantic (shallow) level probably will not produce a more durable memory than would a short time processing at the semantic level (Craik & Watkins, 1973; Rundus, 1977).

A study by Parkin (1984) illustrates the depth-of-processing effect. His subjects were given a word, about which they had to make a semantic-orienting or nonsemantic-orienting decision. The orienting decision refers to a judgment about the word. For example, a semantic-orienting decision might involve a category or synonym judgment. A nonsemantic task might involve making a judgment about how many vowels the word had or whether it had been printed completely in capital letters. Following a series of such trials, the subjects were given a surprise free-recall test. Those who had been semantically oriented recalled significantly more of the target words than did those who were nonsemantically oriented. This result suggests that semantic processing produces a more durable memory code than does nonsemantic processing.

A study by Jacoby, Craik, and Begg (1979) supports this interpretation. Their subjects were given pairs of common nouns (e.g., *horse–goat*) and were told to evaluate the difference in size between the objects on a 1 (not much difference) to 10 (vast difference) scale. The difference between some of the named objects was relatively small, whereas for others the difference was large. After the subjects had made these evaluations, they were given an unexpected memory test in which they were asked to recall as many of the objects as they could. Jacoby et al. found an inverse relationship between the size difference between the objects and the likelihood of their recall. The subjects were more likely to recall the objects when the difference between them was small. Jacoby et al. explained that the task required a semantic analysis of the objects' properties. When the objects were approximately the same size, however, deeper analysis was required, producing a more durable memory code. Notice that the subjects were not aware that a memory test was forthcoming when they evaluated size differences. But their being engaged in a semantic analysis of the words facilitated their retrieval. The implications are clear: Your chances of retrieving a memory depend on the type of processing you do to remember it, not on how *hard* you try to remember.

These effects were shown in a study by Hyde and Jenkins (1973). The subjects saw a list of 24 words, which was presented at the rate of 3 seconds per word. Each subject had one of two tasks. In one condition subjects simply had to check whether each word had an *a* or a *q*. In the second, they had to rate the pleasantness of the word, which presumably required deeper processing than simply looking at the word's physical characteristics. This study had a second variable. Half the group of subjects, the intentional learning group, was told that a memory test would be given after the words were presented, and they were encouraged to learn the words. The other half of the group was not informed about the subsequent memory test, and any knowledge they retained about the words was therefore incidental.

Table 4.3 shows the findings in this study. Notice the strong depth-of-processing effect. When the subjects carried out the semantic analysis, their recall was dramatically enhanced. Notice, too, that intentionality had little effect on the proportion of the words recalled. The levels-of-processing viewpoint thus accounts for something

Table 4.3   Percentage of Words Recalled as a Function of Orienting Task and Whether Subjects Were Aware of Learning Task

	Orienting Task	
Learning-Purpose Conditions	*Rate Pleasantness*	*Check Letters*
Incidental	68	39
Intentional	69	43

Source: From Hyde and Jenkins, 1973.

that vexed multiple-storage models. Our memories are not controlled directly by our intentions (which makes the Atkinson and Shiffrin control processes somewhat misleading) but rather by the type of processing we do.

Maintenance Rehearsal and Elaborative Rehearsal   To help make these processing effects clearer, Craik and Lockhart (1972) distinguished between two kinds of rehearsal. Type I, sometimes called **maintenance rehearsal,** refers to the continual repetition of analyses that have already been carried out. It does not lead to stronger or more lasting memories; its principal function is to retain the availability of an item in memory. Maintenance rehearsal tends to emphasize the phonetic aspects of a stimulus (Wickens, 1984). Type II rehearsal, also known as **elaborative rehearsal,** refers to successively deeper processing of the stimulus and does produce more durable memories. It emphasizes the stimulus's semantic aspects. Both types are under the person's control: they operate on material in working memory, and they compete with other tasks for cognitive resources.

Craik and Watkins (1973) demonstrated that the kind of rehearsal, not how much, determines a memory's durability. The subjects in their study were presented with twelve lists, each with twelve words. The subjects were told to consciously rehearse these words. Moreover, they were told that the last four words in each list were especially important and that these should be remembered at all costs. To emphasize this instruction, the last four words in each list were printed in block letters. The study had two retrieval conditions. Subjects were asked to recall the list either immediately or following a 20-second delay. If recall was delayed, the subjects were told that actively rehearsing the list was permitted. When all twelve lists had been presented, Craik and Watkins sprang a surprise: they asked the subjects to recall as many of the entire set of 144 words as they could. The findings are shown in Figure 4.1.

As the top graph shows, the subjects took advantage of the opportunity to rehearse the last four items in the lists during the 20-second delay. As the lower-left graph shows, an expected recency effect occurred when the words were recalled immediately after presentation or after the 20-second delay. The lower-right graph shows the effects of the surprise. Even though the last four items in each list were rehearsed far more frequently than the others, and even though an immediate recency effect occurred, virtually no long-term effect appeared. In the final recall test, words that had

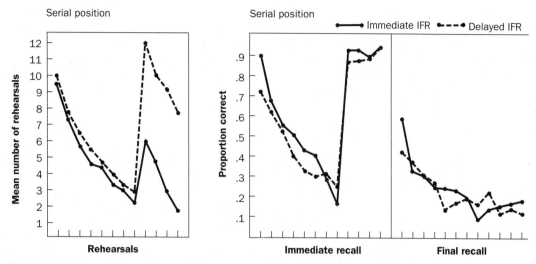

Figure 4.1 Average number of rehearsals (top graph), proportion correct on the immediate free-recall (IFR) test (lower-left graph), and proportion correct on the final recall test (lower-right graph) as a function of serial position. The two lines in the graphs show the results for groups who recalled after no delay or after a 20-second delay in the immediate free-recall test. *Source:* From Craik and Watkins, 1973.

been presented in one of the last four serial positions were not recalled with any greater frequency than words presented in other serial positions. Even though the last four words had been rehearsed more than the others, this was maintenance rehearsal, which did not necessarily lead to more durable memories (Craik & Watkins, 1973).

The distinction between elaborative and maintenance rehearsal sounds plausible, and the Craik and Watkins results make sense. This position implies, however, that *all* semantic processing is equal and thus should create memories of equal durability. But does it?

To answer this question, Craik and Tulving (1975) presented sentences and words tachistoscopically to their subjects. The words and sentences were shown concurrently, and the subject's task was to decide whether the word would meaningfully fit into a blank left in the sentence. The sentence's semantic complexity was varied, too. These three examples show the increasing complexity:

Simple: She cooked the _____ .
Medium: The _____ frightened the children.
Complex: The great bird swooped down and carried off the struggling _____ .

After sixty judgments (twenty at each complexity level), Craik and Tulving sprang the by-now-familiar surprise: a memory test, this time in the cued-recall format. The subjects were given the sentence and asked to recall the word that had been shown concurrently. The surprise now was on Craik and Tulving: subjects remembered more of the complex-sentence fill-ins than the simple-sentence fill-ins. Considering only yes responses, those in which the word could be meaningfully used in the sentence, the subjects recalled about twice as many from the complex sentences. But why? For all answers, semantic processing had been carried out, which is the deepest level according to the theory. Therefore, no differences should have appeared in retrieval as a function of the sentence's complexity. Why, then, did Craik and Tulving observe these differences? The answer must lie in the elaborative rehearsal *and* the larger cognitive structure into which the elaborated code was being fed. In other words, the semantic processing done by subjects on the complex sentences seems to have accessed other cognitive codes richer or more elaborate than those accessed in the simple sentences.

Some Problems with "Levels" of Processing   Although the levels-of-processing account is persuasive, it has been dogged by a few problems. First, the approach has the problem we've just touched on—contradictory findings. Nelson and McEvoy (1979) reasoned that, if words have been processed at the semantic level, then providing a semantic cue should produce better retrieval than a nonsemantic cue. But as it turns out, presenting nonsemantic cues (such as the cue *IME* for the list word *DIME*) is just as effective as presenting semantic cues (such as "an American coin" for *DIME*). Further, Hunt and Elliot (1980) demonstrated that words with irregular and distinctive orthography (such as *phlegm*) are retained better when they are processed as part of a list with words in both regular and irregular orthography than when a whole list is made up of such distinctive words. Even when the task requires semantic analysis, some nonsemantic information—this time orthographic distinctiveness—seems to be retained.

A second problem with this approach is an independent definition for depth of processing. Usually, the level of processing is operationally defined by the orienting task the subject is given to do. For example, if you are given a task involving checking letters or producing rhymes, this processing is considered nonsemantic. But if you are required to produce a synonym, then you must be processing the material at the semantic level. Many commentators have pointed out (Nelson, 1979; Postman, Thompkins, & Gray, 1978) that this operational definition is barely adequate. It's hard to say exactly what the subject is doing when instructed to process the material in a particular way. Furthermore, it's hard to see a way around the problem of defining depth. Linking depth of processing to *time* spent processing is irrelevant by definition, and asking the subjects to self-report their own depth of processing is fraught with difficulty (Seamon & Virostek, 1978).

Yet another problem is the relationship between depth of processing and automaticity. As we saw earlier, highly overlearned tasks become progressively more automatic; that is, they can be executed without heavy demands on cognitive processes. What if subjects become highly practiced at making semantic decisions? According to the levels-of-processing view, the subjects should show good retention of this material because it has been deeply processed. According to the automaticity viewpoint, though, the subjects should show little or no retention of such material. Fiske and Schneider (1984) pitted these viewpoints against each other. Their subjects were extensively trained to categorize materials automatically. Categorization is an orienting task that is usually thought of as semantic. But Fiske and Schneider found that their subjects, who had done well at the categorization task, showed little recognition memory for the categorized materials. This finding contradicts the levels-of-processing approach.

A problem can also be found in the maintenance and elaborative-rehearsal concept. At least in some tasks, maintenance rehearsal does improve memory (Glenberg & Adams, 1978). That kind of finding suggests to many students of memory that a categorical view of rehearsal strategies is probably not correct (Craik, 1979; Jacoby & Craik, 1979). Rehearsal strategies can probably be graded along a continuum of elaboration. This formulation will almost certainly be assessed in future work.

Transfer-Appropriate Processing   Perhaps the biggest complication for the levels-of-processing position comes from a classic study done by Morris, Bransford, and Franks (1977). In this study the experimenter read aloud thirty-two sentences, each missing one word. In the shallow-processing condition, the experimenter might read a sentence such as this: "Blank rhymes with legal." After hearing this sentence, the subjects heard an additional word, the target word, and their task was to decide if the target could be substituted appropriately for the blank. The subjects should say yes if the target word was "eagle" but no if it was "peach." In the deep-processing condition, the task was similar but was modified slightly to demand semantic processing. Now, the experimenter might read a sentence such as, "The blank has a silver engine." Hearing the target word "eagle" after this sentence should produce a no from the subjects, whereas hearing the target word "train" should be answered yes. At test time, half the group of subjects were given a standard recognition task: each of the target words was presented along with additional words that functioned as distractors. The subjects were to pick out the target word. Consistent with the levels-of-processing position, the subjects did a better job recognizing target words that had been presented in the semantic version of the task than those presented in the rhyming version. But a different fate awaited the other half of the group. These subjects were given a rhyming recognition task. They got a series of words and were asked to pick out the word that rhymed with a target word that had been seen before. Continuing the example above, if the original target word had been "eagle," the subject might see a series with the word "regal," and if the original target word had been "train," the subject might now see a series including "brain." Now, something surprising happened: The subjects did a better job of picking out rhyming words of targets originally presented in the rhyming condition than they did for rhyming words of targets presented in the semantic condition. This finding is exactly the opposite of that predicted by the levels-of-processing position; here, when subjects engaged in the shallow, rhyming task, they did better than when they had engaged in the deep, semantic task. How come?

Morris et al. used **transfer-appropriate processing** to explain these effects: the cognitive processes that are used in the initial learning or encoding of some material interact with the cognition used at retrieval time. Thus the best encoding is that based on cognitive processes that most closely match the type of cognitive processing that will be used at retrieval time. Simply, if you have to retrieve something by rhyming, then the best encoding you can make also will involve rhyming. But if you have to retrieve material using semantic processing, then it is probably best for you to use semantic processing at encoding time.

Intrachapter Summary and Interpretation

We've been exploring an alternative to the storage position that we examined in Chapter 3. Although this alternative isn't necessarily explained by an all-encompassing metaphor such as "storage," we might think of it as something like a "recomputation" metaphor. That is, from this perspective, rather than think of the memory as a cognitive device that can store and retrieve things, we might see it as a device for "recomputing" an experience, using the stimulation that we're currently experiencing. As we've seen, this perspective provides us with a good basis for understanding some of the phenomena that Bartlett discovered so many decades ago. Why would students retrieve incorrect elements from the folk tale months or years later? Although it could be true that the students had simply stored and retrieved the wrong information, it might be more congenial to explain their errors as caused by faulty reconstruction of the facts. And it also seems likely that such errors would be at the time of retrieval, rather than at the time of initial storage. From there we went on to consider how context possibly "biased" the memory system to create constructions and therefore pathways toward reconstructing specific memories. We haven't completed our discussion yet, but as we have seen, the type of cognitive processing that you do to remember something strongly biases the likelihood of retrieving (or perhaps I should say, of reconstructing) that memory at retrieval time.

Encoding Specificity

We've been considering the effects of various contextual variables on the likelihood of our retrieving material that we've tried to learn. Beyond the effects of various external stimuli, we've seen that the cognitive processes themselves that we use to learn and to retrieve influence the likelihood of retrieving a specific memory. If you're a student, this finding probably makes sense.

For example, as a student, you're subjected to various tests. Some of these probably are essay tests or oral exams, along with true-false or multiple-choice questions. Essay and oral exams measure your ability to recall material from memory, and multiple-choice questions tap your ability to recognize stored material. The distinction between recall and recognition often boils down to the number of cues or prompts provided. And as you may be aware, knowing which kind of test you have to face strongly influences the way in which you study. That is, knowledge of the retrieval task influences the encoding you do.

This influence was well demonstrated in a study by Leonard and Whitten (1983). Half their subjects studied a list of words with the expectation that they would be given a recognition task. That task would be arranged like a multiple-choice test; the subjects would be required to pick out the listed word from among several alternatives. The other subjects studied the list with the idea that they would be given a free-recall test. But these subjects were deceived. All the subjects were tested with the multiple-choice procedure. On some of the items, the word previously studied was presented in the context of semantically related words. On other items, the studied word appeared in the context of semantically unrelated words. Leonard and Whitten found that the subjects who had studied for recognition showed a decrement in performance when the words were presented in a semantically related context, but this effect was not observed in the subjects who had studied for recall.

This finding makes sense when you think about the task from the subject's point of view. Suppose one of the words in the list was *evil*. Subjects who expected a multiple-choice test may have prepared themselves to pick out a word that means "bad," "cruel," or "rotten." Subjects who expected a free-recall test had to do something different. They had to establish some sort of context for *evil* that they could reproduce from scratch at retrieval time. Consequently, when the alternatives were semantically related to the word studied, the subjects who had expected a recognition task apparently had trouble deciding which was the target word and which was the context.

The Leonard and Whitten (1983) findings have several implications. First, they imply that subjects use different retrieval strategies depending on the memory task. Second, the findings suggest that the subjects know ahead of time that they will use different strategies to retrieve the material depending on the task. (A more thorough discussion of this phenomenon awaits us later in this chapter.) Third, the findings suggest that the intended retrieval strategy affects the actual encoding.

Retrieval processes in recognition and recall have been thought to differ in this way: In a recall test with a word list, the subject generates candidate items and then decides about each candidate's inclusion or exclusion from the list studied (Hulse, Deese, & Egeth, 1975). In a recognition task, this sort of procedure need not take place, because the candidates have already been provided by the experimenter. According to this view of retrieval, performance on recognition tasks should always be superior to performance on recall tasks. To recall something, we have to do two things: generate the candidate and then recognize that it belongs on the list. But to recognize something, we have to do only one thing: recognize it. The generation stage can be bypassed (Wessells, 1982).

When Recall Beats Recognition   A striking series of studies (Flexser & Tulving, 1978; Tulving & Thompson, 1973; Watkins, 1974; Watkins & Tulving, 1975) demonstrates that under some conditions, recall is superior to recognition, and that subjects are sometimes able to recall material that they cannot recognize.

Watkins (1974) gave his subjects lists of paired-associate nonsense words. Each pair had a five-letter A part and a two-letter B part. Although the A and B parts were not meaningful by themselves, the combined seven-letter item was (as in SPANI–SH, or INVOL–VE). After one presentation of the list, recognition memory was assessed by giving the subjects a list of the B parts they had just seen against the context of other two-letter nonsense syllables. In a later assessment of cued-recall memory, the subjects were prompted with the A part and had to recall the B part of the pair. Recognition accuracy was a dismal 9%, but cued-recall accuracy was 67%.

This effect was extended in a study by Watkins and Tulving (1975). Their subjects were given a list of paired associates such as HEAD–LIGHT, but they were told that they would be responsible only for the second word in the pair, which was called the "to-be-remembered" word, or TBR. After the subjects had studied the list, they were given a word and were asked to generate the first four free associates that entered their minds. For example, the subject might be given the word *dark*, and the associates *light, night, shadow,* and *pitch* might be produced. The words given to the subjects were deliberately designed to elicit the TBR. If the subject spontaneously produced the TBR in response to this prompt, the experimenter then showed the subject the four free associates and asked which one was a TBR (subjects had to choose one of them). In this way, their recognition memory was assessed. In the final phase, they were given the first word of the paired associates and were asked to recall the TBR. When the subjects gave the TBR as one of the free associates, they correctly recognized it 54% of the time. In the recall phase, though, accuracy improved to 61%. Perhaps even more startling was that 42% of the words that the subjects successfully recalled had not been recognized when they had seen them a few minutes earlier.

These findings are usually explained by the **encoding specificity** principle (Flexser & Tulving, 1978, 1982), which says that a cue will aid retrieval if it provides information that had been processed during the encoding of the TBR material (Tulving, 1979). When a prompt is presented that wasn't processed at encoding time, then such a prompt doesn't increase the probability of retrieval. In the Watkins and Tulving (1975) study, the prompts that were presented during the recognition task (i.e., the four free associates) weren't present during the initial encoding. Because the prompt presented in the recall task was processed at encoding, however, the probability of successful recall was greater than the probability of successful recognition. We're accustomed to thinking of recall as a harder task than recognition. The Watkins and Tulving study, however, demonstrates that the difficulty of a memory task is really determined by the degree to which the encoding and retrieval contexts match.

More recent empirical and theoretical work on this subject has dealt with the strength of the encoding specificity principle. To this end, a mathematical formulation predicting the degree of encoding specificity has been written (Flexser & Tulving, 1978, 1982). But this formulation has been criticized on several grounds. Bower and Humphreys (1979; Humphreys & Bower, 1980) maintained that the Flexser and Tulving model didn't take into account the considerable priming effects of the recognition task on recall. The force of this criticism is that performance on the recall task is spuriously (i.e., artificially) high because on many of the trials the subjects had actually seen the TBR when they spontaneously generated it in the recognition phase, giving them an unfair advantage on some of the recall trials.

Other criticisms have focused on the generality of recognition failure among different types of verbal materials. Recognition failure is more likely to take place among some verbal materials than others, and this differential effect has some implications for encoding specificity (Horton & Mills, 1984). Gardiner and Tulving (1980) performed two experiments in which the paired associates were either abstract nouns (Honor–Anxiety) or number–word pairs (47–Wet). When subjects were given "typical" instructions, performance on the cued-recall task was poor, and consequently, recognition failure of recallable items was also low. When they were instructed to "elaborate" the pair so that the abstract terms became somehow related, however, cued recall improved and the number of recognition failures also increased.

This finding tells us that when the paired-associate terms are abstract or unrelated to each other, they provide little context for each other, and the effects of encoding specificity will be correspondingly weaker. When the paired-associate terms are strongly related, though, either inherently or by the subject's efforts, then the effects of encoding specificity become stronger. That is, if the encoding context can be reinstated at retrieval time, the probability of recalling the TBR is high.

Implicit Memory

We've examined several studies that show how context influences conscious use of our memory systems. In this and subsequent sections we'll consider nonconscious memories, generally applying this name to phenomena showing that some aspects of our memory systems are operative, even without any intention to use that system. In other words, evidence suggests that our cognitive systems operate a memory device of some sort, even when we are not aware of doing so. Before we begin, two points need to be addressed. First, you may conclude that the existence of such nonconscious memory effects surely demonstrates that the storage metaphor must be at least partially accurate. That is, the typical reasoning goes, how else can we explain that our memories sometimes work without our awareness? We'll have to reserve comment on this subject right now, but in summarizing this chapter I'll try to suggest an alternative to the notion that memory without awareness demands a storage explanation. Second, we've looked at how context affects conscious memory, but this division of memory into conscious and nonconscious components raises a new question. Does context work on nonconscious memory in the same way as it works on conscious memory? Keep that issue in mind as we make our way through the next few sections.

The effects of such nonconscious memory can be seen in the Jacoby and Dallas (1981) study. They showed their subjects sixty words; three subgroups processed the words at several levels (by looking for specified letters in the words, by rhyming the words, or by determining the meaning of the words). Later, the subjects were presented a test list of eighty words; sixty of these were the words they had seen before, and twenty were new. For half the group of subjects, the test list was presented by a conventional procedure that is used in memory labs all over the world: The subject was given each of the eighty words one at a time and simply asked to determine if the word had been on the study list or if it hadn't. This is a straightforward recognition task—a typical memory test. For the other group of subjects, each word in the test list was presented for a 35-msec interval. The subject's task was to correctly identify the word with this brief presentation. Here, the subject is placed in a perceptual identification task, which technically is not a memory task at all by most conventional definitions. If I'm asked to identify briefly presented words, I have no reason to believe that I'll be helped by consciously using my memory of anything. But, surprisingly, Jacoby and Dallas found that a word's status in the study list definitely influenced the likelihood that the subject would identify the word: 80% of the words in the study list were correctly identified, but only 65% of the new words were correctly identified.

Being skeptical, you may think these results don't really provide compelling evidence of memory without awareness, because the subjects could be using conscious retrieval attempts to help them answer the perceptual identification task. Suppose the word "king" is in the study list, and I happen to correctly identify it after a brief presentation. Then, suppose I realize it was in the study list, thus (now) recognizing the word as well. If this sequence happens a few times, I may be inclined to mentally check words whose identity I'm not sure of to see if they correspond to words that I remember in the study list. And if I do that, it certainly seems I'm using my conscious memory-retrieval strategies to help with the perceptual task. But this criticism seems much less valid when we look at the findings in the recognition task. Here, Jacoby and Dallas found that the orienting task given the subjects when the study list was presented (looking for letters, rhyming, etc.) clearly influenced the likelihood that the subjects would correctly recognize the words during the recognition-test phase. Specifically, when a subject was asked about the meaning of a word in the study list, the chance was 95% that the subject would correctly recognize that word when it appeared in the recognition test. This likelihood declined significantly when the subject was asked to rhyme a word in the study list (likelihood of correctly saying yes = 72%) and declined significantly yet again when the subject had hunted for specific letters in the words in the study list (likelihood of correctly saying yes = 51%). Thus, it seems we have a depth-of-processing effect going on in the recognition task: the deeper the subjects processed the words in the study list, the greater their likelihood of being correct when they said yes to a word on the recognition task.

Now why is this finding relevant to the perceptual identification task? If the subjects were using conscious memory processes to influence their responses on the perceptual-identification task, then the depth-of-processing manipulation, which obviously and clearly affected the recognition task, also should affect the perceptual-identification task. But the depth-of-processing manipulation had no effect on the perceptual-identification task. Regardless of whether the subjects had processed the words in the study list deeply or shallowly, their correct identification of previously seen words in the perceptual-identification task remained the same; that is, 80%. What conclusion can we draw? Essentially, the Jacoby and Dallas study (1981) supports the idea of memory without awareness because the subjects in the perceptual-identification task clearly were influenced by their cognitive system's prior processing of the words in the study list, even though the subjects were not aware that this prior processing was influencing the accuracy of their current identifications.

These ideas are seen also in a study by Eich (1984), which involved a shadowing task similar to those discussed in Chapter 2. The subjects wore stereo headphones; they were told to shadow an essay that would be heard in one ear. In the nonshadowed ear, pairs of words were played, the second word in each pair being a homophone of some other English word. Homophones are words that sound alike but have different meanings, such as "meet" and "meat." In the Eich study, the first word in each pair was a contextual word that could bias interpretation of the homophone, just as the word "red" might do in the example above. Subjects heard sixteen such word pairs. In half the cases, the contextual word biased the homophone toward one of its meanings (such as "red–meat"); in the other half the contextual word was chosen to suggest the other meaning of the homophone (such as "track–meet"). The subjects were not instructed to learn these word pairs. As the procedure concluded, the subjects were asked to summarize the essay they had shadowed, just to make sure they had been following directions. Then they were given a recognition task: Eight of the sixteen homophones in each word pair were read to the subjects, who were instructed to rate the word on a scale of 1 (definitely old; i.e., presented in the nonshadowed ear) to 6 (definitely new; i.e., not presented in the nonshadowed ear).

Take a minute to figure out how having heard the words in the nonshadowed ear might affect this task. If you reasoned that this rating is a recognition memory task, like the one Jacoby and Dallas (1981) used, and therefore having heard the words in the nonshadowed ear should not influence rating the word as old or new, then give yourself a small reward. That was the finding. Subjects were no more likely to rate the previously heard words as "old" than they were to rate new words as "old." But then Eich gave the subjects an additional task. Now they were to spell a series of words, some of which were the homophones the subjects had heard in the nonshadowed ear. Consistent with the Jacoby and Dallas findings, the subjects were inclined to spell homophones in a way that was consistent with the bias induced by the contextual word. In other words, the subject who might have heard "track" in the nonshadowed ear was more likely to spell the homophone "meet" than "meat."

Schacter (1987) described the phenomena we've seen in the Jacoby and Dallas (1981) and Eich (1984) studies as **implicit memory.** Implicit memory names situations in which it is clear that a specific previous experience influences a current performance without the performer's awareness of either the specific previous experience or a retrieval attempt. Implicit memory can be contrasted with **explicit memory,** in which we use our memories and become aware of aspects of this use; we may be aware of actively searching our memories, comparing a current stimulus with whatever can be retrieved about specific previous ones to retrieve something not currently available.

One dominant theme in the literature on implicit memory demonstrates that variables or manipulations that influence explicit memory have little or no effect on implicit memory. That is, we frequently observe a dissociation of performance when the effects of specific experience are measured in an explicit memory task versus an implicit one. For example, in the literature on explicit memory, a well-known effect is produced by having a subject generate or produce a to-be-remembered stimulus. Namely, subjects who, for some reason, generate materials that are to be retrieved later show better explicit memory for those materials than do subjects who are simply shown the same materials. Superior retention of self-generated stimuli is called the **generation effect.** But the question before us is how the memory is measured: Do generated materials show the same superior retention when they measured by implicit methods?

Jacoby (1983) explores this question. Some of his subjects were given words to read in varied conditions. One group read one presented word (e.g., "cold") aloud, and other subjects read the word in the presence of some not-very-informative letters (such as "xxx–cold"). Together, these groups made up the "no-context" condition. Another group of subjects read the word in context with an antonym, such as "hot–cold." Finally, a third group did not read the words used in the study. These subjects were told they would see a stimulus such as "hot–????" and their job was to produce (generate) a word that came to mind. Obviously, the target word is "cold"; that is, the study just won't work unless the "generate" subjects produce on their own the same words that the other subjects had read. But this manipulation was quite successful—the subjects generated the target words perfectly. After this procedure, they were placed in either an explicit- or an implicit-memory task. The explicit-memory task was the familiar recognition memory procedure. These subjects were shown words and were asked to judge if the word had been read or generated previously. Here, the dependent measure is the likelihood of correct recognition. The implicit-memory task will also be familiar: this was the perceptual-identification task that we've seen before. These subjects were simply asked to identify the words they saw briefly. Here, the dependent measure is the degree of priming by the previously read or generated word. If the specific previous experience of seeing or generating the word influences implicit

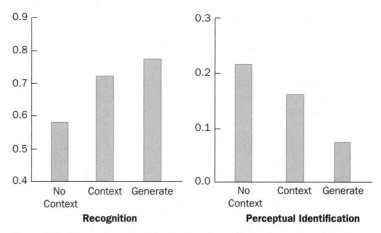

Figure 4.2 The study manipulation produced opposite results on recognition memory (an explicit test) and on primed perceptual identification (an implicit test). *Source:* From Jacoby, 1983.

memory, then we'd expect to see a large priming effect, meaning that the specific previous experience of reading or generating the word speeds up perceptual identification. Figure 4.2 shows the results of this study. In the left panel (labeled "recognition"), you'll see the expected generation effect. The words that the subjects generated from an antonym cue were recognized significantly better than words that had been read in context, which in turn were recognized significantly better than were words that had been read out of context. But now look at the right panel, labeled "perceptual identification." On the Υ axis is a measure of the amount of priming or facilitation. As the graph shows, the priming effect for generated words was quite small. That is, the right panel shows that the words generated were identified significantly more slowly than were words read in context, which in turn were identified significantly more slowly than were words read out of context. The pattern of findings in perceptual identification (once again, this is a measure of implicit memory) shows exactly the opposite ordering of the pattern for recognition (or explicit memory)—very interesting findings!

Now, our next task is to try to explain such dissociations in performance. Some researchers (Schacter, 1989) suggest that performance differs between explicit- and implicit-memory measures because different areas in the brain are involved in explicit and implicit memory.

*P*rocessing Accounts of Implicit-Memory Dissociations

Other researchers have adopted a different perspective on implicit and explicit memory. Roediger (1990) develops an idea known as **transfer-appropriate procedures** to account for these dissociations, and, as you might guess from the name, this idea is clearly based on transfer-appropriate processing, which we examined earlier in the chapter. The idea of transfer-appropriate procedures is based on four assumptions. First, at test time, retrieval will be better if the same cognitive operations used to encode the material in the first place also are involved in the retrieval. Thus, if I used a rhyming scheme to encode some material, then my retrieval will be helped if I use a similar rhyming scheme to retrieve the material, rather than some other procedure. The second assumption is that tests of explicit memory and of implicit memory frequently require either different types of retrieval, or access to different types of information. As you consider this assumption, think back to the way in which retrieval was measured in explicit- and implicit-memory tasks. For explicit memory, the task was almost always recognition, a decision-making task. The alternatives are directly in front of you; all you have to do is decide which item was seen or heard before. But in the studies we looked at, implicit memory was not measured in the same way. Now, according to this second assumption, if the different tasks require different retrieval operations, then these operations will succeed to the extent that they overlap with the original encoding operations. This relationship explains how the dissociations between explicit memory and implicit memory may come about: At retrieval time, different cognitive operations are called into action that may or may not take advantage of the way in which the original encoding was done. If the retrieval operations fit well with the operations used to encode, then retrieval will be good. But if a somewhat different retrieval task is used, then different retrieval operations will be called for, and these may not make a good fit with the cognitive operations used at encoding time; hence, the retrieval effort will suffer.

The third and fourth assumptions in the transfer-appropriate procedures view are extensions of the second assumption. The third assumption states that measures of explicit memory, such as recognition, tend to produce retrieval of semantic, elaborative, or conceptual information. In other words, if you're a subject in an explicit-memory study and you are shown four words and asked to recognize which one appeared on a previous list, you probably will try to think about the meaning of each alternative to see if you might have stored a similar meaning when the list was first presented. You probably wouldn't think about the number of letters or syllables or typeface of each alternative. On the other hand, the fourth assumption states that measures of implicit memory, such as ultrabrief word presentations, tend to produce retrieval based on perceptual characteristics. For example, implicit memory is influenced by the senses that are used to encode and retrieve the material. If a stimulus is presented auditorily, then implicit memory is negatively influenced if the retrieval measure is visual word identification. But this kind of switch does not influence explicit memory as greatly.

Now, the next question is how useful these four assumptions are. Can we use them to help explain the dissociations in performance that we see between explicit and implicit measures of memory? Let's go back to the Jacoby (1983) study. In the explicit-memory condition, you'll recall that the subjects who generated a word from its context outperformed the other subjects. They did so because generating information leads to greater conceptual elaboration than simply reading a word. At test time, the attempt to recognize a word also leads to greater conceptual elaboration than simply reading a word, and so we would expect that the subjects who generated the word "cold" from its context would outperform the subjects who simply read the word. And this is the result that was found. What about the subjects in the implicit task? Here, we would expect that subjects who read a word engaged in greater perceptual processing than did subjects who generated the word. (In fact, the "generate" subjects didn't really see the word at all, and so they did very little perceptual processing compared to the "reading" groups.) Now at test time, the subjects are given an identification task that calls for them to read the words again. We would expect that the group that read the words in the first place would outperform the subjects who simply generated the word, and this is the result found in the perceptual-identification task.

Attention in Implicit Memory   The account given above certainly suggests that implicit-memory effects will be observed in people regardless of whether they have paid attention to a source of stimulation. And this indeed is the classic account (e.g., Eich, 1984). In other words, simply exposing me to a stimulus, even if I direct no attention to it, will enable my cognitive system to respond to a priming stimulus, or to complete a word fragment, such as the word "co_ni_t_v_."

Earlier in the chapter we discussed the notion of transfer-appropriate processing (TAP), which we need here, too. Theorists who endorse a TAP position make a different point about how attention influences implicit memory. We find two suppositions. First, as you recall, the TAP position suggests that retrieval will benefit if the cognitive processes used in retrieval are the same as those used to encode in the first place. In other words, according to the TAP position, the cognitive processes that are used in encoding a memory are themselves part of the context that will influence likelihood of retrieval. One additional point matters. The TAP position distinguishes between two broad categories of cognitive processing (Roediger & McDermott, 1993). On the one hand we have conceptual processing, which analyzes meaning and semantics. For example, if you are asked to name as many vegetables as you can in a limited time, you are engaged in conceptual processing. On the other hand, we have perceptual processing. If you are shown a word briefly, such as "milk," and are asked to determine if the third letter was the tallest, then you are engaged in perceptual processing. The TAP researchers point out that most implicit-memory tasks, such as completing word fragments, are based on perceptual cognitive processes. But some implicit-memory tasks are not perceptual. They are generally called conceptual implicit-memory tasks. Let's consider an example. In a category-exemplar production task, subjects are shown listings of examples drawn from categories. Thus a subject may see a listing of specific birds, such as "robin" or "cardinal," drawn from the category *birds*. Later, the situation is turned around: The subjects are given category names and asked to say as many examples as possible as quickly as they can. This is the production phase in the task. Some of the category names are the same as those from which specific examples came that the subjects have previously seen. Other category names are "new" to the subject, at least in this study's context. What should happen here? From the implicit-memory standpoint, we might expect that when the subjects are asked to generate examples from a category from which they have already seen examples, then they should be expected to generate *more* examples from that category than would a person who has not seen the listing of specific examples previously in the study. Why? The theoretical answer is that, when subjects study the list of specific examples, they engage in some conceptual cognitive processes that subsequently prime or activate related specific members of the category. Even though the subjects are not instructed to search explicitly for these activated members in the production phase of the task, these items will nevertheless be more readily available, and thus likely to be produced than categories whose members have not been primed by the initial presentation.

We are thus led to state the TAP position on attention's influence in implicit memory. Unlike the standard view, which suggests that attention is not required to produce implicit-memory effects regardless of task, the TAP position suggests that this position is not quite right. Attention may not be required to produce implicit-memory effects, provided that the implicit-memory measure used is perceptual. But when the implicit-memory measure that is used requires conceptual processes, then we may not necessarily observe implicit-memory effects, even when conceptual processes are used at encoding time, if attention is then diverted from the task.

To investigate this matter, Mulligan (1997; Mulligan & Hartman, 1996) presented to his subjects one of two tasks, either an implicit-memory task or an explicit task. The implicit-memory task was the conceptual-priming task that we've described. The explicit-memory task was a category-cued recall task in which the subjects were prompted with a category name, and explicitly asked to recall as many specific examples from the studied list as they could. Each of these tasks was carried out under several conditions of attentional load. That is, Mulligan had his subjects carry out an additional task whose trials were interspersed with presentations of the specific examples. His thinking was that this additional task would divert some attention from the cognition that the subjects could bring to bear on encoding the specific examples. Specifically, subjects saw a sequence of digits and letters consisting of one, three, or five elements: a sequence such as "3F4J6" might be presented to the subject, who was instructed to retain this sequence until a "recall" instruction was presented; this instruction was given approximately 3 seconds later. Figure 4.3 shows the findings.

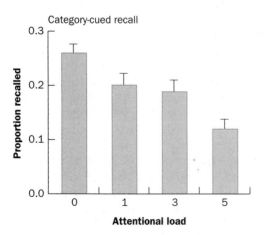
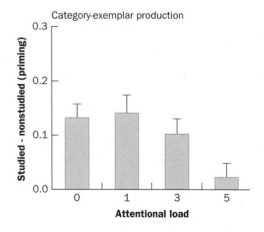

Figure 4.3 Notice that baseline responding (proportion of nonstudied exemplars produced) for the category-exemplar production task was .13. *Source:* From Mulligan, 1997.

The right panel shows the results of the implicit-memory task; the left panel shows the results of the explicit-memory task. It's not news to us to find in the explicit task that increasing the attentional load at encoding time will hurt a person's chance of successfully retrieving something at recall time, and this is what the findings suggest. Specifically, when the attentional load reaches five elements, performance on the category-cued recall task declines appreciably. It is newsworthy and interesting to see, however, that performance on the implicit-memory task (in the right panel) shows essentially the same pattern. Here, the dependent measure is the difference between the proportions of previously studied and unstudied examples that were produced in the production phase of the category task. When the subjects were given only a small attentional load, say, one or three items, they showed almost as large a priming effect as when they had no sequences of digits and letters to store (this is the column labeled "0"). But once again, when the attentional load increases to five elements in the sequence, the subjects' performance in the implicit-memory task declines appreciably. The priming effect was negligible. What do these results suggest about attention in implicit-memory tasks? They suggest that if the measure of implicit memory is perceptual, then attention may not be required at encoding time. But if the measure of implicit memory is conceptual, then diverting attention at encoding time hurts retrieval in an implicit-memory task just as it hurts retrieval in an explicit-memory task.

Remembering and Knowing

We think of our memory systems as a kind of device that we can use or direct to retrieve and reconstitute experiences that we've had. The implicit-memory literature suggests, however, that such a viewpoint underestimates the cognitive system's power to operate without producing awareness of its work. In other words, when we look at either conceptual or perceptual implicit memory, we see that the memory system may clearly leave its mark on our current behavior, even though we may not be consciously trying to direct the system's operation. And this distinction paves the way for another question: Is the memory system's operation always so stark in our conscious experience of its operation? In other words, I may learn something and clearly have a conscious experience that "comes back to me" when I try to remember it. But can other forms of conscious experience take place in addition to, or instead of, this conscious "reliving" of the learning?

Certainly, some cognitive psychologists have thought so. Tulving (1985) distinguishes between autonoetic and anoetic consciousness. **Autonoetic consciousness** is the mental event that most of us think of when we think of remembering something. It is episodic and recollective. **Anoetic consciousness** can be described as semantic and nonrecollective. Here's how these conscious experiences might be experienced if you were a subject in a memory experiment. Suppose you are given a list of words to learn and remember, and you are told that you will be given a recognition task in the future. You study the words. After a time you are given a series of words and asked a simple question after each one, "Was this word on the list, yes or no?" For some words you can remember seeing and thinking about the word and so you answer yes. This is autonoetic, explicit memory. But for other words you may not be able to retrieve the conscious experience of having seen them, yet they seem familiar (and so you've had some kind of conscious experience), and you are pretty sure they were on the list. Again, you would say yes. The latter event is anoetic consciousness. Notice that in the first example we would say, "I remember this word was on the list." In the second we might say, "I know it was on the list, even though I can't remember it exactly." How do these two types of reports interact with each other?

This matter was investigated by Rajaram (1993). In one study, subjects were given a list of words, which they processed in two ways. They processed half the words semantically (that is, they produced semantic associates for these words), whereas they produced rhymes for the other half of the words. No doubt you'll remember from earlier that this is a straightforward levels-of-processing manipulation. This procedure is somewhat unusual, though, in that the same set of subjects engaged in both types of processing; in most such studies, some subjects engage only in semantic processing and others only in rhyming.

Subjects were given 160 such study words, and one hour later they received an explicit-recognition task. But they had more to do than simply write yes if they recognized an item, or no if they did not. Rajaram went on to inquire about this recognition. Here the subjects were tasked with telling whether they actually "remembered" the word or if they "knew" that the word had been presented even though they couldn't explicitly remember it. I excerpt from the instructions to the subjects to show how these judgments were to be made:

> Remember judgments: If your recognition of the word is accompanied by a conscious recollection of its prior occurrence in the study list, then write "R." "Remember" is the ability to become consciously aware again of some aspect or aspects of what happened or what was experienced at the time the word was presented.
>
> Know judgments: "Know" responses should be made when you recognize that the word was in the study list, but you cannot consciously recollect anything about its actual occurrence or what happened or what was experienced at the time of its occurrence.
>
> To further clarify the difference between these two judgments: If someone asks for your name, you would typically respond in the "know" sense; however when asked the last movie you saw, you would typically respond in the "remember" sense, that is, becoming consciously aware again of some aspects of the experience. (Rajaram, 1993)

The results of one study (shown in Table 4.4) revealed a familiar levels-of-processing effect: Words that were processed semantically were significantly more likely to be recognized correctly than were words that had been processed as rhymes. But look at the "remember" and "know" judgments. When the correctly recognized words are broken down into the categories of remembering versus knowing, we see that the basic levels-of-processing result is very strong for words that the subjects remember. But we observe the opposite pattern of findings in the "know" responses. For words to which they had given "know" responses, the subjects gave more "know" responses to the items in the rhyme condition than to words in the semantic condition—just the opposite for the words the subjects remembered!

Let's go through a typical subject's hypothetical thought processes to get a down-to-earth view of this result. The subject sees a word in the recognition test and thinks, "Yeah, I remember that word; I had to come up with a synonym for that word." The subjects are telling us that, when they remember a word, they are a lot more likely to have semantically processed it than to have rhymed it. But for the "know" judgments

Table 4.4   Mean Proportion of Hits and False Alarms as a Function of Study Conditions and Response Type

Study Manipulation	Levels of Processing of Targets		Lures (False Alarms)
	Semantic	*Rhyme*	
Overall			
Recognition	.86	.62	.16
"Remember"	.66	.32	.02
"Know"	.20	.30	.14

Source: From Rajaram, 1993.

("Hmmm, I don't remember it, but I know it was on the study list"), the subjects are more likely to have rhymed the word at study time than to have generated a synonym for it. These findings suggest that for most people it is the conscious experience of "reliving" a specific instance that tells them they are actually remembering something. Without this conscious experience, people may still retrieve something, but then they will tend to make an "I know I saw it" response. Notice too that the "know" response is much more likely to be perceptual or even inferential than a specific reliving: I say that I know something when it seems like I've seen it, or when I think I must have seen it. This finding tells us something important about knowledge: It could be that what I call my knowledge about something refers to information that has been built up by perceptual or inferential processes, rather than by recomputations based on specific events.

Donaldson (1996) provides a useful way to think about the cognition underlying the subjects' reports in studies such as Rajaram's. Considering Figure 4.4, let's think of the triangular distribution B as the quantity of "activation" or intensity provoked by a word actually studied on a recognition memory task. The triangular distribution A represents the quantity of activation that would theoretically be produced by the distractor words at the time the recognition task was given. Overall, the distractors have a weaker activation than the words actually studied (they should—the distractors have not been seen before), but once in a while a distractor will provoke quite a bit of activation, and the subject may be prompted to say yes to that word. Thus the line labeled no–yes represents the subject's decision point for each word that is given. If the activation is high enough (i.e., to the right of the line), then the subject will say yes to that word. Otherwise, the response will be no. But notice that above this decision point is another. This is the line labeled know–remember. If the subject says yes and the activation is high enough, then he or she will say "I remember the word." But suppose the activation is high enough to say yes, but not high enough to say "I remember"? Then the person will fall back to the weaker, anoetic, "I know" response.

Further, from this depiction, we can see that the subject's decision point has some implications for how many words he or she succeeds in recognizing, as well as for the likelihood of saying "know" or "remember." In the top panel in Figure 4.4, the hypothetical subject has a very "strict" criterion for saying yes. Consequently, this hypothetical subject would very seldom say, "I remember it" to a distractor word, and even

Figure 4.4 Effect of response criterion on remember and know responses when considered as stronger and weaker components of recognition. Criteria become more liberal as one moves from top panel to bottom. See text for details. *Source:* From Donaldson, 1996.

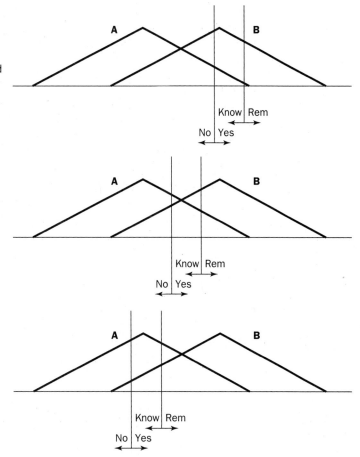

the "know" response would be given to a distractor fairly seldom. Let's consider a hypothetical subject represented by the bottom panel. He or she has a "lax" criterion. In this condition, the area between the two decision lines is occupied mostly by the words from the A distribution. Thus, for such a subject, a "know" response is just as likely, or even more likely, to be given to a distractor as to a previously studied word. Technically, we use the expression "false alarm" to describe a yes response to a distractor, and it's appropriate to say that the hypothetical subject in the bottom panel is false-alarming all over the place. For any given subject, then, if we can determine the yes-or-no decision point, then we can have some confidence about the likelihood of the subject's being correct or producing a false alarm when the "know" versus "remember" judgment is made.

Intrachapter Summary and Interpretation

We've concluded our extensive treatment of context in memory. Since the last intrachapter summary we've seen several phenomena arise. First, the surrounding stimuli present at the same time as we initially learn material can exert a powerful biasing effect at retrieval time. Generally, such stimuli operate in a helpful direction if they are present again at retrieval time. We've seen too that such contextual effects seem to operate on our retrieval attempts, even though we may not have processed those stimuli to the depth required to produce a mental event, or awareness of them. The picture I would like you to consider entails thinking of the memory as a recomputational system that is "driven" by the processing of external and internal stimulation. If those stimuli are present at both learning and retrieval, then we have at least a decent likelihood that the recomputational system will be driven back into the same state as it was in when the learning took place. And if our systems are driven back into that state again, the chance is good that we will report "remembering" the stimulus. The findings about the distinction between actually remembering a stimulus as being on an initial list, versus simply "knowing" that it was there show that the effects of contextual biasing are not necessarily binary (i.e., all or none) in their operation. Thus, contextual cues may not be sufficient to drive the memory system completely back into the state in which an actual memory is reported. But enough stimulation may be present at retrieval time to drive the memory system back into a state of something like "partial knowledge." Although this state may not be sufficient to produce the event that we call "remembering" the original stimulus, it may be strong enough to provide us with a basis for saying, "Well, I know that word was on there, even though I can't actually remember seeing it." I wish I could tell you more about what this partial-knowledge state looks like, at either the cognitive or the neural level of analysis. But the full answer is still on the horizon, and we'll have to content ourselves with the knowledge we have until cognitive scientists' diligent efforts bring the whole story into view. When we see the whole story, this "criterial" interpretation of the remember–know distinction may not be completely accurate. That is, "know" may not be simply a weak "remember"; it may be a completely different state of retrieval, subject to its own principles and effects.

Reconstruction in Retrieval of Events

In Chapter 3, we saw that a simple notion like "forgetting" was not adequate to describe all the sorts of retrieval failures that we may experience. It's true that learned material may sometimes be forgotten in the sense that the person who is trying to retrieve it simply draws a blank. But at other times the person's errors in retrieval are the result of retrieving something that is wrong, rather than of failing to retrieve anything. Moreover, it's sometimes possible to demonstrate that the retrieved "memory" that the person reports is something that did not take place, and perhaps, *could not* have taken place. In this section we consider some of the variables that seem to influence such faulty memory making. Many studies that we'll examine are based on subjects' retrieval of events that they have witnessed, but I suggest that the processes underlying the distortion of witnessed events may be generalizable to other events.

Eyewitness Accounts

In the 1970s, Loftus and her colleagues carried out classic studies (1975, 1977, 1979b, 1979c; Loftus and Palmer, 1974) showing what sometimes happens when subjects encode and retrieve events they have witnessed. The typical paradigm for these studies consists of showing the subjects a film about some event (often a car accident), followed by questions designed to influence the subject's encoding. In the final phase the subjects are asked to retrieve the event.

This procedure was used by Loftus and Palmer (1974). After they saw the film, the subjects were to fill out a questionnaire in which they made several judgments about what they had seen. One of the questions asked, "How fast were the cars going when they _____ each other?" Subjects saw one of five verbs in the blank space: smashed, collided, bumped, hit, or contacted. Loftus and Palmer found that the verb definitely influenced a subject's judgment. Subjects who read the verb *smashed* estimated that the cars were traveling at 40.8 mph. But subjects who read the less violent verb *contacted* estimated that the cars were doing only 31.8 mph—a big difference. Realize that Loftus and Palmer maintained that this sort of leading question truly changed the subjects' memories. That is, no matter how the subjects may have encoded the event when it was visible, after the researchers had biased them with a verb, that original encoding was no longer available; it had been written over by the new encoding.

If the new encoding were really successful in **overwriting** the original encoding, then we'd expect that the subjects would also "know" things about the event that were consistent with this new encoding. That is, we might expect them to make intrusion errors similar to those observed by Owens et al. (1979).

In a second experiment, Loftus and Palmer (1974) tested this idea. Subjects saw a 4-second film in which two cars collided. The subjects were then administered a questionnaire incorporating the critical item about the cars' velocities. One group read the verb *smashed*, a second group, *hit*, and for the third group, this item was deleted. All the subjects returned to the lab one week later to answer additional questions about the film. One of these questions was critical: "Did you see any broken glass in the film?" Although no broken glass had appeared in the film, 32% of the subjects who had read the verb *smashed* said that they remembered seeing broken glass. Only 14% of the subjects who had read the verb *hit* responded in that way, as did 12% of the subjects who had not estimated the car's speed.

This demonstration that the subjects' memories have been overwritten seems convincing. Once subjects read the verb *smashed*, their memories were altered; consequently, at retrieval time they were "accurately" retrieving something they believed to be true: If the cars were traveling at 40 mph, then some broken glass probably would be visible.

As you may have surmised, this study suggests that courtroom and police procedures involving eyewitnesses naming perpetrators may be badly flawed. In fact, Loftus has devoted much of her time in the 1980s and 1990s to a lengthy and convincing demonstration of the caution that is needed in making a conclusion based on eyewitness accounts (Wells & Loftus, 1984).

Wells (1993) documents how some of these processes produce mistaken judgments. In one study, eyewitnesses watched a "crime" that had been staged for their benefit. They were then invited to see if they could pick out the perpetrator (actually the experimenter's accomplice) from a mock lineup. The subjects were told that the criminal might not appear in the lineup, and that they were permitted to make a none-of-the-above response. Wells theorized that people in such a situation begin by assuming that the culprit is indeed before them in the lineup. Because the eyewitnesses know they have seen the crime, pressure is strong to use their memories to determine which of the people before them is the perpetrator.

When the criminal really does appear in the lineup, at least the subjects have a chance of detecting him or her. But when the criminal is not there, then this pressure to detect and name the culprit may increase the likelihood that the eyewitness will name someone else as the criminal. This is exactly the finding that Wells reports. Compared with the situation in which the perpetrator was visible, none-of-the-above responses did indeed increase when the perpetrator was removed from the lineup without replacement. But the most common response by far in this condition was for the subjects to simply select another person as the perpetrator—clearly an inaccurate retrieval. Other evidence suggests that equal care must be taken in selecting "distractors" for the police lineup (Wells, Luus, & Windschitl, 1994). Finally, and you may find this a sobering thought given your studies thus far of cognition and memory, other accounts have estimated that eyewitnesses are considered a major source of evidence in more than 75,000 U.S. cases each year. Incredibly, several studies (e.g., Huff, Rattner, & Sagarin, 1986) provide converging evidence suggesting quite strongly that mistaken eyewitness identification is the most important factor in producing convictions of the innocent.

Retrieving Repressed Memories

The memory-repression concept can be traced directly to Sigmund Freud's writings, although the idea in some form may be older than that: According to the conventional or popular position derived from Freud's work, a memory so painful that it cannot be dealt with is made inaccessible to consciousness, though it may eventually be recovered in psychotherapy. As you can see, such an interpretation is very consistent with the storage metaphor for memory that we considered in Chapter 3. From the storage-metaphor perspective, the **repressed memories** live on somewhere in the "mind," and under a skillful psychotherapist's care it may be possible to bring such memories back to consciousness.

From the point of view we have taken in this chapter, however, we may wonder if other variables could account for the clinical phenomenon of repressed memories without needing to assume that any one experience has been stored. That is, as we have seen in this chapter, retrieving almost any experience seems highly sensitive to the context in which it occurs. Further, as we see in Bartlett's work, the longer the time between encoding and retrieval, the more likely it is that such retrievals will be marked by distortion and inaccuracy. In raising this question I do not imply that such an account would "prove" that repressed memories are neither authentic nor accurate—we have no evidence to prove that. Further, I do not suggest that the childhood sexual abuse that is frequently behind such memories is not real. Several studies have shown (e.g., Daro, 1988) the immeasurably saddening fact that even the lowest estimates indicate that more than 10% of U.S. children may suffer this abuse.

Loftus (1993), considering sources of information that might provide people with the basis for a faulty memory about distant sexual abuse, considered possible factors. Several extremely popular books offer almost recipelike guidelines on symptomatology and behavior. Then too, psychotherapists' testimony in sexual-abuse cases that have gone to trial strongly suggests that the therapists themselves may have hit upon a diagnosis of distant sexual abuse sometime during the psychotherapy, and, acting on this diagnosis, inadvertently coached their clients into eventually recovering the possibly faulty memories.

False Memory   Many laboratory studies show that, even with materials that are much "weaker" than those we have been discussing, and therefore less likely to be subject to distortion, false memories can nevertheless be induced (Haugaard, Reppucci, Laurd, & Nauful, 1991; Loftus & Ketcham, 1991). Further, the false memories that are induced have interesting properties. We'll consider two studies.

Garry, Manning, and Loftus (1996) demonstrate how powerful human imagination can be in creating possibly false memories. They used a three-stage procedure with their subjects. First, subjects were given a forty-item list of possible events that could have occurred to them as children, such as having to go to the emergency room at night. They rated the likelihood that each event occurred to the best of their memories. Two weeks later, the subjects were recalled to the lab and asked to imagine that some of the events had actually taken place. Specifically, they were invited to imagine as thorough a scenario as possible; in the emergency-room event, imagining if an ambulance was involved, whether they remembered being scared, and so on. In this phase, following the subjects' attempts to visualize the event, they also wrote brief answers in response to the experimenter's questions. This manipulation suggests that the subjects were indeed likely to engage in the imagination task. Finally, in the third phase, the experimenter pretended to have misplaced the subjects' original responses to the forty-item form, and asked them if they wouldn't mind filling it out once again. In reality, this second filling out of the form was a posttest, and can be used to see if the subjects have "changed their minds" about the likelihood that any event had occurred. Figure 4.5 shows the percentage of events whose self-reported likelihood decreased, stayed the same, or increased for subjects who had imagined, or not imagined, those events. Keep

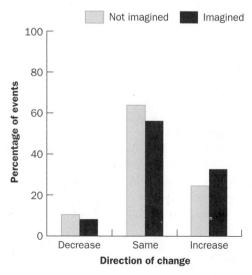

Figure 4.5   Percentage of events staying the same, increasing, and decreasing for subjects who initially responded 1–4 (responses indicating that the critical items probably did not happen). *Source:* Garry et al., 1996.

in mind that each event shown in this figure had originally been given low ratings, indicating that the subjects initially thought these events probably had not actually taken place. The rightmost column in Figure 4.5 is probably the most critical for our discussion. As it shows, the percentage of events whose likelihood increased on the posttest was significantly different for subjects who had imagined that event, compared to those who had not. Although this graph is an aggregate from various scenarios, this pattern was observed more or less for each of the eight items used in the imaginal condition. This finding suggests that the subjects who had imagined that an initially unlikely event had really occurred were now more likely to say that the event had really taken place, compared with subjects who had not engaged in the visualization task. The implications for recovering repressed memories are pretty clear. Because one of the main therapeutic techniques used in this subject involves imaginally reliving abusive episodes, the Garry et al. study suggests some perils in this procedure. That is, using an imaginal technique in psychotherapy may well increase the client's confidence that his or her report of an event that did not occur was accurate.

A growing, substantial body of evidence suggests that imagining an event can lead to "imagination inflation": A person who imagines an event may come to believe that the event has occurred, even when it clearly hasn't. Goff and Roediger (1998) carried out a study demonstrating this effect. Each subject participated in three sessions, the first of which was labeled an *encoding* session. The subjects first either heard, heard and imagined, or heard and performed 72 simple "action statements." They might hear a statement such as "break the toothpick," or hear and imagine a statement such as "bend the wire." Sometimes the subject heard and performed an action statement such as "pull your earlobe."

Second was the *imagining* session, which occurred 24 hours after the encoding session. Some action statements from the encoding session were presented again, along with new action statements. Subjects were asked to imagine these events 0, 1, 3, or 5 times (that is, 0 times meant that they were not asked to imagine those events). Finally, the third session was 15 days after the first—the *testing* session. The subjects were presented all 72 action statements from the encoding session, along with additional items that had been presented only during the imagining session, and some items that had not been presented at all. The subjects were asked if they had heard the action statement. Remember, the subject should answer yes only for the action statements that had been presented in the encoding session, because they were the only ones that had been heard. If the subjects said yes, they were asked to tell if they heard it only, heard it and imagined it, or heard it and performed it. The results were eye-opening. For us, probably the most significant finding is that increasing the number of imaginings in the second session led the subjects to increase their likelihood of judging that they had performed the action in the encoding session—even when they hadn't. The effect worked in two ways: Subjects increased their likelihood of performance estimates for events that had only been heard, and they also increased it for events that weren't even presented in the encoding session. Clearly, imaging these events led the subjects to increase their confidence in reporting that something took place though it had not.

A study by Brainerd, Reyna, and Brandse (1995) adds another angle to this effect. They worked with **fuzzy-trace memory theory** (Reyna & Brainerd, 1995), which postulates that people may break down information into two components for encoding and storage. On the one hand they work with representations of the actual form of the utterances, or sights, or any other stimuli that were present. We can call this the *surface* form of the events. On the other hand, they may store an interpretation of those events, a representation called the **gist.** Fuzzy-trace theory argues that these components in the representation may not be connected, and in fact, frequently they are disconnected. Suppose at the end of a conversation a friend takes leave of you by saying, "Well, I think I'm gonna go have a bite to eat." Suppose also that a cognitive psychologist then rushes up to you and asks you to pick out which, if any, of these statements your friend actually made:

> Well, I think I'm gonna get a snack.
> Well, I think I'm gonna go get something to eat.
> Well, I think I'm gonna go have a bite to eat.

Fuzzy-trace theory argues that the third alternative (which is correct) cues the memory for the actual event. That is, because the third comment is the one your friend actually made, the prompt given above is the only one of the three statements that has an association with the specific memory. You can think of the memory and the prompt as having a lock-and-key relationship, in that only the verbatim statement can be an effective cue for the specific phrasing that was stored. What about the other prompts? In a memory experiment, these prompts function as distractors, and fuzzy-trace theory argues that distractors are effective cues for gist, but not for the actual form of the utterance. In other words, the gist representation is something like this:

> Your friend said he was a little hungry.

Consequently, either one of the distractors may cue this representation because both are things that somebody might say if they were a little hungry. If you picked out the correct response, then we say that the surface form of the representation cued the verbatim memory, and we call this type of response a hit. On the other hand, if you picked out a distractor, we call that a false alarm, and we say that the distractor cued the memory for gist. The false alarm is also, theoretically, a false memory. That is, if you say yes to the "snack" distractor, thinking that was the comment your friend actually made, you have falsely retrieved an event as a memory that was not one.

You've probably noticed a very important point here: Lots of potential distractors can cue gist memory, but only one prompt can cue the actual memory. As we know, the longer the interval between hearing the original statement and hearing its verbatim prompt, the less likely it is that the prompt will succeed in cuing the target memory. But because lots of distractors are available that could conceivably cue the gist memory, we would expect that the longer the interval between hearing the original statement and hearing the verbatim prompt, the lower we'd expect the hit rate to be, and the higher we'd expect the false-alarm rate to be. Brainerd, Reyna, & Brandse extended this viewpoint in an interesting way by showing that such false alarms may actually be more persistent—that is, more durable than hits.

To demonstrate this effect, kindergartners and third-graders heard a list of 60 familiar concrete nouns. After a 5-minute distractor task in which the children played

Table 4.5   Conditional and Unconditional Probabilities of Baseline and Persistent Hits and False Alarms

	Age Level	
Probability	*Younger Children*	*Older Children*
Baseline false alarms	.411	.452
Persistent false alarms	.595	.787
Baseline hits	.608	.642
Persistent hits	.695	.715

Source: From Brainerd et al., 1995.

"Where's Waldo?" the experimenter read a list of 60 words to the subjects. Thirty words were from the original list, and 30 were distractors. The children were instructed to respond yes or no depending on whether they recognized the word from the original list. One week later, the children were brought back into the lab. The experimenter read the list of 30 targets and 30 distractors once again. Several outcomes are interesting. On the second test, anytime a child says yes to a word that wasn't on the list, it's a false alarm. Two kinds of false alarms are possible. First, the baseline rate of false alarms applies to words that the child correctly said weren't on the list in the first test, but now (that is, one week after hearing the words) says yes to. The persistent false-alarm rate applies to words that the child has false-alarmed to on both first and second tests. Similarly, the baseline rate of hits refers to words that the child failed to recognize in the first test, but succeeds in recognizing in the second test, one week later. The persistent hit rate applies to words that were recognized at both test times. The children's responses are shown in Table 4.5.

As you can see in Table 4.5, the baseline hit rate was higher than the baseline false-alarm rate for both the older (third-graders) and younger (kindergarteners) children. Thus the memory system for both ages was functioning appropriately. On the second test, one week after initially hearing the words, the children were more likely to correctly recognize a word that had appeared in the list than they were to falsely say yes to a word that was a distractor. But we get a somewhat different story when we examine the pattern of persistent hits and persistent false alarms. For the younger children, the persistent hit rate remained greater than the persistent false-alarm rate, although the gap had narrowed compared to the difference in baseline rates alone. For the older children, the findings are even more dramatic: the persistent false-alarm rate is significantly higher than the persistent hit rate. Thus, for the older children, once a false-alarm response was produced at first test, the likelihood that the child would emit a second false alarm increases markedly compared to the likelihood of successfully hitting a target word again. In this experiment, a false alarm is a false memory because the child says yes (I remember it) in response to a word that was never presented. Brainerd et al. demonstrate that, once such a false memory is created by a mistake in the older child's memory system, then the false memory is more likely to be retrieved again than is a persistent correct memory. As you can infer, this finding has tremendous implications for the body of knowledge on repressed memory. Typically, most people, especially those who have not studied cognitive psychology, are likely to reason that a memory's persistence and durability is an indication of its accuracy. Here we see that such a widespread, popular belief may be yet another demonstration of how incorrect our intuitions about the cognitive system may be. Not only is the persistence of a memory *not* a good indication of its accuracy, persistence may in fact be a good indication of its falsity.

Reflections of the Environment in Memory

Anderson and Schooler (1991) used this expression as the title for an influential article. They intended to show that our memory systems work something like a mirror, in the sense that the images you can see in a mirror are the things in the world that are in front of the mirror. Anderson and Schooler suggest that our memory systems reflect the things in our world in just this way. When we see that a person can retrieve factual knowledge reliably and accurately, then we can infer that this factual knowledge has been present in the person's world for a long time, and has been presented in a number of contexts. When we see problems in retrieval, then we may be able to infer something different about the status of knowledge in the person's world: it may have been presented in a fragmentary or otherwise incomplete way, or it may reflect some aspect of knowledge that is not stable in time. That is, people's retrieval failure may indicate that some knowledge is being demanded of them that has not generally been a part of their world for a long time, and may or may not be required of them in the future. Parenthetically and without a hint of irony, I report that this is the story many of my students tell me about their retrieval failures in the tests I give them: The things we cover in class are not things that have ever been demanded of them before, and, they believe, will not be asked of them again. In this section we explore the implications of this environmental approach to memory phenomena.

Back to Ebbinghaus Again

As you recall from Chapter 3, Hermann Ebbinghaus showed that retention was a negatively decelerated curve, with a very high initial loss rate but eventually leveling off. Panel *a* in Figure 4.6 is another depiction of the original Ebbinghaus data, and shows this graphic relationship. We've converted the measure on the *x* axis to "hours of delay" rather than the minutes-hours-days scale that we used before, because that scale is more consistent with the approach to the data that we take in this section.

In searching for a way to characterize the data from Ebbinghaus's experiment, Anderson and Schooler built on work by Wickelgren (1976), who wrote that the relationship between performance and retention delay could be expressed as a "power function" in this form:

$$P = AT^{-b}$$

in which *P* stands for a performance measure, *A* is a parameter in the equation that would be fitted to the data (i.e., it's simply a variable number), *T* is the delay time, and $-b$ is yet another parameter. To use this equation to understand the Ebbinghaus finding, Anderson and Schooler transformed the original data.

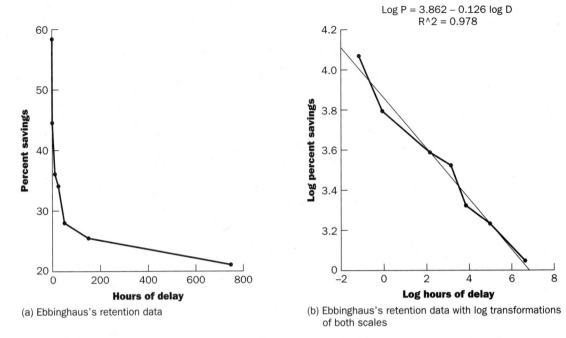

(a) Ebbinghaus's retention data

(b) Ebbinghaus's retention data with log transformations of both scales

Figure 4.6 (a) Ebbinghaus's (1885/1964) retention function, showing percentage of savings as a function of delay. Ebbinghaus used delays from 20 minutes to 31 days. (b) Both performance and delay scales transformed according to a logarithmic function. *Source:* From Anderson and Schooler, 1991.

Specifically, they logarithmically transformed both the performance measure (percentage of savings) and the delay variable (hours since learning). We leave aside discussion of how the logarithmic transformation is carried out for percentage of savings because that's tricky. But explaining transformation of the *x*-axis measure is not too hard. The logarithm of the hours of delay is the power to which you would raise 10 to get that number. Thus, the log of 100 hours of delay (about 4 days in Ebbinghaus's original data) is 2 because 10^2 is 100. Similarly, for 200 hours, the log is 2.3 because $10^{2.3}$ is 200. When the log of performance (percentage of savings) is graphed as a function of the log of hours of delay, we expect to see a linear function (i.e., a straight line), if the relationship between these two variables is really describable in terms of a **power law.** As panel *b* in Figure 4.6 shows, the resulting log-log graph is indeed a straight line. Specifically, once the parameters *A* and *-b* have been fitted to the data, we have this equation:

$$\text{Performance} = 47.56T^{-.126}$$

The value of *b* in this equation, $-.126$, is the forgetting rate. What is the power function telling us about the Ebbinghaus data? First, that the curve in the graph "goes away" when we create the **log-log transformation** shows that we may not need any short- and long-term memory to characterize the rate of loss (Anderson & Schooler, 1991). But another issue faces us here. Why should the retention function be describable as a power law in the first place? To answer this question, Anderson and Schooler next analyzed several aspects of the day-to-day environment in which we use our memories. To anticipate their answer, which we'll see in the next section, the reason our retention function has its shape can be seen in the environment itself, specifically in the likelihood that we will have to retrieve any specific fact in the immediate future.

The Environment "Demands" and We Recompute

To register for classes, fill out your income taxes, or get a car loan, you may be required to list your Social Security number. Every one of these instances can be considered a "demand" placed on you by the environment, because some person in the environment is asking you for a bit of information. As you can see from the example, some information, such as your Social Security number, is demanded by the environment rather often. Other information, such as your mother's maiden name is demanded less often. And finally, information such as the number of foreign-language courses you took in high school is hardly ever demanded. If you paid attention to the examples, you may be aware that the likelihood and speed of your retrieval may have correlated directly with the frequency of environmental demands. Information that is frequently demanded is information that we can retrieve quickly and accurately. Information that is infrequently demanded is less likely to be retrievable at all, and may require more time to do so, even when we succeed.

This analysis suggests that likelihood of retrieval is directly related to likelihood of environmental demand. But here's a problem: How would you go about estimating the likelihood that the environment will demand a specific fact? I quote from the Anderson and Schooler paper to show how they went about solving this problem:

> The basic idea is that at any point in time, memories vary in how likely they are to be needed and the memory system tries to make available those memories that are most likely to be useful. The memory system can use the past history of use of a memory to estimate whether the memory is likely to be needed now. (Anderson & Schooler, 1991, p. 400)

In other words, previous use of a memory strongly determines the likelihood that the environment will demand that memory again. When material is demanded over and over again, the memory system concludes that a safe bet is that it will be demanded again. Consequently, the memory system tries to make those memories available for retrieval. On the other hand, if the environment doesn't demand material very often, then the memory system may not be able to come up with it, if and when it is ever demanded again.

Anderson and Schooler looked at three very different subjects to see if they could support the idea that the likelihood that some memory will be demanded is a function of the likelihood that it has been demanded in the past. They considered words in *New York Times* headlines over two years; words children used, as measured by the CHILDES database (MacWhinney & Snow, 1990); and e-mail messages that had been sent to John Anderson over four years. In other words, every time a word is used in the newspaper headline, this appearance is a demand on readers' memories to retrieve anything they can about the person or thing referred to. Similarly, every time a word is used in communicating with a child, this usage is an environmental demand on the child's memory system to retrieve that word's meaning.

To evaluate how previous usage affects current need, Anderson and Schooler broke down each of the three content areas into 100-day "windows." They then recorded the frequency of each word or e-mail author in that window. For example, over 100 days, the word "Reagan" (who was president when the tabulation was done) might appear in the *New York Times* headlines 52 times. They next used this frequency as a basis for computing the likelihood that the word "Reagan" would appear on day 101 in the *New York Times* headlines. They called this likelihood the "Need Odds." In this context, "odds" is used just as it is in horse racing. When a horse leaves the starting gate at 2 to 1 odds, the bettors are saying, in effect, that they believe the chances are good that horse will win. If a horse leaves the starting gate at 100 to 1 odds, the bettors are saying that they view the horse's winning as somewhat unlikely. Thus "long odds" or "high odds" means the event is unlikely, whereas "short odds" or "low odds" means that the event is likely. They carried out these computations for parents' speech to children, authorship of e-mail messages, and *New York Times* headlines.

To compute a retention interval, Anderson and Schooler next looked at the probability that a word would appear in a *New York Times* headline as a function of the number of days that had elapsed since that word had appeared. We are now considering how likely it is that a word will pop up on day 101, basing our guess on how many days have elapsed since that word appeared in the previous 100-day window. The same tabulations were made for words that were spoken to children by their parents, and for e-mail messages too. Anderson and Schooler went on to compute for messages the probability that an e-mail author would pop up on day 101, given the number of days since that author had been heard from in the previous 100-day window. Panels *a, b,* and *c* in Figure 4.7 show these probabilities for the three subjects we have been considering. As you look at these panels in the diagram, you may be reminded about the original Ebbinghaus data, and why not? Each shows the same negatively decelerated curve that we saw in the untransformed data in Ebbinghaus's study. Thus, the probability that a child will hear and have to retrieve the meaning of any one word as the 101st utterance depends in large part on how many utterances he or she has heard since that word was used. If that was only a couple of utterances ago (that is, the word was used as the 100th or 99th utterance in a 100-utterance window), then the likelihood is reasonably strong that the word will be used again. But if many utterances have gone by since the word was used (thus creating a 40- or 60-utterance delay), then the likelihood diminishes that the child will have to retrieve the word's meaning.

In panels *d, e,* and *f* in Figure 4.7, we have created log-log plots for the three respective areas. On the *y* axis, we took the log of need odds, and on the *x* axis, we used the log of days since last appearance, or the log of the number of utterances since the word was last uttered. You are probably not surprised to find that all are straight lines, strongly suggesting that we can describe the retrieval demands for each of these three very different phenomena with a power function.

What have Anderson and Schooler succeeded in demonstrating in this study? They showed that the odds that you will need to remember something get shorter (remember, that means "become more likely") as that element in your memory has been demanded in your past. It's not clear how your memory system is able to keep track of the demands that have been placed upon it, but it does seem clear that the memory system is better able to retrieve or recompute aspects of memory that have been demanded frequently and recently.

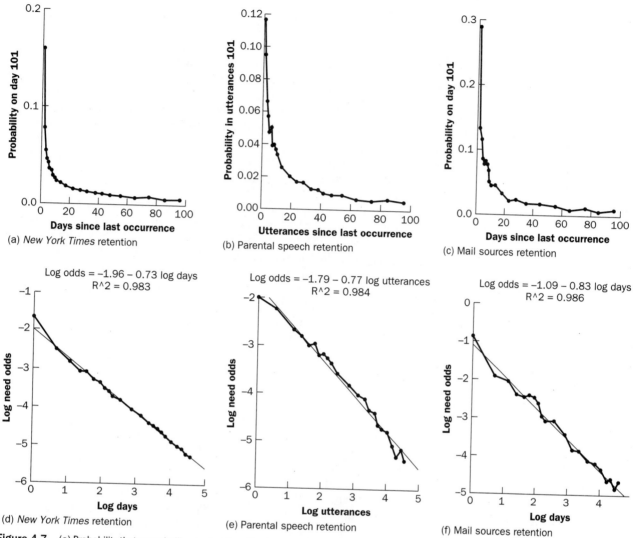

Figure 4.7 (a) Probability that a word will occur in a headline in *The New York Times* on day 101 as a function of how long it has been since the word previously occurred; (b) probability of word occurring in the 101st utterance from a parent as a function of how many utterances it has been since the word previously occurred; (c) probability of receiving an e-mail message from a source as a function of how many days it has been since a message was last received from that source. Panels *(d–f)* provide transformation of *(a–c)* plotting log need odds against log frequency.

Concluding Comments and Suggestions for Further Reading

In many ways, I think of this chapter as something like an "antimemory" essay. That is, in this chapter we take the perspective that the entity we call the "memory" system is not a storage-and-retrieval device, but rather a recomputational device. Here's what I mean by that expression. If you are walking down a corridor in a building, you don't bump into the walls (normally). Why not? On the one hand, we could say that you avoid collisions because your cognitive system "remembers" how to walk down corridors without crashing into the walls. We could say that, but we don't; it seems much more natural to say our perceptual systems know how to take information from the world and process it so that our behavior is congruent, or in synch with our goals. If our goal is to walk safely down the corridor, then we take in the information that we need to accomplish that, and use our perceptual systems to implement our plan. So too with our memories: Our goal is to put ourselves back into the state of knowledge where we need to be to recognize a word in the newspaper, or the origin of an e-mail message. Once launched by cues that may be in the environment, the cognitive system achieves this recomputation (and we may have the feeling that we "remember" something). Or, if the cues are not powerful enough to launch the system in the right direction, we may fail to retrieve.

As we see in this chapter, numerous findings are very difficult to explain from a conventional storage-and-retrieval perspective. Going all the way back to Bartlett's work, we see that people frequently retrieve distorted accounts of stories they have heard, accounts that could not, seemingly, have been encoded at the time they originally encountered the stimulus. Other work shows that humans are exquisitely sensitive to the effects of context on retrieval. The way in which a stimulus is processed at the time we first encounter it powerfully affects our ability to retrieve it. If the context is maintained, or if we use the same cognitive processes to retrieve it that we used when we first encountered the material, then retrieval is likely. But if the context is changed, or if we use cognitive processes at retrieval time that were not used to encode, then the likelihood of correct retrieval is diminished.

Next we looked at the effects of this contextual manipulation on eyewitness testimony. There, we saw that eyewitnesses use their memories very strategically. In a lineup the eyewitness may assume that the culprit is actually in the lineup. By making this assumption the eyewitness has converted the recognition task into a kind of "matching" task in attempting to find the best match between the people in the lineup and the witness's memory. As we've seen, this strategy may work, provided that the police have apprehended the right culprit. But if the culprit is not in the lineup, then the likelihood is strong that the eyewitness will simply match up his or her memory with another person in the lineup. We also examined the phenomenon of repressed and recovered memories. We saw that in the laboratory it is not very difficult to induce a false memory. Moreover, we saw that using the imagination, a technique psychotherapists often apply to help individuals recover repressed memories, in the laboratory increases an individual's confidence that an unlikely event actually occurred. We can't be sure, of course, that the laboratory findings apply to the psychotherapeutic setting, but clearly some caution is called for in assessing the authenticity of memories that have been recovered after months of work with a psychotherapist.

Finally, we looked at the relationship between the frequency of specific environmental events and their retrievability. A very direct relationship connects the frequency with which stimuli have been presented to us in the past and the likelihood that the environment will "demand" those stimuli of us again. Our memory systems try to anticipate the future demand, based on the present demand. As a metaphor, suppose you are CEO in a company that makes three products. Because your manufacturing resources are always limited by time, space, and money, you can't simply make bunches and bunches of all three products. Rather, you have to determine the proportion of resources that should be allocated to each product. How would you go about solving the problem of determining how much of each product to make? You might study customers' demands: If one product was demanded 50% of the time, another 40% of the time, and the third 10% of the time, you might adjust your production schedule to match these proportions. This plan might help to ensure that you always had just enough but not too much of each product. If you noticed that demand for one product lessened, and it grew for another, you might again adjust your production schedule to meet these new demands. This is just a metaphor, but it illustrates your memory system's possible solution to the problem of determining which memories are the ones that need to be reproduced. For memories that are demanded all the time, the memory system keeps them in production. But for a rarely demanded memory, just as for a rarely demanded product, the memory system may say, "Sorry, we're not making that any more." When we say "the memory" is really our ability to retrieve or recompute something, this ability reflects what the environment "expects" of us.

To find out more about these issues, you could start with the lengthy article by Koriat and Goldsmith (1996), which is followed by comments and rebuttals. I'll cite just one negative commentary (McNamara, 1996) and one positive (Neisser, 1996). For those interested in learning more about implicit memory, I recommend the edited volume by Reder (1996). A symposium on implicit learning, which clearly is related to the implicit-memory literature, builds on these two articles: Dienes and Berry (1997) and Neal and Hesketh (1997). Loftus (1993a) is guest editor for a symposium on eyewitness testimony, and in the same issue of *American Psychologist,* Loftus (1993b) writes a very informative article on the reality of repressed memories.

Using Your Knowledge of Cognition
Which Way Is Lincoln Looking?

Does simply seeing a stimulus over and over again ensure that it will enter your memory? Before looking at Figure 4.8, try drawing the head side of a penny, nickel, dime, and quarter. It might be fun to get some of your friends to try this task too. Were your drawings and those of your friends accurate? If you're like most people, you probably found numerous errors in your depiction of the coins.

Rubin and Kontis (1983) asked their subjects to do this task. Figure 4.8a shows how the coins actually appear; Figure 4.8b shows how the subjects typically drew the coins. If you look at the mistakes in the drawings, you'll see that the subjects make the same kind of errors in drawing each of the coins: all the heads are drawn as facing the left; this orientation is generally true to the actual coins, except that Lincoln faces to

Figure 4.8 *(a)* Actual coins now in use. *(b)* Modal coins constructed from recall data. *Source:* From Rubin and Kontis, 1983.

Actual   Modal

Using Your Knowledge of Cognition

the right on the penny. Similarly, subjects seem to think that each American coin says "In God We Trust" at the top of the head side, but actually, only the penny shows this inscription there. For the rest of the coins, the "In God We Trust" inscription appears in various places on the coin's head side. Finally, subjects tend to remember each coin as listing its denomination ("Five Cents") at the bottom on the head side, but in fact no American coins have this feature. Rubin and Kontis (1983) suggest that Americans have a very strong coin schema, or general concept, about American coins. At retrieval time it is this schema that is accessed, and it tells us how coins "ought" to look. Rubin and Kontis (1983) checked this hypothesis by asking subjects to design hypothetical 20-cent coins. The subjects' designs corresponded almost exactly with their recollections of actual coins, suggesting that the schema, rather than the subjects' experience with the coins, was providing the information for retrieval.

Key Terms

Schema
Context
Depth of processing
Maintenance rehearsal
Elaborative rehearsal
Transfer-appropriate processing
Encoding specificity

Implicit memory
Explicit memory
Generation effect
Transfer-appropriate procedures
Autonoetic consciousness
Anoetic consciousness
Overwriting

Repressed memories
Fuzzy-trace memory theory
Gist
Power law
Log-log transformation

Organization of Knowledge

I n Chapters 5 and 6, we focus on knowledge—its description and structure. As you may have surmised, we have several ways of describing knowledge. These approaches can be broadly categorized as one of two types. First, we can describe a number of information-processing positions that are mostly symbolic. According to the symbolic view, my knowledge of Abraham Lincoln is stored in an abstract format that somehow organizes all the facts that I might produce about Lincoln, such as these:

1. Lincoln was president during the Civil War.
2. Lincoln wrote the Emancipation Proclamation.
3. Lincoln was from Illinois.
4. Lincoln was tall.

I could go on, but you get the idea. I really didn't look up any of these four facts that I just wrote about Lincoln. According to the symbolic view, to write these facts, my cognitive system was able to consult something like a mental mini-encyclopedia, in which the relevant information had already been collected and organized. The organization's format is symbolic, however, and that means the cognitive system is using some sort of code to store the information. And what does that code look like? Well, stay tuned—we'll explore that issue in Chapter 5.

One alternative to the idea of symbolic organization is **connectionism.** According to this view, we don't need to talk about a mysterious, abstract language into which the cognitive system's knowledge has been formatted. Rather, proponents of this view argue that the kinds of phenomena observed when people are asked to retrieve knowledge such as the four Lincoln facts above result directly from a brain style computation that is not abstract (or at least not very abstract). Instead of suggesting that knowledge is retrieved by looking something up in a mental encyclopedia, as the symbolic theorists have it, the connectionist view champions the idea that if a large-enough group of neural-like entities interact with each other even in very simple ways, then very complex patterns of information can be stored and retrieved in an organized way. We'll deal with that perspective in Chapter 6.

As you wend your way through these two chapters, be particularly mindful about two issues—representation and formalism. Briefly, representation has to do with the description we give to our knowledge: the properties of knowledge. For example, it's common to say that our knowledge is organized, but what, if any, are the principles behind that organization?

We've considered the formalism issue before, when we looked at the retrieval literature. There we examined models intended to explain retrieval as a rule-based system. Here we're looking at rules again. But this time we're not studying the rules governing retrieval; instead, we're looking at the rules that govern knowledge in general. How can we best characterize the operation of the knowledge that we have? What rules are being followed in acquisition, representation, retrieval, and use of knowledge?

Structure of Knowledge: A Symbolic Approach

Overview

The road I take to my university passes through some of the most productive farmland in the Midwest. In spring, when the farmers start to plant, quite a bit of heavy farm equipment appears, and I enjoy looking at it, especially the gigantic tractors. Sometimes I think it would be fun to ride on one of them. Once, I told a colleague so, and he agreed completely, saying that if he ever saw a sign advertising tractor rides for five dollars, he would be the first in line. Then my colleague, who commuted over the same road, asked if I had ever noticed a particularly huge tractor, the one with twelve wheels, which he said was his favorite. The machine, a Steiger, did indeed sit on a full dozen wheels: six on each axle, three on each side of the cab, each wheel's diameter being about 6 feet. I replied that I had seen it, and that it was one of my favorites too.

One recent morning dawned warm and humid, heralding spring, and I expected that it wouldn't be long before the farmers got busy. Sure enough, on the drive in I saw the Steiger, which I hadn't seen since fall, roaming through a field. And almost with the first sight of the tractor, a mental image of my colleague, who had taken a job at another school some years ago, popped into my mind. Although I had never made any conscious effort to associate him with a tractor, some part of my cognitive apparatus apparently did so anyway.

We usually take for granted the cognitive system's ability to associate two apparently unrelated stimuli, but a moment's thought will show you how remarkable this ability is. For example, a principal technique in psychoanalysis is *free association*. As practiced by Carl Gustav Jung, the analyst supplies a word and the analysand produces the first thing that enters his or her mind. This technique relies upon the apparently associative setup

in our minds, but there's more to it than that. Free association would hardly be a useful technique unless some associations were more or less expected and common, and others were unusual and perhaps deviant. In a sense, then, the success of free association depends upon some commonality of associations from person to person. If associations are produced by experiences, we must conclude that, even though you and I have had plenty of different experiences, we must have had enough similar experiences to generate the associations that we have in common. That people generate the same associations also suggests that they have organized their different experiences in similar ways. In other words, the organization that seems inherent in most people's free associations could indicate how their minds are organized.

This is the sort of analysis that is the foundation for the material we cover in this chapter. The position is that human knowledge must be organized somehow, and if this organization can be discovered, then it can be described and modeled. This modeling refers to one of the researcher's main preoccupations. Among the most important objectives for a cognitive theory of knowledge is creating a mathematical device, a formalism or model, whose performance seems to mimic the characteristics of human knowledge. We explore several such formalisms in this chapter.

*T*he Internal Lexicon

Cognitive psychologists who wish to demonstrate that human knowledge is organized face a difficult problem. Because this knowledge is inherently private and internal, we need a behavioral "window" through which we can see the underlying structure. What collectible data would show convincingly how our knowledge is structured?

One type of task cognitive psychologists use for this purpose is **lexical access.** If a dictionary is a book that defines words and describes how they are related to each other, then we can say that our lexicon is like a mental dictionary. And our position is that our lexicon, our knowledge of words, is inherently organized. Cognitive psychologists attempt to find out something about this organization by asking people questions about words and measuring the time needed to respond. If we vary the words in a systematic way, and see corresponding time differences in access, then we can infer something about the lexicon's organization.

Usually, studies such as those reported here require the subjects to make judgments about words that they must read. Sometimes students therefore believe that these studies can tell us something about how people read words. These studies really aren't about reading, though, because reading makes us interpret meaning constructed over an entire set of sentences. Here, our objective is not to learn how people read but how they organize knowledge.

Accessing the Internal Lexicon

Researchers have agreed on three enduring findings about lexical access. First, lexical units differ in their availability, which seems to be related to the frequency with which the item appears or is used. Second, recent presentation of an item speeds subsequent access, and this phenomenon, known as **repetition priming,** can be observed for lexical elements that are infrequently presented, as well as for more common ones. Finally, lexical items are made more accessible by calling up semantically related elements.

Although such findings underpin semantic memory, several researchers have wondered exactly how the lexicon is organized, building on these findings. First, some researchers (Salasoo, Shiffrin, & Feustel, 1985; Ratcliff, Hockley, & McKoon, 1985) maintain that episodic as well as semantic memory may be involved in many lexical access tasks. Another controversy questions how context influences our access to the lexicon; some researchers maintain that the lexicon itself is relatively uninfluenced by semantic context. That is, our conceptual knowledge's organization is relatively impervious or insensitive to the context in which lexical access is taking place. This view is perhaps most clearly identified with Fodor's (1983) "modularity" approach, which holds that the lexicon is "encapsulated" and therefore resistant to context effects. Other theorists (Glucksberg, Kreuz, & Rho, 1986; Wright & Garrett, 1984) maintain just the opposite, stating that the lexicon itself, and therefore what you get when you access it, is heavily influenced by events occurring at other levels in linguistic processing, such as the syntax used in the prompting or priming sentence, or the theme established by a group of related sentences.

Disagreements aside, most cognitivists seem satisfied that the lexical-access paradigm remains a satisfactory way to describe the relationship among elements in our conceptual knowledge.

Semantic Priming

When a lexical item is called up by the cognitive system, this calling up facilitates (speeds up) the subsequent accessing of semantically related lexical items. This phenomenon, known as **semantic priming** (Foss, 1982), will come into play several times in this chapter, and so we need to spend time with it. A study by Meyer and Schvaneveldt (1971)

Table 5.1   Examples of the Pairs Used to Demonstrate Associative Pairing

Positive Pairs		Negative Pairs		
Unrelated	*Related*	*First Nonword*	*Second Nonword*	*Both Nonwords*
Nurse	Bread	Plame	Wine	Plame
Butter	Butter	Wine	Plame	Reab
940 msec	855 msec	904 msec	1087 msec	884 msec

Source: From Meyer and Schvaneveldt, 1971.

illustrates the effect. (This study is also discussed in Chapter 1.) Subjects were presented pairs of elements, and were to judge as quickly as possible whether both elements in the pair were words. If both were words, they were supposed to respond yes. If either of the elements was a nonword, they were told to respond no. Several kinds of trials were used. On positive trials, both elements were words, and some of these words were highly associated. On other positive trials, the words were unrelated. On negative trials, one or both elements were nonwords. Table 5.1 shows some examples of these trials and the subjects' reaction times.

Response times in the negative trials seem to indicate that the subjects read the top element and made a decision about it before reading the second element. The subjects decided faster when the nonword was the top element. The positive trials demonstrate the effects of semantic priming. When the words were strongly associated, the subjects could read and respond much more quickly than with unrelated words. This effect wasn't produced by any quality inherent in the words themselves—*nurse* isn't more difficult to read, nor is it less common than *bread*. The time difference was apparently produced by the relationship between *bread* and *butter.*

As you can see, these two lexical items share a semantic or conceptual relationship. Meyer and Schvaneveldt's findings suggest that when the cognitive system retrieves a lexical item, it also brings into a state of heightened accessibility other lexical items that are semantically or conceptually related to the initial one.

These effects were explored in a study by Ratcliff and McKoon (1981). Their subjects memorized sentences such as "The doctor hated the book." Then they were given a word-recognition task with a series of nouns and had to determine if the noun had been used in any of the memorized sentences. If the noun *doctor* appeared, the subjects were instructed to say yes. Prior to being presented a previously studied noun such as *doctor,* the subjects were sometimes given a priming noun that had come from the same previously studied sentence (here, "book" would be the priming noun). When they were first given a priming noun, their reaction time to its sentence-mate noun was lowered by approximately 40 msec compared with their performance when the noun was given without a priming stimulus. Let's think about what this finding means. In the Meyer and Schvaneveldt study we saw that established pairs of words such as *bread* and *butter* will produce semantic priming. In the Ratcliff and

Figure 5.1 Difference between primed and control conditions as a function of the interval between priming word and target word. *Source:* Copyright 1981 by the American Psychological Association. Adapted by permission of the publisher and author.

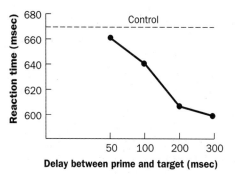

McKoon (1981) study we see that such priming effects can be shown for words that have been linked only in the laboratory. In other words, the words don't have to be "really" semantically related. If we provide the subject with the necessary experiences, his or her cognitive system apparently will make the necessary associations. Ratcliff and McKoon went on to look at the effects of various delays between the priming word and the previously studied target word. That is, the priming word sometimes appeared 50 msec before the target, whereas at other times the delay between the two stimuli was as great as 300 msec. Figure 5.1 shows how delay affected reaction time; here reaction time means the time the subjects took to respond to the target word. This is a very interesting effect. The reaction time grew shorter as the delay between the stimuli was increased. This finding means that the greatest effects of semantic priming do not occur immediately. Rather, they seem to build over at least 300 msec.

In one of the more complex and thorough investigations of the priming phenomenon, Neely (1977) studied the effects of semantic priming on a lexical-decision task. Subjects were given strings of letters, and were to determine as quickly as possible whether the string was a word. In Neely's version of this task, the subjects were given a prompt anticipating the letter string, and the relationship between prompt and target string interests us. In one test, Neely told the subjects that if the target string was indeed a word, it would be an example of the type suggested by the prompt. Thus, if the prompt was BIRD, then if the target string was a word, it might be "robin," or some other bird name. In another condition, the subjects were told to expect a categorical shift between the prompt and the target. That is, they might see the categorical prompt BODY, which was their signal to expect a shift to a target representing part of a building, such as "door." Conversely, they might see the categorical prompt BUILDING, which was their clue to expect a target representing a body part, such as "arm." Now things get really interesting. Although the subjects were told to expect a shift in these conditions, sometimes the shift did not occur. That is, the subject might see the prompt BODY and then a letter string that really was a body part, such as "leg." Finally, the subjects were sometimes told to expect a shift, and the shift did indeed take place. But instead of going to the expected category, as from BUILDING to body part and vice versa, it went to an unexpected category, as from BODY to BIRD.

Before we look at the findings, let's think about what might happen. First, if the subjects are given a prompt such as BIRD and then are actually given a letter string representing a kind of bird, we'd expect the prompt to show a priming or facilitative effect. That is, the subjects who see such a prompt should, as a result of semantic priming, be able to identify the letter string as a word faster than those subjects who have not seen a prompt. For subjects who are given a prompt such as BIRD and are *not* told to expect any category shift, we might expect that if the letter string is a word not drawn from the appropriate category, then it should take the subjects longer to recognize the string as a word. That is, if you are given BIRD and, expecting a bird, you actually get a string such as "arm," it should take you longer to identify the string than if you had no prompt at all. We call this an inhibiting effect of the prompt. This reasoning holds for the "shift" conditions too: If you got a BUILDING prompt, and then a letter string representing a body part, such as "leg," we'd expect to see a facilitative effect from the prompt because you'd been told to expect a shift. But an interesting question is what might happen if we prompt you with BUILDING and the expected shift does *not* occur: You actually see a letter string representing a building part such as "window." If you had not been in the shift condition, we'd expect such a prompt to have a facilitative effect on reaction time because a window really is part of a building. But, because you are in a shift condition, and because the shift does not occur, we'd expect to see an inhibitory effect from the prompt. What happens? Do the two effects, facilitative and inhibitory, cancel each other out? We'll find out in a minute.

Neely had one other variable that we need to discuss. Along with the other conditions already described, Neely varied the time that elapsed between presentation of the prompt and presentation of the letter string in the lexical-decision task. The latency between these two presentations is referred to as **stimulus onset asynchrony, or SOA.** That is, if a 100-msec latency came between presentation of prompt and letter string, then we call this a 100-msec SOA.

Figure 5.2 shows the Neely study findings. Looking first at the left-hand side, we see that the expected priming effects did occur: When subjects were prompted with BIRD, a facilitative effect altered recognition of letter strings such as "robin." Moreover, the longer the SOA, the stronger the facilitative effect, an effect we have also seen in the Ratcliff and McKoon (1981) study. When the subject was not expecting a shift, the prompt BIRD inhibited lexical decisions about unexpected elements such as "arm," and this inhibitory effect also got stronger with longer SOA. Now turning to the right-hand side of Figure 5.2, we see that a prompt such as BODY did facilitate a word such as "door," as long as the subjects were told to expect a shift from the body-part category to the building-part category. When the shift went to a word from an unexpected category, however, such as "sparrow," we see an inhibitory effect by the prompt BODY, even though subjects were expecting to shift categories. This finding means that simply telling the subjects to expect a category shift does not prime all the lexical items in every other category—indeed, how could it? Rather, prompting a category while telling subjects to expect a shift presumably primes only lexical items in the category to which the subjects expect to shift. Now, let's consider the last trial, in which the subject is given a prompt such as BODY, told to expect a category shift, and then sees a letter string that really is a body part, such as "heart." Here we see that the subject's cognitive/neural system temporarily overrides the category-shift

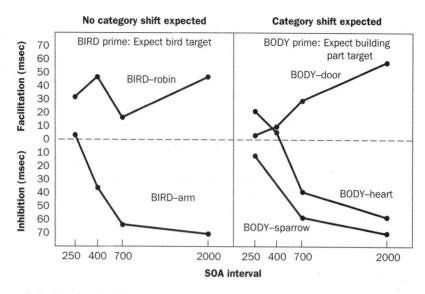

Figure 5.2   Reaction time (RT) to lexical-decision targets. In the left half, subjects saw a prime and did not expect a shift in category; sample stimuli are BIRD—robin for a relevant prime, and BIRD—arm for an irrelevant prime. In the right half, subjects expected the target to come from the building-part category if they saw BODY as a prime, and from the body-part category if they saw BUILDING as a prime. When the shift in category occurred as expected, the RT was facilitated at longer stimulus onset asynchrony (SOA). When the expected shift did not occur, facilitation came when the prime was relevant (BODY-heart). Inhibition occurred when the shift was completely unexpected (BODY-sparrow). *Source:* From Neely, 1977.

instruction. At the briefest SOA (250 msec), such as BODY prompt does facilitate a body-part letter string such as "heart," even though the subject has been instructed to expect a category shift. At longer SOAs, however, this facilitative effect is no longer seen, and in fact the prompt has an inhibitory effect that is similar to the other unexpected category shift. Here we seem to see an interaction between some conscious and some automatic cognitive processing. At the automatic level, subjects know that "heart" is a body part, and at short SOAs this automatic, unconscious processing is likely to occur. When the subjects are given two full seconds to think about the prompt BODY, however, they probably are consciously ready to look for a word in the expected shift category, building parts. Probably this is the conscious expectation that must be overcome for these subjects to recognize that "heart" is indeed a word, even though it does not come from the category they expected.

Repetition Priming   Another way to use the lexical-access phenomenon to show that knowledge is organized comes from studies of repetition priming. Typically, that technique involves a two-stage procedure (Ratcliff & McKoon, 1997). In the first phase, the subject studies a word list. In the second, the subject attempts to identify words presented tachistoscopically for very brief periods. The time is so brief that the subject cannot simply "read" the word and thus identify it. The usual finding is that subjects are more likely to correctly identify words that were studied than new words, and the usual interpretation is that some aspects of the word's representation activated at study time remain active at test time, helping correct identification.

This analysis suggests that a word's representation in the lexicon consists of several more or less independent components. Several phenomena bear witness to this idea. As we have seen, a lexical-access task taps into the word's meaning, or semantic representation, and this activation of the word's meaning can facilitate recognition of semantically related words. Thus the semantic aspects of a word's representation apparently remain active for a time—and that's one component in the word's representation. Repetition priming doesn't depend on semantic priming, however. Rather than activate some aspects in a word's representation of meaning, repetition priming shows that additional aspects of the word are activated by encountering it. Which aspects beyond the semantic ones remain active? Well, components of the word's sound or appearance might remain active.

It is the second of these components that seems to be playing a role in a phenomenon known as the **bias effect** in repetition priming (Ratcliff, McKoon, & Verwoerd, 1989). In this paradigm the subject studies a word list, as usual. At test time a target word is presented ultra-briefly. Then the subject is shown two words, and this time the presentation is long enough for the subject to read each word. The task is to decide which of the two was the briefly flashed target. Suppose the word "died" is one that the subject studies, and it is also the briefly flashed target in one trial. If we then show the subject two words, "died" and "lied," the subject is more likely to choose "died" over "lied," and this is the correct response, because "died" is in fact the word that was flashed. But something funny happens when "lied" is the one that had been studied. Now when the target is "died," subjects show a tendency to choose "lied" over "died," an incorrect response in this trial. The subject seems biased to choose studied words, at least in the presence of similar words (Ratcliff & McKoon, 1997).

Realize though, that the bias effect occurs only when the choice words are visually similar, as "died" and "lied" surely are. Suppose the subject studies the word "died," and the target is "died," and then the subject sees the choices "died" and "sofa." Then prior study of the target doesn't really help; the subject is just as likely to correctly recognize that the target was "died" regardless of whether "died" was studied in the study phase. Furthermore, if "sofa" had been the word studied and "died" had been the target word, the subject given the choices "died" and "sofa" is not more likely to incorrectly choose sofa than is a subject who had not studied that word. The latter finding suggests that the subject's choice of previously studied words is not automatic: The bias effect seems to occur only when the target is similar to a studied word, and in the forced-choice decision phase the subject is given words similar to each other.

One way of explaining the bias effect may involve the subject's use of an explicit strategy. When the choice words are similar to each other, it may cue the subject to consciously try to think back to the presentation of the studied words. If so, Ratcliff and McKoon (1997) reasoned, it should be possible to gauge such a strategy's effects by experimentally manipulating the conditions under which the strategy would be used. Suppose you were a subject in a repetition-priming study. If the similarity of choice words cued you to think back to the words you had studied, and on most trials in the study you were given similar choice words (such as "died" and "lied"), then you would probably use that strategy a lot. On the other hand, if you seldom encountered similar choice words (so that most of the time you were choosing between dissimilar words such as "died" and "sofa"), then chances are you would not use that strategy much, and the bias effect might go away for you—even in the few trials in which similar choice words were presented. This was the logic Ratcliff and McKoon employed. For one of their two groups of subjects, on 80% of the trials the choices were similar, and for the other 20% of the trials, they had dissimilar words to choose between. These proportions were reversed for the second group of subjects. Table 5.2 shows the percentage of correct responses on trials in which the subjects had studied the target word or the distractor, or had studied neither word.

We'll spend time analyzing Table 5.2, but before we do, can you find the bias effect on your own? It shows up very clearly in at least two places. Consider first the situation in which 80% of the trials feature similar alternatives (the top panel). When the target had been studied, the subjects were correct in 85% of those trials. But when the distractor word had been studied, they were significantly less likely to choose correctly on those trials—only 66% of the time. Concretely, when "died" was studied and "died" was the target, the subjects chose "died" over "lied" 85% of the time. But when "lied" was studied and "died" was the target, the subjects correctly chose "died" only 66% of the time. The other 34% of the time they chose "lied"—the word they had studied; that's the bias effect. Notice that the effect also occurs in the bottom panel in Table 5.2. Even when the proportion of trials that have similar alternatives is only .20 (which means that most of the time the subjects are choosing between words such as "died" and "sofa"), we see a similar fall-off in percentage correct from the target-studied to distractor-studied columns when the choice words are similar—and that's the bias effect operating again.

Which component in the word's representation seems to stay active and produce the bias effect? It may be the word's appearance, specifically its "outline." For example,

Table 5.2   Probability Correct in Ratcliff & McKoon Experiment

Similarity Condition	Study Condition		
	Target Studied	*Distractor Studied*	*Neither Studied*
Proportion of similar alternatives = .8			
Similar (*died* vs. *lied*)			
All responses	.85	.66	.75
Dissimilar (*died* vs. *sofa*)			
All responses	.83	.88	.87
Proportion of similar alternatives = .2			
Similar (*died* vs. *lied*)			
All responses	.74	.51	.62
Dissimilar (*died* vs. *sofa*)			
All responses	.78	.77	.79

Source: From Ratcliff and McKoon, 1997.

"died" and "lied," as whole words, have similar contours, with only the loop of the initial *d* in "died" to distinguish them. Similarly, it's possible to produce bias effects with other pairs such as "data" and "date" that share overall contours. This outline of the word, which is also part of our lexical knowledge, apparently remains active once it has been studied, and at test time, people are significantly more likely to get words with similar contours confused with each other, compared to words that do not have the same overall shape.

Symbolic-Network Models of Knowledge

In the preceding section we saw that reaction times to a specific word in a lexical-decision task can be shortened by first prompting the subject with a semantically related word. We also saw that we can make some inferences about the subject's underlying knowledge structure from the pattern of reaction times that we observe. In this section we expand these findings as we attempt to construct models that can represent these knowledge structures. A complete and accurate model of such structures would be equivalent to a theory about our knowledge itself.

Cognitive psychologists working in this subject are likely to build formal models to depict our knowledge structures (SAM, which we've already studied, is a formal model). Formal models are mathematically based and usually are implemented as computer programs; they can be contrasted with a narrative or verbal approach to theory building. The idea in such a formal model approach is to mimic successfully, or "capture" as many phenomena in human knowledge organization and retrieval as possible in the computer implementation.

One extensively used type of formal model is the symbolic network. **Network models** are so named because they specify that the individual elements in our knowledge occur in a patterned array of associations. Figure 5.3 shows a tiny portion in a hypothetical symbolic-network model.

Although Figure 5.3 may give you the impression that the elements of knowledge are just words, strictly speaking they are not. For example, in Figure 5.3 the word *canary* symbolically represents our concept or knowledge about a canary, and this symbolism applies to the other elements in the figure too. Concepts in symbolic-network models are generally referred to as **nodes** (Figure 5.3 shows a canary node and a bird node). Nodes are shown here connected to one another by arrows. Again, this is simply a convention to suggest possible associations between the concepts. Figure 5.3 shows that *canary* and *bird* are concepts that are associated in a specific way. A canary is a member of a higher, more general category called *bird*. We use the expression "superordinate" category to describe this relationship, which is denoted by the arrow "*Isa*." Although Figure 5.3 specifies the canary node as having only one *Isa* relation,

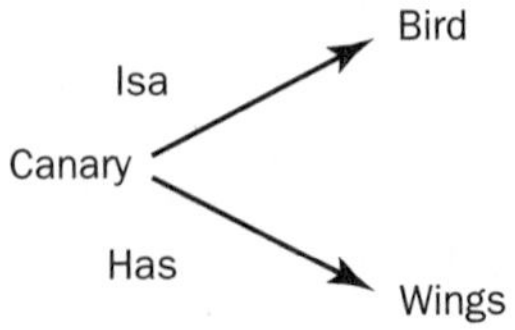

Figure 5.3 A small part of a symbolic-network model.

it could have others. Similarly, the *has* relationship depicts a property of the canary node, but this is not the only property that could be depicted. Notice that the direction of the arrowheads sometimes has theoretical significance in these models, especially in some of the earlier versions that we start with. In other words, the association between *canary* and *bird* can be depicted with an *Isa* linkage, but the relationship between *bird* and *canary* cannot be depicted in that way.

Assumptions in Symbolic-Network Models

One assumption generally made in network models is that the activity we call "searching our memories" is analogous to a search among the model's nodes. In this instance the search refers to a kind of metaphorical movement among the model's nodes, in the direction specified by the arrowhead. This search is considered to proceed node by node—that is, serially—as an unspecified cognitive process that accesses the node and reads out the knowledge there. If that knowledge enables us to answer a specified question, then the search stops. Otherwise, it continues until we find the answer or give up.

Typically, network models assume that the associations constrain the extent or scope of the search. Although this point will be clearer when we look at some specific models, for now we can say that the type of the association is usually assumed to govern the kind of search. Also realize that these models are considered representations of knowledge that cannot be completely expressed verbally. Although all the models we'll look at seem to consist of words and arrows, be aware that the nodes are supposed to represent concepts rather than words. The graphic depictions in these pages are just that: representations (not copies) of mental events that surely must be more complex than words alone.

Finally, most network models make a **type–token distinction.** Broadly speaking, this distinction refers to the differentiation we usually make between general categories (types) and particular, familiar examples drawn from that category (tokens). These relationships are expressed in Figure 5.4.

I know that bikes are two-wheeled vehicles, usually designed to carry only one or two people. This knowledge is semantic. Also, I know that my bike **isa** bike; it's blue and has a 27-inch frame to accommodate my long legs. You wouldn't have known this

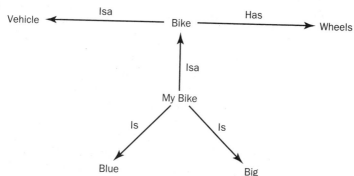

Figure 5.4 Episodic and semantic knowledge in semantic memory.

fact, because this knowledge about my bike is episodic. In other words, the type–token distinction affords the theorist a way of separating semantic from episodic knowledge. Stored at the type nodes are the facts that are true about that category. The facts define the category and consequently are context-free. Stored at the token nodes are facts that are true for that individual. This knowledge is context-dependent and consequently can be distorted, bypassed in the search, or even, as we saw in the Loftus and Palmer (1974) study in Chapter 4, overwritten by later episodic facts. If our objective is to construct a theory of conceptual knowledge, why bother incorporating episodic knowledge into the model?

To answer this question, we need to remind ourselves about the findings in the Hannigan et al. (1980) study. You'll recall their demonstrating that both episodic and semantic memory seem to be involved in almost every act of retrieval from permanent memory. This finding brings us to a related point. People typically use episodic memory as a basis for inference when semantic knowledge is lacking. An example may help clarify this practice. Suppose I were to ask you, "Could a car's battery fail on a hot summer day?" This question involves technical knowledge about battery properties and their relationship to temperature changes. You could get this information from a book, and you might be able to answer without ever having personal experience with car batteries. Because most of us don't possess this knowledge, though, we think about all the car-battery failures we're familiar with. No doubt most, perhaps all, have taken place in wintertime, and so we're inclined to answer no to the original question. To come up with this answer, we've had to search among the token nodes dealing with battery failures to make a logical generalization about what must be true for the type nodes as well. Because such inferences occur routinely, any theory of knowledge would have difficulty predicting some responses if it failed to provide for episodic knowledge. Having examined these general considerations about network models, let's turn to a specific case.

Teachable-Language Comprehender

One of the earliest network models, **Teachable-Language Comprehender (TLC)**, is based on a doctoral dissertation by R. Quillian (1968). Originally, Quillian focused on language rather than on organization of knowledge, and the model was designed to depict some rudimentary comprehension of language. Collins and Quillian (1969) made some modifications and a few simplifying assumptions to create a model of semantic knowledge that could be tested empirically. No one pretends that TLC is a state-of-the-art model; it isn't. From a pedagogical standpoint, however, TLC gives us a good place to get started. Its assumptions have been used in many other models, and its computational mechanisms are accessible for most people taking their first course in cognition. As we'll see, its empirical findings have not all been supported over the past several decades, but I think you'll find something to learn even in its empirical shortcomings.

Assumptions in TLC Part of TLC's network is shown in Figure 5.5. The concepts or nodes each have two kinds of relations. First, each node is related superordinately to some other node, which determines category membership. Although it isn't shown in

Figure 5.5 Memory structure assumed in TLC. One part of the semantic network for animals is depicted. *Source:* After Collins & Quillian, 1969.

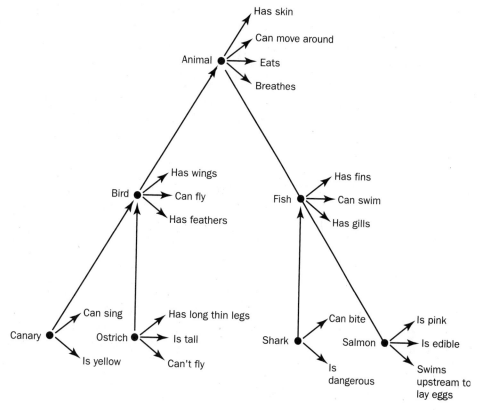

Figure 5.5, the superordinate characteristic expresses the *isa* relationship. For example, a canary is a kind of bird, which in turn is a kind of animal. Second, each node has one or more properties that express the *has* relation. A shark *has* the property *can bite*.

Also assumed in TLC is that semantic knowledge can be expressed in the sort of hierarchic display shown in Figure 5.5. That is, canaries and ostriches are organized by the more general and more inclusive category BIRD. Birds and fish in turn are characterized by the more general category ANIMAL. In TLC it is also assumed that the cognitive system is characterized by *cognitive economy.* You know that nearly all animals have skin, but this fact is mentioned in TLC only once: at the highest—that is, the most general—level. Collins and Quillian designed this model to be stored in a computer and were careful not to tie up too much of the computer's memory by repeatedly storing general animal facts with each specific animal. They reasoned, however, that the cognitive system must have similar storage constraints, and consequently, cognitive economy seemed a plausible assumption.

Also assumed in TLC is that access to knowledge is accomplished by an **intersection search.** This type of search specifies that the search begins from specific nodes and fans out from them. The fanning out is in parallel, meaning that cognitive processes scan all the nodes associated with the entry nodes at the same time. The search is also assumed to have unlimited energy, meaning that the rate of search is not slowed by the number of associations emanating from any one node. In other words, if the cognitive process fans out to three nodes from the entry node, it accomplishes this procedure in the same time that fanning out to only one node would take. With each node accessed in the search, the scanning processor leaves an indicator pointing to (*flagging*) the node where the search originated. If the search processes, which have begun their fanning out from different nodes, ever meet one another during the search, an intersection is then recorded. When an intersection is discovered, cognitive processes check all the flagged nodes until they determine the pathway linking the nodes from which the search originally began. Once this pathway is determined, TLC can use its inference programs to determine if it indeed "knows" that fact.

Let's consider an example. Suppose we give TLC a statement—"A shark is an animal"—and ask it to verify if this statement is true. The search begins from the *shark* and *animal* nodes and fans out from there. At *fish,* the search processes will intersect, and the pathway from *shark* to *animal* will then be evaluated. Here the pathway goes from one node to a superordinate node to another superordinate node, and so TLC would say yes to the statement.

Empirical Findings by TLC Although the intersection search is assumed to take place in parallel, it nevertheless requires time to move the search from node to node. Consequently, the greater the semantic distance between the two originating nodes, the more time TLC requires to verify the sentence.

Consider these sentences from TLC's perspective:

S0: A canary is a canary.
S1: A canary is a bird.
S2: A canary is an animal.

For S0, little time should be required to verify the sentence, because the search processes should intersect quickly, starting as they do from the same place. For S2, however, the search processes have to fan out across two levels, and so we would predict that more time would be required to verify this sentence. These three sentences deal with superordinate relationships, but we would have the same expectation for property relationships. Consider these sentences:

P0: A canary is yellow.
P1: A canary can fly.
P2: A canary has skin.

For P2, the search processes have to fan across two levels. If the mechanism Quillian and Collins propose accurately depicts what goes on when our knowledge is searched, then subjects should require more time to verify P2 than P1 or P0.

These predictions were tested in a study giving a large group of subjects simple sentences whose truth or falsity had to be determined as quickly as possible. They were given an equal number of true and false sentences. Figure 5.6 depicts the findings. Notice that humans performed in a way that was consistent with the theory, lending support to the notion that permanent memory is searched as TLC suggests.

In the tidal wave of research these findings generated, however, some problems were also washed ashore. First, Rips, Shoben, and Smith (1973) found that some superordinate relationships are verified faster than others. Consider these sentences:

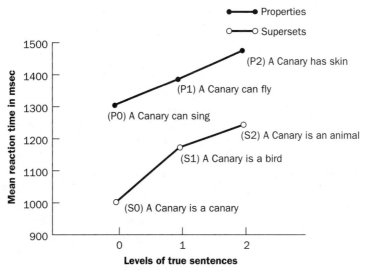

Figure 5.6 The results of Collins and Quillian's (1969) sentence-verification experiment. The data depicted are for true responses only, showing mean reaction time (RT) as a function of the number of levels in the hierarchy that TLC assumes needs to be searched. The sentences shown are only examples, because many sentences were used. Notice that RT increases systematically as the number of levels increases. *Source:* After Collins & Quillian, 1969.

A dog is a mammal.
A dog is an animal.

Collins and Quillian would predict that the first sentence should be verified faster than the second because they assume that semantic knowledge is hierarchically organized. Because mammals are nested (subordinate) within the animal classification, the search processes should intersect sooner when verifying the first sentence. Rips et al. (1973) demonstrated, however, that the second sentence is verified faster.

Now consider these sentences:

A peach is a fruit.
A watermelon is a fruit.

Each sentence mentions a perfectly good example of a fruit, and each example would be nested one level below *fruit* in TLC's knowledge structure. On these grounds we shouldn't expect any consistent differences in verification times for these two sentences. But consistent differences are there: people verify the first sentence faster than they do the second (Smith, Shoben, & Rips, 1974). Why?

Each sentence does mention a perfectly good example of a fruit. Although people recognize that all fruits are equal in a sense, however, some fruits apparently are considered more typical of the category than others. The problem for TLC is that it's too simple to incorporate these effects, meaning that actual human knowledge has other, richer organizational principles than the limited hierarchic ones seen in TLC (McCloskey & Glucksberg, 1978).

Finally, the assumption of cognitive economy seems unwarranted. Recall that Collins and Quillian postulated that specific factual knowledge was stored only once—at the most general possible node. Thus the statement "A canary can sing" required less time to verify than the statement "A canary has skin." Because *skin* is stored only once—at the *animal* node—the search processes require time to fan out and record the intersection. Conrad (1972) questioned this claim, maintaining that the reason for the faster reaction times for the first sentence was simply that the concept *canary* is more strongly associated with the concept *can sing* than it is with the concept *has skin*.

Conrad tested this idea by asking her subjects to describe a series of common nouns, such as *canary, bird,* and *animal.* She found large differences in the properties ascribed to particular nouns. Canaries were often described as being yellow but hardly ever as having skin. Conrad next computed a measure of the association strength based on the frequency-of-mention data she had collected. She then gave her subjects a sentence-verification task similar to the kind used by Quillian and Collins. She found that the reaction times were predictable from the association-strength measure, regardless of how many levels the subjects had apparently searched through. For example, subjects quickly verified statements such as "An orange is edible," even though these expressions are separated by at least one level in the hierarchy. Also, subjects required much time to verify statements whose terms were weakly associated, even when those terms were adjacent in TLC's hierarchy. Conrad's work was influential in closing the door on a pure and simple hierarchic model.

Spreading-Activation Model

As TLC's shortcomings became more widely recognized, Collins and Loftus (1975) developed an alternative model of conceptual knowledge that was not organized hierarchically. Instead, the notion of semantic distance, or semantic relatedness, was the organizing motif. Figure 5.7 shows a small part of their network. The lines connecting nodes indicate that an association connects those concepts. *Daffodils* are associated with *yellow,* which in turn is associated with *bananas. Bananas* and *daffodils,* though, are not associated.

The **spreading-activation model** includes two other assumptions about structure. First, the length of the line connecting two concepts is intended to have theoretical meaning. The shorter the line, the more closely associated the concepts. *Car* and *truck* are closely associated, but *yellow* and *bus* are weakly associated. Second, like TLC, the spreading-activation model assumes that superordinate relationships are labeled with an *isa* link. Thus, the linkage from *bus* to *vehicle* would be of this type. This model, however, represents an advance over TLC in that it also includes some *isnota* links. Thus the model can quickly determine that some strongly associated concepts are nevertheless not superordinate. This point is important. Consider what might take place if subjects were given this sentence:

A school is a bus.

Figure 5.7   A portion of the semantic-memory network proposed by the spreading-activation model. *Source:* From Collins & Loftus, 1975.

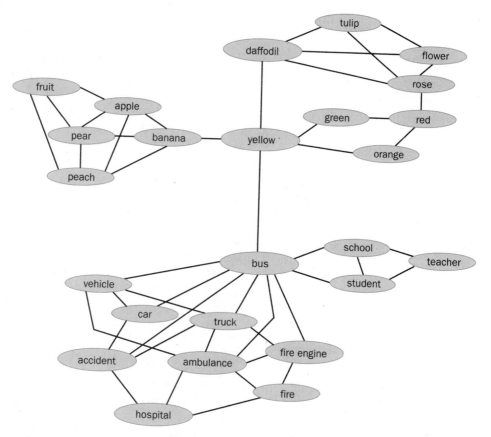

TLC would begin by carrying out a search beginning from the *school* and *bus* nodes, eventually intersecting at some hypothetical *things in the world* node, and finally deciding that the terms were not on a superordinate path. If TLC were a completely accurate model of human knowledge, we would predict that the subjects would take a lot of time before determining that this sentence was false. Although these terms are strongly associated, however, subjects are quick to refute the sentence, indicating that a complete search is probably not carried out. Collins and Loftus came up with **prestored knowledge** to describe such facts that do not require an extensive memory search. Some research (Smith, 1978) indicates that at least some of our knowledge is like this. Knowledge about some relations is stored directly in the network, obviating the need to scan our memories.

This notion of expert knowledge has vital implications, although fuller development is reserved for Chapter 12. Also, you probably know that prestored knowledge wasn't always prestored: small children don't know that a bat isn't a bird. The implication is that our knowledge's organization must be modifiable as people develop. The important point is that some memory processes must do more than simply search the structure of permanent memory in a somewhat passive way. Some processes must go to work on this structure, modifying it to incorporate new knowledge. That is, to be practical, Collins and Loftus must shoulder the burden of specifying which experiences produce the *isnota* link in semantic memory. This objective is not well done in this model. Later in this chapter we'll consider some proposals that accomplish this objective.

Beyond these assumptions about memory structure, the Collins and Loftus model makes some assumptions about the search process, one of which is particularly important. As nodes are searched, the knowledge stored therein undergoes a change in status. Specifically, the search activity is thought to activate searched nodes, meaning that the knowledge is brought into a state of heightened accessibility. Which nodes are activated depends on several factors, including strategic decisions by the person searching her own memory. Evidence suggests, however, that highly associated nodes are activated more or less involuntarily. Having activated one node, the spread of activation radiates outward along strong associative lines to make other nodes more accessible. How far the activation spreads is determined by several factors: strength of the initial activation, time since initial activation, and, of course, semantic distance between nodes all influence the resulting spread of activation. If an unusual or remote concept is the locus for the initial activation, not many other nodes will be activated. If, however, a concept at the center of a richly interwoven network is stimulated, many other nodes will be activated.

Time Course of Activation

One question raised by work on TLC and other spreading-activation models is the **time course of activation,** meaning the status of the node's activation, the resulting search processes, and so on, in reference to passage of time. If we see that it takes a typical subject 1300 or so msec to say "true" to a statement such as "A shark is a fish," we can next ask how many msec were required to activate the nodes, to spread the activation, to verify the connection, and so on. Strictly speaking, according to these models, the subject does not really know the answer in sentence-verification tasks until the search has been completed; that is, not until the "end" of the time course. Thus, according to the theories we have studied thus far, if we were to ask subjects for the answer after, let's say, 600 msec of processing time, their cognitive systems would be unable to answer—and they would simply have to guess. The implication is that we have no "partial" knowledge of the correct answer in sentence-verification tasks prior to the subject's actual answering.

But is this view accurate? Do we have to wait until the search is completed before we know anything about the correct answer? As an alternative, does information about the answer begin to accumulate as soon as we finish reading the stimulus? To answer this question, let's think about how a subject typically responds in sentence-verification tasks. All subjects make a speed–accuracy tradeoff, which varies from trial to trial in sentence-verification tasks such as those used in testing TLC. In general, subjects can be assumed to adopt a high accuracy criterion—they want to get the item right—and so speed is sacrificed. The subjects go as fast as they can without risking inaccuracy. On any trial, however, subjects can lower their accuracy criterion, perhaps from 100% down to 90% accuracy, presumably increasing speed and decreasing time to respond. As cognitive psychologists, our problem is that we don't know on which trials the subjects have lowered their criterion, and so, from these data, we can't begin to estimate how much partial knowledge the subjects have during the trial's time course, because we don't have under our control the subject's response timing. That is, in general, we don't control when the subject elects to respond.

Kounios et al. (1987; Kounios, 1996; Meyer et al., 1988) have, however, designed the **speed–accuracy decomposition technique,** which enables us to estimate the subject's partial knowledge at various points along the trial's time course. Kounios et al. gave the subjects a sentence-verification task, but they used two kinds of trials. The "regular" trial is the kind we're familiar with: the subject reads a sentence and responds as quickly as possible. In the second kind, the speed-stress or "response-signal" trial, a sentence is presented and the subject begins to process it. At some variable time after the stimulus, however, perhaps 400 or 600 msec, the subject hears a tone and is instructed to respond immediately after hearing it, with his or her "best answer" at that moment.

Although the equations and derivations needed to analyze the data are beyond our scope here, we can understand the logic that is used to compare the results from the two kinds of trials. Our objective is to mathematically derive two kinds of estimates. First, we estimate reaction-time distributions for guessing responses; that is, responses in which the subject was responding to the speed signal rather than waiting for processing to be completed (as one would in a "regular" trial). Second, we estimate accuracy in the speeded trials in which the subject is responding to the signal. By comparing the two estimates, we can compute a mathematical index that tells us how accurate the subject was at various 20-msec "slices" during the trial.

If we were to graph accuracy as a function of time course in a trial, what would the TLC model's prediction be? The answer is that the line depicting accuracy would be flat and low (close to 0% accuracy) during the first 1000 or so msec in the trial, and then accuracy would suddenly and dramatically increase to almost 100% near the end of the trial, as the subject got ready to respond. But when Kounios et al. did the experiment and computed accuracy as a function of time, they found that, in fact, accuracy was not flat and close to zero throughout the time course of the trial. In fact, accuracy increased steadily, and was increasing long before (if we can call many hundreds of milliseconds "long") the subject actually responded. What does this finding mean? It suggests that, at least in some trials, as in sentence-verification tasks, the time course of node activation and search is not all or none, as assumed in models like TLC. Instead, we now know that the subject doesn't have to wait until the search is completed before making a response that has at least a respectable chance of being correct.

ACT-R

The theory we are about to describe has been evolving for many years and so warrants a brief history. The "ACT" in ACT-R stands for adaptive control of thought, pronounced like the word "act." The expression has designated versions of an entire family of models developed over the past two decades by cognitive scientist John Anderson and his colleagues. In a 1976 book, Anderson described one of the model's most important early versions, ACT-E. A later, improved offspring, ACT* (pronounced "act-star"), appeared in 1983. ACT-R itself was given birth in books appearing in 1990 and 1993. The "R" in ACT-R stands for "rational," and in more recent work Anderson has argued strongly for a "rational level" in cognition, as well as for an accompanying analysis at this rational level. We'll discuss this analysis and its implications in due time.

The ACT family's early versions had many similarities to TLC and the other spreading-activation models that we've discussed. Thus, in ACT-E, nodes representing concepts could be in one of two states: active or inactive. Active nodes represented concepts, or parts of concepts, which had become accessible to the cognitive system. Once a node was activated, activation spread out to other connected nodes, changing them from inactive to active.

In ACT*, the activation mechanics were changed somewhat. Whereas earlier the linkages between nodes could be in only one of two states, now the linkages between concepts could be at different levels of activation. A light switch and a rheostat, or dimmer, can be seen as metaphors for the theory's early and later versions. In ACT-E, the node is like a light fixture, and its activation is controlled as a conventional light switch is: the light is either on or off. In ACT*, the node's activation can be turned up or down depending on the dimmer setting.

Organization of Knowledge in ACT-R

The development in the ACT family that was seen in both ACT-E and ACT* has continued in ACT-R, resulting in many new ideas on the organization of knowledge and its representation. ACT-R is further developed than ACT-E and ACT* in that it has different representations for procedural and declarative knowledge. If you think back to Chapter 1, you'll remember we distinguished between factlike knowledge that you have in your working memory (declarative knowledge) and the action knowledge that is used when you engage in a skill (procedural knowledge). ACT-R acknowledges these types of knowledge with two completely different formats for representing knowledge. Declarative knowledge is represented in ACT-R as "chunks," whereas procedural knowledge is represented by **production systems.**

Production Systems A production system consists of production rules, each of which can be expressed as an "if-then" rule, or, more formally, as a "condition-action" pair. The "if" part of the rule specifies the "conditions" that govern the rule's use. This could be an example of a production rule in a hypothetical system:

IF   it's raining
THEN   carry your umbrella with you

In other words, under the condition that the weather is rainy, then that's the time to bring along an umbrella. The number of conditions is not limited to one; it may often be greater than one. When the number is greater, then the rule applies only in progressively narrower situations, with the result that the action may be taken with less frequency. Consider this production rule:

IF   it's raining AND
        you have to park far from the office AND
        your raincoat is at the cleaners
THEN   carry your umbrella with you

For the action of umbrella carrying to be taken here, more conditions need to be met than for the preceding production rule. A person who followed the first rule might be seen carrying an umbrella quite a lot (every time it rains). But a person following the second rule may park as close as possible to the office on rainy days, turn up the raincoat collar, and simply run for it, hardly ever bothering with the umbrella.

Production systems are organized by their goals. A production system may have related goals, but at least one goal must be active at any one time, as we can see in the production system for addition shown in Table 5.3. The overall system goal is to arrive at the correct answer to a typical addition problem, and is broken down into subgoals, so that when all subgoals have been solved in a specified sequence, the overall problem will perforce be solved. Let's take a closer look at the first production rule mentioned, NEXT-COLUMN. The "condition" part of this production says that if "c1" is the rightmost column without an answer digit written

---

Table 5.3 Production Rules for Addition[a]

NEXT-COLUMN	
IF	the goal is to solve an addition problem
	and c1 is the rightmost column without an answer digit
THEN	set a subgoal to write out an answer in c1
PROCESS-COLUMN	
IF	the goal is to write out an answer in c1
	and d1 and d2 are the digits in that column
	and d3 is the sum of d1 and d2
THEN	set a subgoal to write out d3 in c1
WRITE-ANSWER-CARRY	
IF	the goal is to write out d1 in c1
	and there is an unprocessed carry in c1
	and d2 is the number after d1
THEN	change the goal to write out d2
	and mark the carry as processed
WRITE-ANSWER-LESS-THAN-TEN	
IF	the goal is to write out d1 in c1
	and there is no unprocessed carry in c1
	and d1 is less than 10
THEN	write out d1
	and the goal is satisfied
WRITE-ANSWER-GREATER-THAN-NINE	
IF	the goal is to write out d1 in c1
	and there is no unprocessed carry in c1
	and d1 is 10 or greater
	and d2 is the ones digit of d1
THEN	write out d2
	and write a carry in the next column
	and the goal is satisfied

Source: From Anderson, 1993.
Note: [a]c1, d1, d2, and d3 denote variables that can take on different values for different instantiations of each production.

under it, then the "action" part of the production says to set up a subgoal to add the rightmost column that doesn't have an answer. In this addition problem,

$$35$$
$$+46$$

we see that the rightmost column (5 + 6) has no answer written under it, and so finding this answer is our first subgoal. Now, where does the production system go from here? The next production rule PROCESS-COLUMN picks up where NEXT-COLUMN left off. The conditions in PROCESS-COLUMN say that if you want to write the sum of the digits in cl, then you must add them up and write the answer below the line. Notice that sums such as this could be greater than 9 (as this one is) or less than 10. If the sum of a column's digits is greater than 9, then the production system goes to the production rule named WRITE-ANSWER-GREATER-THAN-NINE. If a column sum is less than 10, then the system goes to a different production rule: WRITE-ANSWER-LESS-THAN-TEN.

The action that the production system takes from each specific production rule has a lot to do with the specific production rule that the system attempts to implement next, raising a general question: How does the production system determine the appropriate sequence for specific production rules? How does the system know which rule to apply next? The answer is that after the production system executes a specific production rule, it engages in *pattern matching* to determine which production should be executed next. In pattern matching, the system does two things. First it examines the content of working memory and records which parts of the problem have been solved and which still need to be solved. Then the system matches this current state to the production rules that would apply to the problem parts that still need to be completed. Thus the system considers all the "if" statements, the conditions, to see which ones are currently pertinent.

Sometimes more than one production rule can apply. Suppose it is currently raining, and you have these two production rules in your personal production system:

IF   it's raining
THEN   carry your umbrella
IF   it's raining
THEN   wear your raincoat

The conditions for both production rules are met, and so which production rule will be enacted? In other words, will you carry your umbrella or wear your raincoat, or do both? In such conditions, production rules have a *conflict-resolution* system to determine which of these two production rules will be executed. We have lots of ways to accomplish this choice. Sometimes each production rule is given a priority number, and if the conditions for two productions match at the same time, then the production with the higher priority is enacted. Sometimes the system "remembers" which action it took last time these two production rules were in conflict and executes the rule that it did *not* execute last time. In other words, sometimes the systems are designed to alternate between production rules when the conditions for two rules match. In the system's most complicated form, the conflict-resolution procedure may actually try to evaluate which production rule leads to the system's goal faster.

Two other important terms in production systems are "firing" and "cycle." When the action part of a production rule is enacted, we refer to the production as "firing." The sequence of steps from pattern matching, to conflict resolution, through firing is referred to as a "cycle" of activity.

Production systems represent cognitive skills, meaning that we probably will have little or no awareness of actually "running" the production system as we use it. It is true that the *content* of each production is deposited in working memory. And that means the production system content is declarative knowledge. As we solve an addition problem, we should be aware of what we are doing (because that represents the contents of the production system), but we may not have awareness, or be able to talk about, how we are solving the problem, because that represents the actual running of the production system.

Sources of Knowledge for Building Production Systems   In the preceding section, we introduced some of the production-systems terminology, and we described their operation. Now the question we must deal with is how such systems originate: What sort of information could be used for building a production system? One source is a technique known as *task analysis* (Anderson, 1993). To do a task analysis, the experimenter asks what knowledge, actions, and conditions for action are needed to carry out a task. We then write a program in the form of a production system for a specific task. Although this procedure may seem very open-ended, some principles are used in task analyses. First, if the system is to mimic human knowledge, the number of conditions to be matched for each production rule should be reasonable; that is, it should not exceed the number of conditions that a human could have active in working memory at any one time. Generally, this means a limit of three to five conditions for each production rule. A second principle specifies the complexity of the conditions mentioned in each production rule. Generally, most successful production systems do not have production rules that would require humans to make complicated inferences to see if the conditions match some situation in the real world. Most often, determining whether a situation matches the conditions of a production rule can be assessed by a simple observation. Bovair, Kieras, and Polson (1990) have found that these types of guidelines are sufficient to produce a good task analysis for such simple tasks as text editing.

Chunks in Declarative Memory   Production systems deposit their content in working memory, but ACT-R uses a different representation to describe the actual content of working and permanent memory. This representation has various equivalent names: the **chunk,** or the **working-memory element** (**WME,** pronounced wimee). Several aspects of chunks are important to know. First, a chunk can combine several stimuli, but only a limited number of stimuli can be combined in one chunk. ACT-R suggests that three or four elements can be represented by one chunk. Second, the chunk's elements are said to have "configural properties." Suppose I give you the numbers 1776 and ask you to store them. Now, because you have only four elements, you could store these numbers as one chunk, especially if you are familiar with American history. But once you store them as a chunk, shifting the elements around to different positions, such as 7617, would not be recognized as the same chunk that you had stored. When we say that a chunk has configural properties, we mean that the elements' relationship to each other within the chunk is important. Third, chunks can have a hierarchic relationship with each other: two separate chunks can themselves be chunked together to make a superchunk. And we may be able to take two superchunks and put them together to make a supersuperchunk. An example of this phenomenon appears in Chapter 3. Do you recall the runner who learned how to remember and recite random strings of digits up to eighty numbers long? If you go back to that discussion, you'll see that the runner became very skillful in devising a strategy that converted many of the groups of three or four digits into a chunk that might stand for a typical time that could be achieved in a running event.

A Representation for Chunks   We can probably find many ways of depicting cognitive structures that have the property of chunks; the representation chosen in ACT-R is not very difficult. Table 5.4 represents the chunks present at the start of the addition problem described above. Here are several useful points about this representation. First, the "name" for the chunk is the word that is not indented, such as "problem1" and "column0." We probably have no awareness about the "name" of the chunk. Second, beneath each chunk name are no more than three lines representing three features or elements in that chunk. These are the chunk's "content." For example, underneath "problem1" are the statements "isa numberarray" and "columns (column0, column1, column2)". Unlike the name of the chunk, we are aware of the chunk's content. The problem1 chunk says that after looking at the problem, in your working memory you should have the knowledge that this array of numbers represents an arithmetic problem, it consists of two columns of numbers, and the answer is currently unknown. The third important point is how the representation shows the hierarchic relationship between chunks. Notice that the prob-

---

Table 5.4   Schema Representation of the Problem:

$$35$$
$$+46$$

---

problem1
   isa numberarray
   columns (column0 column1 column2)
column0
   toprow blank
   bottomrow +
   answerrow blank
column1
   isa column
   toprow three
   bottomrow four
   answerrow blank
column2
   isa column
   toprow five
   bottomrow six
   answerrow blank

lem1 chunk has in its content the names of the other chunks. This is how this representation shows the hierarchic relationship of the superchunk (problem1) to the normal chunks (column0, column1, and so on). The chunk that is higher in the hierarchy holds the names of chunks that are lower in the hierarchy.

ACT-R in Action: The Navigation Studies

Now we can begin to show how ACT-R models human knowledge. The logical start is to gather information about how humans perform on a reasonably demanding problem. Anderson and colleagues designed several navigation tasks, one of which is depicted in Figure 5.8. In this task a subject looked at a computer screen showing the information in panel *a* and was asked to find a route from the point labeled "start" to the "destination" point. The screen also showed roads (shown as lines) over which the subject could drive a "car" to several intermediate locations. As you can see in Figure 5.8a, no direct road led from the start to the destination. When the subject arrived at an intermediate location, that location turned dark on the computer screen, and all the pathways radiating outward from it, not previously shown on the screen, suddenly became visible. Subjects could move from location to location by two means. First, they could "drive" a simulated car along one of the roads. A car moved across the computer screen at a .25 cm/sec rate. Because the screen was about 24 × 33 cm, you can see that the car moved quite slowly. This low speed was deliberately designed to make subjects think twice about where they were going. In other words, just as in real-world navigation, costs are attached to making wrong turns and other misjudgments. Besides driving a car to a destination, the subject could "walk." Walking was painfully slow; the subject's velocity across the screen was only one-tenth that of the car's speed; that is, .025 cm/sec. As you can imagine, most subjects decided to start walking only when they were quite close to the goal. Walking was necessary, however, because not every destination was reachable by car.

Figure 5.8 b, c, and d show a subject's progress as she attempted to find her way through this "progressive" map. As these panels show, the subject first drove to the location labeled "1." This is a reasonable move, for location 1 clearly is closer to the destination than are the other way points originally shown. As panel *b* indicates, however, no direct linkage leads from location 1 to the destination. Moreover, the only two pathways from location 1 take her either back to the starting point, or to another location that is almost as distant from the destination as the start. Now the subject could have started walking from location 1, but she decided to explore further, driving to location 2 in panel *c*. Here, the situation looked a little more promising. The subject now began to drive to the farthest point on this set of linkages, quite a bit closer to the destination than she previously occupied. In panel *d,* we can see that when the subject arrived at 3, a direct connection between that point and the destination became visible, enabling her to complete the journey. Notice also that a definite memory load was imposed on the subject in this task. Suppose we saw in panel *d* no direct connection between location 3 and the destination. Our subject might have decided to throw in the towel here by driving back to location 1 and walking from there. But from location 3, location 1 was no longer visible because no direct connection linked those two points. To get back to location 1, the subject would have had to retrieve her pathway.

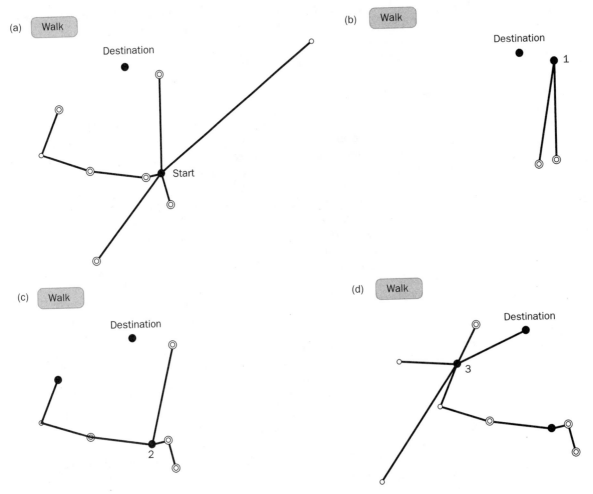

Figure 5.8   The various states observed by a student trying to navigate. *Source:* From Anderson, 1993.

Several types of maps were designed. Some had only fifteen intermediate locations; these were "simple" maps. "Complex" maps had thirty possible intermediate locations that the subject might drive or walk to. Obviously, not all fifteen or thirty points were on view all during the time the subject explored the map, and some locations were irrelevant to finding the solution path. Both simple and complex maps had several subtypes. "Easy" maps had a clear subgoal structure in which the subject's arrival at successive locations revealed routes that led progressively closer to the destination. "Long" maps had a similar feature, but the pathway to the goal was roundabout. On "walk" maps, the subject sometimes had to get out of the car and walk because no direct drivable pathway to the destination appeared. Finally, "backup" maps showed a pathway that led deceptively near, but not directly to, the destination. The subject here was faced with a "walk-or-explore" decision. The map shown in Figure 5.8 is of the simple backup type.

Table 5.5 Productions Involved in the Navigation Task

COMBINE-ROUTES

IF	the goal is to find a route from location1 to location2 and there is a route to location3 and location3 is closer to location2
THEN	take the route to location3 and plan farther from there.

DIRECT-ROUTE

IF	the goal is to find a route from location1 to location2 and there is a route from location1 to location2
THEN	take that route.

WALK

IF	the goal is to find a route from location1 to location2
THEN	walk

GIVE-UP

IF	the goal is to find a route from location1 to location2 and you are getting nowhere
THEN	give up.

Source: From Anderson, 1993.

Anderson and his coworkers next designed a production system to model the knowledge and action of humans on the navigation task. An English-language version of the production system is shown in Table 5.5. Actually, the last production shown in Table 5.5, Give-Up, was not available to the subjects in the study described here. The subjects *had* to find a solution path.

The production system has several interesting features. As you can see, it doesn't seem as complex (at least in overall number of productions) as the addition system that we looked at earlier. Does this simplicity mean the navigation task is not as complicated as addition? The answer is no, not necessarily. First, remember that the production system for navigation is a first approximation; it may become more complicated as deeper analysis is done on people in these types of tasks. Second, the number of productions is somewhat influenced by the number of conditions that have to be matched up before an action can be taken. It could be that a production system holds numerous productions whose conditions are hardly ever matched by stimuli in the real world, and so these productions would "fire" infrequently. Finally, much of a production system's complexity results from its conflict-resolution scheme. A production system with numerous productions might also include a straightforward conflict-resolution scheme that produced very little variation in the system's behavior or performance. On the other hand, a more elaborate resolution scheme might account for much of the complexity in the system's strategy.

Here the production system is designed to "look for" direct routes; these are considered first in this system. In other words, if you are at a location and a direct route lights up between you and the destination, then that's the route you want to take. As

Table 5.6   Summary of Behavior in Navigation Task: Average Number of Moves and Units of Distance (Simulation Averages in Parentheses)

	Simple (15-point)	*Complex (30-point)*
Easy	3.80 moves (3.83)	4.87 moves (5.33)
	28.2 cm (28.4)	25.1 cm (26.8)
Long	3.77 moves (3.50)	4.00 moves (4.00)
	33.4 cm (34.7)	26.3 cm (30.8)
Walk	3.87 moves (4.00)	6.4 moves (7.00)
	31.6 cm (31.4)	20.8 cm (21.0)
Backup	3.57 moves (3.00)	7.37 moves (6.50)
	25.5 cm (18.0)	42.7 cm (37.5)

Source: From Anderson, 1993.

might be expected, walking is considered last. Walking will always get you to your destination, but unless you are at a location that is quite close, it will probably require more time than driving. Between these, we have the "Combine-Routes" production, which looks for locations that are closer to the destination than the current location, evaluating most the closest locations favorably. Of course, you have no guarantee that when you arrive at such a location it will include a further route to the destination. But without actually knowing a direct route, and at the low walking speed, the system will usually try to build a route to the destination by exploring specific segments one at a time.

Now we come to the main question: Does ACT-R do a reasonable job of modeling human knowledge on this type of navigation task? The answer appears to be yes. Table 5.6 compares human performance with ACT-R when ACT-R was run on the navigation problems used in this study (ACT-R's performance is shown in parentheses). As this table shows, human performance and that of ACT-R correlate well both in number of moves taken to solve the problem ($r = .94$) and the distance traveled to get to the destination ($r = .83$). In comparing ACT-R's performance with the typical human, it's interesting that the only substantial difference between the two seemed to take place in the backup problems. Specifically, ACT-R solved both simple and complex backup problems in fewer moves and less distance than people did. What might this superiority mean? The difference between ACT-R and humans in these types of problems might suggest that if humans use something like a "Combine-Routes" production in their production systems, they may overvalue taking a route that gets them closer to the destination, at the expense of exploring further for a direct route. In other words, ACT-R was not as likely to fall for the "trick" in the backup problems as humans were.

The "R" in ACT-R

In this chapter we haven't spoken much about the "R" in ACT-R, the R that stands for rationality. But we'll try to partially redress that problem here. ACT-R's argument

Focus on Research

Repetition Priming—Now You Hear It

We have seen that the visual presentation of a word "primes"—that is, speeds up—recognition of related words and recognition of itself in a lexical-decision task. Compared to visual presentations, a lot less is known about the repetition-priming effects of auditory presentations of words in lexical-decision tasks, but the literature suggests intriguing differences compared to visual presentations.

Mimura, Werfaellie, and Milberg (1997) presented to their subjects one- or two-syllable words and one- or two-syllable nonwords that sounded like possible English words. The subjects heard the digitally recorded stimuli played over headphones; they were to decide, as quickly as possible, if the stimulus heard was an actual word or a nonword. Each trial began 2 seconds after the subject's response on the preceding trial. Mimura et al. systematically varied the number of stimuli that might be heard between two successive presentations of a word or a nonword. The number of stimuli intervening between two presentations of the same stimulus is known as its "lag." In other words, if a

stimulus was repeated with one other different stimulus between its two presentations, then we might refer to that as a "lag 1" trial. Mimura et al. used lags of 0, 1, 4, or 8 stimuli in their study. A zero lag means that no stimuli intervened between the two presentations of a word or nonword. The study addresses several issues. First, how long (in "lags") does the auditory presentation continue to have a priming effect? Second, do nonwords have an auditory priming effect, and does it have the same duration as that of words?

Figure 5.9 shows the findings in their study. As you can see, the top line in each panel shows the subject's initial reaction time (RT) to words and nonwords in the lexical-decision task. Theoretically, this top line should be a straight line in each panel, because lag cannot influence the subject's RT on its initial presentation. And the top line is pretty close to being straight. When we look at the lower line, which shows the subject's RT in response to the second presentation of the stimulus, we should expect to see any priming effects that are going to occur.

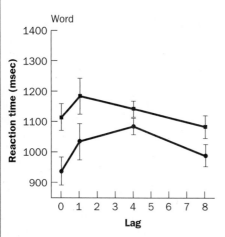
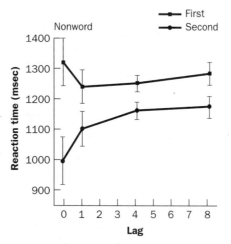

Figure 5.9   Mean reaction time to words and nonwords as a function of lag and presentation. *Source:* From Mimura et al., 1997.

Focus on Research (continued)

The difference between the two lines, measured in msec, represents the extent of priming. In other words, a big difference between the two lines in either panel means a substantial amount of priming was going on. As Figure 5.9 shows, the line depicting the subject's RT to the second presentation of the stimulus is always lower (meaning faster) than RT to the initial presentation. Even out to lag 8, the typical subject is still faster in response to the second presentation of the stimulus than to the first, and this effect is observed for both words and nonwords. As you may have guessed, the bigger effects are at the shorter lags. And there too we see the big difference between processing words and nonwords. For words, the size of the priming effect is about the same at lag 0 and lag 1. But this similarity does not apply to nonwords. For nonwords the priming effect at lag 0 is substantially larger than at lag 1. What might this difference mean? Mimura et

al. suggest that as we try to form a stable of representations of incoming auditory information, nonword phonological and acoustic properties are more readily accessible for nonwords than for words. As soon as a nonword has been identified as such, however, that heightened accessibility diminishes. This interpretation makes sense if you think about how we might use our auditory knowledge of words. If someone says to you,

> Please pick up the broom and use it.

You process those words, infer what is required, and perhaps comply. But if someone says to you,

> Please pick up the proom and use it.

then your cognitive system has to focus on available auditory information to determine what the heck a "proom" could possibly be before it can take any further action.

here is that the human cognitive system is essentially "economical" (I don't mean "miserly"). The cognitive system is economical in that it attempts to determine the type and intensity of demands that will be placed on it in the future. Using this estimation of use, the cognitive system devotes as much of its resources to a problem as it can "afford." The cognitive system's rationality appears as it succeeds in predicting and meeting future demands, just as we would expect a rational person to succeed in budgeting financial resources.

Let's look at a somewhat extended example of a rational analysis applied to human memory. Under this view the memory system tries to estimate the likelihood that a unit of knowledge, or memory, will be needed in the future. If the system concludes that the likelihood is high that the memory will be needed, then a suitable portion of the system's resources will be devoted to encoding and retrieving it. If, on the other hand, the likelihood of a memory's being needed again is low, then our cognitive system may well decide to leave it unencoded. Occasionally the system may not work perfectly: We try to retrieve something and find we can't. When that happens, we may lament our "forgetfulness." But ACT-R invites us to think about the number of times a part of our cognitive system, such as memory, doesn't let us down. You may not be able to remember what you had for lunch two weeks ago today, but I'll bet you can always retrieve your name, your phone number, and your address with little effort. If you were "manager" of a vast cognitive bureaucracy called "your memory," you might decide to encode or not

Using Your Knowledge of Cognition
Likely to Locate a Lamprey on the Sofa?

The semantic or conceptual basis of the declarative permanent memory becomes very clear in this demonstration. First look at your watch and give yourself 10 seconds to write down all the words you can think of that begin with a letter—let's say *L*. Now, having done that, look at your watch again and give yourself 10 seconds to write down as many members of a category—let's say, household furniture, as you can think of. Compare the two lists. More items on the furniture list? I'm not surprised. On the letter list, you probably have *like,* or *love;* you may have *letter* or *list;* you may even have *lima bean* (cheating a little). But you probably don't have *lamprey* or *lugubrious* or very many of the other 6230 words beginning with *L* in my dictionary (and this is surely a low estimate for all the words in English that begin with *L*). On the other hand,

you probably have *sofa, chair, table, lamp, bed, dresser,* etc. on the furniture list. I really doubt that you'll find anything like 6230 household furniture items, which makes the discrepancy between the lists even more interesting because it means that you recalled a much higher percentage of the elements on the hypothetical furniture list than you did on the letter *L* list. Why the difference in performance? You probably can foresee the answer: this is a semantic retrieval task. Prompting with a category name semantically primes the lexical items that are part of that category, increases their accessibility, and therefore makes them easier to recall. Prompting with a letter doesn't cause the same thing to happen, because no underlying conceptual or semantic relationship connects the words that begin with letter *L*.

encode something because it was likely to be asked for at some unspecified time in the future. For any one lunch, you may decide that the need to retain this information is small, because it's unlikely that the memory will be needed in the future. But for your name and other personal information, you may decide to encode the information because likelihood is high that it will be needed again at some time in the future.

Concluding Comments and Suggestions for Further Reading

In investigating the question of knowledge, we first looked at findings from the literature on lexical access. Here we saw that when a concept is called up by the cognitive system, that process speeds up access to related concepts. We saw too that the cognitive system can do any work necessary to relate concepts to each other. Findings like these suggest that much of our knowledge can be modeled as a vast network of related concepts. What organizational principles govern formation and use of these networks? That was the question that occupied us for the rest of the chapter and led us to investigate models such as TLC and ACT-R.

Here's a question to ask yourself about this chapter after you've finished studying: In general, what do formalisms such as ACT-R say about human knowledge? That is, what sort of position about human knowledge is implied by a model such as ACT-R?

Think about this question for a minute before you read further. Many things could be said here, and so if your mental response does not agree completely with what follows, it doesn't mean your response is wrong. First, we say that ACT-R and models like it strongly suggest that the cognitive system has organizational principles and that these principles are orderly and describable. If the model had gone no further, demonstrating just these facts is enough to make most cognitive psychologists giddy. The organizational principles for any cognitive system also seem to be common enough that we can talk about people sharing them. In other words, we can talk about a person as having a typical cognitive system. Finally, the systems that we talk about in this chapter symbolically represent knowledge. This is an advanced idea, but let's delve into it. When we say that ACT-R and models like it are symbolic, we assert the idea that whatever people have going on in their heads when they use their knowledge, we know they don't really, literally, have production systems, or chunks. Instead, we argue that a production system is an accurate, symbolic representation of the computation the neural system makes when people solve puzzles such as the navigation problem. In other words, when we say that a production system is symbolic, we mean that the steps a production system takes as it computes the next action in a problem are abstract depictions of the steps that the real neural system takes as it computes the next action in a problem. And when we say that a production system is accurate, we mean that in some nontrivial way, the correspondence between the abstract depictions of the production system and the "actual steps" of the neural system is close enough to convince us that models like ACT-R are correct.

If you'd like to read more about production systems and their uses, a terrific article by Neches, Langley, and Klahr (1987) will help you get started. In fact, the entire edited book (Klahr, Langley, & Neches, 1987) is a very worthwhile collection of applications of production systems. Some comments on production systems also appear in an excellent, although challenging, book by Newell (1990).

The ACT-R model, its precursors, and its applications are fully described in four surprisingly accessible sources. The beginnings of a general rational analysis of cognition are seen in Anderson (1990). Further developments are described in *Rules of the Mind* (Anderson, 1993). Although each book has some heavy-duty mathematical analysis, the writing and compelling logic are lucid and can be read more or less apart from the mathematical underpinnings. The same can be said for two articles in which Anderson shows how a rational analysis of memory might proceed (Anderson & Schooler, 1991) and how a general production-system-based–model of problem solving and learning might unfold (Anderson, 1993).

 ey Terms

Connectionism	Nodes	Production system
Repetition priming	Type–token distinction	Speed-accuracy decomposition
Lexical access	Teachable-Language	technique
Semantic priming	Comprehender (TLC)	Chunk
Stimulus-onset asynchrony	Intersection search	Working-memory element
(SOA)	Spreading-activation model	(WME)
Bias effect	Prestored knowledge	
Network models	Time course of activation	

Structure of Knowledge: A Connectionist Approach

Overview

Let's try solving this problem (Tank & Hopfield, 1987): Imagine that you are director of an academic library. Part of your job is to supervise the assistants who reshelve books returned by the library's patrons. The library's holdings cover many topics. Each assistant is more or less familiar with all the topics, but their familiarity influences the speed with which they are able to reshelve books. And because the assistants are paid by the hour, it's important to assign them to areas with which they are familiar so that they can reshelve the books quickly. The table shows the number of books per minute that each assistant can reshelve in each of the topics.

Now here's the problem: Assuming that you can assign an assistant to only one collection, and that each of the collections must have one person assigned to it, what is the optimal way of assigning assistants to topics (where optimal means the highest number of books reshelved per minute)? It's a nontrivial problem. You may begin by thinking that because Sarah can reshelve ten books per minute in geology, it's obvious she should be assigned to this topic. But because Tim's fastest subject is also geology, he would have to be assigned to his second-fastest subject, which is physics. But if you do that, then you can't make use of George in physics, and George's rate in physics is two books per minute faster than Tim's. That seems to result in a dead end. For an alternative approach, you may have realized that the number of possible assignments is finite. Therefore you could generate all the assignments, compute the number of books that would be reshelved per minute using each specific arrangement, and simply pick the arrangement with the highest total. This ap-

proach is guaranteed to work, but it has some disadvantages. Although the number of possible arrangements is finite, it's still a large number, 6! (or 720 possible assignments). Even if you could generate and examine one possible assignment scheme per minute, it would take you twelve hours to look at all the possibilities, and so it might take you that long to find the optimal assignment. You might like to try some approaches on your own; I can tell you that the optimal assignment would result in forty-four books per minute being reshelved.

If you found an assignment scheme that results in forty-four books per minute being reshelved, congratulations. If you didn't and you want to know the answer, look at the Concluding Comments section at the end of this chapter. If you tried working this problem, I'm sure you realize that the technique called for here somehow *simultaneously* takes into account each assistant's fastest subject and the effects of that assignment on all the other assistants (Tank & Hopfield, 1987).

Keeping track of these mutual dependencies seems hard for us to do mentally, but cognitively and neurally we must solve problems similar to reshelving all the time. Suppose a friend asks you to take a break from studying and join her for a meal. But suppose you really need to study to earn a decent grade on a test the next day. In resolving this type of problem, sometimes called a double approach-avoidance conflict, we can see that your cognitive system is faced with the same sort of incompatibilities that we dealt with in the reshelving problem. Each course of action (studying or taking a break) has positive and negative aspects that must somehow be simultaneously balanced to make a decision.

Let's look at one more example. We usually don't think of our visual systems as having a "problem" with perception, but in fact almost all the visual information from our retinas could be interpreted in numerous ways by our brains. How does your brain come up with one interpretation from the complicated neural information produced by the retinas? And how does the brain go about making sure that its interpretation is the "right" one? As this example suggests, our brains are frequently faced with the problem of assembling one coherent interpretation from sensory data that are conflicting and "noisy." Further, these examples suggest that the brain and cognitive system may frequently be faced with complex problems that can be successfully resolved only by simultaneously considering many mutual incompatibilities.

We explore in this chapter models of cognition designed to mimic this simultaneity that we see in many cognitive and neural system actions. These models are sometimes called neural-network models, connectionist models, or distributed, nonsymbolic processing. Regardless of the name, the approach is an attempt to produce models of cognition that seemingly have much in common with the neural system's operation.

Assistant's Name	Topic					
	Geology	Physics	Chemistry	History	Poetry	Art
Sarah	10	5	4	6	5	1
Jessica	6	4	9	7	3	2
George	1	8	3	6	4	6
Karen	5	3	7	2	1	4
Sam	3	2	5	6	8	7
Tim	7	6	4	1	3	2

Some Concepts of Distributed Representation

If you look back at Chapter 1, you'll find that we talk there about three levels of psychological analysis: a neural level, a cognitive level, and a mental level. The mental level corresponds to our consciousness or our awareness; it's what you usually mean when you think about your "mind." The neural level is based on a more or less literal description of the nervous system's activity. But we can describe its activities more abstractly too, and then we arrive at the cognitive level. We may not be aware of all our cognitive and neural system activities, but these levels are nevertheless very convenient ways of describing psychological events. When we use the information-processing approach to describe events, the degree of abstraction away from the neural system is marked. Think back to Chapter 5. We were able to characterize some types of memory search as activating a unit or node representing your knowledge of, let's say, your dog. Does this node really exist? The answer is yes: the node exists at the cognitive level of analysis, where activating a node represents summation of a great deal of neural processing. In contrast to the information-processing approach, the connectionist perspective can be understood as an attempt to produce a model that is considerably "closer" to the neural action than are information-processing models. In other words, although all cognitive models are abstract representations of neural events, the degree of abstraction in connectionist models is thought to be much less than it is for information-processing models. Thus connectionist models use terms and procedures that, at least superficially, seem to have a lot in common with actual neural events.

Actual and Idealized Neurons

Let's consider some things that are known about cortical neurons. First, we know that such neurons frequently exhibit the action-potential phenomenon. Second, each neuron is highly connected with surrounding neurons, and finally, these connections between specific neurons might be excitatory or inhibitory. When we say that neurons exhibit an action potential, it is just another way of saying that, theoretically, many cortical neurons are continually in one of only two states. The neuron may "fire" an electrochemical impulse down the length of its axon, and when it does so, we refer to this firing or transmission as the action potential. If the neuron is not currently engaged in an action potential, then it is simply waiting to fire. What causes a neuron to fire? Simply, if the neuron receives from other neurons sufficient input of the right sort, then its firing threshold is exceeded, and the action potential is seen.

Each neuron's impulse may be sent to thousands of surrounding cortical neurons. Each noncortical Purkinje cell in the cerebellum receives inputs from 100,000 neighboring cells (Kalat, 1984). For us, one of the important facts is that the firing neuron's effects on those thousands of surrounding neurons are simultaneous. This is what we mean when we say that cortical neurons typically are highly connected. When a specific neuron fires, it may send its transmission to thousands of other cells, and when a specific neuron receives transmissions, they may come from thousands of surrounding cells. Notice, too, that the strength of the neuron's message is not altered by the number of neighboring cells with which it communicates; the signal is never diluted or weakened by its connections with adjacent cells.

Although the signal strength is not diluted, the signal is not always positive. As you may recall from our discussion in Chapter 1, Rosenblatt (1958) showed that computation among neurons is produced not only by excitatory connections between them, but also by inhibitory connections. Thus, a neuron's firing may increase the likelihood that a neighboring neuron will *not* fire in response to other input. Each neuron then becomes a kind of decision maker by summing up all the excitatory and all the inhibitory transmissions from other neurons and firing (or not firing) depending on whether the total input is positive or negative.

So much for actual neurons. How do the idealized neurons in connectionist models compare with actual neurons? Consider Figure 6.1. The three circles represent three artificial neurons in a tiny neural network. Let's use "neurode" to stand for such neurons (Caudill & Butler, 1992). What are the properties of these neurodes? We might say that, somewhat unlike real neurons, these neurodes are arranged in layers. A convention in neural-network models labels the bottom layer the "input" layer and the top layer the "output" layer. (As we'll see later, frequently layers of neurodes lie between these two.) After we get past this initial artificiality, however, we begin to see some commonalities between neurodes and actual neurons. Each neurode in the input layer communicates with the output neurode. It's true that this isn't exactly like the thousands of inputs that occur in the real nervous system, but some neural networks may have a lot more neurodes and connections. Finally, as the positive and negative signs suggest, the input layer does have excitatory and inhibitory connections with the neurode in the top layer. Thus neurode A apparently will have an excitatory influence on neurode C, and neurode B will tend to have a simultaneous inhibitory influence on the output.

We haven't seen how an analogue of the action potential works in this sort of network (that will come up in the next section), but the action-potential concept is based on the idea of spreading activation discussed in Chapter 5. As you'll recall, in those models activation of a node brought connected nodes into a similar state of activation. Here, linkages between neurodes establish the pathways over which activation will flow. If two neurodes are linked by a line, then some sort of influence occurs between them. If two neurodes are not connected by a line, then they operate mostly independent of each other.

The Transfer Function

In real neural networks, information often is transmitted among neurons by means of the action potential; in connectionist models this transmission is enacted by a transfer function. The action potential therefore is to neurology what the transfer function is to neural networks. The transfer function takes inputs into the system and describes a means for spreading that input throughout the system. In the neural-networks language, we refer to this step as propagating that input throughout the system. Let's go back to Figure 6.1 and describe this little network:

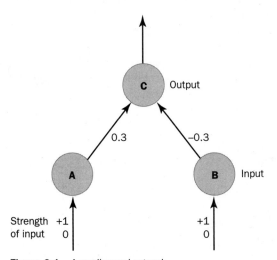

Figure 6.1 A small neural network.

1. If Input Unit A is active (has a strength of 1), then Unit A outputs an activation of 0.3.
2. If Input Unit B is active (has a strength of 1), then Unit B outputs an activation of -0.3.
3. If an input unit is not active, then it outputs no activation.
4. The output of Unit C is always the sum of the activation of all input units.

Now let's describe the strength of the connection between the input units and the output units (0.3 or -0.3 in this example) as the "weight" of the connection between two neurodes. We can then express the output of Unit C:

$$\text{Output}_{\text{Unit C}} = (\text{Input}_{\text{Unit A}} \times \text{Weight}_{AC}) + (\text{Input}_{\text{Unit B}} \times \text{Weight}_{BC})$$

If we assume that both inputs shown in Figure 6.1 are active, then we get:

$$\begin{aligned} \text{Output}_{\text{Unit C}} &= (1 \times 0.3) + (1 \times -0.3) \\ &= (0.3) + (-0.3) \\ &= 0 \end{aligned}$$

On the other hand, if only Input Unit A is active, then we get:

$$\begin{aligned} \text{Output}_{\text{Unit C}} &= (1 \times 0.3) + (0 \times -0.3) \\ &= (0.3) + (0) \\ &= 0.3 \end{aligned}$$

Let's summarize: in this example the transfer function asserts that the neural network we have created will have a positive output if Input Unit A and only Input Unit A is active. If Input Unit B and only Input Unit B is active, then the Unit C output is negative. If both input units are active, then the Unit C output is zero, meaning that there is really no output under that circumstance.

How can we conceptualize this little network? What does it actually "do"? Essentially, this model neural network damps or diminishes incoming stimulation. In other words, the input strength at Input Unit A may be 1, but the system output diminishes it to 0.3. Similarly, if two strong but contradictory inputs are received, their effects are canceled by the network so that no further transmission takes place. We say that no further transmission takes place because the Unit C output is zero under stimulation from both input units. If the Unit C output were fed into another neural network (and there really is no theoretical limit to how many such "layers" of networks we can create), then Unit C would be silent, hence, would transfer no information when both of its inputs were active.

Now we can generalize the transfer function to compute outputs for neurodes with any number of inputs:

$$\text{Output}_j = \Sigma \, (\text{Input}_i \times \text{Weight}_{ij})$$

In other words, the output of a given neurode "j" is equal to the sum of the activation of its inputs 1 through "i" times the weight of the connections between the inputs and the output neurode.

Differences Between Distributed and Symbolic Representation

Typographically, the neurodes we're talking about in this chapter look much like the nodes that we covered in Chapter 5. And the connections between the neurodes seem much like the connections between nodes that we've already seen. And it's true that neural networks can represent knowledge and cognitive actions just as well as the symbolic models did in Chapter 5. But some important differences appear in how the two approaches go about representing cognition. For example, even though neurodes and nodes look similar, the neurode is much "stupider" than the nodes in a symbolic network. A node is capable of housing lots of information. When a node is activated, lots of information can be accessed, perhaps even more than an entire proposition. This capacity makes accessing a node comparable to looking up an entry in an encyclopedia. By contrast, monitoring a neurode is more like watching a traffic light than looking up something in a book. Each individual neurode just doesn't hold much information. A node is a complicated thing; a neurode is a simple thing.

A second difference between nodes and neurodes stems from this first difference. For symbolic models including nodes, it's legitimate to ask: "Where specifically is the knowledge housed?" But this question is much less legitimate for neural models. To see why, consider Figure 6.2, which contrasts two modes for representing a familiar concept.

Figure 6.2a is a typical symbolic representation of the concept "dog." This model asserts that if any one of the specific dog tokens is activated, then activation spreads upward from that token to activate the type node; namely, "dog," at the apex of this hierarchy. Within each token node, quite a bit of information may lie (you may know a lot about cocker spaniels) or very little information (the basenji breed is much less familiar to most people).

Figure 6.2b shows how a distributed representation of specific dogs; that is, dog tokens, might work. At the input layer, we have a set of neurodes representing unitary distinctive features that may be present or absent for a specific dog. If present, then that specific neurode in the input layer becomes activated with an input strength of "1." If the feature is absent, then that specific neurode is not activated and has a strength of "0." Because this network has quite a few neurodes and connections, I did

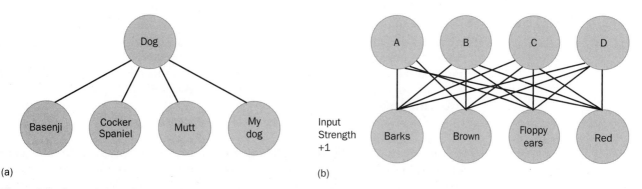

(a) (b)

Figure 6.2 Two depictions of conceptual knowledge: (a) a symbolic depiction, and (b) a correctionist depiction.

Table 6.1	Strength of Connections in a Hypothetical Neural Network			
Feature	Strength of the Connections			
Barks	0.4	0.1	0.3	0.2
Brown	0.2	0.6	0.4	0.5
Floppy ears	0.1	0.3	0.3	0.6
Red	0.5	0.2	0.1	0.2
Connection weight with	A	B	C	D

not put the strength of the connections on the linkages from the input to the output layer, but Table 6.1 shows all sixteen of them.

Suppose that if the "barks" input were activated, activation would flow to each output unit in this way: 0.4 to A, 0.1 to B, 0.3 to C, and 0.2 to D (as another simplification, I used only positive numbers in this example). Let's also say that if the "floppy ears" node were activated, then activation would flow to each output unit in this way: 0.1 to A, 0.3 to B, 0.3 to C, and 0.6 to D. Now what would the network's output be for a dog that barked and had floppy ears, but was neither red nor brown? We can use the generalized rule for calculating the effects of each feature's activation on each output neurode (remember that the weights are just of my own devising; they may not correspond to anything that might exist "in reality"). Only two of the input neurodes will be active; namely, the ones for "barks" and for "floppy ears." Because the other two input neurodes will be inactive, we'll have zeros for their activation. In the equation below, I got the two weights for the effects of "brown" and "red" from Table 6.1. Now, using the generalized rule, we get:

$$\text{Output}_{\text{Unit A}} = (\text{Activation of "barks"} \times \text{weight of "barks" to A}) +$$
$$(\text{Activation of "brown"} \times \text{weight of "brown" to A}) +$$
$$(\text{Activation of "floppy ears"} \times \text{weight of "floppy ears" to A}) + (\text{Activation of "red"} \times \text{weight of "red" to A})$$

$$\text{Ouput}_{\text{Unit A}} = (1 \times 0.4) + (0 \times 0.2) + (1 \times 0.1) + (0 \times 0.5)$$
$$= (0.4) + (0) + (0.1) + (0)$$
$$= 0.5$$

That is, if the dog barks and has floppy ears, then the Output Unit A is active with an activation level of 0.5. Of course, we would have to do the calculations for the other three output neurodes too. Instead of going through that calculation, I'll just list the output from each of the four output units if "barks" and "floppy ears" are the only two active inputs:

$$[0.5\ 0.4\ 0.6\ 0.8]$$

If you look back at Table 6.1, you'll see where each of these terms came from. It's not obvious, but it's very important that you realize that this set of four numbers represents a specific dog—here a barking dog with floppy ears. Now let's complete this exercise with one more question. Suppose the dog in question had activated the feature "barks" and had been "brown" but did not have "floppy ears"? What would the output have looked like then? Using Table 6.1 and the general rule for summing activation, we get:

$$[0.6\ 0.7\ 0.7\ 0.7]$$

As you can see, the output pattern becomes quite different when different input neurodes are activated. In other words, different tokens of dogs are represented in neural networks by different patterns of activation across a set of output units. In contrast to the symbolic representation, in which each node stands for quite a bit of information, in the connectionist approach, the information is not contained in any one neurode, but rather is seen as a pattern of activation across the entire set of interacting neurodes. In response to the question, "Where is the information housed?" the connectionist responds that the information is spread out across the entire network. Sometimes we say that the knowledge is in the connections or in the weights in a neural network.

Some important implications result from this view. According to the symbolic position, losing one node could really incapacitate a system. Just think how disastrous it could be if somehow you lost your "dog" node. But according to the connectionist position, losing one neurode should not bring the system down. In fact, you might have fun playing with the network above to see what would happen if one of the output neurodes, or even if one of the input neurodes, were somehow lost from the system. As you'll find, losing one output neurode leaves the rest of the output pattern intact. According to the connectionist, this finding makes a great deal of sense. However it is that the cognitive system represents and retrieves knowledge, it seems that it should be able to survive the loss of specific, tiny portions of its representation without noticeable deficit in performance.

Let's summarize the differences that we have discussed. Symbolic models emphasize networks whose nodes hold much information. Connectionist models contain neurodes, each of which really can't do much on its own. In symbolic models, it's appropriate to ask at which node in the system specific information is stored, but in connectionist models, knowledge is seen as a pattern of activation across a set of interacting elements. Specific knowledge is not stored in specific locales in connectionist networks. Finally, loss of specific nodes can produce strong decrements in performance in symbolic models, but connectionist models generally are able to survive loss of some, or even many, of their interacting neurodes before serious decrements in performance are seen.

Some Fundamental Networks and Their Computational Properties

Some networks work almost like Lego® building blocks. That is, they are simple in themselves, but they can be put together in various ways to form more complicated arrangements. In this section we look at several such networks.

The Perceptron

The simplest type of building block is the **perceptron,** originating with McCulloch and Pitts (1943). Figure 6.3 shows this simple network.

McCulloch and Pitts defined the transfer function of this neurode:

Figure 6.3 The MuCulloch–Pitts neurode, shown here with two input signals.

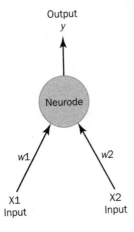

Output
y

Neurode

w1   w2

X1   X2
Input   Input

$$\text{Output}_j = \Sigma\,(\text{Input}_i \times \text{Weight}_{ij})$$
$$y = \{+1, \text{ if Output}_j \geq \text{T}\}$$
$$\{-1, \text{ if Output}_j < \text{T}\}$$

This transfer function is slightly different from the one we considered above. It converts the output neurode's activation into one of two values. If the activation of the output neurode is above a threshold (T), then the output becomes $+1$. If the activation is below a specified threshold, then the output becomes -1. The threshold that usually is used is zero. The output of a perceptron, then, will always be one of two values, $+1$ or -1. This simplicity may make you wonder what a perceptron can actually do.

Rosenblatt (1958) apparently was the first to realize that this one neurode could be "trained," in a sense, to perform various cognitive computations. We'll deal with this notion of training a neural network several times in this chapter. Informally, the first principle in training a neural network goes something like this: To get a neural network to perform differently, change the weights that connect the inputs to the neurodes in the output layer. Here's the rule with which Rosenblatt changed the weights linking the inputs to the outputs in the perceptron:

$$W_{\text{new}} = W_{\text{old}} + Byx$$

where W_{new} = the "new" weights to be used in the perceptron; W_{old} = the weights that have been used in the perceptron until now; $B = +1$ if the perceptron's answer is correct and -1 if its answer is wrong; y = the perceptron's answer; and x = the input pattern.

This learning rule says that if you define the perceptron's output as an "answer," the weights are changed by taking the old weights, adding one to each weight if the perceptron's answer is correct, and subtracting one from the weights if the perceptron's answer is incorrect. In other words, if you treat each computation as an answer that is either right or wrong, and then give the network feedback about whether it was right or wrong, then the network will start to produce the correct output more frequently, in a way "learning" to come up with the correct answer more often. Here, the neurode is learning to take an arbitrary stimulus and categorize it as a member of one or another class of things.

We'll go through a conceptual example to show how this learning occurs. First, imagine that you have a piece of graph paper, on which you draw a standard Cartesian coordinate system. In this system you have an x (horizontal axis) ranging from -1 to 1 in increments of 0.1 and a y (vertical axis) with the same range and increments. Next you plot six or eight points in this space, using the conventional (x, y) coordinates. Then you label each of the six or eight points either "A" or "B." You can label any point either A or B, just so long as when you are finished, it's possible to draw a straight line that separates each and every A from each and every B. Then you arbitrarily decide that the correct answer for the A points will be "1" and the correct answer for the B points will be -1. Thus if you input the Cartesian coordinates of an A point into the perceptron, and the output of the perceptron is "1," then you will call the output of the perceptron "correct," but if you input the coordinates of an A point, and the perceptron's answer is -1, then you'll call that answer incorrect. You can use almost any numbers between 0 and 1 for the initial weights. Regardless of the values you select for the initial weights, they will be changed as a result of the points that you input and the perceptron's answer. But if you go back to the training rule, you'll see that the weights are changed quite a bit differently depending on whether the perceptron's answer is correct or not.

Now for several highly interesting things about the perceptron's behavior. First, as you input more and more of the A and B points, you'll notice that the weights change less and less with each new point. Eventually, you'll get to a point where the weights no longer change because the neurode has "learned" all that it's going to learn. Second, you'll notice that the neurode seems to be getting the "correct" answer more and more frequently. Finally, you may have realized that it's not only the various A and B points that can be graphed. The perceptron's weights too are represented by two coordinates, and the first weight can be treated as an x coordinate and the second as a y coordinate. What happens when you graph the weights? Well, if you graph them and draw a line connecting that point with the origin of the graph (that is, the point whose coordinates are 0, 0), you'll see that this line gradually "rotates" through the space of the points with each change in the perceptron's weights. When the line is finally done rotating, because the weights are no longer changing, you'll see that the line neatly divides all the points on the graph paper. All the A points are on one side of the line and all the B points are on the other. Concretely we might say that the perceptron's weights define a line segment that bisects two arbitrary sets of points, but more abstractly we can argue that the perceptron can be trained with feedback to accurately categorize stimuli as being of one class or another.

The Pattern Associator

In this section we continue to look at neural-network building blocks and their operation. Figure 6.4 shows a **pattern associator**, a commonly used neural network. Pattern associators are neural networks that can reproduce several output patterns when specific input patterns are given. One of pattern associators' most interesting characteristics is their ability to reproduce several distinct output patterns using the same set of weights. Thus different input patterns can be propagated through an identical set of weights to produce output patterns uniquely associated with a specific input pattern. This characteristic enables pattern associators to be used as

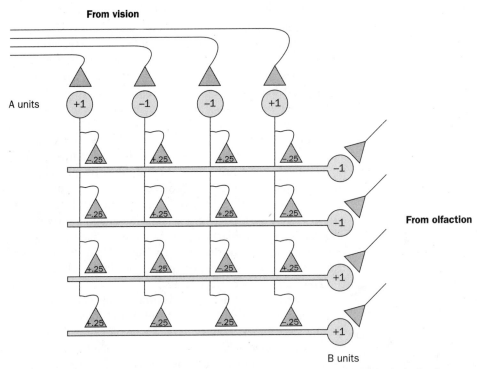

Figure 6.4   A simple pattern associator. The example assumes that patterns of activation in the A units can be produced by the visual system and that patterns in the B units can be produced by the olfactory system. The synaptic connections allow the outputs of the A units to influence the activations of the B units. The synaptic weights linking the A units to the B units were selected so as to allow the pattern of activation shown on the A units to reproduce the pattern of activation shown on the B units without needing olfactory input. *Source:* From Rumelhart and McClelland, 1986.

neural-network models of memory. Here the idea is that having a memory essentially means being able to associate or link a distinct input pattern (as psychologists, we might call this the *stimulus*) with a distinct output pattern. The output pattern might be an actual response, but it doesn't have to be. For example, the stimulus might simply produce an expectation, or a visual image.

The pattern associator in Figure 6.4 is like this. This pattern associator learns to link visual stimuli (such as seeing a rose) with the appropriate olfactory impression that we would expect whenever we see a rose (namely, the rose's pleasant fragrance). Of course, we should also expect this same pattern associator to be able to reproduce the great smell of a barbecued steak from the sight of a T-bone on a smoky grill. We'll go through an example later in this chapter to show how this linking works.

We've already seen an example of a pattern associator, although it was expressed in a format that differs superficially from the one shown in Figure 6.4. If you go back to the network shown in Figure 6.2 (the "dog" network) and compare it to the one shown in Figure 6.4, you'll see that, although the two networks look different, in a formal sense they are the same. That is, each network consists of two layers, both input layer and output layer having four neurodes. Moreover, each input neurode is connected with each output neurode. Now, here's a distinction between the two: If you take a closer look at the vision–olfaction network we're considering, you'll see that it has weights the values of which are negative. We'll explore the implications of that point a little later in this section.

Vector Encoding   One concept most critical in your understanding of how neural networks operate is the **vector-encoding** idea. Informally, a vector is an ordered string of numbers having at least two elements. This arbitrary vector has three elements:

$$[-1\ 1\ 1]$$

Vectors have many interesting mathematical properties, but for cognitive psychologists, one of the best is their ability to encode and represent strings of features. Here's how that might be done. If you look at the representation of speech sounds in Chapter 8, or the representation of alphabetic characters in Chapter 2, you'll see that cognitivists frequently consider a stimulus such as a speech sound or a letter to be nothing more than a bundle of discrete "features." For speech sounds, such features may represent the presence or absence of "voicing" or, for letters, perhaps the presence or absence of "vertical line." As long as the system knows which feature is which, it can represent the presence of a feature by a positive 1 and the absence of a feature by -1. After doing that, the system could "read" a vector as a representation for the stimulus in question, just as the checkout machines in the grocery store can read a bar code to come up with the object's price. At the risk of getting ahead of the story, for the vector above, if the first number represented a -1 for "voicing" absence, the second number indicated "bilabial" (i.e., $+1$ = bilabial, and -1 = "absence of bilabial"), and the third number indicated manner of articulation (let's say $+1$ = stop), then the sequence of three numbers above, $[-1\ 1\ 1]$, would represent a speech sound such as an unvoiced bilabial stop—in other words, the consonant /p/.

It's true that if we really wanted to make a vector representation of all consonantal speech sounds, more than three numbers would be required, because certainly more than three features are involved in consonantal perception. But adding more features doesn't change the underlying concept; it just means the vector would have more elements. As it turns out, most real-life, psychologically interesting variables probably do require a lot more than three or four elements to represent them, and also encoding and representing each feature does require one neurode. The resulting neural networks could become extremely large. But the size of a neural network becomes much less of a problem if you think back to a basic tenet in neural style cognitive computation. Namely, neurodes, like the neurons they are supposed to represent, are rather "inexpensive," in that your head has a lot of neurons, maybe 100 million, each of which has to be kept busy every day. Seen from that perspective, our neurons are really cheap labor, and we probably shouldn't mind so much that it takes so many of them to carry out psychologically relevant and useful computations. Having said that, I'd like to point out that I certainly don't feel that I have any neurons to spare.

The metaphor that will show how we can put all this cheap labor to use requires you to think that vector encoding works just as that bar-code reader in the grocery store checkout line does. Look at a bar code: up to sixteen alternating thin and thick lines can handle the 30,000 or so items in a large grocery store. Each store item requires its own unique bar code, so that the bar-code reader can translate that pattern of lines into the description that you read on the display above the cash register. When the checker scans the 12-ounce jar of Jif® peanut butter that you are buying, you hear a beep and read "Jif® 12-oz" and the price on the cash-register display. I haven't tried it, but I'd like to compare two sizes of Jif® peanut butter to see which line or lines in the bar codes differed. Once you found the difference, you could then say which line or lines coded the size and price of the peanut butter jar. In other words, different "regions" in the set of lines "code" (that is, represent) the brand name, size, and any other variables that matter to purchaser and clerk.

Presumably, our neurons do the same. Instead of a sequence of lines, we have a sequence of neurons. And instead of the thin or thick lines, our neurons can be activated or inhibited. Anderson (1997) shows how we might use such a vector representation to code numbers and operate on those numbers. He sees the vector representing a number as having two regions. Figure 6.5 shows the two regions and the information coded in each region.

In the first region, the neurology codes the "abstract" knowledge of the number, including things such as the number's name. The second region works something like a thermometer. As numbers denote bigger magnitudes, they are coded by groups of active neurons farther to the right of the vector. A representation of the number "1" would include activity in the abstract portion of the vector, and activity in the very leftmost portion in the vector's magnitude region. A representation of the number "2" would include some activity in the abstract region too, but its activity in the magnitude region would be a little to the right of the neurons activated for representing the number "1."

The Pattern Associator at Work   Let's get back to that T-bone steak that we left out on the Weber. What happens when we look at the steak? Looking at Figure 6.4, let the four numbers labeled "A units" be a vector representing a visual encoding of the steak.

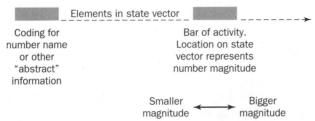

Number representation

Coding for number name or other "abstract" information

Bar of activity. Location on state vector represents number magnitude

Smaller magnitude ←→ Bigger magnitude

Figure 6.5   A neural-network number representation. Each dot is a computing element in a large state vector representing a number. One part of the state vector represents numerical magnitude by the spatial position of a "bar" of activity. The bar's height suggests amount of activity by elements at that location. *Source:* From Anderson and Sutton, 1997.

Moreover, let the four numbers labeled "B units" be a vector representing the steak's aroma. The A units will be our input, and the B units will be the network's output. The connective weights of each A unit to each B unit are shown in the triangles. You'll notice that each weight is either $+0.25$ or -0.25. To operate this network, we convert the visual encoding into a vector, namely $[+1 \ -1 \ -1 \ +1]$, and propagate that encoding through the weights that are shown. To do that, let's begin with the generalized rule to compute the topmost B unit's activation:

$$\text{Output}_j = \Sigma \ (\text{Input}_i \times \text{Weight}_{ij})$$
$$\begin{aligned}\text{Output}_{\text{topmost B unit}} &= (+ \ 1 \times -0.25) + (-1 \times 0.25) + (-1 \times 0.25) + \\ &\quad (+1 \times -0.25) \\ &= (-0.25) + (-0.25) + (-0.25) + (-0.25) \\ &= -1\end{aligned}$$

This is indeed the activation showing on the topmost element in the B units in Figure 6.4. We can use the generalized rule once again to compute the transfer function from the A units to the third-from-the-top B unit (the second from the top is the same as the one we have just done). We can see in Figure 6.4 that the number we're looking for is $+1$. If you look closely, you'll see that the weights from the A units to the third-from-the-top B unit are different than they were for the previous computation. Going through this example,

$$\begin{aligned}\text{Output}_{\text{third-from-top B unit}} &= (+ \ 1 \times +0.25) + (-1 \times -0.25) + (-1 \times -0.25) \\ &\quad + (+1 \times +0.25) \\ &= (0.25) + (0.25) + (0.25) + (0.25) \\ &= +1\end{aligned}$$

And that's the value we're supposed to come up with.

As I've mentioned, one of pattern associators' most useful characteristics is their ability to represent several such associations in the same network; that is, with the same set of weights. To show how they do so, consider the arrangement of numbers shown in Figure 6.6. Now the left-hand side of this figure, labeled "A," shows the pattern associator that we have been discussing. The row vector on the left under "A" represents the sight of the T-bone steak (you'll see that those numbers are the same as those

	A					**B**			
+1	−1	−1	+1		−1	+1	−1	+1	
−.25	+.25	+.25	−.25	−1	+.25	−.25	+.25	−.25	−1
−.25	+.25	+.25	−.25	−1	−.25	+.25	−.25	+.25	+1
+.25	−.25	−.25	+.25	+1	−.25	+.25	−.25	+.25	+1
+.25	−.25	−.25	+.25	+1	+.25	−.25	+.25	−.25	−1

Figure 6.6 Two simple associators represented as matrices. Notice that the weights in the first matrix are the same as those shown in the diagram in Figure 6.4. *Source:* From Rumelhart and McClelland, 1986.

shown as the A units in Figure 6.4), and the column vector (the numbers arranged vertically) represents the aroma of the steak. And once again you'll see that those numbers are the same as those shown as the B units in Figure 6.4. What about the pattern on the right-hand side, under "B"? This pattern represents a different sight–smell combination, perhaps the sight of a rose and its pleasant fragrance. That is, if you use the system described here, you can propagate the row vector under "B" to produce the column vector, where the row vector represents the sight of a rose, and the column vector represents its fragrance. If you look at the weights shown in the Figure 6.6 boxes, you'll notice that they differ from those in the steak example. But could we somehow combine the two sets of weights so that exactly the same set of weights will produce the steak aroma from the visual steak input and the rose fragrance from the sight of a rose?

Figure 6.7 shows how this combination can be accomplished. Figure 6.7 shows only the algebraic sign for the weights (positive or negative). We can get away with this reduced representation because all the weights had the same numerical value. The only thing different about them was their signs. The plus sign linking the two sets of weights shows that they can be added algebraically, with $+0.25$ and -0.25 canceling each other out to make zero. The resulting arrangement, following the equals sign in Figure 6.7, shows each place in the set of weights being held by either a blank (a zero), two plus signs, or two minus signs. Let's now translate the two plus signs as 0.5 (i.e., $0.25 + 0.25$) and two negative signs as -0.5. The resulting arrangement of numbers looks like this:

$$
\begin{vmatrix}
0 & 0 & 0.5 & -0.5 \\
-0.5 & 5 & 0 & 0 \\
0 & 0 & -0.5 & 0.5 \\
0.5 & -0.5 & 0 & 0
\end{vmatrix}
$$

I should be able to take the steak input and get the steak aroma from these weights, and simultaneously be able to get the rose fragrance from the sight of the rose input, without further changes in the set of weights. Let's try it.

I won't go through the entire computation for both outputs, but let's see if we can get the fourth-from-the-topmost output from the steak example $(+1)$ and the fourth-from-the-topmost output from the rose example (-1). For the steak, we have:

$$
\begin{bmatrix}
- & + & + & - \\
- & + & + & - \\
+ & - & - & + \\
+ & - & - & +
\end{bmatrix}
+
\begin{bmatrix}
+ & - & + & - \\
- & + & - & + \\
- & + & - & + \\
+ & - & + & -
\end{bmatrix}
=
\begin{bmatrix}
 & & + & + & - & - \\
- & - & + & + & & \\
 & & - & - & + & + \\
+ & + & - & - & &
\end{bmatrix}
$$

Figure 6.7   The weights in the third matrix allow either row vector shown in Figure 6.6 to recreate the corresponding column vector. *Source:* From Rumelhart and McClelland, 1986.

$$\begin{aligned}
\text{Output}_{\text{fourth-from-top B unit}} &= (+1 \times 0.50) + (-1 \times -0.50) + (-1 \times 0) + \\
&\quad (+1 \times +0) \\
&= (0.50) + (0.50) + (0) + (0) \\
&= +1
\end{aligned}$$

It worked there, then. Let's try the rose example. Now remember, the input will differ from the preceding example, but the weights are the same:

$$\begin{aligned}
\text{Output}_{\text{fourth-from-top B unit}} &= (-1 \times 0.50) + (+1 \times -0.50) + (-1 \times 0) + \\
&\quad (+1 \times +0) \\
&= (-0.50) + (-0.50) + (0) + (0) \\
&= -1
\end{aligned}$$

This is also the desired value.

The pattern associator shows us that a set of weights can be constructed to allow a neural network to compute several outputs from several inputs. This ability is subject to some limitations. You may have wondered how many such associations we could load onto this pattern associator. The answer is that a pattern associator of this type will always compute the right response pattern as long as the set of input vectors has the mathematical property **linear independence.** We don't need to know what this independence means mathematically, but practically speaking, the need for linear independence means that the input vectors must be uncorrelated with each other. In this example, the number of such completely uncorrelated input vectors that could be generated is four, severely limiting this pattern associator as a practical device, because it means that this associator could retrieve only four memories. Limiting this pattern associator as a teaching device, however, in no way implies that our cognitive and neural systems could not have extremely large networks capable of storing many more than four memories.

Three-Layer Systems

The XOR Problem   The building blocks we've considered have consisted of two layers of neurodes: an input layer and an output layer. Although we've seen that such two-layer systems are quite strong, they cannot handle some problems regardless of the system's size. One of these is the "exclusive-or," the **XOR problem** displayed schematically in Table 6.2.

We must construct a neural network such that the input patterns shown can be propagated through a set of weights to come up with their associated output. Let's look more closely at the output patterns. When the system is given the inputs "00," the appropriate output is "0." And when the system is given the inputs "11," the output is exactly the same, "0." We haven't seen anything quite like this before; namely, a system that comes up with the same output from different inputs. Further, if you consider the inputs that produce this output, you'll notice that the inputs are highly dissimilar. In other words, of the four inputs that can be made in this set, "00" and "11" are maximally dissimilar to each other. This is the XOR problem in a nutshell: how to make a neural network produce an identical output when the input conditions

Table 6.2 XOR Problem

Input Patterns		Output Patterns
00	→	0
01	→	1
10	→	1
11	→	0

Source: Copyright 1989 by the MIT Press. Adapted by permission of the publisher and author.

have nothing in common. We'll get to the solution directly, but before doing so, realize that this solution is critical to the ultimate success of neural networks. That is, inability to handle this type of problem would be fatal for neural networks, because the human neural system, and therefore the human cognitive system, can handle the type of situation that the XOR problem represents.

If I'm driving down the street and the traffic light in front of me turns red, I put my foot on the brake. But I may make the same response if I see a child playing with a ball on the sidewalk. In the second scene, I've learned that the ball may get away from the child, who may dart into the street without looking. Here then, my cognitive system computes the same foot-on-brake response from input conditions that are maximally different from each other (traffic signal versus child playing with ball).

Hidden Units The solution to the XOR problem requires adding a third layer of neurodes to the neural network, placing it *between* the input and output layers. Because this layer is never observed as directly as are the input and the output layers, the third-layer neurodes are referred to as **hidden units.**

Figure 6.8 shows a mininetwork capable of solving the XOR problem. The numbers inside the hidden and output units refer to those neurodes' thresholds. If activation of the neurode exceeds its threshold, the neurode fires, but if the activation is not up to the threshold value, then the neurode remains silent.

To see how adding a hidden unit solves the XOR problem, let's operate the network shown in Figure 6.8. Suppose the input units are fed with the [0 0] vector as shown in Table 6.2. Each input unit feeds +1 unit of activation to the hidden unit. Thus, the hidden unit's current activation (+2) exceeds its threshold, and so the hidden unit fires. Before we examine the effects of the hidden unit's firing, however, notice that each input unit is still directly linked to the output unit. The output unit's threshold is +0.5, which here appears to be exceeded because each of the input units is sending +1 units of activation to it. But, as we look further, we see that the hidden unit, which also has been activated, has an *inhibitory* influence on the output unit, to the tune of −2 units of activation. This inhibitory influence completely cancels the positive activation sent by the input units, and so the output unit is silent. And the output unit's activation is zero if the input units too are fed with a [1 1] vector. But when the input units are given different levels of activation, either in the form of a [0 1] or [1 0] vector, something different happens. Consider the [0 1] case. Here the

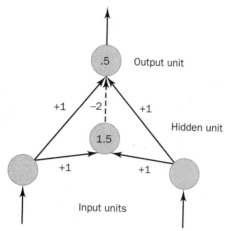

Figure 6.8 A simple XOR network with one hidden unit. *Source:* Copyright 1989 by the MIT Press. Adapted by permission of the publisher

hidden unit is not activated because only one input cell is activated and therefore input to the hidden cell is below the hidden cell's threshold. The hidden unit thus does not exert its inhibitory influence on the output unit. The output cell, however, still receives activation directly from one input unit. This +1 level of activation produced by the active input unit is great enough to raise the output unit above its threshold, and, because the hidden unit is doing nothing to inhibit it, the output unit is in turn activated and fires. Our examination of the XOR problem suggests that if the hidden units in a neural network are arranged in a specified way, then almost any independent input vector can be propagated to produce almost any type of output.

Training a Three-Layer Network

We've seen that a two-layer system, such as a perceptron, can be trained to discriminate specific data points. Three-layer systems can be trained too. When we speak of training a three-layer system, we mean we can modify the weights connecting the various neurodes so that the system becomes progressively better at producing a desired output when a specified input is given. In this section we talk about a commonly used procedure for achieving this and how it works.

The most commonly used procedure for training three-layer systems is the **back-propagation algorithm;** this procedure is said to be used in 80% of neural-network projects (Caudill & Butler, 1992). Figure 6.9 depicts how the algorithm is implemented in a typical three-layer network.

Before we talk about the algorithm, consider some characteristics of the typical network in which a back-propagation algorithm might be used. First, each of the neurodes is connected only with neurodes higher than itself. In other words, input neurodes are connected only with hidden units; hidden units are connected only with output units. It's possible to design a neural network in which the neurodes are connected with other neurodes at their own level (we'll see one later), and certainly our real neural systems have such "intralayer" communication among neurons. But implementing a back-propagation algorithm in such a system is not as straightforward as it

Figure 6.9   A back-propagation network trains with a two-step procedure. The activity from the input pattern flows forward through the network, and the error signal flows backward to adjust the weights. *Source:* Copyright 1992 by MIT Press. Adapted by permission of the publisher.

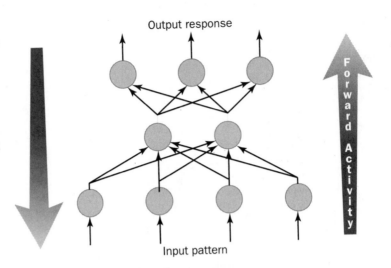

is here. Notice too that the network in Figure 6.9 has no direct connections from the input layer to the output layer, unlike the network used to solve the XOR problem. For the network in Figure 6.9, the input neurodes have no direct influence on the output neurodes; all communication must pass through the hidden units. Finally, each neurode is connected with all the neurodes at the next level. In other words, all the input neurodes are connected with all the hidden units, and all the hidden units are connected with all the output neurodes.

Implementing a back-propagation algorithm in such a network is a two-step procedure. In the first step, an input is given to the system and is propagated upward through the system in the conventional way. When the system arrives at an output, that is compared to the desired or ideal output, which is called the "teacher" because it is used to teach the system how to behave.

Suppose some input is given to the network in Figure 6.9, and it produces this output:

$$[0\ 0\ 1]$$

But suppose this output is actually the one we wanted the system to produce when that input was given:

$$[0\ 1\ 0]$$

It seems the system has not given out what we wanted it to, and we call the difference between the actual and desired output an *error signal*. We then compute the size of that signal:

$$\text{Error signal} = \text{Ideal output} - \text{Actual output}$$
$$= [0\ 1\ 0] - [0\ 0\ 1]$$
$$= [0\ 1\ -1]$$

We now go to the second step. We take the error signal and back-propagate it through the network by treating the output units as the input units. In other words, instead of going from the bottom up with an input, we take the error signal and move from the top of the network back down to the input level, changing the weights between the output units and the hidden units and then changing the weights between the hidden units and the normal input units as we go. Now you can see why all the units at each layer are connected with all those above and below them. The network therefore is symmetrical from top to bottom; any pathway from the input layer to the output layer can be duplicated from the opposite direction. Eventually, as the inputs are propagated forward through the system and error signals are back-propagated, the error signal diminishes and drops to zero. Then we say the network is fully trained; it produces the desired output directly from the input without needing further back-propagation.

Learning Rules and a Bowlful of Error   How does back-propagation work? Without getting into the mathematics of the algorithm, we look at a commonly used learning rule to show how weights are changed under back-propagation. Highly simplified, here's the **delta rule,** which might be used to train a network under back-propagation:

$$\Delta w_{ij} = \epsilon \, E f(I)$$

where Δ (delta) w_{ij} means the change in the weights between two neurodes; ϵ (lowercase epsilon) is the "rate of learning" in the system; E is the error; and $f(I)$ is the input to a neurode. Overall, this rule says that you change the weights between two neurodes depending on how big the error is in relation to the input of a specific neurode and how quickly you want the system to arrive at the target. With ϵ set to a low value (the actual number might be 0.05), the system will take longer to arrive at the target than when ϵ is set to a higher value, such as 0.15, perhaps. Sometimes my students ask why ϵ isn't always set high to maximize the speed of learning. That's a good question. Answering it will be easier if we consider what happens to the system when we back-propagate an error signal through it.

Figure 6.10 shows how a weight vector—that is, the connections between a layer of neurodes and a specific neurode above or below that layer—changes when the delta rule is applied. The solid shape hovering in the three-dimensional space is called an **error bowl.** You have to imagine that the initial vector represents a line drawn directly down from this error bowl onto the two-dimensional plane below it. If we draw this line from a place high on the error bowl, it means that the initial vector is way off the ideal vector. As we draw this line from points that are lower and lower on the error bowl, the network is getting closer and closer to the ideal weight vector, which is always at the bottom of the error bowl. The part of Figure 6.10 labeled "delta vector" shows specifically how much the weights are changed each time we back-propagate the error through the system. As you can tell by looking at Figure 6.10, the fastest way to get to the bottom of the error bowl would be to draw a line straight "down" the outside surface of the bowl. But you'll see that the delta vector in fact seems to be going a little "sideways" instead of straight down. It does so because we have set ϵ either high or low. The bigger the value of ϵ, the more likely it is that the delta vector will go straight down the outside surface of the error bowl. The smaller the value of ϵ, the more likely it is that the delta vector will spiral around the error-bowl surface. Why then shouldn't we set ϵ to a high value and thus cruise straight down?

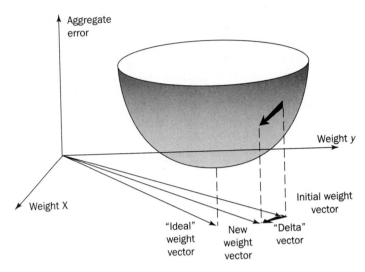

Figure 6.10 The generalized delta rule is a gradient descent system. *Source:* Copyright 1992 by MIT Press. Adapted by permission of the publisher.

The answer is that in real life, because these networks can become very complicated, the actual error bowl may not have nearly so smooth a surface as we see here. Rather it might have numerous small bumps, ridges, and valleys. The valleys can be especially troublesome. If the delta vector were to enter such a valley directly, the network might be fooled into thinking it had reached the bottom of the error bowl. But it's unlikely that such a valley would extend around the entire surface of the error bowl. By moving a little sideways as it heads down, the system may avoid one of these local traps. A sledding metaphor is appropriate. You may know of a steep hill that has a little valley or trough. If you head in directly, you may not have enough energy to sled through it and continue going down the hill. But head into the trough at an angle, and even though you may slow down a little initially, you'll still have enough energy to keep going all the way down the rest of the hill.

Representing and Retrieving Knowledge

When we looked at the symbolic models of knowledge organization in Chapter 5, we considered retrieval and sentence verification in such spreading-activation and search models as TLC. In this chapter we go through a parallel discussion to show how a connectionist network might accomplish these feats.

McClelland (1981; Rumelhart & McClelland, 1986) wrote a classic demonstration depicting a neural network's ability to organize and retrieve knowledge. To show how a neural network could retrieve information, McClelland created a hypothetical microworld—a group of men, each with several associated identifying features. Each man, in fact was a gang member; the hypothetical gang members are listed in Table 6.3. Each member has five facts associated with his name: age, marital status, educational attainment, membership in one of two gangs, and gang-related occupation. Today, of course, the problems associated with urban juvenile gangs seem much more

Table 6.3 Characteristics of Jets and Sharks Members

Name	Gang	Age	Education	Marital Status	Occupation
Art	Jets	40s	J.H.	Sing.	Pusher
Al	Jets	30s	J.H.	Mar.	Burglar
Sam	Jets	20s	Col.	Sing.	Bookie
Clyde	Jets	40s	J.H.	Sing.	Bookie
Mike	Jets	30s	J.H.	Sing.	Bookie
Jim	Jets	20s	J.H.	Div.	Burglar
Greg	Jets	20s	H.S.	Mar.	Pusher
John	Jets	20s	J.H.	Mar.	Burglar
Doug	Jets	30s	H.S.	Sing.	Bookie
Lance	Jets	20s	J.H.	Mar.	Burglar
George	Jets	20s	J.H.	Div.	Burglar
Pete	Jets	20s	H.S.	Sing.	Bookie
Fred	Jets	20s	H.S.	Sing.	Pusher
Gene	Jets	20s	Col.	Sing.	Pusher
Ralph	Jets	30s	J.H.	Sing.	Pusher
Phil	Sharks	30s	Col.	Mar.	Pusher
Ike	Sharks	30s	J.H.	Sing.	Bookie
Nick	Sharks	30s	H.S.	Sing.	Pusher
Don	Sharks	30s	Col.	Mar.	Burglar
Ned	Sharks	30s	Col.	Mar.	Bookie
Karl	Sharks	40s	H.S.	Mar.	Bookie
Ken	Sharks	20s	H.S.	Sing.	Burglar
Earl	Sharks	40s	H.S.	Mar.	Burglar
Rick	Sharks	30s	H.S.	Div.	Burglar
Ol	Sharks	30s	Col.	Mar.	Pusher
Neal	Sharks	30s	H.S.	Sing.	Bookie
Dave	Sharks	30s	H.S.	Div.	Pusher

Source: From McClelland, 1981.

severe than they may have appeared when this model was created early in the 1980s. Passing references to such occupations as pushers and almost lighthearted mentions of gang names such as "Jets" and "Sharks" (inspired no doubt by the Leonard Bernstein musical *West Side Story*) may seem jarring. But our aim is to demonstrate how a neural network may organize and retrieve information, and so let's accept the materials at face value.

Each man here is uniquely specified by the five attributes assigned him. If we can find a way to wire the network so that one of his attributes will activate a man's other right attributes, then the system, given a specific prompt, will show some ability to retrieve the correct information about him. Suppose you were acquainted with these guys, and somebody asked you, say, "Is Earl married?" Suppose moreover that all you knew for sure about Earl was his membership in the Sharks. How might you respond?

Let's think about how a neural system could represent this information and possibly retrieve it. Of the many ways, the one I'll outline is hypothetical, but plausible. Let's start by assuming two neurons, a Shark and a Jet. Moreover, let's assume that, because no man can be in both gangs, as soon as one neuron is activated, its activation inhibits the other. Let the number "1" indicate maximal activation (maximum rate of firing) and the number "0" indicate maximal inhibition (no firing). With these assumptions made, every representation of each man will be in one of two states:

Jet Neuron (or neurode)	Shark Neuron (or neurode)
0	1
1	0

Part of Earl's neural representation would include the elements "01" in the mathematical vector that stands for the pattern of neural energy, which in turn stands for our cognitive representation of Earl. How could this information be used to answer the question about Earl's marital status?

Three marital statuses are possible, taking Single to mean "never married": Married, Divorced, and Single. Suppose we represent these states with three neurons:

$$M \quad D \quad S$$

so that activating one tends to result in that neuron's increasing its rate of firing. Because one can't be married and divorced at the same time, it makes sense to establish an inhibitory linkage separating these neurons. Thus, for each man in the microworld, this part of his representation will eventually wind up in one of three stable states: 100 if he is married, 010 if he is divorced, and 001 if he's single.

Looking at the Sharks listing, we see that six are married, two are divorced, and four are single. How then should the connection between the Shark neuron and the MDS neurons be wired? The answer is that the Shark neuron should have a positive connection to, and therefore a positive weight with, the Married neuron. Once the Married neuron is activated, its activation level will tend to inhibit the Divorced and Single neurons from firing. The correlation between being a Shark and being married is not perfect, and so the Married may not immediately take on a maximal value of "1." But the longer the entire system is active, the more likely it is that the Married neuron will reach that state, other influences being equal. Here's how vector representation of Earl looks thus far:

Person	Gang Status	Marital Status
Earl	01	100

And so, in answer to the question that was asked, you would probably say "Yes, Earl is married."

As Figure 6.11 shows, we can create a graphic representation of the vectors, and have done so for five individuals. Each of the irregularly shaped areas is known as a "cloud." Within each cloud, the elliptical shapes refer to the neurons we have been discussing. When a name is activated, it corresponds to activating one of the dark dots

Figure 6.11 Some of the units and connections needed to represent the individuals shown in Table 6.3. The units connected with double-headed arrows are mutually excitatory. All the units within the same cloud are mutually inhibitory. *Source:* From McClelland, 1981.

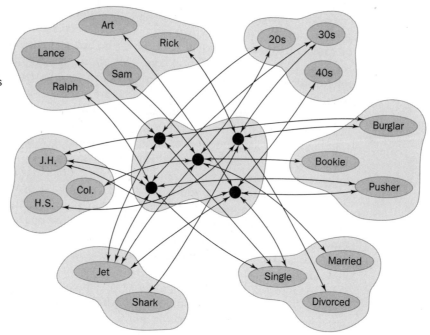

at the center of Figure 6.11; each of those dark dots corresponds to a person, and each is connected by a double-headed arrow to each of the appropriate attributes for that person. These double-headed arrows show the excitatory connections in the model. For clarity, the inhibitory connections are not shown. Activating any specific neuron in a cloud inhibits all the other specific neurons in that cloud. Thus the system arrives at just one unique pattern of activation for each of the men in the microworld. Graphically, we would see a unique activation pattern in the various clouds' neurons. Mathematically, if we wanted to see how that would look, we would have to know how to read the vector representation. For Earl, it might be like this:

Name	Gang Status	Marital Status	Age	Education	Occupation
Earl	01	100	100	010	100

And if we put them all together, as they would be in the "nervous system":

01100100010100

It's hard to tell the difference between Earl and a jar of peanut butter, isn't it?

Neural Networks and Brain Functioning

Can neural networks tell us anything about the brain's organization or operation? In this section we discuss the relationship between connectionist models' operation and the brain to see which processes a neural network could duplicate. In looking at this relationship, researchers have focused on brain damage to see if connectionist models might offer insights into what happens to the damaged brain's computational power.

Brain damage can, of course, arise from a number of causes, and obviously the specific cause may impart its own form of damage. A cerebro-vascular accident (CVA), or stroke may deprive of oxygen almost all the neurons in a relatively small region in the brain. When this deprivation continues, those cells are damaged irreparably. We refer to the site of the damage as a lesion, here a focal lesion. Sometimes, but not always, highly identifiable cognitive functions are lost following the stroke, presumably as a result of the lesion. Other causes, such as shock, may leave more general and diffuse damage to the brain and its computational power. With different techniques (Harley, 1996), neural networks can be used to model both types of damage. Focal damage may be modeled by simply removing neurodes from a trained neural network, or by removing the excitatory or inhibitory connections between specific neurodes. If neurodes are relatively few, and especially if all lesioned neurodes are at the same level in the neural network (Small, 1991), this technique can simulate a focal lesion, provided that the rest of the network is left intact. Diffuse damage may be simulated by randomly adding or subtracting activation throughout the network. Then the entire network is intact, but random activation makes its processing a great deal "noisier" and sloppier.

One approach in rehabilitating stroke victims consists of explicitly retraining them to carry out functions they could achieve with ease before the stroke. Sometimes the retraining focuses on perceptual or motor functions, but often it deals with lost linguistic functions, such as word retrieval, pronunciation, or sentence construction (we'll have a lot more to say about losing linguistic functions in Chapter 7). Several researchers have taken an analogous approach with neural networks. In pioneering research, Sejnowski and Rosenberg (1987) trained neural networks to do word association and retrieval; then the networks were lesioned. The networks were then retrained on the same materials they had previously "known." Consistent with what we know about stroke victims, Sejnowski and Rosenberg found that the lesioned neural networks were able to relearn the original materials, and the relearning was accomplished significantly faster than the original learning. Moreover, the improvement resulting from retraining on some of the original materials carried over to other original materials that were not explicitly retaught. When Sejnowski and Rosenberg divided their original set of twenty associations into two sets (a retraining set of eighteen associations and a "novel" set of two associations), they found that after the network had been retrained on eighteen associations it also showed marked improvement on the other two associations that had not been retrained. This surprising finding is consistent with human performance, and it's difficult to see how a symbolic model might reproduce that effect (Harley, 1996).

Possible Limitations of Neural-Network Models

Although cognitive scientists agree almost unanimously that connectionist models have proved tremendously useful, technical questions have nevertheless arisen about neural-network modeling and the fundamental accuracy of the connectionist approach. We take up the latter question in this section, focusing on a great debate on accuracy in connectionist models.

If you look back at our discussion in Chapter 5 on lexical access as a way of showing how the cognitive system was organized, you may remember that I talked about the "components" in a word's representation. I said we might describe your knowledge about the word's meaning as its semantic component, your knowledge about the word's sound as its phonological component, and so on. There you have the standard position: When we are given a visual word-recognition task, we contact these related components and then call on cognitive routines to determine the word's meaning, to pronounce it, or even to determine if it is a known word (Besner, Twilley, McCann, & Seergobin, 1990). Each of these lexical components must be represented differently; according to the standard approach, each has its own organizational principles and structure. The connectionist account does away with all these components and routines, arguing instead that only one procedure enables us to read words, and it is not based on a "lexicon" at all (Seidenberg & McClelland, 1989). One phenomenon at issue in this discussion was the pseudohomophone effect.

A homophone is a word that is pronounced like another, but shares neither spelling nor meaning with that word: *sum* and *some* are homophones. A **pseudohomophone** is a nonword that is pronounced like a real word (and so you could say it would be a homophone if it were a real word). The nonword *waik* is a pseudohomophone of *wake*. A couple of empirical phenomena are interesting. When humans are given pseudohomophones visually, they can say them more quickly than they can nonwords that are not pseudohomophones. Subjects can say the nonword *waik* faster than they can say the nonword *paik* (*paik* doesn't sound like any known word). But when it comes to making a lexical decision about a word or nonword, people are slower on pseudohomophones than on nonwords that are not pseudohomophones. In other words, the subject who could name *waik* faster than *paik* slows down when the task is to decide if *waik* is a word or a nonword. What's going on here? Again, the standard account suggests that because one can access and use a phonological representation (the sound of the real word *wake*) helps one say *waik*, but because *wake* is a real word that the subject knows, the subject is slowed down when it's time to make a lexical decision about *waik*. In other words, the lexicon's separate components are required to explain the human findings, and each of the lexicons may require its own symbolic representation.

Seidenberg and McClelland (1989) disputed these notions and invented a connectionist model that had neither a lexicon nor pronunciation rules. Instead, their model had:

> . . . a single mechanism that learns to process regular words, nonwords, and other types of letter strings through experience with the spelling–sound correspondences implicit in the set of words from which it learns. (Seidenberg & McClelland, 1989, p. 525)

In other words, Seidenberg and McClelland claim that a lexicon with its several separate components is not needed. Rather, their model learned from its experience with a body of words. This experience would be sufficient to teach the model because enough regularity appears in the irregularity of words to teach the model how to pronounce nonwords such as *waik,* and thus produce the pseudohomophone effect. Their connectionist model could account for these effects because of its knowledge about the words on which it had been trained.

Besner, Twilley, McCann, and Seergobin (1990) wondered how accurate the connectionist model was. They used the same model, first training it with a list of real words such as *brain,* and then testing it with regular nonwords that were pseudohomophones, such as *brane.* The model had not been trained on such pseudohomophones. We can pronounce such nonwords easily, and Besner et al. found that their sample of people correctly pronounced such pseudohomophones 94% of the time. But the Seidenberg and McClelland model did not do nearly so well on the pseudohomophones, "pronouncing" only 59% of them correctly (the model didn't actually speak; its pronunciation was inferred from activity by its phonological units). Besner et al. concluded that the model's performance on letter strings it knew was good, but its performance was very poor on letter strings it did not know.

The findings lead to several implications. First, the connectionist model's relative failure to duplicate a well-known human finding questions how useful a connectionist model is, at least in cognitive psychology. Second, the Besner et al. findings question the connectionist approach in general. Even if the McClelland and Seidenberg model did not duplicate the pseudohomophone effect, another connectionist model might. Maybe so, but suppose that after an exhaustive search among connnectionist models, none can duplicate the pseudohomophone effect. Those failures might point, however indirectly, to the need for a symbolic (i.e., nonconnectionist) model that had lexical knowledge. We can close this story by saying that Seidenberg and McClelland (1990) responded to Besner et al. by focusing on the size of the training set. They point out that it's not altogether fair to compare their model, trained on fewer than 3000 words, with people who had vocabularies of more than 30,000 words. It certainly does seem that people know a lot more than the model does, but the real question may be, do they know more than this kind of model ever could know? We just do not yet have an answer.

Concluding Comments and Suggestions for Further Reading

You've seen plenty of specific findings in this chapter, but, unlike most other chapters here, relatively few human findings. You may wonder why. As you'll recall from Chapter 1, we said that cognitive psychology is simply one of the cognitive sciences, and not all the allied disciplines rely on human subjects as heavily as psychology does. Perhaps more than the other chapters, this one reflects the perspective of some of the other disciplines—although it is extremely difficult to delineate precise borders between cognitive psychology and the other cognitive disciplines.

In Chapters 4 and 5, we've looked at two approaches (local networks and distributed networks) that seem to have a common objective. Both approaches have formal, computational models of human knowledge representation and retrieval. Sometimes students want to know why two approaches are needed, especially when it seems that each approach has been used rather successfully, and I have several responses. First, each approach is needed because the human cognitive system itself seems to operate in that way. That is, cognitive science is fundamentally committed to the idea that cognitive processes can be treated as naturally occurring objects in a natural world. The task of the cognitive scientist, then, is to understand such objects.

Thus, because the cognitive system really does operate in a serial and sequential way, our models of memory should ultimately reflect this reality.

Readers who would like to find out more about parallel distributed processing approaches might read Rumelhart and McClelland (1986). For those who want a hands-on introduction, a handbook by McClelland and Rumelhart (1988) comes with software showing how to build your own neural networks. Levine (1990) offers another hands-on approach, showing how a number of cognitive phenomena might be modeled with a neural-network approach. The Caudill and Butler (1992) volumes are accompanied by software that allows users to build and modify neural networks. Tank and Hopfield (1987) wrote an article-length introduction to distributed networks. Two important articles dealing with connectionism, by Smolensky (1988) and Hanson and Burr (1990), appeared in *Behavioral and Brain Sciences*. One nice feature about articles in this journal is that the "open peer commentary" following each article lets the reader see disagreements and controversy as well as agreements. Books by Nadel et al. (1989) and Churchland (1989) are excellent introductions to this literature. Anderson and Rosenfeld (1988) collected many historically important articles on connectionism, and it's interesting and instructive to trace the modern connectionistic approach in these historical fonts. Gallant (1993) ties the neural-network literature to the literature on expert systems, and volumes edited by Hanson, Drastal, and Rivest (1994) summarize more recent developments. My rendition here mainly supports distributed-network systems, but parallel-processing approaches haven't met with universal acclaim. Those who would like to read two critical and very challenging articles might consider Pinker and Prince (1988) and Fodor and Pylyshyn (1988). Besner, Twilley, McCann, and Seergobin (1990) have questioned such networks' ability to reproduce such empirical outcomes; Seidenberg and McClelland (1990) rebut the questions in the same issue of *Psychological Review*.

Oh, one other thing, I almost forgot: Sarah shelves geology (ten books per minute); Jessica shelves history (seven); George shelves art (six); Karen shelves chemistry (seven); Sam shelves poetry (eight); and Tim shelves physics (six).

Key Terms

Perceptron	XOR problem	Error bowl
Pattern associator	Hidden units	Pseudohomophone
Vector encoding	Back-propagation algorithm	
Linear independence	Delta rule	

PART FIVE

Language

Understanding and producing language are fundamental aspects of our mental lives and our humanity. Without these abilities, we would be cut off from one another. Language enables us to erect complex social structures and to form intimate social bonds.

These claims may seem like overstatements to you. For example, you might point to colonies of insects, such as termites, which have elaborate social structure without having language. However, one striking finding to emerge from the studies of such creatures concerns the complexity of their communication systems, which seems out of proportion to the complexity of the creatures themselves. Termites, for example, signal one another by drumming their heads against the floor of their nests. This action produces a sound like that of sand falling on paper, but a close analysis of the drumming reveals that it is highly organized and complex. By varying the rhythmic phrasing and duration of the drumming, termites send complex codes throughout the whole colony.

In addition to being an apparently essential part of our social structure, language seems to be a crucial ingredient of our mental lives. Our intuitions support this assertion. When we think, we are often aware of some sort of internal speech that seems to accompany our thought processes.

For a variety of reasons, cognitive psychologists have turned their attention to the phenomenon of language. This part of the book considers some of their discoveries and deals with a number of issues. First, defining language is difficult. Second, expressing the essence of language in a set of formal rules has also proved unachievable so far. Almost all linguists believe that our knowledge of linguistic sounds, word order, and meaning can be rewritten as a formal system of rules, and we'll examine some of the reasons for this belief. Not much is known about these rules, although psycholinguists have a good idea of some of the minimum elements that are required in any proposed theory of linguistic knowledge.

Another issue is the origin of language. The concern here is with the role of experience as both a necessary and a sufficient basis for language. As you are probably aware, a number of people believe that experience with language per se is not sufficient to enable the child to learn it. Hence, according to these theorists, the child must be aided in language acquisition efforts by innate linguistic predispositions. We'll cover this question in the next three chapters. We'll also consider some of the cognitive operations that are involved in the comprehension and production of speech, and we'll see that both top-down and bottom-up processes seem to be involved in this form of pattern recognition.

C H A P T E R   7

Structure of Language

*O*verview

In this passage, Denyse, a fourteen-year-old English girl, is conversing with the psycholinguist Richard Cromer. Cromer's colleague, Sigrid Lipka, transcribed the interview and this portion of it appears in Pinker (1994).

Denyse: I like opening cards. I had a pile of post this morning and not one of them was a Christmas card. A bank statement I got this morning!
Cromer: [A bank statement? I hope it was good news.]

No, it wasn't good news.
[Sounds like mine.]
I hate . . . , My mum works over at the, over on the ward and she said "not another bank statement." I said "it's the second one in two days." And she said, "Do you want me to go to the bank for you at lunchtime?" and I went, "No, I'll go this time and explain it myself." I tell you what, my bank are awful. They've lost my bank book, you see, and I can't find it anywhere. I belong to the TSB Bank and I'm thinking of changing my bank 'cause they're so awful. They keep, they keep losing . . . {At this point, another person arrives with tea} Oh, isn't that nice.
[Uhm. Very good.]

They've got the habit of doing that. They lose, they've lost my bank book twice, in a month, and I think I'll scream. My mum went yesterday to the bank for me. She said, "They've lost your bank book again." I went, "Can I scream?" and I went, she went, "Yes, go on." So I hollered. But it is annoying when they do things like that. TSB, Trustees aren't . . . uh the best ones to be with actually. They're hopeless.

How does Denyse come across to you? Reading this passage, I was struck by how sophisticated she seems, despite adolescent expressions such as "I went" for "I said." She seems sophisticated in that, I don't think I knew how to intercede effectively in a bank at age fourteen, if I even had a bank account at that age. This impression of sophistication and precocity is supported by other things Denyse talked about in this interview, among them having a joint bank account with her boyfriend, going for a vacation to Scotland with a boy named Danny, attending her sister's wedding, and being reunited with her long-lost father in a tearful airport scene.

But in fact, none of these things Denyse talked about ever occurred. She has no boyfriend, she has never been to Scotland, her sister is unmarried, and her father has never been away from home for any significant period. She has no bank account at TSB or any other bank, and so could not possibly have lost her bank book, or gotten a statement from a bank that morning. In fact, Denyse, who was born with spina bifida and

hydrocephaly, is retarded. She cannot read or write; neither can she add or subtract. Far from being precocious, Denyse is, and will always be, unable to meet the demands of everyday living.

How then is she able to speak so fluently and with such apparent authority? Unfortunately, we don't yet have a detailed answer to that question. But we do know that other hydrocephalic children like Denyse sometimes exhibit the same pattern, which has been called "chatterbox syndrome" (Pinker, 1994). The syndrome is interesting because it shows that the buildup of internal fluid and resulting pressure that damages the hydrocephalic child's brain may somehow, sometimes leave undamaged either the portion of the brain responsible for language, or the neural processing that language requires. That the cognition supporting language can be left undamaged in spite of a general cognitive deficit means it is appropriate to think of linguistic knowledge as somehow "modularized" or separable from other aspects of our cognitive systems. Explaining how that modularity can occur is one of our tasks in this chapter.

Several varieties of linguistic knowledge must be explained. First, simply to comprehend speech, as Denyse clearly does, requires knowing phonology, or linguistic sounds. Second, we must have models or rules for generating and recognizing appropriate word order, or *syntax.* Finally, effective use of language requires general or semantic knowledge of the type we looked at in Chapters 5 and 6. It is here that Denyse's linguistic performance is perhaps at its shakiest. In talking about her joint bank account, she demonstrated that she did not really understand the expression when she spoke about her boyfriend withdrawing money from her side of the account. Linguists refer to this conglomeration of linguistic knowledge as **grammar.**

For at least the past thirty years, syntax has probably been the most intensively studied component in grammatical knowledge. Many reasons account for this attention, not the least of which is that Noam Chomsky—perhaps the most influential contemporary theoretical linguist—believed that semantics, or meaning, was derived from and secondary to syntax. In this chapter we examine Chomsky's proposition.

Words and phrases can be put together in many ways. And yet, all normal children seem to acquire the appropriate knowledge despite immature intellectual ability. How can they do it? How can children learn language—an extremely complex activity—when they are still more or less incapable of similar intellectual feats? This paradox has led some theorists (Chomsky among them) to argue that children are helped in their linguistic quest by innate predispositions that make them sensitive to regularities in linguistic sounds and phrases. We examine here some of the evidence supporting that proposition and contrast it with the alternative viewpoint—namely, that no innate abilities are required to learn language.

What Is Language?

Whenever I ask the question, "What is language?" in my classes, students usually seem content to let this equation express their belief:

Language = Communication.

Students who hold this opinion are (perhaps unwittingly) asserting that the gesturer's *intention* determines whether language is being displayed. That is, if I make a gesture (broadly speaking, sounds should be considered gestures), and if the gesture seemingly is made in the context of a deliberate mental event, then my students are willing to say that this gesture is linguistic and that my other gestures probably are linguistic, too. This view of language is sometimes called the **continuity theory** (Aitchison, 1983). According to this perspective, human language is a sophisticated calling system not fundamentally different from animal cries and calls. Proponents of this position often describe work by Struhsaker (1967), who studied vervet monkey cries in the wild. They use substantially different vocalizations for different dangerous animals. A *chutter* signals a cobra's arrival, but if an eagle appears, the monkeys produce the *rraup* sound. The argument that these sounds are one step removed from words doesn't seem too far-fetched. That is, among our primitive ancestors, similar danger calls may have been used, and gradually came to represent the animals themselves; they became the animals' names in human language.

The continuity theory suffers from several problems. First, the vervet monkeys may simply be responding to the intensity of the danger rather than to anything specific about the stimulus. That is, the chutter may be used for something extremely dangerous, the rraup for a less frightening stimulus, and so on. This interpretation has been empirically supported; vervet monkeys sometimes chirp on seeing an eagle. This call is usually given too in response to a lion and suggests that the monkey considers lions and eagles equally threatening. The implication is that the apparent specificity observed (heard?) in animal cries doesn't necessarily indicate that such animals have specific referents in mind.

A second problem with continuity theories is that attributing intentionality is often difficult to do in practice. Whale songs are one of the better known illustrations of this problem. As you may know, some species of whales produce sounds that have definite rhythm. These songs change in predictable ways. During a lengthy migration, themes are introduced, become dominant, and eventually are supplanted. No one knows why the whales produce these sounds; consequently, no one knows whether these sounds are communicative.

Although my students may be willing to assume that regularity in gesture indicates both specificity of referent and intentionality (and therefore language), we might do well to modify the equation initially proposed: Language is communicative—at least potentially—but simple communications aren't necessarily linguistic. This statement suggests that, to be considered truly linguistic, a set of gestures must have properties other than simple intent to communicate.

Design Features

Hockett (1963) proposed essential characteristics that seem required in any definition of language. Although many linguists believe that this approach is the only valid way to define language, we should be aware that such an approach nevertheless has problems. Even if Hockett had managed to isolate just the features in communication that determine the essence of language, such a listing wouldn't make clear how those features were *related* to one another. Yet, the relationship among such design characteristics may be the sine qua non of language: We are not necessarily interested in the parts that make up language; we want to know how those parts have been put together.

Figure 7.1 pictorially represents some of Hockett's **design features,** some of which obviously are more important than others. The *vocal-auditory channel* is a desirable but not essential feature of language. Speaking and hearing are more or less nondirectional senses, meaning that our eyes and limbs can be trained on other stimuli while we converse.

Broadcast transmission and *rapid fading* are also aspects of the physics of sound. We are amazingly good at locating sound sources, which can be an aid in communication. Typically, speech is an extremely transitory event. Although having more durable linguistic codes is sometimes advantageous, the speech's transitoriness can also be beneficial. Because this type of communication fades rapidly, privacy is enhanced. The rapid fading also permits duplicity (telling different people different versions), but this isn't all bad, because at times, some messages need editing. Rapid fading also implies a social function. To talk to people, you have to get relatively close to them.

With *interchangeability,* we move closer to a language characteristic that could be called essential. This design feature describes a competent speaker's ability to reproduce any message that she can understand, and the message's content is left undisturbed by this reproduction. This ability isn't present in all animal communication systems. In some, specific gestures are sometimes strongly associated with sex roles and can't be reproduced by the opposite gender.

Total feedback refers to our hearing everything we produce. *Specialization* is applied by linguists in several ways; in this context it means that the usual purpose of human speech is to communicate. The sounds we make are not simply incidental to some

Figure 7.1 A pictorial view of Hockett's design features. *Source:* From Hockett, 1960.

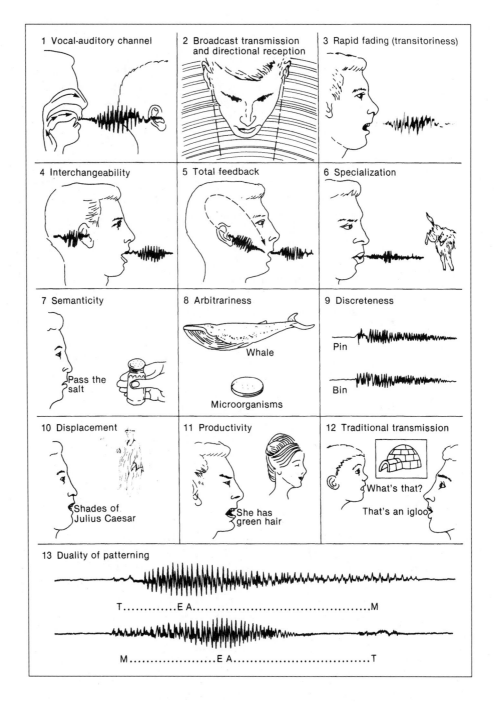

other purpose. In some animal vocalizations, such as whale song, this property is not obviously present. *Semanticity* and *arbitrariness* are related and show that in language no inherent relationship connects linguistic sounds and their referents, even though the sounds clearly mean something.

Discreteness expresses the idea that language consists of **phonemes,** small, separable units of sound, each of which has an identity. Typically, only a few phonemes are used in language. English has about forty phonemes. Standing alone, phonemes have no meaning. They can, however, be combined in many ways. The combination of phonemes according to a language's rules results in creating a **morpheme,** the basic unit of meaning. In English, morphemes are usually words, but not all morphemes are words: the suffix *-ly* is a morpheme.

Duality of patterning describes how an infinite number of meaningful words are created from a few phonemic building blocks. This ability is not unique to humanity. Bird songs are made up of a series of notes, each of which is meaningless by itself. Any meaning the song may have is conveyed only by the entire sequence.

Traditional transmission expresses the idea that many (perhaps most) elements in language are handed down from one generation to the next; some sort of experience within a culture is necessary to acquire language. Children reared in isolation almost invariably seem to show deficits in linguistic ability, some of which seem permanent (Lenneberg, 1964). Traditional transmission is a hallmark of language; experience doesn't seem nearly as clear an influence in animal communication. Bird songs such as that of the thrush appear to be completely innate. For such animals, presence or absence of other members of the species has little or no effect on the acquisition or description of the call. Incidentally, we must avoid thinking of these innate abilities as categorical—that is, either–or. Other birds, such as the chaffinch, seem to hatch with the basic song pattern built in. Details in the song's pitch and rhythm, however, are acquired by experience (Thorpe, 1961, 1963).

Displacement is a language feature that people use and take for granted every day. We often refer to things that are far removed in time and place, but such talk seems acceptable to our listeners. Thus, a movie may begin with the narration, "A long time ago, in a galaxy far, far away"—which doesn't strike us as unreasonable. So common is this feature that we seldom stop to think about its implications. Although animal cries may be truly communicative, can they communicate about things that are no longer present? Your dog may bark at an intruder—perhaps even emit a specific bark—but can the dog bark at a memory, say, of last year's intruder?

Very few bona fide displacement cases have been seen in animal communication, and even these are far more limited than human displacement. Von Frisch (1967) clearly demonstrated that bees have arbitrary communicative gestures, which include displacement. When a bee discovers a source of nectar distant from the hive (at least 200 yards away), she returns to the hive and does a dance (von Frisch's term), which shows the direction to fly from the hive. The scout then does either a "round dance" or a "waggle dance"—the former if the source is relatively close by, the latter if it is far away. The scout bee's dance tells by its vigor something about the quality of the nectar. When the nectar is plentiful and good, the scout bee's dance is energetic. When the rest of the colony leaves the hive to gather the nectar, the bees fly en masse to the indicated spot. This behavior impressively demonstrates displacement in animal communication. Von Frisch (1954) also demonstrated, however, the limitations of this system. A hive was placed near the bottom of a radio tower. As the scout bees flew out, they were collected and taken to a sugar-water container, which had been placed atop the tower. Then the scouts were released. They dutifully returned to the hive and energetically reported (via the round dance) that a good source of nectar was nearby. When the rest of the colony left, the bees flew in all directions except up, because the bee communication system denotes only horizontal, not vertical, distance.

This bee failure bares an extremely important aspect of human communication. We can use our language in novel, creative ways. If we were confronted with the bees' plight, making up a word (or, in bee, a dance) that communicated the idea of altitude would be relatively easy for us. This sort of creativity takes place every day. When actor Lee Marvin's live-in lover sued him some years ago, an anonymous wag created the word *palimony* and we all knew what it meant, even though we hadn't thought of it ourselves. This creativity in language is called **productivity.** Unlike other animals, whose vocalizations seem stimulus bound, we can decide what we want to say and when we wish to say it.

Table 7.1 compares language with several other phenomena for presence or absence of specific design features. As Table 7.1 shows, only language has all the features that have been described. Moreover, the least shared (and therefore the most essential) aspects of language seem to be displacement, productivity, and duality of patterning. This point is important, because these three features seem to be related. Duality in patterning and productivity in language indicate that linguistic rules must be general and abstract. In English, the rules specifying how morphemes are produced from phonemes do not depend in any principled way on the phonemes themselves. Some combinations are not permitted in English (no English word begins with *mg*), but most combinations are permitted, although the patterns thus created are far from random. Similarly, novelty in language is common and is often comprehensible to our listeners. Recall that I demonstrated this receptivity by creating a novel sentence in Chapter 1. Demonstrations such as these show that patterns of morphemes we produce do not depend rigidly on the morphemes we may already have uttered. If they were dependent, we could never produce a creative utterance. Can you see why? Once we had picked a morpheme to begin our comment, that choice would rigidly limit our subsequent choice, which in turn would limit the next choice, and so on. The number of producible utterances would be large, but it would be finite. But we know this limit doesn't apply: the number of producible, and therefore creative, utterances is infinite.

Still, not all novel strings of morphemes are comprehensible to our listeners. Presumably, some novel strings of morphemes are comprehensible, though others aren't because we adhere to some general rules in the former and violate them in the latter. Together, duality in patterning and productivity combine to allow us to expand our ability to refer to objects that are remote. In the extreme these features allow us to refer to things that, strictly speaking, are never present anywhere; I mean ideas such as truth or beauty.

Hockett's work suggests that the design features truly essential to language deal with creativity and flexibility. For some time, a tendency common among linguists has been to think that people's grammatical knowledge can be expressed as rules specific enough to permit us to produce well-formed words and sentences but general enough to give us unlimited creativity.

Table 7.1   Comparing Eight Communication Systems

	(A) Members of the Cricket Family	(B) Bee Dancing	(C) Stickleback Courtship
1. Vocal-audition channel	Auditory, not vocal	No	No
2. Broadcast transmission and directional recognition	_[a]	—	—
3. Rapid fading (transitoriness)	Yes, repeated	?[b]	?
4. Interchangeability	Limited	Limited	No
5. Total feedback	Yes	?	No
6. Specialization	Yes?	?	In part
7. Semanticity	No?	Yes	No
8. Arbitrariness	?	No	—
9. Discreteness	Yes?	No	?
10. Displacement	—	Yes, always	—
11. Productivity	No	Yes	No
12. Traditional transmission	No?	Probably not	No?
13. Duality of patterning	?(Trivial)	No	

Note: Eight communication systems that possess in varying degrees the thirteen design features of language proposed by Hockett.
[a]A line indicates that the feature cannot be determined because another feature is lacking or indefinite.
[b]A question mark means that it is doubtful or not known whether the system has the feature.
Source: From Hockett, 1960.

Grammar and Linguistics

Encountering the heading "Grammar and Linguistics" in a book about cognitive psychology may seem odd, but we have good reason to discuss linguists' theories and modus operandi.

First, as you saw in Chapter 1, linguists were among the first to successfully attack behavioristic psychology. In the 1950s, when this criticism first appeared, psychologists became highly interested in work by theoretical linguists, and the discipline known as psycholinguistics was born. Psycholinguists and linguists have different but complementary ways of doing research. Whereas the psychologist is likely to design experiments that test fairly limited hypotheses about language comprehension in a fairly rigid way, the linguist is much more likely to study sentences that have been produced by speakers in a natural context. The linguist may even compose sentences, which are then studied according to the linguist's intuitions about the sentence's structure and anything that structure may indicate about grammatical knowledge.

The second reason for studying theoretical linguistics derives from one of its stated objectives. Linguists set out to discover **linguistic universals,** which are general principles that are thought to be embodied in every language. The evidence sup-

Table 7.1 (continued)

(D) Western Meadowlark Song	(E) Gibbon Calls	(F) Paralinguistic Phenomena	(G) Language	(H) Western Instrumental Music (Since Bach)
Yes	Yes	Yes	Yes	Auditory, not vocal
—	—	—	—	Yes
Yes	Yes, repeated	Yes	Yes	Yes
?	Yes	Largely yes	Yes	?
Yes	Yes	Yes	Yes	Yes
Yes?	Yes	Yes?	Yes	Yes
In part?	Yes	Yes?	Yes	No, in general
If semantic	Yes	In part Yes, often	—	
?	Yes	Largely no	Yes	In part
?	No	In part	Yes, often	—
?	No	Yes	Yes	Yes
?	?	Yes	Yes	Yes
?	No	No	Yes	—

porting linguistic universals is currently unclear; nevertheless, the linguist makes an interesting claim about them. You may be aware that language and thought seem intimately bound. For this reason, it is often thought that these linguistic universals reveal underlying rules of thought. That is, linguists have maintained that, by fully understanding language and its organization, it will be possible to understand the human mind and its organization.

Early Views About Grammar

Work in experimental linguistics began about thirty years ago when thinkers realized that language has obvious regularities, as in the sentence:

Would you please pass the _____?

The blank is more readily filled with "salt" than with "chilled monkey brains," and the entire sentence is ambiguous when we fill the blank with "skyscraper." This phenomenon occurs in many sentences and suggests to some that the rules for syntax (word order) could be written as a left-to-right grammar. Such grammars were governed by finite-state rules, meaning that the next word choice at any state in the sentence was determined by consulting a finite number of candidates and picking one of them. In other words, the choice made at the leftmost word in the sentence determined the choice made at the next leftmost word, and so on, until the sentence was completed.

What's implied by such a system of syntax? First, this view implies that human grammar consists of rules that limit the word choices that can be made anywhere in producing a sentence. Second, this system implies that people produce sentences word by word. That is, having chosen one word, we consult a mental list of acceptable choices and produce one of them. Having made this choice, we consult the mental list to see which choices are available for the next word, and so on, until the utterance is completed.

Early research with these types of grammars was impressive. Miller (1958) showed his subjects strings of letters, some generated by the finite-state system shown in Figure 7.2. The transition rules are indicated under the drawing. One of two paths can be taken from the node marked *O*. The system could move through *N* to node 1, or through *S* to node 3. From node 1, it could move through *N* to node 3 or through *G* to *O'*, the finish node. These pathways aren't the only ones through this network, but you can see how the strings were created. How many strings could be created by this primitive system? Because the finite-state rules permit a **recursion** at node 3, an infinite number of strings could be generated. All strings produced by these finite-state rules have some things in common: all begin with either an *N* or an *S,* and all end with a *G*.

Miller next used the same four letters to create another set of strings. This time, however, he made the strings with a random-numbers table to determine which letter should come next, the only constraint being that each of the random strings had to be of the same length as one of the grammar-generated strings. Table 7.2 shows the two sets of strings, which look similar. If you hadn't been reading the text, determining exactly what is different about the two sets of lists might be difficult.

The adult subjects attempted to learn all nine strings in two of the lists by looking at each string one at a time. After looking at all nine strings, they tried to write them down. Each pass through the list was a trial. They studied the list for ten trials or until they reproduced all nine strings without error. Figure 7.3 shows the findings. Notice that the subjects learned the grammatical strings much faster than the random strings. These effects carried over to the second list that they learned. Having learned a grammatical list originally seemed to facilitate learning random strings. To see why, compare performance by the *LR* subjects with that by the *RR* subjects. Those who had first learned a grammatical, or *L* list tended to outperform the *RR* subjects (who

Figure 7.2 A finite-state generator. A string is any sequence of letters generated by starting at state *O* and finishing at *O'*. A letter is added to the string by taking the path labeled by that letter from one state to another. *Source:* From Miller, 1958.

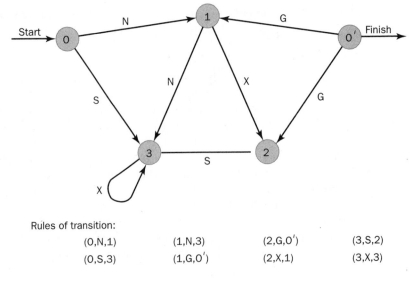

Rules of transition:

| (0,N,1) | (1,N,3) | (2,G,O') | (3,S,2) |
| (0,S,3) | (1,G,O') | (2,X,1) | (3,X,3) |

had learned a random list previously) on each successive trial. Although the differences in the lists seem fairly subtle, the subjects were extremely sensitive to the regularities in the grammar-generated lists. At the time, psychologists were willing to interpret these findings as demonstrating that syntactic knowledge was formally equivalent to a **finite-state grammar.**

Objections to Finite-State Grammars As theories on grammar acquisition, finite-state systems fitted in nicely with the general stimulus-response theories of learning then in vogue. Each word pronounced in a sentence is a response. But because we have total feedback and hear each word we say, hearing a word acts as a discriminative stimulus, a cue to produce the next word in the sentence. At sentence end we are reinforced by our listeners' compliance. This approach reduces learning of a sentence to a much simpler problem—learning a chain of stimulus-response associations. Because researchers had demonstrated many times in laboratories all over the world that animals could learn lengthy stimulus-response chains, and because children surely had to be capable of learning anything that a rat could learn, finite-state grammars were thought to be the definite answer to the problem of how syntax was acquired.

Finite-state systems, however, suffer from theoretical problems, some of which are worth reviewing. First, a competent speaker can embed any syntactic structure into an already formed sentence. We can do this embedding with utterances, too, as demonstrated in Chapter 1. This ability means that the finite state systems' major premise—that a choice of words is constrained by previous choices—is false. Reviewing Figure 7.3, we see that we really don't have to move to any one word in a sentence as a function of the words we have already uttered. We can move from any node to any other node if we wish to. Now we may *typically* produce utterances in accordance with finite-state rules, but we are not obliged to follow them. Because we don't have to follow such rules, our knowledge of syntax must consist of more than simple chaining

Table 7.2 Redundant and Random Strings Used in an Experiment on Learning Structure

Structured (Redundant)		Random	
L_1	L_2	R_1	R_2
SSXG	NNSG	GNSX	NXGS
NNXSG	NNSXG	NSGXN	GNXSG
SXSXG	SXXSG	XGSSN	SXNGG
SSXNSG	NNXSXG	SXNNGN	GGSNXG
SXXXSG	NNXXSG	XGSXXS	NSGNGX
NNSXNSG	NNXXSXG	GSXXGNS	NGSXXNS
SXSXNSG	NNXXXSG	NSXXGSG	NGXXGGN
SXXXSXG	SSXNSXG	SGXGGNN	SXGXGNS
SXXXXSG	SSXNXSG	XXGNSGG	XGSNGXG

Source: From Miller, 1958.

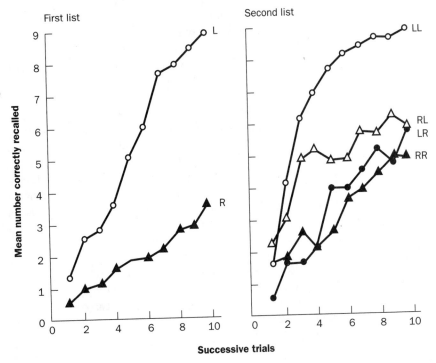

Figure 7.3 The mean number of letters correctly recalled in free recall of random *(R)* and redundant *(L)* lists of letters. Notice that in the second list those exposed to *L* lists at first performed better than those exposed to *R* lists. From Miller, 1958.

rules. In other words, we apparently know how to do a lot more than we typically do when we speak. A complete theory of grammar should specify our capabilities as well as typical usage.

Second, according to finite-state grammar, judgments of grammaticality would depend on the frequency with which individual words have been paired in the past. Grammatical sentences would be those which had many words that had been paired (that is, placed adjacent to each other in preceding sentences), whereas ungrammatical sentences would not have this property. This idea too is wrong, however. Subjects sometimes judge sentences as grammatical even though they include words that probably have seldom been paired. Consider one of Chomsky's most famous demonstration sentences:

Colorless green ideas sleep furiously.

Most respondents judge this sentence to be grammatical (though meaningless). Notice that the sentence is grammatical even though it violates the finite-state grammar assumptions. It's safe to say that not many of us have ever seen the pairs "colorless–green," "green–ideas," and so on, and yet the sentence seems well formed. On the other hand, it's also possible to construct a sentence with words that have frequently been paired. Miller and Selfridge (1950) composed this one:

Was he went to the newspaper is in deep end.

Although the words in the sentence can be grouped in high-frequency pairs (e.g., "was–he," "he–went," and so on), the sentence has no meaning and isn't judged to be grammatical. This result demonstrates that people probably do not form sentences word by word. Instead, sentences apparently are composed and understood in units larger than pairs, which suggests that we look at such large units, called clauses, as the unit of grammatical knowledge. The finite-state system's contribution, though negative, was nevertheless important because it pointed linguists and psychologists toward a path that has been much more productive.

Phrase-Structure Grammars

The linguist Leonard Bloomfield described **phrase-structure grammars** near the turn of the twentieth century. Unlike finite-state grammars, which operate left to right, phrase-structure grammars are organized hierarchically—that is, from the top down. Probably the easiest way to show this hierarchic organization is by analyzing a sentence:

> The boy will hit the ball.

As you recognize, this is a grammatical string of words. But what exactly might that description mean? When we looked at the finite-state grammars we saw that a sentence's grammaticality seems to have nothing to do with the associative links between specific words. Where does that leave us in our search for the meaning of "grammatical"? *Grammatical* is a word that may mean many things, one of which is that each word in this string is a legitimate part of speech in English. Our initial pass at understanding the grammar underlying the sentence may consist of mapping each of the words onto its part of speech (Burt, 1971). Then we get: "The," which is a kind of article called a *determiner;* "boy," which is a noun; "will," which is an auxiliary to the verb "hit"; another determiner; and then the final noun, "ball." Laying this analysis out against the sentence, we have:

> The boy will hit the ball.
> Det noun aux verb det noun

From this pattern it appears that the expressions "Det noun" form larger units, which we can call "noun phrases" (*NP*). And we can use these noun phrases to begin to build the hierarchic structure referred to earlier.

Noun phrase			*Noun phrase*
Det noun	aux	verb	det noun
The boy	will	hit	the ball

This diagrammatic approach implies that equivalent expressions can be substituted for each other and that this operation will maintain grammaticality. Let's test this assertion by substituting the second noun phrase for the first one. We then get the sentence

> The ball will hit the boy.

Obviously, this second sentence means something completely different from the first sentence, but this second sentence is nevertheless grammatical, indicating perhaps that we're on the right track in our attempt to understand something of the structure underlying these sentences. That is, by mapping each of the words in the sentence onto a part of speech, and then grouping parts of speech into higher or more general units, we seem to be getting a clue about the sentence's structure. Now let's go back to the original sentence and take the next step. Just as we grouped two parts of speech to make a noun phrase, we can also group the verb and the second noun phrase to make a "verb phrase." Taking another step, we recognize that the entire string of words can be grouped into another level, which we could call the "sentence." Showing both of these steps diagrammatically, we have

| | | Sentence | |
| | | Verb phrase | |
Noun phrase	Aux	Verb	Noun phrase
Det noun			Det noun
The boy	will	hit	the ball.

Finally, we can convert this diagrammatic structure to a treelike depiction called a *phrase marker.* Figure 7.4 shows the phrase marker for the sentence we have been dealing with. The expressions "verb phrase" and so on appear above the specific words in the sentence. We call these expressions *nonterminal nodes,* and we say that nonterminal nodes dominate the terminal nodes, or the specific lexical entries. The nonterminal nodes make up the "natural" parts in a sentence, which we call its **constituents.** In fact, we have just applied to this sentence a form of constituent analysis: mapping the sentence onto its parts of speech and then grouping and regrouping the components into increasingly general units.

As we see in this analysis, equivalent constituents can be substituted for each other, suggesting that part of the adult's grammatical knowledge consists of rules that specify how constituents can be substituted or "rewritten" for each other. These rewrite rules have the form $X \rightarrow Y$, which specifies when a constituent symbol, Y, can be substituted for a constituent symbol X. To see how this substitution works, consider this sentence (Clark & Clark, 1977):

The likable general collapsed.

This sentence could be divided into two constituents: an NP (noun phrase) standing for "the likable general" and a V (verb) designating "collapsed." The NP can be represented with this formula: $NP = ART + ADJ + N$. If you think about it for a minute, however, you may detect the limitations in such a formula. Although the for-

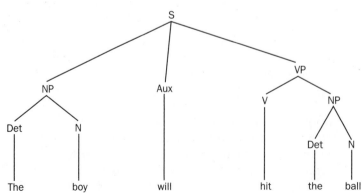

Figure 7.4 This entire diagram is called a *phrase marker,* or *tree,* and the labels *S, NP, Det, N, Aux, VP,* and *V,* which appear above or *dominate* other nodes of the tree, are referred to as *nonterminal* nodes. The words *the, boy, will, hit,* and *ball,* which are not connected by any lines to lower nodes, are called *terminal* symbols.

mula represents some noun phrases perfectly well, it does not represent all noun phrases. Some well-formed noun phrases could be cooked up with this formula: *NP* = *ART* + *N*. And indeed, the phrase "The officer" could be substituted for the noun phrase in the "likable general" sentence (Clark & Clark, 1977). To fully represent the adult's grammatical knowledge, then, we need rewrite rules showing under what circumstances an *NP* of the *Y* type can be rewritten as an *NP* of the *X* type.

You may have noticed that I have been describing phrase-structure grammars as *representations* of or as *expressions* of the adult's grammatical knowledge. This description is intentional on my part. Linguists don't necessarily claim that people actually use phrase-structure grammars to produce or plan their utterances. Rather, they intend to state only that phrase structures are good ways of characterizing the regularities observed in language and *describing* the features that grammatical sentences have in common. If this little proviso can be accepted, phrase-structure grammars offer many powerful advantages over finite-state grammars.

First, phrase structures account for judgments of grammaticality. If the phrase structures and rewrite rules are specified adequately, then all the sentences generated by the phrase-structure grammar will be judged as grammatical, and none of the sentences thus produced will be judged as nongrammatical. Second, phrase-structure grammars have a tidy explanation for ambiguity. What does this sentence mean?

They are cooking apples.

Interpreting the phrase "cooking apples" is the problem. This sentence cannot be mapped onto just one phrase structure; rather, it can be decomposed into two:

They   are cooking   apples.
They   are   cooking apples.

Figure 7.5 shows the two phrase structures that result from the "cooking-apples" sentence. In the first example "cooking" is a part of speech called a *participle,* and when it is included with "are" as a copula, the two words make up the verb in the sentence. In the second, "cooking" maps onto the adjectival role and consequently is part of the final noun phrase in the sentence. Thus, when a sentence cannot be mapped successfully onto any phrase structure, it is judged to be nongrammatical. When it maps successfully onto just one phrase structure, the sentence is judged to be grammatical and meaningful. When the sentence maps onto two phrase structures, however, it is judged to be grammatical but ambiguous. Then the explanation of ambiguity harmonizes nicely with the notions of constituent analysis and phrase structures.

Figure 7.5 Two phrase structures.

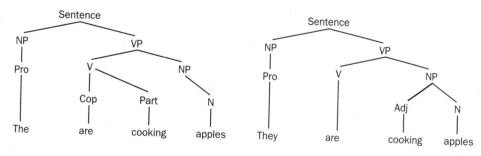

A third advantage is the abstractness of the phrase structures themselves. Having knowledge expressed as phrase structures allows its owner to do at least two things. First, we can accept as grammatical any sentence that maps onto a phrase structure, regardless of whether that sentence has been heard before. Second, the generality of the phrase structure permits some creativity in utterances. I can generate these sentences (assuming that all the words are in my vocabulary):

Rainey parked the car.
Britain ruled the waves.

These sentences don't mean the same thing, but they can be mapped onto the same phrase structure. This principle has implications for children, who are trying to learn appropriate syntax. According to finite-state theories, children build up their knowledge of syntax pair by pair; that is, they learn to associate two words in a specific order. Once formed, this association could be used as a basis for learning successively longer strings. According to this viewpoint, the child acquires syntax in the same way as a tourist in a foreign country might operate—that is, by encoding and storing stock phrases that could be helpful in various situations. With what we know about children's memory, though, it seems unlikely that children could acquire syntactical knowledge in that way.

According to the phrase-structure position, the child's task is simplified somewhat. Phrase-structure grammar proposes that, instead of specific word orderings, children learn general rules that can be used as formulas to generate greatly varied sentences. This possibility simplifies the child's task because, presumably, we'd have fewer rules to learn than specific word orderings. In other words, whereas the number of sentences in the English language is infinite, the number of phrase structures probably isn't. This simplification, though, is purchased at a price. Unlike specific phrasings, the phrase structures themselves are never heard directly. Instead, they must be inferred from all the utterances that the child hears. Because children's inference-making abilities are no better than their metamemories, phrase structure theory's explanation for syntax acquisition is far from complete.

Some other problems also prevent our adopting phrase-structure theory wholesale. First, although not infinite, the number of phrase structures is surely large. Is it reasonable to expect that children somehow infer this large number of rules? Other criticisms are founded on the idea that phrase structures don't tell us the whole story about a sentence. According to the phrase-structure position, sentences that have different phrase structures should be judged as dissimilar. The sentence's meaning depends on the constituent analysis that is carried out upon it. If this analysis points to two different phrase structures, the meaning of the sentence should be altered accordingly. But this phenomenon is not always observed, as this trio of sentences shows:

1. Rainey parked the Renault.

2. It was the Renault that was parked by Rainey.

3. Americans won the gold.

Sentences 1 and 2 don't share the same phrase structure, but sentences 1 and 3 do. And yet, most of us would say that sentences 1 and 3 are more dissimilar than sentences 1 and 2, because the first two have the same *meaning*. This response indicates that a sentence's meaning depends only in part on the results of a constituent analysis. The trio of sentences also shows that we must have some linguistic knowledge that is not expressed in the phrase-structure rule.

A third problem with phrase-structure grammars is their inability to explain some types of sentence ambiguity. The sentence

Visiting relatives can be tiresome.

is ambiguous. What's tiresome—the visits from one's relatives or the act of visiting one's relatives? According to phrase-structure grammars, ambiguity arises because a sentence can be mapped onto more than one phrase structure. Both meanings in that sentence, though, can be mapped onto the same phrase structure:

Visiting relatives   can be   tiresome.

Technically, this sentence should not be ambiguous, because its constituents can be divided up in one and only one way. That the sentence is ambiguous amplifies one of our earlier conclusions; namely, our linguistic knowledge must have more than that which is expressed in phrase-structure grammars.

Transformational Grammar

Transformational grammar is an extension of Bloomfield's ideas and is strongly associated with its originator, Noam Chomsky. In his (1957) *Syntactic Structures,* Chomsky detailed the limitations in both finite-state and phrase-structure grammars and proposed an alternative meant to represent more of the linguistic knowledge that we must have.

Chomsky reasoned that no single-level theory of grammar would ever account for all observed ambiguities in sentences, because these ambiguities were of at least two fundamentally different types. The "cooking-apples" sentence is ambiguous because it can be mapped onto more than one phrase structure. To resolve the ambiguity, all one has to do is ask whether the "cooking" goes with "apples" or with "are." The "visiting relatives" sentence, though, is not ambiguous for that reason and can't be resolved by asking which word "visiting" should be grouped with. The grouping is obvious, but the meaning isn't. Chomsky maintained that these two kinds of ambiguities were evidence that grammatical knowledge is organized in two levels.

He referred to the first of these as **surface structure,** denoting a level of grammatical knowledge that is seen in the sentence's superficial appearance and is instantiated in the rewrite or transformational rules that I alluded to earlier. **Deep structure** denotes a level of grammatical knowledge closely related to a sentence's meaning and is instantiated in the phrase-structure rules that we've examined. Both kinds of rule are required to completely describe our grammatical knowledge. Let's see how these labels are enacted in Chomsky's theory.

First, understand that transformation grammars are said to be *generative.* Because such grammars specify the constituents' relationship to one another, an individual who knows explicitly the grammar's formal properties (the rules in which it is embodied) should be able to apply these rules to a sentence. And an individual who could do that could, in a sense, "prove" that a sentence must be grammatical—that none of the explicit rules had been violated. Such a generation of a grammatical proof of a sentence is referred to as a *derivation* (Carroll, 1986). The mathematical connotations are not wholly far-fetched. That is, although we've seen that our linguistic intuitions seem accurate in creating tree structures such as the one we made from the "boy" sentence, we'd like to have a more formally specified basis for such breakdowns.

To begin, consider this sentence:

The charming professor escorted the visiting dignitary.

We know that we could use our linguistic intuitions to break down this sentence in a hierarchic way. Here, though, our task is to find phrase-structure rules that can be applied to this sentence and, by their application, show how such a sentence could come to be generated. Table 7.3 shows a very simple set of such phrase-structure rules. (This table is modified from one appearing in Carroll, 1986.) For example, PS 1 (phrase-structure rule 1) states that S (a sentence) can be rewritten as an NP (or noun phrase) and a verb phrase. PS 2 means that a noun phrase can be rewritten as an article and a noun. Adjectives are optional, and if they are included, they must be placed between the article and the noun. Phrase-structure rules 4 through 7 are referred to as lexical-insertion rules, describing which elements in our lexicons may be inserted into the slots called for in the first three phrase-structure rules. Armed with these rules, we might derive the sentence above in this way.

Applying PS 1 to the sentence, we would get:

$$NP + VP$$

Next, we can apply PS 2 to the noun phrase *(NP),* rewriting it as:

$$ART + (ADJ) + N + VP$$

Then, we can apply PS 3 to expand the verb phrase *(VP):*

$$ART + (ADJ) + N + V + NP$$

Then we can reapply PS 2 to the noun phrase denoting the object of the sentence:

$$ART + (ADJ) + N + V + ART + (ADJ) + N$$

Table 7.3   A Simple Set of Phrase-Structure Rules

PS 1: *S* (sentence)	⟶	*NP + VP*
PS 2: *NP* (noun phrase)	⟶	*ART + (ADJ) + N*
PS 3: *VP* (verb phrase)	⟶	*VP + NP*
PS 4: *N* (noun)	⟶	professor, dignitary
PS 5: *V* (verb)	⟶	escorted
PS 6: *ADJ* (adjective)	⟶	charming, visiting
PS 7: *ART* (article)	⟶	the

Finally, we can apply the lexical-insertion rules; we apply PS 7 first:

THE + *(ADJ)* + N + V + THE + *(ADJ)* + N

Then we can apply PS 6, the adjective-insertion rule:

THE + CHARMING + *N* + *V* + THE + VISITING + *N*

Following that, we can apply PS 4 and insert the nouns:

THE + CHARMING + PROFESSOR + V + THE + VISITING + DIGNITARY

Last, we can apply PS 5 and insert the verb:

THE + CHARMING + PROFESSOR + ESCORTED
+ THE + VISITING + DIGNITARY

But although such rules make the logic underlying the tree structure clearer, they cannot account for all our linguistic knowledge. Consider the "visiting-relatives" sentence. Our problems in extracting the sentence's meaning were not the result of inappropriate phrase-structure selection; consequently, deriving this sentence in the same manner as the "charming-professor" sentence would not clear up its ambiguity. Rather, the ambiguity in the "visiting-relatives" sentence is produced because elements or constituents in the sentence's deep structure have been (optionally) deleted from the sentence's surface form. Without these elements, the sentence is rendered ambiguous. The rules that operate thus on the phrase structure are known as transformational rules. Here is another important distinction between phrase-structure rules and transformational rules: Whereas phrase-structure rules operate on only one constituent, transformational rules operate on entire strings of constituents. This distinction will be made clearer by taking a look at the transformational rule known as the particle-movement transformation (Carroll, 1986).

Let's consider this sentence:

Billy picked up his date.

We know that this sentence is roughly synonymous with "Billy picked his date up," and we can see that the particle "up" has indeed been moved around with no loss of meaning. Specifically, we see that the particle has been moved around the noun phrase "his date." How can we go about expressing this movement? We could simply add two phrase-structure rules to our previous list that cover such rewrites. We might write these two rules:

PS 8: $VP \rightarrow V + (PART) + NP$
PS 9: $VP \rightarrow V + NP + (PART)$

These rules would permit us to derive both forms of the "Billy" sentence, but the problem is that nothing in these two rules says that the two forms of the "Billy" sentence are clearly related to each other. To show the relationship, let's concoct this transformational rule:

T *1: V* + *PART* + *NP* → *V* + *NP* + *PART*

This rule states that both forms of the "Billy" sentence have the same deep structure and consequently have been built from the same phrase-structure rules. After the initial construction, the particle-movement rule was applied to the initial format to create the second form of the "Billy" sentence, which is superficially, but not meaningfully, different from the first form. Notice also that the particle-movement rule always moves the particle around the entire noun phrase, regardless of how that constituent may itself be rewritten. Thus these pairs of sentences can all be derived:

Billy picked up his attractive date.
Billy picked his attractive date up.
Billy picked up his mysterious, but nevertheless intriguing, date.
Billy picked his mysterious, but nevertheless intriguing, date up.

Let's examine some implications of these transformational rules. Consider these sentences:

He bit her.
Himself bit her.

The first is grammatical but the second one isn't (Fromkin & Rodman, 1978). But why shouldn't the second sentence be grammatical? Its subject is a pronoun, but the same is true for the grammatical sentence. The only difference is that the subject in the first sentence is a "standard" pronoun, but the subject in the second sentence is a reflexive pronoun. We recognize that reflexive pronouns cannot be subjects of sentences, but how do we make our grammatical rules reflect this restriction? The problem here is that pure phrase-structure grammars have no way of distinguishing between these two kinds of pronouns; for them, we can distinguish only among specific lexical entries. In other words, to pure phrase-structure grammars, a pronoun is a pronoun.

But finding transformational rules operating in concert with phrase-structure rules offers us a way out of this problem. Fromkin and Rodman (1978) explain the solution in this way. Let's say that lexical-insertion rules never consider putting reflexive pronouns into a sentence. Rather, each sentence is generated according to the well-defined phrase-structure rules that we have considered. Now suppose that after the string of words has been completely generated by those rules, an entirely different kind of rule "looks" at the whole structure that's been created. If these different rules detect that two identical noun phrases in the same sentence refer to the same individual, then the rules change the second noun phrase to a reflexive pronoun that agrees with the first in person, number, and gender.

Figure 7.6 shows what these transformational rules do to the underlying phrase structure.

To construct the sentence "The girl cheats herself," we would first derive the sentence "The girl cheats the girl." Then looking at the entire sentence, the transformational rule we've been discussing alters the phrase structure by inserting the reflexive pronoun "herself." As Figure 7.6 shows, the effect of these transformational rules is dramatic; they alter the underlying phrase structure, the one used to derive the sentence in the first place, into a different phrase structure, which is used to produce the sentence's surface form.

And with this discussion we come to the insight that may be Chomsky's most essential—namely, that phrase-structure rules can be used to generate a tree structure representing meaning, and to this deep structure, transformational rules then can be

Figure 7.6   This reflexive rule changes or transforms one phrase-structure tree, which the phrase-structure rules specified by the methods discussed earlier, into a different phrase-structure tree. It changed the *NP*, which was specified as *Art + N* (and as *the girl* after the lexical-insertion rules), into an *NP* specified as *Pro* and finally as *herself. Source:* From Fromkin and Rodman, 1978.

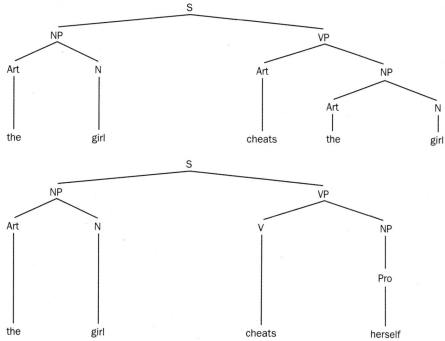

applied to create the specific form of the sentence. This is a radical view because it implies that a speaker cannot have an intention to communicate meaningfully without recruiting some phrase-structure rules. These phrase structures then may be operated on by transformational rules to produce the specific form of the actual utterance, but these sorts of modifications affect only the sentence's surface structure, not its underlying meaning, which is embodied in the phrase-structure rules.

These relationships are expressed in Figure 7.7, which shows the general format of transformational grammar. At the risk of redundancy, Figure 7.7 shows that, according to Chomsky, grammar's syntactic component occupies center stage. Consequently, for Chomsky, it's impossible to study meaning without also studying syntax and, in fact, it's impossible to understand the phonological structure of language without also understanding how syntax shapes these surface considerations. Thus, Chomsky's position is said to espouse the *centrality of syntax*—the idea that syntax is the main ability underlying other grammatical competencies and can therefore be studied more or less in isolation. The rationale underlying this argument is outlined by DeJong:

> Native speakers have syntactic competence: they can judge the syntactic well-formedness of natural language utterances. Furthermore, their syntactic judgments seem to be purely recursive. That is, both membership and nonmembership in the class of syntactically well-formed utterances is decidable. Or, put another way, there is an effective procedure that always halts and assigns an acceptable or unacceptable status to every finite input string of words. Such syntactic competence will necessarily be a part of any complete natural language competence. Thus, it may be studied more or less in isolation and later, after the other components have also been worked out, the various pieces can be connected together in whatever way then seems appropriate. (DeJong, 1982, p. 35)

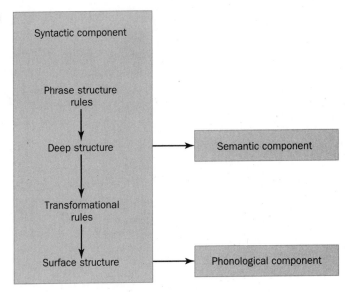

Figure 7.7   Overall form of standard transformational grammar. *Source:* From D. W. Carroll, 1986.

Although DeJong admits that this statement oversimplifies the position, the tenor is crystal clear. According to transformational grammarians of whatever stripe, syntactic knowledge can be studied on its own. This belief has an important implication for psychologists: If Chomsky is correct, no syntax-free grammars could exist. The study of semantics would always be subordinate to the study of syntax.

Implications of Chomsky's Theory

Many ideas in Chomsky's work have implications for cognitive psychology, but space precludes our dealing with more than few of them. First is the notion of linguistic universals. If these truly exist and are discoverable, they may represent a quantum leap in our understanding of the basic rules of language and thought. Second, Chomsky argues that children cannot possibly acquire grammatical knowledge on their own—they must be helped by innate predispositions.

The third implication is the basic premise in Chomsky's theory. Is our linguistic knowledge based fundamentally on syntax? If it is, we should be able to find evidence for deep and surface structure in human judgments of grammaticality. The case for Chomsky's theory would also be strengthened if we could identify some evidence indicating that phrase-structure and transformational rules are a valid form for representing our syntactic knowledge. These issues are dealt with next.

Empirical Support for the Deep–Surface-Structure Distinction

Click Studies   A classic and controversial study by Garrett, Bever, and Fodor (1966) seemed to demonstrate that dividing a sentence into constituents is based on its structure rather than on its sounds. The researchers composed two sentences:

1. In order to catch his train George drove furiously to the station.

2. The reporters assigned to George drove furiously to the station.

Each sentence includes the words "George drove furiously to the station." In the first sentence, however, "George" is the subject of the sentence, and in the second sentence, the subject is "reporters." To understand the sentences, they must be parsed in the correct places:

1. In order to catch his train—George drove furiously to the station.

2. The reporters assigned to George—drove furiously to the station.

That is, in the first sentence the break occurs before "George"; in the second it occurs right after it. Garrett et al. recorded these two sentences and devised an ingenious way to ensure that the utterance's sound would not cue subjects about the correct place to make the division. They cut each of the tapes right before "George" and then connected each "George" clause to the *beginning* of the other tape:

1. In order to catch his train George ⟋ drove furiously to the station.

2. The reporters assigned to George ⟍ drove furiously to the station.

The spliced tapes were then played for the subjects, who heard them via stereo headphones. In one ear, the subjects heard one of the spliced sentences; in the other they heard a click. The click was timed to occur in the middle of "George." What was the purpose for the click? If the subjects were busy allocating cognitive processes to understand the sentence, they would not be likely to have enough processing capability left over to precisely determine the placement of the click. Then the subjects could misperceive the timing of the click. If that timing was misperceived, the researchers were interested in knowing when the subjects thought it had occurred.

After hearing the sentence, the subjects were asked to indicate exactly where the click had occurred. Subjects tended to misperceive its location, and their errors were predictable from analysis of the constituents. In the first sentence, subjects usually thought the click had occurred earlier than it actually had. In the second sentence, they thought the click had occurred after it had actually been presented. These effects can be shown with arrows:

1. In order to catch his train ⟵̶ George drove furiously to the station.

2. The reporters assigned to ⟶̶ George drove furiously to the station.

Notice that in both examples the click was moved closer to the border of the constituent in which "George" was included. Also, the basis for this movement could not have been the sounds of the sentences, because Garrett et al. had controlled for that effect by cutting and editing the tapes. The implication is that the constituent analysis is derived from the structure of a sentence, not from its sounds.

Other studies using the click-displacement paradigm have also supported Chomsky's position. Bever, Lackner, and Kirk (1969) used sentences such as these:

The corrupt police can't bear criminals to confess quickly.
The corrupt police can't force criminals to confess quickly.

These sentences have the same surface structures but different deep structures. Aitchison (1983) suggests a good way to demonstrate that the two sentences have different deep structures (apart from simply realizing that they have different meanings). Try converting each sentence to passive voice. You'll find that conversion is easy for the second sentence with no loss of meaning, but the first sentence cannot be converted without becoming ungrammatical:

Criminals cannot be borne by the police to confess quickly.
Criminals cannot be forced by the police to confess quickly.

If the two sentences had the same deep structure, they could be converted to passive voice with equal ease. Via stereo headphones, the subjects heard the sentence in one ear and a click occurring at "criminals" in the other ear. The results were intriguing. For the first of the two sentences, the subjects displaced the click forward, congruent with Chomsky's theory that a deep-structure break should occur after "bear":

The corrupt police can't bear   criminals to confess quickly.

But in the second sentence the click was not displaced in either direction. This lack of movement is explained in Aitchison's representation of the deep structure in the second sentence, which is shown in Figure 7.8. As Figure 7.8 shows, the deep-structure representation includes "criminals" in both clauses. This representation suggests that the click was not displaced because, in effect, it was being pulled in both directions by the occurrence of "criminals" in both clauses:

The corrupt police can't force criminals   criminals to confess quickly.

These findings are suggestive, but we must be cautious in our interpretation. On the one hand, they are consistent with some aspects of Chomsky's theory; namely, that a sentence is parsed according to its constituents, and that this parsing apparently is consistent with the rules of surface and deep structure. Although the findings are consistent with Chomsky's theory, they don't necessarily *substantiate* it, because other theories of grammar may make the same predictions. Empirically, we have several reasons for caution in interpreting the findings. First, Reber (1973) points out that clausal boundaries are almost always confounded with other aspects of the sentence, such as serial position and intonation pattern. The Garrett et al. tape cutting doesn't appear to control for all these effects.

Figure 7.8 A representation of deep structure. *Source:* From Aitchison, 1983.

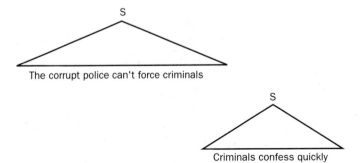

Second, the typical subject is not completely naive about constituents. If she is in doubt about where a click occurred, she must be strongly tempted to push the click toward the nearest clause boundary. Reber and Anderson (1970) demonstrated this effect in a startling way. They used the standard click-displacement procedure but added a twist. They also told their subjects that the experiment involved subliminal perception and that the click would sometimes be almost inaudible. In reality, no clicks of any kind were presented in some of the sentences. And yet, the subjects tended to say that they heard a click, and its location was usually at clause boundaries.

Phoneme-Detection Studies   Other implications of the theory have also had a checkered history in the literature. According to Chomsky, the meaning of a clause is not extracted until the clause boundary has been reached and the clause has been mapped onto a base marker in deep structure. If a word or part of a word has two meanings, this duality of meaning is thought to affect the extraction because the ambiguous term cannot be clearly assigned to one deep structure. This *lexical ambiguity* is not resolved until the clause boundary is reached (Olson & MacKay, 1974); and presumably, only the information from that clause is used to resolve the ambiguity. If all this reasoning is true, then both meanings of the lexically ambiguous term are activated, and they stay activated until the clause boundary is reached and one meaning can be assigned.

These theoretical points have been studied with a so-called *phoneme-detection* paradigm. Recall that a phoneme is a basic unit of linguistic sound. In this paradigm, a subject first hears a phoneme in isolation, the *target phoneme*. Next, the subject listens to a sentence in which the phoneme may or may not occur. If it occurs, the subject is supposed to respond as quickly as possible. When lexically ambiguous words occur right before the target phoneme, the detection latency usually is increased (Cairns & Kamerman, 1975; Danks & Glucksberg, 1980). This finding makes sense, with what we know about activation in permanent memory and allocation of attention. Apparently, the subject waits until the clause boundary to disambiguate the troublesome lexical item; consequently, substantial processing efforts are expended on that task at the clause boundary. When the target phoneme occurs there too, the subject doesn't have quite as many cognitive resources to allocate to processing the target phoneme, and the detection latency increases. Moreover, prior context—that is, information from preceding clauses that could be used to resolve the ambiguity—typically does not eliminate this effect. These findings have been interpreted as supporting the idea that a lexical analysis is carried out clause by clause.

More recent studies, though, have muddied the water here too. Mehler, Segui, and Carey (1978) argue that previous work did not control for all possible contaminating variables, such as the phonemic composition of the words immediately before the target phoneme. Blank and Foss (1978) and Swinney and Hakes (1976) did control for these and other variables and found that information before the clausal boundary could indeed reduce the phoneme-detection latency. Such findings argue against strict interpretation of Chomsky's theory.

Summary   Intuitively, the distinction between surface and deep structure seems valid and necessary. Also, Chomsky bolstered this intuitive argument by composing sentences demonstrating that, rationally, we must have two levels of grammatical knowledge. Although his theory has generated many studies, the empirical findings are mixed. If surface and deep structure are truly represented by different sets of abstract grammatical rules, these rules apparently don't behave in ways that are consistent with other aspects of the information-processing viewpoint. Similarly, on Chomsky's claims for transformational rules that bridge deep and surface structure, several researchers (Fodor, Bever, & Garrett, 1974) have shown that we have no strong empirical reason to believe that Chomsky's position is correct.

In retrospect, it seems that this failure to find empirical support for Chomsky's theory was quite predictable: Chomsky has maintained all along that his is a theory of linguistic competence, not linguistic performance. That is, transformational grammar is a formal device for creating grammatical strings of English words, and for expressing in a formal sense what it is that's similar about sentences that people judge to be similar. He has been careful not to suggest that this theory has any necessary implications for the cognitive operations that we engage in when we speak to each other. Hence, we can see that *grammar* does double duty for Chomsky: Not only does it describe a formal device for generating linguistic strings, but also it describes the knowledge about those strings in human minds, knowledge that can never be tapped directly (Johnson-Laird, 1987).

But we needn't be so glum. People may indeed use their grammatical knowledge indirectly as "strategies" (Clark & Clark, 1977) that may help them understand and produce sentences. You might adopt this strategy to help you process sentences:

> Strategy 1: Whenever you find a function word, begin a new constituent whose length is larger than one word.

A function word is any lexical element that has an almost purely syntactic rather than content function. In the constituent "the green boat," "green" and "boat" are content words, "the" is a function word. One other kind of function word is the relative-pronoun category such as "that," or "which." We may now write one of the many variations of strategy 1 that we could erect and use to help us process sentences:

> Strategy 1a: Whenever you find a relative pronoun (a kind of function word), begin a new clause.

How could this strategy help us? Consider two more sentences:

> The man that the dog bit bought the house.
> The man the dog bit bought the house.

Which is easier to understand? If you're like most people, you probably thought the sentence with the relative pronoun was easier to comprehend than the sentence from which it was missing. If you are using Strategy 1a, this difference is easy to understand. Strategy 1a tells the user that it's time to create a new clause when you hear the "that," thus giving you a good clue to the surface structure that is being used in the sentence. For the sentence with the relative pronoun missing, however, even though it's grammatical, listeners must struggle because they don't get the clue to open a new clause. Instead the second determiner "the" tells them only to open a new noun phrase. Consistent with this interpretation, Fodor and Garrett (1967) found that sentences with the relative pronoun intact were easier to process than those with the pronoun missing. These effects are even clearer when another clause is embedded within the first:

The man that the dog that the cat enraged bit bought the house.
The man the dog the cat enraged bit bought the house.

Sometimes my students try to tell me that the second sentence in this pair isn't even grammatical, even though they'll all acknowledge that, without the "cat" clause, it is. Some researchers (Hakes & Foss, 1970) failed to replicate the Fodor and Garrett findings with sentences having two embedded clauses, suggesting perhaps that even strategies like 1a will fail to help if the memory system is overloaded by the sentence's processing demands.

This lack of empirical support causes some cognitive psychologists to wonder if syntax-based grammars have run their course (Smith, 1982), which brings up the inevitable question, "What's the alternative?" In the last fifteen years, psycholinguists have been likely to turn to semantically based grammars as possible solutions. Charniak (1983) proposed the beginning of a theory of grammar founded on a type of spreading-activation model such as those considered in Chapter 5.

Neurology, Language Structure, and Language Performance

If you look back at Chapter 1, you'll notice that we distinguished between the cognitive and neural levels of analysis. Chomsky's theory is written at the cognitive level—it is an attempt to develop, at an abstract level, a specification of our linguistic knowledge. In this and the following sections, we'll attempt to drop down to a neural level of analysis—we shift from an abstract to a more literal focus: How could a human brain go about making the computations that it must to exhibit the linguistic competence we see in our everyday lives?

To make these computations, the brain has to set about organizing itself, and with the most recent cognitive neuroscience findings, we now know something about how that organization is accomplished (my account here parallels that of Pinker, 1994). At the embryological level, cortical neurons are created on the walls of the ventricles, the fluid-filled spaces inside the brain. They don't remain there; these neurons make their way to their ultimate destination on the brain surface by migrating along highways of glial cells, metaphorically speaking, like a drop of liquid (the neurons) traversing a draped string (the glial cells). The glial cells themselves probably are genetically "aimed" toward specific cortical regions. Once the neurons reach their target areas, their next task is to begin forming connections with other regions in the cortex, both adjacent and distant.

To achieve these connections, the cortex region that will be the ultimate receiving area for the connections begins to emit a chemical signal that acts like a beacon to neurons in a sending area. The neurons begin sprouting additional axon terminals that grow toward the chemical. If you dig up a plant in your garden, you'll see how the root structure is really thick and luxuriant where it has encountered a particularly plentiful underground water supply. Something like that is going on at the neural level, too. As soon as the radiating axons make the chemical connection with their target zone, they begin growing ever more plentifully in that direction. Once the neurons reach the target area, they can begin to form more precise connections with the neurons in that zone as neurons in the target site begin to emit other chemical products that lock the growing neurons onto them. Detailing how these chemical events are turned on and off would take us beyond our scope here, but generally we can say that these chemicals are proteins and that they are activated by DNA itself. Once the brain's development gets started, it's a complicated dance of DNA-driven proteins that accomplish some chemical event, and in so doing activate a new sequence of DNA, which in turn creates a protein, accomplishing some other event. Neuroscientists estimate that 30,000 genes (most of the genes thought to be in the human genome) are involved in building and developing the human brain and the rest of the nervous system (Pinker, 1994).

The embryological account tells us how the brain may go about building areas connected in specific ways to other areas. But the next step we must take is to show how a neural device that is wired in a specific way could go about computing meaningful linguistic functions. Pinker (1994) shows how a neural network might go about making such computations.

We must realize first that simple neural networks can compute some kinds of logical operations. Consider a neuron that receives inputs from exactly two other neurons. Further, assume that this neuron is "on," that is, firing, if and only if the neurons from which it receives input are also both firing. We have thus produced a neural network that computes a logical function known as an "AND" function. That is, for the target neuron to fire, the first input neuron AND the second neuron must both be active. Thus, if the target neuron is firing, the neural system "knows" or can compute that both of its inputs are also firing. Figure 7.9 shows how such an AND gate would be set up. Notice that each of the input neurons has an activation (.4), and the target neuron has a threshold (.5) that must be exceeded if the target neuron is to fire. In an AND gate, the target neuron's activation is represented by the sum of its input neurons' activations. If both are active, then the sum of activation in the target neuron is .8, which does exceed its threshold, and so it fires. But that's the only time it fires. If only one of the input neurons is active, then the target neuron's activation will not exceed its threshold and it will be silent. The AND gate thus is well named: the gate opens up and starts firing if and only if one of its inputs AND one more of its inputs are firing. Figure 7.9 also shows an OR gate and a NOT gate. The OR gate fires if either one OR the other (or both) of its inputs are active. The NOT gate is shown by an inhibitory connection between the input neuron and its target. In the NOT gate, the target is always on, so long as the input neuron is not firing. But as soon as the input neuron begins firing, it inhibits the target neuron from continuing to fire. It turns the target neuron off, and so now it is NOT firing.

Pinker (1994) describes how a neural network made up of these gates might represent and compute a linguistic rule. Consider this grammatical rule: In English, the suffix -s is added when the subject is in the third person, AND is singular, AND the action is in the present time, AND the action is done repeatedly or habitually (this characteristic is referred to in linguistics as the verb's "aspect"—we don't have to

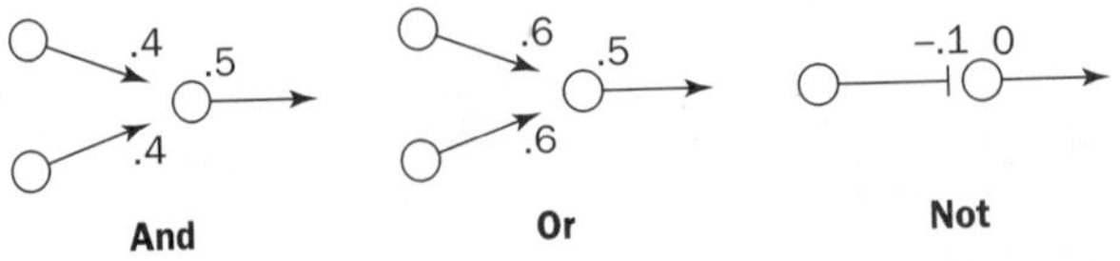

Figure 7.9 Neural networks used as logic gates. *Source:* From Pinker, 1994.

worry about this expression's meaning). There is also a NOT condition: the suffix -*s* should NOT be added when the verb is irregular, such as *do,* or *have.* Figure 7.10 shows how a neural network could carry out these computations. On the lower left in Figure 7.10 is a set of neurons that begin firing upon recognizing specific features, such as detection of third person. Each of these feature neurons is connected via an AND gate to a neuron labeled "3sph" (for third person, singular, etc.). Thus, this target neuron begins to fire only when all its relevant features are firing. The "3sph" combination has an excitatory link to the neuron representing the suffix -*s.* Thus when the "3sph" neuron is active the appropriate suffix is activated. Finally, the -*s* neuron activates the sound of the suffix as "*z*" on the right-hand side of the neural network because, in the condition we have been describing, the "*s*" in the suffix may be pronounced like a "*z.*" If you want to start a sentence with the expression "Bill grabs," then the sequence of neurons described so far will be activated (notice that the "*s*" sound in *grabs* is pronounced like a "*z*").

This system will work fine for regular verbs. The problems begin when we are dealing with an irregular verb, such as "to be." In the "3sph" combination, the verb "to be" is irregular; we shift to the expression "is," as in "Bill is . . ." (not "Bill be's"). How can the system we have outlined compute this combination? In this model, if the person were going to use a form of the verb "to be," it would be activated in the brain, and this activation is shown in the portion of the system labeled *dictionary.* The "be" neuron has an excitatory connection with the appropriate irregular form "is." Notice that the "3sph" neuron too has an excitatory connection with the form "is." Together, they form an AND gate on the "is" neuron. In other words, the "is" neuron becomes active only when the "3sph" and "be" neurons are active. A potential

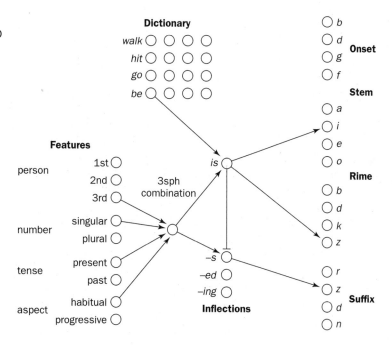

Figure 7.10 A neural network consisting of AND and NOT logic gates that may be used to compute regular and irregular suffixes. *Source:* From Pinker, 1994.

problem lurks here. Have you spotted it? The problem is that for an irregular verb, both forms "is" and "-s" are activated. How do we—or more accurately, how do our brains—know which form is the right one to say? The answer is that when the "is" neuron is activated, it begins to inhibit the "-s" neuron, thus forming a NOT gate on the "-s" neuron. This blockage means that the suffix "z" will not be activated. But if you look carefully at the model you'll see that the "is" neuron has excitatory linkages with the appropriate speech sounds.

Let's review what we've accomplished in this section. Our first objective was to show how the DNA in the human genome authorizes a sequence of protein-based signals to construct a neural network in a brain. What kind of brain do you have when you are born? The "wiring" is decidedly not complete. The embryological program probably builds specific kinds of neural networks in specific regions in the brain. In other words, the kind of neural network that is built in the occipital lobe, and used for vision, probably has different computational properties than does the linguistic neural network that is built in the temporal lobe. Our second objective was to show how a neural network in a human brain could go about computing real linguistic functions, such as suffixes. We've seen here that a neural network certainly no more complicated than the kind that *could* be built in the brain is nevertheless sufficiently complicated to be able to compute at least one linguistic function accurately. The third step would be to show how our experiences in the world enable us to "wire" or configure our neural networks appropriately. Once again, we lack a conclusive answer, although some encouraging work has been done on that front (e.g., Seidenberg, 1997). We'll attempt to show in the next section what happens when the developmental program is derailed by an injury.

Specializations in the Brain   Pioneering work in brain specializations was done by the great French researcher Paul Broca in the 1860s. He discovered that, if an area in the cortex was damaged by a stroke, an **aphasia,** or language disorder, was produced. This section in the frontal lobe is now usually referred to as Broca's area. Broca also discovered that the aphasia appeared only if the stroke had taken place in the brain's left hemisphere; damage to the corresponding area in the right hemisphere did not produce language deficits. These findings confirmed what other researchers had suspected: A specific location in the brain seems to be responsible for producing speech. Most often this language center seems localized in the dominant (i.e., left) hemisphere.

Broca's area is adjacent to the area in the brain that controls muscular movement in the face, and damage to Broca's area usually is accompanied by partial paralysis in the right side of the face. Broca ingeniously demonstrated, though, that the aphasia was not simply the result of this paralysis by asking his patients to sing. Surprisingly, singing ability was unimpaired. The muscles that wouldn't cooperate for speech would work together for singing, suggesting that singing ability was controlled by another part of the brain.

People who suffer damage to Broca's area speak only with great difficulty. Their speech is slow and telegraphic, meaning that some words are left out. Pronunciation of verbs and pronouns is often impaired. Geschwind cites this example of this aphasia, in which a person was asked about a coming dental appointment.

Yes . . . Monday . . . Dad and Dick . . . Wednesday nine o'clock . . . ten o'clock . . . doctors . . . and . . . teeth. (Geschwind, 1980, p. 209)

This type of aphasia isn't the only kind. In 1874, Carl Wernicke identified another type of language disorder, an aphasia resulting from damage to a location in the temporal lobe in the left hemisphere, posterior to Broca's area. People with damage to this location (now known as Wernicke's area) produce speech that is fluent and often syntactically sound. In content, though, the utterance is often meaningless. Here we quote an example of this disorder. The patient was asked to describe a picture that showed two boys stealing cookies behind their mother's back.

Mother is away here working her work to get her better, but when she's looking the two boys looking in the other part. She's working another time. (Geschwind, 1980, p. 209)

Although Broca and Wernicke didn't know it, the two areas named for them are connected by a band of tissue, the *arcuate fasciculus*. This area suggests a view of the brain's function in producing speech that has gone more or less unchallenged in the past century. The meaning of an utterance, or its underlying structure, is first produced in Wernicke's area. This code is next transferred via the arcuate fasciculus to Broca's area, which is responsible for formulating a more detailed speech plan. This plan is next sent on to the motor area in the cortex, which activates the appropriate muscles in lips, tongue, larynx, and so on.

These findings are easily interpretable as evidence that our linguistic ability is "wired into" our brain. We shouldn't be too hasty with that interpretation. The hemispheric organization sometimes differs from the usual, and these people have no trouble speaking. Also, ample evidence suggests that Broca's and Wernicke's areas are simply centers for activity that can be taken up by other structures in the cortex. Following a stroke, most people substantially recover their language ability. Neural tissue adjacent to that which was destroyed apparently is capable of taking on the functions of the original areas.

Closed-Head Injuries and Their Effects on Language Development in Children

We've seen that specific sites in the brain, or perhaps types of brain activities, are associated with linguistic knowledge and linguistic functioning. To argue that such brain specializations reflect innate predispositions to language, then, we must first detail how these sites develop those capacities from the linguistic input that a normal child gets, a task that has proved stunningly difficult. Second, we must also detail how abnormal events, whether injuries or developmental events, alter the processes by which these sites acquire their linguistic capabilities. Finally, we must be able to specify those possible effects on language.

Closed-head injuries (CHIs) are defined as nonpenetrating injuries to the brain. In children, they typically result from motor-vehicle–pedestrian accidents, motor-vehicle–bicycle accidents, falling accidents, or collision sports–related injuries. A CHI's effect on language depends on several variables, including severity of the injury, how diffuse the injury was (across the entire cranium) or how focal (restricted in area), and the size and location of any focal injuries (Chapman, 1997). Consistent with the other effects we have seen, a focal CHI occurring on the left-hemisphere frontal lobe is the most likely type of CHI to result in grammatical simplification and diminished lexicon (Chapman, 1996). Because CHIs occurring in childhood may derail some components in linguistic acquisition in a child whose linguistic abilities would otherwise develop without complication, it is very useful to compare the linguistic development of a CHI child with that of a child whose linguistic impairments seem to result from more general developmental processes.

Chapman (1997; Chapman, Watkins, Gustafson, Moore, Levin, & Kufera, 1997) has undertaken this comparison. Language-impaired (LI) children may show deficits in both comprehending and producing speech. Such deficits are frequently associated with more general cognitive deficits, but even after children with cognitive and perceptual problems are excluded, many linguistic performance deficits remain in LI children. In looking at school-age children between ages eight and eleven, Chapman (1997) found that these two groups differed most strikingly in lexical and grammatical knowledge. In general, LI children use smaller lexicons than do CHI children, and the rate of increase in their lexicons is slower than that of CHI children. Grammatical deficits are both phonological and syntactic. Children who have suffered a CHI do not generally show these deficits. Just like the LI children, though, CHI children suffer from other problems.

Chapman (1997) uses a "narrative" or "retelling" technique to illustrate the problems seen in CHI children. The researcher reads an unfamiliar but comprehensible story to the child, then asks the child to retell the story with as much detail as possible, as if the experimenter had not heard the story. The child's response is scored for content of information (how much, and what level of detail) as well as its structural content. This second score measures how well the child did at representing the episodic content (beginning, middle, and end) of the story. Finally, the child is asked to provide the "moral" of the story. Together, the information and structure scores and moral production indicate how well the child may do at the discourse level in receiving and producing language—that is, representing and reciting the story's objective or "point." Surprisingly, Chapman (1997) finds that CHI children do no better than LI children on these measures of language ability, and both groups do significantly worse than "normal" children. Let's try to bring these abstractly stated findings to a little greater clarity. If you were to listen to an LI child's retelling, you would detect at first hearing the phonological and grammatical difficulties that characterize the disorder. But a CHI child's retelling might sound fine by comparison, until time for the discourse analysis. Then you would see that the CHI child seems to be having difficulty using language in a functional way. Although their phonology and syntax may be appropriate, CHI children extract less information than normal children do, and that knowledge is fragmentary and diffusely organized compared with normals, and no better than that of children who have previously shown language impairment.

Categorical Perception of Speech Sounds The human vocal tract is capable of making many kinds of sounds, some of them linguistic. Moreover, babies are exposed to many linguistic and nonlinguistic sounds. Babies are thus in a bind. To learn to speak, they must be able to distinguish linguistic from nonlinguistic sounds and to distinguish the linguistic sounds from each other. These are large problems, but babies seem to know the basis for distinguishing linguistic sounds from nonlinguistic ones. Babies imitate the sounds made by human speakers, but they don't imitate other sounds (such as that of the refrigerator) that may be present at the same time. Similarly, they stop crying if you speak to them but not if you ring a bell. Ability to make this discrimination appears to be present early—perhaps by two weeks of age (Wolff, 1966). Babies also seem to know how to distinguish one linguistic sound from another. This ability was demonstrated in a classic study by Eimas, Siqueland, Jusczyk, and Vigorito (1971).

Before discussing the study, some background information is necessary. The speech sounds *b* and *p* are produced by closing the lips, then opening them, releasing air. In producing *b,* the vocal cords begin vibrating as soon as the air is released. For *p,* a short latency occurs between release of air and slight vibration in the vocal cords. Speech sounds that involve vibrations in the vocal cords are called *voiced phonemes.* Listeners use the latency between release of air and beginning of vibrations as a cue in determining whether the *b* or *p* sound has been produced. This cue is called *voice onset time* (VOT).

Research with adults demonstrates that VOT strongly influences how some sounds will be heard. Lisker and Abramson (1970) programmed a computer to produce acoustic information that corresponded to the *p* and *b* sounds. In this way, the buzzing sound associated with *b* could be produced separately from the acoustic information heard in *p.* Armed with this technology, they could systematically vary timing of the voicing. The VOT was varied from −150 msec (i.e., the voicing began 150 msec before the simulated release of air) to +150 msec (the voicing began 150 msec after the simulated air release). Lisker and Abramson found that subjects were unanimous in judging that the sound was a *b* unless VOT was 10 msec or greater, when they rapidly shifted opinion. Then the subjects began to hear the stimulus as *p,* and if the VOT was extended to about 30 to 40 msec, the subjects were once again unanimous that the sound being produced was a *p.* Perception of speech sounds is called **categorical perception,** because subjects don't seem aware of any gradual fading away in the "*b*-ness" of the sound as VOT increases. Instead, the subjects seem fairly confident that the sound is a *b* until the critical VOT is reached, and then they are sure that it's a *p.* Clearly, the subjects are imposing a fairly definite mental organization on the somewhat ambiguous speech sounds. This phenomenon is interesting enough, but researchers also wanted to know how old we are when categorical perception of speech sounds begins.

To assess this timing, Eimas et al. used a procedure relying on the infant's ability to become familiar with specific stimuli and to stop responding to them. The infant is given a pacifier enclosing a device that measures the rate of sucking. A sound is then played repeatedly for the infant until the sucking rate is constant, then a new sound is played. If the baby notices anything different about the sound, this interest is translated into heightened activity, expressed by a suddenly increased rate of sucking for a short time. After the baby gets used to the new sound, the rate of sucking gradually declines.

Eimas and his colleagues presented one-month-old babies with various synthetic speech sounds with differing voice onset times. They found that the infants' perception of the speech sounds was indeed categorical. Moreover, the boundary between *b* and *p* was about the same for infants as for adults—approximately 20 msec. In other words, if the babies had gotten used to a sound in which the VOT was 60 msec, and

Using Your Knowledge of Cognition

Who Can Teach Themselves About Pronouns?

We've seen that a transformational grammar has rules that "operate" on the initial phrase structures that are used to derive a sentence, thus creating a surface form of the sentence. We would use this reasoning to say that the sentence:

Betty expects to feed herself.

is "really" (at the phrase-structure level) the sentence:

Betty expects to feed Betty.

You can thus understand the first sentence because your cognitive system knows that the first sentence, with "herself" in it, is really just the second sentence, which has spent some time in the shop being worked on. And the meaning of the second sentence is clear. But we can use the demonstration sentences here to show that your cognitive system can be fooled: it's not always able to recover the underlying structure by working backward from the final surface form. Ask your friends to tell you what this sentence means:

Which one of the older women is it that Betty expects to feed herself?

Is it that Betty, as opposed to someone else doing it, expects to feed one of the older women, or is it that Betty expects one of the older women to be able to feed herself? Your friends probably were confused.

And even if they can come up with an interpretation (and most people can), they nevertheless admit that the other interpretation is plausible. Look what happens if we try to work backward to figure out which noun has been substituted for:

1. Which one of the older women is it that Betty expects to feed Betty? (This version doesn't make much sense.)

2. Which one of the older women is it that Betty expects to feed the older woman? (This version suggests that we have really only one way to understand the sentence.)

3. Which one of the older women is it that Betty expects to feed one? (This form is ambiguous and hard to comprehend, but casts some doubt on the correctness of the interpretation of 2.)

By trying to go backward from the final form of the sentence to the underlying phrase structure, we can get at least a partial handle on why the clause "Betty expects to feed herself," which is clear by itself, becomes ambiguous in the presence of the complete sentence. Essentially, your cognitive system is unable to determine which of the three nouns in the original sentence has been pronominalized by the reflexive pronoun, "herself."

they heard a new sound in which the VOT was 80 msec, the rate of sucking did not increase. Apparently, the infants did not consider these sounds different from each other. If the babies had gotten used to a sound in which VOT was 0 msec, however, and then heard a sound in which it was 20 msec, their rate of sucking increased. The infants seemed to regard these sounds as different from each other.

Infants don't know a *b* from a *p* in the sense that they can refer to these sounds with linguistic labels as more mature people do. For this reason, Eimas et al. (1971) maintain that humans must have some built-in system that is sensitive to the acoustic properties of speech (Clark & Clark, 1977).

Concluding Comments and Suggestions for Further Reading

Two facts are primary in this chapter: describing linguistic knowledge and the foundation of that knowledge in the human mind. We've seen that it's extraordinarily difficult to specify the knowledge that enables us to speak and comprehend utterances by others. No one has written a complete account describing the grammar of any naturally occurring language. Indeed, specifying any part of this knowledge is extremely difficult. No one has specified how people make decisions about acceptable syntax. And yet, the cognitive processes involved operate reliably and quickly, as we know because we quickly make judgments about appropriate syntax, and the consensus about such judgments is good. Perhaps the main point in Chomsky's work is that such knowledge cannot be expressed by rules that work on just one level. For the reasons reviewed in this chapter, grammatical knowledge must be on two—perhaps more—levels. As we saw, extracting the nature of this knowledge has proved extremely difficult for cognitive psychologists and linguists. This difficulty, too, is puzzling. Over the past two decades, researchers have acquired more facts about mentality than they did in the entire history of psychology. Despite many bits of knowledge yielded in many areas, though, the cognitive operations underlying language have proved frustratingly resistant to the research techniques that have been brought to bear upon them. Why?

Responding to this question brings me to the second main point. Many cognitive psychologists have come to believe that the mental operations underlying language will remain obscure precisely because they are not assembled from simpler information-processing routines, as are many of the other cognitive events we have studied. In other words, because the innate knowledge involved in language seems more extensive than for other mental events, how this knowledge operates is correspondingly more obscure. How strongly you believe in this innateness probably depends partly on how persuasive you found the material on innate predispositions. If this evidence seems convincing, you are probably willing to believe that language will remain forever mysterious. On the other hand, some cognitive psychologists don't find this evidence particularly convincing. They maintain that, although it's obvious that some sort of innate influences affect language development, applying the correct research technique, the correct angle on the findings, will demonstrate that language is not necessarily different in kind than the other cognitive processes we have studied. This issue is sure to be surrounded by more debate in the years ahead.

Students who want to learn more about these topics must realize that they cannot be approached by any easy route. Hudson (1984) wrote a pragmatic introduction to linguistics. Chomsky (1972) supplied an introduction to his thinking, which is intended for an educated but nonprofessional audience. Some of his more recent work (Chomsky, 1979) might also be a good starting point. Chomsky (1983) also has contributed a chapter to a volume edited by Mehler and others, and other chapters in that book also make a contribution to Chomskyan theory. Chomsky's formulation is not the only generative grammar system. Horrocks (1987) describes two others, generalized phrase-structure grammar and lexical-function grammar, as alternatives to the traditional transformational approach. For adventuresome souls who want to tackle some of Chomsky's professional writing, try *Aspects of the Theory of Syntax* (1965). One of the issues he raises is the linguistic-universals concept, which is explored in Hawkins (1988).

Focus on Research
Language Acquisition in Feral Children

This chapter discussed categorical perception of speech sounds by infants, and the research suggests that at least the basis for discriminating speech sounds seems to be inborn. But this doesn't mean that children have speech sounds built into their brains. Clearly, some sort of experience with language is necessary to become fluent. But exactly what experiences are necessary, and how much of them are necessary? Perhaps this question is what prompted many theorists to wonder what would happen to a child who wasn't talked to.

Over the years, many cases of so-called feral children have occurred. Feral children are abandoned children who have fended for themselves in the wild, and they invariably have linguistic deficits. Usually, it's not clear how long such children have been left on their own. Neither is it typically known to what extent they were cared for prior to their abandonment. For these reasons, it's difficult to know the extent to which the language deficits were produced by the social deprivation. For obvious ethical reasons, a controlled experiment cannot be done to answer this question, but sometimes the world offers illuminating cases.

Genie was born in April 1957 and was reared under the most abject conditions:

> From the age of twenty months, Genie had been confined to a small room . . . She was physically punished by her father if she made any sounds. Most of the time she was kept harnessed into an infant's potty chair: Otherwise she was confined in a home-made sleeping bag in an infant's crib covered with wire mesh. (Curtiss, Fromkin, Krashen, Rigler, & Rigler, 1974, p. 529)

Genie was fed by her blind mother in a highly routinized way; little or no conversation took place between them. Apparently, her father and older brother never spoke to her. Genie was almost fourteen years old when she was discovered; at that time she could not speak at all. Since then, researchers have followed the course of her language acquisition with interest. Soon apparent was that, in most areas, Genie's development proceeded at a pace much slower than that of other children. For example, normal children begin expressing negatives by simply putting the word *no* in front of already established utterances ("No want go"). Genie also used this form. However, whereas normal children typically pass through this stage quickly, Genie used this primitive form of negation for two years. Normal children begin asking "Wh——" questions ("Where mommy?") around two years of age. However, Genie never mastered this ability, and her attempts were ungrammatical. She did excel in the acquisition of vocabulary. Although her overall language competence seemed to be that of a three-year-old, her vocabulary was much larger than that of a typical three-year-old.

Curtiss (1977) later wrote a follow-up account of Genie, who by then was eighteen years old. Curtiss noted that Genie spoke in short sentences whose grammatical forms were fairly primitive. However, Genie's knowledge of speech, including her knowledge of English word order, seemed fine. Although her production of syntactically correct sentences is limited (and Curtiss apparently believes that these effects are permanent), Genie's comprehension is more or less unaffected by her years of deprivation.

Apparently, some innate linguistic predispositions can survive a traumatic and deprived upbringing. But other specializations, including those that enable people to acquire syntax, can apparently be destroyed if the individual doesn't have adequate opportunities to use them.

Students who want to learn more about language acquisition could start with any of several excellent books. Clark and Clark (1977) wrote a comprehensive introduction to psycholinguistics, as did De Villiers and De Villiers (1978). Aitchison's (1983) book is easy to read and informative, and her later book (1987) could also be read profitably along with this chapter. Ellis and Beattie (1986) give a general, more recent introduction to the cognitive operations involved in communicating. The edited volume by Franklin and Barten (1987) covers various topics from a developmental perspective, including children's understanding of discourse and metaphor. Another edited volume (Kessel, 1988) also covers developmental aspects of language.

Key Terms

Syntax
Grammar
Continuity theory
Design features
Phoneme
Morpheme
Duality of patterning

Displacement (as a design
 feature)
Productivity
Linguistic universals
Recursion
Finite-state grammar
Phrase-structure grammar

Constituents
Surface structure
Deep structure
Aphasia
Categorical perception

Cognitive Processes in Speech and Language Perception

Overview

Recently, my wife bought a series of tapes meant to teach the listener how to understand and speak Italian. Our thinking was that we could listen to these tapes on trips in our car, thus doing something productive during the drive. I had never studied Italian, but I had studied Latin, and so I thought I would be able to follow along right from the start. I was wrong about that; I got absolutely nowhere in my ini-

tial attempts at understanding the typical tourist-ordering-in-a-café conversation. If you've studied a foreign language, you have an idea of what I experienced—profound confusion at seemingly formless babble. The sounds are different, the sequences of sounds are unpredictable, the beginnings and endings of words cannot be discerned, and of course, the meaning is completely lost. But then, after listening for a while, and with a little coaching from the tape, something interesting began to happen. The foreign speech began to take form. I was somehow able to begin to tune in to the different sounds and they started to make some sense. When I first heard a speaker say "ahranjhadah" (that's what it sounded like), I didn't know what to make of it, except that it didn't sound like an Italian word. When I found out that it meant "orangeade," I was able to mentally accomplish a sort of deliberate equivalence, "orangeade" = "ahranjhadah." But then when it dawned on me that the Italians pronounced every vowel, including our silent *e* at the end, I had new comprehension in which "ahranjhadah" sounded like a perfectly natural word for orangeade.

In this chapter we consider some of the numerous issues in perceiving and using speech. Let's think about what's required. First, comprehending speech requires ability to perceive the speech sounds in a language. This question is called feature detection and pattern recognition. What are the features in speech sounds? We'll try to answer that question.

Even after the speech sounds are correctly detected and categorized, the listener's work is far from over. The sounds must be organized into words. Thus the listener must quickly produce a cognitive code that maintains the order in which the sounds were heard. Further, the speaker must have some way of determining the boundaries between words, no easy trick. We seem to be naturally aware of the pauses between words, but most of the pauses we hear are really not there. We'll examine some factors that enable native speakers to determine word boundaries in continuing speech.

We not only comprehend speech, we also produce it. We'll examine speech production, which seems to be accomplished in stages, each consisting of a cognitive code that is modified by successive cognitive operations. Some of these operations can be glimpsed by analyzing errors in speech production. We'll study and interpret some common errors.

As you read this material, keep in mind the top-down–bottom-up distinction first raised in Chapter 2. Probably nowhere else in cognitive psychology are these two modes more intertwined. Understanding and producing speech requires knowing how top-down and bottom-up processes interact. Keep your eyes open for this interaction as you read the chapter.

Perceiving and Comprehending Speech

Speech sounds are not naturally distinct from each other; they usually have no readily distinguishable boundaries between them. Moreover, the pauses we seem to hear between words and phrases are often illusory. For these reasons, Clark and Clark (1977) write that the problems in comprehending speech are similar to the difficulties we have in extracting a signal from a warbling siren. In this section we describe some problems in perceiving and comprehending speech, and discuss some of the approaches various disciplines have taken to understand them.

Why Speech Perception Is Such a Problem: Stream of Speech

Clark and Clark (1977) wrote about the problems posed by speech perception, and my account is built mostly on theirs. Illustrating a complex problem is sometimes best accomplished by analogy, even though the analogy may be incorrect, as it is here.

Let's suppose that speech could be accurately represented by letters. That is, assume that the letters in a sentence such as:

Jim is a hero.

each stood for a unit of sound, or **phoneme.** If this state of affairs were real, then speech comprehension would be easy to understand. Why? Because each phoneme would be distinct from the phonemic segments that preceded and followed it. Assuming that each phoneme is a distinct acoustic event with distinct acoustic properties, the perceiver would simply engage in this sequence of events: (1) map the acoustic signal onto your knowledge of phonetics, (2) determine which phoneme has been signaled, (3) store this representation, and (4) add to it the next phoneme that is detected, and so on.

Although comparing speech to printed matter seems natural, the "theory" of speech perception thus implied unfortunately is almost completely wrong. First, speech flows on. Letters are discrete, separable stimuli. But speech sounds are not discrete and separable. The stream of speech is hardly ever interrupted by periods of silence. Second, unlike letters, phonetic segments usually are influenced by their location within a word. Consider the /m/ sounds in *Tim* and *mink*. The letter *m* designates this sound in both words, and we truly hear the same sound at the beginning of *mink* and at the end of *Tim*. And yet, the acoustic properties of the /m/ sound are markedly different in these two places. In other words, although we hear these sounds as the same, their pronunciation differs. You can readily see the problem here. The symbol /m/ denotes some regularity in our perception of sounds. But this regularity in perception seems to be independent of any regularity in the acoustic patterns themselves.

Third, the opposite problem sometimes appears. We perceive as different speech sounds that aren't different acoustically. Consider the words *writer* and *rider*. Like most people, you probably hear a difference between the /t/ and /d/ sounds. Consequently, it seems reasonable to look at the speech stream with an eye to finding what we do with our mouths to make the /t/ as opposed to the /d/ sound here. But your search would be in vain: here the two sounds have no phonetic distinction. The only difference in pronunciation between the two words is the time the vowel /ay/ (this is how the sound is designated) is held. The /ay/ in *rider* is held slightly longer than the /ay/ in *writer*.

These difficulties are not the only ones that cognitive psychologists must face in grappling with speech perception; they are also faced with the order problem. To identify the word *pill*, we must not only identify the phonetic segments /p/, /i/, and /l/ but also keep their order straight. If this procedure weren't followed, we'd be unable to distinguish *pill* from other words made up of the same phonetic segments arranged differently (such as *lip*).

Warren, Obusek, Farmer, and Warren (1969) played for their subjects sequences of sounds such as a hiss, a vowel, a buzz, and a musical tone. They found that subjects could not accurately report the order of the sounds if they were played at a rate of 1.5 segments per second or greater. Speech, however, typically proceeds at 12 phonetic segments/sec and is intelligible at rates of up to 50 segments/sec. We have two ways of accounting for this finding. First, the appearance of a phonetic segment may constrain the range of phonemes that might appear next. If it did, then hearing a phoneme might enable the perceiver to shrewdly guess which phonemes were likely to appear next, thus narrowing the range of phonemes that would have to be processed. On the other hand, it's possible that phonemes are not processed sequentially but in bunches. This procedure could be accomplished if each phoneme included an acoustic clue about the phoneme or phonemes that were coming up. Thus phonemes are never produced in isolation—they always include information about the phoneme to come, which results in their own pronunciation being altered. This second interpretation seems the more likely explanation for the Warren et al. findings.

How Speech Sounds Are Categorized

Phonetics and Phonology We've just examined some of the reasons making speech perception so complicated. Now we deal with attacks on the problem. Understanding the basics of speech perception is almost impossible without some background in **phonetics** and **phonology.** Phoneticians try to describe linguistic sounds. The two varieties of phoneticians are *acoustic*—they analyze the physical characteristics of speech sounds; the *articulatory phoneticians* try to describe linguistic sounds by determining the patterns of tongue placement, airflow, and vocal-cavity changes that characterize different sounds. Table 8.1 shows the symbols with which phoneticians represent linguistic sounds.

Phonology is a branch of linguistics meant to determine the rules or principles that describe how speech sounds are produced and comprehended. Phonologists don't deal with the sounds directly, just as linguists are not necessarily interested in

Table 8.1 Phonetic Symbols

Consonants				Vowels		Dipthongs	
p	pill	θ	thigh	i	beet	ay	bite
b	bill	ŏ	thy	ι	bit	æw	about
m	mill	š	shallow	e	bait	cy	boy
t	till	ž	measure	ε	bet		
d	dill	č	chip	æ	bat		
n	nil		gyp	u	boot		
k	kill	l	lip	U	put		
g	gill	r	rip	›	but		
η	sing	y	yet	o	boat		
f	fill	w	wet	e	bought		
v	vat	ʌ	whet	a	pot		
s	sip	h	hat		sofa		
z	zip			i	marry		

Source: From Clark and Clark, 1977.

how specific sentences are produced. Rather, phonologists study the more abstract aspects of speech sounds—the general knowledge that enables us to formulate specific utterances. Consider the word *electric*. The final *c* sound, symbolized by /k/, is a "hard" sound. When we change the adjective to a noun (i.e., *electricity*), we know that the hard sound softens to an /s/. Knowing this rule also enables us to pronounce the noun derived from *egocentric*, even if we've never seen or heard that noun before. As this example suggests, both phonetic and phonological knowledge seem to be required for us to successfully comprehend and produce speech.

Articulatory Phonetics   The articulatory gestures involved in speech can be divided into two broad classes: those which produce vowel sounds and those which produce consonants. Producing consonants usually involves a constriction in the oral cavity, which is generally accompanied by movement by the tongue. Vowel sounds are considerably more open and static; little movement is involved during vowel production. Speech proceeds by producing syllables, which are constructed by embedding a vowel sound or sounds within a string of consonants (Clark & Clark, 1977). During the initial part of the syllable's production, movement and constriction in the vocal cavity occur. In the middle of the syllable's production is a short period during which the vowel is sounded; it is heard as a "constant" sound. Finally, in the last part of the syllable, the ending consonantal sound is produced, again with movement and constriction. Because the consonants apparently include information about the sounds to come, pronunciation of the consonant must somehow change to reflect the identity of the coming vowel. The procedure is vividly expressed in this passage:

> Consonants are pronounced as the tongue and mouth move from the vowel of one syllable to the vowel of the next. The consonants hang off one or both sides of each vowel, so to speak, and depend for their very existence on the pronunciation of the vowel. (Clark & Clark, 1977, p. 180)

Consonants can differ in three ways. First, the **place of articulation** describes which part of the mouth is constricted to produce the consonant. In the English language, this constriction can take place at any of seven points, as shown in Table 8.2.

Table 8.2   The Seven Places of Articulation

1. The two lips together (called *bilabial*)
2. The bottom lip against the upper front teeth (*labiodental*)
3. The tongue against the teeth (*dental*)
4. The tongue against the alveolar ridge of the gums just behind the upper front teeth (*alveolar*)
5. The tongue against the hard palate in the roof of the mouth just behind the alveolar ridge (*palatal*)
6. The tongue against the soft palate, or velum, in the rear roof of the mouth (*velar*)
7. The glottis in the throat (*glottal*)

Source: From Clark and Clark, 1977.

Notice that the table shows constriction points from the front of the mouth to the back; the constriction can occur at various places from the lips to the throat.

Consonants can also differ in their **manner of articulation**—the way in which the constriction is produced. Consonants can be classified in one of six categories: *stops, fricatives, affricatives, nasals, laterals,* and *semivowels.* Stops are formed by completely closing the vocal cavity at the point of articulation. Producing /b/ involves briefly but completely closing the lips, followed by release in the pressure that has built up during the closure. Fricatives are the result of incomplete closure. In producing the consonant /s/, you're probably aware that the tongue is touching but is not completely pressed against the alveolar ridge. Affricatives are produced in two steps, involving both complete closure and fricativelike turbulence. Affricatives, such as /j/ as in *judge,* combine stops and fricatives. Nasals, naturally enough, involve the nose. In producing /m/, the tongue is pushed up against the soft palate, closing it. The air is then expelled through the nose. Shutting the nose makes it impossible to produce nasals accurately (if you don't believe it, try humming when you have a cold). The lateral /l/ is produced by flattening the tongue and letting the air flow around its sides. In contrast, the semivowels involve folding the tongue in the middle and letting the air flow through it. If you contrast the pronunciation of /l/ with /r/, you'll feel how the shape of the tongue (rather than its placement, which is the same for both) contributes to the difference in perceived sound.

One other way of distinguishing consonants is the degree of **voicing** present. Voiced consonants are accompanied by vibration in the vocal cords; voiceless consonants are not. In the English language, voicing is the only way in which some pairs of consonants, such as /d/—/t/, can be distinguished. Table 8.3 classifies the phonetic symbols that denote the English consonants.

The information in Table 8.3 tells us a lot about speech perception. If a speech pathologist asked a client to say "cake" and the client's production sounded something like "take," he could readily interpret the client's difficulties. Table 8.3 shows that /k/ is a velar, voiceless stop, and /t/ is an alveolar, voiceless stop. In other words, the child who says "take" for "cake" is "fronting" a "back" consonant, suggesting a breakdown in the articulatory program, which is shown in a front–back confusion.

Table 8.3 Classifying Consonants

	Bilabial	Labiodental	Dental	Alveolar	Palatal	Velar	Glottal
Stops	p b			t d		k g	
Fricatives		f v	θ ð	s z	š ž		h
Affricatives					č j		
Nasals	m			n		ŋ	
Laterals				l			
Semivowels	w			r	y		

Note: Symbols at the left side in each column are voiceless. Those at the right side are voiced.
Source: From Clark and Clark, 1977.

Table 8.4   Two-Way Classification of English Vowels

Height of Tongue	Part of the Tongue Involved		
	Front	Central	Back
High	i beet	ɨ marry	u boot
	ɪ bɪt		ʊ put
Mid	e baɪt	ə sofa	o boat
	ɛ bet		ɔ bought
Low	æ bat	ʌ but	a pot

Source: From Clark and Clark, 1977.

Unlike consonants, which are produced by altering type and degree of constriction, vowels are regulated by curving the tongue. This curvature can vary in two ways. First, the degree of tongue curvature is referred to as its height in the mouth. Tongue placement can be high (as in *bit*), middle level (as in *bet*), or low level (as in *bat*). Second, the part of the tongue that is held highest can also vary. Pronouncing *bit* requires that the front of the tongue be held highest. In pronouncing /ɨ/ as in *marry*, the middle of the tongue is held highest. Finally, in pronouncing some vowels such as the /u/ in *boot*, the back of the tongue is highest. The results of this two-way classification of vowels are seen in Table 8.4.

If you pronounce the word *sofa* and pay attention to your tongue movements, you'll probably become aware that little muscular movement seems to be required to produce the second vowel sound. Indeed, the /ə/ sound, called the *schwa*, never appears in accented syllables, almost as if it can't be pronounced with stress. This phenomenon tells us something about the relationship between tongue movements and accents within a word. Some muscular tension apparently is required if the syllable includes an accented vowel. That is, the muscles involved must pull the tongue away from its central position (see Table 8.4) if the syllable is to be stressed. Without such muscular tension, the tongue returns to its unstressed position, which is used to produce the schwa. If the stops are the most consonantal of the consonants, then the schwa is the most vowel-like of the vowels.

Distinctive Features in Speech   For the past several decades, linguists have maintained that the *organization* of speech sounds enables us to distinguish them from one another. According to this view, the articulatory gestures form the basis for a number of **distinctive features in speech,** some of which can be used to distinguish phonemic segments from one another. Some of these features are closely related to the articulatory gestures we've examined, such as voicing. If a consonant is voiced, it is indicated in this way [+voice]. If the consonant is unvoiced, it is designated with a minus sign: [−voice]. Rather than thinking of the phoneme as an articulatory gesture or acoustic energy, we may grasp the problem of speech perception by thinking of phonemes as bundles of features.

If you produce a speech sound and your vocal cords vibrate as you make that sound, this vibration will cause a change in the acoustic energy coming out of your mouth. Apparently, we have cognitive processes tuned in to detect whatever has changed about the acoustic code. If the vocal cords are vibrating, then the cognitive processes tuned to speech notice a [+voice] feature on that segment of sound. The features are based on articulatory and acoustic aspects of speech sounds, but they are psychological categories nevertheless because they are detected and assigned by cognitive processes. Each phoneme is distinctive because it has a unique pattern of distinctive features.

Chomsky and Halle (1968) performed such an analysis of English speech sounds. They argued that all consonants and vowels can be categorized with thirteen distinctive features, as shown in Table 8.5. Some of the features require explanation. All true consonants are [+consonantal] and [−vocalic], just as all true vowels are the opposite. The liquids /l/ and /r/, however, have properties of both consonants and vowels, making them somewhat ambiguous. Similarly ambiguous are the semivowels /y/ and /w/, which don't have the properties of either consonants or vowels. The anterior feature results when the phoneme is made at the front of the mouth ([+anterior]) or elsewhere ([−anterior]). Similarly, if the phoneme is produced at the top center in the mouth, it is designated [+coronal]. If a feature is [+continuant], it is produced with a continuous sound. All the fricatives are [+continuant]. Phonemes without this quality are marked [−continuant]. Stridency is based on the buzzing quality associated with some phonemes. The vibrations associated with a fricative such as /f/ are apparent; this phoneme is also marked [+strident]. We've already discussed voicing, and nasality is self-descriptive.

The features consonantal and vocalic reappear to distinguish the vowels. The other elements in the cardinal vowel diagram shown in Table 8.4 also reappear in somewhat altered form. The height feature is broken down into two opposed features: high and low. The phoneme /i/ (the vowel sound in *beet*) is marked [+high] and [−low]. The other dimension from Table 8.4 was the front–back distinction, which reappears in Table 8.5 as the features back and round. The vowel /u/, as in *boot,* involves the back of the tongue and is designated in the chart as [+back]. The final feature is tension, which is difficult to get a subjective feeling for, but it is related to the amount of muscular effort needed to produce the vowel. One of the last vowel sounds to appear as children acquire speech is /ɨ/, apparently because of the movement involved. Predictably, this vowel is marked [+tense], whereas a lax vowel such as the schwa is marked [−tense].

Table 8.5 tells us a lot about speech perception. Notice that most of the phonemes have more than one feature distinguishing them. For example, /b/ and /t/ are phonetically distinguishable by their place of articulation. According to Table 8.5, this difference translates into two distinctive features. That is, /b/ is [−coronal], and /t/ is [+coronal]. Also, /b/ is [+voice], and /t/ is [−voice]. This distinction may raise a question in your mind. Why are /b/ and /t/ different in two dimensions, when, technically, a difference in just one dimension should be enough to tell one sound from another? The answer is that some redundancy appears to be built into the speech-recognition system. That is, in a sense, we're giving our speech recognizers two chances to discriminate between /b/ and /t/. If these recognizers miss the coronal

Table 8.5   Distinctive Features of Consonants and Vowels

Consonants and Liquids

Distinctive Feature	p	b	t	d	$č$	$ǰ$	k	g	f	v	$θ$	$ð$	s	z	$š$	$ž$	r	l	m	n	$ŋ$
Consonantal	+	+	+	+	+	+	+	+	+	+	+	+	+	+	+	+	+	+	+	+	+
Vocalic	−	−	−	−	−	−	−	−	−	−	−	−	−	−	−	−	+	+	−	−	−
Anterior	+	+	+	+	−	−	−	−	+	+	+	+	+	+	−	−	−	+	+	+	−
Coronal	−	−	+	+	+	+	−	−	−	−	+	+	+	+	+	+	+	+	−	+	−
Voice	−	+	−	+	−	+	−	+	−	+	−	+	−	+	−	+	+	+	+	+	+
Nasal	−	−	−	−	−	−	−	−	−	−	−	−	−	−	−	−	−	−	+	+	+
Strident	−	−	−	−	+	+	−	−	+	+	−	−	+	+	+	+	−	−	−	−	−
Continuant	−	−	−	−	−	−	−	−	+	+	+	+	+	+	+	+	+	−	−	−	−

Vowels and Glides

Distinctive Feature	$ɨ$	$ι$	e	$ɛ$	$æ$	i	$ə$	$ʌ$	a	u	$∪$	o	$ɔ$	y	w	h
Vocalic	+	+	+	+	+	+	+	+	+	+	+	+	+	−	−	−
Consonantal	−	−	−	−	−	−	−	−	−	−	−	−	−	−	−	−
High	+	+	−	−	−	+	−	−	−	+	+	−	−	+	+	−
Back	−	−	−	−	−	+	+	+	+	+	+	+	+	−	+	−
Low	−	−	−	−	+	−	−	+	+	−	−	−	+	−	−	+
Round	−	−	−	−	−	−	−	−	−	+	+	+	+	−	+	−
Tense	+	−	+	−	+	−	−	−	−	+	+	−	+	−	−	−

Source: From Clark and Clark, 1977.

difference, recognition will still be accurate as long as they catch the voicing difference between the two sounds. This reading also implies that the acoustic information in speech must be fairly subtle. If the features were more perceptible, we probably wouldn't see so much redundancy built into Table 8.5. This fact has other implications for speech recognition, too. If Table 8.5 accurately depicts speech features, we would expect that, if subjects misperceive speech sounds, their confusions should be between sounds that have only one distinguishing feature between them. We next examine a well-known study addressing this matter.

Comprehending Isolated Speech Sounds   Miller and Nicely (1955) answered many basic questions about comprehension and confusion of speech sounds. Their five subjects listened to sixteen consonants, each of which was followed by the vowel /a/, the vowel sound in *pot*. Many of the sounds were masked by white noise. The loudness of the white noise was held constant throughout the study, but that of the speech signal was varied. Seven levels of speech loudness ranged from one-twelfth as loud as the white noise (−18 decibels, expressed as a signal-to-noise ratio) to twelve times louder than the white noise (or +18 decibels). The subjects' task was to correctly identify the

Figure 8.1 Representing the effect of signal-to-noise ratio on confusions among the sixteen Miller and Nicely consonants. *Source:* From Shepard, 1972.

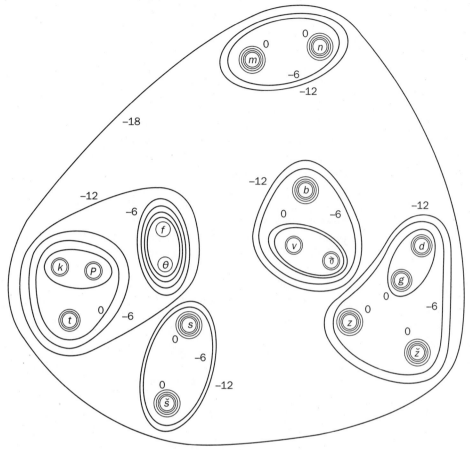

consonant. Their dedication brings tears to the eyes of all but the most hardened researchers: Miller and Nicely asked their subjects to make almost 70,000 consonant identifications over several months.

In their original form, the findings were difficult to summarize, but this task was eased by Shepard (1972), who devised the tableau in Figure 8.1.

The array in Figure 8.1 may seem bewildering at first, but interpreting it is quite straightforward. Consonants depicted as physically close together are more likely to be taken for each other than are consonants that are shown with distance between them. For example, /k/ was very likely to be confused with /p/. The lines around the consonants show the intensity at which the speech signal had to be transmitted before the consonant in question could be correctly identified. Each contour line is labeled numerically; the negative numbers show greater intensity of the masking noise relative to the speech signal. When the speech signal was only one-twelfth as loud as the masking noise (−18 decibel), all the consonants were confused. Consequently, the line labeled "−18" encircles all the consonants in the display. When the intensity of the speech signal was boosted to −12 decibel, however, clusters of consonants could be distinguished from one another. The cluster /s/š/ could now be distinguished from the adjacent cluster /f/θ/k/p/t. Looking within the latter cluster, when the speech signal's intensity was again boosted, this time to −6 decibel, a further discrimination could be made. The consonants /k/p/t/ could be distinguished from /f/θ/.

Analyzing the contour lines in this way produces these clusters of confusion:

m − n f − θ v–ð p − t–k d − g s − š z − ž

That is, these groups required that the speech signal be boosted to at least the same intensity as the noise (0 decibel) before the elements in the group could be discriminated from one another. Referring to Table 8.5, you can verify that, considered as pairs, the members of these groups do tend to differ from one another in only one distinctive feature.

Need for a Phonological Level Students sometimes wonder why we need to know about phonology to understand speech perception. After all, they reason, don't the Miller and Nicely findings tell us which features of speech are attended to, encoded, and used as the basis of perception? The answer is yes and no.

The Miller and Nicely work points out that the articulatory features as conceived by phoneticians by themselves would probably be inadequate to enable speech perception. Rather, the speech signal seems to include more information than the voicing and articulation features shown in Table 8.3. Instead, Miller and Nicely suggest that something like five channels of speech perception pick up as many as thirteen kinds of binary-opposed features as suggested by Chomsky and Halle (1968).

This view is not without its problems, however. First, the Miller and Nicely work clearly implies that the speech signal must have something invariant in various situations, or we would never be able to comprehend speech. That is, they claim that speech must have some invariant acoustic features, which are capable of being detected by some type of feature analyzers. When the acoustic information in the speech signal is analyzed, however, people often perceive different sounds in acoustic events that are identical (Liberman, Cooper, Shankweiler, & Studdert-Kennedy, 1967). Other research suggests that consonant perception must be strongly vowel driven. Blumstein, Tartter, Nigro, and Statlender (1984) artificially enhanced some of the acoustic information in a series of stopped consonants. Next, these consonants were synthesized on a computer and played for subjects. If the subjects are using acoustic information to perceive speech, such enhanced consonants should be easier to detect than they are in natural speech. This hypothesis was not supported. Neither normal individuals nor aphasics found the lengthened consonants any easier to recognize.

Generally speaking, the search for "context-independent" features in speech perception has met with little success (Remez, 1979, 1980). What's the alternative? One way of approaching the problem of relativity in speech sounds is to look for "context-dependent" features (Pisoni, 1978). These are not invariant features that permit immediate recognition in all situations for all speakers. Instead, they are features whose acoustic coding changes depending on the phonetic context in which the sounds appear. According to this view, speech perception proceeds by mapping the acoustic code onto abstract rules flexible enough to adjust for the contextual influences that have distorted the speech sounds from some idealized pronunciation.

Table 8.6 **Phonetic Representation of *Spin* and Its Underlying Phonological Representation**

	S	P	I	N
Underlying phonological representation	+Consonantal	+Anterior −Coronal −Continuant −Strident	+High −Back −Low −Tense	+Anterior +Coronal +Nasal
Final phonetic representation	−Vocalic +Consonantal +Anterior +Coronal −Voice +Continuant −Nasal +Strident	−Vocalic +Consonantal +Anterior −Coronal −Voice −Continuant −Nasal −Strident	+Vocalic −Consonantal +High −Back −Low −Round −Tense	−Vocalic +Consonantal +Anterior +Coronal +Voice −Continuant +Nasal −Strident

Source: From Clark and Clark, 1977.

Linguists have argued that these rules are phonological. Phonological rules are based on the notion of distinctive features, but here the expression is used somewhat differently from the way I've applied it so far. For the phonologist, a sound is made up of distinctive features—whose presence is *not predictable from the other features in the immediate vicinity.*

Consider the word *spin*. It has four phonetic segments, corresponding to each of its letters. Referring to Table 8.5, we can see that looking up each segment's list of features is easy, as done in Table 8.6, which also shows the phonological representation for *spin*.

Notice that the phonological representation has few features; indeed, the initial segment /s/ has only one: [+consonantal]. How can just one feature enable someone to identify the speech sound in question? The answer lies in the two-consonant rule: Whenever a phonetic segment is detected that is [+consonantal] and it's followed by a segment that is [+consonantal] and [−vocalic], then the first segment must also be marked [−vocalic], [+anterior], [+coronal], [−voice], [+continuant], [−nasal], and [+strident]. If you refer to Table 8.5, you will see that this is exactly the set of features that specifies the phonetic segment /s/. If this explanation seems too abstract, the two-consonant rule has a down-to-earth alternative phrasing: If an English word begins with two true consonants (i.e., [+consonantal] and [−vocalic]), then the first one must be an /s/. When I first came across this rule, I was astonished by its implications. I thought some exception must exist—but it doesn't. Try it yourself. Take any true consonant from Table 8.5 and imagine it in the second position of some word to be generated. Then, given that arrangement, try to come up with a word that has anything other than an /s/ in the initial position.

Phonological rules are to speech perception and production as syntactic rules are to sentence comprehension and generation. Just as syntactic knowledge enables us to know which sequences of words are legitimate in our language, phonology enables us to judge which sequences of sounds are legitimate words. From an empirical standpoint, it's easy to see how such phonological rules aid speech perception. The two-consonant rule means that if a word begins with two consonants, the feature analyzers have to pick up only one feature from the initial consonant, [+consonantal], to identify it as an /s/. Thus the acoustic signal need not specify all features of the sound in question. We can rely on our pre-stored knowledge of phonology to fill in information missing or undetected from the stream of speech.

Stages in Speech Perception: From the Bottom Up

Let's review some elements that appear to be required in any theory about isolated speech sounds before we go on to examine the perception of continuous speech.

Speech perception seems to take place in independent stages (Pisoni, 1978), each of which modifies and elaborates the code produced by the preceding stage. How much of this processing is sequential and how much is done in parallel has been controversial (Pisoni & Sawusch, 1975). A reasonable consensus seems to have been reached, though, about the basic components.

1. Auditory Stage.   At the auditory stage, the acoustic signal is converted into a neurological representation that preserves various features of the physical signal. For example, feature analysis at the auditory stage is presumed to encode the sound's fundamental frequency, as well as some details of its harmonic structure. In the auditory stage, too, a code representing the signal's overall intensity and duration is produced. This code is assumed to be stored in some form of sensory storage, and for this reason, the code at the auditory stage is sometimes called "raw." At this stage, no phonetic or phonological information has been extracted from the signal.

2. Phonetic Stage.   The main purpose in the phonetic stage is to name the speech sounds correctly; that is, to assign phonetic labels to the speech signal that are congruent with the speaker's intentions. Here, the listener faces a major difficulty known as the segmentation problem, alluded to in an earlier section in this chapter: Because speech resembles a warbling siren, with hardly any pauses, how is the listener supposed to know where to put the boundaries around phonetic segments to identify them? Fortunately for us, speech is constructed by syllables. Thus the influences that vowels have in producing consonants will probably be limited most often to a range of one syllable. The implication is that some perceptual mechanism must be set, or tuned, to look for patterns of alternating constriction and openness, which are then categorically boxed into syllables whose phonetic names are subsequently determined.

3. Phonological Stage.   At the phonological stage, the phonetic segments that have just been identified are mapped onto underlying (more abstract) phonological rules that extract the true essence from the phonetic segment. This true essence refers to information about the phoneme that permits its other features to be computed from knowledge of phonological rules. As we saw, knowing the two-consonant rule enables us to compute the identity of the first consonant in a two-consonant sequence. Thus, if /s/ happened to be misidentified as /š/ in the phonetic stage, then cognitive processes in the phonological stage would correct this error if the next segment identified was another true consonant.

Phonological rules are inevitably language specific, meaning that the rules of English can be used only to discriminate sounds that make a difference in meaning in English. To understand this point, say *pit* out loud, and pay attention to the /p/ as you do so. Next, contrast the /p/ of *pit* with the /p/ in *spit*. What's the difference? You were probably aware that the /p/ in *pit* is accompanied by a little puff of built-up air, but the /p/ in *spit* wasn't pronounced in that way. Linguists refer to the first /p/ as *aspirated* and the second as *nonaspirated*. The different /p/ sounds in these two examples are said to be *allophones* of each other. Allophones are variations in pronunciation that signal no difference in meaning. *Pit* is still *pit*, regardless of how much air pressure you happen to build up during its pronunciation. Because we don't use aspiration to signal any difference in meaning, phonological rules in English have nothing to say about aspiration. But in other languages, aspiration signals a difference in meaning. In Thai, /p^{h}aa/ (aspirated) means "split," whereas /p^{o}aa/ (nonaspirated) means "forest." Allophonic variations are resolved at the phonological stage. For a speaker of English, during the phonological stage, both /p^h/ and /p^o/ are mapped onto the same underlying phonological segment, /p/, before any further /p/ rules are applied. In Thai, however, this difference is preserved because some phonological rules presumably apply only to the aspirated or nonaspirated /p/.

Perceiving Continuous Speech: From the Top Down

In discussing speech perception so far we've focused on elements in speech that must be extracted more or less directly from the speech signal. Even if all the bottom-up mechanisms go awry, though, we can still use larger units of speech to help us comprehend the message. If you hear someone say,

"She did really well on the test—in fact, she got the highest grade in the whole _____ ."

you know the missing word is *class*, or *section*, or something to that effect. Even before the last word occurs, you can predict what it will be. The sentence is so redundant that much of the speech signal can be left unprocessed with little loss in meaning. It's not clear what proportion of the speech signal is typically processed in this way, but Pollack and Pickett (1964) produced some surprising findings. They covertly recorded people in spontaneous conversations. The participants gave no indication that they misunderstood each other; the replies to questions, jokes, and so on were all appropriate. Pollack and Pickett then cut the tapes to make recordings of isolated words. The tapes were played for the subjects, who were asked to identify the word. The subjects succeeded on 47 percent of the trials—a fairly low percentage. Pollack and Pickett then asked an interesting question: How much context is necessary for a listener to accurately identify a word? As they added larger and larger segments of the original tape to the single words, they found that identification accuracy slowly improved until a critical point was reached, at which accuracy dramatically improved. The subjects' self-reports were congruent with these findings. The word seemed more or less unintelligible until all of a sudden it seemed perfectly clear.

Other research (Sitler, Schiavetti, & Metz, 1983) clarified how context functions in speech perception. Sitler and his colleagues had twenty hearing-impaired speakers pronounce isolated words and the same words in sentences. Recordings of these pronunciations were then played for 100 normal-hearing subjects, whose task was to write down what they understood of the words and sentences. As expected, the subjects performed better when they heard sentences rather than isolated words. This effect was limited, though, to speech produced by the more skilled among the hearing-impaired speakers. When the words were produced by poorer speakers, the subjects did no better in the sentence condition than they did in the isolated-word condition. This result indicates that it is not simply more sound that enables us to comprehend continuous speech better than isolated words. To establish a meaningful context, the acoustic signal cannot vary outside some—presumably wide—boundaries.

A phenomenon that's related to these findings is called the **phonemic restoration effect** (Obusek & Warren, 1973; Warren, 1970; Warren & Obusek, 1971; Warren & Warren, 1970). In the original study, Warren presented to twenty subjects a tape on which this sentence had been recorded:

The state governors met with their respective legi*latures convening in the capital city.

The asterisk marks the point where .12 second was chopped out of the original speaker's utterance and the recording of a cough was substituted. Warren asked his subjects if they detected any sounds missing from the recording. Nineteen of the subjects said no, and the remaining subject misidentified the expunged sound. The subjects did detect the presence of the cough, but they were unable to locate it correctly. Later studies found that a substantial part of a word could be removed without destroying the illusion. Warren found too that a tone or a buzz could be substituted for the /s/ without subjects noticing that any sounds were missing. Subjects were quick to detect a silence, though, and they were also accurate in reporting its placement. This finding tells us something about the illusion. The subjects perceived the sentence as coexisting alongside some extraneous nonspeech sound. Only when the chopped-out sound was not replaced with something else did subjects realize that a gap had occurred in the speech signal.

That subjects were quick to detect a silence, and that they were able to correctly place this silence, suggests that subjects' top-down analysis of speech may not occur at the expense of (in place of) analysis of the acoustic information. Rather, it may be that this is an example of parallel processing, in that the acoustic analysis may occur at the same time as the top-down analysis.

These effects were seen in a study by Samuels (1981), who showed that acoustic as well as contextual information influences the phonemic-restoration effect (and presumably therefore in continuous speech). Several variables were in the study. In some examples a phoneme was expunged from the word and replaced with white noise. In others, the white noise was simply added to the speech signal. A second variable was the familiarity of the words altered by the first variable: some words were familiar; others were more obscure. The length of the word was also a variable: some words were relatively short; others were longer. Finally, Samuels listed the phonetic segments within the words that were replaced or augmented with white noise. In some, the replaced phoneme was a fricative; in others a stop was replaced. These manipulations were designed to produce different effects. Adding white noise affected the acoustic information, and also the phoneme involved had acoustic implications. For example, an /s/ or a /z/ is more acoustically similar to white noise and consequently should be more influenced by it than would a stop consonant such as /b/ or /t/. Other manipulations were designed to influence contextual information; hence, top-down processing. Thus, the word's familiarity, or its length, affects contextual information, in that a longer word provides more context than does a shorter one. The dependent variable was the degree of phonemic restoration these variables produced; that is, the extent to which the subjects continued to hear the expunged sound as present. Samuels found that both classes of variables were involved. The greatest degree of restoration (that is, the greatest tendency to say that speech was present when in actuality it had been replaced with white noise) was observed for longer and more familiar words. In Samuels's interpretation, these words provided more context, thus revealing the expected top-down effects. Samuels also found acoustic or bottom-up effects, however. A strong degree of phonemic restoration was observed for words in which the expunged phoneme was a fricative rather than a stop.

A study by Remez, Rubin, Pisoni, and Carrell (1981) showed that whatever the acoustic information in continuous speech is, it may be more complex than what we've seen. Describing the study requires at least rudimentary understanding of the physics of sound, and of speech sounds in particular.

Speech is a complicated waveform with several components. Every speech sound has a fundamental frequency corresponding to the basic frequency at which our vocal folds are currently vibrating (usually in the range of 250 Hz for males and 450 Hz for females). That the fundamental speech frequency of two people may be the same may lead you to ask: What enables us to differentiate two singers from each other when both are singing the same note? The answer involves the other components of the wave. Everyone is physically unique, and, as a result, our physiques uniquely enhance or deemphasize aspects of the fundamental frequency produced by our vocal folds. These enhancements can also be depicted as separate waves whose frequencies are higher than the fundamental frequencies. The waveform of speech, then, typically consists of the fundamental frequency and usually two or three additional components. When this signal is displayed visually on a special machine, the concentrations of acoustic energy representing the four sound-wave components, which are called **formants,** are clearly visible and, to the untrained eye, look like elongated and rather shapeless blobs. Closer inspection of the formants reveals that they do indeed vary somewhat as a result of the speech sounds produced, and such variation suggests that the formants do bear the acoustic information that we use in our bottom-up analysis of speech.

Remez et al. recorded a natural utterance of the sentence "Where were you a year ago?" and subjected the resulting speech signal to electronic analysis that substantially altered the formants. Simply stated, the amount of acoustic information in the speech signal was reduced in this way: Whereas the normal formant is a concentration of acoustic energy spread over a specific frequency range (giving formants their bloblike shape), the formants as altered by Remez et al. were constricted to a narrow line, showing only the changes in central frequency of the three formants as the utterance was produced. Obviously, much of the acoustic information normally found in continuing speech was sacrificed by this procedure. Remez et al. sought to determine if people could still discern the message despite the impoverished acoustic information in the speech code.

Subjects who were not told what the sounds represented were not aware that they represented altered speech and consequently were wildly inaccurate in identifying the sounds (subjects frequently reported that the sounds resembled computer beeps and chirps or "science-fiction sounds"). When other subjects were told that they would hear a sentence reproduced by a computer and that their task was to try to identify it, recognition accuracy improved substantially, even though, obviously, no change had been made in the signal at the acoustic level. Let's summarize and interpret the Samuels, and Remez et al. findings. Samuels demonstrated that both top-down and bottom-up processes are involved in perception of continuous speech, suggesting that parallel processing of the speech code was taking place. Remez et al. showed that, whatever sort of acoustic information was processed, it was complex. Moreover, the Remez et al. findings suggest that, to engage in top-down analysis of the acoustic information, people require a fairly lengthy sample of speech sounds, perhaps as long as that produced in a typical sentence.

Analysis by Synthesis: Interaction of Top-Down and Bottom-Up Processing

We've covered a great deal of terrain in several pages. Let's catch our breath before winding up the story on speech perception. We've seen that the stream of speech is an extremely ambiguous signal. It offers some acoustic information that is quickly analyzed and categorized into its configuration of features. Probably at the same time as these bottom-up cognitive processes are at work, top-down processes commence their operation, helping the individual infer, or fill in, missing or undetected speech information. These ideas are lucidly expressed by Liberman:

> Some of the distinctive features that specify each phonetic segment probably can be determined from the available acoustic signal. Other distinctive features cannot be uniquely identified. The listener therefore forms a hypothesis concerning the probable phonetic content of the message that is consistent with the known features. However, he cannot test this hypothesis for its syntactic and semantic consistency until he gets a fairly long segment of speech into his temporary processing space. The speech signal therefore remains unintelligible until the listener can successfully test a hypothesis. When a hypothesis is confirmed, the signal abruptly becomes intelligible. The acoustic signal is, of course, necessary to provide even a partial specification of the phonetic signal. However, these experiments [Pollack & Pickett, 1964] indicate that in many instances the phonetic signal that the listener "hears" is internally computed. (Liberman, 1967, p. 165)

This passage implies that speech is analyzed by first synthesizing (hypothesizing) a guess about the utterance's meaning. This synthesis is based on information extracted from the acoustic events and context-based inferences made by the perceiver. Almost all theories of speech perception are based on a version of this **analysis-by-synthesis model,** originally proposed by Halle and Stevens (1964). The essential idea of analysis by synthesis is that the bottom-up processes that act on the acoustic signal cannot do the whole job of speech perception by themselves. By analyzing the context in which the incompletely specified speech signal occurs, we internally compute (synthesize) a likely candidate for the missing phonetic segment. The missing segment thus generated is next checked to make sure that it conforms to phonological, syntactic, and semantic rules.

As we've seen, the analysis-by-synthesis model is a way of summarizing the interaction between two pathways to pattern recognition. Because the acoustic events are so complex, the human perceiver must rely on some top-down, or inferential, processing. On the other hand, the top-down processes must have something—however ambiguous—to work with. Now the bottom-up processes come into play.

Pragmatics: Coherence in Speech

Suppose a casual sports fan watched the final game in the NCAA basketball tournament and then next day said to a colleague, "Great game yesterday, wasn't it?" But suppose the colleague was an avid sports fan who was aware not only of the NCAA final, but also of a closely contested ice-hockey game in which a team was eliminated from playoff contention, a professional basketball game was decided in overtime, and a no-hitter was pitched on the last day in spring training. The colleague might then come back with "Which one?"

We might say that communication suffered a temporary breakdown here, but notice that the problem was not caused by an ambiguous grammatical formulation. Rather, in this situation, and every time we speak, our task is to use such structures coherently to establish a linkage between our intentions and our utterances. Notice also that such linkages are established inferentially from an internal analysis that tells us how much information we have to give our listeners to enable them to make the connection between what we have actually said and what it means. The basis for such an analysis is frequently to be found in societal conventions. Suppose the initial speaker above had known that the listener was a passionate sports fan. Then the first speaker might have reasoned that the listener probably had heard or watched several games the day before and that therefore greater precision was required to specify the one the speaker was talking about. Had the first speaker made such an analysis, the conversation might have opened with, "The NCAA final was super last night, wasn't it?" **Pragmatics** refers to the social rules underlying language use and the strategies speakers use to establish coherence across several sentences.

Direct and Indirect Speech Acts
The relationship between a speaker's intention and his or her actual utterance was explored by Austin (1962), who made several important distinctions. Austin described the speaker's actual utterance as the locutionary act, the interpretation of that utterance by a listener as the illocutionary act, and, finally, the utterance's effect on the listener as the perlocutionary act. Thus if a person says "It's warm in here," the locutionary act is a simple declarative, but it may be interpreted by the listener as a request to open a window or to turn on an air conditioner. And the listener may then get up and do one of those two things, either of which would appear to be the result of the utterance.

The illocutionary act (the interpretation the listener makes) is also called the **speech act** (Bach & Harnish, 1979; Katz, 1977). Speech acts can be organized functionally; that is, they may be organized according to the intentions that are being

Table 8.7   Major Types of Speech Acts

Speech Act	Definition	Examples
Constative	The speaker expresses a belief, intending to create a similar belief in the hearer (*assert, predict, suggest, describe, conclude*)	*I assert the window is open.* *I conclude the case is closed.*
Directive	The speaker expresses an interest in the hearer's future action, with the intention that the utterance provide a reason for such action (*request, question, prohibit, authorize, recommend*)	*I recommend this class to you.* *I prohibit you from taking that action.*
Commissive	Obligates the speaker, by virtue of its occurrence, to do something (*promise, offer*)	*I promise you it will not happen again.* *I offer you the house for $300 a month.*
Acknowledgment	The speaker expresses feelings for the hearer, either true or socially expected feelings (*apologize, congratulate, thank, refuse*)	*I congratulate you on your appointment.* *I apologize for causing you inconvenience.*

Source: From Bach and Harnish, 1979.

conveyed. Table 8.7 shows several speech acts and examples. One conclusion that can be drawn from this table is the relationship between linguistic structure and linguistic function. If we seek to give a congratulatory message, only a few linguistic structures are appropriate ("Let me congratulate you!" or "Congratulations!"). If we were to use an inappropriate linguistic structure, such as an interrogative ("I guess I should congratulate you, shouldn't I?"), the listener might well conclude that we did not really want to acknowledge the event.

Linguistic structure, though, does not constrain linguistic function completely. That is, we can sometimes legitimately use a linguistic structure to convey a speech act that is not normally associated with it. "It looks like you're having trouble performing up to your full potential" is superficially constative but may actually be a directive ("It's time for you to drop the course"). When a linguistic structure is used nonnormatively as a speech act, it is referred to as an **indirect speech act.**

Such usage may suggest that no rhyme or reason governs the intentionality underlying indirect speech. But most researchers (Clark & Lucy, 1975; Searle, 1975) argue that interpretation of indirect speech is governed by principles that are shared by speaker and listener. We now deal with one such rule.

Pragmatics in Comprehending Language   One rule that both speakers and listeners share is the "one-meaning convention." In most situations, we expect that a speaker has only one intention. Further, the one-meaning convention also tells us that the speaker

Table 8.8 Four Conventions for Conversations
1. Quantity: Make your contribution as informative as is required, but not more informative than is required.
2. Quality: Try to make your contribution truthful. That is, do not say anything you believe to be false.
3. Relation: Make your contribution relevant to the aims of the ongoing conversation.
4. Manner: Be clear. Try to avoid obscurity, ambiguity, wordiness, and disorderliness in your use of language.

Source: From Grice, 1975.

who has more than one intention is expected to give us some other clue to start looking for other meanings.

Let's consider a specific example to see how this rule would be used to identify the speech act. One time a colleague of mine, in a somewhat ill-conceived attempt to boost attendance, began giving his students extra-credit points simply for coming to class. When I asked him later how the plan was working, he said that attendance was up, but he had problems nevertheless. Why? "Well," he responded, "they're not coming because they want to be there." I'm sure you can tell what he meant, but if you simply look at what he said, the thought doesn't seem to be expressed very clearly. On the face of it, my colleague's last comment seemed to assert that the students weren't coming to class, but, parodoxically, the reason they weren't coming to class was that they wanted to be in class. Taken in that way, the comment doesn't seem to make much sense, especially because, immediately before making this comment, my colleague asserted that attendance was up. How do we go about figuring out the meaning of such an utterance? Well, we first assume that the speaker does have a meaning—that he or she has not simply and suddenly gone completely insane. Then, applying the one-meaning convention, we can figure that the colleague's second comment was designed to continue and amplify the meaning of this previous comment, unless some other sign was given signaling us that multiple meanings were intended. What might such signals be? We might consider facial expressions, including smiling or laughter, hand gestures, or obvious changes in tone, as cues that additional meanings are intended. Because none of these cues were present in my colleague's utterance, I concluded that its meaning must be an extension of the previous comment. Thus it seemed clear that the only thing he could have intended was that the students were indeed coming to class but that their attendance was motivated not by desire for learning, but by a desire for something else, probably a good grade. The speaker might have said, "Well, they're coming to class, but not for the reasons I had hoped."

Our analysis of this comment suggests that speakers and listeners know specific rules underlying speech acts. In the next section, we look at a related issue—rules that speakers follow to help listeners with the speech act.

Maxims for Conversational Coherence   Grice (1975) has postulated several principles (he refers to them as maxims) for conversational coherence. These maxims (shown in Table 8.8) are offered as guides that speakers might, and do, use to help their listeners interpret their utterances. Of course, we all violate these maxims from time to time, but usually our violations are unintentional.

Cognitive Processes in Speech Production

Our focus in this chapter is speech perception; that is, the cognitive processes that enable us to comprehend speech. But certainly cognitive processes are also involved in producing speech. In Chapter 7, we looked at some of the speech- and language-oriented sectors in the brain, and some of their possible specific functions in both producing and perceiving speech. In this section we'll provide at least an introduction to some of the specific neural and cognitive processes that support production of real-time speech.

What cognitive processes are involved in looking at a picture of a common thing, and saying the name of the object the picture represents? This is a lexical-access task (Van Turennout, Hagoort, & Brown, 1997). To do it, you have to find somehow, somewhere in your cognitive system the name of the object, code that representation onto language, and then produce a plan for articulation; that is, a plan for actually speaking the word. The conventional theory states that this procedure is accomplished in two stages (Dell, 1986; Levelt, 1983, 1989). The first stage is retrieving the **lemma,** the name for the conceptual and syntactic representation of the object: what the object in the picture "is," its neighbors in some conceptual space, and the part of speech for that object. The second stage is phonological. Once the correct lemma has been retrieved, its representation must be coded onto language. Here the item's phonological form is accessed and a phonetic representation of the word is constructed.

One of the theoretical debates has focused on the order and independence of these stages. One position has it that the two stages must really go in the order that I've stated, and they must also be temporally independent of each other (Levelt, 1989). This kind of thinking represents a straightforward information-processing approach to the problem. But other theorists hold a contrasting, interactionist position (Dell, 1986), which suggests that the two stages are not necessarily separate temporally. Thus activation of the phonological stage might occur before the semantic stage is completed. How might we go about settling this issue?

One way is to make use of electroencephalogram (EEG), or brain-wave readings. One well-known reading, the lateralized readiness potential (LRP), is a brain event that begins to develop sometime before a cued voluntary hand movement is executed—it builds in strength and reaches its peak just as the movement is executed. The LRP can be measured by putting two electrodes on the scalp, one over each motor cortex (right at the top of your head). The LRP is strongest on the side of the head opposite that of the cued hand movement, because each hand is controlled by the opposite brain hemisphere.

Several researchers (e.g., Osman, Bashore, Coles, Donchin, & Meyer, 1992) have looked at what happens to the LRP when a subject is in an experiment in which a choice must be made as quickly as possible. If the subject is given an informative signal about which hand to use to respond before the subject makes the choice, then the LRP starts to build up in the interval between this informative signal and the actual stimulus to which the subject is required to respond. In other words, the correct hemisphere starts to get busy, suggesting that the LRP thus measures the hemisphere's readiness to conduct a movement by the hand or other limb.

Van Turennout, Hagoort, and Brown (1997) have used the LRP in an experiment designed to shed light on timing in semantic and phonological processes in a lexical-access task. In the fairly complicated experimental procedure the subjects had two tasks. In the main one, the subjects were shown a picture of an object and asked to say its name as quickly as possible. But the second assignment was actually the critical experimental task. On 50% of the trials, a box or border appeared around the picture stimulus 150 msec after the stimulus. The appearance of this border was the subject's cue to possibly engage in the second assignment, a button-pressing task. The stimulus materials were categorizable by their semantic and phonological properties. On the semantic dimension, the stimuli depicted were living, animate objects such as a tiger, or inanimate objects such as scissors. If the object shown was animate, the subject was to respond with the left hand. But if it was inanimate, such as a picture of a shoe, then the subject was supposed to respond with the right hand. On the phonological dimension, sometimes the name of the objects shown in the picture ended with a sound such as an /r/, as in *tiger* or *scissors*. For other stimuli, the name of the object ended with the sound /n/, as for the words *spider* or *shoe*. Oh, just so you're not confused about that sentence: The experiment was carried out in the Netherlands, and Dutch was the native language of all the speakers. In Dutch, the words for spider and shoe do end with an /n/. Here's an important point: When the word representing the object ended with the /r/ sound, the subject was supposed to go ahead and press the button with either left or right hand, depending on whether the object was animate or inanimate. That is, the subject was requested to make a go decision. But a word representing the object that ended with the /n/ sound was the signal to *suppress* the button-pressing response. In other words, the /n/ sound at the end of the word signaled the subject to make a no-go decision. These trials and their responses are shown in Figure 8.2.

Before we look at these findings, let's think about the logic in their procedure. Figure 8.3 shows the subject's task schematically. Remember, the signal to do the pointing task occurs 150 msec after the picture appears; the subject is still in the early stages of naming. Van Turennout et al. assumed that if semantic activation of the lemma precedes phonological activation, then semantic information should be available to the subject before phonological information, as shown by the a–b time period occurring before the c–d period. Remember too that on some trials the subject is instructed to make the pointing response with a specified hand (the go decision), but on other trials a no-go decision is called for. The "which-hand" decision is made from semantic information, which should be available fairly early in the stimulus processing. The decision to make the pointing response at all, however, is made from phonological information, which should not be available until much later in the time course of processing; that is, during the c–d interval. Thus we see that preparation of the correct response (and the LRP associated with this preparation) can start in the period a–b, but the go/no-go decision can be made only in the later period, c–d. Therefore, where the semantic information is activated before the phonological, we would expect to see an LRP at least begin to develop on both the go trials and the no-go trials. If, however, the semantic information is not completely activated until the phonological

Figure 8.2 Examples of pictures used in the semantic–phonological categorization task in Van Turennout et al. The Dutch picture names (in the international phonetic alphabet) are shown below the pictures. These four pictures represent separate trials for the four experimental conditions. An animal cues a left-hand response, and an object cues a right-hand response. The response has to be executed if the picture name ends with /r/ (go trials) but is withheld if it ends with /n/ (no-go trials). *Source:* From Van Turennout et al., 1997.

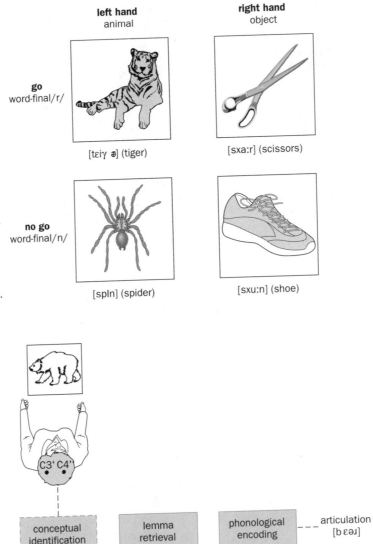

left hand
animal

right hand
object

go
word-final /r/

[tɛiɣ ⱱ] (tiger)

[sxa:r] (scissors)

no go
word-final /n/

[spln] (spider)

[sxu:n] (shoe)

C3' C4'

conceptual identification

lemma retrieval

phonological encoding

articulation
[b ɛəɹ]

a   b   c   d

→ time

Figure 8.3 Processing stages in picture naming using the lateralized readiness potential paradigm. Semantic information about the picture becomes available for response preparation during conceptual identification and lemma retrieval. Phonological information about the picture name becomes available for response preparation during phonological encoding. Under the hypothesis that conceptual identification and lemma retrieval precede phonological encoding, response preparation is first based on semantic information (period *a–b*), and phonological information affects response preparation at a later moment (period *c–d*). C3′ and C4′ are electrode sites. *Source:* From Van Turennout et al., 1997.

Figure 8.4 Grand average (*N* = 16 participants) lateralized readiness potentials (LRPs) on go and no-go trials in Experiment 1. The semantic decision determined response hand; the word-final phoneme decision determined whether a trial was a go or a no-go trial. Significant lateralization of the readiness potential was achieved both on go and on no-go trials. The shaded area shows the time interval in which the go and the no-go LRPs were significantly different from the baseline but not from each other. *Source:* From Van Turennout et al., 1997.

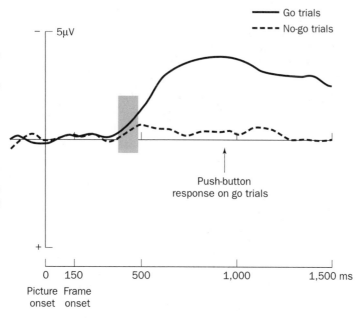

information has begun its activation, then we would not expect to see an LRP develop on the no-go trials, because on those neither hand needs to be prepared to move.

Figure 8.4 shows the study's findings. Notice that on the go trials, the LRP increases dramatically, as we would expect, and reaches its maximum value about 900 msec after the onset of the picture (the graph shows increases as progressively more negative numbers, just because of the way in which these values were computed). Similarly, as we'd also expect, the LRP eventually diminishes to near baseline on the no-go trials. But in the shaded area—that is, a region around 40 msec wide and extending from 450 msec after picture onset to about 490 msec—the LRP is surprisingly elevated on both the go and the no-go trials. Why did the LRP increase during this period, even though it was a no-go trial? The answer is that at that time (i.e., until approximately 500 msec after picture onset) the subjects' cognitive systems apparently had not yet contacted the phonological information that would enable them to determine that the response should be suppressed. Without that phonological information, the appropriate hemisphere had already begun to plan the hand movement, and we see those effects in the LRP readings. In the follow-up studies reported in the rest of their paper, Van Turennout et al. (1997) list additional findings suggesting that the processes might be somewhat more complicated than we've seen here. The study we've examined, however, remains a compelling depiction of how theory and findings explicate the relationship between cognitive and neural levels of analysis.

*R*eading

In some ways it's easier to understand how people read than to face the problem of speech perception. First, to perceive speech, people have to solve the "segmentation problem," which doesn't have to be done in reading. The words are almost always set off from one another, and even when they aren't, reading is still not terribly difficult. And, at first glance, we don't seem to see parallel transmission of information as we did in the speech-perception literature. That is, the characters we use in reading don't seem to be influenced by those preceding them, nor by those which follow. But these factors shouldn't mislead us: understanding reading is still problematic. First, the alphabetic characters are far from a complete specification of their phonetic equivalents. Although the written symbol in an alphabetic system such as ours represents a phoneme (Foss & Hakes, 1978), the correspondence between phonetics and alphabetical symbols is not one-to-one. This lack of correspondence creates some difficulties. We cannot analyze the phonological rules acquired by children as they learn to read and spell because, strictly speaking, our alphabet and its spelling rules are not always phonetic.

Another way of expressing this problem is that English does not have a one-to-one mapping between graphemes and phonemes (Wood, 1983). A **grapheme** is an alphabetic letter, or combination of such letters that stands for a single phoneme. The *s* in *stop* and the *ss* in *kisser* are both graphemes. Coltheart (1978) illustrated several of the problems created by this lack of correspondence. First, when we hear a word, no general rules enable us to make a graphemic representation with certainty: the vowel combinations *oa* and *oe* are both derivable from the same phoneme as in *boat* and *hoe*. These graphemes, however, do not always indicate the same phoneme, as illustrated in the words *boa* and *poem*. The graphemes that previously indicated the same phoneme now point to different phonemes.

Second, even when a series of graphemic units is clearly known, we have no clearly understood, universal way to map them onto a phonetic code. In the word *bread*, which can be broken down into the graphemes *b-r-ea-d*, no rule-based way is available to assign *ea* to a phoneme without considering the other graphemes. You can see why this lack might create problems for the youthful reader. Let's assume for a moment that reading is similar to speech comprehension in that the graphemes must be converted into a phonetic code before they can be processed like speech sounds. If this view of reading is accurate, children with reading difficulties who are asked to sound out the letters have their work cut out for them. Nobody has written a complete specification of grapheme-to-phoneme mappings because the task is impossible. These problems raise an interesting question: How does the typical person go about dealing with these and other issues in order to read effectively?

Generally, cognitivists conceive of reading as involving a series of operations on a written message, called simply "the text." These operations in turn involve creating and successively altering a cognitive code. You might assume that creating this code begins with perceiving individual letters or words and progresses from there to successively larger units of meaning. Such an analysis implies that reading is mostly bottom up or data driven. Yet, as we'll see, readers seldom initiate reading so neutrally. Rather, all reading is done in some context, a context shaped by the reader's skill, purpose, expectations, and the complexity of the written material. At this stage in your reading in this book, words like "purpose" and "expectations" probably are signals telling you to be on the lookout for the phrase "top-down processing"—and so there it is. Top-down processing in reading means that moderately skilled readers are not simply passive spectators but are actively engaged in extracting the desired information from the text.

In the next section, we consider a perspective on reading that we'll use as a model for some of the cognitive operations that seem to be used by skilled readers. In later sections we go into more depth about the specific processes outlined in the general model. As you read, remember to keep in mind the distinction between top-down and bottom-up processing.

Information-Processing Routes in Reading

The numerous theories on reading differ in the number of stages or events required to read, the cognitive processes underlying each stage, and the names given to each stage. We present here something that may approach a "cognitive-consensus" theory (Perfetti & Curtis, 1986) of reading.

Figure 8.5 shows the architecture in Marshall's (1987) model on the routes of information processing in normal reading. As shown, the model postulates three quasi-independent, parallel routes in which the form, meaning, and pronunciation of a printed word are determined. We'll take some time to go through each of these three routes. Visual analysis (VA) determines the features and featural pattern of the text and may operate along the lines of the Pandemonium model that we looked at in Chapter 2. These featural patterns are next assigned to their ultimate graphemic categories by the visual-to-graphemic conversion (VGC) routine. In Marshall's theory, the graphemic code is visual, but nonphonological, and abstract. Thus the line and contour segments have been acquired by the visual and cognitive systems and have been

Figure 8.5 Architecture of normal reading. VA = visual analysis; VGC = visual to graphemic conversion; GB = graphemic buffer; GR = graphemic reparsing; GPC = graphemic to phonologic conversion; IOL = input orthographic lexicon; GM = graphemic morphology; SR = semantic representations; OPL = output phonological lexicon; PB = phonologic buffer. A = phonic route; B = direct route; C = lexicosemantic route. *Source:* From Marshall, 1987.

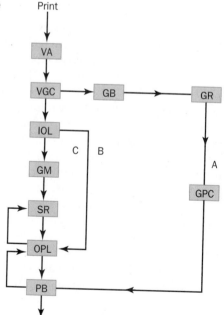

assigned to a grapheme. But these conglomerates of segments have not yet been "named" by the cognitive system with their specific letter names. The literature on this subject is not clear about using so-called transgraphemic features (such as overall orthographic shape) as an aid in letter acquisition. At this place in the system, multiletter strings are represented explicitly by their component letters. The word "cat" is coded as *C* + *A* + *T* in the VGC routine.

Let's now consider what happens when the first major independent route begins to process the code. The phonic route begins when the code is passed to the graphemic buffer (GB), and here the letters are given their specific names. We'll have more to say later in the chapter on how the phonic route typically functions in normal adult reading. From the graphemic buffer, the code is passed to the graphemic reparser (GR), where the code is reanalyzed into its graphemic chunks. These chunks are letters or multiletter strings that map onto a single phoneme. The reparser will leave *D* + *O* + *G* alone, because each chunk maps onto a single phoneme. But *T* + *O* + *E* will be reparsed as *T* + *OE* because the *oe* is a vowel digraph with a specific pronunciation. Notice that the *oe* is not a digraph in the word "poem," meaning that the phonic route will indeed misparse "poem" and other irregular uses of that vowel digraph. In the graphemic to phonological conversion (GPC) routine, the recoded grapheme will be assigned to its most prevalent phonological representation. Thus grapheme *s* will be converted to phoneme /s/. Let's consider, though, what happens to a word like *shoe*. In the GPC the *oe* is assigned its normal phonological representation (as in toe), and so *shoe* comes out of the GPC sounding just like the word *show* and is passed to the phonological buffer (PB) sounding just this way. This statement may seem like a theoretical mistake, but in Marshall's model he seeks to account for the reading of individuals who rely on the phonic route. Such individuals frequently read *shoe* aloud as *show*.

Turning to the direct route, from the VGC, the code also is passed to the input orthographic lexicon (IOL). This routine is the typical word-recognition device that underlies most explanations of "sight vocabulary." This code can be transferred intact to the output phonological lexicon (OPL), which is a repository for phonological information for all words that can be identified by the IOL. Here's how this transfer works. First we have a printed word, let's say, *code*. This word's features are acquired by VA, and then these features are assigned to abstract, unnamed graphemes in VGC. From there the graphemes are passed to IOL, which recognizes the string as an element in the system's lexicon, and finally they are passed to OPL, which assigns a pronunciation to the entire word. Possessing such a route enables me to look at *code* and say *code*, but notice that it doesn't entitle me to know the meaning of *code*.

To know the word's meaning, I would have to use the third and final pathway, the lexico-semantic route. As we've seen, the IOL routine can recognize grapheme strings on sight. When this string, now recognized as a word, is passed to the graphemic morphology (GM) routine, operations are engaged that produce a morphological code suitable as an input for the semantic representation (SR) routine. This routine looks up the meaning of each morpheme in the string and passes this representation to OPL, which, as we've seen, assigns a phonological representation to the code. Understanding the function of the direct and lexicosemantic routes may be easier if you think of them as accessing different kinds of lexical knowledge.

Bottom-Up Cognitive Operations in Skilled Reading

We've looked at a typical model of the routes and stages involved in reading, and we've seen that researchers conceptualize the reader as deploying somewhat independent cognitive processes to read a word and say it out loud. In this section we consider what's involved in each of the stages required by the model.

Feature Processes   If you look back to Chapter 2, you'll see that I talked about feature-extraction processes, and I happened to use features of letters as an example. Now we'll see how such a theory of perception would operate in the reading context.

As we know, a letter can be represented as a related group of features. The letter *E* may be represented by a vertical line with three perpendicular horizontal lines, the letter *P* may be represented by a vertical line and a closed loop, and so on. This is the stage corresponding to the visual analysis in Marshall's model.

At the letter level, this stimulus is represented more abstractly; that is, independently of its configuration. Thus *f* and *F* are both examples of the letter *F*. Finally, the graphemes can be combined and reparsed to form words. A parallel processing model formulated by Johnston and McClelland (1980) is similar to the Marshall model in that it depicts these processes as operating hierarchically (Figure 8.6). As the model shows, once the letters are positioned, their features are extracted, and these features activate the letters composed of those features. Thus, detection of the curved line and the vertical line activates recognition of letter *R*, as shown by the solid lines from the feature detectors to the letter detectors. As you can see, detecting the vertical line in the initial position of the word inhibits the system from detecting this as letter *G*. A similar pattern of activation and inhibition takes place in the interaction of the letter and word detectors. Once letter *R* has been identified, it activates graphemic chunks that begin with *R*. Thus, *road*, *read*, *rend*, and *real* are activated but *head* is inhibited. As shown in Figure 8.6, these processes work for each word in the subject's lexicon: *Read* is the only word that has been activated by all the letter detectors without having been inhibited by any of them.

The Johnston and McClelland model implies that each letter's features are processed more or less independently, and thus, letter recognition is determined by the pattern of activation and inhibition among the features that have been detected. Massaro and Hary (1986) explored these contentions in studying ambiguous letter recognition. Subjects looked at ambiguous letters that varied between *Q* and *G*. The ambiguity was created by varying the openness of the oval and the obliqueness of the straight line in both characters. The results indicated that both sources of featural information were perceived and used by the subjects simultaneously, as predicted by the Johnston and McClelland (1980) model. Moreover, evaluation of each source of featural information was carried out independently. Feature extraction supplied continuous information to another cognitive process, called integration, which weighed the features adding up to "*Q*-ness" against the features adding up to "*G*-ness" and enabled the subjects to label the ambiguous letter either *Q* or *G* in a forced-choice paradigm. In the integration, the least ambiguous letter feature contributes most to the letter judgment.

Figure 8.6 Hierarchic model of word and letter identification.
Source: From Johnston & McClelland, 1980.

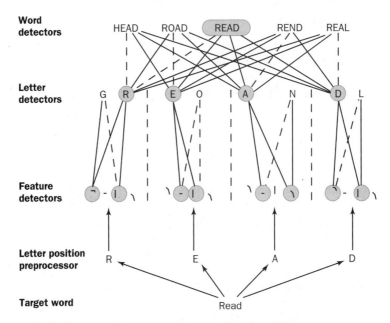

Word detectors

HEAD   ROAD   READ   REND   REAL

Letter detectors

G   R   E   O   A   N   D   L

Feature detectors

Letter position preprocessor

R   E   A   D

Target word

Read

Letter-Recognition Processes   Of course, we use feature-extraction processes to recognize letters, and indications say that they are used in at least two ways, depending on whether we are trying to detect letters in isolation or in their normal context in reading. We'll consider each case in turn.

In Chapter 2, we saw that Neisser (1964) demonstrated that subjects typically found a straight-line letter (a Z) much more quickly when it appeared in a block of curved-line letters than when the target letter appeared in a block of other straight-line letters. (By the way, Chapter 2 will be helpful to us once again in a little while.) The Johnston and McClelland model (1980) offers a good explanation of what produces this effect. According to the model, the straight-line letter was detected quickly among the curved lines because the letter detectors for curved-line letters were all being inhibited by the straight-line letter's features; in a sense, the competing candidates were being suppressed by the straight-line letter's features.

Of course, we don't usually process letters in isolation; we're much more likely to handle them in groups, which leads to a bit of a problem. According to the purely hierarchic information-processing view, processing of words should not begin until all the letters have been processed and identified. But, if you looked back at Chapter 2 a little while ago, you may have seen evidence that the hierarchic view is not completely accurate here. Recall the word-superiority effect? Subjects are more likely to correctly identify a letter when it occurs in the final position in a word than when the letter is presented by itself, or in the context of a nonword letter string. The word-superiority effect, however, is observed only when the readers are at least nominally familiar with the words. Moreover, as also suggested in Chapter 2, the word-superiority effect suggests that we may read in units that are "higher" than individual letters or individual strings. It's not crystal clear yet what some of these higher-order units might be, but some suggest that some whole words might serve as such higher-order units.

Healy (1976) had her subjects scan a prose passage to locate all instances of the letter *t*. She found that subjects were much more likely to miss the letter when it occurred in the word *the* than when it occurred in other words, even in words that begin with *t*, such as *thy*. This finding suggests that the subjects had read *the* as a whole unit and had done so more or less immediately, rather than by detecting features, then letters, then words. If the subjects had engaged in all these processes for all the words, they wouldn't have been able to read over *the* without first contacting its initial *t*. Healy observed this phenomenon even when *the* was embedded in a scrambled-word passage, rather than in coherent prose. Her finding suggests that the phenomenon is not based on *the's* function within a passage, but simply on *the's* status as a word.

Word-Recognition Processes   We can process strings of letters variable in length, but what factors tell us that a string of letters is a word? How do we determine that the word is one we know, or don't know? In our discussion of lexical access, we looked at this expression in its broadest possible sense to include all our semantic knowledge about particular words. Here we will use the expression in its more limited sense. That is, how does letter-string perception access word recognition?

One variable seems to be the string's orthographic structure; that is, the patterns of letter placement within words including constraints of adjacency and vowel–consonant combinations. The reader who encounters *train* knows that it is an English word. Moreover, the skilled reader knows that a slight change in letter placement could produce *trian*. This is not a word, but it is orthographically well formed and thus could be a word. An equally minor variation, *rtian*, is orthographically deviant and so could not be a word (Perfetti & Curtis, 1986). From experience in reading, a skilled reader may encounter thousands of permissible patterns that could be summarized by the rules of English orthography (Venezky, 1970), and such rules could strongly influence word recognition.

Mechanics of Reading   We've focused on some of the cognitive operations that underlie the skilled reader's ability, but we haven't yet seen how such processes are actually used by the reader. It's time to address this issue, and here we have to contact the literature that describes how readers go about engaging the cognitive processes we've been talking about.

During reading, our eyes are not in continuous motion over the page. We're capable of such eye movements, but they can be done only when we are tracking a moving object, such as a tennis ball. But in reading, the eye moves forward in a series of movements called **saccades.** The saccade is a ballistic movement; once launched forward, the eye must come to rest at some point, however briefly, and its movement cannot be altered in midmovement. During these motions, no information from the page can be gathered. Following the saccade, we fixate our eyes at one point on the page. During the fixation, the eyes are relatively motionless, and the cognitive processes we have described go to work. Typically, readers fixate for approximately 200 to 250 msec, and the saccade can be accomplished in 10 to 20 msec. If you look at a skilled reader's eyes during reading, you can easily pick up the regular jump-stop-jump-stop rhythm that characterizes reading skill.

Just and Carpenter (1980) point out, however, that this rhythm is complicated. First, one of their basic findings is that people will occasionally launch a reverse saccade, a **regression.** Regressions seem to be launched when the reader detects some difficulties in comprehension requiring reaccess to previously presented material. The number of regressions launched is one of the features that distinguishes good from poor readers. Poor readers of course are much more likely than good readers to make numerous regressions, and they do so more or less indiscriminately. Second, readers sometimes slow saccadic rate and saccadic "distance" when they encounter difficult material. Intuitively, you may feel that reading consists of "sampling" a relatively small percentage of the words on a page and building from this sample a general idea about the passage's meaning. Certainly our subjective impression that we "skip" some words in prose is accurate. Actually, however, we fixate about 80% of the meaningful content words in a prose passage, and we sometimes fixate the contentless function words (*the, an,* etc.) too. Especially in difficult material, the skilled reader samples much more from the printed page than you may have thought (Perfetti & Curtis, 1986). Because skilled readers are likely to slow down and resample some words more than once in some reading situations, Just and Carpenter (1980) distinguish between the fixation (the time during which the eyes are motionless over a point on the page) and **gaze duration,** the time, summed over fixations, which the subject spends looking at a point on the page.

Figure 8.7 shows the gaze durations for one of Just and Carpenter's subjects who was reading a scientific passage. The subject spent more time fixating on somewhat obscure, but nevertheless important, words such as *flywheels* than on function words such as *the*. With this finding, we might expect a subject's fixation times to be influenced by at least a couple of variables, including status of the word (i.e., content vs. function words) and frequency with which the word currently being sampled occurs in the subject's lexicon.

Some of these variables were included in a study by Rayner and Duffy (1986). They found that when infrequently occurring nouns appeared in a sentence, fixation times were affected—subjects fixated longer on such nouns. The mean length of the first fixation following such nouns also was increased, suggesting that subjects may have used the next word fixated after an infrequent target to help pin down the infre-

Figure 8.7 Eye fixations of a college student reading a scientific passage. Gazes for each word are numbered consecutively, and the gaze time (in msec) is indicated below the sequence number. *Source:* Copyright 1980 by the American Psychological Association. Adapted by permission of the publisher.

1	2	3	4	5	6	7	8	9	1
1566	267	400	83	267	617	767	450	450	400

Flywheels are one of the oldest mechanical devices known to man. Every

2	3	5	4	6	7	8	9
616	517	684	250	317	617	1116	367

internal-combustion engine contains a small flywheel that converts the

10	11	12	13	14	15	16	17	18
467	483	450	383	284	383	317	283	533

jerky motion of the pistons into the smooth flow of energy that powers

19	20	21
50	366	566

the drive shaft.

quent noun's meaning. Curiously, these effects were not observed for infrequent verbs. Rayner and Duffy also analyzed the fixation time that subjects spent on ambiguous nouns, which might have two meanings. They found that, when an ambiguous noun had two equally likely meanings, subjects would fixate on it longer than when an ambiguous noun had one meaning that was substantially more likely than the other.

One other issue in reading mechanics was how much information could be picked up in one fixation. McConkie and Rayner (1974; Rayner, 1975) provided the initial answer to this question with a computer system that adjusted the window of visible text. Subjects wore a contact lens from which a reflection was picked up indicating the subject's current fixation point. This information was fed into a computer, which clearly displayed the characters at the fixation point and for a short distance (measured in letters) around it. But the computer was programmed to mutilate letters beyond a set range, which was accomplished by subtracting some of each letter's features. Letters outside this window of legibility therefore couldn't be read. As the subject's eyes moved across the computer screen, the machine continually updated this window. For all practical purposes, as soon as the subject's eyes moved to a new fixation point, the text around that new point became legible and text that had been legible became mutilated.

Suppose the window was only one character wide. What would happen to your reading speed? We can confidently predict that your reading speed would drop. Now suppose we increased the window to three characters, meaning that the fixation point and one character on each side of it were legible. Your reading speed would pick up. Continuing with this reasoning, if enlarging the window continues to produce increases in reading rate, we can assume that the subjects are picking up the additional information in that fixation. At some stage, expanding the window would not be accompanied by an increased reading rate. We can safely assume that the subject is then extracting as many characters as possible from the fixation. McConkie and Rayner found that the reading rate leveled off when the window of legibility reached about twenty characters—ten on each side of the fixation point. Now for the next question: Do subjects take in all the information they can from the farthest reaches of the window of legibility? Or, do they take in different kinds of information from various points in the window?

Rayner (1975) argued that, if the letters from the window edges were being extracted in the same way as the letters near the fixation center, changes that occurred when the letters were fixated should influence processing time and duration of fixation. One of Rayner's sentences was, "The captain granted the pass in the afternoon." When the subject fixated on the word *granted,* it was presented as shown here. Rayner had modified the computer program, however, so that other elements were present in place of *granted,* before the subject's fixation. For some subjects the word *guarded* was available in the periphery before fixation. As the subject's eyes saccaded their way to *guarded,* though, it was suddenly changed to *granted* at the moment of fixation. Now let's think about what this change might do to you as a subject. If you were not actually extracting letters from the periphery, changing a word at the moment of fixation should have no influence on duration of fixation because, if you haven't extracted any letter information, then you have no reason to suspect that *guarded* has been changed to *granted.* But if you have been picking up at least some of the letters in the periphery, we'd expect that the manipulation would affect length of fixation. Rayner found just that. Moreover, Rayner found that duration could be altered by presenting nonwords such as *gnarbed*.

Using a similar methodology, Pollatsek, Rayner, and Balota (1986) found that visual information is picked up to about nine letter spaces to the right of the fixation point. At such distances, peripheral information affected only the gaze duration (not duration of first fixation) of the target word, but at lesser distances, Pallatsek et al. found that duration of first fixation as well as gaze increased.

Similar effects were observed in a study by Imhoff and Rayner (1986). Their subjects read sentences including a high-frequency or low-frequency target word. In some conditions **parafoveal** (i.e., peripheral) **information** to the right of the target was distorted when the subjects fixated on it; in other conditions, the parafoveal word was left intact. Finally, the status of the parafoveal word was varied. In the intact conditions, some subjects encountered high-frequency parafoveal words, whereas in others a low-frequency parafoveal word was encountered. As expected, readers showed shorter fixations on high-frequency words than they did on low-frequency targets. Also, however, the frequency of the parafoveal word influenced the duration on the target. In other words, when subjects parafoveally encountered a high-frequency word, they were likely to reduce their fixation rate on the target word somewhat, even when the target was a low-frequency word. This finding suggests that subjects were getting at least some contextual, and perhaps semantic, information from beyond the immediate range of the fixation point. This result is consistent with previous research indicating that semantic information is perceived to about four letter spaces to the right of the fixation point (Rayner, 1978).

You may have been curious about what happens to parafoveal information to the left of the fixation point. Because the direction of reading in English is left to right, the reader has access to only about four characters to the left of the fixation point.

The literature we have reviewed suggests, then, that the eye obtains useful information; that is, information that is sufficient by itself to enable lexical access to take place, from only a fairly narrow window surrounding the fixation point.

Recoding in Reading   One of the many controversies in the cognitive psychology of reading is just what happens after readers have engaged an element in the text with their eyes. We know that this information is used for lexical access, but many other questions remain. Looking back at Marshall's model for information-processing routes in reading, we may wonder if all three routes are automatically engaged in by all readers. That is, do skilled readers necessarily rely on the phonic route as much as they do on the direct and lexicosemantic routes? Some cognitive psychologists argue that reading is accomplished by transforming the graphemic code into another, speech-based code, presumably one with acoustic, phonetic, or articulatory properties. This path of course corresponds to Marshall's phonic route. The idea that readers must necessarily do this conversion is called the *recoding* position, named for obvious reasons. Arrayed against these psychologists are others who believe that reading is typically accomplished directly from the graphemic code, without need to access phonological information. These psychologists hold the **direct access** position.

Settling this question has been troublesome. Whatever the phonetic code may look like, it clearly does not involve recasting the graphemic code into a subvocal response, which can easily be demonstrated. First, if we had to subvocalize to read, reading rate would be limited by vocalization rate. Most of the time, though, our speech rate comes nowhere near the reading rate of 250 words per minute that most of us can attain (Kolers, 1970). Similarly, analyzing reaction time indicates that subjects don't have to subvocalize a word to comprehend it. Sabol and DeRosa (1976) have found that people have some semantic knowledge accessed within 200 msec of a word's presentation. And yet, other findings (Cosky, 1975) demonstrate that more than twice that time (i.e., 525 msec) is required to initiate a vocal response for a three-letter word. Also, if subvocalization were required for reading, people who presumably have no phonological or phonetic knowledge—that is, the congenitally deaf—would be completely unable to read. Such individuals can, however, learn to read (but the learning is laborious).

Taken together, these findings suggest that a strict interpretation of the recoding hypothesis is out (Coltheart, 1980). Some phonological encoding may take place nevertheless. Patterson (1982) distinguishes between **assembled phonology** and **addressed phonology.** In reading aloud, once a printed word is recognized, its pronunciation can be looked up or addressed, indicating a sort of phonological lexicon in which the lexical items are catalogued by pronunciation. Presumably, this same lexicon is used to pronounce words in normal speech. This type of phonology is addressed, or *postlexical* phonology, and it apparently does not have much influence on reading. Some phonological information, though, may be, if not necessary, at least helpful in achieving word recognition in the first place. This type is assembled, or prelexical, phonology. The existence of an assembled phonological code does not necessarily disprove the direct-access hypothesis. But it might help clarify reading by specifying the conditions under which people rely more heavily on the graphemic code and under which phonological knowledge aids in word recognition.

Some findings indicate that assembled phonology sometimes influences reaction times in some tasks. First, phonemic similarity seems to affect the time required to make a lexical decision (Coltheart, Davelaar, Jonasson, & Besner, 1977; Rubenstein, Lewis, & Rubenstein, 1971). In these studies, subjects were given a string of letters and were asked to determine as quickly as possible whether the string was a word or a nonword (e.g., *fraze*). When the nonword was homophonic with an actual English word, the subjects required more time to decide than they did when the word was not homophonic. Thus, they'd take longer to decide the fate of a nonword such as *brane* than they would a nonword such as *melp*. The obvious conclusion seems to be that the subjects were slowed by the resemblance of *brane* to *brain*. Although this effect demonstrably involves assembled phonology, it is limited to nonwords. Coltheart (1978, 1980) analyzed the response patterns and concluded that the real words are recognized from visual or graphemic information and recognition is accomplished before the assembled phonology can take effect. Nonwords take longer to recognize as such, giving the assembled phonology time to influence the cognitive processes involved in the recognition.

Dyslexia

Thus far in discussing reading we've emphasized how visual processing influences discrimination of letters and words. And, as suggested in the conclusion to the preceding section, it is almost certain that for competent adult readers most of the perceptual effort in reading is spent on visual processing. But what about people who struggle all their lives to become competent readers? For such individuals, is it reasonable to assume that their reading difficulties simply result from some deficit in visual processing?

Dyslexia is a condition in which a person's reading ability is discrepantly low compared to his or her age, intelligence, and exposure to textual materials (Rutter & Yule, 1975). In schools, this discrepancy is commonly defined as reading ability that is two grades below current grade, with no general intellectual impairment. By this criterion, a third-grader with normal intelligence who reads at first-grade level might be diagnosed as dyslexic. It's a developmental disorder, meaning that it appears in childhood. If you reach young adulthood without becoming dyslexic, you will not become dyslexic then. (But some individuals may not be diagnosed as having the disorder until they reach adulthood; they may have "mild cases" and may find compensatory strategies.)

Many things about dyslexics are interesting from a cognitive psychological standpoint. Children who turn out to be dyslexic frequently show significant delays in phonemic awareness, which is the knowledge a child might have about the relationship between an alphabetic character and the sound that the letter makes. A child who has phonemic awareness may be able to look at the letter "b" and, besides naming it, may be able to make the sound of the letter, saying a syllable such as "buh." A child who does not have phonemic awareness might be able to pick out the letter "b" from a set of letters, and may even be able to say the name of the letter. But without phonemic awareness, the child will not be able to make the sound of the letter, /b/. Beyond delays in phonemic awareness (which, by the way, is the best predictor of reading readiness), children who turn out to be dyslexic have difficulty in detecting rhyme, and they have mild difficulty in speech perception that persists into adulthood (Steffens, Eilers, Gross-Glenn, & Jallard, 1992).

As you've no doubt noticed, all the findings mentioned in the paragraph above have a common theme: the dyslexic's inability to process some characteristics of speech, rather than of letters. These findings do not really contradict the dyslexic's sometimes self-reported judgment of disability—namely, that the letters look as if they are reversing or shifting. That may indeed be going on, too, but even if the letters were reversing, the perception probably is an effect of being dyslexic, rather than a cause of reading difficulty. In other words, one empirical prediction we might make is that if a person were not dyslexic, he or she might still be able to read such reversing letters if they were somehow displayed on a computer screen. The dyslexic person may thus be confusing an effect of dyslexia for its cause.

Several researchers have looked at how auditory or speech processing influences dyslexia. One acoustic characteristic of speech that people use to help themselves understand what is being said is the *amplitude,* or loudness, of the speech signal. As we speak normally, our voices rise and fall in both frequency and loudness throughout a

Figure 8.8 Top trace (a): Example of an amplitude-modulated stimulus (400-Hz carrier, 40-Hz modulation). Lower traces: Example AMFRs recorded to the stimulus above. Each trace is the average of responses to 250 repetitions of the stimulus; (b) The mean amplitude of the AMFR recorded from listeners with dyslexia and from members of the control group. *Source:* From McAnally and Stein, 1997.

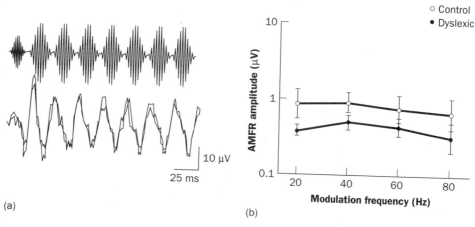

(a)

(b)

sentence. The technical name for this constantly changing level of loudness is *amplitude modulation*. So that we can use it to help us understand speech, the brain must somehow record and represent or "code" amplitude modulation. This recording is accomplished by having a pool of neurons on the central auditory pathway in the brain fire in response to increases or decreases in amplitude. Simplifying somewhat, here's how it works: Let's imagine the pool has 100 cells (obviously, the brain would have thousands of these cells). If a sound is soft, perhaps only 10 cells fire. If a sound is a little louder, twenty cells might be firing. For the loudest sound, as you can imagine, perhaps all 100 cells begin to fire. We would say that the number of cells firing "codes" the sound's loudness. This brain response is called the amplitude-modulation following response (AMFR), which is a good name if you think about it because a portion of your brain is really following or tracking changes in the quantity of physical acoustic energy in the world. Panel (a) in Figure 8.8 shows what the physical stimulus looks like as it modulates, and it also shows the brain's response as more neurons fire in response to increases in amplitude.

McAnally and Stein (1997) looked at the AMFR in dyslexic individuals. They identified fifteen young adults whose reading scores were at least two standard deviations lower than their IQs. They then identified fifteen normally reading young adults whose IQs were equivalent to those in the dyslexic group. Both groups wore several electrodes on their heads while they heard hundreds of amplitude-modulation trials. One thing that makes this study interesting is that, as near as I can determine, the subjects did not actually have to do anything: the dependent measure was the extent of the AMFR, and this response is shown in panel (b) in Figure 8.8. As you see, the average AMFR of the dyslexic subjects was significantly lower than that of normal subjects. What does this difference mean? The dyslexic's brain simply is not tracking or responding to the changes in physical energy with the same force as the normal brain. And what might be the implications of this failure to track the stimulus? If we believe that normal individuals use amplitude modulation to help them perceive speech, and if we believe that in an alphabetic language such as English, effective speech perception is critical to phonemic awareness as a child, then we have good reason to believe that the individual who does not have an effective AMFR will experience difficulty in using the phonological route in reading. And individuals who have delays here may also have difficulty in ever reaching the stage at which the visual-graphemic route dominates.

This interpretation is bolstered by other findings. As we have seen in this chapter, one of the things that effective speech perception requires is ability to represent the incoming speech sounds to preserve their order. If you can't preserve that order, then your speech perception is likely to be impaired. We can assess the likelihood that this problem is a source of speech-perception errors with a temporal-order judgment (TOJ) task, of the type pioneered by Tallal and colleagues (e.g., Tallal & Piercy, 1973, 1974; Tallal, Miller, & Fitch, 1993). In a TOJ task, a listener is presented two consonant–vowel pairs, such as /da/–/ba/. As listener your task is to show that you have represented the order of the stimuli by pointing to one stimulus if you hear the sequence /da/–/ba/, and pointing to a clearly different stimulus if you hear the sequence /ba/–/da/. Mody, Studdert-Kennedy, and Brady (1997) used the TOJ technique in studying second-graders who were selected both for their ability to read and their ability to do TOJ. Figure 8.9 shows the results from one of their studies.

Because the subjects were preselected, it is interesting, but no surprise that the poor readers did markedly worse than the good readers on the TOJ task (in fact, the poor readers did worse on a phoneme-discrimination task too, but that finding doesn't matter here). Another interesting finding does show up in Figure 8.9. Interstimulus interval (ISI) is the name given the time between presentation of stimuli. Here the ISI between the /da/ and the /ba/ could be 10, 50, or 100 msec. Notice that the short ISIs did not bother the good readers at all on the TOJ task: the good readers made zero errors whether the ISI was short or long. But the story was different for the poor

Figure 8.9 Mean number of errors by good and poor readers as a function of ISI on /ba/–/da/ discrimination and temporal-ordering tasks. *Source:* From Mody et al., 1997.

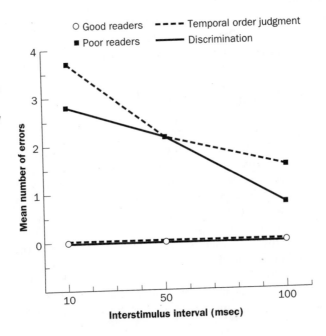

readers. They made significantly more TOJ errors at the short ISIs than they did at the long ISIs, although their error rate was significantly worse than the good readers' at each ISI magnitude.

What do these findings tell us? The poor readers need a lot more time between auditory stimuli to enable the brain to track them, and to make a representation that preserves the order in which the stimuli were presented. It's as if the good readers were not affected at all by short ISIs—they made no errors on the task regardless of whether the ISI was long or short.

Let's close with a few words about the picture that is forming from these studies. It's probably inaccurate to think of the dyslexic's problems as resulting from visual deficits exclusively. We see from these studies that speech perception itself is disrupted in the dyslexic child's brain. Written English is alphabetic, meaning that the visual symbols we read—the letters—actually represent acoustic events and speech sounds. It is the difficulty in processing speech sounds themselves that hinders the dyslexic's ability to connect any representation of the acoustic event to the visual symbols.

Concluding Comments and Suggestions for Further Reading

Using language involves several cognitive processes. Understanding speech requires us to decode ambiguous stimuli, a matter of feature detection and pattern recognition. After the ambiguous stimuli have been recognized, the task of comprehension begins. The lexicon must be addressed, and these processes resemble those involved in activation of nodes in semantic memory. All speech has gaps of which we are usually not aware because the speaker has taken pains to provide the audience with the main points in the discourse. Our inferential processes do the rest of the work. The only reason any narrative, written or told, has main points is that the participants share some mental organization which seems to require more time or experience to develop than does phonological or lexical knowledge. If you doubt this statement, ask a five-year-old to tell you a movie plot. The breakdown in communication won't occur at the phonetic or lexical levels. That which the child sees as important in the story, however, probably will not overlap much with your viewpoint. When we use language to produce speech, we reverse the order of these processes. We start with a broad outline of what we're trying to say, which involves a judgment that our listeners know something about the script we are discussing.

Let's summarize. Using language involves both top-down and bottom-up processes. It also requires perception and memory and some reasoning. Although the organization in this book suggests that language is a separable phenomenon that can be unhitched from the other cognitive processes in the team, this organization is misleading. Language affects and is affected by the other cognitive processes we have studied; work is done because all cognitive processes pull together.

Readers who wish to find out more about speech perception will find no better starting place than Pisoni's article in *Handbook of Learning and Cognitive Processes* (1978). Other material on speech perception can be found in *Psychology and Language* by Clark and Clark (1977). For a good discussion on feature detectors in speech (and the deficiencies in a theory based on them), see the articles by Remez (1979, 1980).

Focus on Research
Disfluent Speech and the Brain

Even though we commit errors in syntax and pronunciation more often than we realize, our errors are unusual. Typically, we seem able to say just what we want to without slip-ups. Unfortunately, some people seldom, if ever, achieve such fluency. Stutterers are plagued by various handicaps, including excessive hesitations, perseveration, and inability to articulate while maintaining normal speech rhythm. For some stutterers, producing speech is such an embarrassing agony they would rather remain silent.

Curiously, however, stutterers seem to have fewer problems when speaking under some conditions. They can sometimes whisper fluently, and their singing ability is usually unimpaired. Also, the stutterer is often able to speak fluently in unison with other people. Some can improve their fluency by tapping their feet rhythmically and speaking one word per tap (Kalat, 1984). These observances suggest that the stutterer's problem is not simply loss of motor control over the tongue or breathing apparatus. The problem seems to be truly linguistic rather than muscular.

Recall that in Chapter 7 we examined the brain's function in normal language. We saw that for most people the left hemisphere is the dominant one, and that in it are Broca's and Wernicke's areas. Could these areas be involved in the stutterer's disfluency? The answer seems to be yes, although the involvement is indirect.

Jones (1966) performed surgery on the left hemispheres of four adults who had tumors near the speech centers. Such surgery would usually not be considered because of the risk it poses for speech. But these patients were unusual. They had speech centers in both hemispheres of the brain (determined by anesthetizing one hemisphere at a time). After the surgery, they were still capable of speech, apparently using the center in the right hemisphere. Another striking finding was that before the surgery, all four patients routinely stuttered, but after the operation, none of them did. What's the interpretation?

For some people, lateral domination is not as great as for others. Essentially, such people have two competing speech centers, and failure to synchronize these centers contributes to the stuttering. When some rhythmic organization is imposed, the two centers have an easier time coordinating their efforts.

Several studies (Pinsky & McAdam, 1980; Rosenfield & Goodglass, 1980) assessed this interpretation. Using a dichotic listening task like the ones we studied in Chapter 2, researchers have found more stutterers than nonstutterers with right-hemisphere speech dominance, mixed dominance, or even fluctuating dominance. This last finding is interesting because it may explain why some stutterers experience lengthy periods of fluent speech followed by disfluencies.

The brain is not the sole cause of stuttering. Plenty of ambidextrous people don't stutter, but they would if hemispheric dominance were the only factor. And yet, competition between speech centers probably influences some people's stuttering.

Garret (1982) presents a complete account of speech production. Deese (1984) wrote a fascinating book in which he analyzed transcripts of naturally occurring speech.

Of the several excellent general reviews on research in reading, see the *Psychological Review* article by Just and Carpenter (1980), who offer complete coverage on the stages in reading. Books by Crowder (1982), Kennedy (1984), and Beech and Colley (1987) also are good. Baker and Brown (1984) wrote an account on the metacognitive influences on reading skill. The volume edited by Britton and Glynn (1987) describes variables that influence top-down control of word recognition and sentence parsing. The edited volume by Tierney, Anders, and Mitchell (1987) deals with the cognitive processes readers use in comprehension.

*K*ey Terms

Phoneme
Phonetics
Phonology
Place of articulation
Manner of articulation
Voicing
Distinctive features in speech
Phonemic restoration effect

Formants
Analysis-by-synthesis model
Pragmatics
Speech act
Indirect speech act
Lemma
Grapheme
Saccade

Regression
Gaze duration
Parafoveal information
Direct access
Assembled phonology
Addressed phonology

CHAPTER 9

Language Acquisition and Cognitive Development

*O*verview

When our younger son was about fifteen months old, he noticed a grass-seed spreader in the garage at his grandparents' house. Looking at the spreader, he called it a "wagon," which of course is wrong, but interesting. I noticed that he did not say "wagon" when he saw an old bicycle wheel hanging on the garage wall. That he called the spreader a wagon but didn't call a bicycle tire a wagon suggested to me that my son knew the difference between a wagon and a wheel. Now you may think that knowing the difference between a wagon and a wheel isn't really much of an accomplishment. But let's consider what must be involved for a cognitive system to recognize and label an unfamiliar object in the world a "wagon."

Calling a spreader a wagon means (possibly) knowing that a wagon is a name that can be applied to things that have specific component structures, such as wheels, an open boxlike entity to which the wheels are attached, and a kind of handle attached to the boxlike entity. In other words, a very sophisticated feature analysis is required to take the object as it is in the world (the spreader) and decompose it mentally into its parts. To attach the label *wagon* to the spreader, however, more than just the parts are required. The parts must stand in specific relationships to each other: the wheels cannot be attached to the handle; they must be attached to the open box. This constraint implies a conceptual structure in the toddler's mind that specifies a number of things: the objects in the world to which names can be attached, the pieces of such objects, and the relationship of these pieces to one another within that concept. Not saying "wagon" when one of the concept's components is presented (the old bicycle wheel) implies that the toddler may also have the "conjunction" concept. That is, the toddler's cognitive system may have some rule that says, "Before you say 'wagon' you must have wheels *plus* box *plus* handle."

This description of the toddler's putative cognitive machinery is interesting for another reason, too. As you may have realized during my description of the conceptual processes underlying the naming of the spreader, a more-than-superficial similarity connects the cognitive events that seem to enable concept formation in toddlers, and the rules by which more sophisticated humans produce grammatical sentences. In Chapter 7 we talked about sentences having structures called noun phrases and so on; we described how sentences can be derived by analyzing the rules that enable parts of sentences to be assembled into larger components. Now, interestingly, we see that the rules that govern syntax may be generalizable to describe how we build all our concepts. For as long as humans have pondered their own mentality, they have wondered about the relationship between language and mind: Do you have to have a mind before you can speak? Or, are there are some concepts that we might call prelinguistic—a person doesn't have to be able to speak before these concepts can be used? What, then, is the relationship between linguistic development and cognitive development in its most general sense? Do these two types of development (if they really are different types of development) almost always go hand in hand, or can one type of development outstrip the other? These are some of the questions that we explore in this chapter.

Stages in Language Development

Table 9.1 shows the "stages" in language development. The word *stages* is in quotation marks as a clue about its meaning. Usually, children are not completely in one stage or another. Because children's behaviors show substantial overlap, the table indicates the dominant linguistic behavior at each age. Also, the ages given in Table 9.1 are only approximations. Some children begin producing their first words before their

Table 9.1   Milestones in Language Development

Language Stage	Beginning Age
Crying	Birth
Cooing	6 weeks
Babbling	6 months
Intonation patterns	8 months
One-word utterances	1 year
Two-word utterances	18 months
Word inflections	2 years
Questions, negatives	2 ¼ years
Rare or complex constructions	5 years
Mature speech	10 years

Source: From Aitchison, 1983.

first birthday; other children's first words don't occur until much later. The range of individual differences is fairly great. Also, a child who "misses" the average onset age for a stage may not necessarily be behind at the next milestone. Children sometimes speed through several stages, only to spend longer than usual later. Other children may go slowly at first and spend less time in the later stages. The order of events listed in Table 9.1 probably is invariant. Once children enter the stage of two-word utterances, they are not likely to revert to babbling.

Crying and Cooing

For the first four weeks in an infant's life, cries are undifferentiated: the same cry is used regardless of the stimulus. During the second month, some differentiation occurs, which may be universal. Ricks (1975) found that English parents could detect various messages in both English and foreign babies' cries. Despite this finding, however, thinking of crying as truly linguistic is probably incorrect. Even babies several months of age don't appear able to use their cries productively, and their behavior seems mainly reflexive. Crying does, however, help lay the foundation for language by strengthening the vocal cords and the lungs (Aitchison, 1983). Also, the baby's cries usually elicit a response, an important point. The baby has an opportunity to find out early that vocalization can be functional, and speech almost always has that property.

Anywhere from six weeks to three months of age, children begin to coo. Cooing is hard to describe. The sounds apparently are vowel-like. And yet, the acoustic properties usually associated with adult vowels are not present in the infant's coos. Cooing seems to be universal. The child seems to be playing with the articulatory apparatus. Generally, this is a time during which the child explores the world, and cooing is probably best understood in that sense. Like crying, cooing is not truly linguistic but it too bolsters development of language. Adults seldom cry when babies cry, but they coo (or try to) when babies coo. Also, babies seem to be able to imitate some adult gestures (such as protruding the tongue) from a very early age (Meltzoff & Moore, 1977). The combination of adults' willingness to coo and babies' ability to detect and mimic various gestures suggests that babies begin to learn about reciprocity in vocalization before they begin to speak. By about six months, the child also uses consonantal sounds in vocalizations. At this stage, the child is said to have begun babbling.

Babbling and Single Words

Babbling has been described as a period of advanced motor play and vocal experimentation for the prelinguistic child. The consonantal and verblike sounds are strung together in lengthy chains that sound like words. Probably for eons, parents have incorrectly assumed that their progeny were addressing them with "dadada" or "mamama," and maybe it's just as well they don't know the truth. No evidence supports the idea that babbling children attach meaning to their utterances. It was once thought that, during the babbling period, children make almost every sound possible for the human vocal apparatus (Jespersen, 1922). This assumption is now known to be untrue; the variety of babbling sounds is not great. Another past belief was that babbling is universal; that is, done by children everywhere, regardless of cultural forces affecting the child. Children have been reported, though, who never babbled yet managed to acquire language. But babbling is widespread and common.

One question that researchers pose is how linguistic culture modifies the child's utterances. If the babbling sounds are not influenced by the language that the child hears, the idea that babbling is programmatic is supported—a more or less innate and rigid stage in development. This idea has been supported by findings (Lenneberg, 1967) showing that congenitally deaf children babble. If, on the other hand, children are affected by the language they are exposed to, whatever the children's innate knowledge, it must be flexible.

Weir (1966) attempted to answer this question by examining how tonality influences children's babbling. Tonal languages are those in which variations in pitch can vary meaning. In Chinese, a word may have different meanings when uttered at different pitches. Weir found that the longer babbling went on, the more likely Chinese babies were to produce monosyllabic utterances with great tonal variation. Nontonal babies (American, Arabian, and Russian) were more likely to show polysyllabic babbling. Interestingly, American mothers were often able to pick out American babies by their babbling sounds, as were Russian mothers able to pick out Russian babies, and Arabian mothers, Arabian babies. Mothers of the three nontonal nationalities, though, could not discriminate babies babbling in languages that were not the mothers' native tongues. This finding has been used to support the idea that, between ages nine and fourteen months, children undergo a **babbling drift** during which they gradually restrict their productions to sounds occurring in the language they will eventually master. Now children's utterances sound particularly like well-formed speech.

At about one year, the child begins to produce single words. From twelve to eighteen months, the child may acquire up to fifty words, although fifteen seems closer to the average. Some children may use as few as four or five words during this period. Babbling may continue briefly after true words are produced, but it tends to disappear fairly rapidly.

This period is also referred to as the **holophrastic stage** in language development because the child seems to use one word to stand for an entire sentence. These words are typically nouns or adjectives (McNeill, 1970) and usually refer to concrete objects that are present or to motivational or emotional states. Nelson (1973) found that animals, toys, and food were the three categories most frequently referred to by children who had learned their first ten words. These utterances have various meanings. The child who says "shoe" may be indicating that the shoe is his, that he wants to have his shoes put on, that someone has been observed who's not wearing shoes, and so on. Only by analyzing the context in which the utterance occurs can we understand the child's intentions.

Greenfield and Smith (1976) state that the content of the child's message may not be as important as the context. When the context is analyzed, the child's utterances are seen to express several functions. Greenfield and Smith followed two children around and recorded their utterances. They found that the children's initial utterances usually named things that were movers or instigators of actions. Later, the children's utterances seemed to name movables, or things that were influenced by actions. Next, they began referring to places, and, finally, to possession, or recipients of actions. These functions and some examples are shown in Table 9.2.

When a child knows only five or so words, picking which one to say may not be too difficult, but by the time the child has learned 100 words, it may be very hard to decide which word to use (Moskowitz, 1991). How then do children go about picking one word, from all those they know, to express a thought in a specific situation? Greenfield and Smith (1976) suggest that children in the holophrastic period understand something about the informativeness of each holophrase in various situations. A child who wants a banana and has the lexical items "want" and "banana" will pick the most informative of these two items to say. That is, the one-year-old will say "banana," not "want." Why is "banana" more informative than "want"? From the child's standpoint, if you say "banana," you may recognize that the adult caretaker will acknowl-

---

Table 9.2   Roles and Actions Talked About in One-Word Utterances

Role or Action	Utterance	Context
Agent	Dada	Hears *someone* come in
Action or state resulting from action	Down	When sits *down* or steps *down* from somewhere
Object affected by action	Ban	When wants *fan* turned off
State of object affected by action	Down	When *shuts* cabinet door
Object associated with another object or location	Poo	With hand on bottom while being changed, usually after bowel movement
Possessor	Lara	On seeing *Lauren's* empty bed
Location	Bap	Indicating location of feces on *diaper*

Source: From Greenfield and Smith, 1976.

edge that only a few relationships could exist between you and a banana with "wanting one" probably being the main relationship. Your caretakers will follow up on your comment by asking if you actually want a banana, to which you can respond "yes." But saying "want" doesn't accomplish the objective nearly as quickly. Once again, from the child's standpoint, you may recognize that dozens or hundreds of things are around the house, or around the kitchen, which you might want. And your caretakers really have no effective clue as to which of these you may want, forcing them to go through a lengthy list ("What do you want? An orange, an apple, a cracker . . ."). This sort of analysis and the findings in Table 9.2 suggest that the child in the holophrastic period is not just learning about word meanings, but is beginning to learn about syntax or word order too.

Overextensions and Underextensions That children use a specific word in specific contexts is no guarantee that this word means the same thing to them that it does to older children or to adults. The deviations in a child's meaning from the standard meaning can be described in several ways. A child who says "doggie" in relation to dogs, and many other four-legged, hairy creatures, has **overextended** the word. A child who uses a general word to refer only to specific examples of its general meaning has **underextended** the word. A child who refers only to his or her cat, but not cats in general, as a "kitty" is underextending the word. Finally, a child may overextend a word sometimes and underextend it at others; this use is an overlap. Anglin (1986) observed an overlap in his daughter, who used "umbrella" to describe only open, not closed, umbrellas (underextension), but who also used the word umbrella to describe kites and a leaf that a character in a book used as a shield from the rain.

Most of us probably are familiar with the overextension phenomenon because it is a fairly noticeable error. Underextensions aren't so obvious. It's hard to tell if a child has restricted the range of a word, because he or she may nevertheless be labeling an object correctly, which may give the impression that overextensions are commoner than underextensions, but that's not true. Kay and Anglin (1982) showed objects to one- and two-year-old children and then asked them questions ("What's this?" or "Is this a _____?"). They found that underextensions were more common, which fits in nicely with other findings by Greenfield and Smith (1976). They found that children are likely to be conservative with their recently acquired words in that they are much more likely to use a recently acquired word as a label for a novel object in the environment than for a familiar object or as a question.

Learning Word Meanings That young children make errors by overextension and underextension shouldn't surprise us greatly because, when you think about it, children in the holophrastic period are faced with a very difficult task in learning the meanings of many words. In the literature on concept formation, which we'll look at more closely in a later chapter, we see that adults who are trying to learn a concept may frequently adopt a "win-stay, lose-shift" strategy. That is, if I'm asked to name elements in some arbitrary category, and I come up with some name that seems to work on an example, then I'll stick with this as a general name until I get feedback indicating that my name has worked on some other example, and then I'll modify my use of the name. Adults can use such a strategy readily, but it's difficult for six-year-olds to generate new hypotheses in the face of negative information. And yet kids as young as two years learn new word meanings quite easily, seemingly doing something that older children can't (Markman, 1990). Children have another, more abstract problem, too. The philosopher Quine (1960) pointed out that for any finite set of data, there is an infinite number of logically possible hypotheses that are consistent with it. Because nobody has infinite time to test all possible hypotheses, technically, nobody, let alone small children, should be able to learn word meanings. Obviously, though, we all seem to have the same meanings for thousands and thousands of words. How do we accomplish this feat?

Markman (1990) indicates that the child does not consider all possible hypotheses about what a lexical item may refer to. Rather, children seem to be constrained in the sorts of hypotheses about word meanings they will consider in the first place. This finding solves the strategy problem described above. Even though children are notoriously poor at modifying hypotheses in the face of negative information, they don't necessarily need such a skill to learn the meanings of words because they are biased in such a way as not to generate "wrong" hypotheses from the start.

Hypotheses about word meanings may be constrained in several ways. First, children seem to follow the dictates of the **whole-object assumption** (Carey, 1978), which means that they assume a new word refers to an entire object, and not to a part of an object, or to a feature or property of the object. But even after children decide that a novel word refers to an entire object, they need some principle telling them how far to extend that term. Here, Markman and Hutchinson (1984) suggest that children are guided by the **taxonomic assumption** which states that children will assume a label can be extended to objects of the same kind, rather than to objects that are thematically related to the newly named object. Thematic relationships are those based on temporal, spatial, or causal properties rather than on categorical properties. Thus, according to the taxonomic assumption, if you say to a one-year-old, "Look, a train," the one-year-old will assume that the label refers to the whole object (the locomotive plus cars) but not to the tracks or the crossing gates (objects that are thematically related to trains). This assumption is especially interesting because some evidence suggests that young children (i.e., toddlers and preschoolers) are very sensitive to thematic relationships and use them in sorting tasks (Gelman & Baillargeon, 1983). The question then is: Children have a propensity to use thematic relationships to sort, but do they also know when to override them to learn new words?

Markman (1990) describes a study in which these elements were played out. Four- and five-year-olds were spoken to by a puppet (controlled by the experimenter) who said, "I'm going to show you something. Then I want you to think carefully and find another one." Next, the puppet showed the children a picture of an object such as a cow. After inviting the children to look at this object, the puppet asked them to find another object that was similar. Then the puppet put up two more pictures, one on each side of the target, and said, "Can you find the other one?" One of the pictures was a pig, which has a taxonomic relationship with the target because they are both farm animals. The second picture was a pail of milk, which has an obvious thematic relationship with the target. In a second exercise, the condition was the same, except that the children were told that the puppet could talk in puppet language, and so they had to listen carefully to what the puppet had to say. In this condition the puppet said, "I'm going to show you a dax, then I want you to think carefully and find another one." Then the two pictures were displayed as before. If the taxonomic bias is operating here, children should be more likely to choose the taxonomic picture when the unfamiliar word is used than when the puppet offers no word. The findings confirmed this prediction. In the no-name condition, children chose the taxonomic category only 25% of the time. But in the name condition, 65% of the time subjects chose the picture that shared a taxonomic relationship with the target.

These findings suggest that the taxonomic bias guides children particularly when it comes to learning new words. Other evidence (Waxman, 1990) suggests that children can use this information that they've learned to form conceptual hierarchies. It appears, however, that some limitations restrict the taxonomic bias's ability to guide language acquisition.

Braine et al. (1990) studied how seven- to ten-year-old children acquired a miniature, artificial language. Their subjects looked at a set of cards, each of which showed a monkey (Frippy) posed in one of three locations in relation to the object depicted on the card. Both the object depicted and Frippy's location relative to it were indicated in the artificial language. The object was represented by a word, and Frippy's location by a suffix attached to the word. The artificial-language word for car was "garth." If Frippy was standing by the car, the suffix "-tev" was attached to the word. Consequently, the expression "Frippy garthtev" means Frippy is by the car. If Frippy was walking away from the car, the expression "Frippy garthgil" was used, and finally, if Frippy was walking over to the car, the expression "Frippy garthfoo" was used. The children attempted to learn twenty-four nouns and suffixes. Of these, eighteen nouns took the "high-frequency" suffix; these nouns took the suffixes described above. The other six nouns took the "low-frequency" suffix. For these nouns, the children had to learn a different set of three suffixes to indicate the *to, from,* and *at* relationships. Of course the children were not told explicitly at the beginning of the study which nouns were in which category. One issue the researchers questioned was the children's ability to recognize that some of the nouns were secondary, and thus required the secondary suffix. This choice turned out to be extremely difficult for children to make. Approximately 80% of the time, children failed to put secondary suffixes on secondary nouns, and almost all the mistakes were the result of the child using the high-frequency suffix inappropriately. Braine et al. (1990) report that this difficulty did not result simply because there were eighteen primary nouns and only six secondary nouns. Even when the number of nouns was balanced (twelve in each category), children had difficulty catching on to the distinction and generalizing to newly learned nouns.

Many other interesting findings came out of this study, but I mention just a few. First, in learning the suffixes, the children almost always learned by rule instead of by rote. That is, very little evidence showed that the children learned simply by "brute-forcing" noun-suffix combinations into their memories. Second, immediate corrective feedback had very little effect. Children who were given explicit information when they were right or wrong did no better than children who were not given such information. Third, when adults were given the same task in a similar format, they did statistically better than the children did. But the adults did not outperform the children in a practical sense; some adults got only about 33% of suffixes correct on the secondary nouns.

In a sense, these findings are quite counterintuitive. As you may know if you've studied foreign languages, many have the category called "gender." That is, in some languages some nouns are "masculine" and others are "feminine"; and adjectives sometimes have to take suffix endings to modify a masculine or a feminine noun. Everyone who takes in such a language as a native learns which nouns are which with no problem. Superficially, learning noun gender seems comparable to the problems faced by the subjects in the Braine et al. study, and this resemblance leads to a question: How is it that native speakers learn the noun genders (which often seem arbitrary) without apparent difficulty, but the Braine et al. subjects had such a hard time learning the arbitrary assignment of suffixes to some categories of nouns? Braine (1987) suggested that the arbitrariness of gender classes in other languages may be more apparent than real. In such languages, a similarity in sound or meaning always clues the language learner how to subclass nouns. Thus the taxonomic bias that guides youthful language learners is not invincible: it can be defeated if we try to teach children languages that are truly arbitrary. In other words, some shared similarity in meaning or in phonological shape is required if the child is to learn that some nouns are members of the same category.

Two-Word Stage

At around eighteen to twenty months, the child begins to produce utterances that are two words long—hence the unimaginative name, the **two-word stage.** All researchers agree that the increase in linguistic capability is dramatic during this period. First, vocabulary increases; the typical two-and-a-half-year-old knows several hundred words. Second, the average length of the child's utterances also increases dramatically. The length of an utterance usually is computed by counting all the basic units of meaning (the morphemes) that have appeared. Morphemes usually correspond to words, but this relationship is not perfect. In English, *sad* is one word and one morpheme. *Sadly,* though still one word, counts as two morphemes, however, because the *-ly* ending denotes meaning by itself. Therefore, the utterance "Daddy go" is counted as three morphemes because the *y* carries meaning by itself. The **mean length of utterance (MLU)** is computed by determining the number of morphemes a child has produced, then dividing that number by the total number of utterances. When MLU is computed for children age two and beyond, a steady increase is seen across the entire period. Figure 9.1 shows the MLU graphed for two children studied by Roger Brown (1973). As mentioned earlier, different children may attain linguistic milestones at widely differing ages. This variation is evident for the two children referred to in Figure 9.1. Adam was three-and-a-half years old before his MLU reached four items; he was a full year behind Eve.

Another important change occurs during this period. Whereas during the holophrastic period, the child's caretakers are willing to analyze the context in which the utterance occurs to deduce the child's intention, caretakers are less likely to analyze context during the two-word stage. The child relies less on the context for meaning and begins to let the word order do some of the work. Using two utterances puts additional linguistic demands on the child, however. As we've seen, the child must now acquire the rules of syntax.

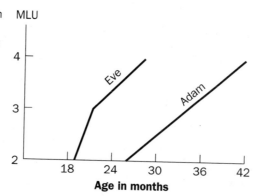

Figure 9.1 Increases in mean length of utterance (MLU) as a function of age for two children. *Source:* From Brown, 1970.

Bloom (1970) was among the first to realize that the child's two-word utterances show syntax. One of her subjects, Kathryn, used the expression "mommy sock" twice in one day. In the first instance, Kathryn produced the utterance while holding her mother's sock; the second time, Kathryn used that expression while her mother put one of Kathryn's socks on. A contextual analysis still must be done to understand the little girl's meaning, but the order of the words helps to express two meaningful relationships. In the first example, Kathryn was expressing the *possession* relationship. In the second, she was making use of the same sort of *agent* construction that also occurs during the holophrastic stage.

These kinds of utterances are called *telegraphic speech.* Just as in a telegram, where inessential words are omitted, the child seems to use only words that are necessary to communicate an intention. Articles, pronouns, and auxiliary verbs have not yet appeared.

Brown (1970) analyzed small children's two-word utterances and found that they typically express one of several meaningful relationships. These **structural relationships** are shown in Table 9.3. Notice that many of these relationships express the same things that children talk about during the holophrastic stage: namely, possession, the agent role, and location.

Braine (1976) examined the two-word utterances of ten children (five were learning English, two Samoan, one Finnish, one Hebrew, and one Swedish). He found that all these children spoke of movers or doers; that is, they all used the agent relationship. Moreover, all the children spoke of movable objects (the action–object relationship) and places (the locative relationship). Some of the other relationships were less commonly used. Braine mentioned that the children did not all use the possessive relationship, and the other relationships were used even less frequently.

The structural relationships Brown described can be used as a basis for longer utterances. Three-word utterances can be made by combining some two-word forms. The child who says "Bobbie take cookie" has combined the agent-action form ("Bobbie take") with the action-object form ("take cookie"). This linkage of primitive forms can take us only so far, however. Generally, after creating three-word utterances, the child seems to differentiate each of the noun classes in the basic utterance. *Differentiation* refers to lengthening a clause by elaboration and expansion. Bloom

Table 9.3   Brown's Structural Description of Two-Word Utterances

Structural Meaning	Form	Example
1. Nomination	that + N	that box
2. Notice	hi + N	hi belt
3. Recurrence	more + N	more cookie
4. Nonexistence	allgone + N	allgone kitty
5. Attributive	ADJ + N	big train
6. Possessive	N + N	mommy lunch
7. Locative	N + N	sweater chair
8. Locative	V + N	walk road
9. Agent–Action	N + V	mommy read
10. Agent–Object	N + N	mommy sock
11. Action–Object	V + N	put book
12. Conjunction	N + N	umbrella boot

Source: From Brown, 1970.

(1970) found that the initial elaboration of a sentence is right to left; that is, the object clause is elaborated first. This elaboration is accomplished by first adding articles or other modifiers to the object of the utterance, and later by including possessive pronouns. In this way, an utterance such as "Mommy read story" might be elaborated into "Mommy, read my story." Although differentiation of a sentence begins with the object clause and is therefore right to left, *within a clause* the differentiation is usually left to right. Articles begin to appear in front of the nouns that are the subjects of the sentence.

Such a view presupposes that all children in the two-word stage express the functional relationships in much the same ways. Braine (1976) pointed out, however, that children in the two-word stage seem to adopt specific formulas to express specific relationships. To talk about the location of an object, some children first mention the object (e.g., "baby") and then the location ("chair"). Other children take the opposite tack, stating the location first, then the object occupying it ("There doggie"). This approach inevitably colors later elaborations. The formula initially picked (which seems to have no rhyme or reason) may constrain the expansion.

Bloom, Lightbown, and Hood (1975) and Nelson (1975) determined another variation that may affect the expansion. They found that their subjects could be reliably grouped in one of two categories. Subjects in the first group used content words very early in the two-word stage, just as the Brown model predicts. A second group of subjects, though, used pronouns in the agent relationship. These children usually used the pronoun *I* in utterances such as "I do" and "I go." They were also likely to use the demonstrative *this* in the object relationship, in utterances such as "try this." This result is not what we would expect, because of the differentiation process just outlined. Anyway, within a few months these early differences seemed to wash out.

The "content" children started to include pronouns in their utterances, and the "I" children began to use content words. These findings suggest substantial individual differences in children's formulaic knowledge in the two-word stage. Whether such individual differences materially affect language development is not now known. These findings also suggest that the initial structural relationships Brown proposed are used by some, but not by all, children. The early use of pronouns by some children seems to confound the notion that the structural relationships are the basis for longer utterances.

In this discussion we have emphasized the syntactic structure in children's two-word utterances, but we should not overlook a problem faced by children at this age that could overwhelm their syntactic structures. Specifically, suppose you are a child at the two-word stage and you have a thought that is just "longer" than any two words you can think of. What do you do then? Conversely, would this problem never come up because children at this age cannot have thoughts that are too complicated for a two-word utterance? The answer seems to be that two-year-old children do have complicated thoughts, and that they are also capable of solving the problem of expressing them in short sentences.

Consider this dialogue between R. Scollon, a language researcher, and two-year-old Brenda:

> Brenda: Tape corder. Use it. Use it.
> Scollon: Use it for what?
> Brenda: Talk. Corder talk. Brenda talk. (Moskowitz, cited in Wang, 1991)

Here we see Brenda expressing a thought that we might translate as, "Turn on the tape recorder because I want to hear myself talking." But Brenda cannot encode this thought directly into a grammatical sentence because her knowledge of syntax is not extensive enough to permit that. What happens? Brenda takes her thought and breaks it down into a series of two-word utterances, which, when interpreted sequentially, give enough information to permit a listener to infer Brenda's intention. The name for this process is **vertical construction** (Moskowitz, 1991), and it can be contrasted with the **horizontal construction** that most speakers use to translate their thoughts into a complete word-by-word specification of their intention. Vertical construction suggests that children have a sophistication about language structure that goes beyond their two-word utterances. Besides the structural relationships that we looked at earlier, children are able to take a fairly complicated thought and break it down into a series of utterances, each of which shows these structural properties.

Word Order and Inflections

As children begin to produce utterances with three and four words, they rely more heavily on word order and **inflections** to signal their intent. In English, inflections are used to show plurality of nouns and possession, among other things. Generally, a language makes a trade-off between stringency in its word-order rules and complexity in its inflections. Because English is not a highly inflected language, word order is quite important to meaning. If the word order is altered, the meaning of the utterance can be drastically revamped. As I recall, Latin is just the opposite: the order of words can

Table 9.4   English Inflections Appear in Two Children's Speech

| Inflection | Age of Appearance (in months) | | Combined Rank Order in Mother's Speech |
	Adam	Eve	
Present progressive, -ing	28	19½	2
Plural on nouns, -s	33	24	1
Past on regular verbs, -ed	39	24½	4
Possessive on nouns, -s	39½	25½	5
Third person on verbs, -s	41	26	3

Source: From Belugi, 1964.

be shuffled around greatly without changing the sentence's meaning. It all works because each word is highly inflected, the ending reveals the noun's case, and adjectives have to agree in case with the nouns they modify.

The appearance of inflections was studied by Bellugi (1964). Her findings are shown in Table 9.4. Once again, we see substantial timetable differences between Adam and Eve. At twenty-six months, Eve began adding -s to the verbs of third-person subjects. Adam was a full fifteen months behind in this ability. The order of appearance, though, is identical for the two children. Moreover, the order of appearance is not strongly related to frequency of use by the children's mothers. The inflection mentioned previously was the last to appear in the children's speech although it was fairly common in their mothers' speech. Notice, too, that three of the inflections involve producing an *s* sound. For Adam, though, the latency between the earliest /s/ inflection and the last to appear was eight months. Even for Eve, whose progress appears much faster, this latency was two months. If use of the inflection depended solely on ability to produce the /s/ sound, no latency would occur between appearance of the first of these inflections and the last. The latency shows that use of these inflections cannot be explained solely by phonemic development.

The development of inflectional markers is researched in a classic study by Berko (1958). Preschool children were shown a card such as the one in Figure 9.2. While the children were looking at the card, Berko would say, "This is a wug." Berko next pointed to the two figures standing together and said, "Now there is another one. There are two of them." Then the child was asked to express this fact by providing the correct term in the statement, "There are two _____ ." Most of the subjects correctly answered with *wugs* even though they were obviously unfamiliar with the word. Berko went on in a follow-up study to demonstrate the power of the plurality rule. The child was shown a picture of a goose and was told, "Here is a goose." Next, a card showing two geese was presented with this statement: "Here are two *geese*. There are two _____ ." Even after hearing the correct form, most children responded with "gooses."

It's possible to identify six stages of development in acquiring plurals. In the first stage, the child uses the singular form when the plural form is required. The child does

Figure 9.2 One of Berko's stimulus cards. *Source:* From Berko, 1958.

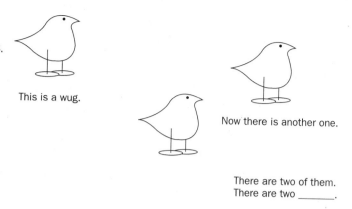

This is a wug.

Now there is another one.

There are two of them.
There are two _____.

not yet appear to know that plurality can be designated linguistically, although certainly the cognitive machinery is available to represent "more than one." Thus, we find children at this stage saying "two cat." At the rather ambiguous second stage, the child seems to have learned that some nouns are irregular, and that to express plurality, a different word altogether may be required. Such a child may say "men" before saying "mans." At the third stage in development, in which many of Berko's subjects found themselves, the child adds an /s/ or a /z/ to various words to express more than one. Consequently, the child may say "feets" or "gooses" and overgeneralize this rule, now saying "mans." In the third stage, though, children do not routinely alter words that already end in an /s/ or /z/ sound to make them plurals. A child in stage three may not discriminate between one house and two house(s). Adults have a way of dealing with such words, and it consists of adding a /schwa-z/ to get the "ehz" effect that adults pronounce in words like "houses," "roses," and "bushes." (Remember, the schwa is the unaccented vowel sound that we hear in "sofa.") When children catch on to this distinction, a very short fourth stage may follow in which they add the /schwa-z/ ending indiscriminately to all words, thus getting something like "boyzez" or "manzez." After perhaps only a few days children begin to shift back to the simple "add /s/ or /z/" formula they used earlier. Rapidly ditching the /schwa-z/ formulation suggests that children probably had been working on such a rule during the third stage, mentally trying it out on all plural forms to see if it conformed to the linguistic rules that the community seemed to be playing by. When children conclude that it's only the "end-in-/s/" singulars that take the /schwa-z/ plural ending, they've learned just about everything there is to know about forming English plurals. The only remaining bit of business is to memorize the truly irregular forms such as "men" or "mice." Moskowitz (1991) points out that this task may seem like small potatoes to the five-year-old who may still have more interesting linguistic problems to work on, and so the child may remain at stage five ("housez," "ducks," "mans") for quite some time before entering stage six, when his or her knowledge and use conform to the adult's.

This sort of overregularization is interesting for several reasons. First, many of the forms thus created by children are not copies of adult speech, and so cannot be explained as imitations. Second, the developmental pathway is similar for various overregularization errors. For verbs, children at age three are fairly likely to use the correct past tense of some irregular verbs. The small child might say, "We went bye-bye." By age four or five, though, the child who had been producing the correct form now shifts to the incorrect form *goed*—a seeming regression. Usually by age six, the child once again consistently produces the correct form. Overregularization is sometimes called a "smart error" because it indicates that the child has mastered an inflection rule.

That overregularization errors are often not imitative (what adult says "goed"?) has attracted researchers' attention. Parents are not neutral toward these utterances, and parents sometimes try to get the child to imitate their correct usage. To produce such novel utterances, then, the child sometimes has to counteract the caretakers' will. Children seem remarkably resistant to these pressures:

> Child: My teacher holded the baby rabbits and we patted them.
> Adult: Did you say your teacher held the baby rabbits?
> Child: Yes.
> Adult: What did you say she did?
> Child: She holded the baby rabbits and we patted them.
> Adult: Did you say she held them tightly?
> Child: No, she holded them loosely. (Cazden, 1972, p. 92)

More often, attempts to influence the child are **expansions** such as these:

> Child: Daddy office?
> Adult: That's right, Daddy's gone to the office.

Such expansions are omnipresent in the child's linguistic environment. Brown and Bellugi (1964) estimated that expansions make up more than a third of parental responses. Until Cazden (1972) completed her landmark study, it was commonly thought that such expansions helped the child acquire syntactic knowledge. Now the issue is not so clear.

The subjects in this study were children who were less than three years, six months old at the beginning. In one group, an adult caretaker responded to the child's utterances with expansions. In a second group, the caretaker deliberately responded with well-formed utterances that did not expand the child's remarks. The caretaker might respond, "Yes, but he'll be back soon" to the child's earlier utterance. If expansions are useful for syntax learning, we'd expect that the expansion group would outperform the nonexpansion group. But after three months, the children in these groups continued to perform at the same level, a somewhat puzzling finding. The various explanations tend to have one theme in common. Language is a richly varied phenomenon, and language development seems to proceed faster when children are exposed to a good measure of this richness and variety. The Cazden finding also has a practical implication. Parents who overexpose their children to simple expansions or who subtly try to coerce them into correct speech may be doing their children a disservice. Some errors, such as overregularization, seem an important part of the overall language-development scheme. Well-meant interventions may be more disruptive than effective.

Later Development

By age five or six, children appear to have mastered most rules of syntax and inflection, and so their knowledge of language seems complete. This apparent mastery is an illusion, however. Five-year-olds are readily able to interpret a sentence, but their interpretations are not always correct, as Carol Chomsky (1969) demonstrated by show-ing a blindfolded doll to a group of five- to eight-year-olds. They were then asked, "Is the doll hard to see or easy to see?" Chomsky found that all the five- and six-year-olds thought that the doll was hard to see, and many of the seven- and eight-year-olds agreed. Although this study has been criticized, replications of it (e.g., Cromer, 1970) confirmed the finding. Apparently, children at ages five and six don't realize that sen-tences such as "The rabbit is nice to eat" and "The rabbit is eager to eat" have com-pletely different meanings (Aitchison, 1983). Language development apparently con-tinues until age ten or eleven.

Development in Reading Ability

In the first part of this chapter, we have focused on how spoken language matures. We have seen that language ability develops rapidly from onset to the end of the first six years and continues at a somewhat slower pace perhaps for the first ten years. During this period, reading and writing develop in parallel. In reading, some of the improve-ment comes from better mechanics: Older children are better than younger at mov-ing their eyes forward on the page. They have better visual scanning strategies in gen-eral, and in reading are less likely than younger children to launch their eyes in a reverse saccade. But most of the improvements in reading ability in older children do not result from purely mechanical changes. A host of cognitive processes are brought to bear by the older or better reader, and in this section of the chapter I present what we know about some of those processes.

One of the reader's most important tasks consists of building a mental represen-tation of the information as it is being read, on the fly. This is not an easy task. Consider this sentence:

To do all that, a lot of spades would be required.

By itself, this sentence is sort of ambiguous, isn't it? But now, let's take the sentence and put it into two contexts:

Context 1: The bridge player reviewed the bidding thus far. Her partner's bid set the contract rather high, and to make it, quite a few tricks would have to be taken. To do all that, a lot of spades would be required.
Context 2: The landscaper turned next to the estimates for the equipment needed. Some topsoil would have to be spread, and a watercourse would be established to drain into the culvert. To do all that, a lot of spades would be required.

In each context, the identical sentence takes on two meanings, and it appears to do so effortlessly. That is, it doesn't seem like we have to work too hard to figure out the meaning of the initially ambiguous sentence when it occurs in context, regardless of which context it appears in. Cognitive psychologists have attempted to explain this phenomenon by suggesting that when we first read the final sentence in the passages above, both meanings of the ambiguous word *spades* are accessed and made available. Readers are helped because now all they have to do is decide which of the available meanings of the word *spades* is the one intended in the passage.

Supporting this interpretation, Gernsbacher et al. (1990) asked their subjects to read a short sentence ending with a homograph or a nonhomographic word. *Spade* is a homograph; a word whose spelling is identical to that of another word, but which has a completely different meaning here—either the name for a suit of cards or the name for a tool. After the subjects read the sentence, they saw a test word. They were to indicate yes or no if the test word was related to the sentence's overall meaning. Suppose the subject saw this sentence:

He dug a hole with the shovel.

Then suppose the subject saw this test word:

ACE

The subject should respond no this time because the word ACE has nothing to do with digging a hole. Some sentences ended with a homograph:

He dug a hole with the spade.

If the subject sees the test word ACE after this sentence, the correct answer is still no because ACE still has nothing to do with digging holes. But if the subjects had contacted all the meanings of the word *spade* immediately after reading the sentence, it might take them longer to correctly say no for the spade sentence than for the shovel sentence because the word ACE is related to the word *spade*, even though it is not related to the sentence as a whole. Gernsbacher and colleagues varied the time between offset of the sentence and onset of the test word. In the short-delay situation, only 100 msec elapsed between the sentence's offset and the test word's appearance. In the long-delay condition, 850 msec elapsed between these two events. The findings are very interesting. In the short-delay condition, all the readers experienced interference between test word and homograph. That is, they all required more time to say no in the homographic sentence condition (*spade*) than the nonhomographic word condition (*shovel*). But in the long-delay condition (850 msec), only the poor readers still showed this effect. When the delay between sentence and test word was 850 msec, the good readers responded no to the homographic sentence just as quickly as they did to the nonhomographic sentence. What does this finding mean?

It suggests that both meanings of the word *spade* are initially activated. Because both meanings are activated, if we hit the subjects with a test word that relates to the "unwanted" meaning of the word (here "suit of cards"), they will require more time to answer no because they have to override the relationship between the homograph and the test word. In the long-delay condition, the relationship between the test word and the homograph isn't a problem for the good readers because, after 850 msec, their cognitive and neural systems have suppressed the unwanted meaning of the homograph, and have kept active only the appropriate meaning in that sentence. That the poor readers are still getting some interference after 850 msec suggests that their cognitive and neural systems have not yet decided which of the homograph's two meanings should be kept active, and which should be put away.

Gernsbacher and Robertson (1995) theorize that this effect is not limited to homographs, but may extend to homonyms. The syllable /red/ when spoken might mean the color *red* or the past participle of the verb *to read*. Yuill and Oakhill (1991) report that less-skilled elementary-school readers have some difficulty mentally ditching the unwanted meaning in riddles such as, "What is black and white and /red/ all over?" When they are told that the answer is a "a newspaper," these students tend not to get the riddle because they perseverate on the homonym's color meaning, saying things such as "I don't understand; a newspaper would look funny if it was red."

Language Development Summarized

In looking at language acquisition, we've seen evidence suggesting that infants and toddlers have incredible cognitive sophistication enabling them to learn or know that there are such things as speech sounds and words, that words may mean something, that producing some words in some contexts is efficient in getting needs met, that words can be strung together to communicate even more complicated thoughts, and so on. Paradoxically, though, we also see that it's very difficult to teach small children other things that are no more complicated than language. From a strictly informational point of view, learning calculus is probably not as difficult as learning your native language at age two. (My sympathies are with you if you're now in a calculus course and thus find my assertion hard to swallow.) Even though learning one's native language is harder than learning calculus, we recognize that children will learn their language pretty much on their own, but they probably could not be taught calculus at age two no matter how intensively we worked with them. How is it that the cognitive machinery that seems so sophisticated for language doesn't seem nearly so smart when it comes to learning other things?

We can respond to this paradox in several ways. First, Markman (1990) points out that children are guided in learning the meanings of words by a taxonomic bias that guides them to put the stimulus that we call a word in a special class, and to hunt for similarities among the members in this class. In other words, from the evidence supporting the taxonomic bias, it seems that children already know where to look to find the regularities inherent in word meanings. A second way of responding to the paradox of children's language learning is advanced by Newport (1990), who has formulated a position labeled the **less is more (LIM) position.** Newport believes that, yes, children are relatively disadvantaged cognitively for many kinds of learning, but their general cognitive shortcomings actually help them learn language. According to this position, a cognitively sophisticated learner faced with language's problems would have quite a bit of work to do. In trying to learn the meaning of a word, such a learner might try to encode, in both short- and long-term memory, all the features that had been present at the time a novel object was named. But suppose the language learner had a relatively low-capacity short-term memory, as small children do. Such a learner would not bother trying to encode all the features that were presented, but rather might encode only the most salient feature in the stimulus. But this feature is probably most likely to correspond to the actual meaning of the word. Consider this example: Suppose a caretaker is holding a small child, and both are looking at a large tractor right next to them in a field. When the caretaker says, "That's a tractor," the child (technically) may not know for sure if "tractor" refers to the large thing sitting there, or the field itself, or the sky, or a bug crawling on the tractor. But the tractor is the most salient aspect in the scene, and the other elements will overcrowd the child's short-term memory and thus be eliminated. The child is left with the correct label for the most salient object presented.

This discussion focuses on the relationship between language and more general properties of cognition such as memory and attention. Moreover, in Newport's (1990) account, we've seen evidence suggesting that children's language acquisition is paced by their general level of cognitive development. In the remainder of this chapter we explore several issues in cognitive development, and see some of the parallels in cognition and language.

Cognitive Development

Conceptual Basis of Language

We might argue, as many have, that language's function is to express some interior or cognitive event, and that the fundamental elements in such an event can be described as concepts. According to such a view, concepts are the atoms of thought, which can be arranged and rearranged in infinite ways to represent intentions. The rules of language enable this arrangement, and every particular arrangement, of conceptual atoms to be mapped onto a structured temporal code that preserves its underlying intentionality. According to such a view, it would be hard to imagine that much real language learning could take place early in a human life, unless a theorist also wished to argue that infants have a fairly strong conceptual basis for such language.

We have some evidence for such a point of view. Antell and Keating (1983) showed infants who were less than one week old arrangements of dot patterns. Antell and Keating used a habituation paradigm to measure the infants' interest in the dot patterns. That is, infants will suck harder on a pacifier if such sucking is followed by new and interesting sights, but their sucking rate declines if the same picture is on view too long. The habituation phenomenon enables researchers to make inferences about the infant's conceptual apparatus: If we show infants different stimuli, and their sucking rate continues to decline, we can infer that such young children do not detect the difference in the stimuli. The Antell and Keating subjects habituated to dot patterns showing three dots, even when the specific configuration of the dots was altered. But the subjects' interest perked right back up when they were shown dot patterns consisting of either two dots or one dot. This finding suggests that even very young children have a primitive number concept that can be used as the basis for later linguistic communication. In other words, when the child begins to develop the idea that language can reflect plurals, or more-than-oneness, it is perhaps this primitive concept of numerosity that is the conceptual underpinning of the linguistic code.

A similar idea is seen in research by Golinkoff and Kerr (1978). They presented to fifteen- and eighteen-month-old children short film clips showing a man A (an agent or actor) pushing a recipient B (either another man, or a chair). The subjects' heart rates were monitored as individual clips were shown, and the children eventually habituated. But when Golinkoff and Kerr showed the subjects a different clip, with B now pushing A, the children's heart rates accelerated, suggesting to the researchers that these children had at least a primitive concept of "agency," or cause and effect. Once again, when we think back to the "agent–object" structural relationships that children express linguistically beginning around this time, we see a strong suggestion that such linguistic events are anchored on a conceptual framework that has been previously developed.

A lot of questions, though, are left unanswered in this account. Gross (1985) points out that these studies don't explain what becomes a concept in the first place. For something to be a concept, it must have boundaries or borders specifying what's to be included and what's to be excluded. In other words, a "car" is defined just as much by what it's not as by what it is. Once these features are established, only then do we have a basis on which to categorize or conceptualize objects that we encounter in the natural world. But—and this is important—nothing about the natural world tells us which concepts are the natural ones. Of the infinite ways in which we could use aspects of the world as a basis for grouping things, people seem to show both consensus and diversity. That is, there are probably some universal concepts, but certainly we have many concepts that seem to be culturally generated and bound. The taxonomic bias that we discussed before doesn't help us solve this problem, either. It's true that bias helps children tremendously with the problem of mapping the child's interior, conceptual world onto language. But the taxonomic bias should not be understood as a way of enabling children to build their conceptual furniture in the first place. Another issue is modification or development of concepts. However they do it, children build concepts. But the concepts they build may not always be the same as the adult version, a phenomenon we saw in my son's calling the seed spreader a wagon. Because we know that children almost invariably do eventually attain the adult forms of the concept, they must have some reliable means for modifying their initial attempts in such a way as to get closer to the adult forms. We'll discuss some theories on this process in a later chapter, but for now we'll just say that this issue is far from settled.

Theory of Mind

In at least one location in the cognitive–psychology domain these ideas come together very directly, and that is "theory of mind." This idea has been around for a while; Premack and Woodruff (1978) first used it to describe their notion that chimpanzees acted as though they were making inferences that others, including chimpanzees and perhaps people, also had mental states and these others were acting in accordance with their presumed mental states. In other words, the chimpanzee recognized its own mental states and apparently believed that others had them too—this was the chimpanzee's theory of mind. Attention soon shifted from chimps' mental life to that of small children. Several studies (e.g., Bretherton & Bates, 1979; Wimmer & Perner, 1983) showed that children as young as three years use many mental expressions such as "want," "know," and "think" to describe internal states. In one extensive analysis Bartsch and Wellman (1995) thoroughly analyzed more than 200,000 separate utterances produced by ten children between eighteen months and six years. (These utterances have been gathered in the CHILDES database, MacWhinney & Snow, 1985.) Several findings were interesting. Children use terms indicating a want or desire long before they use expressions that would designate a belief. All ten of the children referred to wants and desires in utterances produced between their second and third birthdays. Children's talk about beliefs did not occur until almost a year later, on the average.

Wellman (1990) has devised a theory on such beliefs and desires. In the theory's first stage, children at age two have a concept of desire that is described as "mentalistic, but nonrepresentational" (Astington, 1997). For the two-year-old, a "want" is simply a drive toward some object. If people act differently, it is because they want different things. A three-year-old may have a belief about something (and such beliefs are usually indicated in the words "know" or "think"). But according to Wellman, the three-year-old has only a limited concept of beliefs, and these beliefs must be in congruity with desires. To see this point, imagine that we tell a typical three-year-old this brief story:

> Sally is looking for her lost puppy. She wants to get the puppy back. Sally thinks the puppy is in the back yard; the puppy is really in the basement. Where will Sally look first for her puppy?

The three-year-old probably will say that Sally will look in the basement, because, according to Wellman, the three-year-old does not yet have the concept of a mistaken or false belief. Not until children reach four years do they realize that, although people will act to fulfill their wants, their actions are nevertheless based on their beliefs, some of which could be erroneous. Thus it is that when three-year-old children are placed in this situation, if they are told where Sally looked for her puppy (in the back yard), they can explain why Sally looked there ("because she wanted to find her puppy"). But even the children who can explain why Sally looked there can't successfully predict where Sally will actually look. According to Wellman, they can't do so because the concepts "want" and "belief" are congruent in the mind of the three-year-old. It doesn't occur to the three-year-old that a person may have a belief that's false. And so they do not yet see the problem caused by their contradictory answers in explaining and predicting the searcher's behavior.

It is when we begin to consider the origin of these concepts that we may see how language can be influential. From the Bartsch and Wellman (1995) standpoint, expressions such as "want" and "know" designate elements in children's conceptual lives that they use to predict behavior just as a physicist may use "electron" and "quark" to understand the natural world. As an alternative, Astington (1997) suggests that it may be precisely because children are linguistic creatures who interact with others in their culture and milieu that these specific conceptual labels are developed. This alternative raises the possibility that other cultures who use language differently may come up with entirely different concepts on which to base their "theory of mind." If they were correct, any talk about a theory of mind would be applicable only to the culture in question; a different culture could have a different theory of mind. At present, we simply don't know enough about how other cultures use such mental constructs to know if differences in language usage might imply differences in theory of mind.

Memory and Metamemory Development

Flavell (1971) used **metamemory** to name any aspect in the relationship between awareness and memory. Later, Flavell and Wellman (1977) refined the expression and described metamemory as any of several kinds of knowledge that people may have about their storage or retrieval processes. Specifically, metamemory can be broken down into three categories of memory knowledge (Wingfield & Byrnes, 1981):

1. Knowledge About One's Own Characteristics   that are relevent to remembering. This kind of knowledge comprises our attitudes toward our memories,
as well as knowledge about our own capacities and abilities. You may know that you
do better on essay tests than on multiple-choice tests because you find that retrieving
information you've organized on your own is easier than making a judgment about
the correctness of teacher-organized material. Similarly, you may know that remembering something that someone has explained to you is easier than remembering
something you've read about. On the other hand, you may know that the mode of
input is not especially important to you. Then we remember what has worked for us
in the past, and we retrieve this knowledge to guide us in encoding new material.

2. Knowledge About Differences Among Tasks   that are important in storage and retrieval. This category includes the knowledge we have about a task's
memory demands and how well our memory will be able to meet those demands.
You know what happens when you are introduced to many people at a party. As the
introductions drone on, you become aware that you won't recall all the names
you've just heard. The people being introduced sometimes challenge you to retrieve
their names, which brings up a related point. If everyone knows that a long series of
introductions imposes an almost impossible demand on someone's memory, then
why do people persist in doing it? Most adults have a fairly large fund of such task
knowledge. You probably know that you will remember the meaning and tone from
a conversation but not the exact wording. You know too that memorizing a list of
related words is easier than memorizing unrelated words, and so on.

3. Strategic Knowledge   is our ability to direct encoding and search
processes. You probably know many retrieval strategies. If asked what you had for
lunch yesterday, you may try to retrieve this information by thinking about the day
of the week it was, who your companions were, where you went for lunch, and so
on. If one of these approaches doesn't work, you know that you can try an alternative retrieval strategy that may succeed.

Metamemory is implicit knowledge. Most people don't know where they learned
about their memories or how they came by this knowledge; nevertheless, they're often fairly certain that their knowledge is accurate. This statement prompts two questions. First, can cognitivists outline how metamemory is acquired? Second, is the as-
surance people have about their metamemorial knowledge well founded, or does
people's knowledge of their memories include inaccuracies?

Development of Metamemory

Ample evidence indicates that small children have little knowledge in any of the three
categories just mentioned. Flavell and Wellman (1977) found that their five-year-old
subjects didn't rehearse a string of digits during a short-term retention task, an interesting result. Children can easily be taught to rehearse strings of digits or lists of words,
and when they do, their retention improves substantially. Even though children know
the meaning of the phrase, "Say these to yourself, over and over," and they're able to
rehearse, they don't rehearse unless explicitly instructed. This type of failure is referred
to as a **production deficiency**—failure to use a strategy that one is able to execute.
Production deficiencies can be contrasted with **process deficiencies** (Craik & Simon,

1980). The latter expression is defined as inability to execute some activity, because a memory process or capacity has not yet been fully developed.

Some findings suggest that, early in the school years, children's knowledge about the memory demands imposed by different tasks increases significantly. Yussen and Levy (1975) asked their five- and eight-year-old subjects to estimate how many things from a list they could recall without a mistake—in essence, estimating their memory span. Both groups overestimated the number of elements they could recall. The subjects then heard strings of nine or ten elements and attempted to recall them immediately after the presentation. Working memory was clearly overburdened by these demands. After several trials, the experimenters again asked the subjects to estimate their memory span. The eight-year-olds revised their estimates appropriately—that is, downward. But the preschoolers didn't revise their estimates and were optimistic that they'd get all right during the next trial. The preschoolers apparently were unable to tell that their working memories were being overburdened.

This finding has implications for other memory processes. In a series of studies, Brown and Smiley (1977, 1978; Brown, Smiley, & Lawton, 1978) found that children learn to pick out important factors in a story and use them as a basis for retrieval. First, the experimenters had a group of raters determine the structural importance of idea units in Japanese fairy tales translated into English. The structural importance was a rating given to each of the passage's ideas and can be interpreted as indicating how necessary remembering that idea was to understanding the passage as a whole. Table 9.5 shows some of the idea units and their rated importance.

Next, Brown and Smiley gave the passage to third-, fifth-, and seventh-graders, and to college students. After the story was read, the subjects were asked to recall as much as they could. When the proportion of recalled ideas was analyzed as a function of the idea's importance, the researchers found that all the subjects tended to recall the important ideas better than the less important ideas. Sixty-nine percent of the subjects recalled the most important idea, but only 23% of them recalled the least important idea. Although this finding was true for all age levels, an age effect was nev-

---

Table 9.5   Idea Units and Their Rated Importance

Unit	Rated Importance
1. Once upon a time	162
2. there was a rich lord	356
3. who liked to collect carvings of animals	321
4. (those are like little wooden dolls)	106
5. He had many kinds	150
6. but he had no carved mouse	294
7. So he called two skilled carvers to him and said	341
8. "I want each of you to carve a mouse for me."	397

Source: From Brown and Smiley, 1977.

ertheless found. Older subjects recalled more of the material regardless of its importance. That is, even in the less important material, the older subjects recalled more
than the younger ones. Superficially, this finding suggests that the younger subjects
had a process deficiency, meaning that they hadn't yet developed the ability to store
large amounts of material.

Other findings suggest a deeper interpretation. In an additional experiment,
Brown and Smiley (1977) asked their subjects to make the structural-importance ratings originally done by the college students alone. The researchers discovered that the
younger subjects were not very skilled in distinguishing important from peripheral
ideas. Whereas the college students could distinguish four levels of importance in the
passage, seventh-graders could distinguish only three, fifth-graders two, and third-
graders only one. Table 9.6 shows the numerical evaluation of the least important and
most important ideas in the passage by third-graders and college students. Notice that
no appreciable difference appears among the ratings made by the third-graders. If the
younger subjects indeed have a process deficiency, it is inability to detect the important aspects in a story. This apparent inability is bound to affect the subjects' encoding and comprehension of the story, because meaning in such a passage depends heavily on readers' ability to abstract important or thematic ideas.

Smiley, Oakley, Worthen, Campione, and Brown (1977) extended this idea in
studying retrieval among seventh-graders. They found that good readers' recall patterns corresponded closely to ratings of idea importance. Important ideas were consistently recalled by good readers. This correspondence was not as good, though, for poor
readers. This finding suggests that the poor readers were not as sensitive to the story's
structure as good readers were. Perhaps more significant, it suggests that poor readers
were not as sensitive to the story's structure as a vehicle, or medium, to aid memory.

Comparing college students' performance with that of school-age children may
give the impression that metamemory is fully developed among young adults and that
their knowledge is invariably accurate. These impressions are false, however.
Shaughnessy (1981) asked college students to predict which of two learning conditions would produce better performance on a memory test. In one condition, a list of
words was to be learned by simple rote repetition. In the second, the list of words was
to be learned by a procedure that prompted the subjects to elaborate the words' meanings. Subjects predicted that the two techniques would produce equivalent learning,

Table 9.6 Ratings of Structural Importance by Subjects of Different Ages in the Brown and Smiley Study

Subjects	Importance Rating	
	Least Important Fact	*Most Important Fact*
Third-graders	2.41	2.56
College students	1.61	3.52

Source: From Brown and Smiley, 1977.

but they performed much better in the elaboration condition. The subjects' memory knowledge obviously was incomplete and inaccurate. They persisted in their belief that rote repetition was an effective rehearsal strategy even though their own behavior provided evidence to the contrary. Subjects who were given permission to learn the list in any way they wanted reported frequently that they learned by rote repetition. This knowledge also seems inaccurate, because these subjects outperformed the group that had been instructed to memorize the list using rote repetition.

Earlier, I phrased two questions about metamemory, and now I'll summarize my answers. First, cognitive psychologists have provided a reasonably detailed outline of improvement in metamemory. Specifically, improvement during the grade-school years occurs in both the second and third categories of memory knowledge discussed earlier. That is, grade-school children begin to get a better idea about the demands that various memory tasks impose, and they begin to get more effective encoding strategies as their sensitivity to story structures increases. In response to the second question, adults apparently are not infallible about their metamemories. Some evidence (Klatzky, 1984) suggests that people are strongly influenced by folk beliefs about memory, some of which are incorrect.

The Brown and Smiley studies suggest that as subjects become more knowledgeable about text, they will start to remember more about the material than they had. This implication in turn suggests that what happens during childhood could be interpreted as an improvement in learning about knowledge generally, and its organization. I suppose we could call this a general kind of metaknowledge. But, in addition to these organizational improvements, we have evidence that during their middle childhood years children simply become more skilled in using memory strategies.

Other findings suggest a developmental pathway in acquiring such strategies. That is, children acquire different, and perhaps more complex, strategies at different times in their school years. A classic study by Moely, Olson, Halwes, and Flavell (1969) shows these effects. Children aged five to eleven were shown pictures of objects drawn from categories such as animals and articles of clothing. The pictures were arranged in a circle; no picture was placed next to another from the same category. The children were asked to learn the names of the objects in the pictures, and, while the experimenter was gone for a few minutes, they were invited to move the pictures around in any way they thought might help them remember the names of the things shown. The variable of interest was how well the children had learned that putting pictures of category members together would help them remember names of the objects. Only the ten- and eleven-year-olds used this grouping strategy spontaneously, which is interesting because, as we've seen, children who are much younger, perhaps as young as seven, know that subvocal rehearsal will help them remember a list. Here we see that even children who have learned something fundamental—that there are things you can do to help you remember—don't seem to know that the picture situation offers the possibility of using such a strategy.

Developing Ability to Reason

When we looked at the issue of memory development, we saw that children's memory capabilities change in at least two ways during their school years. First, their conceptual knowledge of the world grows dramatically, enabling them to recognize connections and relationships among natural objects. Second, children's strategic knowledge also grows, enabling them to encode and organize these new found connections among objects with greater flexibility. When we look at how reasoning or problem solving develops, we see a similar phenomenon unfold. In part, older children reason better than younger ones because older children just know more about the world. It also seems that older children know more because they are able to reason about their knowledge in ways that younger children cannot. In other words, it's as if the improvement in reasoning schemes seen in the school-age years enables children to widen their cognitive horizons and thus take in more information than they did when they were younger. And from all this knowledge that's been taken in, school-age children learn how to build schemes that are more effective in reasoning. If this discussion suggests to you that knowledge and reasoning have something like a "braided" relationship, that's probably right. In this section we'll explore some of the findings that bear on this relationship.

It's not too difficult to demonstrate that children frequently know less about the world than adults do. In one study by McCloskey and Kaiser (1984), subjects watched a toy electric locomotive pull a flatcar carrying a ball. At one point, the ball fell through a hole in the moving flatcar and through the tracks to the floor several feet below. The children were told that the ball would fall; their task was to predict the path it would take in its descent to the floor. Seventy percent of the children thought it would fall straight down, rather than in a parabolic trajectory. When they were asked to reconcile their predictions with what they had observed, many claimed that the ball had indeed fallen straight down just as they had predicted! Some claimed the train had given the ball a small push just before it was released. Both of these explanations show that the children were trying to make their observations fit what they "knew" to be true about the world.

But as children learn more about the world, their ability to reason about it also increases. Most adults use cause and effect to reason about some events in the world, and children also have this concept in some form. But, as the philosopher David Hume observed more than two centuries ago, "causes" are never observed in nature; they are inferred. Hume went on to discuss three factors that seem to be involved in making a causal inference. The events must be close together in time and space (contiguity); the event labeled the cause must occur before the event labeled the result (precedence); and the presumed cause and effect must have occurred reliably together in the past (covariation). As you would probably hypothesize, the degree to which we can infer cause and effect seems to depend in part on how well we can observe and make inferences from contiguity, precedence, and covariation.

Some good evidence suggests that even very young children are sensitive to the effects of contiguity. Leslie (1982) demonstrated that four- and five-month-old children look longer at passive objects that begin moving without first being struck than they do at objects that begin moving after another object has collided with them. Presumably, the children's longer looking means they sense that something is "wrong" or "odd" about this violation of contiguity. By age three, when children observe three sequential events A, B, and C, and they're asked to tell "what made B happen," these preschoolers are almost as likely to say "C" as they are to say "A." By age five, though, kindergartners seem to have the concept of precedence well established; now on various tasks, children always respond with the initial event. At this time in their lives, children will

Using Your Knowledge of Cognition

That Reminds Me! (But It Wouldn't Remind a Five-Year-Old)

If you want to remember to do something, but you fear you might forget, you may use a reminder. A reminder can be almost any sort of stimulus, but usually it's (1) something visible that you're pretty sure you'll see, and (2) something that you'll see before you have to do whatever it is you're trying to remind yourself about. For most of us, it's not too hard to think of reminders and to use them. But using reminders requires more sophistication than we might think. Just as memory itself develops, the ability to recognize and use reminders also develops, implying that younger children may have to learn what to do to remind themselves of something. If you have nieces or nephews or younger siblings, you may be able to track such development with fairly simple apparatus.

Get four identical paper cups and show a four- or five-year-old that you are hiding a penny under one of the cups. Now tell the child that you are going to move two of the cups and slowly slide the cup with the penny under it into the position of another cup, while sliding that cup to the position that's now vacant. Ask the child where the penny is. He or she should know and be able to pick out the cup. If the child accomplishes this choice, then increase the number of switches by one on

each consecutive trial until the child's short-term memory is overloaded, and he or she can no longer tell where the penny is. Then produce a paper clip and tell the child you will put the paper clip on top of the cup hiding the penny. Ask the child if this will help him or her remember, and the child's answer will almost certainly be yes. Does it help? Yes, now the child recognizes that the visible paper clip is an excellent reminder of the penny's whereabouts, and can still find the penny after numerous switches. But it's also easy to demonstrate that many children at this age don't truly understand the reminding concept. Take the paper clip off the cup and ask the child if the paper clip would help them remember if it were placed inside the cup along with the penny. Surprisingly, Beal (1985) found that almost half the four- and five-year-olds thought that this trick too would be a good reminder. In contrast, none of the eight-year-old children Beal tested thought that putting the paper clip in with the penny would help them remember. This demonstration points out that the kindergartners may have an incomplete notion of reminding: They recognize that a visible stimulus may help them remember, but they don't realize that then the stimulus *must* be visible if it is to be of any use.

overlook the effects of covariation, especially when these conflict with contiguity. If one event always follows another after a five-second interval, thus establishing covariation but not contiguity, five-year-olds will not necessarily see the causal connection. By age eight, though, children will see the temporally separate but covariate events as causally connected (Mendelson & Schultz, 1976). Evidence from this developmental pathway suggests that children at various ages should be strategically different from each other in attempting to draw inferences about cause and effect, and that, by age eight or so, they should be relatively able to reason about cause and effect.

An interesting study by Schauble (1990) bears on this issue. The subjects were children aged nine to eleven; their task was to predict the speed of race cars generated by a computer. Five variables could be manipulated by the child-as-experimenter, who would then observe how the designs performed on a "track." The variables were engine size, wheel size, tail fins, presence or absence of a muffler, and color. Before the experiment, the children expected that cars with large engines, large wheels, and a muffler would be fastest. In fact, large engines and medium-sized wheels were associated with faster cars; muffler and color had no causal influence. Tail fins helped a car go faster when the engine was large, but had no effect when the engine was small. Technically, this was not a difficult task. The children were given eight sessions to learn about the cars, and the cars' performance did not vary. Given the children's age range, they should have been able to draw on their knowledge of the concepts of contiguity, precedence, and especially covariation to figure out what made some cars go faster than others. But it turned out to be a hard task for them. Although they had a good scheme for causal reasoning, this task necessitated that they design mini experiments, holding all but one feature in a design intact while varying the one remaining feature. That is, the children had to design a situation in which they could bring their causal reasoning schemes to bear. But that is just the challenge the children found difficult. Schauble (1990) found that most of their experiments were invalid. They typically manipulated two variables simultaneously, making a clear inference impossible. Even when they succeeded in designing a valid experiment, they often seemed to ignore its conclusions if these disagreed with their prior expectations. Even after they had developed a good scheme for interpreting events in a causal way, they still had to learn how to apply such schemes.

Concluding Comments and Suggestions for Further Reading

We began this chapter with questions about the relationship between language acquisition and general cognitive development. After reviewing some of this literature, we can see that in some ways, at some stages in the life span, some aspects of language acquisition seem to move "faster" than the child's overall cognitive development. Word acquisition from eighteen months to age five or six grows explosively. Other rule-based aspects of language, such as plural learning, inflections, and syntax generally, are also acquired at a terrific pace from about age two to age six. But these findings show another picture too. We also saw that often language acquisition is supported by—that is, aided by—cognitive changes in concept formation, memory, and reasoning. That is, although two-year-olds may not be able to string lengthy sentences together—a linguistic problem—helped by vertical construction and a short-term memory whose capacity has grown just large enough, the child is able to express fairly complicated thoughts at a speed that is close to real time.

For those interested in language development, and the interplay between language development and other forms of cognition, here are several excellent and very accessible books. First, Gross (1985) surveys cognitive development, comparing the information-processing viewpoint with the Piagetian perspective. Siegler's (1991) *Children's Thinking* is more comprehensive than the title implies, and it's very readable too. On language acquisition, Wang (1991) has edited a volume of articles from the magazine *Scientific American* dealing with many issues, including the cultural origins of language. On a narrower front, a special issue of the journal *Cognitive Science* (14(1), 1990) is about constraints on learning, especially because these memory and attention constraints may actually help the child acquire language and concepts. Kail

Focus on Research
Children's Addition

How do children go about adding two numbers, as in a problem such as "solve 2 + 9"? For many years, the standard answer was the one provided by Groen and Parkman (1972), who discovered that children used the **"min" strategy.** To use it, a child looks at the two numbers to be added (the addends), determines which is smaller, and counts up that number of times beginning from the larger addend. To solve the problem shown above, the child's mental event would be something like "9, 10, 11—and so the answer is 11." According to the min strategy, the only variable that should influence solution times is the size of the smaller addend, because the children count internally at a constant rate.

This hypothesis has been supported many times. Thus, children who are asked to add "9 + 6" require more time to get the answer than when they are given the problem "9 + 3," because it takes them longer to count up six places from the number nine than it does to count up three places. Educators have long reported, however, that the children themselves maintain that they are capable of using various strategies to solve such problems.

Could it be that the children were inaccurately reporting their use of strategies? Or, could it be that the chronometric analysis simply masked the children's arriving at the answer via a number of routes?

Siegler (1987) asked his subjects, who were kindergartners, first-graders, or second-graders, to solve addition problems and to describe what they were doing to get the answer. The data were remarkable. When the children reported that they were using the min strategy (which they actually used on only 36% of the problems), their solution times correlated beautifully with the size of the smaller addend. But when the children said they were using a different strategy (such as simply counting from 1, which they might do if both addends were small), their solution times were correlated rather poorly with the size of the smaller addend, suggesting that when the children said they had used a non-min strategy, they indeed had used a non-min strategy to solve the problem. As this study shows, even these rather young children were capable of making a sophisticated decision from a menu of strategic choices that were available to them.

(1990) has written a comprehensive book on memory development in children. Finally, two books deal with children's reasoning and their strategies for reasoning. Siegler and Jenkins (1989) present a coherent picture of children's arithmetic strategies. Bjorklund (1990) has edited a more general volume that includes chapters on children's strategies in reading, paying attention, and solving problems.

*K*ey Terms

Babbling
Babbling drift
Holophrastic stage
Overextensions
Underextensions
Whole-object assumption
Taxonomic assumption

Two-word stage
Mean length of utterance (MLU)
Structural relationships
Vertical construction
Horizontal construction
Inflections
Expansions

Less is more (LIM) position
Metamemory
Production deficiency
Process deficiency
Min strategy

Thinking

I n the book's final chapters we discuss the so-called higher mental processes in human beings. The word *higher* is in quotation marks for these reasons. Generally, thinking, reasoning, and problem solving have been called higher processes because traditionally it's been thought that such events come at the end of the information-processing chain. This view of cognitive activity became particularly entrenched during the 1960s. Because perception and memory were strongly rooted in sensory and physiological psychology, they were thought to be closely related to neural processes. The cognitive activity related to thinking and reasoning, however, did not seem synonymous with any neural-processing pattern and in that sense seemed "higher" than other cognitive processes.

We now know the picture is much more complicated. First, as we've seen, information-processing theories of perception and memory have been formulated. These theories are abstract; that is, they do not deal with these phenomena as explicitly neural. Second, the idea that a chain of events occurs in cognition is also simplistic. Although the information-processing paradigm often treats mental events as though they occurred sequentially, we know they do so just as a theoretical convenience. In reality, the so-called higher processes don't necessarily occur after the so-called lower processes. What we perceive does form the basis for our thoughts, but our thoughts also influence what we perceive. The sequences of information processing are quite tangled, and they constantly loop and double back on each other. From this perspective, the label *higher mental processes* is really only a teaching or organizational device.

One important issue dealt with in this section is representation, or problem understanding. How a problem is represented or understood by the problem solver seems to powerfully influence the problem solver's effectiveness. Thus reasoning is much like problem solving. Although the principles of logic can be delineated clearly, people often don't perceive these principles, which means that their representations of logic problems sometimes differ from those logicians use. Earlier, we talked about the schema as an encompassing cognitive structure that organizes incoming information and suggests which information should be forthcoming. In this context, the schema influences how problems are represented. In this section we examine schematic influences in both reasoning and problem solving.

C H A P T E R   1 0

Reasoning and Deciding

*O*verview

All the first-year students in my undergraduate college were required to take a course in logic. I remember looking forward to the course and thinking that I would soon possess some penetrating analysis that would enable me to immediately see the truth or falsity of things. Thus armed, I would be able to demolish my friends' arguments on any matter. My expectations were probably incorrect; the course turned out to be disappointing. First, I wasn't thrilled with the prospect of memorizing the form of all sixty-four categorical syllogisms—they didn't seem like any argument winners to me. Further, I found that logic didn't always seem logical. Logicians have designed truth tables that can be used to verify the truth of complex remarks. One of the truth tables applies to the truth of implications, such as "If P, then Q." I was surprised to find out that if P and Q were both false, the whole statement (If P, then Q) was nevertheless true! How could the whole statement be true when both of its parts were false? I had a realization: if this was logic, then my mind certainly wasn't logical all the time, because this statement didn't make much sense to me.

To what extent is this realization common to other people as well? In this chapter we consider the question of human reasoning. Success in **formal reasoning** seems to depend somewhat on educational level. Individuals from cultures that don't emphasize Western education often perform poorly (by Western standards) on formal-reasoning tasks. Even highly educated Westerners, though, sometimes perform poorly on such tasks. Do people therefore have to be trained to be logical? We'll examine some of the findings from research on conditional syllogisms, and we'll see that people often seem to interpret logical information differently from the logician's way. We'll also consider natural reasoning—reasoning on problems that seem closely related to the kinds of judgments that are required of us every day. How do people accomplish such reasoning? Apparently, people typically apply general rules of thumb that usually work quickly and efficiently. Here we consider some situations in which these rules of thumb are pushed past their limits. Such situations occur more frequently than we think; reasoning that looks plausible and logical sometimes isn't.

*L*ogic and Formal Reasoning

In this section we consider some of the findings that result when people try to solve formal problems by using **logic.** Several issues surface here: Do people without formal training in logic nevertheless use logic to solve such problems? From failures to solve such problems, is it legitimate to conclude that people are illogical?

Human Thought and the Rules of Logic

If we think about all the people we know, we find that it is easy to categorize each individual as "logical" or "not logical." By "logical" we usually mean that individuals are capable of giving plausible reasons for events, or capable of making inferences implied by other facts. We seldom try to describe the behavior of the people we call illogical, but their actions need to be explained, too. Are such individuals following different rules of thought than logical people? If so, how did they learn those illogical rules of thought? Perhaps the problem should be turned around. Maybe people are inherently illogical, and must be explicitly taught to use logic.

The idea that people are inherently illogical would not have been accepted a century ago. Mill (1874) viewed the laws of logic as synonymous with the laws of thought. According to Mill, logical principles were not really discovered and developed. He understood logical principles as simply a formal account of the same principles used by people in their everyday thinking and reasoning. Mill was aware that people sometimes made logical errors, but he explained these as simply nonsystematic "slips." Similarly, James (1890) maintained that the two principal components in logical reasoning were analysis and abstraction. Analysis was our ability to break down an object into its components, letting one of the parts represent the entire object. In the statement, "Freud is a man," the thinker must represent Freud using only one of Freud's components—his maleness. Abstraction was our ability to designate a specific component as part of a broader classification. Thus from the statement, "All men are mortal," it follows that Freud must be mortal. That is, Freud can be represented by his maleness, which can be grouped into the broader classification "mortal." Therefore, "Freud" can also be grouped in this broader classification. According to James, these two mental processes enabled logical reasoning to occur.

Validity, Truth, and Soundness

Logical analysis can take many forms, some of which we will deal with in this chapter. A few terms, though, are common to all logical systems. One of these is **validity.** A logical argument is valid if, according to the rules established by logicians, the conclusion of the argument necessarily follows from the earlier statements. Sometimes students think an argument's validity is synonymous with its **truth,** but that's a mistake. A logical argument can be valid but untrue. Consider these statements:

> All dinosaurs are animals.
> All animals are in zoos.
> Therefore, all dinosaurs are in zoos.

The conclusion is valid according to the rules logicians use. Not all dinosaurs are in zoos, however, and so the conclusion is not true. On the other hand, if the argument's initial statements *are* true and the reasoning is valid, then the conclusion will also be true. All logical systems have this property, which is referred to as **soundness,** which simply means that, given the truth of the argument's initial statements, valid reasoning will produce a truthful conclusion.

Soundness in reasoning doesn't necessarily imply that logical reasoning has taken place. If we are given true initial statements, we may be able to determine a valid, true conclusion with regularity. Under these circumstances, our reasoning would be sound. But if we accomplish this feat by applying an idiosyncratic reasoning system that we cannot explain, our reasoning is not logical. Logical reasoning implies that we have followed the rules of logical inference as established by logicians and described in textbooks. In other words, logical reasoning is defined as much by its methods as by its outcome. If we deviate from this method, our reasoning is not logical no matter what other properties it may have.

Researchers face difficulty in trying to determine human logical abilities. Even if we succeed in determining an argument's validity or invalidity, this achievement does not necessarily mean that we used logic to arrive at the conclusion. This assertion was clearly demonstrated in a well-known study by Henle (1962), who gave graduate students who had no formal training in logic problems such as this:

> A group of women were discussing their household problems. Mrs. Shivers broke the ice by saying: "I'm so glad we're talking about these problems. It's so important to talk about things that are in our minds. We spend so much time in the kitchen that of course household problems are in our minds. So it is important to talk about them." (Does it follow that it is important to talk about them? Give your reasoning.)

Henle found that subjects often treated the logical problem as an empirical task. That is, they attempted to assess whether spending a great deal of time in the kitchen would necessarily imply that kitchen events would really be on the homemakers' minds. Frequently, subjects gave the correct answer (Mrs. Shivers is logically correct when she states that talking about such problems is important), but their reasoning was usually not logical. Although being able to give the correct answer implies that the answer has been derived logically, this implication is deceptive. Henle's subjects did not perform in a logical way. Some commentators (Howard, 1983) suggest that the subjects may have performed illogically because everyday reasoning does not demand the knowledge that we know and apply formal logical principles. When confronted with practical problems, we usually behave pragmatically or probabilistically. We know that if we run over a skunk on the highway, a characteristic, intense odor will be produced. If we're driving along some night and smell this scent, we're likely to conclude that a skunk has been hit, and we'll probably feel that this conclusion is valid. But it isn't. The skunk may have been warding off an intruder, or perhaps a sensory psychologist had been conducting a field study on the effects of skunk scent on some aspect of driving performance. Henle's study implies that people do not typically distinguish between the everyday sort of probabilistic reasoning and logic.

Cross-Cultural Studies   If the laws of thought were truly synonymous with the rules of logic, then logic should be observable wherever human thought occurs. Specifically, individuals who are reared and educated in non-Western ways should nevertheless be capable of reasoning logically. Debate on this issue was initiated by Lévy-Bruhl (1910), who maintained that the "primitive mind" thinks in a "prelogical" way, governed by emotion, magic, and inability to distinguish between mental and external events. Although Lévy-Bruhl probably overstated the case, more recent anthropological studies (Cole & Scribner, 1977) indicate that nonliterate, non-Western people employ reasoning strategies that are somewhat different from those observed among educated Westerners. Such individuals are capable of reasoning in an orderly way; consequently, their deductions are often sound. These nonschooled people, however, seem to accomplish this reasoning without formal logic. When Sylvia Scribner asked members of the Vai (a West African tribe) to respond to logical arguments as part of a literacy program, she found that their answers, although reasonable, were not logical. Here is a problem and response by one of the Vai:

> All women who live in Monrovia are married.
> Kemu is not married.
> Does she live in Monrovia?
> Answer and Explanation: Yes. Monrovia is not for any one kind of people, so Kemu came to live there. (Scribner, 1977)

Notice that the respondent answered the question by ignoring or discounting the first statement and insisted upon giving the correct answer, based on what is known to be true: Anyone is permitted to live in Monrovia. This little protocol illustrates well a finding that Scribner found to be general in her work. As little as two years of schooling dramatically increased the likelihood that an individual would be able to reason logically. The protocol also shows a process that Henle observed in her Western subjects: The Vai tribesperson treated the task as an empirical problem—one that could be answered from one's observation of the world.

Are people inherently logical? The answer appears to be a qualified no. Human reasoning may be inherently orderly and sound, but logical ability seems to be a byproduct of education. But even people who are educated are not always logical. Their reasoning processes have offered cognitive psychologists a good "window" on what might be called the rules of thought.

Conditional Reasoning

One formal reasoning task that has been studied extensively by cognitive psychologists is **conditional reasoning,** which takes place when an individual is given statements called *conditions*—a rule for determining what outcomes can be expected if specified conditions are present, and a conclusion whose validity the reasoner tries to assess, using the information previously given:

> If you have studied hard, you will do well in this course.
> You have studied hard.
> Therefore, you can expect to do well in this course.

Generally, the rule is expressed in an if-then format: If P (some sort of antecedent condition), then Q (some sort of consequent condition). One of the other statements establishes the truth or falsity of P or Q. The reasoner must establish the truth or falsity of the remaining term, or determine that its truth or falsity can't be established from the information given. Logicians have two inference rules that can be used to reason validly in these circumstances. The first is **modus ponens.** In situations such as "If P, then Q" and "P is true," modus ponens allows us to validly infer that "Q is true." In other words, when we're given "if P, then Q," modus ponens enables us to infer that the presence of P implies the presence of Q. The studying example just used represents the valid use of modus ponens. The second rule is **modus tollens.** Consider this argument:

> If it snows on Thursday, I'll go skiing.
> I did not go skiing.
> Therefore, it did not snow on Thursday.

The conclusion is valid, and represents the correct use of modus tollens, which can be expressed in this general format: Given, "if P, then Q" and "Q is false" or "not Q," then modus tollens allows us to validly infer that "P is false" or "not P." Where P implies Q, the absence of Q implies the absence of P.

In addition to modus tollens and modus ponens, conditional reasoning can take place in two other forms, both of them kinds of logical errors. Look at this argument:

> If she likes me, she'll go out with me.
> She likes me not.
> Therefore, she won't go out with me.

If the conclusion looks valid to us, then we have made an error in reasoning known as "denying the antecedent." Notice that the error is named after the antecedent, the first part of the conditional rule. When we deny the antecedent, we assume that the consequent will be true *only if* the antecedent is true. That's an error because the consequent could be true even if the antecedent is false. That is, she may go out with you for some other reason even if she doesn't like you. Denying the antecedent is not the only error our love-stricken friends are likely to commit. Consider this reasoning:

> If she likes me, she'll go out with me.
> She goes out with me.
> Therefore, she likes me.

Not necessarily. This time the reasoner has assumed that the truth of the consequent implies the truth of the antecedent, an error that is known as "affirming the consequent." These forms of conditional reasoning are summarized in Table 10.1.

We can be pretty sure that subjects who are untrained in logic are not familiar with these expressions, but can educated people nevertheless reason successfully on formal conditional reasoning problems? Rips and Marcus (1977) presented their subjects, who were students untrained in using inference rules, with eight "concrete" (more about this label later) examples of conditional reasoning, such as this:

> If a card has an A on the left, it has a 7 on the right.
> The card does not have a 7 on the right.
> The card does not have an A on the left.

They asked their subjects to judge whether the conclusion was always true, never true, or sometimes true. What's your answer? Perhaps the best way to proceed here is to

Table 10.1   Conditional Reasoning

Form	Name	Example
If P, then Q P ――――― Therefore Q	Modus ponens (valid inference)	If the object is square, then it is blue. The object is square. The object is blue.
If P, then Q not Q ――――― Therefore not P	Modus tollens (valid inference)	If the object is square, then it is blue. The object is not blue. The object is not square.
If P, then Q not P ――――― Therefore not Q	Denying the antecedent (invalid inference)	If the object is square, then it is blue. The object is not square. The object is not blue.
If P, then Q Q ――――― Therefore P	Affirming the consequent (invalid inference)	If the object is square, then it is blue. The object is blue. The object is square.

Source: Adapted from *Cognitive Psychology: Memory, Language, and Thought* by Darlene V. Howard, copyright © 1983. Reprinted by permission of Prentice-Hall, Inc., Upper Saddle River, NJ.

convert the preceding "concrete" phrases to a more general format compatible with the information in Table 10.1. Thus, the "A on the left" phrase becomes "P," and the "7 on the right" phrase becomes "Q." Logicians have devised a symbol, ⊃, sometimes called the horseshoe, to designate the idea of implication. The first line in the prior example then becomes "A on the left implies 7 on the right," or "P ⊃ Q." Logicians also make use of a symbol to designate "not" or "the absence of." This is the *tilde*, written like this: ~. The phrase in the second line in the prior argument then becomes "not Q" or "~ Q." Logicians sometimes use a three-dot pattern, ∴, to indicate "therefore." Making the conversion for the prior argument, then, we have:

$$P \supset Q$$
$$\sim Q$$
$$\therefore \sim P.$$

Looking back to Table 10.1, we see that this is indeed a valid inference that shows correct use of modus tollens. If we were one of the Rips and Marcus subjects, the correct answer here would be "always true." Table 10.2 shows the percentage of subjects responding "always true," "sometimes true," and "never true" for each of the eight types of problems used. The problems shown here are in the "abstract" format, but they were given to the subjects in the concrete form shown before. Problems 1 and 2 require use of modus ponens, and as Table 10.2 indicates, subjects were quite adept in applying this inference rule. No errors at all were made on those two problems. Problems 7 and 8 also permit a valid inference using modus tollens. That is, modus tollens enables us to say that problem 7 could never be true and problem 8 (the example used earlier) would always be true. The subjects were much less successful in applying modus tollens than in using modus ponens. More than a fifth of the subjects believed that the conclusion of problem 7 could sometimes be true. And more than 40% made a reasoning error on problem 8.

No valid inferences can be drawn from the information in problems 3 through 6, and so the correct answer to each of those should be "sometimes true." We see, however, that subjects sometimes insisted that valid inferences could be drawn. In problems 3 and 4, about 20% of the subjects believed that some valid inference could be drawn about Q from ~P. This result represents denial of the antecedent. Similarly, about 20% of the subjects believed that valid inferences could be drawn in problems 6 and 7, which represents an affirmation of the consequent. From Q, we can't draw any valid inference about P or ~P.

The errors on problems 3 through 6 can be explained by examining the subject's understanding of the logical term "if" when it is used in "if P, then Q" statements. People who have not been trained in logic apparently use this word differently than do logicians. Logicians distinguish between the term "if," which is called the *conditional*, and the expression "if and only if," which is called the *biconditional*. The sentence

I will win if and only if I practice.

implies that practice is a necessary condition for my victory to take place, which wouldn't be so if I had used the connective "if."

To analyze the truth of implications including the conditional or biconditional statement, logicians use truth tables. A truth table offers us a way of determining the

Table 10.2   Percentage of Total Responses for Eight Types of Conditional Syllogisms

Syllogism	Always	Sometimes	Never
1. P ⊃ Q 　P ∴ Q	100[a]	0	0
2. P ⊃ Q 　P ∴ ~Q	0	0	100[a]
3. P ⊃ Q 　~P ∴ Q	5	79[a]	16
4. P ⊃ Q 　~P ∴ ~Q	21	77[a]	2
5. P ⊃ Q 　Q ∴ P	23	77[a]	0
6. P ⊃ Q 　Q ∴ ~P	4	82[a]	14
7. P ⊃ Q 　~Q ∴ P	0	23	77[a]
8. P ⊃ Q 　~Q ∴ ~P	57[a]	39	4

[a]The correct response
Source: From Rips and Marcus, 1977.

truth of a complex remark based on the truth of its component statements. Table 10.3 shows the truth tables for both the conditional "if," which is indicated by the horseshoe symbol, and the biconditional "if and only if," which is shown by the double-headed arrow.

To see how this table would be used in practice, let's consider an example:

If the switch is turned on, then the light will go on.
The switch is not turned on.
Therefore, the light does not go on.

Using the conditional truth table, we see two conditions in which the complex remark is true but P, the antecedent, is false. In one of these two conditions, Q, the consequent, is false. In the other condition, it is true. All we can say about the conclusion is that sometimes it might not be true and sometimes it might be. Turning to the biconditional truth table, however, we see a different story. If P is false (i.e., ~P) and P

Table 10.3 Truth Tables

Implication or Conditional			Biconditional		
P	Q	P ⊃ Q	P	Q	P ↔ Q
T	T	T	T	T	T
T	F	F	T	F	F
F	T	T	F	T	F
F	F	T	F	F	T

⊃ Q is true, then Q must be false. Also, if P is true and P ⊃ Q is true, then Q must also be true. If you go back to the preceding example and change the word "if" to "if and only if," then you'll see that the conclusion is now valid. Thus neither denial of the antecedent (as seen in the Rips and Marcus problems 3 and 4) nor affirmation of the consequent (as in problems 5 and 6) is a fallacy in reasoning if one has interpreted the conditional as the biconditional.

Staudenmayer (1975) gave his subjects conditional-reasoning problems similar to those used by Rips and Marcus. He was able to demonstrate that subjects typically decide how the connective "if" is to be interpreted, and the subsequent reasoning processes are consistent with whatever interpretation the subjects make. When an "if then" phrasing was used, 59% of the subjects treated the "if" connective as though it were the biconditional, "if and only if." This misuse increased to 77% when phrasings such as "P causes Q" were used in the problems. Once the interpretation of the "if" connective had been made, subjects' reasoning was fairly sound. Staudenmayer concluded that errors in these conditional-reasoning problems were not errors in reasoning but failures to realize the distinction between the conditional and the biconditional phrasings.

The Wason Selection Task Although such an analysis accounts for the errors made on problems 3 through 6 in the Rips and Marcus study, it does not explain the considerable number of errors on problems 7 and 8. These errors seem to result from inability to apply modus tollens. This inability is rather well documented, dating back to a study by Wason (1966). Wason presented to his subjects four cards showing these symbols:

The subjects were told that each card had a number on one side and a letter on the other. Their task was to turn over the minimal number of cards necessary to verify (an important term) this rule: If a card has a vowel on one side, then it has an even number on the other side. You might try solving this problem. While you're thinking about it, realize that this problem, now known to everyone as the Wason selection task, is a mainstay in the literature on reasoning, prompting Tweney and Doherty (1983) to comment that research on it and other logical tasks has become "... somewhat of a small industry, spawning a host of variations, dozens of studies, and more than its share of interpretational controversies."

In Wason's study, 46% of the subjects turned over both the *E* and the *4*. This response is incorrect and is another example of affirming the consequent. We're really not interested in what's behind the *4* because, even if we found a consonant, that wouldn't invalidate the rule. Many subjects turned only the *E* over. This response is on the right track, but it's incomplete. Only 4% of the subjects got the problem right, by turning over the *E* and the *7*. Turning over the *7* is an application of the important modus tollens step called **disconfirming the consequent.** If "vowel" implies "even number," the absence of an even number (for the *7*) implies the absence of a vowel on the reverse side of the card.

Readers who are still in the dark on this problem are probably not alone. Wason and Johnson-Laird (1970) have pointed out that many people did not see why the *E* and *7* had to be turned over even after it had been explained to them. Some subjects who picked the *E* and *4* initially seemed to have been "blinded" by their initial choices and seemed unable to consider the implications of the other cards. To see if the subjects were indeed blinded by their initial picks, Wason and Johnson-Laird (1970) presented to their subjects a specific form of the Wason selection task in which four cards were partially covered with cardboard masks, thus concealing some of the information on the cards. The subject's task was to determine which cards had to be unmasked to validate a conditional rule. When subjects got the problem wrong, the experimenters unmasked the correct cards and asked subjects if they would like to change their minds, given what they could now observe. Seventy-four percent of the subjects who failed to get the answer initially also failed to correct themselves when the correct cards were unmasked! During an interview with these subjects that followed, 48% failed to correct themselves after the experimenter pointed out their logical error.

What makes the subjects do so poorly on this problem? One reason may be that the subjects simply don't have the logical competence to do the task. That is, unless you've studied logic, you can't possibly do well. Markovits (1985) found that, when subjects were given a conditional statement to interpret that was embedded in the context of other conditional statements, they performed better overall than when they were given only one conditional-reasoning problem. Subjects who profited most from the additional information, however, were those who had already documented reasonable understanding of conditional rules on a pretest problem.

On the other hand, sheer logical competence, or lack of it, may not be the only explanation for most subjects' poor performance. The weakness might result from the subjects' use of poor reasoning. According to this view, people actually have the reasoning competence necessary to solve the problem, but they deploy faulty reasoning strategies. Supporting this position, Pollard (1985) found that subjects seem to use a matching strategy to solve the task. Subjects who use the matching strategy turn over whichever cards are mentioned in the problem. When the rule is, "A card that has a vowel on one side doesn't have an even number on the other side," subjects still turn over the *E* and the *4*—which happens to be the correct answer. When the rule is, "A card that doesn't have a vowel on one side has an even number on the other side," subjects may still turn over the *E* and the *4,* although now the *K* and the *7* are the cards that should be flipped.

Further complications were introduced by Johnson-Laird, Legrenzi, and Legrenzi (1972) who demonstrated that these sorts of errors don't have to occur. That is, the context in which the inference is demanded apparently influences the likelihood that a person will get the problem right. In their study, the subjects were given **thematic materials.** Subjects were shown the envelopes depicted in Figure 10.1, and were asked to imagine that they were postal workers sorting letters. Specifically, they were to determine if this postal regulation had been violated: "If a letter is sealed, then it has a 50-lire stamp on it." Subjects were asked to turn over the minimal number of envelopes necessary to verify the rule; 88% of the subjects were correct, turning over the sealed envelope and the envelope with the 40-lire stamp on it.

The so-called thematic-materials effect is quite dramatic, altering for most people the likelihood of getting the correct answer from something under 10% to almost 90%. Given that people seem to be rather poor on the selection task, what accounts for the thematic effect? Needless to say, intense theorizing and experimentation have questioned the necessary and sufficient causes of the effect. For clarity, I enumerate some possible explanations:

1. **Concreteness of the Materials.** Some commentators (e.g., Mayer, 1983) have pointed out that the envelope task is more concrete than the original letter–numeral selection task.

2. **A Sense of Reality.** Johnson-Laird et al. (1972) thought thematic materials established a natural, or down-to-earth, real-world context that enabled the subjects to reason about what they would do if they were in that situation.

3. **Instructional Set.** Some researchers point out that we might be dealing with a linguistic phenomenon here. In other words, the subjects simply interpret words like "verify" and "falsify" differently depending on the context.

4. **Memory.** Other researchers maintain that the thematic-materials effect extends as far as the subject's memory of the task. In other words, if the subjects can remember being in a situation that corresponds closely to the "cover story," they do well on the task. But if they've never been in such a situation, or if they can't retrieve their memory about it, they will fail.

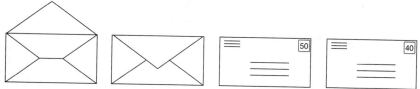

Figure 10.1 Material used in the envelope experiment by Johnson-Laird, Legrenzi, and Legrenzi (1972). Subjects were asked which envelopes should be turned over to test the rule, "If a letter is sealed, then it has a 50-lire stamp on it." (Copyright 1977 by the British Psychological Society. Adapted by permission of the publisher and author.)

5. **Something Else in Addition to, or Instead of, These.** Some researchers argue that some altogether different variables may be involved.

Let's consider each of these. First, "concreteness" of the materials probably isn't relevant here. After all, looking at pictures of envelopes can hardly be considered more "concrete" than looking at pictures of cards.

On the "sense of reality" established by the envelopes, some evidence suggests that simply giving people thematic materials won't improve reasoning unless the sense of reality established by the theme agrees with knowledge that people have stored in memory. Thus, Griggs and Cox (1982) thought it wasn't the thematic material in the envelope study that enabled the subjects to do so well; rather, the subjects were using remembered knowledge about the British postal system to help them make the deduction. Indeed, Griggs and Cox found a defunct regulation specifying that a sealed envelope required more postage than did an envelope with flap simply tucked in. Griggs and Cox repeated the Johnson-Laird et al. study with University of Florida undergraduates as subjects, and found that these subjects performed no better on the envelope problem than they did on the abstract letter–number problem. Next, Griggs and Cox constructed a problem representing facts and relationships that their subjects might have experienced directly. Subjects saw four cards labeled "beer," "Coke," "22 years," and "16 years." They were told to turn over the minimal number of cards necessary to verify this rule: "If a person is drinking beer, then the person must be over 19 years of age." Here, subjects performed much better than people who had received the letter–number task. Griggs and Cox concluded that performance on card-selection problems was enhanced when the thematic material cued retrieval of directly experienced knowledge stored in permanent memory.

Chrostowski and Griggs (1985) supported this interpretation. Subjects who were given a memory-cuing context outperformed subjects who were not given such a context; thus memory cuing was established as a necessary and sufficient condition to enhance performance on the selection task. The degree of improvement was influenced, however, by the instructions that the subjects were given. Subjects who were given true–false instructions were not helped by the memory-cuing conditions as much as subjects given falsification instructions.

This last finding does indeed suggest that the instructional set at least modifies in some way the cognitive processes that the reasoners bring to bear on this problem. Other studies provided some evidence for this contention. In a study by Yachanin (1986), subjects in some conditions were told to establish whether the rules were true or false (considered the most ambiguous instructional set), and in other conditions, the subjects were given a falsification instruction. For one of the rules, they had direct experience; for the other rule, they did not. Performance was best when the subject had direct experience and falsification instructions; moreover, most of the effect seemed to be based on the instructions. That is, when subjects were given falsification instructions for a rule with which they were completely unfamiliar, their performance was nearly as good as in the condition in which they were given falsification instructions for a familiar problem. This finding agrees fundamentally with that of Chrostowski and Griggs (1985), although Yachanin's work seems to emphasize the linguistic component more than does the Chrostowski and Griggs study. We have some reason to suspect the strength of the instructional effect, however, if only for its volatility. In some studies the instructional effect was very strong; in others it was weak. In still other studies the subjects' behavior was opposite that which we would theoretically predict. Valentine (1985) argued that, if the subjects were to check the cards that were necessary to see if the rule was being violated, such an instructional set should induce a falsification strategy and thus produce a reasonable chance for success. But the subjects misbehaved: the instructions instead produced a verification bias. Because of the falsification instructions, subjects were likely to turn over the cards that would be needed to *verify* the rule.

Margolis (1987) describes how these factors may produce poor performance. First, Margolis distinguishes between open and closed scenarios in reasoning tasks. An **open scenario** is one in which the subjects are given no information about how to search for an answer. In a **closed scenario** the person is simply presented a limited number of options. Margolis believes that in real life we encounter closed reasoning tasks only after we have gone through an open phase. Consequently, Margolis believes that subjects in the selection task misinterpret it as an open task, when it really is a closed task. Suppose you were told that each card in a collection of cards has either a "swan" or a "raven" on one side, and the other side is either "white" or "black." Then, suppose you are given a rule: "If a card says swan on one side, then it must say white on the other side of that card." Now, of the four categories of cards (swan, raven, white, black) you are asked to choose any category of cards (not just a specific card) that must be checked to see if the rule has been violated. When you pick a category, you are able to look at all the cards in that category; that is, all the cards that are black, or all the cards that have "swan" on them, or whatever. What would you do? The correct response is to look at either the cards that have "swan" on them, or the cards that are "black," but not both sets of cards! Looking at all the cards in either category would find any example of a black swan, and that's the only combination that would violate the rule. Now, let's add one other variable: Suppose subjects make the logical error of reversing the rule (if swans are white, then ravens are black). Under these circumstances the two categories of cards that would be searched are "swans" as above and "white" cards, and, as we've seen, these are exactly the most common choices. When these sources of ambiguity are fixed (that is, when the subject understands that the scenario is closed and that the rule is not reversible), Griggs (1989) found that subjects averaged 74% correct answers in an abstract form of the selection task. Other research in support of Margolis's ideas (Griggs & Jackson, 1990) shows that when the subjects are given the instruction set, "Figure out which two cards violate the rule and circle them," their attention is drawn to the not-P and not-Q cards, even though these are not the answer to the problem. As Margolis would predict, Griggs and Jackson (1990) found that 65% of the subjects getting these instructions looked at the not-P and not-Q cards. Without these instructions, these alternatives are rarely chosen by the subjects, typically by not more than 20%. Thus, volatile as the instructional phenomenon seems, the weight of the evidence suggests that it indeed has its effect.

Returning to the memory-cuing issue, Hoch and Tschirgi (1983) found that the effects of thematic materials were not limited to situations with which the subjects were familiar. They argued that people have general knowledge about circumstances that should make one wary or suspicious. One circumstance that might make a person suspicious is missing information. Hoch and Tschirgi reasoned that this *extralogical* information could be used as a basis for solving a card-selection problem even in a situation outside the person's expertise. To test this assertion, they created this scenario. Subjects were told to imagine themselves as quality-control inspectors for a firm that manufactured pocket calculators. Subjects in the no-relation condition were given information telling them how to decide if the calculators were acceptable, including a rule that could be verified by turning over some of the calculators. Next, the subjects looked at four drawings of calculators and circled the ones they thought should be turned over. Subjects in the blank condition were given similar instructions, including a rule that could be verified by turning over some of the calculators. Next, these subjects looked at drawings of calculators, one of which was left blank. Again, the subjects' task was to circle calculators that needed to be turned over to verify the rule. Figure 10.2 shows the instructional set and drawings for these two conditions. In the blank condition, you need to turn over the XT-10 calculator and the blank. In the no-relation condition, you need to turn over the XT-10 calculator and the technical instructions. Which problem did you find easier?

The Hoch and Tschirgi subjects found the blank problem substantially easier than the no-relation problem. Seventy-six percent of the subjects in the blank condition solved the problem, whereas 44% of those in the no-relation condition succeeded. What accounts for the discrepancy? Hoch and Tschirgi maintain that the subject notices the missing information in the blank condition, which may help to establish a "detective" orientation (van Duyne, 1974). That is, the subjects begin to suspect that something is wrong, and they turn over the calculator to investigate it. In so doing, Hoch and Tschirgi say that the subject is obviously not relying exclusively on personally experienced knowledge retrieved from memory to solve the problem.

Along the same lines, Hoch and Tschirgi (1985) suggested that "cue redundancy" might be used as an alternative to personally experienced knowledge in solving the selection task. According to their theoretical perspective, to solve the task, subjects could generate all possible antecedent–consequent pairs plus the four reverse orderings. Next, they could identify the truth value for each pair [(p,q), $(-p,q)$, $(-p,-q)$ are true and $(p,-q)$ is false] and the reverse orderings. These two steps, according to Hoch and Tschirgi, are the psychological equivalent of the mental construction of a truth table. Finally, the subjects select the two cards that represent the false pair. Hoch and Tschirgi argue that typically subjects are kept from doing so by the generative difficulty: they don't stop to think about generating all four pairs, and they don't think about the reverse orderings. In their study, they gave some subjects information that could be used to help generate the pairs; this information could be understood as an elaborate prompt. As part of the instructions, some of their subjects read these two sentences: "A card with a vowel showing, though, may have only an even number on the back side. A card with a consonant showing may have either an odd or an even number on the back side" (Hoch & Tschirgi, 1985, p. 455).

When these redundant cues were used with subjects who had at least a master's degree (most of these degrees were in technical subjects), 72% got the problem right. When nonredundant instructions were used with master's-degree subjects, only 48% got the correct answer. For those who had a bachelor's degree, 4% of subjects with the nonredundant instructions got the problem right, versus 36% who were correct when

(A) Imagine that you are a quality-control clerk for Microdigit, Inc. Your job is to inspect different models of pocket calculators moving along a conveyor belt. Your company markets two different calculator models: the XT-10 and XT-11. The two models are basically the same, but the XT-10 is sold in the United States and the XT-11 is exported to Canada.

Model numbers appear on the front side and a brief set of instructions can be glued to a panel on the back side. The instructions come in two versions, one technical (for the business market) and one quite simple (for the consumer market). The calculators move along a conveyor belt, some face up with the model number showing and some face down with the instruction panel showing. Clerks must make sure that the following rule is obeyed:

If a calculator is a model XT-10, then the simple instructions must be on the panel on the back side.

Clerks must work as quickly as possible, so you want to turn over the fewest number of calculators while making sure that the rule is followed in all cases. Below is a sample of 4 calculators on your conveyor belt. Circle the calculator or calculators that you would turn over to verify the rule.

(B) Imagine that you are a quality-control clerk for Microdigit, Inc. Your job is to inspect different models of pocket calculators moving along a conveyor belt. Your company markets two different calculator models: the XT-10 and XT-11. The two models are basically the same, but the XT-10 is sold in the United States and the XT-11 is exported to other countries.

Model numbers appear on the front side and a brief set of instructions can be glued to a panel on the back side. The instructions are quite simple (directed toward the consumer market). In some cases, no instructions have been glued onto the panels. These are cases where different language instructions are supplied by the distributor at a later date. The calculators move along a conveyor belt, some face up with the model number showing and some face down with the instruction panel showing. Clerks must make sure that the following rule is obeyed:

If a calculator is model XT-10, then a set of instructions must be on the panel on the back side.

Clerks must work as quickly as possible, so you want to turn over the fewest number of calculators while making sure that the rule is followed in all cases. Below is a sample of 4 calculators on your conveyor belt. Circle the calculator or calculators that you would turn over to verify the rule.

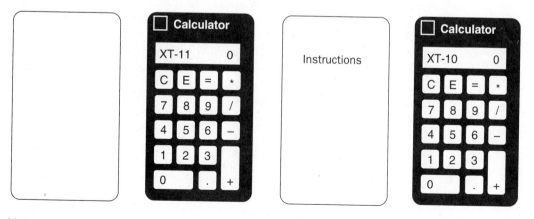

Figure 10.2 The materials and instructions used in the Hoch and Tschirgi (1983) study: (A) "no relation" condition; (B) "blank" condition.

the redundant instructions were given. Finally, for subjects who had a high-school education, 8% of those who received the nonredundant instructions got the problem right, versus 24% who were correct when the redundant instructions were given. Hoch and Tschirgi concluded that many of the master's-degree subjects had adequate logical knowledge to solve the problems without added redundant cues, but that high-school subjects had so little logical knowledge about the structure of conditional statements that they couldn't be helped much by adding redundant cues.

Finally, another line of evidence suggests that these sorts of extralogical strategies and linguistic effects may be subsumed into an altogether different type of cognitive structure. Cheng and Holyoak (1985) agreed that individuals might solve the selection task with internally generated and computed logical steps. They referred to this concept of internal logic as the "syntactic view." Alternatively, people may solve the problem because its cover story has cued a previously stored memory. They call this the "specific-experience view." Although either of these might work in the selection task, Cheng and Holyoak proposed that people are more likely to use **pragmatic-reasoning schemas** to solve such reasoning problems. These are clusters of rules that are highly general and abstract, but nonetheless they are defined for classes of goals and types of relationships. An example of a pragmatic-reasoning schema is the set of abstracted rules for situations involving "permission"; that is, situations in which some action A may be taken only if some precondition B is satisfied. If the semantic aspects of a problem suggest to people that they are dealing with a permission situation, all the rules about permissions in general can be called on, including, "If action A is to be taken, then precondition B must be satisfied," "Action A is to be taken only if precondition B is satisfied," and so on. In one of their studies, subjects were given a selection problem based on an abstract description of a permission situation: "If one is to take action A, then one must first satisfy precondition B." Subjects also were given an arbitrary card version that was syntactically (i.e., logically) identical to the permission problem. About 60% of the subjects solved the abstract permission problem correctly, whereas only 20% solved the abstract selection problem.

Realize that Cheng and Holyoak maintain that these effects will be observed only if the permission schema is "triggered" by the problem's semantic content. In the problem above, to trigger the permission schema, the subjects were given instructions about converting if-then conditional statements, which are normative in the Wason selection task, to permission-triggering statements in the form only if. Thus, subjects were told in the instructions that statements such as "If the tablecloth is brown, then the wall is white" could be converted to "The tablecloth is brown only if the wall is white."

Cheng, Holyoak, Nisbett, and Oliver (1986) reasoned that, if people are indeed using the pragmatic-reasoning schemas, perhaps to the exclusion of logical principles, training in logical principles alone should have little influence on performance on the selection task because presumably the subjects would not know how to map the formal rules onto the selection-task situation nor might they in fact even realize that such rules could be mapped onto that task. Their results confirmed this hypothesis: Training was effective only when abstract principles were coupled with examples of selection problems that enabled the subject to map abstract principles onto concrete instances. On the other hand, a brief training session on pragmatic-reasoning schema dealing with obligation was sufficient to enable subjects who received "obligation" problems (such as "If one works for the Armed Forces, then one must vote in the elections") to lower their error rate to only 8%, versus a 36% rate for subjects who did not get the schema training.

Deontic Reasoning

Cheng and Holyoak's use of permission schemes to explain performance on the Wason selection task implies that people must have sensitivity to, and ability to reason about, situations in which they may, must, or must not, engage in specified activities. We refer to reasoning about such situations as **deontic reasoning;** that is, reasoning about situations that are permissible or impermissible. Some evidence suggests that we become sensitive to demands for such reasoning at a very early age.

Cummins (1996) considered the question of deontic reasoning in preschoolers (ages three and four) by presenting to children this situation. Children first examined a model playhouse and an adjoining model back yard. Toy mice were at play in the house and in the yard. Some mouse toys made a squeaky noise when squeezed; others were silent when squeezed, as demonstrated for the children with toy mice. Children were then randomly assigned to one of two conditions. In the deontic condition, they heard the experimenter describe how the mice get very excited when they play out in the back yard. Further, when they get excited, they squeak, which draws unwelcome attention from a neighborhood cat. Next the children were told that when the Queen Mouse (a stuffed Minnie Mouse) heard, she worried about safety for the mice playing outside. The Queen Mouse made a rule that "All squeaky mice must stay in the house," and this rule was repeated for the subjects. The child was then asked about which mouse or mice would need to be squeezed to make sure that no mouse was disobeying the Queen. In the second, *indicative* condition, after demonstrating that some mice squeak when squeezed, the experimenter simply said, "Now I'm going to tell you something, but I might be tricking you . . . I know that all squeaky mice are in the house." Notice that this phrasing is not at all deontic; it avoids language implying "must" or "might." In the indicative condition, the subjects were invited to squeeze a mouse or mice to determine if they were being tricked by the experimenter.

If we set up the indicative and deontic statements in if-then format, we can see that they are formally equivalent:

> If a mouse is squeaky then it [must stay in—deontic] or [is in—indicative] the house.

And so, in both conditions it is the same kind of mouse that we need to investigate to determine if the Mouse Queen's rule was being followed, or that the experimenter was not tricking the subject. That is, in both conditions we would need to look at a mouse that was not in the house (these are our "~q mice") to make sure that none of the mice not in the house squeaked. Any toy mouse that was in the back yard then was an appropriate candidate for squeezing. Table 10.4 shows the number of three- and four-year-olds who chose a ~q mouse in the deontic and indicative conditions. As you can see in the table, the deontic language tremendously affected the likelihood that the child would answer the problem correctly. Pooling across the two age groups, we see that 76% of the children in the deontic condition squeezed a mouse that was in the back yard, but only 33% of the children in the indicative condition did so. This finding suggests that,

Table 10.4   Number Correct (−q) Selections Among 3- and 4-Year-Olds in Deontic and Indicative Reasoning Contexts (Experiment 1)

	Reasoning Context			
	Deontic		Indicative	
Age	−*q*	*n*	−*q*	*n*
3	15	22	7	22
4	17	20	7	20

Source: From Cummins, 1996.

consistent with the Cheng and Holyoak position, a pragmatic-reasoning scheme involving permission may be triggered by using the language of permission and obligation. And such a triggering response can occur in very youthful individuals.

Mental Models

We've looked at two ways in which people might accomplish formal reasoning tasks. First, it may be that people have a kind of built-in "psycho-logic." Although such rules may not always be equivalent to the formal rules logicians use, these psychological equivalents are nevertheless good enough to accomplish most of the reasoning tasks we are faced with. As an alternative account, some theorists argue that we reason by means of pragmatic-reasoning schemes. Finally, other theorists argue that we reason deductively by creating mental models (Johnson-Laird & Byrne, 1991; Johnson-Laird, Byrne, & Schaeken, 1992).

Mental models are built on the idea that we reason by creating a representation of the world that is neither totally abstract (a truth table would be a totally abstract representation) nor completely specific (if our representation of the world were completely specific, we would not show any transfer of previous experience to new situations). Let's consider an example to show how a conditional statement could be represented at this level of abstraction. According to Johnson-Laird and Byrne (1991), the statement, "If my son wakes up in time, then he watches 'Biker Mice from Mars' " would be represented:

My son wakes up in time.	He watches "Biker Mice from Mars."
My son does not wake up in time.	He watches "Biker Mice from Mars."
My son does not wake up in time.	He does not watch "Biker Mice from Mars."

Each of the three lines represents a situation that could occur in the world, or we say that each line represents a possible model of the world. You may have noticed that one model seems to be missing; namely, the situation in which my son wakes up in time, but for some reason does not watch the show. Why isn't this model included in the representation? Because the theory assumes that only models consistent with the utterance's meaning are created. In the original statement, "If my son wakes up in time, then he watches 'Biker Mice from Mars,' " the meaning has to do with what he does if he wakes up or, by implication, what happens if he doesn't wake up. That's why only those situations are shown in the representation.

Now, let's move on to the next step, "reducing" the models. We'll use "a" to stand for "awaken" or "wakes up in time" and "w" to stand for "watches 'Biker Mice from Mars.' " Then we have

```
    a      w
   ~a      w
   ~a     ~w
```

where the "~" or tilde means just what it meant earlier in the chapter; that is, either "not" or "the absence of."

We have a little more terminology to deal with before we can go on to discuss how the mental-models approach explains the ease of modus ponens and the difficulty of modus tollens. According to mental-models theory, the limitations on working memory that we all face impose an order on the way in which these models will be generated when we are given a proposition. In this situation,

```
[a]  w
 . . .
```

the top line represents the "exhaustive" representation of the statement, "my son awakes in time." When a statement is "exhausted," it cannot occur in any model without the statement, "then he watches 'Biker Mice from Mars' " also occurring. In other words, when the "a" is exhausted, the "a" cannot occur without the "w," which we show by putting brackets around the "a." The three dots, or ellipses, tell a different story. Because our working memory is almost inevitably filled up when we begin to reason with these models, we may try to represent some models implicitly rather than explicitly. That's the function of the model in the second line above, the ellipses, which represent all the other models about a conditional-reasoning situation that I could create, but haven't yet created. In other words, the ellipses are like a mental place holder that says, "I know there's more information to be represented, but I haven't gotten into the details of it yet."

Now we're ready to understand the model's explanation about the ease and difficulty in some conditional-reasoning tasks. Consider this syllogism:

If the Cubs win the division, then they'll go to the playoffs.
The Cubs win the division.

The first premise is modeled:

```
[w]  p
 . . .
```

and the second premise is modeled simply:

```
w
```

Now to make an inference from these models, we must have a way of combining the two models, and in this example, that is not very difficult. The information is combined by adding the information from the second model to the first and then eliminating the ellipses. When the information is combined, we have

w   p

which might be translated back into English as "The Cubs win the division and go to the playoffs." As you can see, making the modus ponens conclusion from this set of models is not very difficult because the set includes all the information that is needed.

Something different happens when we think about modus tollens. Consider this syllogism:

If the Cubs win the division, then they'll go to the playoffs.
The Cubs didn't go to the playoffs.

Once again, the first premise may be represented by the model

[w]   p

and the second premise might be represented by the model

~p

Notice that we have no obvious way of combining the information from the second model with that of the first. According to the mental-models position, this lack of an obvious linkage from the second model to the first stops most people from reasoning successfully in modus tollens situations. To combine the information from the two models, the first model must be fleshed out more extensively. Here's how that would look:

w   p
~w   p
~w   ~p

Now, using the same procedure we used before to combine models, we can see a linkage from the ~p model to the first set of models. Specifically, we can link the ~p model to the ~w model to arrive at

~w   ~p

Translating this model back into English, we might get a statement such as, "If the Cubs don't go on to the playoffs, it means that they haven't won the division."

As this analysis shows, modus tollens is difficult according to the mental-models approach for two reasons. First, modus tollens requires that the initial model be "fleshed out" or expanded from its first appearance. Cognitive effort is required to detect that the initial model must be expanded. As you'll recall, in the modus ponens example the initial model does not have to be fleshed out in this way. Second, modus tollens is difficult because, for at least a short time, the reasoner must keep several distinct alternative representations in mind simultaneously. Doing so imposes a cognitive load on the reasoner's memory. Once again, this cognitive load is not imposed in modus ponens reasoning.

Summary of Formal Reasoning

Studying conditional-reasoning tasks tells us several interesting things about human reasoning. First, the untrained person's use of logical terms is sometimes far different from the logician's use. We've seen that people typically take the term "if" to mean "if and only if." Such transformations, however, usually are orderly. Once subjects decide how they will interpret the "if" statement, they tend to stick with this interpretation, and their reasoning is appropriate, given their misinterpretation. It also seems that skill in formal reasoning depends somewhat on Western education. Both logic and Western education may have been designed to meet the needs of a culture that emphasizes some modes of thinking while deemphasizing others. In cultures emphasizing other systems of thought, we might expect the culture to educate its people to reason accordingly. In other words, logic and education may simply be the byproducts of a culture. If our culture were different, we would expect both logic and education to be different.

The modus tollens literature offers a fascinating picture of the ways in which people can circumvent, or somehow make up for, shortcomings in formal reasoning ability. When we looked at work by Rips and Marcus (1977) and Wason (1966), we saw that people typically don't do well on tasks that require explicit knowledge about the modus tollens inference rule. In real life, though, people have several strategies they can use to solve such problems. First, they can check their memories for situations that seem similar to the one they encounter in the problem. Thus, the Johnson-Laird et al. subjects could use knowledge about the British postal system to help solve the problem. Although such knowledge was not available to the Griggs and Cox subjects, they could nevertheless imagine that they were checking identification at a bar. By mapping the problem's conditions onto an easily visualizable action, these subjects also circumvented their apparent lack of explicit modus tollens knowledge. Finally, Hoch and Tschirgi demonstrated that in some conditions people's suspicion or curiosity is piqued. People then often choose to investigate further, and by doing so they often solve a modus tollens problem. One condition that seems to produce these general **extralogical inferences** is the search for missing information.

This search brings us to a related issue—an important one, although we've alluded to it obliquely so far: reasoning is "rule based" (Rips, 1990). Is reasoning always accomplished by applying some sort of rules? If it is, what kinds of rules? Are these rules hard and fast or fuzzy? It's not very difficult to get evidence for the hard-and-fast position. If I tell you that Joe is taller than Bob, and Bob is taller than Alex, I'm sure you can tell me about Joe's height in relation to Alex's. It certainly seems in such examples that you are consulting some internal calculus that has converted the specific statement into some more abstract rule in the form "If $A > B$, and $B > C$, then $A > C$," and moreover, built into the reasoning scheme is a tag that says "must be true." That is, besides knowing the rule and applying it, your cognitive system can access that tag and know that whatever you substitute for A, B, and C, if the first two statements are true, the third must also be true. On the other hand, having access to hard-and-fast rules doesn't mean that we might not also use fuzzy rules. Here, the cognitive system's tag might read "could be true," or "not too confident that this is true," or "usually true," or whatever. Behaviorally, we would expect that reasoners who are using fuzzy rules should not be as confident of their reasoning as those who are using hard-and-fast rules, but the form and structure of the reasoning is identical for both. Of course, we find opposition to the basic premise here. Plenty of theorists argue that reasoning is always "just" retrieving and comparing the current situation with some previously experienced one. According to this view, errors in reasoning may result from poor analogies, inexperience, failure to encode or retrieve previous encounters, or whatnot. Can you see the difference between the two positions? The rule-based theorist seeks the underlying syntactic grammar of reasoning; the opposing camp maintains that there are only mere instances or examples of reasoning, and any behavioral similarities in reasoning outcomes are produced superficially by appearances of similarity in the reasoning tasks themselves. As you can see, this issue hinges somewhat on the notion of similarity across reasoning tasks.

Natural Reasoning

Most people don't know about logical inference rules, and so they can't possibly apply them explicitly when reasoning is required. In the preceding section I pointed out some of the tricks people use to overcome this lack of formal knowledge. One technique that can be used to study these strategies is to give people problems that are similar to the ones they are likely to encounter in real life. That is, although reasoning is still studied in the laboratory, the problems involve making estimates about events that could take place in the real world. Thus, the objective here is not to see if people can reason their way to a valid conclusion. Instead, we are trying to find out whether people can reason their way to a true conclusion, given premises that could be true. In this sense, the emphasis in **natural reasoning** is on conditions that foster soundness in human reasoning. From the pattern of responses, the cognitive psychologist hopes to be able to say something about the underlying reasoning processes.

Inferences About Causality

One of the most useful properties in our cognitive systems is the ability to make inferences about cause and effect that are reliable, at least sometimes. I'm sure some creatures on the surface of this planet get along just fine in their evolutionary niche without having to make such inferences, but I think it's safe to say that we would have a very difficult time functioning in our own niche without having this ability. One of the things about cause-and-effect inferences that makes them especially interesting is that they are inherently cognitive. That is, as philosophy has recognized for some time, no sensory information is sufficient by itself to produce a causal judgment. Such knowledge must then be the result of the cognitive system's carrying out operations on our sensory knowledge to yield a causal inference. Just how do we go about this exercise?

Almost every psychological theory of causal inference (e.g., Cheng, 1997; Cheng & Novick, 1992; Shanks, Holyoak, & Medin, 1996) begins with our ability to notice, store, and use types of covariations or co-occurrences. If I notice that "lilacs bloom in the spring," I've spotted a co-occurrence or covariation in the sense that I have seen that the lilacs' appearance coincides with springtime weather's onset. Moreover, it appears that the lilacs do not bloom at any other time in the year. To the extent that this covariation appears to be constant, I may eventually infer that springtime, or something about springtime, causes the lilacs to bloom. My willingness to make such an inference is influenced in part by the extent to which the presumed causes and effects conform to a rule known as the ΔP ("delta P") rule (Spellman, 1996). Here's the rule:

$$\Delta P = P(E/C) - P(E/{\sim}C)$$

where $P(E/C)$ is the probability that the effect will be observed when the presumed cause is observed and $P(E/{\sim}C)$ is the probability that the effect will be observed even when the presumed cause is not observed. The difference between these two probabilities, ΔP, is a number bounded by the values -1 and 1, and is referred to as the "strength of the contingency." Let's first consider the condition in which the contingency strength is close to 1. For that to happen, $P(E/C)$ has to be close to 1 itself. Thus the probability that the effect will be observed when the presumed cause is observed is large. At the same time, for the contingency strength to be close to 1, the second term, $P(E/{\sim}C)$, must be close to zero, which occurs when the probability that the effect will be observed without the cause also being observed is very low. When the strength of the contingency is zero, or close to it, the probability that the effect will be observed in the presence of the cause hardly differs from the probability that the effect will be observed in the absence of the cause. In other words, when the contingency strength is zero, the implication is that the presumed cause really has little causal power. Let's consider an example. Suppose I have twenty tomato plants in my garden, and I wonder if applying a fertilizer will hasten their maturity. I select ten plants and apply the fertilizer, and let nature take its course for the other ten. Suppose eight of the ten fertilized plants have early tomatoes, but only one of the ten nonfertilized plants has early tomatoes, then,

$$\Delta P = P(E/C) - P(E/{\sim}C)$$
$$\text{or}$$
$$.7 = .8 - .1$$

I probably would conclude that the fertilizer was pretty effective in hastening the tomatoes' maturity, because the strength of the contingency was pretty close to 1.

The typical finding in studies of causal inferences is that people are fairly accurate in using such information on covariation to make reliable inferences about presumed causes, as long as an event has only one cause. That is, as long as an effect is covarying with only one presumed cause, people can compute the contingency strength pretty accurately. (When I say "compute," I'm not trying to suggest that people are really doing the math, but rather that whatever the form of the computation, it seems close to the answer they would get if they did do the math.) Thus, peoples' judgment of contingency strength tends to agree with the rule.

The picture changes dramatically, however, if an event has multiple causes. Then we frequently observe large deviations from the ΔP rule. A study by Baker, Mercier, Vallée-Tourangeau, Frank, and Pan (1993) shows these effects. In their study, subjects were asked to play a video game in which they attempted to drive a tank across a minefield. Two potential variables could influence the tank's success in getting across. The

Table 10.5   Results from Experiment 1 of Baker, Mercier, Vallée-Tourangeau, Frank, and Pan (1993)

Condition	ΔP_{plane} (unconditional contingency)	$\Delta P_{camouflage}$ (unconditional contingency)	Camouflage rating
.5/0	0	.5	49
.5/1	1	.5	−6

Source: From Spellman, 1996.

subjects were allowed to push a button that sometimes succeeded in camouflaging the tank, presumably affecting the tank's ability to get through the mines. Second, sometimes a spotter plane of unknown origin flew overhead, which could also presumably influence the tank's success. Subjects viewed forty trials presenting various combinations of camouflage, spotter plane, and tank success. After the forty trials, the subjects were asked to estimate the effectiveness of the camouflage in helping the tank get across the minefield. They used a −100 to +100 scale, using larger positive numbers to indicate greater confidence that the camouflage actually helped the tank. The results of their study are shown in Table 10.5.

In the condition labeled .5/0, the .5 refers to the camouflage's contingency strength, and the 0 to the plane's contingency strength. In other words, in this condition, the camouflage had moderate causal strength, and the plane had no effect whatever on the tank's chances. Subjects very accurately estimated the camouflage's effectiveness in this condition. But let's now consider the subjects in the .5/1 condition. Here, the plane's ΔP was 1, meaning that when the plane was present, the tank always succeeded, and when the plane was absent the tank always failed to get across the minefield. The ΔP for the camouflage was unchanged in this condition; it was kept at .5. But the subjects' mean evaluation of −6 for the camouflage's effectiveness is very close to zero, suggesting that the subjects perceived the camouflage as not very effective. The subjects in this condition deviated quite a bit from the outcome that the ΔP rule suggests. We refer to this phenomenon as **discounting:** In the presence of multiple causes, subjects discount or deemphasize a moderate contingency strength when a strong contingency strength is present. The implication in this study is that in a single-cause world, in which all effects were produced by one cause, people would be able to discern those causes. But in a multiple-cause world, in which effects are produced by several causes, people may tend to discern the strongest cause, and perhaps deemphasize or dismiss weaker, but still present, causes.

World Knowledge and Judging Causal Effects

One principle that a student must realize is that the reasoning tasks that cognitive psychologists give to, say, us as their subjects might better be understood as invitations to reason, rather than as demands or requirements to reason. In other words, the task is an opportunity for us to enter a "logical" world in which the principles of validity and necessity are the only variables operating. As with any invitation, if we are subjects in a reasoning experiment, we may decline to reason, preferring instead to think about the task in a way that suits us. Rather than enter a logical world, we may be more comfortable remaining in a world in which truths that we have personally observed, or know about, are the principles. Cummins (1995) has investigated these issues.

Cummins argues that, in making causal inferences, people access and use two kinds of world knowledge, each of which may influence a person's likelihood of and willingness to make a causal deduction. These varieties of world knowledge are **alternative causes** and **disabling conditions.** An alternative cause is simply a different cause which we may know of, which we may believe could produce the effect in question. A disabling condition is an event that may prevent an effect from being observed, even though its actual cause is present. In this example,

> If the brake pedal is pressed, the car will slow down
> The brake pedal is pressed
> And so the car will slow down

the causal inference (pressing the brake pedal causes the car to slow down) is supported because the argument has been cast in a modus ponens form. The conclusion is logically valid. And so, if I were a subject in a cognitive psychology study, and I understood the problem as an invitation to enter into the "logical" world I described above, I might be willing to endorse the conclusion as necessarily true. But suppose I decline that invitation and instead use my world knowledge to think of events that may prevent a car from slowing down, even though its brake pedal has been pressed (e.g., the road is icy, the brake lines have been cut, the master cylinder is broken). If I contact that knowledge, I may not be so willing to endorse a causal connection between pressing the brakes and slowing the car, because it no longer seems that pressing the pedal will be sufficient to always slow the car down. On the other hand, consider this argument:

> If Larry grasps the glass with his bare fingertips, then his fingerprints will be on the glass.
> Larry grasps the glass with his bare fingertips
> Larry's fingerprints will be on the glass.

Once again, the causal inference (grasping a glass with one's bare fingertips causes fingerprints to remain on the glass) is supported because the argument has been cast in a modus ponens format, and so this conclusion is valid. In fact, the two arguments are identical in format. But unlike the preceding example, I may not have any world knowledge that I can contact to disable the inference. Thus, if I can't think of any event that would prevent one's fingerprints from remaining on a glass after it has been grasped with bare fingers, then, according to Cummins's argument, I may be more likely to endorse the conclusion from this second argument as necessarily true compared to the conclusion from the first argument, even though in a logical sense, the arguments are identical in format.

Alternative causes and disabling conditions work in this way to influence causal deduction: Thinking of alternative causes reduces the *necessity* that any one cause will bring about an effect, and thinking of disabling conditions (as we did in the brake-pedal example) reduces the *sufficiency* of the cause to bring about the effect. These two variables lead to two mechanisms that may undermine causal reasoning's success.

If I'm able to contact many alternative causes, I may reject a causal deduction because I may believe that the purported cause doesn't really have to be present to produce the effect. And if I'm able to contact many disabling conditions, I may again reject a causal deduction—this time, though, because I may believe that even if the cause is present, the effect may not always follow. Cummins (1995) has worked out how these variables should theoretically influence causal deductions for each of the four conditional-reasoning formats (i.e., modus ponens—MP, modus tollens—MT, denying the antecedent—DA, and affirming the consequent—AC), and this analysis is shown in the top panel in Figure 10.3. The drawings suggest that both MP and MT inferences should be influenced by the number of disabling conditions that a person may be able to access, and both of these inferences should be relatively uninfluenced

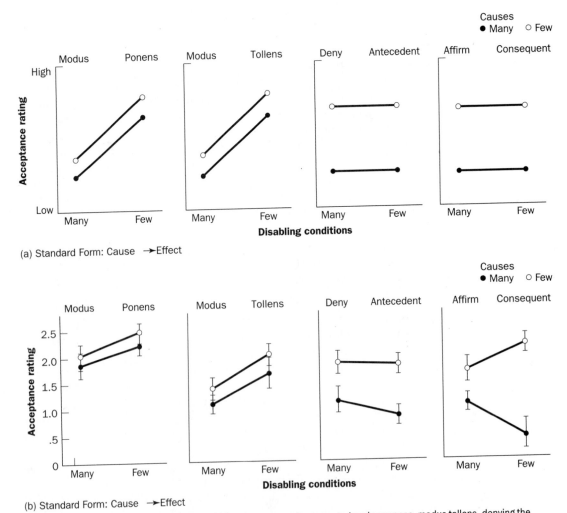

Figure 10.3 Predictions of acceptability ratings for four types of arguments (modus ponens, modus tollens, denying the antecedent, and affirming the consequent) based on a causal analysis (a) and actual findings (b). *Source:* From Cummins, 1995.

by the number of alternative causes that the person may contact. On the other hand, the situation is exactly reversed for DA and AC inferences. In other words, if the number of alternative causes that I can access is relatively small, then, regardless of how many disabling conditions I can think of, I'll be likely to accept as genuinely causal an argument that is logically an error.

Returning to the Larry-fingerprints and brake-pedal arguments, both of which were cast into MP arguments, according to Figure 10.3, I should be more likely to accept the Larry-fingerprints argument as causal, compared to the brake-pedal argument, because it seems easier to think of disabling conditions for the latter argument than it does for the former. To test these assertions, Cummins (1995) had an initial set of subjects evaluate arguments for the number of alternative causes and disabling conditions they could think of. Then, after developing materials that varied on these dimensions, she had a second sample of subjects read and evaluate the arguments on a seven-point scale of the Likert type, with higher numbers indicating greater sureness that the conclusion could logically be drawn. The bottom panel in Figure 10.3 shows these acceptance ratings for each of the four argument types, as a function of the number of alternative causes and disabling conditions in each.

It's interesting to compare the actual findings to the theoretical predictions, and observe, generally, a good degree of matching up. Consistent with Cummins's predictions, both MP and MT arguments were more or less likely to be accepted for the number of disabling conditions, whereas DA and AC arguments were more or less likely to be accepted for the number of alternative causes (the sole exception is that AC arguments appear to be influenced by both mechanisms). Notice a couple of points in interpreting these findings. First, it could be that none of the reasoning done by the subjects in the study is really "deductive." Rather, when they run their "reasoning program" in a study like this, they get a measure of how many alternative causes and disabling conditions were contacted or found in thinking about the problem. If a lot turn up, then the subjects may be reporting the result of a naive probabilistic analysis. Or the reasoning may be deductive. Then, the number of alternative causes and disabling conditions that are found may influence subjects' confidence that they have run the reasoning program correctly. Cummins (1995) suggests that more research will be needed to disentangle these two viewpoints.

Representativeness

A series of studies by Kahneman and Tversky is the basis for much of what we know about natural reasoning and decision making. In one study (Kahneman & Tversky, 1973), subjects were divided into two groups. Subjects in the "engineer-high" group were told that a person had been picked at random from a sample of 100 people, 70 of them engineers, and the remaining 30 lawyers. Subjects in the "engineer-low" group were told that the sample had consisted of 30 engineers and 70 lawyers. Subjects in both groups faced the same task: they were required to estimate the odds that the person picked at random from the sample of 100 was an engineer. Subjects in both groups were generally accurate. The engineer-high group correctly estimated that the chances were about 70% that the person picked was an engineer, and those in the engineer-low group correctly estimated that the chances were about 30%. The subjects were then told that another person had been picked at random from the sample, and they were given this thumbnail sketch:

> Jack is a 45-year-old man. He is married and has four children. He is generally conservative, careful, and ambitious. He shows no interest in political and social issues and spends most of his free time on his many hobbies, which include home carpentry, sailing, and mathematical puzzles. (Kahneman & Tversky, 1973)

The subjects in both groups were asked to estimate the odds that this person was an engineer. Subjects in both groups now maintained that the odds that this person was an engineer were greater than the representational proportions in the sample. Both the engineer-high and engineer-low groups estimated that the odds that Jack was an engineer were greater than 90%. As you can see from the description, Jack has hobbies and interests that are somewhat stereotypical for an engineer, but more unusual for a lawyer. In that sense, Jack's profile represents an engineer more than it does a lawyer, and the subjects apparently were swayed by this stereotype. Because Jack was typical of engineers, they concluded that the odds were great that he *was* an engineer. The engineer-low subjects did not take into account that the odds of selecting an engineer were only 30%.

A *heuristic* is a term psychologists use to denote general problem-solving procedures that often work in solving everyday problems. A heuristic is a rule of thumb—a general, rather than precise guide for coming up with a solution. Subjects in the Kahneman and Tversky study apparently were using the **representativeness heuristic.** To make a quick judgment about odds, people compare the question with a concept that is at least similar to a prototype and compute its deviation from that. If the deviation is small, people tend to assume that the odds are good that their judgment is true. In this study the subjects in the engineer-low group overlooked important information when they used the representativeness heuristic; namely, that engineers were not very common in the original sample. Generally, people seem to have difficulty evaluating how influential the *base rate* is in making such judgments. When the base rate is low, the representativeness heuristic can lead to serious misestimations. To see why, read this problem and make the judgment that's called for:

> Pretend that a stranger told you about a person who is short, slim, and likes to read poetry, and then asked you to guess whether this person is more likely to be a classics professor in an Ivy League university or a truck driver. Which would be your best guess (Myers, 1986)?

The preceding problem has tipped you off, but those who are naive are likely to guess that the person is a classics professor rather than a truck driver. But this assumption is almost certainly wrong. To begin with, the Ivy League probably has about 40 to 50 classics professors. Perhaps half of these fit the description, which yields 25 people. Compared with this result, the number of truck drivers is overwhelmingly large—perhaps 500,000. Truck drivers who fit the description may be relatively rare—let's say one in 1,000, but we still have 500 cases in the truck-driver pool against 25 in the Ivy League pool. The odds are rather good that the person is a truck driver rather than a professor, even though the description is typical for the latter.

Availability

The Kahneman and Tversky work also found that people's reasoning is influenced by availability of material in memory. In other words, when things come readily to mind, we assume they are more common than things that don't come to mind as easily. This heuristic is usually suitable for estimating likelihoods; that is, common things usually do come to mind more readily than rare things. But like the representativeness heuristic, the **availability heuristic** can go astray.

Kahneman and Tversky (1973) asked their subjects to estimate the proportion of words in English that begin with *k* and the proportion of words in which *k* is the third letter. One way in which we might try to accomplish this task is by generating a list of words that begin with *k* and comparing this list with some hypothetical, uncomputed list of words that don't begin with *k*. Once this proportion has been estimated, we might generate a list of words that have *k* as their third letter and compare this list with another, not fully computed list of words without this property. Spend a minute or two making these obviously speculative estimates. If you're like most people, producing the list of words beginning with *k* seems easier than producing the list of words with *k* in the third position, which may result in your saying that *k*-beginning words are more common. In reality, words with *k* in the third position outnumber *k*-beginning words by a ratio of about 3:1. This misestimation is thought to be related to the processes that we considered in Chapter 5 (Anderson, 1980). A reasonable assumption is that words are more likely to be coded by initial letters rather than third letters. If they are, then the spread of activation of *k*-beginning words to one another is likely to be stronger than the spread from words with *k* as their third letter. What happens is that more *k*-beginning words are likely to enter our awareness, and thus we mistakenly figure that the contents of our minds are a good reflection of the proportions in reality.

This explanation is supported in work done by Slovic, Fischoff, and Lichtenstein (1976), who asked their subjects to estimate the likelihood of various occurrences. Which do you believe is more frequent: death resulting from all forms of accidents or resulting from strokes? From homicide or from diabetes? From all forms of cancer or from heart disease? Most people estimated that death was more likely from accidents, homicide, and cancer, but this assumption is incorrect. Although these events are often publicized, the less recognized killers (strokes, diabetes, heart disease) actually take more lives. We see that the publicity surrounding homicide and cancer victims apparently makes these events more memorable and available.

The availability heuristic is also influenced by the ease with which some computations can be made. Events that are easily computed are perceived as more common, and consequently they are more available than events whose likelihood is hard to compute. In another problem given by Kahneman and Tversky (1973) to their subjects, people were asked to form subcommittees from a group of ten. In one group, the subjects were asked to estimate how many subcommittees of two people each could be formed from the original group of ten. In a second group, the subjects were asked to estimate how many subcommittees of eight people each could be formed from the original ten. The median estimate for subjects in the first group was seventy subcommittees, and the median estimate for subjects in the second group was twenty subcommittees. The number of subcommittees that can be formed is actually the same for each—forty-five. Do you see why? Every group of two that is formed leaves a remainder of eight people who could make up a different subcommittee. Every subcommittee of eight that is made up also leaves a remainder of two from the original group. The subjects apparently didn't realize this point. Kahneman and Tversky maintain that the subjects probably began to compute the various groupings and succeeded in producing a fairly large number of two-people subcommittees in a short time. Subjects who started in the eight-person condition had a harder task. Computing the members of the subcommittee is difficult, as is storing the result. After a time, subjects in the eight-person condition probably hadn't generated as many subcommittees as the subjects in the other group, and so were inclined to estimate that there weren't that many of them.

Framing Decisions

As implied in the preceding section, the way in which a question is asked can influence our reasoning. Kahneman and Tversky (1982) refer to this effect as **framing.** Essentially, framing refers to steering the reasoning processes by increasing the availability or representativeness of the desired outcome. Subjects read information such as this:

> Imagine that the U.S. is preparing for the outbreak of an unusual Asian disease, which is expected to kill 600 people. Two alternative programs to combat the disease have been proposed. Assume that the exact scientific estimate of the consequences of the program are as follows:
> If Program A is adopted, 200 people will be saved.
> If Program B is adopted, there is a ⅓ probability that 600 people will be saved and a ⅔ probability that no people will be saved.

When asked which program they would pick, about 75% of the subjects chose Program A. They were then given this choice:

> If Program A is adopted, 400 people will die.
> If Program B is adopted, there is a ⅓ probability that nobody will die, and a ⅔ probability that 600 people will die.

In the latter choice, about 75% of the subjects favored Program B. In the first, the two-thirds probability that no people will be saved seems like a steep price to pay for the one-third probability (fairly low odds) of saving all the people. In contrast, 200 people saved seems like a tangible, solid, and beneficial result. In the second choice, the one-third probability that everyone can be saved looks like a long shot, but it seems better than ensuring the deaths of 400 people if Program A were adopted.

How Biases Influence Decision Making

Suppose you were given a statement such as, "Membership in a fraternity or sorority affects a student's likelihood of completing college in four years," and you were asked to indicate whether you thought the relationship between these variables was positive or negative. You might mentally record your own position on this matter. Now, suppose you had access to various facts. What numerical data would you have to know to accurately evaluate your position? We need to know four facts, and we can easily imagine laying out these four bits of data in a table that we call a 2 × 2 contingency table.

The numerical data should include the number of students who graduated in four years and who participated in the Greek system (let's call this cell "*A*" in the table), the number of students in the Greek system who did not graduate in four years (cell "*B*"), the number of independent students who did graduate in four years (cell "*C*"), and finally, the number of independent students who did not succeed in graduating in four years. Then, if you divide *A* by the sum of *A* + *B*, you get the percentage of Greek students who graduated in four years. Similarly, if you divide *C* by the sum of *C* + *D*, you get the percentage of independent students who got out in four years. If these two percentages are the same, then participating in a fraternity or sorority has no effect on the likelihood of on-time graduation. If the first percentage is greater than the second, we could argue that participating in a fraternity or sorority has a beneficial effect on graduation likelihood, whereas if the first percentage is less than the second, then we would say that participating in a fraternity or sorority might impair the chances of graduating in four years. Notice that to accurately evaluate your position, you need to have the data from all four cells before any argument becomes logically compelling: just knowing one percentage or the other really doesn't allow you to make any inferences about the relationship between the two variables. Because you need all four cells to compute the two percentages, technically and logically, each of the four cells is equally important mathematically. Levin, Kao, and Wasserman (1991) found, though, that people typically don't think each cell is equally important. For the problem given above, university students who thought that the relationship was positive felt that cell *A* was more important than cell *B*, which in turn was more important than cells *C* and *D*. The opposite was true for students who thought that the relationship was negative: these students thought cell *D* was more important than any of the other three. These findings demonstrate clearly the **confirmation bias** that is frequently seen in human reasoning. People often seek information that may confirm what they expect to be true. Thus, even without any explicit framing information, people seem to "self-frame." That is, prior to reasoning, they may access any a priori biases they may have; if such biases are present, they will color decisions and reasoning.

Summary of Natural Reasoning

In one sense, people apparently perform little better on everyday reasoning tasks than they do on formal reasoning tasks. When we look at people's ability to estimate probabilities, we see that they seem to rely on several rules of thumb, and more or less uncritically. People seem to think that if a person or event is representative of some category, then the likelihood is great that the person or event *is* a member of that category even though the base rate of such an event may be low. The representativeness heuristic produces errors when people fail to take base rates into account. People are also influenced by the ease with which some events can be computed. That which is easily computed and stored is thought to be more common than rare or unusual things. Generally, the Kahneman and Tversky findings can be interpreted as showing that people seem pretty insensitive to these biases; they are unaware that they have them. As a general finding, therefore, we might say that people are far from optimal reasoners when asked to reason formally, or to estimate the likelihood of outcomes (Wickens, 1984). This finding may seem discouraging, but we have to realize that using heuristics in reasoning

Focus on Research

Brain Activity During Reasoning

Throughout the book, we have set out to show the relationship between events at the neural level of analysis and events at the cognitive level. Through most of cognitive psychology's history, various cognitive functions, such as memory or language, have gradually yielded to analysis focusing on their underlying neural activity. One of the least yielding has been the relationship between the functions of rea-

soning and problem solving and brain activity. But in recent years, this picture has begun to change.

To see the relationship between specific kinds of reasoning and underlying neural processes, Prabhakaran, Smith, Desmond, Glover, and Gabrieli (1997) used a nonverbal reasoning test, the Raven Progressive Matrices (RPM) test. Figure 10.4 shows an example of the kinds of

Figure 10.4 Types of problem used in the Prabhakaran et al. experiment: (a) Match problem: Participants were instructed to select one of the eight response alternatives that matched the bottom-right pattern. (b) Figural problem, and (c) analytic problem: Participants were instructed to use the eight patterns in the upper array to determine which one of the eight response alternatives should appear in the bottom-right position. *Source:* From Prabhakaran et al., 1997.

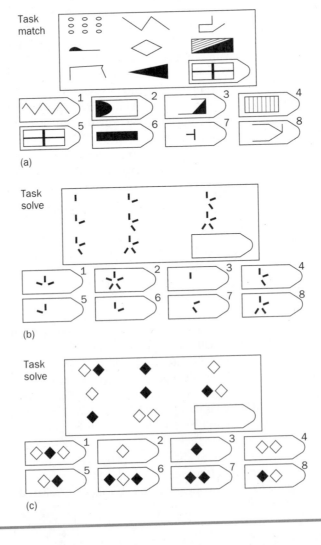

Focus on Research

problems you may encounter in the RPM. To solve the problems, you need to look at the eight patterns in the rectangle, and then pick out the one pattern from among the wedge-shaped boxes below that best completes the pattern established in the rectangle. Prabhakaran et al. chose three types of matrices in their task. In one type of task (labeled "match"), the subject's was perceptual scanning—all that was required was to find the pattern that matched the pattern in the rectangle. As we'll see, this task served as the basis of comparison for the two other tasks in the study. In the second task (under panel b), the subject had to engage in a kind of visual–spatial processing called figural processing. In the example, you'll see that in each column, one more line is added to each pattern. And looking across the rows, the same thing applies. The solver's task then consists of finding a pattern that has the right number of lines among the alternatives. The third task (under panel c) is the most complicated. Here the subject had to simultaneously analyze all the patterns in the rectangle, rather than a simple pairwise comparison such as that needed for the figural task. This third type of task was "analytic" processing.

The subjects were then placed inside a full-body MRI scanner, where they viewed the various problems, and where the researchers viewed the subjects' brains in action as they tried to figure out the answer. As expected, the analytic problems were more difficult than the others; the subjects were correct on 100% of the match problems, performing somewhat lower on the figural problems, and

finally getting only 74% of the analytic problems correct. This increase in difficulty was accompanied by dramatic increases in brain activity when the figural or analytic problems were attempted. When the subject was given the match problems, most of the increase in neural activity (compared to the brain's simple baseline activity) was concentrated in the occipital lobe, where visual stimuli are coded and processed. When subjects attempted the figural problems, brain activity increased greatly compared to that during the match problems. The activity increased only in the right hemisphere, but was quite widespread through all four lobes in the right hemisphere. Finally, when the analytic problems were attempted, brain activity increased even more compared to that occurring for the figural problems. The big story here is that, for the analytic problems, all the lobes except for the parietal lobe in the *left* hemisphere are involved in addition to all the lobes in the right hemisphere. This picture is really interesting: solving the analytic problems requires successive activity in various centers across your whole brain. One of the things that's interesting about this finding is that some of the centers involved in solving the analytic problems are active in verbal working-memory tasks. Does this mean that your brain "converts" the analytic problems into verbal representations to solve them? We don't have a definitive answer to that question, but, as we've seen for other cognitive functions, how things look to us, and how things look to our brains are often very different.

doesn't guarantee anything. A heuristic is a tool, or reasoning device, that has the advantages of simplicity and speed. This ease of use requires a price to be paid. Sometimes the heuristic produces a biased estimate, and people are usually unaware of this bias.

Concluding Comments and Suggestions for Further Reading

I think we can identify three themes in the literature on reasoning. The first is the tremendous difficulty in specifying the content of human knowledge. Thus, a very appropriate and seemingly answerable question such as "Are human beings logical or not?" becomes extremely difficult to answer in practice. On the one hand, we can sometimes give responses that are congruent with those of logicians, suggesting that people can assemble some basic cognitive processes in a logical way. Of course, as we've seen, people are also subject to innumerable biases in reasoning. Sure, cognitive scientists have gotten very good at naming biases in reasoning, at predicting when people are likely to fall victim to a bias, and when they may overcome one. But the bigger question remains. If humans can assemble logical operations sometimes, and sometimes override their biases in doing so, why can't they override their biases all the time? Human knowledge must be very strange if sometimes we have enough knowledge to chart a straight course in reasoning (assuming, that is, that the logical course is really "straight"), but sometimes we wander around pointlessly. A subtheme has to do with the question of strategies in reasoning. We saw that people sometimes devise strategies that may compensate for their inability to use "logical" processes. But, are different strategies really different? That is, do such strategies really involve different cognitive processes? If we can establish that some basic cognitive operations are used in reasoning, and that using different strategies involves assembling different components, then (I think) we will have met the requirement of "discontinuity" implied by the term *strategy*. We'll take this issue up again in Chapter 12.

The second theme is related to the first; the specificity or generality of the rules used in reasoning. The issue is this: Do we have general-purpose, "contentless" reasoning schemes that we can use in various situations? We did offer evidence to that effect. But what happens to such schemes? One possibility is that, as such general reasoning schemes continue to "inhabit" a reasoning task, the schemes eventually conform themselves to the idiosyncrasies in that task. To see how, suppose you give me a reasoning task that's unfamiliar to me. I analyze the task and call up what I think is the most appropriate general reasoning scheme. The next time I see this task, I'll be likely to call up this scheme again, and with repeated use in that task, the generality of the scheme gradually fades, replaced with specific reasoning schemes for dealing with problems of that specific sort. Thus my reasoning schemes could be said to "evolve" so that, as I work with them in specific tasks, they no longer resemble the general reasoning scheme that was their progenitor.

Many students find these topics among the most interesting in cognition, and fortunately, many excellent papers and books summarize this field in cognitive psychology. Rips (1990) has one of my favorite chapters for introducing the student to some issues in understanding reasoning. Kuhn (1989) treats the development of reasoning ability; her research deals with adults as well as children. Along these lines, Voss,

Perkins, and Segal (1991) discuss "reasoning skills," especially as such skills may be teachable in schools. Biases in reasoning are covered in detail in Evans (1989). A couple of very thorough, excellent textbooks are Evans, Newstead, and Byrne (1993) and Garnham and Oakhill (1994).

*K*ey Terms

Formal reasoning
Logic
Validity
Truth
Soundness
Conditional reasoning
Modus ponens
Modus tollens

Disconfirming the consequent
Thematic materials
Open scenario
Closed scenario
Pragmatic-reasoning schemas
Deontic reasoning
Extralogical inferences
Natural reasoning

Discounting
Alternative causes
Disabling conditions
Representativeness heuristic
Availability heuristic
Framing
Confirmation bias

CHAPTER 11

Concepts and Categories

*O*verview

Here's a simple episode that shows how complicated and rich our knowledge of the world is. The other day, on my way to get lunch, I passed by a trash can in the parking lot at a fast-food place that had the words "Thank you" embossed on its hinged lid. I didn't think anything about this remark. In the lot, though, was a large delivery van with a magnetically attached sign on its door reading, "Want to lose weight? Ask me for details." I was able to see some humor in this suggestion because, without apparent effort on my part, it seemed natural to shift the "me" reference to the truck because the driver wasn't around. How was my world knowledge involved in enabling this humor to arise? Here's a possible analysis. Clearly, the two messages have an intended context. That is, we can imagine that someone really is thankful if the trash can is used for its intended purpose, and we can similarly imagine that the van driver would be able to answer questions about weight-loss programs. In their intended contexts, neither message is at all funny; each is simply informative (although the trash can message is not very informative). Moreover, the trash can seems to be operating within its intended context, and perhaps that's why I paid no attention to it. But the missing driver suggests a context shift for the delivery van, and this (I think) is where the humor might arise. It's not necessarily the idea of a vehicle referring to itself that's funny, but that a large vehicle would refer to itself as expert in weight loss is sort of funny. In other words, the sign invites the rejoinder, "I don't think you're in any position to give advice." Notice that the humor seems to depart partially or completely depending on this kind of contextual analysis. If the sign were rewritten to read, "Ask driver for de-

tails," I don't think it would produce a context shift, and wouldn't be funny. Second, and sort of oddly, if the sign were stuck to a compact car or sports car, I think it wouldn't seem funny there, either.

What kind of world knowledge do we use to establish a context for, and thus interpret such statements and signs? The answer is surely multifaceted, involving at least the use of our memories and our knowledge about the owners' goals in both examples. But one part of that world knowledge that may not seem to be involved is our categorical knowledge. Once that knowledge has been applied, we have some idea about the object's range of action, and we may have expectations about its behavior. Thus, if I'm working in my garden at twilight, and I see from the corner of my eye a dark shape moving in the yard, I may devote some attention to trying to categorize it. It might be an opossum or a raccoon, which would inspire in me some caution; or it might be a rabbit, which might impel me to take some action to protect my plants from a nocturnal rabbit raid. Although I surely used other forms of world knowledge in finding the humor in the sign, it nevertheless does seem that something about my categorical knowledge was called into play. That is, because the sign's phrasing invited a self-reference to the truck, if I had not also categorized the truck as a "large and weighty thing," I doubt that I would have found the sign on its side at all funny.

In this chapter we see how much cognitive psychologists have learned about our concepts and our categories, and how those are organized. As we review the theoretical perspectives and research, I think you'll see how influential world knowledge and context are in making these kinds of categorical judgments.

Classical View of Concepts

Many of our concepts, especially the simpler ones, can be embodied or expressed linguistically, but our conceptual knowledge differs from our linguistic knowledge. To see this distinction, let's take the linguistic term "dog." Your definition of this term might well be an attempt to specify what it is that is both necessary and sufficient to qualify an object as a dog. That is, in trying to define "dog" in this way, you are trying to specify under just what conditions this term can and should not be used. Thus, if your friend gets a Saint Bernard or a Doberman for a pet, then you know he got a dog, because those objects qualify. But if he got a Himalayan, that's something else. Beyond your attempt to define the term in this way, you may have a great deal of knowledge from your own experience with dogs, but not all this knowledge, or perhaps any of it may come into play in your attempt to define the linguistic term. If you've ever been bitten by a dog, you may remember it, and thus know it, but you may not use this knowledge in defining "dog," because you may recognize that (1) not all dogs would bite, and (2) other things too could bite you. Thus "biting" does not really help you much in defining "dog," because it specifies nothing about dogs, although it may clearly be categorical knowledge that you would associate with dogs.

This distinction between conceptual and categorical knowledge on the one hand and linguistic knowledge on the other seems basic and natural to us. But the first cognitive psychologists to think about concepts and their structure would not have been so quick to make this distinction. Rather, their position on concepts and their structure held that definitional characteristics could be observed at the conceptual as well as the linguistic level. This is the essence of the "classical view" of concepts (Smith & Medin, 1981). According to such a view, our concept of a dog consists of exactly the knowledge that enables us to specify what it is about a dog that makes it a dog, and not something else. Consequently, if I were to show you a specimen of a creature that you had not seen before, you would be able to contact a package of knowledge that would enable you to determine that the creature is, or is not, a dog.

This position's intellectual history is traceable to its origins in the work of cognitive developmental psychologist Jean Piaget. From Piaget's perspective, children built conceptual structures by engaging in a kind of question-and-answer game with their parents and caretakers. Thus a child who sees a flying creature and uses the word "bird" to describe it is actually producing a hypothesis about what it is that makes a bird a bird. If the flying object really is a bird, the child's vocal hypothesis may be confirmed by the caregivers. But if the creature is a butterfly and not a bird, then the child may be corrected by the caregivers, and the child must revise his or her concept. Children proceed in this way until they arrive at the definitional or criterial elements that make a monarch a butterfly and not a bird, and make a blue jay a bird and not a baseball player.

Artificial Concepts

The classical position has several essential elements. One is that our conceptual and categorical knowledge is definitional and criterial: Our categorical knowledge should enable us to take each object that we encounter in nature, determine its features, and then use those features to accurately put that object in its appropriate mental slot. A second element is the cognitive system's ability to engage in the kind of hypothesis testing that is necessary to determine which features are indeed criterial in the first place. We've seen that the hypothetical child finds out soon enough that simply being able to fly does not make an object a bird, but all that really tells the child is that flying is not criterial for determining that an object is a member of the bird category. The classical view maintains that the child has the ability to determine which features are in fact criterial.

How would we go about determining the correctness of the classical view? The approach taken by Bruner, Goodnow, and Austin (1956) clearly extended the Piagetian position on concepts. In their study, subjects saw a set of eighty-one cards, as shown in Figure 11.1. The cards had four dimensions, and each dimension had three values, or levels. Shape was one dimension; its three values were circle, cross, or square. Color was another dimension (values: red, black, green). Border number was the third dimension (values: 1, 2, or 3). Object number was the final dimension; its values were also 1, 2, or 3. The set of cards could be used as a "universe" in which a number of specific concepts could be embodied. Each concept was expressed as a rule. If a card conformed to the rule, then that card was a member of the category. If a card did not conform to the rule, then it was out of the concept, or not in the category. The subject's task was to determine the rule, which would enable him or her to then categorize all the cards as either in or out of the concept.

Several types of rules were used in the study; among them were single-value concepts, which specified that all cards having one particular value of one specific dimension were in the concept. A rule specifying all green cards is a single-value concept. Somewhat more difficult for the subjects were the *conjunctive* concepts. These rules specified the concept as having one value on one dimension *and* one value on some other dimension (e.g., green crosses). More difficult were the *disjunctive* concepts—rules specifying that the concept had one value of one dimension or one value of some other dimension. Thus if a card had either a green symbol of any type, or a cross of any color, then it was a member of the category.

The stimuli were presented to the subjects in one of two ways. In the **reception paradigm,** the subjects were shown one card and were asked to state whether or not it was in the concept. The experimenter then informed the subjects that the response was correct or incorrect. In the other procedure, the **selection paradigm,** the entire set of eighty-one cards was on view, and the subjects each selected a card, stating whether or not it was in the concept. Following the selection and judgment, the experimenter informed the subjects about the correctness of the response.

The Bruner et al. study is perhaps best known for discovering the strategies that subjects used in the reception and selection paradigms. In the reception paradigm, two strategies were recorded:

1. Wholist strategy. The subject using this strategy attempted to remember all the attributes common to instances in which the experimenter gave the response "Correct." Everything else was to be ignored. This is an elimination method, because it eliminates attributes that are not part of a positive instance.

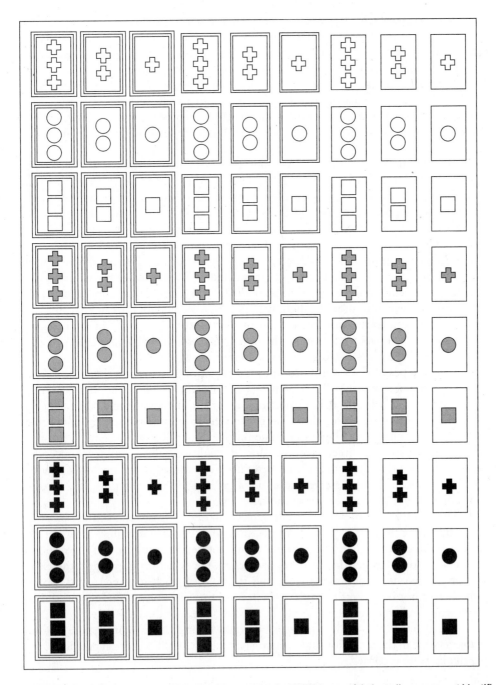

Figure 11.1   Material used by Bruner, Goodnow, and Austin (1956) in one of their studies on concept identification. The array consists of instances of combinations of four attributes, each exhibiting three values. *Source:* Copyright 1957 by John Wiley & Sons, Inc. Adapted by permission of the publisher and author.

2. Partist strategy. Subjects using the second strategy focused on one hypothesis at a time (color green = yes), kept the hypothesis if it correctly predicted that a card was in the category, or formed a new hypothesis if the hypothesis was not correct in its prediction.

These strategies are shown in Table 11.1. Of these two strategies, the wholist strategy is the optimal one and was used more or less by 65% of the subjects. This example shows the wholist strategy in operation. Suppose the first card the subject sees is

two borders, two red squares

Assume that the subject is trying to determine a conjunctive rule. Assume also that the subject correctly guesses that this card is in the concept. This card then becomes the

---

Table 11.1   Strategies in Concept Learning

When subjects are presented a series of instances selected from those shown and told whether each is a positive or negative instance, they may adopt one of these strategies or a combination.

Wholist Strategy

Take the first positive instance and retain all the positive attributes as the initial hypothesis. Then, as more instances are presented, eliminate any attribute in this set that does not occur with a positive instance.

	Positive Instance	Negative Instance
Confirming	Maintain the hypothesis now in force.	Maintain the hypothesis now in force.
Infirming	Take as the next hypothesis what the old hypothesis and the present instance have in common.	Impossible unless one has misreckoned. If one has misreckoned, correct from memory of past instances and present hypothesis.

Partist Strategy

Begin with part of the first positive instance as a hypothesis (for example, choose just one attribute). Then retain or change it in this way.

	Positive Instance	Negative Instance
Confirming	Maintain hypothesis now in force.	Maintain hypothesis now in force.
Infirming	Change hypothesis to make it consistent with past instances; that is, choose a hypothesis not previously infirmed.	Change hypothesis to make it consistent with past instances; that is, choose a hypothesis not previously infirmed.

Source: From Bruner, Goodnow, and Austin, 1956.

initial positive instance. The subject now attempts to encode all its features, which this time are two border lines, two objects, red colors, and square shapes. Suppose the subject is next given the card

one border, one red square

In this example, the subject would judge that this card is not in the concept. If the subject is informed that the response is correct, then the current hypothesis is maintained. If the subject is told that the response is incorrect; that is, that the second card *is* in the concept, then the subject makes up a new hypothesis based on whatever the old hypothesis and the current card have in common, namely

red squares

The wholist strategy is the optimal one for the reception paradigm because it puts a minimal load on memory. The subject has only the current hypothesis to remember. Thus the wholist strategy is easy to use because the only time the subjects must take action is when they guess incorrectly.

Bruner et al. also discovered that subjects use a number of strategies in the selection paradigm. They described four possible strategies:

1. Simultaneous scanning. Here the subject begins with all possible hypotheses and eliminates the untenable ones after feedback from each instance.

2. Successive scanning. To use this strategy, the subject begins with just one hypothesis, which is kept if it correctly predicts concept membership, and discarded if it does not.

3. Conservative focusing. Here the subject guesses until hitting upon a card that was correctly hypothesized as in the concept. Then the subject selects subsequent cards that change only one attribute at a time from this initial positive instance.

4. Focus gambling. Here the subject guesses until hitting upon a card that was correctly hypothesized as in the concept. Unlike the solver who uses conservative focusing, however, the gambler now selects subsequent cards in which more than one attribute is altered from the initial positive instance.

Let's consider only the focusing strategies in this discussion. Once again, let's assume that the subject is working on a conjunctive rule. Suppose the subject picks the card

three red circles and three borders

and correctly guesses that it is in the concept. The subject using the conservative-focusing strategy will not attempt to find out which dimensions are the relevant ones, and which are irrelevant. Suppose the subject now selects

two red circles and three borders

Notice that this selection represents a change in only one attribute from the preceding card that was identified as a member of the concept. The subject who finds that this card too is in the concept then can infer that the number of shapes is not a relevant dimension in this rule, because when shapes were changed from two to three, the card was still considered a member of the concept. Thus the solver can stop worrying about the number of objects and can begin to concentrate on finding out about the remaining three dimensions. On the other hand, the subject who discovers that this second card is not in the concept then can infer that the number of shapes on the card is relevant in the concept. Either way, the solver using a conservative-focusing strategy is in a position to determine something conclusive about the status of at least one of the dimensions.

As stated above, the focus gambler changes more than one dimension after finding the initial positive trial. Suppose a subject made the same initial selection as did the preceding subject. Using the focus-gambling strategy, the subject might now select

two black circles and three borders

If this trial is positive, the subject is in a position to eliminate two dimensions (number of objects and color of objects) in one trial. Can you see why? If you change both the number from three to two, and the color from red to black, and your card is still in the concept, then you can infer that neither of the changed dimensions, number or color, is relevant in the concept. Thus, you can now focus on the two remaining dimensions. A gamble is involved in changing more than one dimension at a time, however. If the guess above is negative—that is, the solver finds out that the two-black-circles card is not in the concept—then the solver must back up to figure out which of the two changed dimensions is relevant. It's also possible that both of the changed dimensions are relevant. Thus the subject may have to spend the next two trials clarifying the status of the changed dimensions, in addition to the one that was spent gambling. Ultimately, this approach may require more trials than would have been required if the subject had stuck to the conservative-focusing strategy.

Let's summarize the information about strategies. The scanning strategies in the selection paradigm are similar to the partist strategy in the reception paradigm in that both impose a fairly heavy load on the subject's memory. For that reason, focusing strategies are usually more efficient and most subjects eventually settled on conservative focusing as their preferred approach for determining conjunctive concepts.

Critique of the Classical Position

The work by Bruner et al. and the numerous studies that it spawned can certainly be understood as demonstrating that naive human beings can come into a cognitive psychology laboratory and learn to make subtle differentiations among the elements in a set of highly artificial and arbitrary stimuli. This realization amounts to a "sufficiency analysis" for the underlying Piagetian position on concepts. A sufficiency analysis shows simply that something can be done; it doesn't necessarily prove how it is done. Piaget's position stipulates that people can learn an underlying conceptual structure from their confirmatory and disconfirmatory experiences with stimuli in the real world. Thus, according to the Bruner et al. interpretation, concepts could be acquired in the real world in the same way as their subjects acquired the artificial concepts in the lab; namely, by strategically driven hypothesis tests, over which inferences can be logically drawn. We need to review several points here.

First, it's interesting that the subjects were able to select cards that seemed to be excellent choices for making inferences about the specific form of the rule that determined the concept's boundary. This finding is, however, somewhat at odds with the literature we reviewed in Chapter 10. When we examined the literature on conditional reasoning, we saw numerous studies suggesting that people are not particularly good at making valid inferences about abstract and artificial materials. Those findings suggest a contradiction that would require some resolution.

Second, a sufficiency analysis can be criticized for at least a couple of reasons. First is the problem of specifying how something is accomplished. Bruner et al. suggest that people use a fairly sophisticated hypothesis-testing strategy to acquire their conceptual knowledge. Even assuming that they could sometimes do so, have we any reason to believe that all our conceptual knowledge could be acquired by strategic hypothesis testing? Think back to the anecdote at the beginning of this chapter. Do you see any evidence to suggest that I used a hypothesis-testing strategy to construct a concept for "large and weighty" objects? The existence of such a strategy becomes even more problematic when you begin to think about what good it might do us to have a category for large and weighty objects. I can tell you that I cannot now consciously retrieve any situation in my life in which I thought forming such a category would do me any good. It's not the existence of such ad hoc, or temporary categories that I'm attacking. In fact, later in this chapter we'll see that people form such goal-driven categories in lots of situations, and they do so with relative ease. The basis of the criticism here is how strategy is used in forming such categories.

Finally, a sufficiency analysis can be criticized for its content. In the Bruner et al. study, the materials consisted of artificial concepts defined by abstract rules and cards. By definition, these concepts exist nowhere in nature. Thus these concepts did not refer to anything familiar to the subjects, nor did the materials mean anything to them. But natural categories such as "bird" or "car" do exist in nature, and they refer to things with which the subject is familiar. Thus we must question the correspondence between the artificial concepts used in the Bruner et al. study and our everyday, real-world concepts.

From Laboratory Concepts to Real-World Concepts

Fuzzy Borders and Unclear Cases

Medin (1984; Medin & Smith, 1989) has discussed several important differences between artificial and natural concepts. One of these variations is the division between category members and noncategory members. According to the classical view, and critical in the Bruner et al. study is the idea that an object is either clearly in, or clearly not in the concept. Thus, if the concept was "two red squares" in the Bruner study, it would be a simple matter to determine if it was in or out of the concept. But in the real world, we must make allowances for cases that are "sort of" in a category, and "sort of" not. Medin (1989) invites us to think about a rug as a member of the category "furniture." Rugs may not seem like furniture, in the sense that tables and chairs clearly are, but if rugs are not furniture, then what are they? Or how about this one: A long time ago, my brother owned a vehicle known as an El Camino. Kiddingly, I used to give him a hard time about owning a vehicle that had the worst features of both a car and a pickup truck. Like the rug that was "sort of" a piece of furniture, the El Camino was sort of a car, and sort of a pickup truck too. These unclear examples (and I'm sure you can think of others in almost any category you can think of) suggest that we should modify our view of a concept's boundaries and divisions. Rather than thinking of a category as bound by a rigid rule that clearly separates members from nonmembers, it may be more helpful to think of natural categories as having an indistinct or "fuzzy" border (Rosch, 1973).

A study by Sokal (1977) illustrates how fuzzy boundaries operate in natural categories. Three experts (an entomologist and two paleontologists) created a taxonomy, or categorical structure for the imaginary animals shown in Figure 11.2. Although

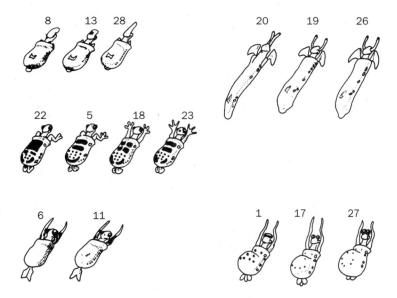

Figure 11.2 Caminalcules, imaginary animals created by J. H. Camin, illustrate individual differences in taxonomic judgment. Three taxonomists were asked to group the organisms by their similarities. Taxonomists A and C thought 13 was more similar to 8, but B placed it closer to 28. All three taxonomists thought 6 was most similar to 11. Whereas taxonomist C placed 5 and 18 together, taxonomist A grouped 5 with 22, and 18 with 23, and B did not form a close group with any of these Caminalcules. Taxonomist A thought 17 was most similar to 1, C held it most similar to 27, and B described the three organisms as equally similar. Taxonomists A and C recorded 19 most similar to 26, but B considered it closer to 20. By multiple regression of the similarities implied by the taxonomists on 112 objectively defined criteria differentiating the twenty-nine animals, the relative importance of various criteria in judging taxonomic similarity can be inferred. The judgments by persons A and C were more similar to each other than either was to B; most dissimilar were B and C. Table 11.2 shows which features of the organisms appeared important to each of the three taxonomists. No one feature was important to all three persons. *Source:* From Sokal, 1974.

these experts mostly agreed on each animal's classification, important differences arose about which features or aspects of the creature determined its classification. No one feature determined classification status, and the "weight" given to different aspects of the creatures varied for each of the experts. These effects are shown in Table 11.2. Of course the Caminalcules are not real creatures; nevertheless, Medin's (1989) point is good. If the Caminalcules could be real, we'll find no hard and fast divisions between members of the subcategories.

Criterial Features and Family Resemblance

According to the classical position, concepts and categories are defined by criterial features. A criterial feature is an aspect of a concept that is necessary or sufficient to categorize a specific example as a member of the category. In all the experiments done in the tradition of the classical position, the artificial concepts had this property. Medin (1989) points out, however, that natural categories do not have this property. Natural categories therefore have no features that must be present (any specific feature could be missing, and the example might still belong to a category), nor are any specific fea-

Table 11.2 Features of Caminalcules That Appeared Important to Three Taxonomists[a]

	Taxonomists		
Feature of Caminalcules	*A*	*B*	*C*
Horns on head		+	
Stalked eyes	+		+
Groove in neck		+	
Anterior appendage			
Length	+		+
Flexion		+	
Subdivision	+		
Bulb		+	
Posterior appendage			
Disklike	+		+
Platelike	+		
Anterior abdomen spots			+
Posterior abdomen bars	+	+	
Abdomen			
Width	+		
Large pores	+		+
Small pores		+	

[a]A plus sign indicates a feature that the taxonomist considered important.
Source: From Sokal, 1977.

tures sufficient. That is, natural categories have no feature guaranteeing that a specific example will be categorized in a specific way.

That natural categories are not marked by criterial features raises a question about their organization. Here cognitive psychologists have built on work by the philosopher Ludwig Wittgenstein (1953), who argued that natural concepts and categories exhibit a property he called "family resemblance." Like members of an extended family who physically resemble each other, the specific elements in a category share features that seem to co-occur. You may have your grandfather's nose and your great-aunt's earlobes, your sister may have your uncle's eyes, and both of you may have your dad's forehead. No one facial feature is essential, or even shared among all family members.

If you think about a natural category, you may see the principle of family resemblance in operation. Here's one I like to give my students: What is a "sport"? As we work through this question in class, we find some of the shared features. A sport is an activity that at least had its origins in recreation. Sports tend to be competitive events, and the participants tend to be athletes. Frequently, a ball is involved in the conduct of the sport. Thus, my students are able to name a number of specific examples such as "basketball," "football," "mountain climbing," and "golf" as sports. The point here is that each of these four examples seems to have nothing specific in common with the other three (or at least I can't think of anything).

Family resemblance has an interesting function in classifying or sorting tasks done in the laboratory. As the examples above suggest, it seems clear that people are sensitive to, and respond to, pools of weakly or strongly correlated features that are shared among the specific examples in a category. But when sorting specific, novel examples, people do not typically behave as though they were constructing their categories on family resemblances. Rather, people are most likely to take all the stimuli and simply divide them into two exclusive categories according to one dimension. Medin, Wattenmaker, and Hampson (1987) had their subjects sort novel animals that varied in such dimensions as shape of head, number of legs, body markings, and length of tail. Sorting for family resemblance would have involved using each of these dimensions. But not one subject chose family resemblance to sort the creatures into their most natural categories. Instead, they took only one dimension, such as spotted versus striped markings, to make their sorts. And this pattern of behavior has been observed in numerous studies (e.g., Ahn & Medin, 1992; Regehr & Brooks, 1995). Going back to the extended-family example, if we were to relate this sorting strategy to the extended-family members, it would be like putting all who had grandfather's nose into one category, and anybody who didn't have his nose into another. As you can see, such a scheme ignores that which we would know to be true about family resemblance; namely, that the people who were sorted together for only one dimension may actually be more different than alike for all other dimensions. Here then is our first question about family resemblance: If we see that natural categories are marked by a family-resemblance principle, then why don't people behave in that way when they are asked to sort novel examples? The answer may lie in the demands placed on individuals prior to sorting the novel stimuli, the approach taken by Lassaline and Murphy (1996). Their subjects read descriptions of twenty animals that had a categorical structure, shown in Table 11.3. The "exemplar" column applies to the twenty

Table 11.3   Stimulus Structure Used in Experiments 1 and 2

Exemplar	Feature							
	A	B	C	D	E	F	G	H
Category 1								
1	1	1	1	—	—	1	1	—
2	1	1	—	1	—	1	0	—
3	1	—	1	1	—	0	1	—
4	—	1	1	1	—	0	0	—
5	1	1	—	—	1	1	1	—
6	1	—	1	—	1	1	0	—
7	—	1	1	—	1	—	0	1
8	1	—	—	1	1	—	1	0
9	—	1	—	1	1	—	1	1
10	—	1	—	1	1	—	0	0
Category 2								
11	0	0	0	—	—	1	1	—
12	0	0	—	0	—	1	0	—
13	0	—	0	0	—	0	1	—
14	—	0	0	0	—	0	0	—
15	0	0	—	—	0	1	1	—
16	0	—	0	—	0	1	0	—
17	—	0	0	—	0	—	0	1
18	0	—	—	0	0	—	1	0
19	—	0	—	0	0	—	1	1
20	—	0	—	0	0	—	0	0

Note: Features A–E are relevant for family-resemblance categorization; features F–H are irrelevant. The two possible values of each attribute are represented by 0 and 1. Absence of an attribute is represented by a hyphen.
Source: From Lassaline and Murphy, 1996.

animals. The letter designates a specific feature of the animal: A might refer to "teeth," a "1" designates one value of that feature (such as "sharp teeth") and a "0" designates the only other value that the feature could take on ("flat teeth"). A dash means that the description of the creature did not mention either value in that dimension. If feature B refers to a creature's tail length, then exemplar 3 would not mention whether the animal's tail was long or short. As you can see, two categories clearly are embedded in the twenty examples, and these two categories can be defined by a family-resemblance principle. Each of ten examples in category 1 is defined by the presence of a value on three of the five dimensions from A to E, and each of the ten examples in category 2 is defined similarly, except that the value is "opposite" to that in category 1. If category 1 animals had sharp teeth and long tails, then category 2 animals had flat teeth and short tails (among other things). Notice feature G, which is completely uncorrelated with the family-resemblance principle because there are just as many 1s

Table 11.4   Sorting as a Function of Question Condition

Type of Sort	Experiment 1 Question Condition		
	Induction	*Frequency*	*None*
Family-resemblance sort (%)	54	17	19
Undimensional sort (%)	21	50	52
Other sort (%)	25	33	29
Mean deviation from family-resemblance sort	4.17	7.00	7.52

Source: From Lassaline and Murphy, 1996.

and 0s in category 1 on feature G as in category 2 (namely, five 1s and five 0s in each category). A subject who used feature G to categorize animals clearly is not using the family-resemblance principle. Feature G, however, is the only one for which we know the value for each of the twenty animals, and so a subject who used only one dimension to sort the animals might wish to focus on feature G.

Before the subjects did the sorting task, Lassaline and Murphy asked them to do one of two preliminary tasks. After one group of subjects looked at each of the animals once, they were asked questions such as, "If an animal has a long tail, what kind of teeth does it have?" Notice that this series of questions essentially asks the subject to make an inductive inference about the population of animals. A second group saw the animals' descriptions once, but they were asked different questions, such as, "How many animals had a long tail?" This question does not invite the subject to make inductive inferences about the relationship among the animals' properties. Questions such as these focus the subjects' attention on the frequency with which specific properties were observed. Finally, the control group saw the animals once, and then went directly to the sorting task.

The results of this study are shown in Table 11.4. As you can see, subjects who responded to the "frequency" instructions were essentially no different in their sorting than the subjects in the baseline condition (this is the group under the heading "None" in the table). But the subjects who responded to the induction questions behaved quite differently, most of them using the family-resemblance principle to sort the animals. These findings are interesting for several reasons. First, they offer a solution to an empirical puzzle: If our natural concepts seem to be based on family resemblances, then why don't people use family-resemblance principles when they sort novel stimuli into categories? The answer taking shape is that the family-resemblance structure seems to happen only when people engage in a specific kind of "work" before sorting. Without that work, people are much more likely to take the easy way out and sort for one dimension, a strategy that requires little cognitive effort. Second, these findings are our first intimation that the categorical structure people acquire may be highly influenced by the activities they do in forming the categorical structure in the first place. We'll follow up on this idea later in the chapter.

Centrality and Prototypes

One major difference between natural and artificial categories is that natural categories exhibit a property called **centrality** and artificial categories do not. Centrality in natural categories is the idea that some category members seem to be "better" examples of that category than others. To see the contrast between this and the situation in artificial concepts, think back to the Bruner et al. study. Consider the conjunctive concept *black squares*. Any card with a black square on it would be in the concept, and all such cards would be equally good members of the concept. Not all members of a natural category, though, seem to be equally good members of that category. Which creature seems more birdlike to you, a robin or an ostrich? Effects like these are extensively documented in classic work by Rosch and her colleagues (Rosch, 1973, 1975, 1977; Rosch & Mervis, 1975). Rosch (1975) presented to her subjects several lists of words referring to objects that shared category membership. The subjects rated each example on a 1 to 7 scale, with 1 designating a "better" example of the category than 7. The subjects showed a reasonable degree of consensus in each category; the ratings for the category "fruit" are shown in Table 11.5. These findings seem to suggest that people see oranges and apples as more fruitlike than coconuts and avocados.

From findings such as these, Rosch argued that our natural categories have an internal structure, an extension of the family-resemblance principle. Family resemblance suggests that categories are formed around a pool of specific features that seem to be correlated. Even though this correlation may not be perfect, people are nevertheless

Table 11.5   Goodness-of-Example Ratings for Fruits

Member	Rank	Specific Score[a]	Member	Rank	Specific Score[a]
Orange	1	1.07	Lemon	20	2.16
Apple	2	1.08	Watermelon	23	2.39
Banana	3	1.15	Cantaloupe	24	2.44
Peach	4	1.17	Lime	25	2.45
Apricot	6.5	1.36	Papaya	27	2.58
Tangerine	6.5	1.36	Fig	29	2.86
Plum	8	1.37	Mango	30	2.88
Grapes	9	1.38	Pomegranate	32	3.05
Strawberry	11	1.61	Date	37	3.35
Grapefruit	12	1.77	Raisin	39	3.42
Cherry	14	1.86	Persimmon	41	3.63
Pineapple	15	1.99	Coconut	43	4.50
Blackberry	16	2.05	Avocado	44	5.37
Raspberry	19	2.15	Tomato	46	5.58

[a]1 means highly typical; 7 means least typical.
Source: From Rosch, 1975.

sensitive to this relationship of one feature to another, and they can use such relationships to make predictions about the likelihood that other features will co-occur with any specific feature. As you probably can tell from Table 11.4, some category members simply have more of these features from the pool. According to this view, oranges and apples receive their high goodness ratings because they have more of the features being used to form the category. Rosch named the member of any category that has more of the features than any other member the **prototype** for that category.

The prototype occupies a special position in a category according to Rosch's position because it is the "center" of that category. Thus, the orange is the center of the fruits category, and is the prototype of a fruit. It is the prototype that gives any category we are considering its mental coherence, because mental coherence depends on the number of featural differences between the specific members of the category and the category's prototype. Here's how we might visualize our conceptual structure, using Rosch's theory as a guide. Imagine that your conceptual domain is a landscape, marked by hills rising above a plain. Each hill in this landscape indicates a specific category. At the top of this hill, and most salient, is the prototype of that category. Lower down on each hill are less feature-laden category members. The farther down the hill you go, with greater and greater distance from the prototype, the less "good" that specific example is. Finally, you may arrive at the fuzzy border itself, on the floor of the plain. There, people may or may not judge the specific example to be a member of the category. From Rosch's perspective, the prototype is therefore "summary representation" of the concept (Medin, 1989).

Here are some additional implications. We would expect the prototype and other central members of the category to be more readily accessible than would distant or peripheral members. Rosch (1973) examined this possibility in a study in which both children and adults responded to such questions as "Is a _____ fruit?" The blank was sometimes filled in with a central member of the fruit category; in other blanks, a peripheral member appeared. If the central members are more accessible than the peripheral members, we would expect the central members to be verified more quickly. Figure 11.3 shows the findings of the study. As you can see, Rosch's predictions were supported. A moderate effect of peripheral category members appears for adults, but for children this effect is particularly dramatic, and suggests that a category's coherence is developmental.

Hierarchic Structure and the Basic Level

We've been talking about the category "fruit" and its examples. We realize, however, that we can take the category "fruit" and use it as an example rather than a category at a more general, less specific level of organization. From this perspective, "fruit" becomes a specific example in the more general category "food." Figure 11.4 shows the relationship among several levels of categorization. We refer to categories in the intermediate zone in these hierarchies as being at the **basic level** of categorization (Lassaline, Wisniewski, & Medin, 1992). Higher levels are referred to as **superordinate levels** of categorization, and levels of categorization that are more specific than the basic level are **subordinate levels** of categorization. The basic level of categorization has a number of interesting properties that we explore in this section.

Figure 11.3 Reaction times for correctly answered sentences about central-category and peripheral-category members. *Source:* Copyright 1975 by Academic Press, Inc. Adapted by permission of the publisher and author.

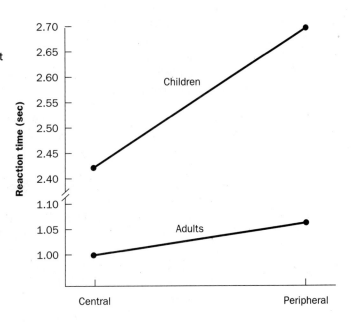

Figure 11.4 Category Hierarchies. Nearly all categories have a built-in hierarchic structure—categories within categories within categories. Most objects, such as that shown to the left, fit nicely into several of these natural-category levels. But when people refer to an object during normal conversation, they tend to use its intermediate, or *basic-level,* category label. They call this object a cat rather than a living thing, an animal, or an 18-year-old Siamese cat who likes salmon. *Source:* From Nairne, 1997.

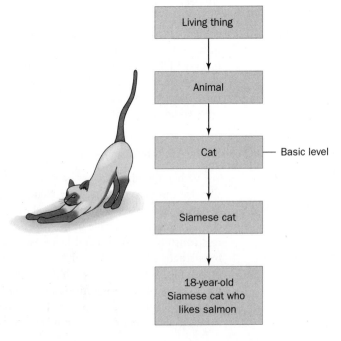

First, we might describe the basic level as including "most information for lowest cost." Here's an example based on one appearing in Markman and Wisniewski (1997): Suppose I tell you about an object on my desk at home that is rectangular, weighs a pound, has a hard cover, includes pages of printed text, and relates the events in a fictional murder. How would you categorize this object? Did you think of it as a "book"? I'm not too surprised. You could have categorized the object as a member of a more general category called "reading material," which includes magazines, newspapers, letters, postcards, greeting cards, and so on. But using a general label such as "reading material" doesn't tell anyone much about the object; thus, even though it's not wrong to label the object in that way, it's not very informative, either. On the other hand, you could have categorized the object as a "British murder mystery involving a well-known fictional detective who has appeared in several of this author's works." Notice that this statement is informative, in that it is narrow, but at a cost. First, it's effortful to code all that information onto language in the first place. Second, a lengthy coding such as that one imposes a memory burden on the categorizer. Call it a book, and you have a label that differentiates the object most, relative to the rather small computational load in coding and memory.

In other words, basic-level categorizing maximizes both informativeness and distinctiveness (Murphy, 1991). The greater a concept's specificity the more information it holds. A subordinate category such as "coffee-table book" is more specific and therefore more informative than the basic-level category "book." Within the category "coffee-table book," however, the specific cases may be rather similar to each other: A coffee-table book dealing with "art" might have quite a bit in common with a coffee-table book dealing with "architecture." In that sense, their commonality means that these subordinate levels of categorization differ little, and so are low in distinctiveness. The basic level of categorization is relatively high in both informativeness and distinctiveness—not as informative as the subordinate level, but more distinctive. Conversely, the basic level is not as distinctive as the superordinate level ("reading material" is quite different from other categories at that level), but the basic level is more informative.

Ample evidence documents that the basic level of categorization is privileged, or has special properties. It's been known for some time that pictures of isolated objects are categorized faster at the basic level than they are at other levels (e.g., Murphy & Wisniewski, 1989). Further, basic-level terms predominate in adult discourse, at least compared to superordinate categories (Wisniewski & Murphy, 1989). Children acquire basic-level terms more readily than they do other levels (Horton & Markman, 1980), and evidence also shows that different cultures use the same basic-level terms, as least for some things.

"Parts" of a Category—Does the Basic Level Require Them? Despite this agreement on many issues, cognitive psychologists have strenuously debated the structure, content, and operation of concepts at the basic level (Murphy, 1991; Tversky & Hemenway, 1991). One debate has focused on how "parts" or sometimes attributes, function at the basic level (Tversky & Hemenway, 1984). Parts are perceptually distinct segments that make up an object; a chair has a seat, a back, legs, and so on. When individuals are asked to list parts of a concept, the number of parts they list depends on the level of categorizing. When individuals are asked to list all parts in a superordinate concept, they list rather few, but when asked to list all the parts they can for a basic-level category, the number of parts listed goes up dramatically. When the concept is moved to the subordinate level, the number of parts goes up again, but only a little. The basic levels of categorization thus have lots of parts compared to higher levels. In the parts lists themselves, the subordinate levels show many of the same parts, but the basic levels show different lists of parts. That is, the parts themselves overlap very little at the basic level. Let's consider an example: Both basic-level categories "sailboat" and "bicycle" have lots of parts, but right now, I can't think of one part that my sailboat and my bicycle have in common. Tversky and Hemenway's (1984) conclusion is that "the natural breaks among basic-level categories are between clusters of parts." To examine this position in greater detail, Murphy (1991) created artificial categories using the examples and organization shown in Figure 11.5. This organization is an attempt to discover all we know to be true about natural categories in a set of artificial stimuli. At the highest level, the categories are not very informative. All you know about a NOP is that it's blue or yellow, and that's not saying much, is it? At the middle level are quite a few clusters of features, again similar to natural categories. Finally, at the bottom level in each category are the most specific, hence most informative examples. But these specific elements are not very distinct from each other, making them like the subordinate level in natural categories. A PIM and a HOB could both be blue, have squares, and have a solid, wavy edge. The only difference between them is that a PIM is large and a HOB is small.

Another characteristic in this set of stimuli is important: Murphy deliberately created stimuli that do not seem to consist of "parts" of things that have been put together. Now it's true that the stimuli have edges, and the edges may seem like a "part" of the stimulus. But the edges themselves differ in that they are wavy or jagged or straight, and these characteristics do not seem like a "part" of the edge (at least not in the same way as a mast seems clearly part of a sailboat). To verify that these categories do not have parts that might cluster at the middle, basic level of categorization, Murphy asked judges to list the parts they saw in the stimuli, and then defend their judgments. The finding was that, indeed, the judges perceived these stimuli as made up of very few parts, and moreover the number of parts was not markedly different in going from superordinate down to subordinate levels of categorization.

Let's think about the implication: If we give people natural categories and ask them to list the parts, we find they can produce longer lists of parts for objects that were given at the basic level of categorization than at the superordinate level. I could create a much longer list of parts for a "sailboat" (basic level) than I could for a "transportation vehicle" (superordinate level). Theoretically, this difference creates the advantage in informativeness for the basic level of categorization. Moreover, we find that the list of parts for different basic-level categories is itself different, unlike the list of parts for subordinate-level categories, which is similar. This difference creates the distinctiveness advantage for the basic level.

And now we arrive at this question: What would you expect to happen if you asked people about the informativeness and distinctiveness of the stimuli Murphy created, even though they apparently do not consist of parts? The theoretical answer is that, under those conditions, the basic-level categories should show no advantage in informativeness or distinctiveness compared to the superordinate or subordinate

Figure 11.5 Examples of stimuli and names and hierarchic structure of categories used in Murphy's experiment. *Source:* From Murphy, 1991.

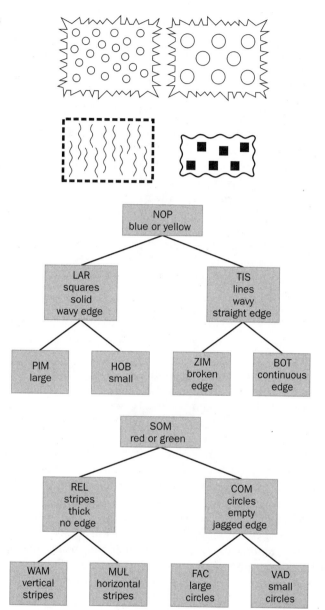

categories. If the basic-level categories still do show such advantages, however, that finding suggests that having separable parts is not essential to produce the basic level's special effects. Murphy's subjects compared the artificial stimuli for similarity and dissimilarity and found that, unlike the result we might expect theoretically because of their parts, stimuli compared at the basic level still showed higher levels of informativeness and distinctiveness combined, in relation to stimuli compared at either the superordinate or subordinate levels. This finding suggests that subjects do not need to perceive a set of common parts for categories to show the basic-level effects. This conclusion has not met with universal agreement (see, e.g., Tversky & Hemenway, 1991), but regardless of how it turns out, it's sure to be an interesting topic in the years ahead.

Basic, Superordinate, and Subordinate Categories—What's the Difference?

We've seen that basic-level categories differ from both superordinate and subordinate categories in their informativeness and distinctiveness. The combination of informativeness and distinctiveness differences at the basic level is referred to as **differentiation.** We can say that the basic level is highly differentiated compared to the superordinate and subordinate levels because categories at the basic level maintain the high information value of the subordinate level, and, simultaneously, the high distinctiveness of the superordinate level. Turning this statement around somewhat, in some ways the basic level of categorization is similar to the subordinate level (because both levels are informative); in other ways the basic level is similar to the superordinate (because both levels are distinctive).

Several researchers have wondered about the basis for these judgments of similarity. Let's consider what happens when we attempt to judge how similar two things are. According to an influential view (Markman & Gentner, 1996; Medin, Goldstone, & Gentner, 1993), we arrive at several conclusions when we compare things. Not necessarily in chronological order, we become mindful of the **commonalities** between the two objects or categories. We may also become aware of **alignable differences** as well as **nonalignable differences.** A commonality is a feature, part, or attribute that two things share. An alignable difference is based on a commonality; a nonalignable difference is not based on a commonality. To see this distinction in operation, let's think about the basic-level categories "car" and "motorcycle." Both categories include objects that have wheels and engines; these would be commonalities. That most motorcycles have two wheels, but most cars have four, is an alignable difference, because it is based on the commonality of having wheels in the first place. But that most cars use a steering wheel to change or maintain direction and most motorcycles accomplish the same thing with handlebars is a nonalignable difference because the difference between steering wheels and handlebars is not based on a commonality. As this analysis suggests, a pair of categories may differ from each other in at least two ways. First, they may have only a few commonalities. Second, they may have many alignable differences.

To see how patterns of commonality, alignable differences, and nonalignable differences might affect representation of concepts, Markman and Wisniewski (1997) carried out a study using the superordinate and basic-level categories shown in Table 11.6. Their subjects saw pairs of superordinate categories (such as "disease–vegetable"), pairs of basic-level categories drawn from the same superordinate level (such as "spoon–fork"), or pairs of basic-level categories drawn from different superordinates (such as "sword–bus"). The subjects attempted to list the commonalities and differences they could find between the two category names. Table 11.7 shows the findings of their study. Let's examine these findings. As expected, when basic-level categories such as "horse and cow"—which are drawn from the same superordinate category "animal"—are compared, the subjects find many similarities between them (6.68 commonalities on the average). Notice too that almost all the differences the subjects found

Table 11.6 Superordinates and Their Basic-Level Categories

Superordinate	Basic-Level Categories
clothing	tie–scarf
musical instrument	trumpet–saxophone
weapon	sword–spear
vehicle	bus–truck
furniture	bed–couch
reading material	magazine–newspaper
kitchen utensil	spoon–fork
human dwelling	apartment–hotel
tool	screwdriver–drill
beverage	coffee–tea
fruit	apple–pear
vegetable	onion–radish
animal	horse–cow
insect	ant–termite
bird	robin–canary
disease	measles–chickenpox

Source: From Markman and Wisniewski, 1997.

Table 11.7 Mean Number of Commonalities, Alignable Differences, Nonalignable Differences, and Proportion of Alignable Differences Listed by Participants

Condition	Mean Commonalities	Mean Alignable Differences	Mean Nonalignable Differences	Mean Proportion of Alignable Differences
Basic/basic–diff	2.86	2.55	2.68	.48
Basic/basic–same	6.68	3.07	0.78	.81
Super/super	3.13	2.06	2.14	.50

Note: Basic/basic–diff = pairs of basic-level concepts from different superordinates; basic/basic–same = pairs of basic-level concepts from the same superordinate; super/super = pairs of superordinates.
Source: From Markman and Wisniewski, 1997.

between these two categories were alignable differences. But this pattern was not observed for basic-level categories that were drawn from different superordinates. First, the number of commonalities that were found dropped dramatically, down to 2.86 on the average. Equally important was that although the number of alignable differences did not decline substantially in shifting to basic-level categories from different superordinates, the subjects were nevertheless significantly more likely to find nonalignable differences when the basic-level categories were not drawn from the same superordinate. To put this in concrete terms, if you listed the differences between "robin" and "parakeet," most of the differences you would find would be alignable. Thus you might list "pointed beak" for the robin and "rounded beak" for the parakeet. This is an alignable difference, because it's based on the fact that both birds have a part, namely a beak, in common. However, in comparing two basic-level categories from different superordinates, such as my favorite, "coffee" (from the superordinate "beverage") and "screwdriver" (from the superordinate "tool"), it becomes somewhat harder to find alignable differences, but much easier to find nonalignable differences. In other words, "coffee" and "screwdriver" have quite a few differences, but they are not based on any common parts. Our conclusion is that basic-level categories can contrast with other basic-level categories in two ways. Basic-level categories drawn from the same superordinate contrast with others for their few nonalignable differences. But basic-level categories drawn from different superordinates contrast because of their fewer commonalities and higher proportion of nonalignable differences.

Prototypes in Natural Categories: A Summary

The pathfinding work by Rosch and her colleagues suggested that natural categories and concepts are very much unlike the artificial concepts that had been studied in the lab. First, natural categories are not organized around criterial or decisive features. Rather, category members have a family resemblance. Then too, no hard-and-fast boundaries separate members in one category from those in another. Rather, the border between categories is fuzzy, with some specific examples occupying a position neither completely in, nor completely out of, a category. The category members also exhibited centrality, some members of the category being regarded as "better" examples of that category. The literature we have reviewed suggests that centrality depends on the number of features from the shared pool that a category member possesses (assuming that all specific features are equally valuable in forming a category). As a specific category member acquires more features, it becomes more central. The category member with most features becomes the centermost member of the category, and we refer to it as the prototype of that category.

Concepts have a "vertical" or hierarchic structure, too, in addition to this lateral structure. From this perspective, concepts at the intermediate level of generality, or basic level, appear to be special in a number of ways, making them the most "natural" of the natural categories. We examined several issues on how the basic level was organized, including composition of basic-level categories by parts, and kinds of differences among basic-level categories.

Exemplar-Based View of Categories

We have presented the prototype as the category's "summary representation" (Medin, 1989), which implies that the prototype is the "last word" in category representation. The prototype is where your cognitive system ends up, at least for that category.

Several theorists have challenged the notion that our prototypes are truly summaries of our categories. According to the exemplar viewpoint, we actually maintain in our cognitive systems a collection of specific cases and situations (Smith & Medin, 1981). These are stored without any particular organization. What then becomes of the prototype? Exemplar theorists argue that the prototypes are computed at retrieval or decision time, rather than being used as a basis for storing or encoding. From this perspective, I can use my cognitive system to figure out which example has more features than any other, if that's what the task requires, but that doesn't mean I use my cognitive system in that way all the time. The **exemplar theory's** position on categorization suggests that to categorize an object, I compare it to all the individual and specific examples in the category, rather than just to the prototype.

Implementing Exemplar Theories

A number of people have attempted to show how exemplar theories operate using connectionist networks of the sort that we examined in Chapter 6. (If you have forgotten some neural-networks details, it might be wise to review them before you try reading the rest of this description. I will spare you as many of the mathematical details as I can.) In this section we describe the ALCOVE model (Kruschke, 1992; Nosofsky, Gluck, Palmeri, McKinley, & Glauthier, 1994). Here's how ALCOVE works. When people encounter objects in the world, they store a representation of each according to its features in a large multidimensional space. Let's imagine a simplistic space consisting of only three dimensions (it would create a space like the inside of a typical room). Each object would be placed somewhere in the room, depending on how that object "scored" on each of the three dimensions that define the space. Each object in the room also has two other relevant components. First, it has an association with each of the other objects in the room. Second, the object has an association with each of the possible categories in which it can be placed. Take a concrete example: Suppose the first object that we want to place in the multidimensional space is a medium-sized teddy bear. Having evaluated that object on each of the dimensions that define the space, the teddy bear occupies some position in the room. (To avoid making the example horribly complicated I leave out how we evaluate the teddy bear according to any dimensions that might define this space.) After the teddy bear is placed, we encounter a Beanie Baby (a small plush animal filled with plastic beads, beloved by children—let's leave it at that). Presumably the Beanie Baby should be evaluated in some way similar to the teddy bear, and so these two objects would occupy similar positions in the multidimensional space; that is, they would be close together in that space. Numerically, both the Beanie Baby and the teddy bear would have associations to each other, so that when the teddy bear's representation was encountered, it would also increase the Beanie Baby's activation level. Moreover, representations of both Beanie Baby and teddy bear would have numerical strengths indicating the degree of association between each of these specific examples, and specific categories in which these objects could be placed. Specifically, we would expect that both examples might have strong connections to a category such as "children's toys." But having strong associations to each other does not mean that both exemplars must have strong associations to every category. It might be possible for the teddy bear, but not the Beanie Baby to have a strong association with some other category as well. Thus I can imagine using the teddy bear, but not the Beanie Baby, as a pillow if I had to do so. For ALCOVE to model my personal categorical structure, my teddy-bear exemplar would require at least a moderately strong weight with the category "pillow" in addition to the category "children's toys." Figure 11.6 depicts these processes in a schematic formula.

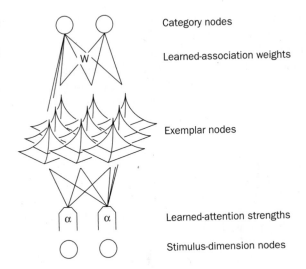

Figure 11.6 Structure of the ALCOVE model.
Source: From Nosofsky et al., 1994.

Category nodes

Learned-association weights

Exemplar nodes

Learned-attention strengths

Stimulus-dimension nodes

In connectionist networks, inputs to the system are usually at the bottom of the figural representation, and that's true here. The stimulus-dimension nodes take each exemplar that is encountered and represent it numerically on the dimensions that define the multidimensional space. The figure shows two stimulus-dimension nodes; our example would require three of them. The attention strengths represent the effect of learning. As we pay attention to the exemplars we encounter, we gradually learn to use some of an object's dimensions more effectively. These dimensions will have a higher weight than dimensions that are not so important in categorizing an object. "Color" might be a dimension that would be highly important, and thus have strong weight in categorizing some things, but would be relatively unimportant in categorizing children's toys, because we have learned that those can be of any color. As the schematic diagram shows, each specific exemplar node can be associated with more than one actual category, and that weight can vary. Going back to the example we've been working through, my teddy-bear exemplar node might have at least a moderately strong weight with my "pillow" category, but my Beanie-Baby exemplar node almost certainly has no strong association with that category.

Theory-Based View of Concepts

We have considered a couple of alternatives to the classical view of conceptual structure. The prototype-based view suggests that concepts are organized around a summary representation, the prototype, which includes more features, or more salient features, of a category than any other member. The exemplar view treats the prototype as a computational phenomenon that is produced at retrieval time in cognitive psychology laboratories. According to the exemplar view, we keep a representation of each category member in our memories. Thus the category is not reduced to just a prototype. In this section, we consider the method that has come to be called the **"theory-based" view** of conceptual structure (Medin, 1989). This perspective is based on several ideas, the first of which is the notion of "similarity," which has been running like a musical leitmotif throughout this chapter. All the theories we have examined so far have been attempts to specify what it is about category members that makes them seem alike. The theory-based view suggests that similarity is not necessarily a property of the world, but might be more like a concept itself, whose components come and go, depending on the situations in which we find ourselves. From this perspective, it's not so much what it is about the members of a category that makes them seem alike; it's more like what it is about us that produces a judgment of similarity when confronted with specific stimuli. A second key idea according to the theory-based view is the notion that personal knowledge and context must be important in our categorical structures. This is the "theory" in the theory-based view, the idea that our concepts and categories are our explanations to ourselves of what we see as the members of a category (Komatsu, 1992). We'll see each of these ideas played out in greater detail as we examine this perspective over the next several sections.

Ad Hoc and Goal-Derived Categories

The exemplar view suggests that each example, or member of a category, may have a function in other categories too. According to the exemplar view, you and I maintain representations of all the specific examples of objects that we have encountered, each one of them "weighted" more or less strongly to a number of categories. My categorical structure may not be identical to yours, because my specific examples could differ in weighting slightly, or massively, from yours, but the exemplar view has another implication. That is, the exemplar view suggests that specific examples are not locked in to any specific categorical structure; rather, each example or representation can do some sliding around in our categorical structure, by being a member of this or that category at various times. A robin may almost always be a member of my "bird" category, which is another way of saying that the robin has a strong weight with my "bird" category. But the specific example, robin, may function in other categories that are in no way superordinate to the "bird" category. Here's an example: What do crocuses, robins, and muddy ground have in common? The answer is that each is a member of the category "signs that winter is over."

Baraslou (1987) shows that categories such as this, which can be created on the spur of the moment, have a graded structure, just like more enduring categories. By graded structure we mean that the members of these ad hoc categories can be rated or judged for their "goodness" in the category. Consider the ad hoc category, "things to do to escape being killed by the Mafia." When Baraslou presented subjects with two "members" of that category, such as

1. Change your identity and move to the mountains in South America.
2. Stay where you are presently living in Las Vegas.

subjects agreed that option 1 was a better member of the category than option 2. Clearly, option 1 is not more typical or prototypical compared to the other members of the category, because there is no center, or summary representation of such categories. Rather, the goodness rating seems to be derived by the member's agreeing with a goal or an ideal (Barsalou, 1991). Thus, the members of the category "things to eat while on a diet" might be rated for their conformity to a goal of having as few calories as possible, the ideal number of calories being zero. Consistent with the theory-based view of concepts, the person's goal establishes a context that in turn influences the likelihood that specific elements will be understood as members of particular categories.

Similarity

Both the prototype view and the exemplar-based view of categories (and the classical view too) are based on the idea that category members are similar to one another (Komatsu, 1992; Medin & Wattenmaker, 1987). This statement doesn't seem at all controversial, does it? After all, why else would the category members exist together if they weren't similar to each other in some way? According to theory-based views of categories and categorical structure, however, **similarity** is itself a very slippery term (Goldstone, Medin, & Gentner, 1991; Medin, Goldstone, & Gentner, 1990). Medin (1989) suggests several components in similarity. First, the similarity between two things should increase as the number of shared features increases, and should decrease as the number of shared features decreases. Second, the features should be independent of one another, and they must contribute to similarity in an additive way. Third, the features that contribute similarity should be at the same level of abstractness. Fourth, these principles should be sufficient to describe the structure of a concept or category: a concept should be more or less a list of its features.

Stating that the features are independent of one another suggests that typicality judgments, and with such judgments, the appearance of prototypes, should be relatively invariant across different contexts. Thus, if the features that contribute to my "bird" concept are independent and additive, then my judgement of "robin" as prototypical should occur whether I'm sitting in cognitive science lab, or sitting on a bench looking at a collection of stuffed birds in a natural-history museum. It has been determined, though, that context does influence typicality judgments. Roth and Shoben (1983) found that tea is the prototypical beverage in the context of secretaries taking a break, but milk is a more typical break beverage than tea when the context is shifted to truck drivers taking a break.

About additivity: Some evidence suggests that the features of prototypes are not additive, either. Medin and Shoben (1988) found that small spoons are judged to be more typical of spoons than are large spoons. Similarly, metal spoons are thought to be more typical of spoons than wooden spoons are, leading one to think that large wooden spoons would not be likely to be judged as typifying spoons. But no—people find large wooden spoons more typical than they do small wooden spoons, or large metal spoons. Could it be, then, that similarity really isn't the engine in our conceptual structure, as the prototype view and the exemplar-based view would have it?

Let's consider experimental work by Rips (1989) showing the effects of this dissociation between judgments of similarity and categorical judgments. In one study, Rips presented to his subjects a rather terse oral description of an object; in fact, subjects were told about only one feature of the object—perhaps its diameter. This feature was previously determined to be between the values of two categories. If you think of a car wheel as perhaps 14 inches in diameter, and a soup can as 3 inches in diameter, then the value 8.5 inches is between these two values. Then Rips asked his subjects in which of the two categories the object in question should be placed. If the subjects were told the object was 3 inches in diameter, they might be asked if this object is more likely to belong in the category "pizzas" or the category "U.S. quarters." Now, even though an object that is 3 inches in diameter is closer to the size of a quarter (about 1 inch in diameter), and thus more similar in size to a quarter than to a pizza (perhaps 12 to 16 inches in diameter), the subjects nevertheless judged the object to be a pizza rather than a quarter. You may be thinking, Well, sure they did: Pizzas can be of different sizes, but official U.S. quarters can't. But let's think about what the study is telling us. The subjects applied their background knowledge and beliefs to consider the effects of variability and then to use this knowledge to override what they could perceive was only a superficial similarity.

In a second study, Rips (1989) told the subjects that an animal had started in life having many birdlike features (but it was not labeled a bird in the account that the subjects saw). Then, in an accident, the creature ingested contaminated food, and its properties mutated to insectlike features. This creature then mated with a normal member of its species, and the young produced were normal in appearance. Subjects were more likely to judge that the creature was a bird (that was its category) than an insect, but they were more likely to judge that it was more nearly similar to an insect than to a bird. This study shows the dissociation that can occur between the knowledge that is used to categorize a thing, and the perceptual appearances that may be at the basis of similarity judgments. That is, we apparently believe that the creature's essence determines its categorization, and thus, if the creature started out with birdlike qualities, then these were probably indicative of having the essence of a bird. The accidental changes that the presumed bird underwent altered its appearance, though, and with it, seemed to alter judgments of similarity as well. This study suggests that people may not always use similarity (in the sense of feature lists) to judge categorical structure. Rather, sometimes at least, people may apply theoretical, explanatory, background knowledge to make a categorical judgment. For this example, we might encapsulate that knowledge in the statement: "creatures produce young of the same species as themselves."

Thus we see that a strong relationship may connect conceptual structure and our reasoning schemes. Together, these findings suggest that, although the prototype and exemplar views have been very influential among cognitive psychologists, these approaches may nevertheless have embarrassing shortcomings, because both approaches are based on a concept of similarity that has not proven completely reliable empirically.

According to the theory-based view, concepts have the structure they do, not because people routinely build prototypes of similar things, but because people's experiences have provided them with a kind of theory about motives, reasons, "real" changes and "surface" changes, and so on. Similar things are judged to be in the same category only because some theoretical knowledge has been called up. But this kind of similarity can be overridden at any time by invoking a different theoretical perspective.

Interactions with Instances

We haven't discussed how our theories begin, but one place to look might be the interactions we have with the instances that we categorize. Ross (1996) suggests that our interactions with specific exemplars may lead us to pay more attention to specific features, to notice new features, or to appreciate relationships among features. Any one of these specific mechanisms may produce different categorizations. To investigate these effects, Ross gave his subjects algebra problems such as this:

$$a + \left(\frac{bx}{c}\right) = p$$

How would you go about solving for x in this problem? If you are like many people, you might first subtract (S) a from both sides of the equation. Then you might elect to multiply (M) both sides by c to remove the c from the denominator on the left side. Finally, you would divide (D) both sides by b to isolate the x on the left side of the equation. Ross thus referred to these as SMD problems, referring to the typical order of operations in solving it. Now, consider this problem:

$$\frac{(q + mx)}{b} = s$$

How would you go about solving for x in this problem? You might first multiply (M) both sides of the equation by b, then subtract (S) q from both sides, and finally divide (D) both sides by m to isolate the x on the left side. This is therefore an MSD problem, and we see that the subtraction operation has moved from the first to the second step in MSD problems. These two categories of problems differed in other ways, too. The SMD problems tended to use variables drawn from letters that appeared early in the alphabet, whereas the MSD problems involved variables drawn from letters at the end of the alphabet. The SMD problems also had parentheses that covered only a portion of the variables on one side of the equation, but the MSD problems had parentheses covering all the variables on one side of the equation.

The study involved two groups of subjects. One group simply studied the problems in the learning set one at a time, and then categorized them using a neutral term, such as "type 1" or "type 2." A second group studied each problem in the set, categorized it, and then solved it. Then the experiment moved to a second stage, in which the subjects were given additional problems varying from those they had already studied. A test problem might be of the SMD type but with letters from the end of the alphabet rather than the beginning, or it might be an MSD problem with letters from the beginning of the alphabet. The location of the parentheses might also be varied, so that an SMD problem might have parentheses covering one entire side of the equation, more like an MSD problem. Some examples of the problems initially presented for study and some test problems are shown in Table 11.8.

The results indicated that the subjects who classified and then solved the study problems were better able to successfully categorize the test problems than were those who simply categorized the problems. Specifically, the solution group was not at all affected by letter changes (front to back of the alphabet, or vice versa); they successfully categorized just about 100% of the test problems that had the "wrong" letters in them. The solution group was influenced somewhat by location of the parentheses. That is, when an SMD problem had the parenthetical structure of an MSD problem, or vice versa, the solution group miscategorized about 18% of such problems. But both of these variables much more strongly affected the categorization-only group.

Table 11.8   Sample Materials for Ross's Experiment

Phase of Experiment	Type	
	SMD	MSD
Study	$a + \left(\dfrac{bx}{c}\right) = p$	$\left(\dfrac{q + mx}{b}\right) = s$
Test	$f = \left(\dfrac{cnx}{6}\right) + 1$	$r = \left(\dfrac{dx + 7}{sp}\right)$
P+L+	$b = \left(\dfrac{gsx}{9}\right) + 2$	$a = \left(\dfrac{m + px}{r}\right)$
POL−	$\dfrac{4x}{m} + q = s$	$g = \dfrac{6x + b}{7f}$
P−LO	$k = \left(j + \dfrac{ix}{9h}\right)$	$\dfrac{i + (hx)}{k} = j$
P−L−	$n = \left(\dfrac{3x}{t} + p\right)$	$e = \dfrac{(7x) + 6}{9d}$

Note: SMD = subtract, multiply, divide; MSD = multiply, subtract, divide. P = parentheses; L = letter; and +, 0, and − refer to whether the test assignment was consistent, neutral, or inconsistent with the study assignment, respectively.

Source: From Ross, 1996.

When the problems used the "wrong" letters, the categorization-only group miscategorized about 21% of the test problems. Moreover, when both letters and parenthetical structure differed from the study problems, they miscategorized fully 40% of the test problems.

What does this study tell us about the "theories" that we use to categorize specific examples? The findings suggest that the interactions we have with the stimuli become important sources of information that we can use to help explain or justify our classifications. Second, they also suggest that our own individual categorical structure is probably influenced by the experiences that we have had with the members of various categories. And perhaps the influence these interactions exert in determining our categorical structure is even greater than that of the correlations of the features themselves.

This last point suggests that, as individuals become familiar with a category's exemplars from their experience in dealing with those exemplars, their categorical structure itself may change in predictable ways. A few tantalizing studies suggest that this process does go on. Boster and Johnson (1989) asked novice and expert sport anglers to categorize groups of fish. The newcomers to the sport used obvious and superficial morphological (i.e., shape-based) dimensions to sort the fish. But the expert anglers created groupings based on their interactions with the fish, sometimes using the difficulty of catching them ("superb sport fish"), and sometimes the quality of the meat ("inshore meat fish") as bases for categorizing them.

In another study, Medin, Lynch, Coley, and Atran (1997) asked three types of tree experts to categorize or sort the names of forty-eight broadly representative tree species from the U.S. Midwest. The three groups included taxonomists, engaged in research and teaching about trees at the university level; landscapers, who focus on the aesthetic and utilitarian aspects of trees as design elements for city streets or parks; and maintenance workers, whose job involves planting, pruning, and sometimes healing urban trees. The various experts' specialties strikingly affected their sorting of trees. The taxonomists never put members of the same genus of trees into different categories, which makes a great deal of sense. The genus names are the scientific identities of the trees, and this was the standpoint they were most likely to endorse, for they were, after all, scientists. Both landscapers and maintenance workers, though, put trees from the same genus into different categories, and also put trees from different genera into the same category. The genus *Fraxinus* includes the trees known as white ash and green ash. Landscapers and maintenance workers preserved this scientific taxonomy in their sorts by putting these trees into the same category. But they also included another tree, American mountain ash, in this category, even though it is in a completely different, and distantly related genus *(Sorbus)*. None of the taxonomists included the mountain ash in their categories with white ash and green ash. In other words, both landscapers' and maintenance workers' categories clearly seem influenced by their knowledge and use of a basic-level linguistic term "ash tree," whereas taxonomists were not at all affected by this term.

In another part of their study, Medin et al. asked the experts to "justify" or give the reason they used to categorize the trees in the way they did. Table 11.9 shows the percentage of experts in each of the three types who used specific sorts of terms to explain their categories. Notice that of the eight reasons that could be given, the taxonomists tended to stick with only the scientific taxonomy as a justification for sorting. Scientific taxonomy was also used by 90% of the maintenance workers, and 90% of the landscapers. But each of these groups used other, nonscientific aspects of the trees in explaining why they sorted the trees as they did. For example, 60% of the landscapers mentioned "size" as a justification for their categories, as did 20% of the maintenance workers. This choice makes sense, too: Landscapers have to be sure that a tree won't get too big for its allocated space, and I'm guessing that most maintenance workers would rather prune a small tree. One of the most interesting justifications was the ref-

Table 11.9   Proportion of Experts in Each Subgroup Using the Various Types of Justifications for Any Category in Their Initial Sort

Type of Justification	Taxonomist	Expert Group Maintenance	Landscaper
Taxonomic	1.00	0.90	0.90
Morphological	0.25	0.80	0.40
Weed	0.00	0.60	1.00
Landscape utility	0.00	0.10	0.80
Aesthetic	0.00	0.40	0.60
Size	0.00	0.20	0.60
Distribution	0.00	0.20	0.40
Native/nonnative	0.00	0.10	0.50

Source: From Medin et al., 1997.

erence to "weed" or "garbage" trees: they have weak wood, drop a lot of vegetation and twigs to the ground, reproduce quickly, and are generally difficult to maintain and control. They include weeping willows and white poplars. Notice that the taxonomists didn't use this term at all in their justifications, but all the landscapers did so, as did 60% of the maintenance workers. Clearly, if a person has to actually deal with the tree, then the tree's overall "friendliness" becomes an issue in categorizing it. I can relate well to this finding: Our near neighbors have a white poplar on their property, and I've spent too many summer evenings grumbling as I pick up the twigs and branches in our yard, and dig up the endlessly propagating "runners" that emanate from the tree. I may not know much about the scientific basis for tree categorization, but I would be happy to use the "weed-tree" label to describe the white poplar.

Knowledge Effects in Categorization

According to the theory-based view of categorization, we will use our knowledge, and our analysis of the current context, to help us categorize. These effects are seen in some classic work by Labov (1973), who showed his subjects the objects labeled 1 through 4 in Figure 11.7. Going from 1 to 4, the object's width increases in proportion to its height. The ratio of width to height is 1 to 1 for Object 1; it is 1.9 to 1 for Object 4. The subject's task was to label the object. As Figure 11.8 shows, the wider the object became, the more likely the subjects were to label the object a bowl. A second group of

Figure 11.7 Cuplike objects used in experiment by Labov (1973), studying boundaries of the cup category. *Source:* From Labov, 1973.

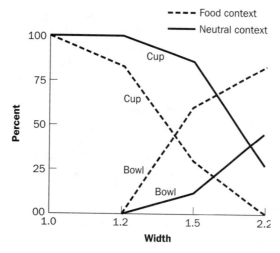

Figure 11.8 Percent of different name types applied to objects as the width increases and as a function of the verbal set. *Source:* From Labov, 1973.

subjects engaged in the same task, but they were invited to imagine that the vessel contained mashed potatoes, a food we typically think of as served in a bowl. As the graph shows, the subjects in this condition were willing to use the "bowl" label for vessels that were not nearly as wide as those labeled "bowl" by subjects in the first condition. Another way of looking at the graph is to consider the points at which the percentage of subjects using the "cup" label equaled the percentage using the "bowl" label. For the subjects in the neutral condition (that is, when the vessel was empty), this point was not reached until the vessel was about 2.4 times wider than it was tall. But for the subjects in the mashed-potatoes condition, the point was reached much sooner. Subjects were equally likely to label the vessel a "cup" or a "bowl" when its width-to-height ratio was only 1.3 or so. It seems clear that subjects' use of the "bowl" term was influenced by their knowledge about how such vessels are used. You might ask a family member to please pass you the bowl of mashed potatoes, but I think few ask their dinner companions to pass the cup of mashed potatoes. As a check on your comprehension of this study, you might ask yourself what would have happened if Labov had asked his subjects to imagine the vessel to be filled with coffee instead of mashed potatoes.

Concluding Comments and Suggestions for Further Reading

Where did we begin, and where have we gone over the last forty years in understanding concepts and categories? As part of our answer to the first question, it's interesting that research on this subject predates the information-processing model that became dominant in cognitive psychology through the 1960s and 1970s. Before that, the Swiss psychologist Jean Piaget operated from the perspective that the human mind was an intrinsically rational or logical hypothesis-testing device. According to this view, our categories were the result of a procedure that was metaphorically similar to a town's zoning ordinances. That is, just as a town's government limits the type of structures and establishments that can be set up in proximity to each other, so too our cognitive system has strict procedures determining how an object will be categorized. To accomplish this mental zoning, the child uses the medium of language to play a kind of guessing game with parents. As a result of this linguistic process, the child builds a representation of the world into which all the world's objects can eventually be placed. Unlike real zoning laws, though, which are arbitrary, according to Piaget's view, our conceptual knowledge is really knowledge about the world's structure. That is, the way in which we categorize things is most likely to be the "right" and only way to categorize them.

Rosch's essential points are in some ways similar to this approach, and in other ways different. Compared to Piaget's mental zoning ordinances, which strictly determine and limit how objects are categorized, the mental landscape according to Rosch is much more "pastoral" or unfenced and unbordered. That is, Rosch's work clearly suggests that no boundary lines separate concepts. We saw this point amplified in Labov's work, too. If you look back to his findings, you can see that no "magic" point appears at which the subjects dramatically shifted their judgment of "cup" to "bowl" or vice versa. In both, the proportion of judgments using either term gradually shifts up or down, depending on the ratio of width to height. In some ways, though, Rosch's position is similar to the Piagetian one. Both have a developmental perspective suggesting that children must build a representation, and this process probably occupies the child for some years. Second, both the Piagetian position and the prototype view have the idea that the categorizer-as-learner is learning about properties of the world. When Rosch speaks of the cognitive system as exploiting the "correlational structure" of the world, she is suggesting that our cognitive system is capable of attuning itself to which features in the world typically are found in the presence of which others, and thus of building a representation based on such co-occurrences.

Things change somewhat when we come to the exemplar view, which questions the notion that the categorical structure we report really depicts "the" world. Rather, the exemplar view suggests that our categorical structure may be more accurately understood as depicting our history with specific sets of stimuli. Here's an example to show what I mean. Just to give you some context, I'll provide you with a partial list of the objects on my desk right now (it's a big desk): phone, two staplers (don't ask), in-box and out-box trays, box of tissues, two coffee cups, tape dispenser, plastic box of floppy disks, stacks of photocopied papers that I'm reading for courses that I'm teaching, manila folders with data and notes for studies that I have in progress arranged in piles of paper, stacks of books, current issues of scientific journals, flyers from publishing companies, a daily calendar, and an appointment book. Along with all this stuff are the "focal objects" to which I wish to draw your mental gaze: a bound volume of issues of the journal *Memory & Cognition,* and an authored, nonfiction book with a dust jacket. Can you picture them among those other stimuli? I think most people might be inclined to call both focal objects "books." I can certainly get to a basic level of categorization for both focal objects in which I would call them both books. But doing so is a little hard for me, because the volume of journal issues is only superficially a book in my world, but the other focal object clearly is a book. My judgment about these objects reflects my involvement with them, and thus might tell someone more about me, and my history with things like this, than it would about the "real" world out there.

Beyond these points about the differences among the various perspectives, we can make at least a couple of points about ourselves. First, although I haven't made this point explicitly in the chapter, we can see several indications that our conceptual structure is under a great deal of strategic control. In other words, in summarizing work by Ross (1996), Boster and Johnson (1989), and Medin et al. (1997), we can see that our conceptual structure reflects our environment, and also that we can direct aspects of the environment that our cognitive system may attend to for categorizing. We are not simply passive recipients of our categorical structure; we are active agents in creating it. The second point is how context works, as it directs these strategic effects. Under the Piagetian and "classical" views of concept formation each person, to form a category, does something like "run a category program," which runs in about the same way for each person in each situation, and, after it's finished running, establishes pretty much the same categories for each person. The point here is that there really isn't any such program. Instead, each of us forms categories according to our unique goals, and in our unique context. If you as an experimenter were to change the context for an individual, chances are good that you would change the categorizing scheme that person is using.

Focus on Research
Kids Have the Darndest Concepts (About the Origin of Species)

Clearly, a developmental theme runs through this chapter. Both prototype and exemplar theorists suggest that the child must build a representation of a concept by interacting with instances in the world. Other theorists have wondered about that interaction and the resulting conceptual world that children erect. At least two schools of thought consider these issues. On the one hand, such researchers as diSessa (1993) believe children's concepts are frequently like "novice knowledge," characterized by conceptual beliefs that are weakly organized, internally inconsistent, and self-contradictory. Novices' conceptual knowledge and by extension, that of all children, may be particularly unstable. On the other hand, some (e.g., Vosniadou & Brewer, 1992) suggest that kids and novices may be able to develop systematic ways of thinking about certain concepts. As a result, children's conceptual knowledge may share quite a few features with that of adults.

These researchers draw upon an "explanatory framework" to describe the structure of children's conceptual knowledge. This framework is a network of prestored, related beliefs that enable children to construct some mental representations, which are then used to answer questions put to them (Samarpungavan & Wiers, 1997). Suppose a seven-year-old has a concept of "gravity" as a force that pulls things together. That seven-year-old may be able to explain why people don't float off the earth, and why the earth doesn't fly away from the sun. Now suppose such a child sees a demonstration of magnets being attracted to each other. The child may be able to infer that, whatever it is that the magnets are doing, it may have something to do with gravity. Notice that a child whose explanatory framework for gravity is that it is "some-thing that makes things heavy" may also be able to explain why people don't float away from the earth, but will have some difficulty in interpreting and explaining the magnet demonstration.

Samarpungavan and Wiers (1997) looked at an especially rich explanatory framework; namely, children's knowledge about and explanations for the origin of animals and species of animals on our planet. Their subjects were Dutch schoolchildren who were eight to nine or ten to eleven years old. These children were interviewed in a structured series of questions to find out about their concept of speciation. Samarpungavan and Wiers had expected to find four possible explanatory frameworks among children. They listed and explained these frameworks:

1. The Greek or Essentialist framework: The ancient idea that the animals we see today are those which have been here forever. They are unchanging and, in fact, they cannot change. These children explain the varieties of species by saying that's just the way things are.

2. The Lamarckian framework: The idea that animals change in response to their own activities. A child who explains the giraffe's long neck by saying that it acquired this long neck to help it reach high leaves in trees is Lamarckian.

3. The Creationist viewpoint: The idea that the animals we see were created in their present form by a deity. The explanation for speciation is that God made them that way.

4. The Darwinian viewpoint: The idea that helpful adaptations have a survival advantage. This viewpoint explains the varieties of species by saying that the current form of the species might have the best chance for survival.

Focus on Research

Of the thirty-five children, twenty-eight had some sort of explanatory framework, but only twelve of these frameworks fit into the researchers' expectations. They identified twelve Essentialists, three Creationists, three Lamarckians, and no (!) Darwinians. In fairness to the researchers, eight more kids were categorized as slightly modified Essentialists, whom the researchers labeled Dinosaur Essentialists. These kids acknowledged that the dinosaurs are no longer around (meaning that these kids cannot be categorized as pure Essentialists), but they more or less insisted that was the only change. These kids went on to argue that all the animals that exist now were somehow related to dinosaurs: dinosaur birds, dinosaur horses, and so on. Here's an example of how an Essentialist child responded to part of the interview in which the researcher asked about the peacock's tail:

"I can tell you that the peacock's tail helps him to attract wives. And now you will surely ask me how this tail originated. It just is that way. Peacocks always had long tails just like giraffes always had long necks." (Samarpungavan & Wiers, p. 161)

Some issues are left unaddressed here that we would certainly like to have answered. First, we don't know what percentage of people are content to stick with an adult version of one of these frameworks, and so we don't know how many of the kids' concepts about speciation change. Are you surprised by the percentage of children who are Essentialists? I was, but until we know more about adults, I don't know how surprised I have a right to be. Second, to the extent that they do change (and they must change somewhat, because certainly some adults are Darwinians), we don't know which experiences, if any, may be most critical in giving the kids the idea that it's time to change their concept on the origin of species.

Students who wish to read more about categorization and conceptual structure might begin by looking at the survey of the theoretical perspectives in Komatsu (1992). The chapter by Smith (1990) is also an excellent introduction to categorization, particularly on the difficulty in measuring the concept of similarity. Finally, Smith and Medin (1981) remains a classic that is well worth your time.

Key Terms

Reception paradigm	Prototype	Alignable differences
Selection paradigm	Basic level	Nonalignable differences
Conservative focusing	Superordinate level	Exemplar theory
Focus gambling	Subordinate level	Theory-based view
Centrality	Differentiation	
Similarity	Commonality	

Problem Solving

*O*verview

What comes to mind when you think about the prototypical intelligent person's actions? In other words, what behaviors do you usually associate with being smart? This was essentially the question Sternberg (1982) asked his subjects, many of whom were not experts on intelligence. To get people's everyday notions about intelligence, Sternberg went into the real world and approached people in natural settings, such as commuter trains and supermarkets. Persons who agreed to participate in the study were given a blank sheet of paper and were asked to write down behaviors that were characteristic of **intelligence**. Sternberg found a substantial consensus about these behaviors. People's responses clustered around three categories of activities indicative of intelligence. Sternberg found that people think of social competence as one component of intelligence. He also found that people consider verbal ability to indicate intelligence. But according to many people, the most important indicator is practical problem-solving ability. A person who could "size up the situation accurately," "get to the heart of the problem," and then "reason logically" had the skills most often identified as indicating intelligence. When experts on intelligence research were asked the same questions, Sternberg got similar findings. The experts listed "verbal intelligence" as the most important indicator of intellectual ability, but "problem-solving ability" was still mentioned as the second most important component of intelligence.

Both lay people and experts seem to agree that problem solving is one hallmark of intelligence, and so it seems natural for cog-nitive psychologists to be interested in the mental events that take place when a person tries to attain a goal in an unfamiliar situation. In this chapter we consider the phenomenon of problem solving from several perspectives. First, we examine a European psychological tradition, **Gestalt psychology**. The Gestaltists believed that thinking was much like perceiving. Finding a solution to a problem was like trying to see things from a different perspective. The information-processing approach to problem solving, which originated in this country about forty years ago, really isn't an outgrowth of the Gestalt position. And as we'll see, studies using the information-processing orientation indicate that many of the Gestaltists' basic beliefs about thinking and problem solving have turned out to be inaccurate. Some important studies, though, have supported some of the Gestaltist's ideas.

In Chapter 1, I mentioned that cognitive psychologists have become interested in exploring cognition in natural situations. Nowhere is this more true than in the area of problem solving. In the real world, an expert is a person skilled at solving problems in some domain. Cognitive psychologists have asked themselves several questions about the expert. How can expertise be described? What does the expert's knowledge consist of, and how does it differ from the novice's knowledge about the same material? All experts were novices once. How, then, does expertise develop? How does a person go from being a novice to being a pro? In the last section in this chapter we try to answer these questions.

Gestalt Heritage

Before going on to examine the Gestalt psychologists' work, we need a definition for problem solving. A problem is a situation in which a person is trying to reach some goal and must find a means for arriving at it (Chi & Glaser, 1985). In Europe early in this century, the Gestalt tradition flourished as several thinkers began to work on problem solving and other forms of creative thinking. According to members of the Berlin group, such as Max Wertheimer, Kurt Koffka, and Wolfgang Köhler, the goal of problem solving was to achieve a *Gestalt,* a German word with no precise equivalent in English, but usually translated as "form" or "configuration." According to the Gestaltists, the end result of all perceptual processes was formation of a Gestalt, and Gestalts were also the end result of all thinking processes. Thus, the Gestaltists believed that problem solving was much like perceiving. When we look at something, our task as perceivers is to arrange the separate elements in the visual field into a coherent whole. As problem solvers, our task is to mentally recombine the elements in a problem over and over until a stable configuration, or Gestalt, is achieved.

The Gestaltists were intrigued by how frequently we use perceptual terms to describe our thinking processes. A friend who doesn't understand a concept in physics says, "I don't see it." Similarly, we may encourage someone who is stumped by a problem to "try to look at it from a different perspective." We've probably all heard a confused person bemoan having a problem with the words "I can't get a handle on it."

The Gestaltists were not too precise about how Gestalts were achieved. They were quite influential in their time, though, and they outlined the issues that modern workers have sought to map more precisely. In this section we examine the Gestalt approach to problem solving.

Stages in Thinking

All problem solving necessarily begins with the recognition that a problem exists. The solver must perceive a discrepancy between the current state of affairs and some desired state of affairs. The desired state becomes the goal, and the solver undertakes mental operations with the intention of achieving the goal. Problem solving, then, consists of recognizing a problem and doing mental work to achieve a goal. The Gestaltists customarily thought that problem solving proceeded in a sequence of fixed stages. According to Wallas (1926), these stages were:

1. Preparation.   In the preparation stage of problem solving, the solver has recognized that a problem exists, and some preliminary attempts have been made to understand and solve the problem.

2. Incubation.   If the preliminary attempts fail, the solver may then put the problem aside for a while. At least on a conscious level, the thinker is no longer working on the task. At some unconscious level, though, work proceeds.

3. Illumination.   Illumination is the famous flash of **insight** that ends the unconscious work and brings the answer to the surface of consciousness.

4. Verification.   The verification stage confirms the insight. Generally, this stage is the least complicated and usually is nothing more than simply checking to make sure that the insight worked.

In retrospect, this sequence of operations seems almost too rigid. We definitely have times when we put a problem aside, return to it, solve it, and never experience a flash of insight. Further, Wallas makes some assumptions about which some modern psychologists might be unhappy. One is the reference to unconscious thought. Another is the notion that problem solving is discontinuous. Like all stage theories, Wallas's model assumes that activities in the different stages are qualitatively different from one another, meaning that mental operations at the preparation stage somehow differ fundamentally from operations at the other stages. Modern theories of problem solving, though, have emphasized that problem solving is continuous and accumulative. Despite these reservations, Wallas's position has received support from artists and mathematicians maintaining that their own creative endeavors followed the course outlined by Wallas (Ghiselin, 1952; Harding, 1940). In particular, the concept that a period of unconscious work might follow the initially unsuccessful preparation phase has provoked a fair amount of research.

Incubation   Several researchers have demonstrated the so-called **incubation effect.** Fulgosi and Guilford (1968) asked subjects to first imagine some unusual event (e.g., all the power stations closing down) and then to list all possible consequences. Although subjects' performances were improved when they got a twenty-minute waiting interval before producing consequences, these improvements were limited to more obvious but not remote consequences. Curiously, a ten-minute interval produced no effect.

Silveira (1971) demonstrated a similar effect when she presented to her subjects the cheap-necklace problem, shown in Figure 12.1. Here are the instructions to this problem:

> You are given four separate pieces of chain, each three links in length. It costs two cents to open a link and three cents to close a link. All links are closed at the beginning of the problem. Your goal is join all twelve links of a chain into a single circle at a cost of no more than fifteen cents.

Figure 12.1 The cheap-necklace problem.

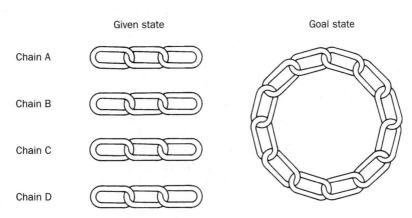

Given state

Chain A

Chain B

Chain C

Chain D

Goal state

You might try to solve this problem before reading further. Silveira's control group worked on the problem for half an hour; 55% of these subjects were successful. Four experimental groups also worked on the task. Two groups worked briefly on the problem; one was then interrupted for four hours. Two other groups had a longer preparation period for uninterrupted work before one of them got a half-hour interruption and the other a four-hour interruption.

Can you guess the findings? The two experimental groups who worked briefly on the problem showed no evidence of incubation; their performance was similar to that of the control group. The other two experimental groups, however, showed the incubation effect. In the long-preparation–short-interruption group, 64% of the subjects solved the problem, and 85% of those in the long-preparation–long-interruption group were successful. (If you're still stumped, the answer to this and the other examples in this chapter can be found in the appendix.) According to the Gestalt position, this is the expected pattern of results. The long-preparation groups had ample time to develop familiarity with the problem, and this familiarity in turn facilitated unconscious processing of the task. But not all cognitive psychologists would agree with this reasoning. Indeed, Silveira presented evidence arguing against the unconscious-thought hypothesis. She had her subjects talk aloud as they solved the cheap-necklace problem, and she tape-recorded what they said. She found that when the subjects returned to the problem after the break, they tended to pick up where they had left off. If the Gestalt position were completely correct, we should expect the subjects to show some progress during the interruptions; they should appear to be closer to the answer when they return from the break. But they didn't.

The Gestalt reasoning apparently requires modification, but what alternative explanations can we offer? Simon (in Hunt, 1982) suggests that the incubation effects might best be explained by selective forgetting. He hypothesized that solving a problem is at least a two-stage task. Initially, we devise a plan for solving the problem that is held only in working memory. As our solution efforts proceed, we encode and store in permanent memory additional information that could easily be formulated into a successful plan, if only our attention could be shifted away from the initial plan in our working memory. During incubation, that's exactly what happens. We allocate our attention to permanent memory (thus letting the content of working memory decay) and use the knowledge represented there to create a successful plan.

A second explanation for the incubation effect is offered by Anderson (1981), who suggests that the effect is related to another Gestalt term, *set,* which is our tendency to perceive events and objects in a way that our prior experiences have led us to expect. That is, our perceptions are somewhat predetermined (set) by our experience. According to Anderson, when we begin to solve a problem, our prior knowledge is used as a resource that can be called up, or activated, to suggest at least an outline of effective procedures for solving the problem. If our set is appropriate, we'll call up effective procedures. If our set is inappropriate, though, we'll remain stuck with a list of ineffective procedures. During incubation, solvers are freed from these inappropriate procedures, giving them a chance to call up more effective ones. One important aspect in Anderson's argument is its suggestion that problem solving should not always be improved by interrupting it. To understand this idea, consider what might happen if we began to solve Silveira's problem and our set *was* appropriate. Following the interruption, we have no guarantee that we'll succeed in calling up the same appropriate set once again. And if we fail to do so, we'll probably get stuck using an inappropriate set of operations, which may compromise our chance for solution. This difficulty helps explain why several studies (Dominowski & Jenrick, 1972; Murray & Denny, 1969) show decrements in problem solving following an interruption.

Insight and Creativity   The Gestaltists maintained that problem solving often resulted in sudden awareness of the correct relationship among the problem's elements. This perception was often accompanied by the "aha!" experience—the solver is positive that she has discovered the problem's answer. In a famous passage, the mathematician Poincaré (1913) describes one of his great insights:

> Just at this time, I left Caen, where I was then living, to go on a geological excursion under the auspices of the school of mines. The changes of travel made me forget my mathematical work. Having reached Coutances, we entered an omnibus to go some place or another. At the moment when I put my foot on the step the idea came to me, without anything in my former thoughts seeming to have paved the way for it, that the transformations I had used to define the Fuschisan functions were identical with those on non-Euclidean geometry. I did not verify the idea; I should not have had time, as, upon taking my seat in the omnibus, I went on with a conversation already commenced, but I felt a perfect certainty. On my return to Caen, for conscience' sake I verified the result at my leisure. (pp. 387–388)

Some comments in this passage are striking. Poincaré says that "the idea came to me, without anything in my former thoughts seeming to have paved the way for it." His insight was not continuous with his previous thinking. We see here anecdotal evidence of discontinuity in problem solving: When the insight would take place could not be predicted. He also refers to the effortlessness of the new thought; it was unforced and unbidden. This passage thus points out one of the Gestaltists' most cherished beliefs. Truly creative thought could never be predicted by previous behavior, because the creative work was essentially a break in the stream of problem solving. Such a break could be accomplished only by insight. We've all had experiences similar to Poincaré's, but is there any empirical evidence to substantiate such discontinuities in human thought?

Katona (1940) compared the roles of memory and creativity (or as the Gestaltists called them, reproductive and productive thinking) in solving schematic matchstick problems, as shown in Figure 12.2. The lines are drawn so that five squares are represented. The solver's task is to move three—and only three—matchsticks to create an array of four squares. The memory group was presented the series of moves that would solve the problem. They were shown the sequence seven times and were told to memorize it. The creative group was given hints that might be helpful in fostering understanding of what was involved in solving the problem. The presumption was that such hints might encourage the subjects to find general principles that could be used to solve other problems in this class. Along with the memory and creative groups, a control group solved the matchstick problem and was given no help. All three groups were tested on the same and different matchstick problems after intervals of one and three weeks.

The Problem
Given matchsticks which form five squares, move three sticks to form four squares.

Group Mem
The complete solution steps are presented to the subject in order, moving one stick at a time, and repeating six times. For the above problem, the required moves shown are:

Group Help
The second method involves giving a series of hints to the subject accompanied by the comment "Try to understand what I am doing."

Results
Typical proportions correct on retention and transfer tests were as follows:

	Test after one week		Test after three weeks	
	Practice	New	Practice	New
Group	tasks	tasks	tasks	tasks
Mem	.67	.25	.53	.14
Help	.58	.55	.52	.55
Con	.12	.12	.12	.12

Figure 12.2   Katona's matchstick problem. *Source:* From Katona, 1940.

The results are also shown in Figure 12.2. The control group's performance was remarkably constant across the board, arguing that apparently little learning is generalized from one problem to the next. Similarly, the memory group had good retention of the original task after both one and three weeks, yet it hardly outperformed the control group after a three-week interval. The creative group's performance is quite different from that of the other groups, however. Notice that its members performed as well on new matchstick problems as they did on the original problem. The conclusion appears to be that Katona's hints were successful in prompting the subjects to develop a structural understanding of this type of problem. Thus, to the extent that the solution of these problems requires an insight, the creative group's experiences with matchstick problems did pave the way for future insights in solving this kind of problem.

Other researchers have used this procedure of giving their subjects hints in an effort to foster insight. Duncker (1945) gave his subjects this problem: Why can you divide all numbers of the form abc,abc (e.g., 456,456) by 13? You might think about this question for a while—it's a hard problem. Duncker found that general hints were not helpful! (e.g., if a divisor of a number is divided by p, then the number itself is divisible by p), but only specific hints were helpful. An important hint was that the subject's attention be drawn to the number 1001, for this is the key to the problem. If the subjects were given the hints "The numbers are divisible by 1001" or "1001 is divisible by 13," then they were likely to realize that each of the original numbers could be factored abc times into 1001, and 1001 is factored by 13.

We need to realize about the Katona and Duncker findings their implication about insight and creativity. Rather than think of creative work as being accomplished by some discontinuous insight, which seems to arrive at unpredictable times and in unpredictable ways, a more reasonable approach is to emphasize the *continuity* of problem solving. The creative act is one of finding original arrangements of accumulated experiences.

Some research by Weisberg and Alba (1981) makes this point dramatically. They gave their subjects the well-known "nine-dot" problem: nine dots arranged in three rows of three dots each. Each dot is placed so that it is equidistant from its row and column neighbors. The subject's task is to connect the nine dots using four and only four straight lines, without lifting the pencil from the paper. This task can be done, but most solutions involve drawing a line "outside" the boundary implied by the arrangement of the nine dots. According to the Gestaltists, most people assume that they must stay within the implied borders, and this set makes it impossible for them to solve the problem. According to the Gestaltists, success on this problem is achieved when the problem solver realizes that the boundary is an artificial one that must be crossed. Weisberg and Alba contested this theorizing by simply telling the subjects that they had to go outside the implied square (this advice came after the subjects had worked on the problem unsuccessfully for a while). The Gestaltists would argue that the nine-dot problem should now become trivially easy; as soon as the subjects drew a line outside the imaginary square, they would restructure their representation of the problem and solve it. Weisberg and Alba found that the Gestaltists' predictions were wrong: Only 20 to 25% of the subjects who were given the "insight" succeeded in solving the problem. Analyzing the lines that were drawn indicated that the "insight" was little or no help in figuring out the answer. In fact, several of the Weisberg and Alba subjects drew a line more or less randomly outside the dots and then said something like, "Okay, I'm outside the square. Now what do I do?" Such findings argue that insight is not the mechanism of creativity, nor is thinking in general, creative or otherwise, accomplished in discontinuous leaps.

Consider this final example. In 1797, Coleridge composed "Kubla Khan," one of the finest examples of English romantic poetry. Coleridge had fallen asleep while reading about Khan and (as he told it) composed the poem in his sleep without conscious effort. Upon awakening, he immediately began to write down the whole 200-line poem he had composed in his sleep. Unfortunately, at line 54, he was interrupted by a bill collector, whom it took an hour to get rid of. When Coleridge returned to his work . . . well, you guessed it, the rest of the poem had vanished. Not until many years after, when Lowes (1927) conducted a close analysis of Coleridge's notebooks, did the real origin of "Kubla Khan" come to light. Lowes was able to demonstrate that Coleridge had seen or read and, in many cases, had written down almost every image or metaphor that occurred in "Kubla Khan." In other words, the raw material had already been encoded by Coleridge. He had taken medication prior to his nap, and it was probably in his slightly disinhibited state that he was able to organize the material that made up the poem.

The Importance of the Correct Representation

According to the Gestaltists, perhaps no aspect of problem solving was more important than the activity involved in understanding or **representing the problem.** Consider this problem (Wickelgren, 1974):

> You are given a checkerboard and thirty-two dominoes. Each domino covers exactly two adjacent squares on the board. Thus, the thirty-two dominoes can cover all sixty-four squares of the checkerboard. Now suppose two squares are cut off at diagonally opposite corners of the board [as shown in Figure 12.3]. Is it possible to place thirty-one dominoes on the board so that all of the sixty-two remaining squares are covered? If so, show how it can be done. If not, prove it impossible.

You might enjoy spending a few minutes solving this problem. If you became engrossed in this task, you are probably aware that you spent time visualizing various configurations of dominoes being placed on the altered checkerboard, mentally noticing whether any part of the domino would stick out over the edge of the checkerboard. Thus, your representation of the problem included information about area and edges. But until your representation of the problem includes at least one other important fact, you're unlikely to solve this problem.

The answer is that the checkerboard cannot be covered by the thirty-one dominoes. To see why, realize that each domino must cover one white and one black square on the checkerboard. Covering two squares of the same color with one domino is impossible. But the checkerboard has been altered by taking away two white squares—leaving thirty-two black but only thirty white squares. We've solved this problem when we realize that the parity as well as the number of squares on the checkerboard have been altered. Notice that the problem's difficulty is not the result

Figure 12.3 The mutilated checkerboard.

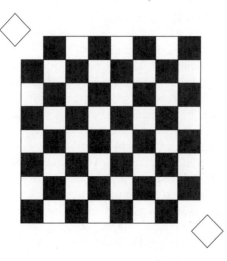

of logical or inferential complexity; it's difficult because one important element (what gets covered by every domino) is usually left out of most people's representations. As the Gestalt psychologists realized, the act of representation is done by the solver, and different solvers may arrive at equally valid representations.

Consider the game known as number scrabble (Newell & Simon, 1972), which has these rules:

> A set of nine cardboard squares (pieces) like those used in the game of Scrabble is placed face up between the two players. Each piece bears a different integer, from 1 to 9, so that all nine digits are represented. The players draw pieces alternately from the set. The first player who holds any subset of exactly three pieces from among those drawn, with digits summing to 15 wins the game. If all the pieces are drawn from the set without either player obtaining three whose digits sum to 15, the game is a draw.

I have played this game against students in my cognitive psychology classes, and I often win. When I watch the students to see how they may have represented this task, I usually find that they begin by listing all the combinations of three digits whose sum is 15. They then check off as "gone" any combination that involves a number that I have picked. Such a representation doesn't afford them many possibilities for victory. Can you see any representations that might be somewhat more efficient?

When you were a child, you probably played tic-tac-toe, a game whose interest is generally limited to children. Although not apparent, tic-tac-toe and number scrabble are formally the same game. Figure 12.4 makes this relationship clear. The games are formally identical in the sense that a winning tic-tac-toe player would always have three digits from the "magic square" whose sum was 15. The converse is also true. Winning-number scrabble players would also always have a winning tic-tac-toe configuration. My mastery of number scrabble now stands revealed: my superior representation of the game enables me to play a child's game against my students, who don't have the same representation.

The Gestaltists believed that improvements in thinking ability were accompanied by, or in fact depended on, improvements in representation. The expert thinker was superior because he could see things that the novice problem solver could not. We'll come back to this point again later, but apparently the Gestaltists were essentially correct about it.

De Groot (1965, 1966) conducted studies that have helped clarify how perception works in problem solving. He showed his subjects, most of them chess masters, a tactical position taken from an actual tournament game that had taken place between two grand masters. A tactical position is one in which many of the chess pieces are still on the board, and their arrangement is such that several moves are possible. In other

Figure 12.4 Magic square for tic-tac-toe.

2	7	6
9	5	1
4	3	8

words, in many tactical situations the "correct" move is not obvious, and coming up with a good move involves fairly lengthy analysis of the board.

The subjects were asked to analyze the board to determine what they thought would be white's best move. You might expect that chess masters would be much better able to do this task than class A players, the next lower rank. But when de Groot compared masters' responses with those of class A players, he had a surprise. The masters were not overwhelmingly better than class A players in selecting the "correct" move. The class A player could analyze the board almost as well as the master; yet, if a game were staged between players of the two ranks, the outcome would not be in doubt. The master would win an overwhelming proportion of such games. De Groot wanted to analyze the method used by the players to reach their decisions, and so had his subjects **think out loud** as they examined the chessboard. These comments were tape-recorded and analyzed. When de Groot compared the method of analysis used by the masters and class A players, he found similarities there as well. In both classes, the player looked at the board and selected a move as the basis for a continuation—a series of alternating white and black moves that the player would try to imagine. If you play chess, you're probably familiar with this type of "I'll do this, then they'll do this, then I'll do this" thinking. Generally, the continuation went on until the player felt that some clear evaluation point had been reached, such as capturing an opponent's piece or achieving some identifiable, strong position. After one continuation ended, the player selected another base move and explored a different continuation until another evaluation point was achieved. After several continuations had been explored, the player evaluated the outcomes and picked the base move that led to the best one.

Although the method of analysis and the move picked by the players were similar for players of different abilities, de Groot found that the differences between the two classes were in the number of moves that were selected for continuation. Surprisingly, masters explored fewer moves than did less able players. In other words, the masters seemingly had a good idea about which moves should be explored in the first place. According to de Groot, the masters were able to see some moves better than class A players because their interpretation and organization of the chessboard were more likely to be deadly accurate, when accuracy was defined by independent postgame analysis by other masters.

De Groot and other researchers (Chase & Simon, 1973) also learned something about this organization when they asked chess masters to reproduce tournament positions (i.e., configurations of chess pieces that had occurred in a tournament) from memory. As you might expect, chess masters are quite good at this task. De Groot found that his masters could reproduce a position of greater than twenty pieces after only five seconds of study. De Groot noticed that when the players reconstructed the position, they did not put down pieces on the board one at a time at a constant rate. Rather, in retrieving the position from memory, the master placed a group of four or five pieces on the board in their correct locations. A short latency then occurred, followed by another group of four or five pieces being placed.

What does this finding mean? The masters apparently had encoded the position in several chunks, where each chunk consisted of a group of pieces that were somehow related to one another. One such chunk was the pawn chain, a group of mutually supporting pawns (Chase & Simon, 1973). Realize too that the relationships between the pieces were expressible in chess terms. For example, fianchettoed bishops are those which operate on long diagonals on the chessboard and consequently have freedom of movement. The masters might retrieve the fianchettoed bishops simultaneously, even though the bishops themselves were not necessarily close to one another on the chessboard. The chess masters were not simply using a geographic code to organize the pieces on the basis of their place on the board. Rather, they apparently were using a much more abstract coding scheme, which depended on their extensive knowledge of chess configurations.

This contention was supported in another study by Chase and Simon (1973). They showed chess masters and novices chess positions that were produced by random assignment of pieces. In that situation, chess masters were no better than novices in reconstructing the position. Simon and Gilmartin (1973) have speculated that the typical chess master, after countless hours of examining and analyzing chess positions, has encoded perhaps 50,000 such chunks of related pieces.

Very similar findings have been reached in a different domain, computer programming. McKeithen, Reitman, Rueter, and Hirtle (1981) asked their subjects, who were computer programmers of differing skill levels, to recall programs that had been briefly presented on a computer screen. Both meaningful and meaningless programs were presented; the latter were created by scrambling the lines of code in a meaningful program. As you might expect, expert programmers were quite good at recalling the meaningful programs. Experts did no better than novices, though, in recalling the scrambled programs. McKeithen et al. hypothesized that the experts' superiority was based on their organization of the elements in the computer program, and they tested this assertion by having experts and novices memorize and recall lists of programming "keywords" such as "string," "while," "do," and "step." The dependent variable was the order in which the terms were recalled by various groups. Interestingly, they found that experts often retrieved words in an order that might correspond to the words' use in a computer program (e.g., "while—do," "for—step"). This organization was not observed in the novices' retrieval patterns; they tended to recall words in an order corresponding to natural-language associations (e.g., "bits"—"of"—"string"). Such findings intriguingly foreshadow the literature on expertise that we'll take up later in this chapter.

Summarizing the Gestalt Position

The Gestaltists emphasized **discontinuity in thinking.** That is, they believed problem solving was accomplished in stages that were qualitatively different from one another. Moreover, problem solving could sometimes be accomplished by unconscious work that would be terminated by insight. These matters have supplied modern researchers with a host of interesting questions to explore, and as we've seen, these explorations have generally shown the Gestalt account to be lacking as an empirical prediction of what takes place when someone tries to solve a problem. That is, contemporary research seems to indicate that problem solving is not accomplished by insight, but rather is continuous. In emphasizing the correct representation, however, the Gestaltists were clearly on to something, a theme for this chapter. Later, when we consider expertise in problem solving, we'll see that the expert seems to have a representation of the problem that includes elements missing from the novice's representation. In the next section we examine some of the modern research in problem solving.

omain-Free Problems and General Strategies

Much of the contemporary research on problem solving has dealt with so-called **domain-free problems,** which have a clearly specifiable answer but require no explicitly specialized training to solve. You may be familiar with any number of river-crossing problems in which people or animals are to be transported across a river in a limited-capacity boat. Some constraints are usually imposed about who can be transported with whom. Such problems are used for several reasons. First, they are usually complicated enough to be challenging for most adults, but not so complicated as to be undoable. Second, the properties of such problems can often be specified in some formal way, as in a mathematical representation, or embodied in a computer program. Thus it is possible to compare human performance on such problems with some idealized performance. The advantage in such an approach is that we may be able to discern commonalities in problems in which human performance deviates significantly from ideal performance. If we find such deviations, they may tell us much about the characteristics of the human information-processing system in general. Finally, if we see commonalities among people's attempts to solve such problems, we may be able to draw inferences about their strategies and, in turn, their representations of the problem.

Generally, cognitive psychologists have taken two complementary approaches to studying domain-free problems. First, some psychologists have attempted to classify domain-free problems. This approach focuses on the problems themselves in the hope of finding out the cognitive skills that seem to be required to solve that class of problem. The ultimate—and perhaps unrealizable—objective in such a program would be to catalogue problem types, each type demanding different cognitive skills.

An alternative approach is to look at problem solvers who are trying to solve many kinds of domain-free problems. Here, the objective is to find commonalities among people rather than among problems. The hope is that general strategies might be discovered that people use to solve a number of domain-free problems. Part of the reason for searching for such general strategies is practical. If they could be found, perhaps they could be taught to people, possibly enhancing their problem-solving ability. In this section we explore the findings produced by both approaches.

Well-Defined and Ill-Defined Problems

One simple way of categorizing a problem is to determine whether it is well or ill defined. Most of the problems we have considered thus far in this chapter could be considered well defined (Reitman, 1964). A **well-defined problem** begins with a clearly defined start state and has clearly defined goals. If the problem is well defined, every proposed solution can be evaluated against the criteria implied by the goal. If the proposed solution matches the criteria implied by the goal, the problem is solved; if the criteria have not been achieved, the problem is still unsolved. Getting to the football game from your house in time for the kickoff is a well-defined problem. The chess game offers us another good example. The game starts from a clearly prescribed arrangement of pieces. Moreover, the goal can be precisely stated: in chess we're trying to checkmate the opposing king. Checkmate has been achieved if one of our pieces is checking the opposing king and our opponent is unable to (1) move his or her king to a safe square, or (2) interpose a friendly piece between the king and the checking piece, or (3) kill the checking piece. Can you think of some other well-defined problems? Is the board game Monopoly well defined? The answer is yes. Monopoly and other board games such as Clue or Stratego are almost always well defined. Notice that a well-defined problem does not have to specify every path to the goal state; finding such a path is the solver's task.

Not all problems are well defined. The goal state or the start state or both are sometimes left partially specified. A problem that has some component missing in this sense is said to be **ill defined.** Plenty of ill defined problems confront us in this world; indeed, most of our interesting problems, such as achieving success in life, are ill-defined. That is, how will you know when you're a success? Our intuitions tell us that our concepts of success will vary throughout our lifetimes, and so we can have no precise criteria for determining its presence or absence. Generally, specifying the actions that should be taken to solve ill-defined problems is much more difficult than it is for well-defined problems (Chi & Glaser, 1985). Generally speaking, then, a problem is ill defined if the start state is vague or unspecifiable, if the goal state is unclear, or if the operations required to change the start state into the goal state are unclear.

Little research has been done on ill-defined problems, but the few discoveries are interesting. Voss and his colleagues (Voss, Greene, Post, & Penner, 1983; Voss, Tyler, & Yengo, 1983) asked their subjects to imagine that they were minister of agriculture for the Soviet Union. They were told to imagine that crop productivity had been too low for the past several years and that they were to come up with a plan to increase crop production. Notice that this problem is quite ill defined. All three components in a well-defined problem are missing from the description given the subjects. They are told crop production is low, but the problem is far greater. To specify what has made crop production low, subjects need to know something about the Soviet Union, agriculture, and so on. Similarly, the subjects were told to increase crop production, but were given no clue about how to do so. Finally, the goal is also unclear. How much of an increase is reasonable and significant? Would a 5% increase solve the problem, or is a 50% increase required?

Three groups of subjects were used, differing in their knowledge about the Soviet Union. One group of subjects were political scientists specializing in Soviet affairs. A second group were students taking a course in Soviet domestic policy, and the third group were chemistry professors. Voss et al. found that predictable effects resulted from prior knowledge. In 24% of their solutions, the Soviet experts mentioned that the problem's initial state needed to be elaborated more fully to achieve a solution. This need was mentioned in only 1% of the solutions offered by students and chemistry professors. Some commonalities were seen, however, in the approaches the various subjects chose. They usually realized that the best way to solve a problem of this sort is to eliminate its causes. They generally tried to determine the causes behind low productivity and then thought about ways of counteracting those effects. Typically, they realized that the problem wasn't produced by one cause but possibly by a series of separate causes. Subjects who recognized this multiplicity usually proposed various ways for dealing with such causes. One expert identified three causes of low productivity: the Soviet bureaucracy, Soviet farmers' attitudes toward modernizing, and lack of infrastructure (e.g., production of pesticides and farm equipment and transportation deficiencies). Notice that these problems are somewhat more precise than the original one.

This research therefore suggests that people solve ill-defined problems by performing transformations that result in breaking down the problem into smaller, more manageable subproblems. The more knowledge we have about a subject, the better able we seem to be in creating such solvable subproblems. That is, problem solvers seem to rely on knowledge to create more or less well-defined subproblems from the original ill-defined problem.

We should be aware, though, of several other aspects of the well-defined–ill defined distinction. First, the boundary between the two classes of problems is occasionally blurry (Simon, 1973). The proof of a theorem in logic is usually considered a well-defined problem. Simon writes, however, that a person may not restrict problem solving to the symbols of formal logic, but may use analogy to other logic problems. Thus, although the proof of a logic theorem may be well defined, the rules for going about such proofs are themselves ill defined. Second, some evidence suggests that unless people perceive a rigid procedure for converting start states into goal states, they are likely to treat well-defined problems as ill defined—just the opposite of what Voss et al. found.

Greeno (1976) presented to high-school students in geometry problems involving proof of various theorems. He asked them to think out loud as they solved the problems, and tape-recorded their comments. Analyzing these utterances indicated that the subjects tended to break down the problem into subproblems, as Voss and his colleagues had found. The surprise in the findings, however, was the apparent vagueness of the subjects' subgoals. When asked if he had any specific theorems in mind, one student answered:

> I don't know. I was just sort of letting . . . I was just sort of letting the information . . . I shouldn't have said that I was running through all the theorems, I was just letting this stuff, the given information, sort of soak through my head, you know. (p. 483)

Typologies of Problems

As we've seen, the well-defined–ill-defined distinction offers us one way of categorizing problems, but its usefulness is somewhat limited. An alternative scheme for classifying problems was developed by Greeno (1978). He analyzed several problems that he maintains can be considered examples of the three basic forms of problem solving. He argues too that each of these three basic forms can be associated with a cognitive operation or skill necessary to solve problems of that type.

Problems in Inducing Structure   The first of Greeno's three basic forms he calls **problems in inducing structure,** which consist of determining the relationship among several elements of the problem. A common example is the analogy problem, in which four elements are supplied, and the solver must determine whether they can be related in some way that fits the structure $A:B::C:D$ (i.e., A is to B as C is to D). Greeno states that the principal cognitive ability required for problems of this type is some form of understanding. What processes are required to do analogy problems successfully?

Pellegrino (1985) theorized that three classes of cognitive skills are necessary to do analogy problems. The first class of cognitive operations consists of attribute discovery or encoding processes. If verbal items are presented, encoding consists of activating some aspects of semantic memory. If the analogy consists of figural or pictorial elements, the encoding processes are based on feature extraction. In either class, a representation of the elements is created and stored. This representation is critical because subsequent operations are carried out on it. After the elements in the analogy have been encoded, the problem solver begins comparing the encoded attributes. This process is the second cognitive skill needed to solve analogies. The attributes might be compared in several ways. The subject might use inference making to determine what the first two elements in the analogy have in common with each other, as well as some of the things that differ between them.

Mapping the attributes is another way in which the encoded attributes might be compared. This method refers to the solver's attempts to find a comparison between the first and third terms in the analogy. If the analogy were Dog:Wolf::Cat: ? the solver must first activate the semantic nodes of *dog* and *wolf*, noticing perhaps that both are canine, and also that dogs are domestic whereas wolves are wild. In mapping, the solver would activate the *cat* node, noticing that cats are feline and domestic.

Another way of comparing the encoded attributes is application. Here, the solver attempts to relate the inference drawn from the A–B comparison to the differences found in the C term, in an effort to generate what the "ideal" D candidate might be. The solver working on the prior analogy might convert its form thus: Domestic Canine is to Wild Canine as Domestic Feline is to (perhaps) Wild Feline. Thus, the ideal candidate as produced by application might be lion, tiger, or panther.

After the solver has encoded the analogy's attributes and compared them, it's time to engage in the final class of processes necessary to do analogies, which is evaluation. In the example just given, determining the ideal candidate was fairly simple, and so making a response or picking out the most appropriate response from among several alternatives would be easy. In other situations, however, the complexity of the analogy might be increased if the elements differ in many features. Then, evaluating the alternatives to pick the best one may be a complicated cognitive act in its own right.

According to Pellegrino's account, these processes should be enacted sequentially; that is, you cannot go to evaluation until you have completed all the attribute comparisons. Moreover, attribute comparison should be affected by the complexity of the elements in the analogy and by the degree of difference between features among the elements in the analogy. If the analogy has many features, or if the elements in the analogy share few features, the analogy should be harder.

A study by Mulholland, Pellegrino, and Glaser (1980) tested these assertions. Subjects were shown the analogies depicted in Figure 12.5 and were asked to state whether the analogy was true or false (the analogy had to be exact to be true). Notice that the analogies had been varied in complexity by altering both the number of elements in the figures and the number of transformations between the elements. Figure 12.6

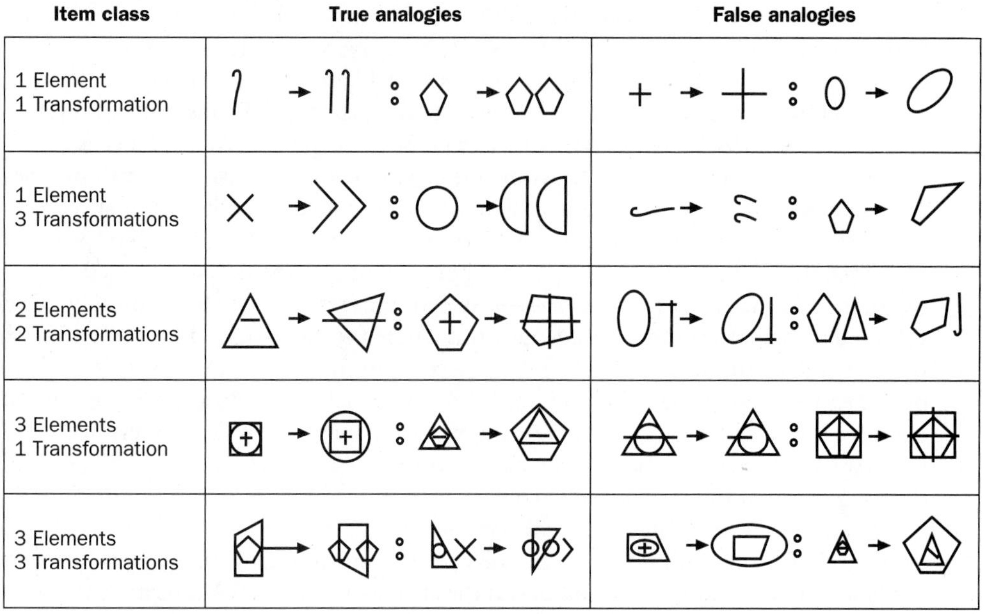

Item class	True analogies	False analogies
1 Element 1 Transformation		
1 Element 3 Transformations		
2 Elements 2 Transformations		
3 Elements 1 Transformation		
3 Elements 3 Transformations		

Figure 12.5 Examples of true and false figural analogies varying in complexity of items. *Source:* From Mulholland, Pellegrino, & Glaser, 1980.

Figure 12.6 Reaction times for figural-analogy solution, showing the separate effect of elements and number of transformations. *Source:* From Mulholland, Pellegrino, & Glaser, 1980.

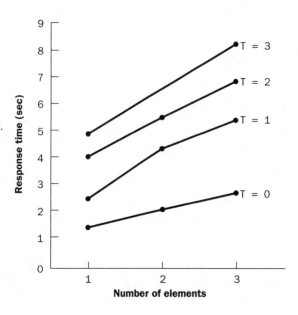

shows the findings in this study, which support Pellegrino's predictions. The two factors affecting complexity combined in an orderly way to produce increases in latency for more complex analogies. Each element in the original analogy added about 300 msec to the average subject's solution time, and each transformation added about 400 msec.

In our everyday problem solving, we rely on analogies quite a bit; generally we use the analogy to take us from one domain of knowledge to another, or from one kind of problem to another within a domain. Novick and Holyoak (1991) theorize that, in addition to the mapping process that we've already discussed, people must engage in a separate adapting process to complete an analogy. In other words, even after a problem reminds us of another that we might use as the basis for our solution efforts, we still must endeavor to see if the solution procedure that we used in the reminded problem can be tailored to work for the problem at hand. According to Novick and Holyoak (1991), it is this adaptation that often spells the difference between success and failure in using analogies. To show these effects, Novick and Holyoak first gave their subjects a problem like this one to solve:

> Mr. and Mrs. Renshaw were planning how to arrange vegetable plants in their new garden. They agreed on the number of plants to buy, but not on how many of each kind to get. Mr. Renshaw wanted to have a few kinds of vegetables and ten of each kind. Mrs. Renshaw wanted more kinds of vegetables, and so she suggested having only four of each kind. Mr. Renshaw didn't like that because if some of the plants died, there wouldn't be many left of each kind. They agreed to have five of each vegetable. But then their daughter pointed out that there was room in the garden for two more plants, although then there wouldn't be the same number of each kind of vegetable. To remedy this imbalance, she suggested buying six of each vegetable. Everyone was satisfied with this plan. Given this information, what is the smallest number of vegetable plants the Renshaws could have in their garden?

Would solving such a problem permit some "general" learning to take place that might enable a person to solve other problems? To find out, Novick and Holyoak gave their subjects additional problems, one of which was the Marching Band Target Problem:

> Members of the West High School Band were hard at work practicing for the annual Homecoming Parade. First they tried marching in rows of twelve, but Andrew was left by himself to bring up the rear. The band director was annoyed because it didn't look good to have one row with only one person in it, and of course Andrew wasn't very pleased, either. To get rid of this problem, the director told the band members to march in columns of eight. But Andrew was still left to march alone. Even when the band marched in rows of three, Andrew was left out. Finally, in exasperation, Andrew told the band director that they should march in rows of five to have all the rows filled. He was right. This time all the rows were filled and Andrew wasn't alone any more. Given that there were at least 45 musicians on the field but fewer than 200 musicians, how many students were there in the West High School Band?

Some subjects were given additional information. Some got a simple retrieval hint; others were given a number-mapping hint but were given no conceptual information. These subjects got a statement similar to this one: The 12, 8, and 3 in the band problem are like the 10, 4, and 5 in the garden problem. Also, the 1 in this problem is like the 2 in the garden problem. Finally, the 5 in this problem is like the 6 in the garden problem. Other subjects got a conceptual hint but did not get specific numerical information. These subjects read this passage:

> In particular, your goal in this problem is to arrange band members into rows or columns so that each row (or each column) has the same number of people in it, with no one left over. That's like the goal you had in the garden problem of grouping plants into different types so that there were the same number of plants of each type, with none left over. In the garden problem the major difficulty encountered was that once the Renshaws finally figured out how many plants they had room for in their garden, all the arrangements they had thought of failed to accommodate two plants. A similar difficulty is found in the marching-band problem. There, each formation the band director thought of failed to accommodate one person. In summary, the band members are like plants, the rows and columns of band members are like kinds of plants, and the number of band members per row or column is like the number of plants of each kind.

Both problems can be solved with a least common multiple (LCM) approach. In each problem, the solver must generate the lowest common multiple of the first three divisors mentioned in the problem that leaves a constant remainder, generating multiples of this LCM, adding the constant remainder to each multiple, and then selecting from this set the generated multiple that can be evenly divided by a fourth number—the divisor that is mentioned last in the problem.

The subjects wrote down the approach that they used, and all their mathematical work was shown. A score of 2 was given to a subject who used the LCM procedure on the band problem; a 1 was given if the subject partially transferred the LCM procedure to the band problem, and a zero went to those who showed no transfer. The number-mapping subjects showed the greatest degree of transfer (mean transfer score = 1.4); the concept-mapping subjects had a significantly lower transfer score (mean = 0.84). This finding suggests that understanding the numerical relationships in the two problems was crucial for success. But understanding the numerical relationships was not sufficient for successful transfer. In other words, simply knowing that "12" in one problem is like "10" in another doesn't enable subjects to apply the LCM procedure in the second case. Indeed, Novick and Holyoak found that even in the "number-mapping" condition, which had the highest mean transfer score, still only 50% of the subjects successfully transferred the LCM procedure intact to the band problem. As the researchers suggested, the major source of difficulty in transferring knowledge across to the target problem may be the adaptation process rather than the mapping process.

Analogy and Memory

No doubt some instances of using analogy in problem solving do not involve a particularly heavy memory component. Let's imagine that the problem solver is a student in a statistics course who must compute an ANOVA homework problem. Suppose she proceeds to do it by getting out her stat book and using the example of the ANOVA computation there as a model for her own homework. It's clear that the student is using the book as the basis for an analogy, but there is relatively little retrieval in that situation. Most of the work of making this analogy consists of mapping and adapting the textbook example to the homework problem.

But much more typically, using an analogy to solve a problem involves some form of retrieval. Then we don't have the basis for the analogy right in front of us, and so we either have to search our memory explicitly for an analogy, or perhaps something about the current problem suggests an analogy we might explore and use. This choice brings us to a question: What in a current problem's features or aspects reminds us of another problem that could be used analogically? In other words, what is it about a current problem that points us to a specific example in our memory that could be used as the basis for an analogy? As you'll read in the Focus on Research in this chapter, several cognitive psychologists (Gentner, Rattermann, & Forbus, 1993; Reeves & Weisberg, 1994) have found that memory access is guided by similarity at the level of surface cues. Surface cues are superficial aspects of the problem as it is presented to a solver, and they may include such elements as names of the people or objects in the problem, or the specific activities or locations around which the problem's story revolves. Let's say my neighbor tells me about a problem he has getting water to come out of his kitchen faucet. It's most likely that his problem would remind me of a problem I had with my kitchen faucet. This episode of memory access seems to be based on a superficial similarity, because the same objects (kitchen faucets) are involved. On some other bases, though, the neighbor's problem might be very different from mine. His problem could be caused by a break in the water line, whereas mine may have been caused by a mechanical failure in the faucet itself. Wharton, Holyoak, and Lange (1996) outline several possible kinds of similarity that could potentially be used as the basis for a reminding and an analogy. These kinds of similarity include object similarity, which is based on using similar objects or characters in different problems. The faucet problem is an example of this type of similarity. Situational similarity describes problems that may involve actors engaged in similar activities, or playing similar roles. A problem in which an individual performs as a drama coach may remind an individual of a problem in which another individual performed as a tennis coach. Unlike these forms of similarity, thematic similarity is based on abstract types of correspondences, including similarities in plans, goals and objectives, and conclusions. But about reminding, are we limited to object and situational similarity? Or, could we also be reminded by an abstract thematic similarity? This was the issue on which Wharton et al. focused.

Consider the stories in Table 12.1. Two target stories are shown, each focused on a theme. For each target story we see a close cue that has both situational elements similar to those of the target (similar characteristics and role of the actor, for example) and thematic elements. For each target story we also have a remote cue that does not share situational elements with the target, but nevertheless has the same thematic structure. Elle the unicorn is very different situationally from John's story. But Elle discounts her failure with a sour-grapes attitude in a way that is similar to John's discounting his failure to get into Yale. Notice that each close and remote cue also functions as a "disanalog" for the alternative target story. That is, the Jennifer story is a disanalog of the John story in the sense that, although it has a situational similarity to the John story, at the thematic level, the stories are different. John experiences sour grapes, but Jennifer turns her failure into a chance to blame herself for her perceived inadequacies.

The subjects read these and other targets and then, after a five-minute filler task, were given close and remote analogs and disanalogs. For each of these, they were asked

Table 12.1   Example of Stories in the Close Condition and in the Remote Condition

Theme 1: Sour Grapes

Target: John was very confident about himself. He did a lot of homework to get good marks. John had only a B–GPA in his first year in high school. He was sure he could do better. Earlier, a counselor had arranged for him to meet with the recruiter from Yale. When he got home from class, he opened the thin rejection letter from Yale. That night he mentioned to his father how he believed that people from Ivy League schools were pretentious.

Close Cue: Lisa spent long hours trying to make her corporation successful. She was very sure about herself. Lisa had broken up with her fiancé a year ago. She wanted to meet someone new. A coworker set her up to go out with someone he knew well. She waited at the fancy restaurant until 8:30 and then left without ordering dinner. She told her friend that she thought her date probably wasn't that handsome and that investment bankers are really boring, anyway.

Remote Cue: Elle was a unicorn who wanted to see what was on the other side of the river. She thought the lands over there were enchanted and rich with meadows and fruit trees. One day she set out to cross the river. Unfortunately, the water was very fast and too deep. Elle swam as hard as she could but after 20 minutes she had to turn back because of fatigue. Elle decided that the stories about the land on the other side of the river were just false rumors and that probably nothing of worth was over there.

Theme 2: Self-Blame

Target: Derrick had failed to make the gymnastics team last fall. He practiced a lot to make the team. He wanted to try again. Derrick was positive he had a lot of potential. His PE teacher had gotten him a tryout with the gymnastics team coach. The coach watched him perform and then told his PE teacher that he didn't want him on the team. Derrick confessed to his teacher that the coach undoubtedly thought he, Derrick, didn't have the talent for gymnastics.

Close Cue: Jennifer worked hard attempting to create a new business venture. She had divorced her husband some time before. She wanted to start socializing again. A friend fixed a blind date for her with one of his friends, Henry, from work. Jennifer was very excited. She waited alone at the entrance to the museum for 2 hours. She confessed to her friend that her date thought she wasn't that attractive and that software engineers aren't interesting.

Remote Cue: Jane was a unicorn who wanted to see what was on the other side of the river. She thought the lands over there were enchanted and rich with meadows and fruit trees. One day she set out to cross the river. Unfortunately, the water was very fast and too deep. Jane swam as hard as she could but after 20 minutes she had to turn back, exhausted, Jane decided that she wasn't worthy of being in the magic lands.

Source: From Wharton et al., 1996.

to write down as accurately as possible which, if any, of the earlier stories they were reminded of by the current stories. In other words, we will see in this study the extent to which close and remote analogs and disanalogs reminded subjects of the target.

The results are shown in Figure 12.7. The subjects were reminded of the target more by the analog than by the disanalog, regardless of whether the analog and disanalog were close or remote in situational similarity. Expressed as in Table 12.1, the subjects were more likely to be reminded of the Derrick story by the Jennifer story than by the Lisa story. And they were more likely to be reminded of the Derrick story by the Jane story than by the Elle story. As previous research has shown, the close or situational cues, which are superficial, are powerful. The subjects were reminded of the target more by the close disanalog than by the remote analog. The thematic resemblance is not just as strong as the situational resemblance in producing a remind-

Figure 12.7 Reminding for target stories in Experiment 1. *Source: Wharton et al., 1996.*

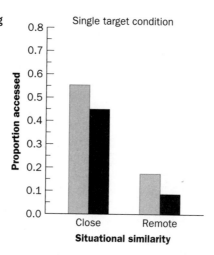

ing. In fact, the thematic resemblance is probably weaker. But the point is that the subjects were nevertheless representing abstract aspects of the stories at the time they first read them, and then later, they used abstract resemblances as the basis upon which the analogy was built. It's also true that the subjects in the Wharton et al. study were not actually solving problems, and so the analogy process may be directed differently when the subject is using the reminding in the service of solving a problem.

Problems in Transformation   The second of Greeno's three types is the transformation problem. **Problems in transformation** involve finding a sequence of operations that transform the initial situation into a goal state. A characteristic example is the well-known **Tower of Hanoi** problem. Figure 12.8 illustrates a four-disk version of the Tower of Hanoi. The four disks have holes in them so that they can be placed on the three pegs. The disks may be moved one at a time to any other peg provided that no disk is ever stacked on top of a smaller disk. Only the top disk in a stack may be moved. The goal is to move the entire stack on peg 1 over to peg 3. You can duplicate the Tower of Hanoi with different-sized coins placed on pieces of paper labeled "peg 1" and so on. If you try it, you'll see that the problem is far from trivial. According to Greeno, the major cognitive skill required to do this task is means-end analysis (Newell & Simon, 1972): perception of differences between current and desired states. Moreover, means-end analysis suggests some sort of action that will reduce the discrepancy.

The Tower of Hanoi puzzle has been extensively studied for various reasons. First, although usually not clear initially to the subjects, the puzzle has an orderly structure that significantly constrains the subjects' choices. Figure 12.9 shows this organization.

As the drawing shows, each move in the Tower of Hanoi can be thought of as producing a different configuration of disks, or a different state. This version of the Tower of Hanoi problem has 27 states. In general, a Tower of Hanoi has 3^n states, where n is the number of disks. The minimal number of moves necessary to solve a Tower of Hanoi problem is $2^n - 1$. You can therefore see that increasing the number of disks in a Tower of Hanoi by 1 essentially triples the number of states that could be entered, but it only doubles (more or less) the minimal number of moves necessary for solution.

Figure 12.8   The four-disk version of the Tower of Hanoi problem.

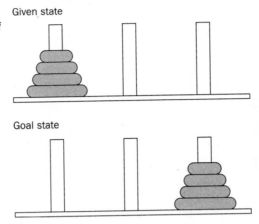

Given state

Goal state

Figure 12.9   Problem graph of the legal moves and states for the three-disk Tower of Hanoi problem. Disks are represented by the numbers 1, 2, and 3, 1 being the smallest disk. *Source:* From Karat, 1982.

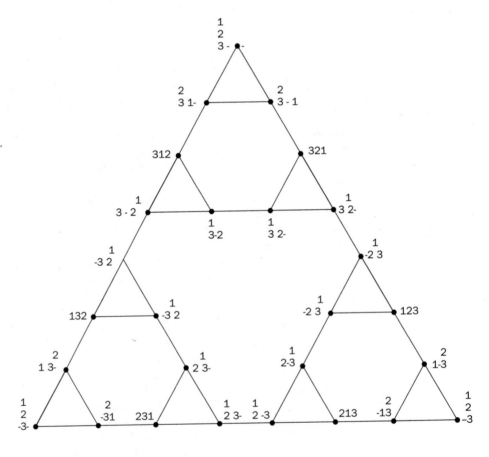

What produces this discrepancy? Again, it's not apparent, but the Tower of Hanoi problem has a feature known as *recursion,* which means that the larger versions of the problem include the smaller versions. In other words, on the way to solving a four-disk version of the problem, the solver actually solves two three-disk versions. Solving the five-disk version consists of solving two four-disk problems, and so on.

This organization is not initially clear to the problem solver, but Karat (1982) has determined that subjects do have limited understanding of how to solve the problem. This understanding, however, is not enough to permit the subject to generate the complete solution. Subjects quickly realize that moving the same disk on two consecutive moves is not useful, because such a movement could always be accomplished in one move. This realization is often followed by the solver's understanding that the smallest disk in any Tower of Hanoi should be moved on the odd-numbered moves, and some other disk should be moved on the alternate, even-numbered moves. Together, these realizations suggest this pattern for movement: (1) move the smallest disk, (2) move disk 2 (the second smallest disk) to the only available peg, (3) put disk 1 on disk 2, and (4) move the only other disk possible. Any deviation from this sequence of moves leads to undoing the most recently attained state (Polson & Jeffries, 1982). Although most solvers quickly latch on to these concepts, which Karat has called local knowledge, there's one thing that the four-step sequence doesn't indicate. That is, to which peg should the smallest disk be moved initially? This move requires some additional knowledge—broader, or global knowledge of Tower of Hanoi problems.

Karat contends that both types of knowledge can be represented in three types of cognitive processes, which he has formalized as a three-stage model: execute, propose, and evaluate. The executive system describes a group of cognitive processes that examine working memory to see if any from a list of approved moves (such as moving the smallest disk on an odd-numbered move) is available. If one such move is available, the person will make that move. If no such move is detected, the propose system is activated. The propose system considers the current condition of the array and tries to figure out if some approved moves would become possible if the disks were rearranged somewhat. Here, Karat maintains that the solver has two kinds of knowledge. The first we might call understanding; the solver knows what has to be done to rearrange the array so that the four-step sequence previously outlined can be executed. If understanding is not present, the solver will make available moves probabilistically, which constitutes the second kind of knowledge the solver might have. The final system, evaluation, simply checks the proposed move for legality. When Karat's model is compared with naive human performances, its predictions about move choice and move latency agree closely with actual behavior. Although such findings don't prove that human subjects are endowed with and use the processes Karat has theorized, they suggest that we have a few basic operations that are involved in these sorts of transformation problems.

Karat's research suggests that human behavior on these types of tasks is fairly simple because the task constrains people's choices. This finding may give you the idea that for most people it is not hard to come up with a strategy or plan for dealing with the Tower of Hanoi. That is, because most people act in a very local sense, without seeming to take into account where they're ultimately going in the problem, you might get the idea that people are content simply to take baby steps in problems such as the Tower of Hanoi. But actually, coming up with a strategy in these problems may be harder than it seems. Anzai and Simon (1979) asked their subjects to make oral statements of their thoughts while they were solving the Tower of Hanoi. Anzai and Simon found that people may actually use four strategies in solving problems. Two strategies were particularly advanced. Many subjects' comments indicated the presence of a disk-moving strategy consisting of several moves that were designed to move a particular disk to a particular peg. Many subjects also had an even more advanced pyramid-moving strategy in which the subject produces a series of individual moves designed to move a stack of several disks to a specific peg.

VanLehn's (1991) work supports these notions. Using the same procedure as that of Anzai and Simon in a case study on one subject, VanLehn found that the subject explicitly worked on developing particular strategies eleven times in a problem-solving session on the Tower of Hanoi. One particularly interesting aspect of VanLehn's findings is that the strategies were usually discussed in terms of rules; moreover, these rule-acquisition events were not always driven by the subject's reaching an impasse. Sometimes the subject examined her strategies simply because she was seeking a more efficient (that is, fewer-moves) solution.

Problems in Arrangement   Finally, in Greeno's third type of problem, that of arrangement, the solver is given some element that must be rearranged according to some criterion. A typical example of **problems in arrangement** is the anagram, and the principal cognitive skill needed to do such a problem is constructive search. That is, the solver must develop some way of systematically examining reasonable combinations of letters until the solution is found. This task is not easy. A five-letter anagram has 5 or 120 possible combinations. If you were to search through this number of combinations at the rate of one per second, coming up with the answer might take as long as two minutes. Because most people can solve such anagrams faster than that, however, the subjects don't seem to be searching the combinations randomly.

For most subjects not all 120 possibilities are examined. Consider this anagram:

AIFMA

If you are even moderately aware of your own thought processes, you know you quickly became aware that the first two letters in the anagram almost certainly had to be separated. Few English words begin with the letters *AI*. Similarly, you know that the letters *MA* form a fairly common syllable in English that occurs at the beginning or ending of words (probably more often at the beginning). Perhaps you mentally shifted the *MA* combination around while visualizing various combinations of the remaining three letters. Greeno calls this type of thinking "generating partial solutions" (Greeno, 1978). That is, the problem solver produces what are believed to be the components of the entire solution, and these components are fabricated on the basis of the solver's knowledge.

This process is roughly analogous to the **local–global distinction** we made for transformation problems. The person who is generating partial solutions has some local knowledge, but not complete global knowledge, about the task, which implies that an anagram would be more difficult if its letters could be combined systematically in many ways. This hypothesis was supported in a study by Ronning (1965), who determined that anagrams are harder to solve if their letters can be organized in various ways that are consistent with English phonology. In addition to this phonetic knowledge, other evidence indicates that knowledge of the anagram's semantic category (knowing, for example, that the anagram can be rearranged to make "a form of transportation") also facilitates the search (Dominowski & Ekstrand, 1967; Richardson & Johnson, 1980), probably because it somewhat constrains the search.

Greeno's work is an endeavor to identify classes of problems that seem to require different classes of cognitive skills. We have seen that the problems Greeno has identified as prototypical do require some different skills, but the skills required also seem to overlap. For example, constructive search is brought into play both for transformation and arrangement problems, which has led some cognitive psychologists to wonder if perhaps the problem should be turned around. Instead of trying to identify classes of problems that differ from one another, perhaps we should focus on what takes place in the solver's mind. This realization has resulted in a search for what we might call general problem strategies that can be used for many problems. In the next section we review the outcome of this line of investigation.

Tactics for Solving Problems

Greeno's work suggests that different types of problems can best be solved with relevant and particular skills. Are any general strategies available that might be useful in solving widely varied problems?

Before we examine some of these all-purpose strategies, we need a definition for **strategy,** which is derived from the Greek *strategos,* which originally meant "trick" or "deception." The Greeks later used this word to describe army generals; that is, a general was one who could trick the enemy. Notice that although a trick or ruse is *indicated* by some behavior, a trick is more than *just* behavior. The trick implies that some mental action or planning has preceded it. Unintentional tricks are not possible.

A modern definition of strategy must take these things into account. Strategies are seen in behavior, but the behavior implies some sort of mental effort. A strategy can therefore be defined as a move, trial, or probe designed to effect some change in the problem and provide information by so doing. That is, the change is considered informative. Cognitive psychologists have described two broad classes of strategies: **heuristics** and **algorithms.**

An *algorithm* is a procedure that is guaranteed to produce an answer to the problem. Algorithms may not always be efficient, but they always work. We make use of algorithms whenever we multiply numbers together with paper and pencil or with a calculator. Similarly, we can solve any anagram problem if we follow the algorithm of arranging the letters in every possible combination until a word is found. If algorithms are so powerful, why don't we use them all the time? The answer to this question can be found by referring to the well-defined–ill-defined distinction made earlier. Successful solutions to ill-defined problems often can't be specified ahead of time; thus, no procedure can be developed that will necessarily produce solutions to them. We can't have algorithms for ill-defined problems. Even for well-defined problems, we are sometimes defeated in our attempts to find an algorithm because the problem itself is so large. Chess and checkers are examples of problems that are too vast to permit easy discovery of an algorithm. Even the IBM RS/6000 SP computer "Deep Blue" that defeated the human chess master Garry Kasparov in a celebrated match in May 1997 can consider "only" 200 million chess moves per second. This sounds like a gigantic number, and it is, but in the context of the number of chess games that can be played (10^{40}), it is just a tiny fraction of the chess moves that could be made. Even Deep Blue cannot consider every possible chess move, with every possible countermove, with every possible counter-countermove, all the way to the end of the game, in a reasonable time. What happens when we don't have an algorithm to help us solve a problem? We turn to heuristics.

Heuristics are rules of thumb that have been developed from experience in solving problems. If you've ever changed the tire on a car, you're probably aware of some useful heuristics such as loosening the bolts slightly *before* you jack up the car. Similarly, if you play chess, you probably know some of its heuristics, such as keeping the queen at the center of the action, keeping the knights away from the edge of the board, and so on. Unlike algorithms, heuristics don't guarantee attainment of a solution. But they often make up for this shortcoming by being easy and fast to use. Over the past several years, cognitive scientists have discovered that humans often use several all-purpose heuristics that don't appear closely tied to specific problems. Much of this knowledge comes from work by Newell and Simon.

The Newell and Simon Research   Perhaps the most imposing theory of problem solving to be erected by cognitive psychologists is that of Newell and Simon, which they developed over the past thirty-five years (Newell, 1962, 1965, 1966, 1967; Newell, Shaw, & Simon, 1958; Newell & Simon, 1961, 1972; Simon, 1969, 1978). This is an information-processing theory that begins with the concept of problem representation. Newell and Simon discuss two sorts of problem representations. The term **task environment** describes how a problem is represented thoroughly and neutrally as possible. The task environment therefore is an attempt to represent the problem objectively. In trying to understand human problem solving on a task, Newell and Simon invariably begin by attempting to map out the problem's task environment. Why?

They have two major reasons. First, completely understanding a problem's task environment can be equated with understanding all the ways in which that problem could be represented. Clearly, for anything more than trivial problems, this ideal cannot be reached. But the solver, in the act of problem solving, chooses some representations as more desirable than others. Knowing which representations were chosen from an array of all possible representations affords a great deal of knowledge about the solver's psychology.

A second reason for understanding the task environment stems from the task environment's powerful influence on the apparent complexity of the solver's behavior. According to Newell and Simon, the human information-processing system is not very complicated. Consequently, if its behavior appears complex, it's probably because the task environment in which it is operating is complex.

The solver does not typically have complete knowledge about the task environment. Confronted with an unfamiliar problem, the solver must encode the relevant features of the problem to construct an internal representation of it. Newell and Simon label the solver's internal representation the **problem space;** and thinking of the problem space as a subset of the task environment is appropriate.

Operators Newell and Simon conceptualize the problem space as a collection of nodes, similar in form to those we looked at in the TLC model. In the problem space, each node stands for a state of knowledge. The nodes are linked by cognitive processes called **operators,** which convert one node into another. For Newell and Simon, problem solving consists of moving through the nodes in the problem space. The solver working on the problem accesses or enters different states of knowledge. Newell and Simon describe this movement as controlled by an executive system, and the movement itself is similar to the search processes that we looked at for models like TLC.

How does a solver go about selecting an operator? The evidence amassed thus far suggests that solvers are sensitive to both their current context, or location in the problem, and to their history, or success or failure with certain operators. This view suggests that some operators may become more or less preferred as the solver moves from the early to the later stages in a problem or sequence of similar problems. Second, this view suggests that solvers may be sensitive to which operators have "worked" and which haven't. Both effects can be seen in work by Lovett and Anderson (1996).

Solvers in this study were confronted with a set of problems called the building-sticks task (BST). On their computer screens, they saw an initial array that looked like the topmost box in Figure 12.10. The subject's task was to select one of the three sticks shown at the bottom of the box as a first step toward building the "desired" stick shown in the box. From this initial selection, the subjects could add or subtract lengths from the three sticks shown at the bottom of the box. The three boxes below the topmost box show three hypothetical choices that subjects could make in attempting to build the desired stick. After making this initial choice, they could add to it or subtract from it by clicking on the three sticks. The "R" ellipsis was a "reset" or "start-over" button that the subject clicked on if it seemed impossible to solve the problem with the sticks that had been selected. Solvers have two operators that they may use in their

Figure 12.10 Initial and successor states in the building-sticks task. The circled R represents reset. *Source:* From Lovett and Anderson, 1996.

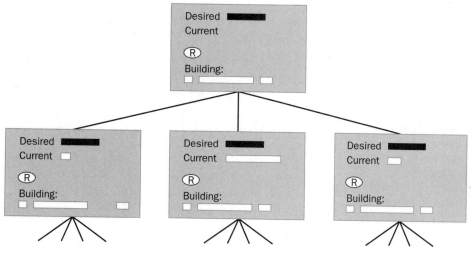

initial selection of sticks. The leftmost and rightmost boxes show how the *undershoot* operator is used. The solver using the undershoot operator tries to build the desired stick by adding small segments together. The box at the middle shows the response by a subject who is using the *overshoot* operator. The solver initially selects a stick that is clearly too long compared to the one desired and then tries to create the desired stick by subtracting either or both of the small sticks to end up with the desired one.

The subjects were given an eight-problem training phase, followed by a three-problem variable phase. In the variable phase, subjects solved three problems of one type: either "o," "u," or "U" problems (all problems in the training phase were "o" problems). Let's examine this terminology. A solver given the "o" problems saw one building stick that was longer than the desired stick and two building sticks that were shorter than the desired one. Such problems could be solved only by overshooting; that is, by selecting the long stick at some stage in the problem. For the "u" problems, the solver saw the same initial configuration of building sticks, but "u" problems could be solved only by undershooting. That is, no solution path included the longest stick. The "U" problems presented a starting configuration of three building sticks that were all shorter than the desired stick, and so these problems could be solved only by undershooting, because overshooting was impossible in these problems. After the three-problem variable phase, the solvers saw a four-problem test phase.

Figure 12.11 shows the percentage of subjects using the overshoot operator as their initial selection on each problem in the learning, variable, and test phases. The initial phase shows quite a bit of variability in use of the overshoot operator as the solvers were trying out the two operators to see which, if either, was generally more useful. I think the most important comparison takes place at problem 12, the first in the test phase. The subjects who had seen the "o" problems all along continued to select the longest stick first. The "U" subjects behaved similarly. That is, after coming out of the three-problem variable phase in which they had to undershoot (i.e., select a little stick because no long sticks were available), these subjects seemed to be

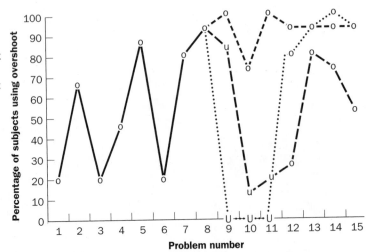

Figure 12.11
Percentage of subjects using overshoot for Lovett and Anderson's experiment 1. Each data point is labeled by its problem type: "o" problems have one stick longer than the desired stick and are solved by overshoot; "u" problems have one stick longer than the desired stick and are solved by undershoot; "U" problems have no sticks longer than the desired stick and are solved by undershoot. *Source:* From Lovett and Anderson, 1996.

content to revert to the overshoot operator. But consider the "u" subjects, who experienced success in the variable phase only when they used the undershoot operator. In the test phase, the subjects have their choice of either over- or undershooting, and as the drawing shows, these subjects seem reluctant to take their chances with an initial use of the overshoot operator. And their initial use of this operator for the four problems in the test phase remains significantly lower than that of either of the other two groups. Consistent with the Newell and Simon predictions, the solvers appear to take into account their recent history in selecting an operator. As the conditions in the problem space change, the most effective solvers change along with those conditions by selecting an operator that moves them through the problem space effectively.

Using Operators and Moving Through the Problem Space   A concrete example from the Newell and Simon research will help anchor some of this theorizing. Newell and Simon frequently used the case study as a method for investigation. Their procedure often involves making tape recordings of a subject who has been instructed to think out loud while solving a problem. Consider this "cryptarithmetic" problem (Bartlett, 1958). (The answer to this problem is in the appendix. You might want to try it—but I'm warning you, it's not easy.)

> DONALD
> +GERALD
> ROBERT

The subject is informed that each letter represents one numeral and that the correspondence between the numerals and letters is one-to-one. The subject is asked to deduce the correspondence, so that when numerals are substituted for letters, the resulting addition problem is mathematically correct. The subject is given one correspondence ($D = 5$). The resulting output, a protocol, is then broken down into short behavior phrases labeled B1, B2, and so on. Finally, the behavior phrases are coded by fairly rigid criteria. Newell and Simon argue that such coded behavior phrases can be used as markers to indicate something about the state of knowledge or cognitive process that was taking place at the time the utterance was made. If the subject remarks:

> B74: "But now I know that G has to be 1 or 2"

we know that the solver is capable of considering disjunctive sets; that is, either–or assignments of numbers. When the protocol has been completely coded in this way, Newell and Simon use it to generate two representations of the subject's problem space. The first representation is depicted in Figure 12.12.

These expressions probably won't be too meaningful to you at first. They are written in a formal notation known as Backus Normal Form (BNF). If you take a close look at Figure 12.12, you'll see that the expressions formally define both the symbols that must be constructed in solving cryptarithmetic problems and the four operators that move the solver through the problem space. In other words, the BNF representation is a condensed, or collapsed form of the subject's problem space. Thus, if Figure 12.12 accurately depicts the solver's internal representation, we should be able to expand, or unpack it. In other words, we should be able to use the rules implied by the

Figure 12.12 Problem space for S3. *Source:* From Newell and Simon, 1972.

```
<digit> :: = 0 |1|2|3|4|5|6|7|8|9
<digit-variable> :: = x|y
<general-digit> :: = <digit>|<digit-variable>
<digit-set> :: = <general-digit>\/ <general-digit:>|<general-digit>\/ <digit-set>
<letter> :: = A|B|D|E|G|L|N|O|R|T
<letter-set> :: = <letter>|<letter> <letter-set>
<carry> :: = c <column-number>
<variable> :: = <letter>|<carry>
<column> :: = column.<column-number>
<column-number> :: = 1|2|3|4|5|6|7
<column-set> :: = <column>|<column><column-set>
<assignment-expression> :: = <variable><—<general-digit>|
    <variable> = <general-digit>
<constraint-expression> :: = <variable><parity>|<variable> = ;<digit-set>|
    <variable><inequality><general-digit>|<variable><qualifier>
<parity> :: = even|odd
<inequality :: = >| <
<qualifier> :: = free|last
<expression> :: = <variable>|<assignment-expression>|<constraint-expression>
<state-expression> :: = <expression>|<expression><tag>
<tag> :: = new□|unclear|unknown|note
<knowledge-state> :: = <state-expression>|<state-expression><knowledge-state>
<operator> :: = PC[<column>]|GN|AV|TD
<goal> :: = get <expression>|get <letter-set>
    check <expression>|check <column-set>
Particular sets:
all-letters, free-letters
all-digits, free-digits
all-columns
```

BNF representation to develop a graph that charts the subject's movement through his problem space during problem solving. This is the second of Newell and Simon's representations of the problem space, and they refer to it as a problem behavior graph (PBG). Understand the PBG as tracing the subject's trajectory through a problem; that is, a record of movement from state to state.

Table 12.2 lists the rules that Newell and Simon give for unpacking the PBG from the BNF notation, and Figure 12.13 shows the condensed version of a subject's PBG for the Donald + Gerald problem.

As the PBG in Figure 12.13 implies, the subject's search is generally trial and error, particularly starting the solution attempt. This method is evident because the subject, S3, has to back up fairly often, much like a novice chess player who cannot carry the continuations very far forward and so must constantly return to the base move. Sometimes S3 has to back up to nodes occurring early in problem solving. The bottom third of the PBG reveals how S3's search changes in the late stages of problem solving. The graph shows much more horizontal than vertical movement, meaning that S3 apparently has latched onto the solution path. Newell and Simon have carried out extensive analyses of problem solving in chess (Newell & Simon, 1965; Simon & Simon, 1962), logic problems (Newell & Simon, 1956), and cryptarithmetic. Their

---

Table 12.2   Rules for Problem Behavior Graph (PBG)

A state of knowledge is represented by a node.

The application of an operator to a state of knowledge is represented by a horizontal arrow to the right; the result is the node at the head of the arrow.

A return to the same state of knowledge, say node X, is represented by another node below X, connected to it by a vertical line.

A repeated application of the same operator to the same state of knowledge is indicated by doubling the horizontal line.

Time runs to the right, then down; thus, the graph is linearly ordered by time of generation.

Source: From Newell and Simon, 1972.

---

work suggests that solvers' internal representations have invariant qualities, which are shown in Table 12.3.

A problem solver's effectiveness is determined by two major variables: the quality of the problem space and the mode of search. The solver is said to be searching for a solution path—a series of knowledge states—that leads through the problem space. Using the thinking-out-loud methodology, Newell and Simon were able to isolate a limited number of search modes—calling them heuristics—which seemed to have wide applicability for a number of domain-free problems. Generally, the solver operates by working forward from the initial knowledge state to the goal state. In such situations, Newell and Simon describe two general heuristics—means-end analysis and subgoal analysis—that seem to describe the mode of search. The solver may sometimes elect to work backward from the goal state. In the next sections we consider examples of these search modes and their implications.

Subgoal Analysis   Consider this problem (Wickelgren, 1974):

> Nine men and two boys want to cross a river, using a raft that will carry either one man or the two boys. How many times must the boat cross the river to accomplish this goal? (A round trip equals two crossings.)

This problem can be solved in a number of ways, but like many people, you probably intuitively adopted a subgoal approach. If you haven't solved the problem, try it again with the idea of determining how many crossings are necessary to get just one man across the river. Without too much difficulty, you've probably determined that getting one man across and returning the boat to the original bank takes four crossings. First, the two boys cross; then one boy brings the boat back. Next, the man crosses by himself, and finally, the boy on the far bank returns with the boat. To get all nine men across requires that this sequence be repeated eight more times for a total of thirty-six crossings. The boat will then be on the original bank, and only the two boys will remain. They cross together, making the total thirty-seven crossings. The key to this problem is realizing that the actions needed to get one man across can be duplicated to solve the entire problem; this problem can be broken into parts (Wickelgren, 1974, p. 91).

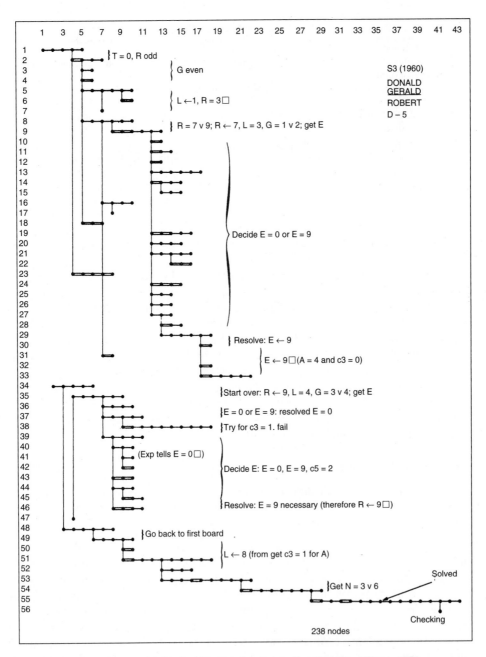

Figure 12.13   Problem Behavior Graph of S3—overview. *Source:* From Newell and Simon, 1972.

Table 12.3 Invariant Features of Problem Spaces

1. The set of knowledge states is generated from a finite set of objects, relations, properties, and so on, and can be represented as a closed space of knowledge.

2. The set of operators is small and finite (or at least finitely generated).

3. The available set of alternative nodes in the space to which the problem solver might return is very small; in fact, it usually includes only one or two nodes.

4. The residence time in each knowledge state before generation of the next state is of the order of seconds.

5. The problem solver remains within a given problem space for times of the order of at least tens of minutes.

6. Problem solving takes place by search in the problem space—i.e., by considering one knowledge state after another until (if the search is successful) a desired knowledge state is reached. The moves from one state to the next are mostly incremental.

7. The search involves backup—that is, return from time to time to old knowledge states and hence abandoning knowledge-state information (although not necessarily path information).

8. The knowledge state typically is only moderate in size—containing at most a few hundred symbols, more typically a few dozen.

Source: From Newell and Simon, 1972.

To understand the power of the subgoal heuristic more fully, another term must be introduced into our description. Imagine that the initial description of the problem is represented by a dot with some appropriate notation on a piece of graph paper. Also imagine that every action that can be taken from this initial point is represented by a line radiating from the original dot. Again, imagine that each line can be labeled with some notation to show the sort of action it represented (one boy crossing, one man crossing, or whatever). Each such line would terminate in another dot, which would represent the state of the problem as it had been transformed by the preceding action. Indeed, all the achievable states of the problem and all the actions possible from each state could be represented in a diagram of this sort. Such a representation is referred to as the state-action space, or **state-action tree.** You've probably recognized that the PBG and the diagram of the Tower of Hanoi are both versions of state-action trees. A hypothetical state-action tree is shown in Figure 12.14.

The power of the subgoal heuristic becomes clearer when we consider problem solving as movement through a state-action tree. Suppose we consider a hypothetical problem that has m alternative actions at each dot or state and requires a sequence of n actions for solution. If we mindlessly plow through the state-action tree in such a problem, we could well wind up pursuing some m^n alternative paths or action sequences needlessly. Assume, though, that you know just one state that could serve as a subgoal, and this state is on the correct path to the goal and is halfway through the sequence of n actions. Thus we now have $m^{n/2}$ paths to be investigated from the start state to the subgoal and a similar number from the subgoal to the final goal. The complexity of the entire problem has thus been reduced from m^n action sequences to $2m^{n/2}$ action sequences that are $n/2$ steps long.

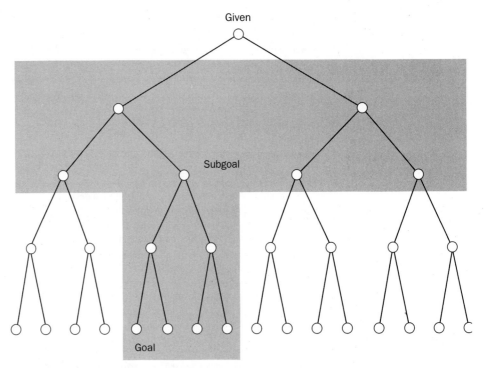

Given

Subgoal

Goal

Figure 12.14   **State-action tree for simple problem solving showing how defining a subgoal on the correct path (action sequence) to the goal can reduce the search.** Here the search is limited to the region inside the two boxes, which is eight action sequences, each two steps long, instead of sixteen action sequences, each four steps long. Some simplifying assumptions are made, such as that one knows that the subgoal is two steps from the beginning and two steps from the end. The average problem is much longer, however, and the degree of reduction in search by defining subgoals is far greater than in this simple example.

The authenticity of this reduction becomes clear if you consider a problem in which $m = 10$ and $n = 10$. The number of possible action sequences to be investigated is awesome: 10^{10}. Knowing just one subgoal with the conditions just described reduces the number of action states to $2(10^5)$, which is $1/50,000$ of the original number. This heuristic will not prove useful all the time. Often we're stumped in our search for subgoals, and being sure that the subgoal is on the correct path to the goal is sometimes difficult. Nevertheless, the subgoal heuristic can be a remarkable way to prune the state-action tree. In the Tower of Hanoi problem, it may have occurred to you that the movement of the bottom disk to the appropriate peg is a subgoal that is halfway to the final goal state. Accordingly, this move makes the movement of the bottom disk a reasonable subgoal for that problem.

Working Backward   Consider this problem (Wickelgren, 1974):

Three people play a game in which one person loses and two people win each game. The one who loses must double the amount of money that each of the other two players has at that time. The three players agree to play three games. At the end of the three games, each player has lost one game, and each player has eight dollars. What was the original stake of each player?

This problem can be devilishly difficult unless you work backward from the goal state, which in this problem is the only known state. That is, the goal state, or *n*th state of the action sequence, is known, and our task could be represented as moving *backward* through the state-action tree from the *n*th state to the *n* − 1th state.

If you haven't solved this problem yet, stop here and try it again. We know what the state of affairs is after three games have been played; what happened in the third game? One person lost, and two won. The person who lost doubled the money of those who won. Because everyone has ended up with eight dollars, the two people who won the third game must have had only four dollars after two games. Consequently, the person who lost the third game had to pay out eight dollars to the two winners, and so the loser of the third game must have had sixteen dollars after two games had been played. If you haven't solved the problem yet, I'll leave it up to you to use this same reasoning to determine what happened on the second and, finally, the first games. What conditions of the state-action tree must hold if the working-backward method is to succeed?

According to Wickelgren, these techniques will be useful if the problem satisfies two criteria. First, the problem should have a uniquely specified goal. The problem should have one ending state that can be clearly described. The heuristic is particularly powerful in situations that involve many plausible initial states. Here, the advantage of working backward accrues because the goal tells you where you must start to solve the problem, whereas the more conventional working-forward techniques do not tell you which of the many initial statements will lead to the goal. Working forward in such a problem has been compared to finding a needle in a haystack (Newell, Shaw, & Simon, 1962), and working backward is analogous to letting the needle find its way out of the haystack.

General Problem Solver These general heuristics that Newell and Simon discovered have been incorporated into a computer program known as the **General Problem Solver**, or **GPS.** The program is intended to simulate human problem solving, meaning that it is supposed to duplicate the outcome of human thought by duplicating the process of human thought. How does it work?

First, GPS has to be fed a description of the problem to be solved. In this sense, the program does not really form its own problem space (although this shortcoming has been partially corrected in recent editions of GPS). Once the problem is presented, GPS proceeds by applying general heuristics, such as those we have been considering, to the state-action tree and evaluating its progress. The heuristic most typically used is means-end analysis, which we have examined before. When confronted with the Tower of Hanoi problem, several activities are undertaken. First, the program represents the goal. Next, the difference between the current state of affairs and the goal is recorded. After that, the program looks for a method that will reduce this discrepancy. The result of this processing is that a subgoal is set up, and generally the subgoal is accomplished by means-end analysis. GPS has been quite successful on the Tower of Hanoi and more difficult problems.

Summary and Comments on the Newell and Simon Theory   Newell and Simon's theory emphasizes the relative invariance seen in people's strategies on domain-free problems. They argue that the similarity among people's strategies reflects that the human information-processing system is not very complex: people have a few basic, general heuristics for dealing with many kinds of problems. The Newell and Simon approach also emphasizes the correct representation. Building a problem space is probably the most important constructive act during problem solving, given that the mode of search is often fairly limited. If your problem space doesn't include the "right" elements, this technique is like trying to solve the problem with a representation that may not include an adequate specification of the goal and may therefore be inadequate for attaining a solution. In essence, the problem solver may be searching through a problem space that is a poor subset of the task environment. No matter how thorough the search is under those circumstances, the solver will not succeed. The corollary of this assertion is that what differentiates an effective problem solver from a poor one is probably the quality of the internal representation used. We can examine de Groot's work as evidence.

Numerous questions have been raised about the Newell and Simon approach. One is the appropriateness of verbal reports as data. Nisbett and Wilson (1977) maintain that humans have little or no introspective access to higher mental processes. This conclusion is based on several facts. First, people are sometimes unaware of the existence of a stimulus that influenced their response. Second, they are sometimes unaware of all the responses they have made. Third, even if they are aware of the stimulus in question, they are unaware that they have been influenced by it. Nisbett and Wilson cite studies in which the subjects are given hints that are designed to facilitate their finding a solution. Typically, the subjects are not aware that hints have been given. Perhaps even more important, when false hints (which have previously been demonstrated to be ineffective) are given along with genuine hints, people are not very accurate in determining which hints are useful.

Several researchers (Ericsson & Simon, 1980; Kellogg, 1982) have commented on these findings. Ericsson and Simon (1980) point out that the Nisbett and Wilson findings do not deal with consciousness. Instead, the subjects in their studies could not be expected to have awareness of their mental processes because of the judgments they were being asked to make. They argue that introspective evidence will be valid when the subjects are reporting about something that they are truly aware of; namely, something that is currently being stored in working memory. In their view, subjects are capable of commenting on knowledge not currently stored in working memory, but this comment is an inference, not a report. Consequently, if people are probed correctly and at the correct time, then subjects' introspections will be accurate on all except highly practiced tasks.

Perhaps a more serious trouble is the problems used by Newell and Simon in their investigations. Be aware that much of the research on problem solving has been based on fairly artificial games and puzzles that might have no genuine relationship with problem-solving ability in the real world. If you take your bill stubs, receipts, W-2 forms, and so on to a tax person to prepare your income-tax statement, we can imagine that the preparer uses knowledge about tax laws and other expertise to solve the problem of preparing your statement. My guess is that the preparer does not explicitly use general heuristics to do this task. Thus, even if we ask the person to think out loud à la Newell and Simon, the tax person is not likely to make statements such as, "Now I'm going to use a subgoal analysis to see what should be entered on Schedule A." This speculation implies that the sort of strategizing we have seen on problems such as the Tower of Hanoi may not routinely occur in the knowledge-rich domains of everyday thinking. In the next section we take up the question of problem solving in knowledge-rich domains.

Problem Solving in a Domain of Knowledge

How Knowledge Guides Search

In Chapter 4 we examined the notion of schema as a coherent body of knowledge that can channel perception by producing expectations about the stimuli that will be displayed. The schema is therefore an active knowledge structure, and it has a function in problem solving in knowledge-rich domains. That is, we can think of prior knowledge as activating slots, or nodes, in semantic memory. Naturally, these slots are organized. When enough nodes in an area of semantic memory are activated, this condition will activate that area's organizing principle—its schema. Once the schema is activated, the subject is able to fill in some of the gaps observed in the display of stimuli. This sort of knowledge is exactly what enables the experienced pilot to bring a plane in for a landing when weather is poor and enables a physician to make an accurate diagnosis from a few presenting symptoms. In both examples, schematic knowledge enables the problem solver to extrapolate, thus going beyond the information given. Once activated, the schematic knowledge suggests that the solver search the problem space in specific ways, looking for characteristics of the problem.

Hinsley, Hayes, and Simon (1978) present findings that are consistent with this interpretation. They asked their subjects, who were high-school and college students, to classify—not solve—algebra problems. The problems could be categorized in any way the subjects wished. Hinsley et al. found that the subjects' categorizations were similar and that the classification schemata were based on the solution procedures for the various kinds of problems. In other words, problems that were solved in similar ways were categorized together. Such a categorization schema is developed as a result of problem-solving experience with algebra problems.

The schematic form of this knowledge became even clearer when Hinsley et al. asked the subjects to classify the problems as quickly as they could. They found that subjects were able to classify the problems after hearing only the initial sentence. They might hear a sentence such as "An airplane with a tailwind takes two hours to fly 230 miles." After hearing this sentence, subjects could quickly and reliably classify it as belonging to a "river-current" problem in which some velocity has to be computed under aided and hindered conditions. The speed at which the problems are classified seems to rule out the possibility that the subjects are actually figuring out the solution plan and categorizing accordingly. A more likely explanation is that they are able to guess accurately about the problem's forthcoming information, which enables them to guess what the solution procedure will be.

Unlike the general heuristics mentioned by Newell and Simon, however, the schemata learned in knowledge-rich domains are apparently highly specific to the types of problems encountered. That is, little generalization occurs from one domain of knowledge to another. This inability to transfer schematic knowledge from problem to problem has been studied using problem isomorphs. Recall that problem isomorphs were discussed earlier in this chapter, when I described the number scrabble problem as formally similar to tic-tac-toe. Generally, isomorphs are problems whose underlying structures and solutions are the same, but whose context may be quite different (Chi & Glaser, 1985).

Hayes and Simon (1974) studied transfer of schematic knowledge using the tea-ceremony problem. In this problem, three people are conducting an oriental tea ritual in which the responsibility for aspects of the ceremony is shared among the participants according to an elaborate etiquette. The solver's task is to specify a sequence in which the aspects of the ritual can be enacted in a way that does not violate the etiquette. The tea-ceremony problem is isomorphic with the Tower of Hanoi, and anyone who realizes the **isomorphism** can easily solve the tea-ceremony problem. Hayes and Simon found, though, that almost none of their subjects, who were familiar with Tower of Hanoi problems, noticed the resemblance.

Simon and Hayes (1976) wondered why. They investigated the variables that seem influential in activating the solver's schematic knowledge. They used the Tower of Hanoi once again as the basis for nine so-called Monster problems. The structure of all nine isomorphs is shown in Table 12.4.

As Table 12.4 depicts, sentence 3 in each problem refers to two classes of objects (for example, problem 5, sentence 3 refers to monsters and globes). In each problem, sentence 4 designates the objects of one class as fixed and the other as variable. Again, in problem 5, the globe held by each monster is fixed, and the monster's name is variable. Sentence 7 in each problem indicates that the legality of moves depends on the ordering in one of the attributes (e.g., in problem 5, the names are ordered by length). If the ordering referred to the variable objects, the problem was designated a transfer problem. If the ordering referred to the fixed objects, the problem was a change problem. Problems 1, 2, 5, 6, 8, and 9 are transfer problems, and 3, 4, and 7 are change problems.

Although some of the subjects in this problem were run through the typical thinking-out-loud procedure, others were given paper and pencil and allowed to record their moves. Of the 117 subjects who were presented these isomorphs, more than half spontaneously used some form of state-matrix notation that offers strong evidence for the kind of representation in use. A state-matrix notation is a two-dimensional table showing the monsters on one dimension and the states of the problem on the other. Here, the states in the problem refer to the successive changes or transformations made by the problem solver. In the body of the table are entries showing the size of the globe each monster is holding, the size the monster has become, and so on. A typical state-matrix notation used by the subjects in both transfer and change problems is shown in Table 12.5.

Of sixty-two subjects presented a transfer problem, thirty-seven used a state matrix, as did thirty of the fifty-five subjects presented a change problem. Of the sixty-seven subjects who used this notation to represent the problem, none used a notation

Table 12.4 Monster Problem 1 and the Phrasing of the Nine Isomorphs

S1. Three five-handed extraterrestrial monsters were holding three crystal globes.

S2. Because of the quantum-mechanical peculiarities of their neighborhood, both monsters and globes come in exactly three sizes with no others permitted: small, medium, and large.

S3. The medium-sized monster was holding the small globe; the small monster was holding the large globe; and the large monster was holding the medium-sized globe.

S4. Because this situation offended their keenly developed sense of symmetry, they proceeded to transfer globes from one monster to another so that each monster would have a globe proportionate to his own size.

S5. Monster etiquette complicated the solution of the problem because it requires:

S6. (1) that only one globe may be transferred at a time.

S7. (2) that if a monster is holding two globes, only the larger of the two may be transferred, and

S8. (3) That a globe may not be transferred to a monster who is holding a larger globe.

S9. By what sequence of transfers could the monsters have solved this problem?

Problem

Number	Type	Sentence 3	Sentence 4	Sentenc 7
1	T	The small monster held the larger globe.	. . . to teleport globes . . . monster should have a globe proportionate to its own size.	If a monster is holding two globes . . . can transmit only the larger.
2	T	The small monster stood on the large globe.	. . . to teleport themselves . . . monster would have a globe proportionate to its own size.	If two monsters are standing on the same globe, only the larger . . . can leave.
3	C	The small monster was holding the large globe.	. . . to shrink and expand the globes . . . monster would have a globe proportionate to its own size.	If two globes are of the same size, only the globe held by the larger monster . . . can be changed.
4	C	The small monster was holding the large globe.	. . . to shrink and expand themselves . . . monster would have a globe proportionate to its own size.	If two monsters are of the same size, only the monster holding the larger globe can change.
5	T	The monster with the small name was holding the large globe.	. . . to transfer names . . . monster would have a globe proportionate to the size of its name.	If a monster has two names . . . can transmit only the longer.
6	T	The monster with the small tail was holding the large globe.	. . . to transfer tails . . . monster would have a globe proportionate to the size of its tail.	If a monster has two tails . . . can transfer only the longer.
7	C	The small monster was originally large.	. . . to shrink and expand themselves . . . monster would have its original size back.	If two monsters are of the same size . . . only the monster that was originally larger can change.
8	T	The monster with the small name originally had the large name.	. . . to transfer names . . . monster would have its original name back.	If a monster has two names . . . can transmit only the longer.
9	T	The small monster was originally large.	. . . to transfer sizes . . . monster would have its original size back.	If a monster has two sizes . . . can transfer only the larger.

Source: From Simon and Hayes, 1976.

Table 12.5   State-Matrix Notations Used by Subjects[a]

	Transfer Type				Change Type		
	M	*L*	*S*		*M*	*L*	*S*
0	L	S	M	0	L	S	M
1	–	L,S	M	1	L	L	M
2	M	L,S	–	2	L	L	S

[a]The columns correspond to the fixed attribute; the rows correspond to the successive problem situations after each move (0 is the starting situation). Within the cells are shown the current values of the variable attributes, which either (1) migrate from column to column (transfer type) or (2) change value within a column (change type).

Source: From Simon and Hayes, 1976.

form inconsistent with the isomorphs they were given, as we can see by looking at the entries in Table 12.5. In the transfer problems, the variable attributes migrate from column to column. But in the change problems, the variable attributes change their values within the column. Clearly, although the form of the problems was structurally the same, the instructions seemed to powerfully influence the schema-guiding search. Using the transfer terminology apparently resulted in activating a schema in which the variable attributes were thought of as being passed around from monster to monster, whereas the change instructions resulted in calling up a schema in which the subject apparently imagined the monster as changing the size of the globe it was holding. Little or no evidence appeared that the subjects attempted to alter the form of their internal representations once problem solving began. This observation was surprising because the change problems were quite difficult, requiring almost twice as much time as the transfer problems. Also, no formal indications suggested that the subjects realized the equivalence of the Monster problem with the Tower of Hanoi problem, even though some of the subjects may have been familiar with the latter problem.

We've seen that schematic knowledge accrued from problem solving appears to be effective only when dealing with a particular class of problems—or maybe even a particular problem. This limitation has led some researchers to wonder if an expert's organization of this highly specific knowledge differs from that of a novice.

Expertise

For the last several years, cognitive psychologists have come to appreciate that the expert's knowledge probably is organized differently from knowledge in the novice's mind. Reif (1979) analyzed this problem from the standpoint of hierarchic organization. According to Reif, the expert's knowledge is based on years of experience in which specific bits of information have been associated with other specific bits, which together have been placed in a more general category. This category in turn is placed under a more general category of knowledge. The expert's speedy and efficient problem solving is not necessarily the result of better using general heuristics. Rather, ex-

Figure 12.15 How knowledge is organized in an expert's mind. *Source:* From Reif, 1979.

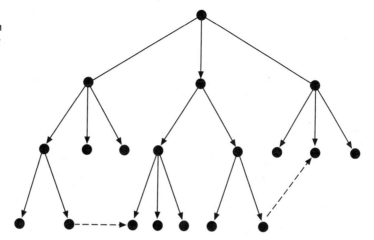

perts' organization of material enables them to quickly get to the heart of the matter. Figure 12.15 will help clarify this point.

Reif (1979) refers to the dotted lines as pointers. These are associations between specific elements of knowledge that connect the lower branches of this tree and provide mental shortcuts in the expert's mind. If Figure 12.15 could be compared with a state-action tree, we can see that actions within this tree are not neutral for the expert, as they might be for the novice. Because the expert's knowledge suggests which branches of the state-action tree are the "right" ones, reliance upon general problem-solving heuristics is lessened. One implication of Reif's position is that if specific facts were fed to the novices in a way that was similar to their representation in the expert's mind, knowledge and problem solving in that domain might be improved.

Such a study was undertaken by Eylon (1979), who developed two versions of a chapter on buoyancy and presented them to students in an introductory physics class. One account was organized conventionally; that is, like other physics texts on the market. The second chapter presented the information hierarchically, based on analyzing experts' knowledge about buoyancy. Students who used the hierarchic text showed a 40% improvement in retention of the material and 25% better scores in problem solving than did students who used the conventional text.

Eylon and Reif (1984) and Heller and Reif (1984) amplified these findings. They found that subjects who were taught with hierarchic materials that mimicked an expert's organization of the material outperformed subjects who were taught with traditional "linear" models. They constructed a model incorporating the procedures that experts use to organize and solve problems in mechanics. Nonexpert subjects were induced to act in accordance with the model's prescriptions, and these subjects showed marked subsequent improvement in describing and solving such problems.

The organization of experts' knowledge was studied further by Chi, Glaser, and Rees (1982). They asked eight experts (Ph.D. students in physics) and eight novices (undergraduates who had a semester of mechanics) to classify twenty-four physics problems from a well-known physics text. Chi et al. found no major quantitative differences between the groups. The members of both groups used about eight categories to classify the problems, and each required about 40 seconds to make the classification. Major qualitative differences, showed up, though, between experts' and novices' performance. Essentially, the novices saw some problems as quite similar to one another, but the experts did not use this resemblance.

Figure 12.16 shows the diagrams for two pairs of problems that all eight novices grouped together. As this diagram shows, the novices were heavily influenced by the diagram that accompanied the problem. The bottom two problems were considered the same because both showed an inclined plane. Notice in Figure 12.17, however, that these diagrams did not strongly affect the experts' sorting.

The problems grouped together by the experts have no superficial similarity, but they can be solved using the same principle of physics, such as Newton's second law of motion. Thus the organizational principles the experts used could be understood only by a physicist. In other words, because the problems that the novices grouped together looked alike, we might say that the basis of the grouping was perceptual appearance. But the basis of the experts' grouping was more abstract and resulted from their knowledge of physics. Chi et al. compare this difference to the deep–surface-structure distinction examined in Chapter 7. The novices are influenced by the appearance of a problem—its surface structure; and the experts seem better able to extract the underlying meaning from the problem—its deep structure.

This finding suggests that the novices' classification procedures would be sensitive to variations in surface, but not deep, structure. Chi et al. corroborated this analysis in a follow-up study. They designed twenty problems in which they systematically varied the problems' appearance and objectives. When these specially designed problems were categorized by novices and experts, Chi et al. found once again that the novices were more influenced by the appearance of the problem than by the underlying physical principle. But the experts were not affected by this manipulation. Regardless of the problem's text and diagram, the experts categorized it according to abstract physical principles.

Other research (de Jong & Ferguson-Hessler, 1986) corroborates these basic findings. In categorizing a problem, nonexperts are likely to be influenced by its appearance, and experts perceive its underlying structure.

The schematic and hierarchic nature of this knowledge was made apparent in another study by Chi et al. Here, the subjects had three levels of expertise. Experts were graduate students in physics. Intermediate subjects were fourth-year physics majors, and novices were students who had been in an introductory physics course and received grades of A, B, or C. The subjects were asked to sort forty physics problems, but in this study, several passes through the set were made. In the first step, the subjects simply sorted the problems. In the second step, the subjects were asked to look at their groups, and if they wished, they were permitted to further subdivide their original groups. In the third step, the subjects who had created subgroups were asked to examine them, and if they wished, they could further divide these subgroups they had just created. Finally, in the fourth step, the subjects reexamined their original groups and tried to combine them on whatever basis seemed appropriate.

Figure 12.18 shows the resulting hierarchic structure that was created for two novices and two experts. The circles represent the original sorting; the squares, the first subdivision; and the hexagons, the second subdivision. The final, combined stage is shown by the triangles. The numbers inside the geometric forms represent the number

Diagrams depicted from problems categorized by novices within the same groups

Novices' explanations for their similarity groupings

Problem 10 (11)

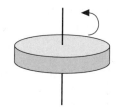

Novice 2: "Angular velocity, momentum, circular things"
Novice 3: "Rotational kinematics, angular speeds, angular velocities"
Novice 6: "Problems that have something rotating: angular speed"

Problem 11 (39)

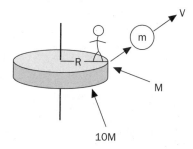

Problem 7 (23)

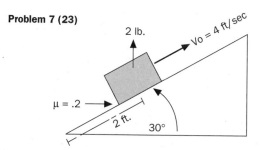

Novice 1: "These deal with blocks on an inclined plane"
Novice 5: "Inclined plane problems, coefficient of friction"
Novice 6: "Blocks on inclined planes with angles"

Problem 7 (35)

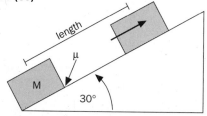

Figure 12.16 Examples from novices' problem categories. Problem numbers represent chapter and problem number. (From Halliday and Resnick, 1974. Copyright 1982 by Lawrence Erlbaum Associates, Inc. Publishers. Adapted by permission of the publisher and author.)

Diagrams depicted from problems categorized by experts within the same groups	Experts' explanation for their similarity groupings

Problem 6 (21)

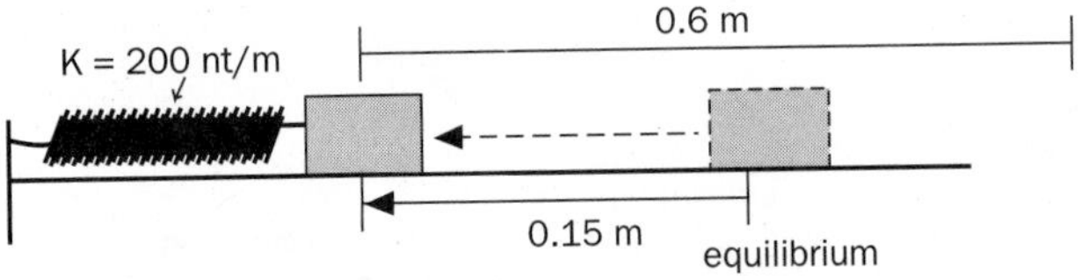

Expert 2: "Conservation of Energy"
Expert 3: "Work-Energy Theorem: They are all straightforward problems."
Expert 4: "These can be done from energy considerations. Either you should know the Principle of Conservation of Energy, or work is lost somewhere."

Problem 7 (35)

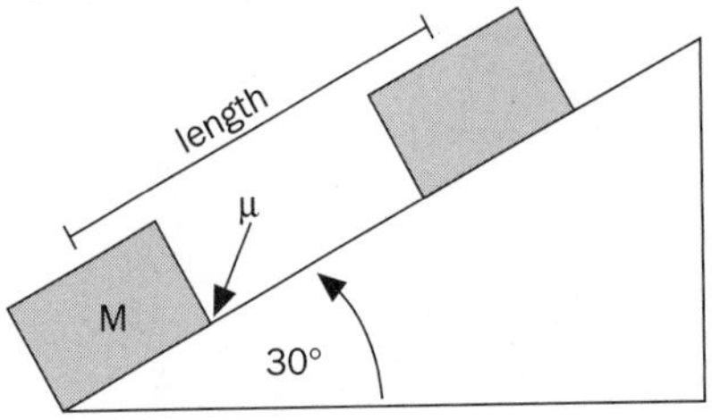

Expert 2: "These can be solved by Newton's Second Law."
Expert 3: "F = ma; Newton's Second Law"
Expert 4: "Largely use F = ma; Newton's Second Law"

Problem 5 (39)

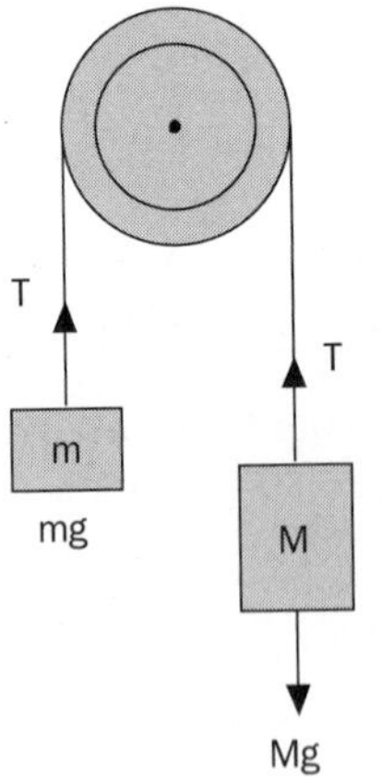

Problem 12 (23)

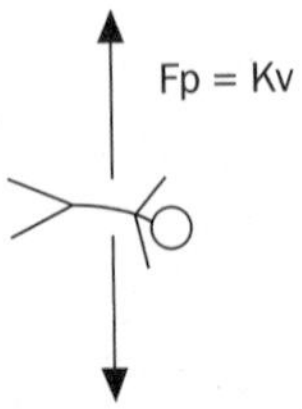

Figure 12.17 **Examples from experts' problem categories.** Problem numbers represent chapter and problem number. (From Halliday and Resnick, 1974. Copyright 1982 by Lawrence Erlbaum Associates, Inc., Publishers. Adapted by permission of the publisher and author.)

Novice R.R.

Novice J.T.

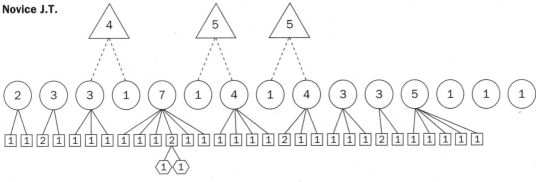

Expert C.D.

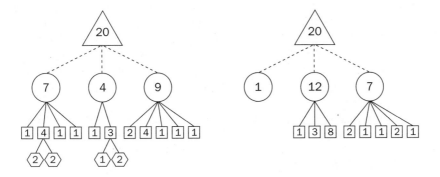

Expert M.F.

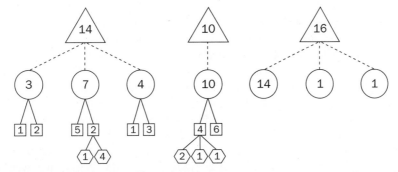

Figure 12.18 **Groupings made by novices and experts on a hierarchic sorting task.** *Circular nodes,* the preliminary groups; *squares* and *hexagons,* subsequent discriminations; *triangles,* the combinations. *Source:* From Chi, Glaser, & Rees, 1982.

of problems sorted into that category. Figure 12.18 is a good way of showing the differences in the organization of knowledge in the minds of experts and novices. First, as we learned earlier, subjects typically needed eight categories to sort the problems. Here we can see that one of the novices required nine categories, which he could divide no further. The other novice required fifteen categories. In contrast, both the experts required fewer than eight categories in their initial sorts.

The drawing also shows that the organization of knowledge is similar for both of these experts, but the novices' organization of knowledge is quite different from each other. One novice was unable to divide the problems into subcategories, suggesting that the categories were already at their lowest level (Chi, Glaser, & Rees, 1982). In the other novice's groupings shown in Figure 12.18, the problems were so finely divided that each problem almost became its own category. This result also suggests inability to perceive any sort of abstract organizing principle. The experts' knowledge is not like this. Notice in Figure 12.18 that both experts were able to group all forty problems by some unifying principle. In expert C.D.'s initial sort, the left group of circles represents problems dealing with conservation of energy, conservation of momentum, and conservation of angular momentum. The three groups of circles on the right represent problems dealing with force (i.e., $f = ma$), using $f = ma$ to find the resultant force, and simple harmonic motion. The leftmost circles in turn were combined into the superordinate category *conservation laws,* whereas the rightmost group of circles was collapsed into the category *equations of motion.* By contrast, only one of the novices was able to indicate any superordinate categories, and these accounted for only fourteen of the forty problems classified. This finding suggests that the hierarchic structure of knowledge seen in the experts is a developmental phenomenon. That is, the vertical organization seen in Figure 12.18 is produced by the expert's experience with physics problems.

Thus far in this book we have focused on acquisition of expertise in academic subjects, such as physics, probably giving you the impression that expertise is usually acquired by formal training in some subject. Actually, the importance of academic training, or even its usefulness for expertise, has been debated. Voss et al. (1986) compared the economics knowledge of college-educated subjects with that of people who hadn't gone to college. Perhaps to no one's surprise, subjects who had been to college did better in answering questions requiring economics knowledge (interest rates, the federal deficit, and so on) than did those who hadn't gone to college. Voss et al. determined, however, that classroom instruction in economics did not necessarily help the college-educated subjects in day-by-day dealing with economics, suggesting that academic training was of limited use in acquiring hands-on economic knowledge. This finding implies that our intuitions about everyday experience may be correct. That is, experience may be a good teacher.

Some support for this notion comes from research by Ceci and Liker (1986), who studied the ability of fourteen expert horse-racing handicappers over a three-year period. They defined expertise as the ability to predict race-time odds using factual information about the horses (their lineage, the weight they were carrying, their ability to run under different track conditions, and so on). They asked these experts to handicap ten actual races and fifty fictitious ones contrived to elucidate some of the variables the experts may have used in picking horses, as well as the importance

Using Your Knowledge of Cognition
Using a Notation to Find an Algorithm

One easy way to discover a problem's algorithm is to devise notation that shows the problem's transformations. Sometimes this notation also shows regularities in the problem's structure, and when these are revealed, an algorithm may also become apparent.

I've devised a notation for Tower of Hanoi problems. First, number the pegs 1, 2, and 3. Next, give each disk a name. In the convention I use, the disks have letter names; the biggest is always A, the next biggest B, and so on. Thus the (trivial) problem of transferring three disks from peg 2 to peg 3 could be written in this way:

$ABC_{(2)}–ABC_{(3)}$

All disk moves can be shown as a letter with a numerical subscript indicating the disk's destination. Thus, the solution to the prior problem could be written:

$C_3B_1C_1 \ A_3 \ C_2B_3C_3$

Of the seven moves, the first (C_3) involves taking the smallest disk and transferring it to peg 3. If you make an arrangement of coins and duplicate each move, you'll see that this string of letters indeed represents a solution to the problem.

What about a four-disk problem? That is, how would we solve this one?

$ABCD_{(2)}–ABCD_{(3)}$

I'll show the solution to this problem and then we'll compare the two we've seen to see if they suggest an algorithm for all Tower of Hanoi problems. Here's the answer to the four-disk problem:

$D_1C_3D_3 \ B_1 \ D_2C_1D_1 \ A_3 \ D_3C_2D_2 \ B_3 \ D_1C_3D_3$

Do you see any similarities between the two solutions? You may have noticed that each problem has one A move, and it is at the midpoint in both problems. The clusters of moves on both sides of A are symmetrical. Also, the smallest disk in each problem is in motion on exactly every other move. In both examples, the next to the smallest disk periodically moves between moves of the smallest disk. These regularities can be summarized:

1. The A disk moves once in a Tower of Hanoi problem.

2. The B disk moves exactly twice as frequently as the A disk, and these moves are symmetrically distributed around the A disk move.

3. The C disk moves exactly twice as frequently as the B disk, and these moves are symmetrically distributed around the A and B disk moves.

4. The D disk moves exactly twice as frequently as the C disk, and these moves are symmetrically

---

of those variables in relation to each other. The researchers found that expertise in handicapping horses depends on a very complex internal calculus in which several variables are related to one another in multiplicative, as opposed to additive, ways. Ceci and Liker administered a Wechsler Adult Intelligence Scale (WAIS) to the expert subjects and to several nonexpert handicappers. They found that the experts were not necessarily more intelligent (as measured by the WAIS) than were the nonexperts, even though the experts consistently outperformed the nonexperts in handicapping ability. Cognitivists haven't determined yet what produces expertise, but it doesn't seem that classroom education, or vast amounts of intelligence, are crucial to attaining it.

*U*sing *Y*our *K*nowledge of *C*ognition (*continued*)

distributed around the A, B, and C disk moves. (Hence, the D disk move will always precede and follow C disk moves on a four-disk problem. By extension, the smallest disk will always precede and follow the moves of the next smallest disk.)

These rules enable us to expand any Tower of Hanoi problem—that is, write the string of letters that shows which disk is to be moved next. This is the first step in solving a Tower problem. These expansion rules don't indicate the subscript pattern, though. To determine this pattern, the solution to the five-disk problem shows how the subscripts are derived:

$$ABCDE_{(2)}\text{--}ABCDE_3$$

$$E_3D_1E_1 \ \ C_3 \ \ E_2D_3E_3 \ \ B_1 \ \ E_1D_2E_2 \ \ C_1 \ \ E_3D_1E_3$$

$$A_3$$

$$E_2D_3E_3 \ \ C_2 \ \ E_1D_2E_2 \ \ B_3 \ \ E_3D_1E_1 \ \ C_3 \ \ E_2D_3E_3$$

Looking at the three- and five-disk problems, you'll see that the subscript pattern of the smallest disk (C in the three-disk and E in the five-disk problem) is the same. Specifically, the sequence repeats the sequence 3, 1, 2 over and over. Looking at the four-disk problem, we see a different pattern, but it also repeats. The D disk

moves in the sequence 1, 3, 2 over and over. The first step in determining the subscript pattern is to count the disks in the tower. If odd, number all the smallest disk moves in the 3, 1, 2 sequence. If even, number all the smallest disk moves in the 1, 3, 2 sequence. In both steps, you'll end with a 3. You'll also notice that the moves of the next to the smallest disk always take the subscript of the following disk move. Number all these moves next. We see too that there are always only two B moves, and these go in the order 1, 3. Looking at the C disk moves, we see that they always move in the same sequence: 3, 1, 2. Similarly, the D disk moves are always the same: 1, 3, 2.

Do you see the subscript pattern? Besides the A and B disk moves, which are always locked in, and the two topmost disk moves, whose subscripts are derivable by counting the disks, all intervening disks have either a 3, 1, 2 pattern (if they're an odd-numbered disk up from the bottom) or a 1, 3, 2 pattern (if they are an even-numbered disk up from the bottom). Knowing these facts enables you to write a string of letters representing the minimal solution to any Tower of Hanoi problem. You can demonstrate this result for yourself by writing the solution to the six-disk problem.

*C*oncluding Comments and Suggestions for Further Reading

We began this chapter by discussing the Gestaltists. They were a tremendously productive group of thinkers whose diverse opinions nevertheless concentrated on a few key ideas. One of these ideas was that perception and thinking were very similar. In both, the person mentally recombined and rearranged elements in a problem or visual array until a stable configuration, or Gestalt, was achieved. A second important idea was that thinking and problem solving took place in stages qualitatively different from one another. Thus problem solving was seen as a discontinuous process. When insights would come along was hard to tell in advance. Yet another idea was that the solver's representation of the problem could be critical for success. Although we didn't explore the Gestalt literature on creativity, it generally discusses the creative person's ability to overcome the effects of seeing the problem in a new way.

Time (and subsequent research) have put many of these ideas on the shelf. Information-processing accounts of problem solving, though, have seemed to converge on the notion that representation is perhaps the most critical act in problem solving. We've seen that cognitive psychologists have undertaken two different but complementary ways of understanding problem solving. One of these ways consists of isolating prototypical problems that seem to require particular cognitive skills. The second approach focuses on the solver in an effort to find cognitive skills that seem general enough to be usable in many kinds of problems. Recently, psychologists have turned away somewhat from studying games and puzzles and have begun to study expertise in solving real-world problems. As we've seen, such research seems to indicate that one important outcome of experience in a domain of knowledge is restructuring knowledge in the expert's mind. Exploring this organization is sure to become one of the hot issues in problem solving in the foreseeable future.

Students who wish to find out more about the Gestaltists' work should read Wertheimer's (1959) book *Productive Thinking*, which is the classic Gestalt account. Weisberg (1986) has written something of a rebuttal of the Gestalt position. The vast and challenging book by Newell and Simon (1972) has been the basis for much of the research in problem solving for the past twenty-five years.

The literature on expertise is surveyed by Ericsson and Lehmann (1996). Problem solving is frequently discussed in the context of creativity. This relationship is explored in John-Steiner (1997), and in Runco (1994). In speaking of problem solving, we are inevitably drawn to the question of thinking more generally. Sometimes my students wish to explore the notion of thinking in its broadest possible context, wondering if machines like computers can think, or if nonhuman animals can think. For an exploration of the issues in machine thought, try Millican and Clark (1996). On the existence of animal minds and thought, you might enjoy reading Dennett (1996).

Focus on Research

A Strategy for Solving a Problem Is a Very Specific Thing

If you go all the way back to Chapter 2, you'll see that we talked about what happens when we create a log-log graph of performance in a problem-solving task. That is, when we take the logarithm of some performance measure and graph it on the vertical axis, and then take the logarithm of practice or time spent with the task and graph it on the horizontal axis, the result is a straight line, and it continues to improve as long as the individual continues to engage in the task. Newell and Rosenbloom (1981) demonstrated that this finding held for all sorts of problem-solving tasks, including the solitaire card game that they apparently made up, called Stair. Now that we're in the last chapter in this book, it's appropriate for us to revisit that finding.

Delaney, Reder, Staszewski, and Ritter (1998) have shown that this general effect is contingent on the strategy that we use to solve the problem. If we change strategies, we will continue to improve at a

linear rate—but the improvement may be at a different linear rate than that at which we were improving before. Here's how they demonstrated these effects. They used only one subject; his initials are G.G. His task was to learn how to solve mental-arithmetic problems, specifically mental multiplication. For problems that were cast in this format: (Multiplicand = 2-place number) times (Multiplier = 5-place number), such as 47 × 10,482, G.G. learned an unconventional but accurate strategy commonly used by mental-multiplication experts. It's a novel strategy for most other people because you multiply from right to left instead of in the way we are accustomed to. A dedicated research subject, G.G. practiced this strategy for 500 sessions, and he got significantly better at it. Then, on his 501st session, G.G. was taught a new strategy for these problems that was somewhat more efficient than the older one because it reduced memory load in comparison to the old strategy, and G.G.

Figure 12.19 The data from the Delaney et al. (1998) analysis of G.G.'s performance on mental-arithmetic problems. The regression line with the Os shows G.G.'s performance on his first 500 practice sessions. The line with the Xs shows the next 100 practice sessions, in which he shifted strategies. As the bottom regression line shows, the rate of G.G.'s improvement changed with the strategy shift. *Source:* From Delaney et al., 1998.

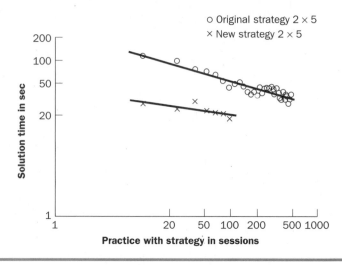

Focus on Research

was instructed to use this strategy for the remainder of the study.

Figure 12.19 shows these effects. Two regression lines have been fitted to these data. The line with the Os shows the improvement that G.G. accomplished in his first 500 practice sessions using his initial strategy. The line with the Xs shows G.G.'s solution times with the new strategy (to visualize what's going on here, imagine the line with the Xs as continuing the regression line with the old strategy because G.G's first 20 sessions with the new strategy were actually his 500th to 520th sessions overall). You can see the slight but almost immediate effect of strategy shift on the dependent measure, solution time. This effect goes in the direction opposite that which you might expect—that is, it took him slightly longer at first to use the new strategy. But initial slowdown resulting from the shift to a new strategy dissipates within a very few practice sessions, and then G.G. begins to go faster with the new strategy than he did with the old.

Notice that the interesting thing is that the slope of the regression line for the new strategy clearly differs from the one for the old strategy. What's the interpretation? As long as G.G. used his old strategy he continued to improve over the 500 practice sessions. This effect is predictable, recalling the results that we examined in Chapter 2. But when he shifted to the new strategy, the rate of his improvement continued at a faster pace than it had before. This is an interesting finding. Some theorists might argue that when you learn to solve a kind of problem, what you are "really" learning, and *all* you are learning about, is the domain itself. That is, if you were G.G., all you would be learning about is the mental-arithmetic domain. But these findings show us that something more is going on. It's clear that, if you have a strategy, in addition to domain knowledge, you are learning about how to use your head to operate that strategy more effectively, and those effects are independent of the effects of any domain knowledge that you are acquiring as you continue to solve problems.

Key Terms

Intelligence
Gestalt psychology
Insight
Incubation effect
Representing the problem
Thinking out loud
Discontinuity in thinking
Domain-free problems
Well-defined problems

Ill-defined problems
Problems in inducing structure
Problems in transformation
Tower of Hanoi
Problems in arrangement
Local–global distinction
Strategy
Heuristic
Algorithm

Task environment
Problem space
Operator
State-action tree
General Problem Solver (GPS)
Isomorphism
Expertise

Appendix

1. Answer to the cheap-necklace problem. Realizing that a chain must be completely disassembled is the key to solving this problem. First, open a link in one of the three-link chains, let's say chain A. Take this open link and connect two three-link chains, for example chains B and C. Then close this connecting link. Now we have one seven-link chain, one three-link chain, and one two-link chain. Next open a second link in chain A. Use this link to connect the seven-link chain with the remaining three-link chain (i.e., chain D). Then close the link. Now we have one eleven-link chain and just one closed link left from chain A. Open the last remaining link in chain A and link both ends of the eleven-link chain through it. Then close that link. We have opened and closed three links for a total cost of 15 cents.

2. Answer to DONALD + GERALD = ROBERT:

$$\begin{array}{r} 526485 \\ +197485 \\ \hline 723970 \end{array}$$

The real key to cracking this problem is deducing E = 9.

3. Answer to the "working-backward" problem. Let's list the players using the notation P1, P2, and P3. Moreover, let's assume that P3 lost the final game. From the material in the text, we have already deduced that after playing two games, P1 and P2 each had $4 and P3 had $16. Now, what happened in the second game? Because each player lost one game, we know that the second game was lost by either P1 or P2, and because they have the same amount of money, it doesn't matter which one we designate as the loser of game 2. Let P2 be the loser of the second game. We know that P2 had to double the current stakes of P1 and P3. Because P3 had $16 after two games had been played, and because P3's stake had been doubled in game 2, P3 must have gotten $8 as a result of the second game, paid by P2. Similarly, we already know that P1 had $4 at the end of game 2 and this player's stake was also doubled by P2's losing in game 2. Thus P1 must have had $2 going into game 2 and earned $2 as a result of P2's loss. In game 2, then, P2 paid $8 to P3, $2 to P1, and still had $4 remaining. Therefore, at the conclusion of game 1, P2 must have had $4 + $10, or $14. We've now established that at the end of the first game P1 had $2, P2 had $14, and P3 had $8. What took place in the first game? The only player whose loss is not accounted for is P1. Given that P2 had $14 at the end of game 1, this player must have been paid $7 by P1 in game 1 as a result of P1's loss. Similarly, we know that P3 had $8 at the end of game 1, and so this player must have been given $4 as a result of P1's losing the first game. This result establishes that the initial stake of P2 was $7 and P3 was $4. P1 paid out $7 + $4 = $11 dollars as a result of losing game 1 and still had $2 left, and so P1's initial stake must have been $11 + $2 = $13.

References

Ahn, W., & Medin, D. L. (1992). A two-stage model of category construction. *Cognitive Science, 16,* 81–121.

Aitchison, J. (1983). *The articulate mammal: An introduction to psycholinguistics* (2nd ed.). New York: Universe.

Aitchison, J. (1987). *Words in the mind.* New York: Blackwell.

Aitkenhead, A. M., & Slack, J. M. (Eds.). (1985). *Issues in cognitive modeling.* Hillsdale, NJ: Erlbaum.

Anderson, J. A., & Rosenfeld, E. (1988). *Neurocomputing.* Cambridge, MA: MIT Press.

Anderson, J. R. (Ed.). (1981). *Cognitive skills and their acquisition.* Hillsdale, NJ: Erlbaum.

Anderson, J. R. (1990). *The adaptive character of thought.* Hillsdale, NJ: Erlbaum.

Anderson, J. R. (1993). *Rules of the mind.* Hillsdale, NJ: Erlbaum.

Anderson, J. R. (1993). Problem solving and learning. *American Psychologist, 48,* 35–44.

Anderson, J. R., & Paulson, R. (1977). Representation and retention of verbatim information. *Journal of Verbal Learning and Verbal Behavior, 16,* 439–452.

Anderson, J. R., & Ross, B. H. (1980). Evidence against a semantic-episodic distinction. *Journal of Experimental Psychology: Human Learning and Memory, 6,* 441–466.

Anderson, J. A., & Sutton, J. P. (1997). If we compute faster, do we understand better? *Behavior Research Methods, Instruments, & Computers, 29,* 67–77.

Anderson, J. R., & Schooler, L. J. (1991) Reflections of the environment in memory. *Psychological Science, 2,* 396–408.

Anderson, R. C., & Pichert, J. W. (1978). Recall of previously unrecallable information following a shift in perspective. *Journal of Verbal Learning and Verbal Behavior, 17,* 1–12.

Anglin, J. M. (1986). Semantic and conceptual knowledge underlying the child's words. In S. A. Kuczaj and M. D. Barrett (Eds.), *The development of word meaning* (pp. 85–97). New York: Springer-Verlag.

Antell, S. E., & Keating, D. P. (1983). Perception of numerical invariance in neonates. *Child Development, 54,* 695–701.

Anzai, Y., & Simon, H. A. (1979). The theory of learning by doing. *Psychological Review, 86,* 124–140.

Astington, J. W. (1997). Talking of mind: theoretical or social construction? *Contemporary Psychology, 42,* 688–691.

Atkinson, R. C., & Shiffrin, R. M. (1968). Human memory: A proposed system and its control processes. In W. K. Spence & J. T. Spence (Eds.), *The psychology of learning and motivation: Advances in research and theory* (Vol. 1, pp. 89–195). New York: Academic Press.

Austin, J. L. (1962). *How to do things with words.* New York: Oxford University Press.

Awh, E., Jonides, J., Smith, E. E., Schumacher, E. H., Koeppe, R. A., & Katz, S. (1996). Dissociation of storage and rehearsal in verbal working memory: Evidence from positron emission tomography. *Psychological Science, 7,* 25–31.

Bach, K., & Harnish, R. M. (1979). *Linguistic communication and speech acts.* Cambridge, MA: MIT Press.

Baddeley, A. D. (1982). Reading and working memory. *Bulletin of the British Psychological Society, 35,* 414–417.

Baddeley, A. D. (1983). Working memory. *Philosophical Transactions of the Royal Society of London, 302B,* 311–324.

Baddeley, A. D. (1990). *Human memory: Theory and practice.* Boston: Allyn and Bacon.

Baddeley, A. A. (1992). Working memory. *Science, 255,* 556–559.

Baddeley, A. D., & Dale, H. C. (1966). The effect of semantic similarity on retroactive interference in long- and short-term memory. *Journal of Verbal Learning and Verbal Behavior, 5,* 417–420.

Baddeley, A. D., & Lewis, V. J. (1981). Inner active process in reading: The inner voice, the inner ear, and the inner eye. In A. M. Lesgold & C. A. Perfetti (Eds.), *Interactive processes in reading* (pp. 107–129). Hillsdale, NJ: Erlbaum.

Bahrick, H. P. (1984). Semantic memory content in permastore: Fifty years of memory for Spanish learned in school. *Journal of Experimental Psychology: General, 113*, 1–29.

Bahrick, H. P., Hall, L. K., Goggin, J. P., & Bahrick, L. E. (1994). Fifty years of language maintenance and language dominance in bilingual Hispanic immigrants. *Journal of Experimental Psychology: General, 123*, 264–283.

Baker, A. G., Mercier, P., Vallee-Tourangeau, F., Frank, R., Pan, M. (1993). Selective associations and causality judgments: Presence of a strong causal factor may reduce judgments of a weaker one. *Journal of Experimental Psychology: Learning, Memory, and Cognition, 19*, 414–432.

Baker, L., and Brown, A. L. (1984). Metacognitive skills and reading. In D. Pearson (Ed.), *Handbook of Reading Research* (pp. 353–394). Newark, DE: International Reading Association.

Banaji, M. R., & Crowder, R. G. (1989). The bankruptcy of everyday memory. *American Psychologist, 44*, 1185–1193.

Barsalou, L. W. (1987). The instability of graded structure: Implications for the nature of concepts. In U. Neisser (Ed.), *Concepts and conceptual development* (pp. 101–140). Cambridge, UK: Cambridge University Press.

Barsalou, L. W., (1991). Deriving categories to achieve goals. In G. H. Bower (Ed.), *The psychology of learning and motivation*, Vol. 27 (pp. 1–64). New York: Academic Press.

Bartlett, F. C. (1932). *Remembering: A study in experimental and social psychology*. Oxford: Cambridge University Press.

Bartlett, F. C. (1958). *Thinking*. New York: Basic Books.

Bartsch, K., & Wellman, H. M. (1995). Children talk about the mind. New York: Oxford University Press.

Beal, C. R. (1985). Development of knowledge about the use of cues to aid prospective retrieval. *Child Development, 56*, 631–642.

Beech, J. R., & Colley, A. M. (Eds.). (1987). *Cognitive approaches to reading*. New York: Wiley.

Bellugi, U. (1964). *The emergence of inflections and negation systems in the speech of two children*. Paper presented at New England Psychological Association Meetings.

Berko, J. (1958). The child's learning of English morphology. *Word, 14*, 150–177.

Besner, D., Twilley, L., McCann, R. S., & Seergobin, K. (1990). On the association between connectionism and data: Are a few words necessary? *Psychological Review, 97*, 432–446.

Bever, T. G., Lackner, J. R., & Kirk, R. (1969). The underlying structures of sentences are the primary units of immediate speech processing. *Perception and Psychophysics, 5*, 225–231.

Biederman, I. (1987). Recognition-by-component: A theory of human image understanding. *Psychological Review, 94*, 115–147.

Biederman, I., Cooper, E. E., Hummel, J. E., & Fiser, J. (1993). Geon theory as an account of shape recognition in mind, brain, and machine. In J. Illingworth (Ed.), *Proceedings of the fourth British machine vision conference* (pp. 175–186). Guildford, Surrey, U.K.: BMVA Press.

Biederman, I., & Cooper, E. E. (1991). Priming contour-deleted images: Evidence for intermediate representations in visual object recognition. *Cognitive Psychology, 23*, 393–419.

Bjorklund, D. F. (Ed.). (1990). *Children's strategies*. Hillsdale, NJ: Erlbaum.

Blank, M. A., & Foss, D. J. (1978). Semantic facilitation and lexical access during sentence processing. *Memory and Cognition, 6*, 644–652.

Bloom, L. (1970). *Language development: Form and function in emerging grammars*. Cambridge, MA: MIT Press.

Bloom, L. M., Lightbown, P., & Hood, L. (1975). Structure and variation in child language. *Monographs of the Society for Research in Child Development, 40* (Serial No. 160).

Bonebakker, A. E., Bonke, B., Klein, J., Wolters, G., Stijnen, T., Passchier, J., & Merikle, P. M. (1996). Information processing during general anesthesia: Evidence for unconscious memory. *Memory & Cognition, 24*, 766–776.

Boster, J. S., & Johnston, J. C. (1989). Form or function: A comparison of expert and novice judgments of similarity among fish. *American Anthropologist, 91*, 866–899.

Bovair, S., Kieras, D. E., & Polson, P. G. (1990). The acquisition and performance of text-editing skill: A cognitive complexity analysis. *Human Computer Interaction, 5*, 1–48.

Bower, G. H., & Humphreys, M. S. (1979). Effect of a recognition test on a subsequent cued-recall test. *Journal of Experimental Psychology: Human Learning and Memory, 5*, 348–359.

Braine, M. D. S. (1976). Children's first word combinations. *Monographs of the Society for Research in Child Development, 41* (Serial No. 164).

Braine, M. D. S. (1987). What is learned in acquiring word classes/M/A step towards an acquisition theory. In B. MacWhinney (Ed.), *Mechanisms of language acquisition* (pp. 65–87). Hillsdale, NJ: Erlbaum.

Braine, M. D. S., et al. (1990). Exploring language acquisition in children with a miniature artificial language: Effects of item and pattern frequency, arbitrary subclasses, and correction. *Journal of Memory and Language, 29*, 591–610.

Brainerd, C. J., Reyna, V. F., & Brandse, E. (1995). Are children's false memories more persistent than their true memories? *Psychological Science, 6*, 359–364.

Bretherton, I., & Bates, E. (1979). The emergence of intentional communication. In I. C. Uzigiris (Ed.). *Social interaction and communication during infancy: Vol. 4, New directions for child development*. San Francisco: Jossey-Bass.

Britton, B., & Glynn, S. M. (Eds.). (1987). *Executive control processes in reading*. Hillsdale, NJ: Erlbaum.

Broadbent, D. E. (1954). A mechanical model for human attention and immediate memory. *Psychological Review, 64*, 205.

Broadbent, D. E. (1958). *Perception and communication*. London: Pergamon Press.

Brooks, L. R. (1967). The suppression of visualization by reading. *Quarterly Journal of Experimental Psychology, 19*, 289–299.

Brown, A. L., & Smiley, S. S. (1977). Rating the importance of structural units of prose passages: A problem of metacognitive development. *Child Development, 48*, 1–8.

Brown, A. L., & Smiley, S. S. (1978). The development of strategies for studying texts. *Child Development, 49*, 1076–1088.

Brown, A. L., Smiley, S. S., & Lawton, S. Q. C. (1978). The effect of experience on the selection of suitable retrieval cues for studying texts. *Child Development, 49*, 829–835.

Brown, H. D., Kosslyn, S. M., Breiter, H. C., Baer, L., & Jenike, M. A. (1994). Can patients with obsessive-compulsive disorder discriminate between percepts and mental images? A signal-detection analysis. *Journal of Abnormal Psychology, 103*, 445–454.

Brown, R. (1970). *Psycholinguistics*. New York: Free Press.

Brown, R. (1973). *A first language: The early stages*. Cambridge, MA: Harvard University Press.

Brown, R., & Bellugi, U. (1964). Three processes in the child's acquisition of syntax. In E. H. Lenneberg (Ed.), *New directions in the study of language*. Cambridge, MA: MIT Press.

Bruner, J. S., Goodnow, J., & Austin, G. A. (1956). *A study of thinking*. New York: Wiley.

Buckner, R. L. (1996). Beyond HERA: Contributions of specific prefrontal brain areas to long-term memory retrieval. *Psychonomic Bulletin and Review, 3*, 149–158.

Buckner, R. L., Petersen, S. E., Ojemann, J. G., Miezin, F. M., Squire, L. R., & Raichle, M. E. (1995). Functional anatomical studies of explicit and implicit memory retrieval tasks. *Journal of Neuroscience, 15*, 12–29.

Burt, M. K. (1971). *From deep to surface structure: An introduction to transformational syntax*. New York: Harper & Row.

Cairns, H. S., & Kamerman, J. (1975). Lexical information processing during sentence comprehension. *Journal of Verbal Learning and Verbal Behavior, 14*, 170–179.

Cantwell, D., & Baker, L. (1987). Differential diagnosis of hyperactivity. *Journal of Developmental & Behavioral Pediatrics, 8*, 159–165.

Carey, S. (1978). The child as word learner. In M. Halle, J. Bresnan, & A. Miller (Eds.), *Linguistic theory and psychological reality* (pp. 264–293). Cambridge, MA: MIT Press.

Carroll, D. W. (1986). *Psychology of language*. Monterey, CA: Brooks/Cole.

Caudill, M., & Butler, C. (1992). *Understanding neural networks* (Vol. 1). Cambridge, MA: MIT Press.

Cazden, C. (1972). *Child language and education*. New York: Holt, Rinehart & Winston.

Ceci, S. J., & Liker, J. K. (1986). A day at the races: A study of IQ, expertise, and cognitive complexity. *Journal of Experimental Psychology: General, 115*, 255–266.

Chapman, S. B. (1996, February). *MRI and SPECT correlates of cognitive/linguistic ability in brain-injured children*. Paper presented at the meeting of the American Association for the Advancement of Sciences, Baltimore, MD.

Chapman, S. B. (1997). Cognitive-communication abilities in children with closed head injury. *American Journal of Speech-Language Pathology, 6*, 50–58.

Chapman, S. B., Watkins, R., Gustafson, C., Moore, S., Levin, H. S., & Kufera, J. A. (1997). Narrative discourse in children with closed head injury, children with language impairment, and typically developing children. *American Journal of Speech-Language Pathology, 6*, 66–76.

Charniak, E. (1983). Passing markers: A theory of contextual influence in language comprehension. *Cognitive Science, 7*, 171–190.

Chase, W. G., & Simon, H. A. (1973). The mind's eye in chess. In W. G. Chase (Ed.), *Visual information processing*. New York: Academic Press.

Cheng, P. W. (1997). From covariation to causation: A causal power theory. *Psychological Review, 104*, 367–405.

Cheng, P. W., & Holyoak, K. J. (1985). Pragmatic reasoning schemas. *Cognitive Psychology, 17*, 391–416.

Cheng, P. W., Holyoak, K. J., Nisbett, R. E., & Oliver, L. M. (1986). Pragmatic versus syntactic approaches to training deductive reasoning. *Cognitive Psychology, 18*, 293–328.

Cheng, P. W., & Novick, L. R. (1992). Covariation in natural causal induction. *Psychological Review, 99*, 365–382.

Cherry, E. C. (1953). Some experiments on the recognition of speech with one and with two ears. *Journal of the Acoustical Society of America, 25*, 975–979.

Cherry, R. S., & Kruger, B. (1983). Selective auditory attention abilities of learning disabled and normal achieving children. *Journal of Learning Disabilities, 16*, 202–205.

Chi, M. T. H., & Glaser, R. (1985). Problem-solving ability. In R. J. Sternberg (Ed.), *Human abilities: An information processing approach* (pp. 227–248). New York: Freeman.

Chi, M. T. H., Glaser, R., & Rees, E. (1982). Expertise in problem solving. In R. J. Sternberg (Ed.), *Advances in the psychology of human intelligence* (Vol. 1, pp. 7–76). Hillsdale, NJ: Erlbaum.

Chomsky, C. (1969). *The acquisition of syntax in children from 5 to 10*. Cambridge, MA: MIT Press.

Chomsky, N. (1957). *Syntactic structures*. The Hague: Mouton.

Chomsky, N. (1959). Review of Skinner's verbal behavior. *Language, 35*, 26–58.

Chomsky, N. (1972). *Language and mind* (enlarged ed.). New York: Harcourt Brace Jovanovich.

Chomsky, N. (1979). *Language and responsibility*. Hassocks, Sussex, England: Harvester.

Chomsky, N. (1983). On the representation of form and function. In J. Mehler, E. C. T. Walker, & M. Garrett (Eds.), *Perspectives on mental representation* (pp. 3–38). Hillsdale, NJ: Erlbaum.

Chomsky, N., & Halle, M. (1968). *The sound pattern of English*. New York: Harper & Row.

Chorover, S. L., & Schiller, P. H. (1965). Short-term retrograde amnesia in rats. *Journal of Comparative and Physiological Psychology, 59*, 73–78.

Chrostowski, J. J., & Griggs, R. A. (1985). The effects of problem, content, instructions and verbalization procedure on Wason's selection task. *Current Psychological Research and Reviews, 4*, 99–107.

Churchland, P. M. (1989). *A neurocomputational perspective: The nature of mind and the structure of science*. Cambridge, MA: MIT Press.

Clark, A. (1989). *Microcognition: Philosophy, cognitive science, and parallel distributed processing.* Cambridge, MA: MIT Press.

Clark, H. H., & Clark, E. V. (1977). *Psychology and language.* New York: Harcourt Brace Jovanovich.

Clark, H. H., & Lucy, P. (1975). Understanding what is meant from what is said: A study in conversationally conveyed requests. *Journal of Verbal Learning and Verbal Behavior, 14,* 56–72.

Cole, M., & Scribner, S. (1977). Cross-cultural studies of memory and cognition. In R. V. Vail, Jr., & J. W. Hagen (Eds.), *Perspectives on the development of memory and recognition.* Hillsdale, NJ: Erlbaum.

Collins, A. M., & Loftus, E. F. (1975). A spreading activation theory of semantic processing. *Psychological Review, 82,* 407–428.

Collins, A. M., & Quillian, M. R. (1969). Retrieval time from semantic memory. *Journal of Verbal Learning and Verbal Behavior, 8,* 240–247.

Coltheart, M. (1978). Lexical access in simple reading tasks. In G. Underwood (Ed.), *Strategies of information processing.* New York: Academic Press.

Coltheart, M. (1980). Iconic memory and visual persistence. *Perception and Psychophysics, 27,* 183–228.

Coltheart, M. (1980). Reading, phonological recoding, and deep dyslexia. In M. Coltheart, K. Patterson, & J. C. Marshall (Eds.), *Deep dyslexia.* London: Routledge & Kegan Paul.

Coltheart, M., Davelaar, E., Jonasson, J. T., & Besner, D. (1977). Access to the internal lexicon. In S. Dornic (Ed.), *Attention and Performance* (Vol. 6). New York: Academic Press.

Conrad, C. (1972). Cognitive economy in semantic memory. *Journal of Experimental Psychology, 92,* 149–154.

Conrad, R. (1964). Acoustic confusions in immediate memory. *British Journal of Psychology, 55,* 75–84.

Conway, M. A. (1990). *Autobiographical memory: An introduction.* Philadelphia: Open University Press.

Conway, M. A., Cohen, G., & Stanhope, N. (1991). On the very long-term retention of knowledge acquired through formal education: Twelve years of cognitive psychology. *Journal of Experimental Psychology: General, 120,* 395–409.

Conway, M. A., Cohen, G., & Stanhope, N. (1992). Why is it that university grades do not predict very-long-term retention? *Journal of Experimental Psychology: General, 121,* 382–384.

Cosky, M. J. (1975). *Word length effects in word recognition.* Unpublished doctoral dissertation, University of Texas, Austin.

Cowan, N. (1993). Activation, attention, and short-term memory. *Memory & Cognition, 21,* 162–167.

Cowan, N. (1994). Mechanisms of verbal short-term memory. *Current Directions in Psychological Science, 6,* 185–189.

Cowan, N., Wood, N. L., & Born, D. N. (1994). Reconfirmation of the short-term memory concept. *Psychological Science, 5,* 103–106.

Cowan, N., Day, L, Saults, J. S., Keller, T. A., Johnson, T., & Flores, L. (1992). The role of verbal output time in the effects of word length on immediate memory. *Journal of Memory and Language, 31,* 1–17.

Craik, F. I. M. (1979). Human memory. *Annual Review of Psychology, 30,* 63–102.

Craik, F. I. M., & Lockhart, R. S. (1972). Levels of processing: A framework for memory research. *Journal of Verbal Learning and Verbal Behavior, 11,* 671–684.

Craik, F. I. M., & Simon, E. (1980). Age differences in memory: The roles of attention and depth of processing. In L. W. Poon, J. L. Fozard, L. S. Cermak, D. Arenberg, & L. W. Thompson (Eds.), *New directions in memory and aging: Proceedings of the George Talland memorial conference.* Hillsdale, NJ: Erlbaum.

Craik, F. I. M., & Tulving, E. (1975). Depth of processing and the retention of words in episodic memory. *Journal of Experimental Psychology: General, 104,* 268–294.

Craik, F. I. M., & Watkins, M. J. (1973). The role of rehearsal in short-term memory. *Journal of Verbal Learning and Verbal Behavior, 12,* 559–607.

Cromer, R. F. (1970). Children are nice to understand: Surface structure clues for the recovery of deep structure. *British Journal of Psychology, 61,* 397–408.

Crowder, R. G. (1982). *The psychology of reading.* New York: Oxford University Press.

Crowder, R. G. (1993). Short-term memory: Where do we stand? *Memory & Cognition, 21,* 142–145.

Crowder, R. G., & Morton, J. (1969). Precategorical acoustic storage (PAS). *Perception and Psychophysics, 5,* 365–373.

Cummins, D. D. (1995). Naive theories and causal deduction. *Memory & Cognition, 23,* 646–658.

Cummins, D. D. (1996). Evidence of deontic reasoning in 3- and 4-year-old children. *Memory & Cognition, 24,* 823–829.

Curtiss, S. (1977). *Genie: A psycholinguistic study of a modern-day "wild child."* New York: Academic Press.

Curtiss, S., Fromkin, V., Krashen, S., Rigler, D., & Rigler, M. (1974). The linguistic development of Genie. *Language, 50,* 528–554.

Danks, J. H., & Glucksberg, S. (1980). Experimental psycholinguistics. *Annual Review of Psychology, 31,* 391–417.

Daro, D. (1988). *Confronting child abuse.* New York: Free Press.

Dawson, M. E., & Schell, A. M. (1982). Electrodermal responses to attended and nonattended significant stimuli during dichotic listening. *Journal of Experimental Psychology: Human Perception and Performance, 8,* 315–324.

Dawson, M. E., & Schell, A. M. (1983). Lateral asymmetries in electro-dermal responses to nonattended stimuli: A reply to Walker and Ceci. *Journal of Experimental Psychology: Human Perception and Performance, 9,* 148–150.

Deese, J. (1984). *Thought into speech: The psychology of a language.* Englewood Cliffs, NJ: Prentice-Hall.

Deese, J., & Kaufman, R. A. (1957). Serial effects in recall of unorganized and sequentially organized verbal material. *Journal of Experimental Psychology, 54,* 180–187.

de Groot, A. (1965). *Thought and choice in chess.* The Hague: Mouton.

de Groot, A. (1966). Perception and memory versus thought: Some old ideas and recent findings. In B. Kleinmuntz (Ed.), *Problem solving*. New York: Wiley.

DeJong, G. (1982). On communications between AI and linguistics. In D. L. Farwell, S. C. Helmreich, & W. D. Wallace (Eds.), *Perspectives in cognitive science* (pp. 33–41). Urbana, IL: Linguistics Student Organization.

de Jong, T., & Ferguson-Hessler, M. G. (1986). Cognitive structures of good and poor novice problem solvers in physics. *Journal of Educational Psychology, 78,* 279–288.

Delaney, P. F., Reder, L. M., Staszewski, J. J., Ritter, F. E. (1998). The strategy-specific nature of improvement: the power law applies by strategy within task. *Psychological Science, 9,* 1–7.

Dell, G. S. (1986). A spreading activation theory of retrieval in sentence production. *Psychological Review, 93,* 283–321.

Dennett, D. C. (1996). *Kinds of minds: Toward an understanding of consciousness*. New York: Basic Books.

Deutsch, F. A., & Deutsch, D. (1963). Attention: Some theoretical considerations. *Psychological Review, 70,* 80–90.

De Villiers, J. G., & De Villiers, P. A. (1978). *Language acquisition*. Cambridge, MA: Harvard University Press.

Dienes, Z., & Berry, D. (1997). Implicit learning: Below the subjective threshold. *Psychonomic Bulletin and Review, 4,* 3–24.

diSessa, A. (1993). Toward an epistemology of physics. *Cognition and Instruction, 10,* 105–225.

Dominowski, R. L., & Ekstrand, B. R. (1967). Direct and associative priming in anagram solving. *Journal of Experimental Psychology, 74,* 84–86.

Dominowski, R. L., & Jenrick, R. (1972). Effects of hints and interpolated activity on solution of an insight problem. *Psychonomic Science, 26,* 335–338.

Donaldson, W. (1996). The role of decision processes in remembering and knowing. *Memory & Cognition, 24,* 523–533.

Drewnowski, A. (1980). Attributes and priorities in short-term recall: A new model of memory span. *Journal of Experimental Psychology: General, 109,* 208–250.

Drewnowski, A., & Murdock, B. B., Jr. (1980). The role of auditory features in memory span for words. *Journal of Experimental Psychology: Human Learning and Memory, 6,* 319–332.

Duncker, K. (1945). On problem solving. *Psychological Monographs, 58* (5, Whole No. 270).

Ebbinghaus, H. (1885). Uber das Gedachtnis. Leipzig: Dunker. (Translated by H. Ruyer and C. E. Bussenius, (1913), *Memory,* New York: Teachers College, Columbia University.

Eich, E. (1984). Memory for unattended events: Remembering with and without awareness. *Memory & Cognition, 12,* 105–111.

Eimas, P. D., Siqueland, E. R., Jusczyk, P., & Vigorito, J. (1971). Speech perception by infants. *Science, 171,* 303–306.

Ellis, A., & Beattie, G. (1986). *The psychology of language and communication*. New York: Guilford.

Ericsson, K. A., Chase, W. G., & Faloon, S. (1980). Acquisition of memory skill. *Science, 208,* 1181–1182.

Ericsson, K. A., & Lehmann, A. C. (1996). Expert and exceptional performance: Evidence of maximal adaptation to task constraints. *Annual Review of Psychology, 47,* 273–305.

Ericsson, K. A., & Simon, H. A. (1980). Verbal reports as data. *Psychological Review, 87,* 215–251.

Evans, J. St. B. T. (1989). *Bias in human reasoning: Causes and consequences*. Hillsdale, NJ: Erlbaum.

Evans, J. St. B. T., Newstead, S. E., & Byrne, R. M. J. (1993). *Human reasoning: The psychology of deduction*. Hillsdale, NJ: Erlbaum.

Eylon, B. (1979). *Effects of knowledge organization on task performance*. Unpublished doctoral dissertation, University of California at Berkeley.

Eylon, B., & Reif, F. (1984). Effects of knowledge organization on task performance. *Cognition and Instruction, 1,* 5–44.

Feldman, J. A. (1985). Connectionist models and their applications: Introduction. *Cognitive Science, 9,* 1–2.

Fiske, A. D., & Schneider, W. (1984). Memory as a function of attention, level of processing, and automatization. *Journal of Experimental Psychology: Learning, Memory, and Cognition, 10,* 181–197.

Fivush, R., & Hamond, N. R. (1990). Autobiographical memory across the preschool years: toward reconceptualising childhood amnesia. In R. Fivush and J. A. Hudson (Eds.), *Knowing and remembering in young children*. New York: Cambridge University Press.

Flavell, J. H. (1971). First discussant's comments: What is memory development the development of? *Human Development, 14,* 272–278.

Flavell, J. H., & Wellman, H. M. (1977). Metamemory. In R. V. Kail & J. H. Hagen (Eds.), *Perspectives on the development of memory and cognition*. Hillsdale, NJ: Erlbaum.

Flexser, A. J., & Tulving, E. (1978). Retrieval independence in recognition and recall. *Psychological Review, 85,* 153–171.

Flexser, A. J., & Tulving, E. (1982). Priming and recognition failure. *Journal of Verbal Learning and Verbal Behavior, 21,* 237–248.

Fodor, J. A. (1983). *The modularity of mind*. Cambridge, MA: MIT Press.

Fodor, J. A., Bever, T., & Garrett, M. (1974). *The psychology of language*. New York: McGraw-Hill.

Fodor, J. A., & Garrett, M. F. (1967). Some syntactic determinants of sentential complexity. *Perception and Psychophysics, 2,* 289–296.

Fodor, J. A., & Pylyshyn, Z. W. (1988). Connectionism and cognitive architecture: A critical analysis. *Cognition, 28,* 3–71.

Foss, D. J. (1982). A discourse on semantic priming. *Cognitive Psychology, 14,* 590–607.

Foss, D. J., & Hakes, D. T. (1978). *Psycholinguistics: An introduction to the psychology of language*. Englewood Cliffs, NJ: Prentice-Hall.

Franklin, M. B., & Barten, S. B. (Eds.). (1987). *Child language: A reader*. New York: Oxford University Press.

Fromkin, V. A. (1971). The non-anomalous nature of anomalous utterances. *Language, 47,* 27–52.

Fromkin, V., & Rodman, R. (1978). *An introduction to linguistics* (2nd ed.). New York: Holt, Rinehart, and Winston.

Fulgosi, A., & Guilford, J. P. (1968). Short-term incubation in divergent production. *American Journal of Psychology, 81,* 241–246.

Gabrieli, J. D. E., Desmond, J. E., Demb, J. B., Wagner, A. D., Stone, M. V., Vaidya, C. J., & Glover, G. H. (1996). Functional magnetic resonance imaging of semantic memory processes in the frontal lobes. *Psychological Science, 7,* 278–283.

Gallant, S. L. (1993). *Neural network learning and expert systems.* Cambridge, MA: MIT Press/Bradford.

Gardiner, J. M., & Tulving, E. (1980). Exceptions to recognition failure of recallable words. *Journal of Verbal Learning and Verbal Behavior, 19,* 194–209.

Garner, W. R. (1979). Letter discrimination and identification. In A. D. Pick (Ed.), *Perception and its development: A tribute to Eleanor J. Gibson.* Hillsdale, NJ: Erlbaum.

Garnham, A., & Oakhill, J. (1994). *Thinking and reasoning.* Cambridge, MA: Blackwell.

Garrett, M. F., Bever, T., & Fodor, J. A. (1966). The active use of grammar in speech perception. *Perception and Psychophysics, 1,* 30–32.

Garret, M. F. (1982). Production of speech: Observations from normal and pathological language use. In A. W. Ellis (Ed.,), *Normality and pathology in cognitive functions* (pp. 19–76). New York: Academic Press.

Garry, M., Manning, C. G., Loftus, E. F., & Sherman, S. J. (1996). Imagination inflation: Imagining a childhood event inflates confidence that it occurred. *Psychonomic Bulletin and Review, 3,* 208–214.

Gelman, R., & Baillargeon, R. (1983). A review of some Piagetian concepts. In J. H. Flavell & E. M. Markman (Eds.), *Handbook of child psychology* (Vol. 3). New York: Wiley.

Gentner, D., Rattermann, M., & Forbus, K. (1993). The roles of similarity in transfer: Separating retrievability from inferential soundness. *Cognitive Psychology, 25,* 524–575.

Geschwind, N. (1980). Specializations of the human brain. In R. C. Atkinson & R. L. Atkinson (Eds.), *Mind and Behavior* (pp. 206–215). San Francisco: Freeman.

Gernsbacher, M. A., & Robertson, R. R. W. (1995). Reading skill and suppression revisited. *Psychological Science, 6,* 165–169.

Gernsbacher, M. A., & Varner, K. R., & Faust, M. E. (1990). Investigating differences in general comprehension skill. *Journal of Experimental Psychology: Learning, Memory, and Cognition, 16,* 430–445.

Geyer, L. H., & DeWald, C. G. (1973). Feature lists and confusion matrices. *Perception and Psychophysics, 14,* 471–482.

Ghiselin, B. (1952). *The creative process: A symposium.* Berkeley: University of California Press.

Gibson, E. J. (1969). *Principles of perceptual learning and development.* New York: Prentice-Hall.

Glenberg, A. M., & Adams, F. (1978). Type I rehearsal and recognition. *Journal of Verbal Learning and Verbal Behavior, 17,* 455–463.

Glucksberg, S., Kreuz, R. J., & Rho, S. (1986). Context can constrain lexical access: Implications for models of language comprehension. *Journal of Experimental Psychology: Learning, Memory and Cognition, 12,* 323–335.

Goff, L. M., & Roediger, H. L. III. (1998). Imagination inflation for action events: Repeated imaginings lead to illusory recollections. *Memory & Cognition, 26,* 20–33.

Goldstone, R. L., Medin, D. L., & Gentner, D. (1991). Relational similarity and the nonindependence of features in similarity judgments. *Cognitive Psychology, 23,* 222–262.

Golinkoff, R. M., & Kerr, J. L. (1978). Infants' perception of semantically defined action role changes in filmed acts. *Merrill-Palmer Quarterly, 24,* 53–61.

Greenfield, P. M., & Smith, J. H. (1976). *The structure of communication in early language development.* New York: Academic Press.

Greeno, J. G. (1976). Indefinite goals in well-structured problems. *Psychological Review, 83,* 479–491.

Greeno, J. G. (1978). Natures of problem-solving abilities. In W. K. Estes (Ed.), *Handbook of learning and cognitive processes* (Vol. 5, pp. 239–270). Hillsdale, NJ: Erlbaum.

Grice, H. P. (1975). Logic and conversation. In P. Cole & J. L. Morgan (Eds.), *Syntax and semantics: Vol. 3, Speech Acts* (pp. 41–58). New York: Seminar Press.

Griggs, R. A., & Cox, J. R. (1982). The elusive thematic-materials effects in Wason's selection task. *British Journal of Psychology, 73,* 407–420.

Griggs, R. A. (1989). To "see" or not to "see": That is the selection task. Quarterly Journal of Experimental Psychology, 41 A, 517–529.

Griggs, R. A., & Jackson, S. L. (1990). Instructional effects on responses in Wason's selection task. *British Journal of Psychology, 81,* 197–204.

Groen, G. J., & Parkman, J. M. (1972). A chronometric analysis of simple addition. *Psychological Review, 79,* 329–343.

Gross, T. F. (1985). *Cognitive development.* Monterey, CA: Brooks/Cole.

Grossberg, S. (1988). *Neural networks and natural intelligence.* Cambridge, MA: MIT Press.

Hakes, D. T., & Foss, D. J. (1970). Decision processes during sentence comprehension: Effects of surface structure reconsidered. *Perception and Psychophysics, 8,* 413–416.

Halle, M., & Stevens, K. N. (1964). Speech recognition: A model and a program for research. In J. A. Fodor & J. J. Katz (Eds.), *The structure of language: Readings in the philosophy of language.* Englewood Cliffs, NJ: Prentice-Hall.

Halliday, D., & Resnick, R. (1974). *Fundamentals of physics* (2nd ed.). New York: Wiley.

Hammond, N. R., & Fivush, R., (1991). Memories of Mickey Mouse: Young children recount their trip to Disneyworld. *Cognitive Development, 6,* 443–448.

Hannigan, J. L., Shelton, T. S., Franks, J. J., & Bransford, J. D. (1980). The effects of episodic and semantic memory on the identification of sentences masked by white noise. *Memory and Cognition, 8,* 278–284.

Hanson, S. J., & Burr, D. J. (1990). What connectionist models learn: Learning and representation in connectionist networks. *Behavioral and Brain Sciences, 13,* 471–518.

Hanson, S. J., Drastal, G. A., & Rivest, R. L. (Eds.). (1994). *Computational learning theory and natural learning systems* (Vol. 1). Cambridge, MA: MIT Press/Bradford.

Harding, R. (1940). *An anatomy of inspiration.* London: Cass.

Harley, T. A. (1996). Connectionist modeling of the recovery of language functions following brain damage. *Brain and Language, 52,* 7–24.

Hasher, L., & Zacks, R. T. (1979). Automatic and effortful processes in memory. *Journal of Experimental Psychology: General, 108,* 356–388.

Haugaard, J. J., Reppucci, N. D., & Laurd, J., & Nauful, T. (1991). Children's definitions of the truth and their competency as a witnesses in legal proceedings. *Law and Human Behavior, 15* 253–272.

Hawkins, J. A. (Ed.). (1988). *Explaining language universals.* New York: Blackwell.

Hayes, J. R., & Simon, H. A. (1974). Understanding written problem instructions. In L. W. Gregg (Ed.), *Knowledge and cognition.* Hillsdale, NJ: Erlbaum.

Healy, A. F. (1976). Detection errors on the word *the:* Evidence for reading units larger than letters. *Journal of Experimental Psychology: Human Perception and Performance, 2,* 235–242.

Healy, A. F., & McNamara, D. S. (1996). Verbal learning and memory: Does the modal model still work? *Annual Review of Psychology, 47,* 143–172.

Hebb, D. O. (1949). *The organization of behavior.* New York: Wiley.

Heller, J. I., & Reif, F. (1984). Prescribing effective human problem-solving processes: Problem description in physics. *Cognition and Instruction, 1,* 177–216.

Henle, M. (1962). On the relation between logic and thinking. *Psychological Review, 69,* 366–378.

Hilgard, E. R. (1987). *Psychology in America: A historical survey.* San Diego, CA: Harcourt Brace Jovanovich.

Hinsley, D. A., Hayes, J. R., & Simon, H. A. (1978). From words to equations: Meaning and representation in algebra word problems. In P. A. Carpenter & M. A. Just (Eds.), *Cognitive processes in comprehension.* Hillsdale, NJ: Erlbaum.

Hintzman, D. L. (1965). Classification and aural coding in short-term memory. *Psychonomic Science, 3,* 161–162.

Hintzman, D. L. (1967). Articulatory coding in short-term memory. *Journal of Verbal Learning and Verbal Behavior, 6,* 312–316.

Hirst, W., Spelke, E. S., Reaves, C. C., Caharack, G., & Neisser, U. (1980). Dividing attention without alternation or automaticity. *Journal of Experimental Psychology: General, 109,* 98–117.

Hoch, S. J., & Tschirgi, J. E. (1983). Cue redundancy and extra logical inferences in a deductive reasoning task. *Memory & Cognition, 11,* 200–209.

Hoch, S. J., & Tschirgi, J. E. (1985). Logical knowledge and cue redundancy in deductive reasoning. *Memory & Cognition, 13,* 453–462.

Hockett, C. F. (1960). The origin of speech. *Scientific American, 203,* 89–96.

Hockett, C. F. (1963). The problem of universals in language. In J. H. Greenberg (Ed.), *Universals of language.* Cambridge, MA: MIT Press.

Horn, B. K. P. (1986). *Robot vision.* Cambridge, MA: MIT Press.

Horrocks, G. (1987). *Generative grammar.* White Plains, NY: Longman.

Horton, D. L., & Mills, C. B. (1984). Human learning and memory. *Annual Review of Psychology, 35,* 361–394.

Horton, M. S., & Markman, E. M. (1980). Developmental differences in the acquisition of basic and superordinate categories. *Child Development, 51,* 708–719.

Houston, J. P. (1986). *Fundamentals of learning and memory* (3rd ed.). New York: Harcourt Brace Jovanovich.

Howard, D. V. (1983). *Cognitive psychology: Memory, language, and thought.* New York: Macmillan.

Hudson, R. (1984). *Invitation to linguistics.* New York: Blackwell.

Huff, R., Rattner, A., & Sagarin, E. (1986). Guilty until proven innocent. *Crime and Delinquency, 32,* 518–544.

Hulse, S. H., Deese, J., & Egeth, H. (1975). *The psychology of learning* (4th ed.). New York: McGraw-Hill.

Humphreys, G. (1963). *Thinking: An introduction to its experimental psychology.* New York: Wiley.

Humphreys, M. S., & Bower, G. H. (1980). Sequential testing effects and the relationship between recognition and recognition failure. *Memory and Cognition, 8,* 271–277.

Hunt, M. (1982). *The universe within.* New York: Simon & Schuster.

Hunt, R. R., & Elliott, J. M. (1980). The role of nonsemantic information in memory: Orthographic distinctiveness effects on retention. *Journal of Experimental Psychology: General, 109,* 49–74.

Hyde, T. S., & Jenkins, J. J. (1973). Recall for words as a function of semantic, graphic, and syntactic orienting tasks. *Journal of Verbal Learning and Verbal Behavior, 12,* 471–480.

Imhoff, A. W., & Rayner, K. (1986). Parafoveal word processing during eye fixations in reading: Effects of word frequency. *Perception and Psychophysics, 40,* 431–439.

Jacoby, L. L. (1983). Remembering the data: analyzing interactive processes in reading. *Journal of Verbal Learning and Verbal Behavior, 22,* 485–508.

Jacoby, L. L., & Craik, F. I. M. (1979). Effects of elaboration of processing at encoding and retrieval: Trace distinctiveness and recovery of initial context. In L. S. Cermak & F. I. M. Craik (Eds.), *Levels of processing in human memory.* Hillsdale, NJ: Erlbaum.

Jacoby, L. L., Craik, F. I. M., & Begg, I. (1979). Effects of decision difficulty on recognition and recall. *Journal of Verbal Learning and Verbal Behavior, 18,* 585–600.

Jacoby, L. L., & Dallas, M. (1981). On the relationship between autobiographical memory and perceptual learning. *Journal of Experimental Psychology: General, 110,* 306–340.

James, W. (1890). *The principles of psychology.* New York: Holt, Rinehart & Winston.

James, W. (1890/1983). *The principles of psychology.* Cambridge: Harvard University Press. (Original work published 1890).

Jenkins, J. G., & Dallenbach, K. M. (1924). Oblivescence during sleep and waking. *American Journal of Psychology, 35,* 605–612.

Jespersen, O. (1922). *Language: Its nature, development and origin.* New York: Allen & Unwin.

John-Steiner, V. (1997). *Notebooks of the mind* (rev. ed.). New York: Oxford University Press.

Johnson-Laird, P. N. (1987). Grammar and psychology. In S. Modgil & C. Modgil (Eds.), *Noam Chomsky: Consensus and controversy* (pp. 147–156). New York: Falmer Press.

Johnson-Laird, P. N., & Byrne, R. M. J. (1991). *Deduction.* Hillsdale, NJ: Erlbaum.

Johnson-Laird, P. N., Byrne, R. M. J., & Schaeken, W. (1992). Propositional reasoning by model. *Psychological Review, 99,* 418–439.

Johnson-Laird, P. N., Legrenzi, P., & Legrenzi, M. (1972). Reasoning and a sense of reality. *British Journal of Psychology, 63,* 395–400.

Johnston, J. C., McCann, R. S., & Remington, R. W. (1995). Chronometric evidence for two types of attention. *Psychological Science, 6,* 365–369.

Johnston, J. C., & McClelland, J. L. (1980). Experimental tests of a hierarchical model of word identification. *Journal of Verbal Learning and Verbal Behavior, 19,* 503–524.

Johnston, W. A., & Heinz, S. P. (1978). Flexibility and capacity demands of attention. *Journal of Experimental psychology: General, 107,* 420–435.

Jones, R. K. (1966). Observations on stammering after localized cerebral injury. *Journal of Neurology, Neurosurgery, and Psychiatry, 29,* 192–195.

Just, M. A., & Carpenter, P. A. (1980). A theory of reading: From eye fixations to comprehension. *Psychological Review, 87,* 329–354.

Kahneman, D. (1973). *Attention and effort.* Englewood Cliffs, NJ: Prentice-Hall.

Kahneman, D., & Tversky, A. (1973). On the psychology of prediction. *Psychological Review, 80,* 237–251.

Kahneman, D., & Tversky, A. (1982). On the study of statistical intuitions. In D. Kahneman, P. Slovic, & A. Tversky (Eds.), *Judgements under uncertainty: Heuristics and biases* (pp. 493–508). Cambridge: Cambridge University Press.

Kail, R. (1990). *The development of memory in children* (3rd. ed.). New York: Freeman.

Kalat, J. W. (1984). *Biological psychology* (2nd ed.). Belmont, CA: Wadsworth.

Karat, J. (1982). A model of problem solving with incomplete constraint knowledge. *Cognitive Psychology, 14,* 538–559.

Katona, G. (1940). *Organizing and memorizing.* New York: Columbia University Press.

Katz, J. J. (1977). *Propositional structure and illocutionary force.* New York: Thomas Y. Crowell.

Kay, D. A., & Anglin, J. M. (1982). Overextension and underextension in the child's expressive and receptive speech. *Journal of Child Language, 9,* 83–98.

Kellogg, R. T. (1982). When can we introspect accurately about mental processes? *Memory and Cognition, 10,* 141–144.

Kennedy, A. (1984). *The psychology of reading.* London: Methuen.

Keppel, G., & Underwood, B. J. (1962). Proactive inhibition in short-term retention of single items. *Journal of Verbal Learning and Verbal Behavior, 1,* 153–161.

Kessel, F. (Ed.). (1988). *The development of language and language researchers.* Hillsdale, NJ: Erlbaum.

Kihlstrom, J. F. (1980). Posthypnotic amnesia for recently learned material: Interactions with "episodic" and "semantic" memory. *Cognitive Psychology, 12,* 227–251.

Kintsch, W., Miller, J. R., & Polson, P. G. (Eds.). (1984). *Methods and tactics in cognitive science.* Hillsdale, NJ: Erlbaum.

Klahr, D., Langley, P., & Neches, R. (1987). *Production system models of learning and development.* Cambridge, MA: MIT Press.

Klahr, D., & Kotovsky, K. (Eds.). (1989). *Complex information processing: The impact of Herbert A. Simon.* Hillsdale, NJ: Erlbaum.

Klatzky, R. L. (1980). *Human memory: Structures and processes* (2nd ed.). San Francisco: Freeman.

Klatzky, R. L. (1984). *Memory and awareness.* San Francisco: Freeman.

Kolers, P. A. (1970). Three stages of reading. In H. Levin & J. P. Williams (Eds.), *Basic studies on reading.* New York: Basic Books.

Komatsu, L. K. (1992) Recent views of conceptual structure. *Psychological Bulletin, 112,* 500–526.

Koppel, S. (1979). Testing the attentional deficit notion. *Journal of Learning Disabilities, 12,* 52–57.

Kounios, J. (1996). On the continuity of thought and the representation of knowledge: Electrophysiolgical and behavioral time-course measures reveal levels of structure in semantic memory. *Psychonomic Bulletin and Review, 3,* 265–286.

Kounios, J., Osman, A. M., & Meyer, D. E. (1987). Structure and process in semantic memory: new evidence based on speed-accuracy decomposition. *Journal of Experimental Psychology: General. 116,* 3–25.

Koriat, A., & Goldsmith, M. (1996). Memory metaphors and the real-life/laboratory controversy: Correspondence versus storehouse conceptions of memory. *Behavioral and Brain Sciences, 19,* 167–228.

Kuehne, C., Kehle, T. J., & McMahon, W. (1987). Differences between children with attentional deficit disorder, children with specific learning disabilities and normal children. *Journal of School Psychology, 25,* 161–166.

Kruschke, J. K. (1992). ALCOVE: An exemplar-based connectionist model of category learning. *Psychological Review, 99,* 22–44.

Kuhn, D. (1989). Children and adults as intuitive scientists. *Psychological Review, 96,* 674–689.

Labov, W. (1973). The boundaries of words and their meanings. In C. J. N. Bailey, & R. W. Shuy (Eds.), *New ways of analyzing variation in English* (pp. 340–373). Washington, DC: Georgetown University Press.

Larkin, J. H. (1989). Display-based problem solving. In D. Klahr & K. Kotovsky (Eds.), *Complex information processing: The impact of Herbert A. Simon* (pp. 319–341). Hillsdale, NJ: Erlbaum.

Lashley, K. S. (1929). *Brain mechanisms and intelligence.* Chicago: University of Chicago Press.

Lashley, K. S. (1950). In search of the engram. *Symposia of the Study of Experimental Biology, 4,* 454–482.

Lassaline, M. E., & Murphy, G. L. (1996). Induction and category coherence. *Psychonomic Bulletin and Review, 3,* 95–99.

Lassaline, M. E., Wisniewski, E. J., & Medin, D. L. (1992). Categories, concepts, and learning basic levels in artificial and natural categories: Are all basic levels created equal? in B. Burns (Ed.), *Percepts concepts and categories: The representation and processing of information.* (pp. 327–378). Amsterdam, Netherlands: Elsevier Science.

Leahey, T. H. (1987). *A history of psychology: Main currents in psychological thought.* Englewood Cliffs, NJ: Prentice-Hall.

Leahey, T. H., & Harris, R. J. (1985). *Human learning.* Englewood Cliffs, NJ: Prentice-Hall.

Lenneberg, E. H. (1964). *New directions in the study of language.* Cambridge, MA: MIT Press.

Lenneberg, E. H. (1967). *Biological foundations of language.* New York: Wiley.

Leonard, J. M., & Whitten, W. B. (1983). Information stored when expecting recall or recognition. *Journal of Experimental Psychology: Learning, Memory, and Cognition, 9,* 440–455.

Leslie, A. M. (1982). The perception of causality in infants. *Perception, 11,* 173–186.

Levelt, W. J. M. (1983). Monitoring and self-repair in speech. *Cognition, 14,* 41–104.

Levelt, W. J. M. (1989). *Speaking: From intention to articulation.* Cambridge, MA: MIT Press.

Levin, I. P., Kao, S-F., & Wasserman, E. A. (1991, November). *Biased information usage in contingency judgments.* Paper presented at the meeting of the Midwestern Psychological Association, Chicago.

Levine, D. S. (1990). *Introduction to neural and cognitive modeling.* Hillsdale, NJ: Erlbaum.

Levy-Bruhl, L. (1966). *How natives think.* New York: Washington Square Press. (Original work published 1910.)

Lewis, J. L. (1970). Semantic processing of unattended messages using dichotic listening. *Journal of Experimental Psychology, 85,* 225–228.

Liberman, A. M., Cooper, F., Shankweiler, D. P., & Studdert-Kennedy, M. (1967). Perception of the speech code. *Psychological Review, 74,* 431–461.

Lieberman, P. (1967). *Intonation, perception, and language.* Cambridge, MA: MIT Press.

Light, L., & Carter-Sobell, L. (1970). Effects of changed semantic context on recognition memory. *Journal of Verbal Learning and Verbal Behavior, 9,* 1–11.

Lindsay, P. H., & Norman, D. A. (1977). *Human information processing* (2nd ed.). New York: Academic Press.

Ling, X., & Sanocki, T. (1995). Major axes as a moderately abstract model for object recognition. *Psychological Science, 6,* 370–375.

Lisker, L., & Abramson, A. S. (1970). The voicing dimension: Some experiments in comparative phonetics. *Proceedings of the Sixth International Congress of Phonetic Sciences.* Prague: Academia, 1970.

Loftus, E. F. (1975). Leading questions and the eyewitness report. *Cognitive Psychology, 7,* 560–572.

Loftus, E. F. (1977). Shifting human color vision. *Memory & Cognition, 5,* 696–699.

Loftus, E. F. (1979a). Reactions to blatantly contradictory information. *Memory & Cognition, 7,* 368–374.

Loftus, E. F. (1979b). The malleability of human memory. *American Scientist, 67,* 312–320.

Loftus, E. F. (1993a). Psychologists in the eyewitness world. *American Psychologist, 48,* 550–552.

Loftus, E. F. (1993b). The reality of repressed memories. *American Psychologist, 48,* 518–537.

Loftus, E. F., & Ketcham, K. (1991). *Witness for the defense.* New York: St. Martin's Press.

Loftus, E. F., & Palmer, J. C. (1974). Reconstruction of automobile destruction: An example of the interaction between language and memory. *Journal of Verbal Learning and Verbal Behavior, 13,* 585–589.

Logan, G. D. (1990). Repetition priming and automaticity: Common underlying mechanisms? *Cognitive Psychology, 22,* 1–35.

Long, G. M. (1980). Iconic memory: A review and critique of the study of short-term visual storage. *Psychological Bulletin, 88,* 785–820.

Lovett, M. C., & Anderson, J. R. (1996). History of success and current context in problem solving. *Cognitive Psychology, 31,* 168–217.

Lowe, D. G., & Mitterer, J. O. (1982). Selective and divided attention in a Stroop task. *Canadian Journal of Psychology, 36,* 684–700.

Lowes, J. L. (1927). *The road to Xanadu.* London: Constable.

MacKay, D. G. (1973). Aspects of the theory of comprehension, memory, and attention. *Quarterly Journal of Experimental Psychology, 25,* 22–40.

MacWhinney, B. & Snow, C. (1990). The child language data exchange system. *Journal of Child Language, 12,* 271–296.

Marcus, G. F. (1996). Why do children say "breaked"? *Current Directions in Psychological Science, 5,* 81–85.

Margolis, H. (1987). *Patterns, thinking and cognition: A theory of judgment.* Chicago: University of Chicago Press.

Markman, A. B., & Gentner, D. (1996). Commonalities and differences in similarity comparisons. *Memory & Cognition, 24,* 235–249.

Markman, E. M., & Hutchinson, J. E. (1984). Childrens' sensitivity to constraints on word meaning: Taxonomic vs thematic relations. *Cognitive Psychology, 16,* 1–27.

Markman, A. B., & Wisniewski, E. J. (1997). Similar and different: The differentiation of basic level categories. *Journal of Experimental Psychology: Learning, Memory, & Cognition, 23,* 54–70.

Markman, E. M. (1990). Constraints children place on word meanings. *Cognitive Science, 14,* 57–77.

Markovits, H. (1985). Incorrect conditional reasoning among adults: Competence or performance? *British Journal of Psychology, 76,* 241–247.

Marr, D. (1982). *Vision.* San Francisco: W. H. Freeman.

Marshall, J. C. (1987). Routes and representations in the processing of written language. In E. Keller & M. Gopnik (Eds.), *Motor and sensory processes of language* (pp. 237–256). Hillsdale, NJ: Erlbaum.

Massaro, D. W., & Cowan, N. (1993). Information processing models: Microscopes of the mind. *Annual Review of Psychology, 44,* 383–425.

Massaro, D. W., & Hary, J. M. (1986). Addressing issues in letter recognition. *Psychological Research, 48,* 123–132.

Mathieson, C. M., Sainsbury, R. S., & Fitzgerald, L. K. (1990). Attentional set in pure versus mixed lists in a dichotic listening paradigm. *Brain & Cognition, 13,* 30–45.

Matlin, M. (1983). *Cognition.* New York: CBS College Publishing.

Mayer, R. E. (1983). *Thinking, problem solving, cognition* (2nd ed.). San Francisco: Freeman.

McAnally, K. I., & Stein, J. F. (1997). Scalp potentials evoked by amplitude-modulated tones in dyslexia. *Journal of Speech, Language, and Hearing Research, 40,* 939–945.

McCann, R. S., & Johnston, J. C. (1992). Locus of the single-channel bottleneck in dual-task interference. *Journal of Experimental Psychology, Human Perception and Performance, 18,* 471–484.

McCarthy, R. A., & Warrington, E. K. (1990). *Cognitive neuropsychology: A clinical introduction.* San Diego: Academic Press.

McClelland, J. L. (1981). Retrieving general and specific knowledge from stored knowledge of specifics. *Proceedings of the Third Annual Conference of the Cognitive Science Society,* 170–172.

McClelland, J. L., & Rumelhart, D. E. (1988). *Explorations in parallel distributed processing: A handbook of models, programs, and exercises.* Cambridge, MA: MIT Press.

McCloskey, M. E., & Glucksberg, S. (1978). Natural categories: Well-defined or fuzzy sets? *Memory & Cognition, 6,* 462–472.

McCloskey, M., & Kaiser, M. (1984). The impetus impulse: a medieval theory of motion lives on in the minds of children. *The Sciences.*

McConkie, G. W., & Rayner, K. (1974). Identifying the span of the effective stimulus in reading. *Final Report OEG 2-71-0531.* U.S. Office of Education.

McCulloch, W. S., & Pitts, W. (1943). A logical calculus of ideas immanent in nervous activity. *Bulletin of Mathematical Biophysiology, 5,* 115–133.

McGaugh, J. L., Weinberger, N. L., & Lynch, G. (1995). *Brain and memory: Modulation and mediation of neuroplasticity.* Oxford: Oxford University Press.

McKeithen, K. B., Reitman, J. S., Rueter, H. H., & Hirtle, S. C. (1981). Knowledge organization and skill differences in computer programmers. *Cognitive Psychology, 13,* 307–325.

McNamara, T. P. (1996). False dichotomies and dead metaphors. *Behavioral and Brain Sciences, 19,* 203.

McNeill, D. (1970). *The acquisition of language: The study of developmental psycholinguistics.* New York: Harper & Row.

Medin, D. L. (1989). Concepts and conceptual structure. *American Psychologist, 44,* 1469–1481.

Medin, D. L., Goldstone, R. L., & Gentner, D. (1990). Similarity involving attributes and relations: Judgments of similarity and difference and not inverses. *Psychological Science, 1,* 64–69.

Medin, D. L., Goldstone, R. L., & Gentner, D. (1993). Respects for similarity. *Psychological Review, 100,* 254–278.

Medin, D. L., Lynch, E. B., Coley, J. D., & Atran, S. (1997). Categorization and reasoning among tree experts: Do all roads lead to Rome? *Cognitive Psychology, 32,* 49–96.

Medin, D. L., & Shoben, E. J. (1988). Context and structure in conceptual combination. *Cognitive Psychology, 20,* 158–190.

Medin, D. L., & Smith, E. E. (1981). Strategies and classification learning. *Journal of Experimental Psychology: Human Learning and Memory, 7,* 241–253.

Medin, D. L., & Smith, E. E. (1984). Concepts and concept formation. *Annual Review of Psychology, 35,* 113–138.

Medin, D. L., & Wattenmaker, W. D. (1987). Category cohesiveness, theories, and cognitive archaeology. In U. Neisser (Ed.), *Concepts and conceptual development* (pp. 25–62). Cambridge, UK: Cambridge University Press.

Medin, D. L., Wattenmaker, W. D., & Hampson, S. E. (1987) Family resemblance, conceptual cohesiveness, and category construction. *Cognitive Psychology, 19,* 242–279.

Mehler, J., Segui, J., & Carey, P. (1978). Tails of words: Monitoring ambiguity. *Journal of Verbal Learning and Verbal Behavior, 17,* 29–37.

Meltzoff, A. N., & Moore, M. K. (1977). Imitation of facial and manual gestures by human neonates. *Science, 198,* 75–78.

Mendelson, R., & Schultz, T. R. (1976). Covariation and temporal contiguity as principles of causal inference in young children. *Journal of Experimental Child Psychology, 13,* 89–111.

Meyer, D. E., Irwin, D. E., Osman, A. M., & Kounios, J. (1988). The dynamics of cognition and action: Mental processes inferred from speed-accuracy decomposition. *Psychological Review, 95,* 183–237.

Meyer, D. E., & Schvaneveldt, R. W. (1971). Facilitation in recognizing pairs of words: Evidence of a dependence between retrieval operations. *Journal of Experimental Psychology, 90,* 227–234.

Mill, J. S. (1874). *A system of logic* (8th ed.). New York: Harper.

Miller, G. A. (1956). The magical number seven, plus or minus two: Some limits on our capacity for processing information. *Psychological Review, 63,* 81–97.

Miller, G. A. (1958). Free recall of redundant strings of letters. *Journal of Experimental Psychology, 56,* 485–491.

Miller, G. A., Galanter, E., & Pribram, K. H. (1960). *Plans and the structure of behavior.* New York: Holt, Rinehart & Winston.

Miller, G. A., & Nicely, P. (1955). An analysis of perceptual confusions among some English consonants. *Journal of the Acoustical Society of America, 27,* 338–352.

Miller, G. A., & Selfridge, J. A. (1950). Verbal context and the recall of meaningful material. *American Journal of Psychology, 63,* 176–185.

Millican, P., & Clark, A. (Eds.) (1996). *Machines and thought: Vol. 1.* New York: Oxford University Press.

Mimura, M., Werfaellie, M., & Milberg, W. P. (1997). Repetition priming in an auditory lexical decision task: Effects of lexical status. *Memory & Cognition, 25,* 819–825.

Minsky, M., & Papert, S. (1969). *Perceptrons.* Cambridge, MA: MIT Press.

Mody, M., Studdert-Kennedy, M., & Brady, S. (1997). Speech perception deficits in poor readers: Auditory processing or phonological coding? *Journal of Experimental Child Psychology, 64,* 199–231.

Moely, B. E., Olson, F. A., Halwes, T. G., & Flavell, J. H. (1969). Production deficiency in young children's clustered recall. *Developmental Psychology, 1,* 26–34.

Moray, N. (1959). Attention in dichotic listening: Affective cues and the influence of instructions. *Quarterly Journal of Experimental Psychology, 11,* 56–60.

Morris, C. D., Bransford, J. D., & Franks, J. J. (1977). Levels of processing versus transfer appropriate processing. *Journal of Verbal Learning and Verbal Behavior, 16,* 519–533.

Moskowitz, B. A., (1991). The acquisition of language. In W. S-Y. Wang (Ed.), *The emergence of language: Development and evolution* (pp. 131–149). New York: Freeman.

Mowbray, G. H. (1953). Simultaneous vision and audition: The comprehension of prose passages with varying levels of difficulty. *Journal of Experimental Psychology, 46,* 365–372.

Mulholland, T. M., Pellegrino, J. W., & Glaser, R. (1980). Components of analogy solution. *Cognitive Psychology, 12,* 252–284.

Murdock, B. B., Jr. (1962). The serial position effect of free recall. *Journal of Experimental Psychology, 64,* 482–488.

Murphy, G. L. (1991). Parts in object concepts: Experiments with artificial categories. *Memory & Cognition, 19,* 423–438.

Murphy, G. L., & Wisniewski, E. J. (1989). Categorizing objects in isolation and in scenes: What a superordinate is good for. *Journal of Experimental Psychology: Learning, Memory, & Cognition, 15,* 572–586.

Murray, H. G., & Denny, J. P. (1969). Interaction of ability level and interpolated activity (opportunity for incubation) in human problem solving. *Psychological Reports, 24,* 271–276.

Myers, D. (1986). *Psychology.* New York: Worth.

Nadel, L., Cooper, L. A., Culicover, P., & Harnish, R. M. (1989). *Neural connections, mental computations.* Cambridge, MA: MIT Press.

Neal, A., & Hesketh, B. (1997). Episodic knowledge and implicit learning. *Psychonomic Bulletin and Review, 4,* 24–37.

Neches, R., Langley, P., & Klahr, D. (1987). Learning, development, and production systems. In D. Klahr, P. Langley, & R. Neches (Eds.). *Production system models of learning and development* (pp. 1–54). Cambridge, MA: MIT Press.

Neely, J. H. (1977). Semantic priming and retrieval from lexical memory: Roles of inhibitionless spreading activation and limited-capacity attention. *Journal of Experimental Psychology: General, 106,* 226–254.

Neisser, U. (1964). Visual search. *Scientific American. 210(6),* 94–102.

Neisser, U. (1967). *Cognitive psychology.* New York: Appleton-Century-Crofts.

Neisser, U. (1976). *Cognition and reality: Principles and implications of cognitive psychology.* San Francisco: Freeman.

Neisser, U. (1978). Memory: What are the important questions? In M. M. Gruneberg, P. E. Morris, & R. N. Sykes (Eds.), *Practical aspects of memory* (pp. 3–24). London: Academic Press.

Neisser, U. (1982). *Memory observed.* San Francisco: Freeman.

Neisser, U. (1996). Remembering as doing. *Behavioral and Brain Sciences, 19,* 203–204.

Neisser, U., & Harsch, N. (1992). Phantom flashbulbs: False recollections of hearing the news about Challenger. In E. Winograd, & U. Neisser (Eds.), *Affect and accuracy in recall: Studies of "flashbulb" memories* (pp. 9–31). New York: Cambridge University Press.

Neisser, U., & Winograd, E. (Eds.). (1988). *Remembering reconsidered: Ecological and traditional approaches to the study of memory.* New York: Cambridge University Press.

Nelson, D. L. (1979). Remembering pictures and words: Appearance, significance, and name. In L. S. Cermak & F. I. M. Craik (Eds.), *Levels of processing in human memory.* Hillsdale, NJ: Erlbaum.

Nelson, D. L., & McEvoy, C. L. (1979). Encoding context and set size. *Journal of Experimental Psychology: Human Learning and Memory, 5,* 292–314.

Nelson, K. (1973). Structure and strategy in learning to talk. *Monographs for the Society of Research in Child Development, 38* (Serial No. 149).

Nelson, K. (1975). The nominal shift in semantic-syntactic development. *Cognitive Psychology, 7,* 461–479.

Nelson, K. (1993). The psychological and social origins of autobiographical memory. *Psychological Science, 4,* 7–14.

Newell, A. (1962). Some problems of basic organization in problem-solving programs. In M. C. Yovits, G. T. Jacobi, & G. D. Goldstein (Eds.), *Self-organizing systems* (pp. 293–423). Washington, DC: Spartan Books.

Newell, A. (1965). Limitations of the current stock of ideas for problem solving. In A. Kent & O. Taulbee (Eds.), *Conference on electronic information handling* (pp. 195–208). Washington, DC: Spartan Books.

Newell, A. (1966). *On the representations of problems*. Computer Science Research Review, 18–33. Pittsburgh: Carnegie Institute of Technology.

Newell, A. (1967). *Studies in problem solving: Subject 3 on the cryptarithmetic task: DONALD + GERALD = ROBERT*. Pittsburgh: Carnegie-Mellon University.

Newell, A. (1990). *Unified theories of cognition*. Cambridge, MA: Harvard University Press.

Newell, A., & Rosenbloom, P. S. (1981). Mechanisms of skill acquisition and the law of practice. In J. R. Anderson (Ed.), *Cognitive skills and their acquisition* (pp. 1–56). Hillsdale, NJ: Erlbaum.

Newell, A., Shaw, J. C., & Simon, H. A. (1958). Elements of a theory of human problem solving. *Psychological Review, 65*, 151–166.

Newell, A., Shaw, J. C., & Simon, H. A. (1962). The processes of creative thinking. In H. E. Gruber, G. Terrell, & M. Wertheimer (Eds.), *Contemporary approaches to creative thinking* (pp. 63–119). New York: Atherton Press.

Newell, A., & Simon, H. A. (1956). The logic theory machine: A complex information processing system. *IRE Transactions on Information Theory, IT-2* (3), 61–79.

Newell, A., & Simon, H. A. (1961). GPS: A program that simulates human thought. In H. Billing (Ed.), *Lernende Automaten* (pp. 109–124). Munich: R. Oldenbourg.

Newell, A., & Simon, H. A. (1965). An example of human chess play in the light of chess playing programs. In N. Weiner & J. P. Schade (Eds.), *Progress in biocybernetics* (Vol. 2, pp. 19–75). Amsterdam: Elsevier.

Newell, A., & Simon, H. A. (1972). *Human problem solving*. Englewood Cliffs, NJ: Prentice-Hall.

Newport, E. L. (1990). Maturational constraints on language learning. *Cognitive Science, 14*, 11–28.

Nisbett, R. E., & Wilson, T. D. (1977). Telling more than we can know: Verbal reports on mental processes. *Psychological Review, 84*, 231–259.

Norman, D. A. (1968). Toward a theory of memory and attention. *Psychological Review, 75*, 522–536.

Norman, D. A., & Bobrow, D. G. (1975). On data-limited and resource-limited processes. *Cognitive Psychology, 7*, 44–64.

Nosofsky. R. M., Gluck, M. A., Palmeri, T. J., McKinley, S. C., & Glauthier, P. (1994). Comparing models of rule-based classification learning: A replication and extension of Shepard, Hovland, and Jenkins (1961). *Memory & Cognition, 22*, 352–369.

Novick, L. R., & Holyoak, K. J. (1991). Mathematical problem solving by analogy. *Journal of Experimental Psychology: Learning, Memory, and Cognition, 17*, 398–415.

Nyberg, L., Cabeza, R., & Tulving, E. (1996). PET studies of encoding and retrieval: The HERA model. *Psychonomic Bulletin and Review, 3*, 135–148.

Obusek, C. J., & Warren, R. M. (1973). Relation of the verbal transformation and the phonemic restoration effects. *Cognitive Psychology, 5*, 97–107.

Olson, J. N., & MacKay, D. G. (1974). Completion and verification of ambiguous sentences. *Journal of Verbal Learning and Verbal Behavior, 13*, 457–470.

Osman, A., Bashore, T. R., Coles, M. G. H., Donchin, E., & Meyer, D. E. (1992). On the transmission of partial information: Inferences from movement-related brain potentials. *Journal of Experimental Psychology: Human Perception and Performance, 18*, 217–232.

Owens, J., Bower, G. H., & Black, J. B. (1979). The "soap opera" effect in story recall. *Memory and Cognition, 7*, 185–191.

Palmer, J. (1990). Attentional limits on the perception and memory of visual information. *Journal of Experimental Psychology: Human Perception and Performance, 16*, 332–350.

Palmer, S. E., & Kimchi, R. (1986). The information processing approach to cognition. In T. J. Knapp, & L. C. Robertson (Eds.), *Approaches to cognition: Contrasts and controversies* (pp. 37–77). Hillsdale, NJ: Erlbaum.

Parkin, A. J. (1984). Levels of processing, context, and facilitation of pronunciation. *Acta Psychologia, 55*, 19–29.

Parkin, A. J. (1993). *Memory: Phenomena, experiment and theory*. Oxford: Blackwell Publishers.

Pashler, H. (1994). Divided attention: Storing and classifying briefly presented objects. *Psychonomic Bulletin and Review, 1*, 115–118.

Patterson, K. E. (1982). The relation between reading and phonological encoding: Further neuropsychological observations. In A. W. Ellis (Ed.), *Normality and pathology in cognitive functions* (pp. 77–112). New York: Academic Press.

Pellegrino, J. W. (1985). Inductive reasoning ability. In R. J. Sternberg (Ed.), *Human abilities: An information processing approach* (pp. 195–226). San Francisco: Freeman.

Perfetti, C. A., & Curtis, M. E. (1986). Reading in R. F. Dillon & R. J. Sternberg (Eds.), *Cognition and instruction* (pp. 13–57). Orlando, FL: Academic Press.

Perner, J. (1991). *Understanding the representational mind*. Cambridge, MA: MIT Press.

Perner, J. (1992). Grasping the concept of representation: Its impact on 4–year-olds' theory of mind and beyond. *Human Development, 35*, 146–155.

Peterson, L. R., & Peterson, M. J. (1959). Short-term retention of individual verbal items. *Journal of Experimental Psychology, 58*, 193–198.

Pinker, S. (1994). *The language instinct*. New York: Morrow.

Pinker, S., & Prince, A. (1988). On language and connectionism: Analysis of a parallel distributed processing model of language acquisition. *Cognition, 28*, 73–193.

Pinsky, S. D., & McAdam, D. W. (1980). Electroencephalographic and dichotic indices of cerebral laterality in stuttering. *Brain and Language, 11*, 374–397.

Pisoni, D. B. (1978). Speech perception. In W. K. Estes (Ed.), *Handbook of learning and cognitive processes* (Vol. 6, pp. 167–234). Hillsdale, NJ: Erlbaum.

Pisoni, D. B., & Sawusch, J. R. (1975). Some stages of processing in speech perception. In A. Cohen & S. G. Nooteboom (Eds.), *Structure and process in speech perception* (pp. 16–34). Heidelberg, Germany: Springer-Verlag.

Poincare, H. (1913). The value of science. In *The foundations of science* (G. B. Halsted, Trans.). New York: Science Press.

Pollack, I., & Pickett, J. M. (1964). Intelligibility of excerpts from fluent speech: Auditory vs. structural context. *Journal of Verbal Learning and Verbal Behavior, 3,* 79–84.

Pollard, P. (1985). Nonindependence of selections in the Wason selection task. *Bulletin of the Psychonomic Society, 23,* 317–320.

Pollatsek, A., Rayner, K., & Balota, D. A. (1986). Inferences about eye movement control from the perceptual span in reading. *Perception and Psychophysics, 40,* 123–130.

Polson, P. G., & Jeffries, R. (1982). Problem solving as search and understanding. In R. J. Sternberg (Ed.), *Advances in the psychology of human intelligence* (Vol. 1, pp. 367–412). Hillsdale, NJ: Erlbaum.

Posner, M. I., & Boies, S. J. (1971). Components of attention. *Psychological Review, 78,* 391–408.

Posner, M. I., & Snyder, C. R. R. (1975). Attention and cognitive control. In R. Solso (Ed.), *Information processing and cognition: The Loyola symposium.* Hillsdale, NJ: Erlbaum.

Postman, L., & Phillips, L. W. (1965). Short-term temporal changes in free recall. *Quarterly Journal of Experimental Psychology, 17,* 132–138.

Postman, L., Thompkins, B. A., & Gray, W. D. (1978). The interpretation of encoding effects in retention. *Journal of Verbal Learning and Verbal Behavior, 17,* 681–705.

Prabhakaran, V., Smith, J. A. L., Desmond, J. E., Glover, G. H., & Gabrieli, J. D. E. (1997). Neural substrates of fluid reasoning: An MRI study of neocortical activation during performance of the Raven's Progressive Matrices Test. *Cognitive Psychology, 33,* 43–63.

Premack, D., & Woodruff, G. (1978). Does the chimpanzee have a theory of mind? *Behavioral and Brain Sciences, 1,* 515–526.

Quine, W. V. O. (1960). *Word and object.* Cambridge, MA: MIT Press.

Quillian, M. R. (1968). Semantic memory. In M. Minsky (Ed.), *Semantic information processing,* Cambridge, MA: MIT Press.

Raajmakers, J. G. W., & Shiffrin, R. M. (1981). Search of associative memory. *Psychological Review, 88,* 93–134.

Rajaram, S. (1993). Remembering and knowing: Two means of access to the personal past. *Memory & Cognition, 21,* 89–102.

Ratcliff, R., Hockley, W., & McKoon, G. (1985). Components of activation: Repetition and priming effects in lexical decision and recognition. *Journal of Experimental Psychology: General, 114,* 435–450.

Ratcliff, R. A., & McKoon, G. (1981). Does activation really spread? *Psychological Review, 88,* 454–462.

Ratcliff, R., & McKoon, G. (1997). A counter model for implicit priming in perceptual word identification. *Psychological Review, 104,* 319–343.

Ratcliff, R., McKoon, G., & Verwoerd, M. (1989). A bias interpretation of facilitation in perceptual identification. *Journal of Experimental Psychology: Learning, Memory, and Cognition, 15,* 378–387.

Rayner, K. (1975). The perceptual span and peripheral cues in reading. *Cognitive Psychology, 7,* 65–81.

Rayner, K. (1978). Eye movements in reading and information processing. *Psychological Bulletin, 85,* 618–660.

Rayner, K., & Duffy, S. A. (1986). Lexical complexity and fixation times in reading: Effects of word frequency, verb complexity, and lexical ambiguity. *Memory & Cognition, 14,* 191–201.

Reber, A. S. (1973). What clicks may tell us about speech perception. *Journal of Psycholinguistic Research, 2,* 287–288.

Reber, A. S., & Anderson, J. R. (1970). The perception of clicks in linguistic and nonlinguistic messages. *Perception and Psychophysics, 8,* 81–89.

Reder, L. (Ed.). (1996). *Implicit memory and metacognition.* Hillsdale, NJ: Erlbaum.

Reed, E., & Jones, R. (Eds.). (1982). *Reasons for realism: Selected essays of James J. Gibson.* Hillsdale, NJ: Erlbaum.

Reeves, L. M., & Weisberg, R. W. (1994). The role of content and abstract information in analogical transfer. *Psychological Bulletin, 115,* 381–400.

Regehr, G., & Brooks, L. R. (1995). Category organization in free recall: The organizing effect of an array of stimuli. *Journal of Experimental Psychology: Learning, Memory, and Cognition, 21,* 347–363.

Reicher, G. (1969). Perceptual recognition as a function of meaningfulness of stimulus material. *Journal of Experimental Psychology, 81,* 275–280.

Reif, F. (1979). *Cognitive mechanisms facilitating human problem solving in a realistic domain: The example of physics.* Unpublished manuscript.

Reitman, W. (1964). Heuristic decision procedures, open constraints, and the structure of ill-defined problems. In M. W. Shelley & G. L. Bryan (Eds.), *Human judgements and optimality.* New York: Wiley.

Remez, R. E. (1979). Adaptation of the category boundary between speech and non-speech: A case against feature detectors. *Cognitive Psychology, 11,* 38–57.

Remez, R. E. (1980). Susceptibility of a stop consonant to adaptation on a speech-nonspeech continuum: Further evidence against feature detectors in speech perception. *Perception and Psychophysics, 27,* 17–23.

Remez, R. E., Rubin, P. E., Pisoni, D. B., & Carrell, T. D. (1981). Speech perception without traditional speech cues. *Science, 212,* 947–950.

Reyna, V. F., & Brainerd, C. J. (1995). Fuzzy-trace theory: An interim synthesis. *Learning and Individual Differences, 7,* 1–75.

Richardson, J. T., & Johnson, P. B. (1980). Models of anagram solution. *Bulletin of the Psychonomic Society, 16,* 247–250.

Ricks, D. M. (1975). Vocal communication in pre-verbal, normal, and autistic children. In N. O'Connor (Ed.), *Language, cognitive deficits, and retardation.* London: Butterworth.

Rips, L. J. (1989). Similarity, typicality, and categorization. In S. Vosniadou & A. Ortony (Eds.), *Similarity and analogical reasoning.* Cambridge: Cambridge University Press.

Rips, L. J. (1990). Reasoning. *Annual Review of Psychology, 41,* 321–353.

Rips, L. J., & Marcus, S. L. (1977). Supposition and the analysis of conditional sentences. In M. A. Just & P. A. Carpenter (Eds.), *Cognitive processes in comprehension.* Hillsdale, NJ: Erlbaum.

Rips, L. J., Shoben, E. J., & Smith, E. E. (1973). Semantic distance and the verification of semantic relations. *Journal of Verbal Learning and Verbal Behavior, 12,* 1–20.

Roediger, H. L. (1980). Memory metaphors in cognitive psychology. *Memory & Cognition, 8,* 231–246.

Roediger, H. L. (1990). Implicit memory. *American Psychologist, 45,* 1043–1056.

Roediger, H. L., III, & McDermott, K. B. (1993). Implicit memory in normal human subjects. In F. Boller & J. Grafman (Eds.), *Handbook of neuropsychology* (pp. 63–131). Amsterdam, Netherlands: Elsevier Science.

Ronning, R. R. (1965). Anagram solution times: A function of the "ruleout" factor. *Journal of Experimental Psychology, 69,* 35–39.

Rosch, E. H. (1973). On the internal structure of perceptual and semantic categories. In T. E. Moore (Ed.), *Cognitive development and the acquisition of language.* New York: Academic Press.

Rosch, E. H. (1975). Cognitive representations of semantic categories. *Journal of Experimental Psychology: General, 104,* 192–233.

Rosch, E. H. (1977). Classification of real-world objects: Origins and representation in cognition. In P. N. Johnson-Laird & P. C. Wason (Eds.), *Thinking: Readings in cognitive science* (pp. 212–222) Cambridge: Cambridge University Press.

Rosch, E. H., & Mervis, C. B. (1975). Family resemblances: Studies in the internal structure of categories. *Cognitive Psychology, 7,* 573–605.

Rosenblatt, F. (1958). The perceptron: A probabilistic model for information storage and organization in the brain. *Psychological Review, 65,* 386–408.

Rosenfield, D. B., & Goodglass, H. (1980). Dichotic testing of cerebral dominance in stutterers. *Brain and Language, 11,* 170–180.

Ross, B. H. (1996). Category representations and the effects of interacting with instances. *Journal of Experimental Psychology: Learning, Memory, and Cognition, 22,* 1249–1265.

Ross, B. M. (1992). *Remembering the personal past: Descriptions of autobiographical memory.* Oxford: Oxford University Press.

Roth, E. M., & Shoben, E. J. (1983). The effect of context on the structure of categories. *Cognitive Psychology, 15,* 346–378.

Rubenstein, H., Lewis, S. S., & Rubenstein, M. A. (1971). Evidence for phonemic recoding in visual word recognition. *Journal of Verbal Learning and Verbal Behavior, 10,* 645–657.

Rubin, D. C., & Kontis, T. C. (1983). A schema for common cents. *Memory & Cognition, 11,* 335–341.

Rumelhart, D. E., & McClelland, J. L. (1986). *Parallel distributed processing: Explorations in the microstructure of cognition* (Vol. 1). Cambridge, MA: MIT Press.

Runco, M. A. (Ed.) (1994). *Problem finding, problem solving, and creativity.* Norwood, NJ: Ablex.

Rundus, D. (1977). Maintenance rehearsal and single-level processing. *Journal of Verbal Learning and Verbal Behavior, 16,* 665–681.

Russell, W. R., & Nathan, P. W. (1946). Traumatic amnesia. *Brain, 69,* 280–300.

Rutter, M., & Yule, W. (1975). The concept of specific reading retardation. *Journal of Child Psychology and Psychiatry, 16,* 181–197.

Sabol, M. A., & DeRosa, D. V. (1976). Semantic encoding of isolated words. *Journal of Experimental Psychology: Human Learning and Memory, 2,* 58–68.

Salame, P., & Baddeley, A. D. (1982). Disruption of short-term memory by unattended speech: Implications for the structure of working memory. *Journal of Verbal Learning and Verbal Behavior, 21,* 150–164.

Salasoo, A., Shiffrin, R. M., & Feustel, T. C. (1985). Building permanent memory codes: Codification and repetition effects in word identification. *Journal of Experimental Psychology: General, 114,* 50–77.

Samarapungavan, A., & Wiers, R. W. (1997). Children's thoughts on the origin of species: A study of explanatory coherence. *Cognitive Science, 21,* 147–177.

Samuels, A. B. (1981). Phonemic restoration: Insights from a new methodology. *Journal of Experimental Psychology: General, 110,* 474–494.

Schacter, D. L. (1989). On the relation between memory and consciousness: Dissociable interactions and conscious experience. In H. L. Roediger & F. I. M. Craik (Eds.), *Varieties of memory and consciousness: Essays in honour of Endel Tulving* (pp. 355–389). Hillsdale, NJ: Erlbaum.

Schauble, L. (1990). Belief revision in children: The role of prior knowledge and strategies for generating evidence. *Journal of Experimental Child Psychology, 49,* 31–57.

Schneider, W., Dumais, S. T., & Shiffrin, R. M. (1984). Automatic and control processing and attention. In R. Parasuraman & R. Davies (Eds.), *Varieties of attention* (pp. 1–27). New York: Academic Press.

Schneider, W., & Shiffrin, R. M. (1977). Controlled and automatic human information processing: I. Detection, search, and attention. *Psychological Review, 84,* 1–66.

Scribner, S. (1977). Modes of thinking and ways of speaking: Culture and logic reconsidered. In P. N. Johnson-Laird & P. C. Wason (Eds.), *Thinking: Readings in cognitive science* (pp. 483–500). Cambridge: Cambridge University Press.

Seamon, J. G., & Virostek, S. (1978). Memory performance and subject-defined depth of processing. *Memory and Cognition, 6,* 283–287.

Searle, J. R. (1975). Indirect speech acts. In P. Cole & J. L. Morgan (Eds.), *Syntax and semantics: Vol. 3. Speech Acts* (pp. 59–82). New York: Seminar Press.

Seidenberg, M. S. (1997). Language acquisition and use: Learning and applying probabilistic constraints. *Science, 275,* 1599–1603.

Seidenberg, M. S., & McClelland, J. L. (1989). A distributed, developmental model of word recognition and naming. *Psychological Review, 96,* 523–568.

Seidenberg, M. S., & McClelland, J. L. (1990). More words but still no lexicon: Reply to Besner et al. (1990). *Psychological Review, 97,* 447–452.

Sejnowski, T. J., & Rosenberg, C. R. (1987). Parallel networks that learn to pronounce English text. *Complex Systems, 1,* 145–168.

Selfridge, O. (1959). Pandemonium: A paradigm for learning. In *Symposium on the mechanization of thought processes.* London: HM Stationery Office.

Shanks, D. R., Holyoak, K. J., & Medin, D. L. (Eds.). (1996). *The psychology of learning and motivation: Vol. 34. Causal learning.* San Diego: Academic Press.

Shaughnessy, J. J. (1981). Memory monitoring accuracy and modification of rehearsal strategies. *Journal of Verbal Learning and Verbal Behavior, 20,* 216–230.

Shepard, R. N. (1972). Psychological representation of speech sounds. In E. E. David & P. B. Denes (Eds.), *Human communication: A unified view* (pp. 67–113). New York: McGraw-Hill.

Shiffrin, R. M. (1993). Short-term memory: A brief commentary. *Memory & Cognition, 21,* 193–197.

Shiffrin, R. M., & Dumais, S. T. (1981). The development of automatism. In J. R. Anderson (Ed.), *Cognitive skills and their acquisition* (pp. 111–140). Hillsdale, NJ: Erlbaum.

Shiffrin, R. M., Murname, K., Gronlund, S., & Roth, M. (1989). On units of storage and retrieval. In C. Izawa, (Ed.), *Current issues in cognitive processes: The Tulane Flowerree symposium on cognition* (pp. 25–68). Hillsdale, NJ: Erlbaum.

Shiffrin, R. M., & Schneider, W. (1977). Controlled and automatic human information processing: II. Perceptual learning, automatic attending, and a general theory. *Psychological Review, 84,* 127–190.

Shulman, H. G. (1971). Similarity effects in short-term memory. *Psychological Bulletin, 75,* 399–415.

Shulman, H. G. (1972). Semantic confusion errors in short-term memory. *Journal of Verbal Learning and Verbal Behavior, 11,* 221–227.

Siegler, R. S. (1991). *Children's thinking.* Englewood Cliffs, NJ: Prentice-Hall.

Siegler, R. S., & Jenkins, E. (1989). *How children discover new strategies.* Hillsdale, NJ: Erlbaum.

Siegler, R. S. (1987). The perils of averaging data over strategies: An example from children's addition. *Journal of Experimental Psychology: General, 116,* 250–264.

Silveira, J. (1971). *The effect of interruption timing and length on problem solution and quality of problem processing.* Unpublished doctoral dissertation, University of Oregon, Eugene, OR.

Simon, H. A. (1969). *The sciences of the artificial* (1st ed.). Cambridge, MA: MIT Press.

Simon, H. A. (1973). The structure of illstructured problems. *Artificial Intelligence, 4,* 181–202.

Simon, H. A. (1978). Information processing theory of human problem solving. In W. K. Estes (Ed.), *Handbook of learning and cognitive processes* (Vol. 5, pp. 271–295). Hillsdale, NJ: Erlbaum.

Simon, H. A., & Gilmartin, K. A. (1973). A simulation of memory for chess positions. *Cognitive Psychology, 5,* 29–46.

Simon, H. A., & Hayes, J. R. (1976). The understanding process: Problem isomorphs. *Cognitive Psychology, 8,* 165–190.

Simon, H. A., & Simon, P. A. (1962). Trial and error search in solving difficult problems: Evidence from the game of chess. *Behavioral Science, 7,* 425–429.

Sitler, R. W., Schiavetti, N., & Metz, D. E. (1983). Contextual effects in the measurement of hearing-impaired speakers' intelligibility, *Journal of Speech and Hearing Research, 26,* 30–35.

Skinner, B. F. (1957). *Verbal behavior.* New York: Appleton-Century-Crofts.

Slovic, P., Fischoff, B., & Lichtenstein, S. (1976). Cognitive process and social risk taking. In J. S. Carroll & J. W. Payne (Eds.), *Cognition and social behavior.* Hillsdale, NJ: Erlbaum.

Small, S. (1991). Focal and diffuse lesions of cognitive models. *Proceedings of the 13th annual conference of the Cognitive Science Society, USA,* 85–90.

Smiley, S. S., Oakley, D. D., Worthen, D., Campione, J. C., & Brown, A. L. (1977). Recall of thematically relevant material by adolescent good and poor readers as a function of written versus oral presentation. *Journal of Educational Psychology, 69,* 381–387.

Smith, E. E. (1978). Theories of semantic memory. In W. K. Estes (Ed.), *Handbook of learning and cognitive processes* (Vol. 6, pp. 1–56). Hillsdale, NJ: Erlbaum.

Smith, E. E. (1990). Categorization. In D. N. Osherson & E. E. Smith (Eds.), *Thinking: An invitation to cognitive science* (Vol. 3, pp. 33–53). Cambridge, MA: MIT Press.

Smith, E. E., & Medin, D. L. (1981). *Categories and concepts.* Cambridge, MA: Harvard University Press.

Smith, E. E., Shoben, E. J., & Rips, L. (1974). Structure and process in semantic memory: A featural model for semantic decisions. *Psychological Review, 81,* 214–241.

Smith, S. M., Glenberg, A., & Bjork, R. A. (1978). Environmental context and human memory. *Memory and Cognition, 6,* 342–353.

Smith, T. (1982). Chomsky's cognitivism at twenty-five from the perspective of Skinner's "behaviorism at fifty." *Papers in the Social Sciences, 2,* 23–32.

Smolensky, P. (1988). On the proper treatment of connectionism. *Behavioral and Brain Sciences, 11,* 1–74.

Snoddy, G. S. (1926). Learning and stability. *Journal of Applied Psychology, 10,* 1–36.

Sokal, R. R. (1977). Classification: Purposes, principles, progress, prospects. In P. N. Johnson-Laird & P. C. Wason (Eds.), *Thinking: Readings in cognitive science* (pp. 185–198). Cambridge: Cambridge University Press.

Spellman, B. A. (1996). Acting as intuitive scientists: Contingency judgments are made while controlling for alternative potential causes. *Psychological Science, 7,* 337–346.

Sperling, G. (1960). The information available in brief visual presentations. *Psychological Monographs, 74* (Whole No. 498).

Staudenmayer, H. (1975). Understanding conditional reasoning with meaningful propositions. In R. J. Falmagne (Ed.), *Reasoning: Representation and process in children and adults.* Hillsdale, NJ: Erlbaum.

Steffens, J. L., Eilers, R. E., Gross-Glenn, K., & Jallard, B. (1992). Speech perception in adult participants with familial dyslexia. *Journal of Speech and Hearing Research, 35,* 192–200.

Sternberg, R. J. (1982, April). Who's intelligent? *Psychology Today,* pp. 30–39.

Struhsaker, T. T. (1967). Auditory communication among vervet monkeys (Cercopithecus aethiops). In S. A. Altmann (Ed.), *Social communication among primates* (pp. 285–324). Chicago: University of Chicago Press.

Swinney, D. A., & Hakes, D. T. (1976). Effects of prior context upon lexical access during sentence comprehension. *Journal of Verbal Learning and Verbal Behavior, 15,* 681–689.

Tallal, P., Miller, S., & Fitch, R. H. (1993). Neurobiological basis of speech: A case for preeminence of temporal processing. In P. Tallal, A. M. Galburda, R. R. Llinas, and C. von Euler (Eds.), *Temporal information processing in the nervous system* (Vol. 682, pp. 27–47). New York: Annals of the New York Academy of Sciences.

Tallal, P., & Piercy, M. (1973). Defects of non-verbal auditory perception in children with developmental aphasia. *Nature, 241,* 468–469.

Tallal, P., & Piercy, M. (1974). Developmental aphasia: Rate of auditory processing and selective impairment of consonant perception. *Neuropsychologia, 12,* 83–93.

Tank, D. W., & Hopfield, J. J. (1987). Collective computation in neuronlike circuits. *Scientific American, 257* (6), 104–114.

Theeuwes, J. (1992). Perceptual selectivity for color and form. *Perception and Psychophysics, 51,* 599–606.

Thorpe, W. H. (1961). *Bird song: The biology of vocal communication and expression in birds.* Cambridge: Cambridge University Press.

Thorpe, W. H. (1963). *Learning and instinct in animals* (2nd ed.). London: Methuen.

Tierney, R. J., Anders, P. L., & Mitchell, J. N. (Eds.). (1987). *Understanding readers' understanding.* Hillsdale, NJ: Erlbaum.

Treisman, A. M. (1960). Contextual cues in selective listening. *Quarterly Journal of Experimental Psychology, 12,* 242–248.

Treisman, A. M. (1964a). Verbal cues, language, and meaning in selective attention. *American Journal of Psychology, 77,* 206–219.

Treisman, A. M. (1964b). The effect of irrelevant material on the efficiency of selective listening. *American Journal of Psychology, 77,* 533–546.

Treisman, A., & Gormican, S. (1988). Feature analysis in early vision: Evidence from search asymmetries. *Psychological Review, 95,* 15–48.

Treisman, A. (1990). Variations on the theme of feature integration: Reply to Navon (1990).

Treisman, A., & Gelade, G. (1980). A feature integration theory of attention. *Cognitive Psychology, 12,* 97–136.

Tulving, E. (1972) Episodic and semantic memory. In E. Tulving & W. Donaldson (Eds.), *Organization of memory.* New York: Academic Press.

Tulving, E. (1979). Relation between encoding specificity and levels of processing. In L. S. Cermak & F. I. M. Craik (Eds.), *Levels of processing in human memory.* Hillsdale, NJ: Erlbaum.

Tulving, E. (1983). *Elements of episodic memory.* Oxford: Clarendon Press/Oxford University Press.

Tulving, E. (1985a). How many memory systems are there? *American Psychologist, 40,* 385–398.

Tulving, E. (1985b). Memory and consciousness. *Canadian Psychology, 26,* 1–12.

Tulving, E. (1986). What kind of a hypothesis is the distinction between episodic and semantic memory? *Journal of Experimental Psychology: Learning, Memory and Cognition, 12,* 307–311.

Tulving, E., Kapur, S. Craik, F. I. M., Moscovitch, M. & Houle, S. (1994). Hemispheric encoding/retrieval asymmetry in episodic memory: Positron emission tomography findings. *Proceedings of the National Academy of Science, 91,* 2016–2020.

Tulving, E., & Thompson, D. M. (1973). Encoding specificity and retrieval processes in episodic memory. *Journal of Experimental Psychology: Learning, Memory, and Cognition, 8,* 336–342.

Tversky, B., & Hemenway, K. (1984). Objects, parts, and categories. *Journal of Experimental Psychology: General, 113,* 169–193.

Tversky, B., & Hemenway, K. (1991). Parts and the basic level in natural categories and artifical stimuli: Commens on Murphy (1991). *Memory & Cognition, 19,* 439–442.

Tweney, R. D., & Doherty, M. E. (1983). Rationality and the psychology of inference. *Synthese, 57,* 139–161.

Usher, J. A., & Neisser, U. (1993). Childhood amnesia and the beginnings of memory for four early life events. *Journal of Experimental Psychology: General, 122,* 155–165.

Valentine, E. R. (1985). The effect of instructions on performance in the Wason selection task. *Current Psychological Research and Reviews, 4,* 214–223.

Vallar, G., & Shallice, T. (1990). *Neuropsychological impairments of short term memory.* Cambridge: Cambridge University Press.

van Duyne, P. C. (1974). Realism and linguistic complexity in reasoning. *British Journal of Psychology, 65,* 59–67.

Van Turennout, M. Hagoort, P., & Brown, C. M. (1997). Electrophysiological evidence on the time course of semantic and phonological processes in speech production. *Journal of Experimental Psychology: Learning, Memory, and Cognition, 23,* 787–806.

VanLehn, K. (1991). Rule acquisition events in the discovery of problem-solving strategies. *Cognitive Science, 15,* 1–47.

Venezky, R. L. (1970). *The structure of English orthography*. The Hague: Mouton.

von Frisch, K. (1954). *The dancing bees*. London: Methuen.

von Frisch, K. (1967). *The dance and orientation of bees* (L. E. Chadwick, Trans.). Cambridge, MA: Harvard University Press.

Vosniadou, S., & Brewer, W. F. (1992) Mental models of the earth: A study of conceptual change in childhood. *Cognitive Psychology, 24,* 535–585.

Voss, J. F., et al. (1986). Informal reasoning and subject matter knowledge in the solving of economics problems by naive and novice individuals. *Cognition and Instruction, 3,* 269–302.

Voss, J. F., Greene, T. R., Post, T. A., & Penner, B. C. (1983). Problem solving skill in social sciences. In G. Power (Ed.), *The psychology of learning and motivation: Advances in research and theory* (Vol. 17). New York: Academic Press.

Voss, J. F., Perkins, D., & Segal, J. (Eds.). (1991). *Informal reasoning and education*. Hillsdale, NJ: Erlbaum.

Voss, J. F., Tyler, S. W., & Yengo, L. A. (1983). Individual differences in the solving of social science problems. In R. F. Dillon & R. R. Schmeck (Eds.), *Individual differences in cognition.* (pp. 205–232). New York: Academic Press.

Walker, E., & Ceci, S. J. (1983). Lateral asymmetries in electrodermal responses to nonattended stimuli: A response to Dawson and Schell. *Journal of Experimental Psychology: Human Perception and Performance, 9* (1), 145–147.

Wallas, G. (1926). *The art of thought*. New York: Harcourt Brace Jovanovich.

Wang, W. S-Y. (Ed.). (1991). *The emergence of language: Development and evolution*. New York: Freeman.

Warren, R. M. (1970). Perceptual restoration of missing speech sounds. *Science, 167,* 392–393.

Warren, R. M., & Obusek, C. J. (1971). Speech perception and phonemic restorations. *Perception and Psychophysics, 9,* 358–362.

Warren, R. M., Obusek, C. J., Farmer, R. M., & Warren, R. P. (1969). Auditory sequence: Confusions of patterns other than speech or music. *Science, 164,* 586–587.

Warren, R. M., & Warren, R. P. (1970). Auditory illusions and confusions. *Scientific American, 223*(6), 30–36.

Wason, P. C. (1966). Reasoning. In B. M. Foss (Ed.), *New horizons in psychology* (Vol. 1), (pp. 135–151). Harmondsworth, Middlesex, England: Penguin.

Wason, P. C., & Johnson-Laird, P. N. (1970). A conflict between selecting and evaluating information in an inferential task. *British Journal of Psychology, 61,* 509–515.

Watanabe, I. (1980). Selective attention and memory. *Japanese Psychological Review, 23* (4), 335–354.

Watkins, M. J. (1974). When is recall spectacularly higher than recognition? *Journal of Experimental Psychology, 102,* 161–163.

Watkins, M. J., & Tulving, E. (1975). Episodic memory: When recognition fails. *Journal of Experimental Psychology: General, 104,* 5–29.

Waugh, N. C., & Norman, D. A. (1965) Primary memory. *Psychological Review, 72,* 89–104.

Waxman, S. R. (1990). Linguistic biases and the establishment of conceptual hierarchies: Evidence from preschool children. *Cognitive Development, 5,* 123–150.

Weaver, C. A. III. (1993). Do you need a "flash" to form a flash bulb memory? *Journal of Experimental Psychology: General. 122,* 39–46.

Weir, R. H. (1966). Some questions on the child's learning of phonology. In F. Smith & G. A. Miller (Eds.), *The genesis of language*. Cambridge, MA: MIT Press.

Weisberg, R. W. (1986). *Creativity: Genius and other myths*. New York: Freeman.

Weisberg, R. W., & Alba, J. W. (1981). An examination of the alleged role of "fixation" in the solution of several "insight" problems. *Journal of Experimental Psychology: General, 110,* 169–192.

Wellman, H. M. (1990). *The child's theory of mind*. Cambridge, MA: Bradford Books/MIT Press.

Wells, G. L. (1993). What do we know about eyewitness identification? *American Psychologist, 48,* 553–571.

Wells, G. L., & Loftus, E. F. (1984). *Eyewitness testimony: Psychological perspectives*. New York: Cambridge University Press.

Wells, G. L., Luus, C. A. E., & Windschitl, P. D. (1994). Maximizing the utility of eyewitness identification evidence. *Current Directions in Psychological Science, 6,* 194–197.

Wertheimer, M. (1959). *Productive thinking*. New York: Harper & Row.

Wessels, M. G. (1982). *Cognitive psychology*. New York: Harper & Row.

Wharton, C. M., Holyoak, K. J., & Lange, T. E. (1996). Remote analogical reminding. *Memory & Cognition, 24,* 629–643.

Wheeler, D. D. (1970). Processes in word recognition. *Cognitive Psychology, 1,* 59–85.

Wickelgren, W. A. (1965). Size of rehearsal group and short-term memory. *Journal of Experimental Psychology, 68,* 413–419.

Wickelgren, W. A. (1974). *How to solve problems*. San Francisco: Freeman.

Wickelgren, W. A. (1976). Memory storage dynamics. In W. K. Estes (Ed.), *Handbook of learning and cognitive processes* (pp. 321–361). Hillsdale, NJ: Erlbaum.

Wickens, C. D. (1984). *Engineering psychology and human performance*. Columbus, OH: Merrill.

Wiener, N. (1948). *Cybernetics*. Cambridge, MA: MIT Press.

Wimmer, H., & Perner, J. (1983). Beliefs about beliefs: Representation and constraining function of wrong beliefs in young children's understanding of deception. *Cognition, 13,* 103–128.

Wingfield, A., & Byrnes, D. L. (1981). *The psychology of human memory*. New York: Academic Press.

Winograd, E., & Killinger, W. A. (1983). Relating age at encoding in early childhood to adult recall: Development of flashbulb memories. *Journal of Experimental Psychology, 112,* 413–422.

Wisniewski, E. J., & Murphy, G. L. (1989). Superordinate and basic category names in discourse: A textual analysis. *Discourse Processes, 12,* 245–261.

Wittgenstein, L. (1953). *Philosophical investigations*. Oxford, UK: Blackwell.

Wolfe, J. M. (1998). What can 1 million trials tell us about visual search? *Psychological Science, 9,* 33–39.

Wolff, P. H. (1966). The natural history of crying and other vocalizations in early infancy. In B. M. Foss (Ed.), *Determinants of infant behavior* (Vol. 4, pp. 81–109). London: Methuen.

Wood, G. (1983). *Cognitive psychology: A skills approach*. Monterey, CA: Brooks/Cole.

Wright, B., & Garrett, M. (1984). Lexical decision in sentences: Effects of syntactic structure. *Memory & Cognition, 12,* 31–45.

Wundt, W. (1900–1920). Volkerpsychologie (Vols. 1–10). Leipzig: Englemann.

Yachanin, S. A. (1986). Facilitation in Wason's selection task: Content and instructions. *Current Psychological Research and Reviews, 5,* 20–29.

Yantis, S. (1993). Stimulus-driven attentional capture. *Current Directions in Psychological Science, 2,* 156–161.

Yantis, S., & Jonides, J. (1990). Abrupt visual onsets and selective attention: Voluntary versus automatic allocation. *Journal of Experimental Psychology: Human Perception and Performace, 16,* 121–134.

Yuill, N., & Oakhill, J. (1991). *Children's problems in text comprehension: An experimental investigation*. Cambridge, England: Cambridge University Press.

Yussen, S. R., & Levy, V. M., Jr. (1975). Developmental changes in predicting one's own span of short-term memory. *Journal of Experimental Child Psychology, 19,* 502–508.

Zechmeister, E. B., & Nyberg, S. E. (1982). *Human memory: An introduction to research and theory*. Pacific Grove, CA:

Glossary

Addressed phonology Postlexical phonology. Knowledge of pronunciation represented in a cognitive code produced after the specific word is recognized.

Affordance A combination of the properties of a substance and its surfaces taken with reference to an animal.

AI Artificial intelligence. A discipline that attempts to create software capable of executing actions thought to require intelligence when done by people.

Algorithm A procedure that specifies a correct solution to any particular example from a class of well-defined problems.

Alignable differences Differences that can be contrasted on the same dimension are alignable: The fact that a motorcycle usually has two wheels while a car typically has four is an alignable difference.

Allocation policy In capacity theories of attention, refers to the process of dividing cognitive resources among competing stimuli.

Alternative causes In causal conditional reasoning, the appearance of alternative causes may diminish the reasoner's judgment of the perceived necessity of the stated cause.

Analog representation A representation made by the nervous system that preserves many of the elements of a stimulus in a way that is closely related to the elements' appearance in the natural world.

Analysis by synthesis model A general model of speech perception and pattern recognition that maintains that bottom-up processes suggest to top-down processes the information that should be filled in or internally computed.

Angular disparity The difference, in degrees, in the orientation of stimuli.

Anoetic consciousness The experience of knowing something in the absence of being able to retrieve a specific memory to support that knowledge.

Anterograde amnesia A general inability to encode durable memories following a trauma.

Aphasia A general term designating a wide variety of language disorders.

Articulatory loop A component of working memory having at least two parts: a phonological input store, and a rehearsal process capable of operating upon and extracting elements from the phonological store.

Assembled phonology Prelexical phonology. A cognitive code that may amplify graphemic information useful in reading.

Attenuation model This model suggests that a non-shadowed ear is not completely "turned off" as it is in the Broadbent model of attention, but that it's simply attenuated, which is what we do when we turn down the volume on a stereo.

Attenuation theory A theory of attention that maintains that unattended-to stimuli are damped down but not completely screened out.

Automatic processes Cognitive processes that can be initiated and run off without the allocation of attentional resources.

Automaticity The establishment of automatic processing on some specific cognitive task.

Autonoetic consciousness A conscious experience of having retrieved a specific memory.

Availability heuristic   A rule of thumb used to make estimates of likelihoods based on their commonness or ease of computation.

Babbling drift   In infants, the tendency to restrict the production of linguistic sounds of those of the language they will eventually learn.

Babbling   Prelinguistic motor play and vocal experimentation characterized by the production of both vowels and consonants.

Back-propagation algorithm   A procedure used to train neural networks by running an error signal "backwards" through the network, that is by beginning with the output units.

Backward masking   The presentation of a visual stimulus that prevents the recognition of a previously presented stimulus.

Bartlett tradition   An orientation in memory research concerned with qualitative changes in the contents of retrieved material.

Basic level   In categories, basic level terms combine generality and specificity in an optimal way.   Calling an object a "book" (the basic level term) is more general but less specific than calling it a "British murder mystery," but it is also less general and more specific than calling it simply "reading material."

Bias effect   When given two words and asked to choose which one had been a briefly flashed target, people show a tendency to choose the word that may have been present on a study list, seen prior to briefly flashed target.

Binary code   A representation of information using strings of symbols that can take on either of two values.

Brain writing   Refers to the position that new memories produce some physical change in the brain's structure.

Canalization   Refers to the idea that the contents of our minds are influenced and bounded by our affordances.

Capacity   The volume of cognitive codes capable of being retained by a memory store.

Categorical perception   The perception of phonemes as either-or. When ambiguous sounds are presented, subjects "hear" them as being a member of one category or another, not as having features of two categories.

Central attention   A form attention that is required to process stimuli in order to make the called-for response.

Centrality   Many naturally occurring categories have members that seem more typical of that category than do other members. For example, in the category of sports, baseball, football, and basketball seem more typical and central than do curling, yachting, and skeet shooting.

Chunking   Refers to associated elements being retained in short-term storage.

Chunk   Items that become associated and therefore unitized in memory.

Closed scenario   Type of reasoning that takes place when subjects are presented with a limited number of options for solving a particular problem.

Cognitive capacity   Refers to the number of cognitive processes or resources that can be brought to bear on sensory stimulation.

Cognitive codes   Representations of physical energy by the nervous system that are potentially capable of entering our awareness.

Cognitive maps   Internal representations of spatial layouts.

Cognitive resources   Cognitive programs, or routines, that process sensory stimulation or elaborate existing cognitive codes.

Commonality   In categories, commonality refers to shared features.

Comprehension   The reception, analysis, and interpretation of an utterance.

Computer simulation   The creation of software capable of executing actions in a way thought to mimic the cognitive processes of people.

Conceptual complexity   Pauses in the stream of speech that seem to be associated with the translation of a thought into a linguistic code.

Conceptually driven processes (top-down processes)   Cognitive processes involving feature abstraction and categorization that begin with expectations derived from context.

Conditional reasoning   Logic problems involving the conditional, or "if-then," statement.

Confirmation bias   Wason found that subjects in hypothesis evaluation tasks had a tendency to find evidence supporting particular hypotheses. This tendency to support hypotheses rather than refute them is called the confirmation bias.

Connectionism   The position that argues that cognitive processes can best be modeled using neural networks.

Connectionist approach   Essentially, connectionists approach the problem of cognition from an *analog* position in trying to show that cognitive events are the result of computations that could take place in neural-like systems that are organized in certain ways.

Conservative focusing   A strategy useful in solving artificial concept attainment problems. It involves changing only a single element of an array and observing the outcome of the change.

Constituents Components of a sentence that can be arranged in a hierarchical structure. They loosely correspond to linguistic parts of speech.

Constructivist theory of perception A position that emphasizes the formation of prototypes and schemata used in recognition and categorization.

Content addressability The ability of our memory system to access or reinstantiate particular memories given specific probes. In other words, we don't have to search through an entire set of material to discover whether or not we know a particular fact.

Context Information surrounding stimuli being recognized, categorized, or searched for.

Continuity theory A theory of language that maintains that speech developed from the apparently intentional cries of animals.

Control processes The information-processing theory of memory maintains that control processes transfer material from one storage to another.

Controlled processes Effortful cognitive processes that seem to require the allocation of attention to sustain them.

Convolution A matrix algebra process that can be used in parallel distributed processing models of memory. In such models, convolution can be used to show how a network of neuronlike entities may store and retrieve information.

Correlational world structure Refers to the notion that distinctive features are not randomly assigned to objects in the world. Rather, such features can be useful in predicting the appearance of other features.

Data-driven processes (bottom-up processes) Cognitive processes involving feature abstraction that begin with sensory stimulation.

Data-limited processes The processing of ambiguous stimuli is limited by the poverty of information that can be extracted from them. Performance decrements are produced by limitations in the stimuli.

Decay The loss of a cognitive code resulting from the passage of time.

Declarative knowledge Typically refers to factual, describable information whose organization is flexible and, to some extent, under our control.

Deep dyslexia The ability to read silently without being able to convert a graphemic code into a phonological one.

Deep-surface structure distinction The distinction between meaning and its expression in a wide variety of phrase structures.

Delta rule The delta rule governs weight changes in neural networks. As a network is trained, the weights are changed more when the system makes a large error than when it makes a small one.

Demand characteristics Subtle aspects of the experimental situation that provide the alert subject with clues about the desired findings or outcome.

Deontic reasoning Deontic reasoning is reasoning about forms of permission, usually involving the terms "might" or "may."

Depth of processing The nature of encoding is controlled by the subject. Semantic coding involves deeper processing than acoustic coding, because more knowledge is required to produce a semantic code.

Depth of search In chess-playing programs, refers to the number of moves and responses considered consecutively from some base move.

Design features Refers to attempts to define language in terms of presumed necessary characteristics.

Dichotic listening Listening to two unrelated messages played over stereo headphones.

Differentiation In categories, basic level terms are highly differentiated in comparison to both subordinate and superordinate terms because they combine the information value of the subordinate terms, with the distinctiveness of the superordinate terms.

Direct access This refers to the idea that the meaning of lexical elements can be contacted during reading without first contacting any of the element's phonological properties.

Direct theory of perception A position that emphasizes the ability of the perceiver to pick up sensory information as it truly exists in the world.

Disabling conditions In causal conditional reasoning, disabling conditions are events that may block the effectiveness of the stated cause in producing an effect. Thus, alternative causes may diminish the reasoner's judgment of the perceived sufficiency of the stated cause.

Disconfirming the consequent Refers to the application of modus tollens in conditional reasoning. If P implies Q, then the absence of Q implies the absence of P.

Discontinuity in thinking Refers to the Gestalt notion that problem solving could be accomplished by insight, a phenomenon that the Gestaltists believed was unrelated to prior cognitive effort.

Discounting In causal reasoning, people de-emphasize, or discount, the effect of a moderately strong cause when a very strong cause is also present.

Displacement All natural languages enable their possessor to refer to things that are distant in time or space.

Distinctive features in speech This refers to the idea that phonemes might be marked by a unique constellation of particular features.

Distributed network models Theories that postulate that the phenomenon in question can be modeled by a system of interacting "neuronlike" entities that represent concepts and other knowledge as patterns of activity.

Domain-free problems Problems whose solutions do not require extensive expertise.

Dual code position The theoretical position that holds that our nervous system is capable of producing and sustaining two kinds of memories: verbal memories, and analog memories that have visuospatial properties.

Duality of patterning One of Hockett's design features that described language as consisting of "small" elements such as sounds that could be put together in an infinite variety of ways.

Echo Refers to the representation of acoustic events in the sensory register.

Ecological approach to visual perception A position that emphasizes the information about the world that can be seen by moving through it.

Ecological validity Refers to the trend in cognitive science to explain cognitive processes in everyday terms and to study mental processes in their "natural habitats."

Elaborative rehearsal Rehearsal whose objective is to meaningfully associate incoming stimuli with previously learned material.

Electrodermal responses Changes in the skin's electrical conductance, used as indicators of ongoing cognitive processing.

Encoding specificity At retrieval time, a cue will aid retrieval if the cue provides information that was also processed during the encoding of the to-be-remembered material.

Encoding Transforming a stimulus into a format that can be retained by the cognitive system.

Episodic knowledge This refers to a memory that is based on particular experience.

Episodic memory Memories that are autobiographical, personal, and sensitive to the effects of context.

Equipotentiality As far as memory is concerned, all cortex areas seem to be equally important.

Error bowl The error bowl is a mathematically defined space that shows the nature of the corrections that need to be made in the weights of a neural network.

Exemplar theory According to this viewpoint, individual category members are retained in memory, as opposed to retaining only the category's most central member.

Expansions A form of linguistic response to a child in which the intended meaning of the child's utterances is reformulated in the standard and complete form by the caretaker.

Expertise Human knowledge or the representa- tion of such knowledge in machines. In humans, such knowledge is acquired directly through experience.

Explicit memory When a subject is asked to recognize or recall presented materials in a study, the subject must deliberately use his or her memory system. In these cases, the subjects are making use of their explicit memory.

Extralogical inferences Inferences that are based on a person's general knowledge of the world. Although outside the realm of formal reasoning, such inferences can be useful as heuristics.

Fan effect In ACT, the time required for acti- vation to spread to associated nodes is inversely related to the number of associated nodes being activated.

Feature abstraction Refers to the cognitive processes that take complex stimuli and abstract—that is, draw out from them—their simplest components.

Feature detection theory A position that maintains that pattern recognition is accomplished by the abstraction and reassembly of specific aspects of sensory stimulation.

Filter theory A theory of attention that maintains that unattended-to stimuli are completely screened out.

Finite state grammar An attempt to formulate grammatical knowledge in left-to-right rules that specify the transitions between words.

Flashbulb memories Vivid, seemingly accurate memories produced by unexpected, emotionally charged events.

Focus gambling A strategy used on artificial concept attainment tasks. It involves simultaneously changing more than one element of the problem array and then observing the outcome.

Formal reasoning Refers to the use of logical inference rules that have been developed by logicians.

Formant Refers to the visual representation of a particular concentration of acoustic energy in the speech signal. Formants are typically distinguished by number. The fundamental frequency of speech (as produced by the vibrations of our vocal folds) is referred to as the first formant. The concentration of acoustic energy in the next higher frequency range, and the one produced by changes in the vocal cavity itself, is referred to as the second formant.

Framing Refers to the influence of context on likelihood estimations.

Fuzzy borders Refers to the fact that people treat many natural categories as though they were ill defined. The borders of the concept shift according to the context in which the category member appears.

Fuzzy-trace memory theory This position states that we maintain a verbatim representation of an experience along with a general representation of the gist of that experience.

Gaze duration Refers to the total amount of time that the reader has spent fixating on a particular point of text; if there has been only fixation on that particular point, then gaze duration is equal to fixation.

Generate and recognize models Models of this class maintain that retrieval is accomplished by two component activities. First, plausible candidates for the searched-for memory are internally generated. Then the list of candidates is examined and the most likely candidate is picked from among those generated.

Generation effect Subjects who generate materials that will be explicitly searched for later in a memory task outperform those subjects who have not generated the materials themselves.

Gestalt psychology A European movement emphasizing the primacy of construction in perception and problem solving.

Gist The representation of general semantic content or meaning.

GPS The General Problem Solver, a computer program designed by Newell and Simon whose purpose was to show how general heuristics could solve a wide variety of problems.

Graceful degradation Used to describe cognitive systems that remain relatively efficient at least up to a certain point under some adversity induced either by processing overloads or by impoverishment of incoming stimuli.

Grammar Our total linguistic knowledge, consisting of phonological, syntactical, and semantic components.

Grapheme A letter or combination of letters that stands for a single phoneme.

Höffding step The step between sensation and perception. The conversion of a cognitive code representing a stimulus into a code that enables the categorization of the stimulus.

Habituation The tendency to cease responding to familiar, or extensively processed, stimuli.

Heuristic A rule of thumb for solving problems or reasoning in everyday situations.

Hidden units In a neural network, hidden units are those neurodes that intervene between input and output neurodes.

Higher-order invariances Regularities in patterns of stimuli that are available to be seen as we move through the world or as elements in the world move around us.

Hippocampus A large forebrain structure located between the thalamus and the cortex.

Holophrastic stage At about one year of age, the child begins to produce single words that seem to symbolize entire sentences.

Horizontal construction This is the "normal" process of coding a thought into language. The "larger" or more complicated the thought, the longer and more complicated the syntax coding might be.

Human factors research A discipline that studies information processing by humans and machines in an attempt to find their optimal relationship.

Icon Neisser's name for the visual contents of sensory storage.

Ill-defined problems A problem is ill defined if the start or goal states are unclear, or if the operations required to change states are unspecified.

Implicit memory When a subject shows priming effects of materials that have been presented but not studied, and these priming effects occur in the absence of any deliberate attempt by the subject to use his or her memory system, we say that the subjects are making use of their implicit memory.

Incubation effect According to the Gestalt psychologists, incubation wa a period of unconscious problem solving. The incubation effect refers to the sudden appearance of an answer.

Incubation Refers to the unconscious work done by problem solvers who have left off conscious solving of the problem.

Indirect speech act When a speaker uses a linguistic structure nonnormatively, that is, to carry out a function for which the structure is not typically used, the speaker is relying upon the listener's ability to "go beyond" the typical use of the structure. This event is referred to as an indirect speech act.

Infantile amnesia This term describes the fact that most of us do not have very many vivid memories from the earliest period of our lives.

Inferential intrusion errors   Recall failures produced by general knowledge of the world. These errors occur when general knowledge is used to logically infer what must have taken place when a particular memory cannot be retrieved.

Inflection   The process of adding linguistic markers to words to indicate plurality, possession, or case.

Information-processing approach   The metatheory of cognitive psychology that holds that mental events can be understood as complex cognitive codes that are often serially transformed.

Information   As defined by Shannon, the function of information is to reduce the uncertainty of future events.

Input attention   A form of attention that appears early in the processing of stimuli and is used to assess and evaluate the nature of the task, possibly to determine its place in a queue of information processing tasks.

Insight   A conscious experience consisting of a sudden awareness of the correct organization of a problem's elements.

Intelligence   Capabilities that seem to be reflected in the apparent purposiveness and goal orientation inferred from the behavior of humans and some animals. Intelligence can be represented as an organized amalgamation of cognitive structures and processes.

Intentionality   Describes mental events that are the antecedents of certain actions and that perhaps play a causal role in producing those actions.

Interference   In memory research, refers to the inability to retrieve material resulting from its confusion with other cognitive codes.

Intersection search   In attempting to verify a relationship between two nodes in semantic memory, an intersection search fans out from both entry nodes until some path is found or until the search has verified that no common path exists.

Inter-stimulus interval   In Sperling's study, the time interval between the offset of the stimulus and the onset of the cue to begin reporting.

Intrinsic characteristics   The light reflected from an object carries with it information about the boundary characteristics and surface homogeneity of the object. These are the intrinsic characteristics.

Intrusion errors   This term describes the retrieval of nontargeted information. If I'm given two lists of words to learn and I'm asked to retrieve the second list, any first list word I retrieve is an intrusion error.

Invariant features   Information contained in the visual field that does not change regardless of our movement through it.

Isomorphism   Formal equivalence. Usually used to describe the relationship between problems whose deep structure is the same, although their appearance, or surface structure, differs.

Late selection   A theory of attention that maintains that almost all incoming stimuli are sent to working memory before any screening out is done.

Layout of perceivable space   Knowledge of the apparent alteration of the shapes of geometric objects in the visual field, acquired by motion.

Lemma   This is the technical term that refers to the portion of the word's meaning that is contained in its gloss or its theme.

Less is more (LIM) position   The fact that the attention spans and memory capacities of children are limited may actually help them constrain the meanings of words to only their intended referent.

Lexical access   Our ability to cognitively contact and retrieve the meanings of words and to be able to express the relationship of these elements to one another.

Lexical uncertainty   Refers to pauses in the stream of speech occurring just prior to the appearance of unusual words.

Linear independence   A mathematical property of a set of vectors in which each item in each vector is uncorrelated with all other items in all other vectors.

Linguistic universals   Used in two senses: the boundaries of language and characteristics of language that all languages share.

Local network models   Theories of semantic memory that postulate that such knowledge is represented by a system of nodes, each one standing for a concept, and connections that show the associations among such concepts.

Local-global distinction   In problem solving, answering the question 'What to do next?' involves local knowledge. Understanding the big picture—the problem's underlying structure—is global knowledge.

Logic   Any one of a variety of systems of reasoning used to determine the validity of certain premises.

Log-log transformation   In a graph, taking the logarithm of the values on both the ordinate and on the abscissa results in a log-log transformation.

Long-term storage   The information-processing theory of memory maintains that long-term storage is semantically organized and has an infinite capacity. Retrieval failures are produced by interference.

Maintenance rehearsal   Rehearsal whose objective is simply to retain information in working memory. This rehearsal seems to be accompanied by subvocalization.

Mand function   Skinner's term for the function of language referring to verbal operants reinforced through compliance.

Manner of articulation   In uttering consonants, refers to the way in which the constriction is produced.

Mass action   As far as memory is concerned, the brain seems to work en masse.

Mastermind   A logical deduction game in which the problem solver must deduce the color and location of a string of hidden buttons using only the ambiguous feedback provided.

Mental rotation   The creation and inspection of a rotating image.

Mental size   The amount of mental space that seems to be taken up by an image.

Mentalism   A term used as a criticism by behaviorists for phenomena that seemed neither public nor reproducible.

Metamemory   Personal knowledge about the operation of the memory system.

Metatheory   A set of basic presumptions thought to operate in a general domain. A metatheory is a schematic plan for building specific theories in particular domains.

Min strategy   Children using the min strategy to add two numbers count up from the larger number the number of steps represented by the smaller number.

MLU   The mean length of a child's utterance. Determined by counting the number of morphemes produced, then dividing the total by the number of separate utterances.

Modality specific   Each sense loads information into its own compartments in the sensory register, making the sensory register sense specific or modality specific.

Modus ponens   An inference rule stating that, if P implies Q is true, then the presence of P implies the presence of Q.

Modus tollens   An inference rule stating that if P implies Q is true, then the absence of Q implies the absence of P.

Morpheme   The basic unit of meaning.

Müller-Lyer illusion   Refers to the famous "fins-out–fins-in" illusion.   The length of the middle bar seems to vary as the direction of the fins is changed.

Natural categories   Unlike the categories used in artificial concept tasks, everyday categories are ill defined, have fuzzy borders, and are sensitive to the effects of context.

Natural reasoning   The study of human reasoning in life-like situations involving the estimation of likelihoods.

Network models   Depictions of knowledge, usually cast into either a symbolic network model or a neural network model.

Neural code   A pattern of neural activity that represents a particular event.

Nodes   The locations in a symbolic knowledge network in which specific lexical entries are stored.

Nonalignable differences   Differences that cannot be contrasted on the same dimension.   The fact that a sailboat is steered by a tiller while a car is usually steered by a wheel is a nonalignable difference.

Nonstrategic processing   The notion that some information such as the frequency of occurrence of some stimuli is encoded automatically, that is, without effort by the subject.

Open scenario   Type of reasoning that takes place when the subjects understand the task as one that involves searching for a particular method or form of reasoning.

Operator   A cognitive process that transforms one state of knowledge into another. Although a solver may access dozens of such states during the course of problem solving, the number of distinct operators is thought to be limited.

Optical flow pattern   The arrangement of changing and invariant aspects of the visual field.

Overextensions   A child who overextends a word's meaning applies a basic level term such as "dog" to a superordinate category, "furry four-legged creatures."

Overregularization   A "smart error" in which a child treats an irregular noun or verb form as if it were regular. This indicates knowledge of general inflectional rules.

Overwriting   A position that maintains that inferences made at retrieval wipe out previous encodings.

Parafoveal information   Refers to information that can be picked up beyond the fixation point and used for word recognition, or lexical access.

Parallel processing   Refers to the simultaneous transformation of several different cognitive codes.

Partial-report technique   Used by Sperling, a technique that involves cuing the subject to report only certain elements of an array.

Pattern associator   In distributed network models, a pattern associator is a matrix of elements that, when premultiplied by specific vectors representing particular associated experiences, reproduce other vectors representing particular associated experiences, or memories.

Perceptron The perceptron is a simple neural network that can learn to categorize certain types of arbitrary input.

Perceptual cycle Neisser's attempt to synthesize the direct and constructive viewpoints by conceiving of perception as on ongoing activity.

Perceptual fluency The ability to recognize a particular stimulus under impoverished presentation conditions.

Phoneme A separable, identifiable unit of sound. Phonemes are the basic acoustic building blocks of spoken language.

Phonemic restoration effect A speech illusion that occurs when a nonspeech sound is substituted for a deleted phoneme. The listener usually fails to detect the deletion.

Phonetics The discipline that attempts to categorize speech sounds. There are two approaches. Articulatory phonetics focuses on the movements of the tongue, and acoustic phonetics deals with linguistic sounds as physical energy.

Phonology The discipline that attempts to express the regularities in linguistic sounds as being rule based and principled.

Phrase structure A hierarchical, abstract formula, written in terms of constituents that can be used to generate and analyze utterances.

Place of articulation In speech, refers to the point of constriction in producing consonants.

Power law The notion that some psychological dimension or characteristic can be explained by taking a numerical value on some other psychological dimension and raising that value to a certain power.

Pragmatic reasoning schemas Clusters of highly generalized, and therefore abstract, rules that are organized on the basis of certain goals and conditions.

Pragmatics Describes the socially derived rules, principles, and conventions that speakers and listeners use to establish coherence across groups of sentences.

Preattentive analysis An analysis of stimuli that may extract acoustic, phonetic, and possibly prior semantic information prior to the material's entry into awareness.

Prestored knowledge Knowledge of "isnota" links in semantic memory that limit the extent of search.

Primal sketch A representation of the two-dimensional image that makes explicit the amount and disposition of the intensity changes or discontinuities present. The representation consists of place tokens and is hierarchical. The primitives at the lowest level represent raw intensity changes and their local geometry. Higher level primitives represent groupings and alignments among the lower level primitives.

Primary component Refers to the first part of the serial position effect seen in free-recall studies—presumably the result of material retrieved from long-term storage.

Primary memory Refers to the memory of those stimuli whose recent appearance we are conscious of, and whose representation feels fragile or prone to fading.

Proactive interference Interference that results when some previously learned material hinders the formation of a memory for some recently learned material.

Problem space A theoretical term that denotes the problem solver's internal representation of the problem.

Problems of arrangement In Greeno's classification, refers to problems in which the elements of the problem must be rearranged according to a specific criterion.

Problems of inducing structure In Greeno's classification, refers to problems in which a relationship must be discovered among the problem's components.

Problems of transformation In Greeno's classification, refers to problems in which a sequence of moves or alterations must be determined to change the problem's initial state into the goal state.

Procedural knowledge Refers to knowledge that no longer enters awareness. Usually expressed as a skill.

Process deficiencies The inability to execute some cognitive process resulting from immaturity of the cognitive system.

Production deficiency A failure to use a memory strategy that one has the ability to execute.

Production rules Rules that can be used to guide intelligent actions. They have two parts. The state part lists conditions that might be observed in the world. The action part dictates the actions that should be taken if the conditions in the state part have been observed.

Production system A production system is a formalism that shows how procedural knowledge might be represented in an abstract format.

Production Refers to the planning, lexical choice, and execution of speech.

Productivity All natural languages permit their possessor to create novel utterances.

Propositional analysis Breaking down complex remarks into propositions, which are the smallest units of knowledge that can possess a truth value.

Prototype The prototype is the most feature-laden member of a category; it is the most central member of the category.

Prototype The psychological center of a category; the most typical instance of a category.

Pseudohomophone A pseudohomophone is a non-word that is pronounced like an actual word. For example, "phude" is a pseudohomophone of "food."

Psycholinguistics The study of language from a psychological rather than from a linguistic perspective.

Psychological refractory period The presentation of two stimuli that each demand a specific response temporarily overwhelms the cognitive system, disabling its capacity to respond to both stimuli. This period of time is referred to as the psychological refractory period.

Recency component Refers to the second part of the serial position effect seen in free-recall studies—presumably the result of material retrieved from short-term storage.

Reception paradigm In artificial concept formation tasks, the reception paradigm describes situations in which the subject has no control over which exemplars will be examined.

Recursion Complete linguistic structures can be embedded within others. This process can theoretically be continued indefinitely.

Reductionist viewpoint A theoretical position that maintains that complex phenomena can be thought of as consisting of simpler, although qualitatively different, events.

Referential communication This occurs when a listener gathers additional information from a speaker in order to clarify a meaning previously produced by the speaker.

Regression When a reader launches a **saccade** leftward during reading, this type of saccade is called a regression.

Rehearsal The two types of rehearsal are maintenance rehearsal, which keeps a cognitive code intact for limited periods, and elaborative rehearsal, which establishes contact with semantic memory.

Repetition effect The perception of nonwords primes or facilitates their later perception.

Repetition priming The initial presentation of a recognized word speeds up, or primes subsequent access of that word.

Representation problem To solve unfamiliar problems, a person must construct an internal representation of the problem. The difficulty involved in constructing such a representation is known as the representation problem.

Representativeness heuristic A rule of thumb used in estimating likelihoods. It is based on a subjective computation of the person or event's similarity to a prototype.

Repressed memories The conventional doctrine suggests that there are experiences that we have representations of, but whose retrieval is inhibited by their traumatic nature.

Resource-limited processes Demanding, or unpracticed, tasks that require the heavy allocation of cognitive resources. Performance decrements are produced by unavailability of additional resources.

Response competition This phenomenon occurs when an individual cannot determine which of several associations is correct.

Retinal image The raw code produced by the retina and sent to the brain for perceptual processing.

Retrieving Cognitive processing that recovers or elaborates stored cognitive codes.

Retrograde amnesia Retrieval failure involving material encoded just prior to the occurrence of a traumatic shock.

Saccade A rhythmic, ballistic eye motion used in reading.

Schema A term that denotes what is essential in category membership and connotes a plan or expectation that can be used to receive or organize incoming stimulation.

Script A general, context-free mental framework that can be used to organize particular sequences of common and familiar actions.

Secondary memory Refers to the memory of those stimuli whose representation seems both durable and capable of being retrieved under a variety of circumstances.

Secondary recall cues Recalled material capable of cuing the recall of additional material.

Segment-and-label An AI approach to computer vision that emphasizes bottom-up processes such as feature abstraction.

Selection paradigm As used in artificial concept attainment tasks, refers to experimental procedures in which the subject picks the next exemplar in the series. The subject's choices indicate the nature of the strategy being used.

Selective attention The capacity to focus cognitive processes on a narrow band of sensory stimulation.

Selective filter Broadbent's model of attention postulated that any stimulus must pass through a selective filter in order to be detected.

Selectivity In attention, whatever is being attended to is processed to a deeper extent than is nonattended information.

Self-schema A cognitive structure used to represent and assimilate information about the self.

Semantic knowledge This term refers to general knowledge, "world" knowledge, or context-free knowledge.

Semantic memory General, encyclopedic knowledge of the world and language.

Semantic priming The activation of a word in semantic memory facilitates or primes the activation of subsequent, conceptually related words.

Semantics Linguistic knowledge of meaning.

Sensory register A storage location that retains an almost complete representation of sensory stimulation for a brief time.

Sequential processing Sequential processing occurs when some cognitive processes are dependent on the output of previous processes. This term can be contrasted with parallel processing.

Serial exhaustive search Refers to a complete, one-at-a-time search of the elements in working memory.

Serial position effect When a subject's memory is tested in a free-recall situation, initial and final items are more likely to be recalled than items presented in the middle of the list.

Serial processing Refers to the sequential transformation of a cognitive code.

Serial self-terminating search In a search of short-term memory, this refers to the ability of the subjects to conclude a search immediately upon encountering the target probe.

Shadowing Reciting a message played over stereo headphones, as soon after hearing it as possible.

Short-term storage The information-processing theory of memory maintains that this storage is acoustically organized, has a limited capacity, and loses material through decay.

Similarity For a time, it was thought that judgments of similarity were based on the degree to which features were shared. However it appears that similarity is more than simply an appreciation of common features.

Soundness A system of reasoning is sound if, given true premises, it always produces true conclusions. All formal logical systems have this property.

Specializations for languages Refers to certain features of the brain and larynx that may indicate innate predispositions for language ability.

Speech act This refers to the interpretation by a listener of a speaker's intention. In other words, the speech act is the utterance as received and comprehended by a listener.

Speed-accuracy decomposition technique A technique used to determine the extent to which a subject's response was dependent on a need to respond quickly, versus the extent to which a subject's response was dependent on a need to respond accurately.

Spreading activation model Retrieval from permanent memory can be thought of as activating elements in a semantic network.

State-action tree A method of representing move problems in which the problem states are shown as nodes, and the actions transforming successive states are shown as connecting lines.

State-dependent learning Retrieval is enhanced if the subjects are in roughly the same psychological state at both retrieval and encoding times.

Stimulus onset ayanchrony Refers to a difference in time between the appearance of two stimuli.

Storage The capacity of the nervous system to retain cognitive codes.

Strategy A move, or probe, designed to effect some change in the problem and provide information by so doing.

Structural relationships Various sorts of underlying meanings, such as agent role, location, possession, and so on, that seem to be expressed by children in the holophrastic and two-word stages.

Structuralism A theoretical position that regards the mind as an organized set of decomposable mental acts.

Subordinate level In categories, subordinate level terms (such as "Abyssinian cat") are more specific and thus more informative than are basic level terms (such as "cat").

Sufficiency analysis An analysis that focuses on how a particular cognitive process *may* be carried out.

Superordinate level In categories, superordinate level terms (such as "pet") are more general and thus less informative than are basic level terms (such as "cat").

Surface dyslexia The ability to read out loud more or less normally without being able to recognize the words or their meanings.

Surface structure This term refers to the form of a sentence as it is actually uttered.

Syntax Linguistic knowledge of word order and inflections.

Tact function Skinner's term for the function of language referring to verbal operants cued by discriminative stimuli.

Task environment Theoretically, a neutral and complete representation of a problem that includes all possible problem spaces.

Taxonomic assumption In learning the meaning of words, children seem to assume that a given word might be extended to things that seem to fall in the same category.

Teachable language comprehender (TLC) This is a symbolic network model of semantic knowledge in which the individual nodes are arranged hierarchically.

Template-matching theory A position that maintains that pattern recognition is accomplished by comparing incoming stimuli with a fixed mental model of an ideal pattern.

Text model The reader's internal representation, or understanding, of the text.

Texture gradient The orderly and gradual loss of surface detail and clarity as we scan the visual field from nearby to distant objects.

Thematic materials Sometimes reasoners are more likely to produce the correct answer in the Wason selection task when the task is cast in the context of a real-world problem.

Theory-based view This viewpoint refers to the idea that we bring our background knowledge into play both in making judgments of similarity, and in making categorical decisions.

Thinking out loud Verbalizing the contents of working memory. A tape recording of the resulting utterances, known as a protocol, can be useful in analyzing a subject's problem solving.

Time course of activation Cognitive psychologists are interested in what components of a lexical item are accessed first, and how long that access takes relative to the access of item's other components.

TLC Teachable Language Comprehender, one of the earliest models of semantic memory.

TOT phenomenon William James referred to the "tip of the tongue" phenomenon as an "intensely active gap."

Tower of Hanoi A transformation problem in which a stack of disks, situated on one of three pegs, must be transferred to another peg. Constraints limit the size of the disks that may rest on top of each other.

Transfer appropriate processing The cognitive processes that are used to encode a stimulus interact with the processes that are used to retrieve it. When the retrieval processes match those that were used at encoding, retrieval may be enhanced.

Truth In logic, refers to the reality of premises. An argument can be valid but untrue if the initial premises describe unreal situations.

Two-word stage A period in which the child typically produces utterances of two words. This period indicates the beginning of syntactical knowledge.

Type-token distinction The elements of semantic memory consist of nodes representing general categories (types) as well as specific examples of those categories (tokens).

Unattended speech effect The processing of visually presented text is impaired by the presence of concurrent speech sounds. This impairment is observed even when the subject is told to ignore the speech sounds. This is not an acoustic effect per se because the presence of white noise does not produce the impairment in processing the visual materials.

Underextensions A child who underextends a word's meaning applies the word to only a single example of a category, such as a child who refers to only his or her dog as "doggy."

Unlearning This is similar to extinction of conditioned responses. The acquisition of new associations suppresses the associative strength of older associations.

Validity An argument is valid if, according to the principles of reasoning developed by logicians, a conclusion necessarily follows from certain premises.

Vector encoding This refers to the representation of a complex object by a string of numbers designating values of a number of dimensions.

Vertical construction Children who do not possess enough syntactic knowledge to code their entire thought into a single sentence may break the thought down into a series of one- or two-word utterances. When taken cumulatively, this series of utterances may be understood as a sentence.

Visuospatial scratch pad A component of working memory having at least two parts: an active storage for stimuli with visual properties or spatial extension, and a rehearsal process capable of extracting such material.

Voicing The degree to which the vocal cords are involved in the production of a consonant. Voiced consonants are those in which the buzzing of the vocal cords is detected.

Well-defined problems Those in which the start and goal states are clearly specified. A procedure that transforms the start state into the goal state must be at least potentially available.

Whole-object assumption In learning the meaning of words, children seem to assume that a given word refers to an entire object, rather than to a part of that object.

Whole-report technique Sperling's original methodology involved asking his subjects to report as much information as they could retrieve following the brief presentation of visual stimuli.

Widrow-Hoff rule Describes the rate of change in the connective strength among elements in a distributed network model.

Width of search In AI research, refers to algorithms that try to limit the number of different search pathways explored.

Word superiority effect Subjects are better at identifying a letter when it appears in the context of a word rather than when it appears by itself.

Working memory element (WME) In ACT-R, the working memory element corresponds to a "chunk" in short-term memory.

XOR problem The XOR ("exclusive or") problem refers to the fact that it is impossible for two layer neural networks like pattern associators to compute identical outputs from inputs that are completely uncorrelated.

Zero-crossing The point where a function's value changes its sign from positive to negative or vice versa.

Name Index

Subject Index

Credits

This page constitutes an extension of the copyright page. We have made every effort to trace the ownership of all copyrighted material and to secure permission from copyright holders. In the event of any question arising as to the use of any material, we will be pleased to make the necessary corrections in future printings. Thanks are due to the following authors, publishers, and agents for permission to use the material indicated.

2.12 From "Visual Search" by Ulric Neisser in *Scientific American,* June 1964. Copyright © 1964 by Scientific American. Reprinted by permission. **76:** Figure 2.11 Adapted from Eleanor Gibson, *Principles of Perceptual Learning and Development,* © 1969, p. 88. Reprinted by permission of Prentice-Hall, Inc., Englewood Cliffs, New Jersey. **77:** Figure 2.13 Based on "Human Image Understanding: Recent Research and a Theory," by I. Biederman, 1985, *Computer Vision, Graphics and Image Processing,* 32, 29–73. **78:** Figure 2.14 From "Human Image Understanding: Recent Research and a Theory," by I. Biederman, 1985, *Computer Vision, Graphics and Image Processing,* 32, 29–73. Copyright © 1985 Academic Press. Reprinted by permission. **79:** Table 2.1 From *Vision* by David Marr. Copyright © 1982 by W. H. Freeman and Company. Used with permission. **81:** Figure 2.15 Ling, X., & Sanocki, T. (1995). "Major axes as a moderately abstract model for object recognition" in *Psychological Science,* 6, 370–375, fig 1, page 371. Reprinted by permission. **82:** Figure 2.16 Ling, X., & Sanocki, T. (1995). "Major axes as a moderately abstract model for object recognition" in *Psychological Science,* 6, 370–375, fig 2, page 371. Reprinted by permission. **83:** Figure 2.17 From *Psychology Today, 3rd ed.* Copyright 1975 by Random House, Inc. Reprinted by permission.

Chapter 3: 96: Figure 3.2 From Atkinson & Shiffrin, 1968. Copyright 1968 by Academic Press. Adapted by permission of the publisher and author. **99:** Figure 3.3 From Peterson & Peterson, 1959. Copyright 1959 by the American Psychological Association. Reprinted by permission of the publisher and author. **101:** Figure 3.4 From "Short-term temporal changes in free recall" by L. Postman and L.W. Phillips, *Quarterly Journal of Experimental Psychology,* 17, 132-138. Copyright © 1965 by Lawrence Erlbaum Associates Publishers. Adapted by permission. **108:** Figure3.5 Copyright 1983 by The Royal Society. Adapted by permission of the publisher and author. **109:** Figure 3.6 Copyright 1983 by The Royal Society. Adapted by permission of the publisher and author. **111:** Figure 3.7 Cowan, N. (1994). "Mechanisms of verbal short-term memory" in *Current directions in Psychological Science,* Vol 3, 185–189. Fig 1, p. 187. Reprinted with the permission of Cambridge University Press. **113:** Figure3.8 From "Semantic Confusion Errors in Short-Term Memory," by H.G. Shulman in *Journal of Verbal Learning and Verbal Behavior,* 1972, 11, 221–227. Copyright 1972 by Academic Press, Inc. Adapted by permission of the publisher and author. **120:** Table 3.1 Weaver, C.A. III. (1993). "Do you need a 'flash' to form a flash bulb memory?" in *Journal of Experimental Psychology:* General. 122, 39–46, Tab. 3, p. 43. Reprinted by permission. **126:** Figure 3.9 Buckner, R. L. (1996). "Beyond HERA: Contributions of specific prefrontal brain areas to long-term memory retrieval" in *Psychonomic Bulletin and Review,* 3, 149–158, Fig 2, p. 152. Reprinted by permission.

Chapter 4: 133: Table 4.1 Adapted from *Remembering* by F. C. Bartlett, Cambridge University Press, 1932. Reprinted by permission. **134:** Table 4.2 Adapted from *Remembering* by F. C. Bartlett, Cambridge University Press, 1932. Reprinted by permission. **138:** Table 4.3 From "Recall for Words as a Function of Semantic Graphic and Syntactic" by T.S. Hyde and J.J. Jenkins in *Journal of Verbal Learning & Verbal Behavior,* 12 (5), October 1973 pp. 471–480. Copyright © 1973 Academic Press, Inc. Reprinted by permission. **139:** Figure 4.1 From "The Role of Rehearsal in Short-Term Memory," by F.I.M. Craik and M.J. Watkins in *Journal of Verbal Learning and Verbal Behavior,* 1973, 12, 599–607. Copyright 1973 by Academic Press, Inc. **148:** Figure 4.2 From "Remembering the Data: Analyzing Interactive Processes in Reading" by L. L. Jacoby in *Journal of Verbal Learning and Verbal Behavior,* 1983, vol. 22, page 493. Copyright © 1983 by Academic Press. Reprinted by permission. **151:** Figure 4.3 Mulligan, N.W. (1997). "Attentional load and implicit memory tests: The effects of varying attentional load on conceptual priming" in *Memory & Cognition,* 25, 11–17, Fig. 1, p. 14. Reprinted by permission. **154:** Table 4.4 From Rajaram, 1993. Copyright 1993 by the Psychonomic Society, Inc. Adapted by permission of the publisher and author. **155:** Figure 4.4 Donaldson, W. (1996). "The role of decision making processes in remembering and knowing" in *Memory & Cognition,* 24, 523–533, Fig 1, p. 524. Reprinted by permission. **159:** Figure 4.5 Garry, N., Manning, C.G., Loftus, E.F., & Sherman, S.J. (1996). "Imagination inflation: imagining a childhood event inflates confidence that it occurred" in *Psychonomic Bulletin and Review,* 3, 208–214, Fig. 1, p. 211. Reprinted by permission. **162:** Table 4.5 Brainerd, C.J., Reyna, V.F., & Brandse, E. (1995). "Are children's false memories more persistent than their true memories?" in *Psychological Science,* 6, 359–364, Tab. 1, p. 361. Reprinted by permission. **164:** Figure 4.6 From John R. Anderson and Lael J. Schooler, "Reflections of the environment in memory," *Psychological Science* 2, 396–408. Copyright © 1991 American Psychological Association. Reprinted by permission. **167:** Figure 4.7 From John R. Anderson and Lael J. Schooler, "Reflections of the environment in memory," *Psychological Science* 2, 396–408. Copyright © 1991 American Psychological

Association. Reprinted by permission. **170:** Figure 4.8 From Rubin and Kontis, 1983. Copyright 1977 by Academic Press. Adapted by permission of the publisher and author.

Chapter 5: 178: Table 5.1 From Meyer and Schvaneveldt, 1971. Copyright 1971 by the American Psychological Association. Adapted by permission of the publisher and author. **179:** Figure 5.1 Copyright 1981 by the American Psychological Association. Adapted by permission of the publisher and author. **181:** Figure 5.2 From Neely, J. H. "Semantic priming and retrieval from lexical memory: Roles of Inhibitionless spreading activation and limited-capacity attention" in *Journal of Experimental Psychology:* General, 106, 226–254. Copyright © 1977 by the American Psychological Association. Adapted by permission of the author. **183:** Table 5.2 Ratcliff, R., & McKoon, G. (1997). "A counter model for implicit priming in perceptual word identification" in *Psychological Review,* 104, 319–343, Table 1, p. 323. Reprinted by permission. **187:** Figure 5.5 After Collins & Quillian, 1969. Copyright 1969 by Academic Press. Adapted by permission of the publisher and author. **189:** Figure 5.6 After Collins & Quillian, 1969. Copyright 1969 by Academic Press. Adapted by permission of the publisher and author. **191:** Figure 5.7 After Collins & Quillian, 1969. Copyright 1969 by Academic Press. Adapted by permission of the publisher and author. **195:** Table 5.3 From *Rules of the Mind* by J. R. Anderson. Copyright © 1993 by Lawrence Erlbaum Associates. Reprinted by permission. **200:** Figure 5.8 From *Rules of the Mind* by J. R. Anderson. Copyright © 1993 by Lawrence Erlbaum Associates. Reprinted by permission. **201:** Table 5.5 From *Rules of the Mind* by J. R. Anderson. Copyright © 1993 by Lawrence Erlbaum Associates. Reprinted by permission. **201:** Table 5.6 From *Rules of the Mind* by J. R. Anderson. Copyright © 1993 by Lawrence Erlbaum Associates. Reprinted by permission. **203:** Figure 5.9 Mimura, M., Verfaellie, M., & Milberg, W.P. (1997). "Repetition priming in an auditory lexical decision task: Effects of lexical status" in *Memory & Cognition,* 25, 819-825, Figure 1, p. 820. Reprinted by permission.

Chapter 6: 214: Table 6.1 Copyright © 1989 by the MIT Press. Adapted by permission of the publisher and author. **218:** Figure 6.4 From Rumelhart and McClelland (Eds.), *Parallel Distributed Processing.* Vol. I. Copyright 1986 MIT Press. Adapted by permission of the publisher and author. **220:** Figure 6.5 Anderson, J.A., & Sutton, J.P. (1997). "If we compute faster, do we understand better?" in *Behavior Research Methods, Instruments, & Computers,* 29, 67–77, Fig 2, p. 70. Reprinted by permission. **221:** Figure 6.6 From Rumelhart and McClelland (Eds.), *Parallel Distributed Processing.* Vol. I. Copyright 1986 MIT Press. Adapted by permission of the publisher and author. **222:** Figure 6.7 From Rumelhart and McClelland (Eds.), *Parallel Distributed Processing.* Vol. I. Copyright 1986 MIT Press. Adapted by permission of the publisher and author. **224:** Table 6.2 Copyright 1989 by the MIT Press. Adapted by permission of the publisher and author. **225:** Figure 6.8 Copyright 1989 by the MIT Press. Adapted by permission of the publisher and author. **226:** Figure 6.9 Copyright 1992 by MIT Press. Adapted by permission of the publisher. **228:** Figure 6.10 Copyright 1992 by MIT Press. Adapted by permission of the publisher. **229:** Table 6.3 From "Retrieving General and Specific Knowledge From Stored Knowledge of Specifics" by J.L. McClelland, 1981, *Proceedings of the Third Annual Conference of the Cognitive Science Society,* Berkeley, CA. Copyright 1981 by J.L. McClelland. Adapted by permission of the author. **231:** Figure 6.11 From "Retrieving General and Specific Knowledge From Stored Knowledge of Specifics" by J.L. McClelland, 1981, *Proceedings of the Third Annual Conference of the Cognitive Science Society,* Berkeley, CA. Copyright 1981 by J.L. McClelland. Adapted by permission of the author.

Chapter 7: 243: Figure 7.1 From *The Origin of Speech,* by C.F. Hockett. Copyright © 1960 by Scientific American, Inc. All rights reserved. Reprinted by permission. **246:** Table 7.1 From *The Origin of Speech,* by C.F. Hockett. Copyright © 1960 by Scientific American, Inc. All rights reserved. Reprinted by permission. **259:** Figure 7.6 Excerpt from *An Introduction to Language, Second Edition* by Victoria A. Fromkin and Robert Rodman, copyright © 1978 by Holt, Rinehart and Winston, Inc., reproduced by permission of the publisher. **260:** Figure 7.7 From *Psychology of Language,* by D.W. Carroll, p. 43. Copyright © 1986 Brooks/Cole Publishing Company. All rights reserved. **262:** Figure 7.8 From *The Articulate Mammal: an Introduction to Psycholinguistics, 2d ed.* by Jean Aitchison. Copyright © 1976, 1983 by Jean Aitchison. Reprinted by permission of Routledge. **266:** Figure 7.9 From *The Language Instinct* by Steven Pinker. Copyright © 1994 by Steven Pinker. Reprinted by permission of William Morrow and Company, Inc. **267:** Figure 7.10 From *The Language Instinct* by Steven Pinker. Copyright © 1994 by Steven Pinker. Reprinted by permission of William Morrow and Company.

Chapter 8: 279: Table 8.1 Tables from *Psychology and Language: An Introduction to Psycholinguistics* by Herbert H. Clark and Eve V. Clark, copyright © 1977 by Harcourt Brace & Company, reproduced by permission of the publisher. **280:** Table 8.2 Tables from *Psychology and Language: An Introduction to Psycholinguistics* by Herbert H. Clark and Eve V. Clark, copyright © 1977 by Harcourt Brace & Company, reproduced by permission of the publisher. **281:** Table 8.3 Tables from *Psychology and Language: An Introduction to Psycholinguistics* by Herbert H. Clark and Eve V. Clark, copyright © 1977 by Harcourt Brace & Company, reproduced by permission of the publisher. **282:** Table 8.4 Tables from *Psychology and Language: An Introduction to Psycholinguistics* by Herbert H. Clark and Eve V. Clark, copyright © 1977 by Harcourt Brace & Company, reproduced by permission of the publisher. **284:** Table 8.5 Tables from *Psychology and Language: An Introduction to Psycholinguistics* by Herbert H. Clark and Eve V. Clark, copyright © 1977 by Harcourt Brace & Company, reproduced by permission of the publisher. **285:** Figure 8.1 From R.N. Shepard, "Psychological Representation of Speech Sounds" in *Human Communication, a Unified View,* E.E. David, P.B. Denes, eds, © 1972 by McGraw-Hill. **287:** Table 8.6 Tables from *Psychology and Language: An Introduction to Psycholinguistics* by Herbert H. Clark and Eve V. Clark, copyright © 1977 by Harcourt Brace & Company, reproduced by permission of the publisher. **294:** Table 8.7 Bach and Harnish. Copyright 1979 by the MIT Press. Adapted by permission of the publisher and author. **295:** Table 8.8 Grice. Copyright 1975 by Academic Press. Adapted by permission of the publisher and author. **298:** Figure 8.2 Van Turennout, M., Hagoort, P., & Brown, C.M. "Electrophysiological evidence on the time course of semantic and phonological processes in speech production" in *Journal of Experimental Psychology: Learning, Memory and Cognition, 23,* 787–806, Fig 2, p. 792. Copyright © 1997 by the American Psychological Association. Reprinted with permission. **298:** Figure 8.3 Van Turennout, M., Hagoort, P., & Brown, C.M. "Electrophysiological evidence on the time course of semantic and phonological processes in speech production" in *Journal of Experimental Psychology: Learning, Memory and Cognition, 23,* 787–806, Fig 1, p. 790. Copyright © 1997 by the American Psychological Association. Reprinted with permission. **299:** Figure 8.4 Van Turennout, M., Hagoort, P., & Brown, C.M. "Electrophysiological evidence on the time course of semantic and phonological processes in speech production" in *Journal of Experimental Psychology: Learning, Memory and Cognition, 23,* 787–806, Fig 3, p. 794. Copyright © 1997 by the American Psychological Association. Reprinted with permission. **301:** Figure 8.5 From "Routes and represntations in the processing of written language" by J. C. Marshall in E. Keller & M. Gopnik (eds.), *Motor and sensory processes of language.* Copyright 1987 by Lawrence Erlbaum Associates, Inc. Adapted by permission. **304:** Figure 8.6 Adapted from "Experimental Tests of a Hierarchical Model of Word Identification" by J.C. Johnston and J.L. McClelland in *Journal of Verbal Learning and Verbal Behavior,* vol. 19, pp. 503–24. Copyright © 1980 Academic Press, Inc. Adapted by permission. **306:** Figure 8.7 Copyright 1980 by the American Psychological Association. Adapted by permission of the publisher. **311:** Figure 8.8 McAnally, K. I., & Stein, J.F. (1997). "Scalp potential evoked by amplitude-modulated tones in dyslexia" in *Journal of Speech Language and Hearing Research,* 40, 939–945, Fig. 2, p. 942. © American Speech-Language-Hearing Association. Reprinted by permission. **312:** Figure 8.9 Mody, M., Studdert-Kennedy, M., & Brady, S. (1997). "Speech perception deficits in poor readers: Auditory processing or phonological coding?" in *Journal of Experimental Child Psychology,* 64, 199–231, Fig 1, p. 215. Reprinted by permission.

Chapter 9: 318: Table 9.1 From *The Articulate Mammal: an Introduction to Psycholinguistics, 2nd ed.* by Jean Aitchison. Copyright © 1976, 1983 by Jean Aitchison. Reprinted by permission of Routledge. **320:** Table 9.2 From *Structure of Communication in Early Language Development* by P.M. Greenfield and J.H. Smith pg. 34. Copyright © 1976 by Academic Press. Reprinted by permission. **325:** Figure 9.1 Adapted with the permission of the Free Press, a Division of Simon & Schuster from *Psycholinguistics* by Roger Brown. Copyright © 1970 by the Free Press. **326:** Table 9.3 Adapted with the permission of the Free Press, a Division of Simon & Schuster from *Psycholinguistics* by Roger Brown. Copyright © 1970 by the Free Press. **338:** Table 9.5 Brown and Smiley, 1977. Copyright 1977 by the Society for Research in Child Development, Inc. Reprinted by permission. **339:** Table 9.6 Brown and Smiley, 1977. Copyright 1977 by the Society for Research in Child Development, Inc. Reprinted by permission.

Chapter 10: 352: Table 10.1 Adapted from *Cognitive Psychology: Memory, Language And Thought* by Darlene V. Howard., copyright © 1983. Reprinted by permission of Prentice-Hall, Inc., Upper Saddle River, NJ. **354:** Table 10.2 From "Supposition and the analysis of conditional sentences" by L.J. Rips and S.L. Marcus in M.A. Just & P.A. Carpenter (eds.), *Cognitive processes in comprehension.* Copyright © 1977 by Lawrence Erlbaum Associations, Inc. Reprinted by permission. **357:** Figure 10.1 Copyright 1977 by the British Psychological Society. Adapted by permission of the publisher and author. **364:** Table 10.4 Cummins, D. D. (1996). "Evidence of deonic reasoning in 3- and 4-year old children" in *Memory & Cognition*, 24, 823–829. Table 1, p. 825. Reprinted by permission. **370:** Table 10.5 Spellman, B.A. (1996). "Acting as intuitive scientists: Contingency judgments are made while controlling for alternative potential causes" in *Psychological Science*, 7, 337–342, Table 1, p. 338. Reprinted by permission. **372:** Figure 10.3 Cummins, D.D. (1995). "Naive theories and causal deduction" in *Memory & Cognition*, 23, 646–658, Figure 2, p. 650. Reprinted by permission. **378:** Figure 10.4 Prabhakaran, V., Smith, J.A.L., Desmond, J.E., Glover, G.H., & Gabrieli, D.E. (1997). "Neural substrates of fluid reasoning: An fMRI study of neocortical activation during performance of the Raven's Progressive Matrices Test" in *Cognitive Psychology*, 33, 43–63, p. 48. Reprinted by permission.

Chapter 11: 386: Figure 11.1 Copyright 1957 by John Wiley & Sons, Inc. Adapted by permission of the publisher and author. **387:** Table 11.1 From Bruner, Goodnow, and Austin, 1956. Copyright 1957 by John Wiley and Sons. Adapted by permission of the publisher and author. **392:** Figure 11.2 Reprinted from "Classification: Purposes, principles, progress, prospects," by R. R. Sokal, with permission from *Science*, 185, 27 Sept. 1974, pp. 1115–1123. Copyright © 1974 by The American Association for the Advancement of Science. Reprinted by permission. **392:** Table 11.2 From Sokal, 1977. Copyright 1977 by Cambridge University Press. Adapted by permission of the publisher and author. **394:** Table 11.3 Lassaline, M.E. & Murphy, G.L. (1996). "Induction and Category coherence" in *Psychonomic Bulletin and Review*, 3, 95–99, Tab. 1, p. 97. Reprinted by permission. **395:** Table 11.4 Lassaline, M.E. & Murphy, G.L. (1996). "Induction and Category coherence" in *Psychonomic Bulletin and Review*, 3, 95–99, Tab. 3, p. 98. Reprinted by permission. **396:** Table 11.5 From Rosch, E.H., "Cognitive representations of semantic categories" in *Journal of Experimental Psychology: General*, 104, 192–233. Copyright © 1975 by The American Psychological Association. Reprinted by permission of the author. **398:** Figure 11.4 From *Psychology: The Adaptive Mind*, by J.S. Nairne, p. 331. Copyright © 1997 Brooks/Cole Publishing Company. All rights reserved. **398:** Figure 11.3 Copyright 1975 by Academic Press Inc. Adapted by permission of the publisher and author. **401:** Figure 11.5 Murphy, G.L. (1991). "Parts in object concepts: Experiments with artificial categories" in *Memory & Cognition*, 19, 423–438, Fig. 1 on p. 425 and Fig. 2, p. 426. Reprinted by permission. **403:** Table 11.6 Markman, A.B., & Wisniewski, E.J. "Similar and different: The differentiation of basic-level categories" in *Journal of Experimental Psychology: Learning, Memory, and Cognition*, 23, 54–70, Tab. 3, p. 60. Copyright © 1997 by the American Psychological Association. Reprinted with permission. **403:** Table 11.7 Markman, A.B., & Wisniewski, E.J. "Similar and different: The differentiation of basic-level categories" in *Journal of Experimental Psychology: Learning, Memory, and Cognition*, 23, 54–70, Table 4, 61. Copyright © 1997 by the American Psychological Association. Reprinted with permission. **406:** Figure 11.6 Nosofsky, R.M., Gluck, M.A., Palmeri, T.J., McKinley, S.C., Glauthier, P. (1994). "Comparing models of rule-based classification learning: A replication and extension of Shepard, Hovland, and Jenkins" (1961) in *Memory and Cognition*, 22, 352–369, Fig 4, p. 358. Reprinted by permission. **411:** Table 11.8 Ross, B. H. (1996). "Category representations aand the effects of interacting with instances" in *Journal of Experimental Psychology: Learning, Memory, and Cognition*, 22, 1249–1265, Tab 1, p. 1252. Reprinted by permission. **412:** Table 11.9 Medin, D.L., Lynch, E.B., Coley, J.D., & Atran, St. (1997). "Categorization and reasoning among tree experts: Do all roads lead to Rome?" in *Cognitive Psychology*, 32, 49–96, Tab 1, p. 72. Reprinted by permission. **413:** Figure 11.7 Reprinted with permission from W. Labov, "The boundaries of words and their meanings" in *New ways of analyzing variations in English*, edited by C.J.N. Bailey and R. W. Shuy. Washington, DC: Georgetown University Press, page 354. Copyright 1973 by Georgetown University Press. **413:** Figure 11.8 Reprinted with permission from W. Labov, "The boundaries of words and their meanings" in *New ways of analyzing variations in English*, edited by C.J.N. Bailey and R. W. Shuy. Washington, DC: Georgetown University Press. Copyright 1973 by Georgetown University Press.

Chapter 12: 434: Figure 12.5 From Mulholland, Pellegrino, & Glaser. Copyright 1980 by Academic Press, Inc. Adapted by permission of the publisher and author. **434:** Figure 12.6 From Mulholland, Pellegrino, & Glaser. Copyright 1980 by Academic Press, Inc. Adapted by permission of the publisher and author. **438:** Table 12.1 Wharton, C.M., Holyoak, K.J., & Lange, T.E. (1996). "Remote analogical reminding" in *Memory & Cognition*, 245, 629–643, Table 1, page 631. Reprinted by permission. **439:** Figure 12.7 Wharton, C.M., Holyoak, K.J., & Lange, T.E. (1996). "Remote analogical reminding" in *Memory & Cognition*, 245, 629–643, Figure 3, page 634. Reprinted by permission. **440:** Figure 12.9 From

John Karat, *Cognitive Psychology, 14* (4), October 1982, pp. 538–559. Copyright 1982 by Academic Press, Inc. Adapted by permission of the publisher and author. **445:** Figure 12.10 Lovett, M.C. & Anderson, J.R. (1996). "History of success and current context in problem solving: Combined influence on operator selection" in *Cognitive Psychology,* 31, 168–217, fig. 1, p. 175. Reprinted by permission. **446:** Figure 12.11 Lovett, M.C. & Anderson, J.R. (1996). "History of success and current context in problem solving: Combined influence on operator selection" in *Cognitive Psychology,* 31, 168–217, fig. 2, p. 179. Reprinted by permission. **448:** Figure 12.12 From Allen Newell, Herbert A. Simon, *Human Problem Solving.* Copyright 1972, p. 168. Reprinted by permission of Prentice-Hall, Inc. Englewood Cliffs, N.J. **449:** Table 12.2 From Allen Newell, Herbert A. Simon, *Human Problem Solving.* Copyright 1972, p. 173. Reprinted by permission of Prentice-Hall, Inc. Englewood Cliffs, N.J. **450:** Figure 12.13 From Allen Newell, Herbert A. Simon, *Human Problem Solving.* Copyright 1972, p. 181. Reprinted by permission of Prentice-Hall, Inc. Englewood Cliffs, N.J. **451:** Table 12.3 From Allen Newell, Herbert A. Simon, *Human Problem Solving.* Copyright 1972, p. 811. Reprinted by permission of Prentice-Hall, Inc. Englewood Cliffs, N.J. **457:** Table 12.4 Simon and Hayes. Copyright 1976 by Academic Press, Inc. Adapted by permission of the publisher and author. **458:** Table 12.5 Simon and Hayes. Copyright 1976 by Academic Press, Inc. Adapted by permission of the publisher and author. **459:** Figure 12.15 From Reif. Copyright 1979 by Frank Reif. Adapted by permission of the author. **461:** Figure 12.16 From Halliday and Resnick, 1974. Copyright 1982 by Lawrence Erlbaum Associates, Inc. Publishers. Adapted by permission of the publisher and author. **462:** Figure 12.17 From Halliday and Resnick, 1974. Copyright 1982 by Lawrence Erlbaum Associates, Inc., Publishers. Adapted by permission of the publisher and author. **463:** Figure 12.18 From "Expertise in problem solving" by M.T.H. Chi, R. Glaser & E. Rees in R.J. Sternberg (ed.), *Advances in the psychology of human intelligence,* Vol. 1. Copyright 1982 Lawrence Erlbaum Associates, Inc. Reprinted by permission. **468:** Figure 12.19 Delaney, P.F., Reder, L.M., Staszewski, J.J., & Ritter, F.E. (1998). "The Strategy specific nature of improvement: The power law applies by strategy within task" in *Psychological Science,* 9(1), 1–7, Fig 3, p. 6. Reprinted by permission.